"Furthermore, we have not even to risk the adventure alone, for the heroes of all time have gone before us. The labyrinth is thoroughly known. We have only to follow the thread of the hero path, and where we had thought to find an abomination, we shall find a god. And where we had thought to slay another, we shall slay ourselves. Where we had thought to travel outward, we will come to the centre of our own existence. And where we had thought to be alone, we will be with all the world."

Joseph Campbell[1]

Nigel,
I hope, over the years, you find value in my book

Kind Regards
Richard Clark
July 2016

---

[1] *The Power of Myth*, Joseph Campbell with Bill Moyers, Doubleday, 1988, p. 123.

between the confusing, complex, and subtle aspects of both the psychological and spiritual work necessary to recover. I vouch for the integrity of the material in the book because I constantly utilize it. It is a constant source of clarity. Much of the quality of my recovery is due to Richard Clark's vast knowledge and experience, and his passion and dedication to the field of addictions recovery. This is a "must read" book.

C.J., British Columbia

It's a powerful book. It's a bit scary, too... and it's hard to believe that so many people are so messed up in their recovery—especially me.

D.L., Maine

I've been wandering in twelve-step programs for ten years. I've tried AA and CODA and Alanon and ACOA, and spent most of that time being hit on by men and given all sorts of "advice" that never really made sense. I could never put my finger on how not to get hooked into more insanity. This book straightened all that out for me. I feel a relief that now I know what is supposed to be going on and how to really make the twelve steps work for me.

L.B., California

I just passed twenty years of sobriety and during the twenty years my recovery was repetitious and confusing. I wish I'd had this book twenty years ago.

R.W., Washington

Finally it all makes sense to me. I was so lost and confused with everything I was hearing in twelve-step meetings, I felt like I was drowning and now I'm not. It's an amazing book.

J.M.B., British Columbia

A book like this is long overdue. Addicts trying to get recovered really need to get back on track. I really need it. I can't think of anyone in this field that doesn't need it. Really, everyone should have a copy of this book.

J.R., British Columbia

I wasn't expecting what I got when I bought this book. As a woman and former client of several therapists, I always felt a little patronized. I was reading this and realized I wasn't being patronized or spoken down to. Very refreshing. I am actually shocked at how clear addictions are to me now. As a woman struggling to find recovery from sex and relationship addiction I know what I need to do. It's difficult and frightening at times, but I'm doing it. After looking through many, many self-help books, I have finally found a real one.

S.T., Alberta

I purchased your book in July 2008 for my husband who is incarcerated due to a heroin addiction. After studying your book, he has been clean now since Sep. 2008. Praise God and your book. Your book has done more for him than the twelve step programs he tried prior to his arrest. Thank you so much.

B.O., New Jersey

This book is an invaluable resource when read with the original AA literature. I find it inspiring and profound. This book contains extraordinary insights that, for me, dismantle the traps and foolishness and pitfalls that kept me away from sincere spiritual integrity and recovery. I know this may seem like too much praise, but I cannot recommend it enough.

P.J., British Columbia

This book has inspired me and given me hope. It has exposed the misperceptions about healing from addictions and explained what spiritual recovery really entails. It clearly illustrates what twelve-step programs were meant to do. This book has guided me into a more spiritual lifestyle, which for me is both beautiful and frightening. I am sure, without this book's insights, I would have remained lost.

R.A., British Columbia

Spiritual Transformation

Making Twelve-Step Recovery More Effective

Richard W. Clark

Spiritual Transformation
Making Twelve-Step Recovery More Effective
Copyright © Richard Clark

Library and Archives Canada Cataloguing in Publication

Clark, Richard W., 1950 –

Cataloguing data available from
Library and Archives Canada.

Spiritual Transformation
Making Twelve-Step Recovery More Effective
ISBN 978-0-9867724-0-5

Printed and bound in Canada by Friesens

Editor: Gerda Wever, www.thewriteroom.net

Cover: Zabolotney Graphic Design / Vancouver

Published by Iguana Press, Vancouver

For
Michael George Perry
1951-2003

Welcome to this book . . .
It was conceived, and my decision to write it was made, in April of 1986. After eleven years of research, in the fall of 1997, I finally put pen to paper and started the first draft. What followed were many more years of research and writing. Finally, after six major rewrites, four earlier editions, and two publishers, the book is now complete. I do hope you find value in it.

Richard Clark
Vancouver, Canada
September, 2010

Permission

The author is greatly indebted to Alcoholics Anonymous World Services, Inc., for their generous permission to quote at length from their published material. The material quoted and excerpted from *Alcoholics Anonymous*, *Twelve Steps and Twelve Traditions*, and other material they hold copyright on is used with permission of Alcoholics Anonymous World Services, Inc. Permission to use this material does not mean or imply that AA has reviewed or approved the contents of this work, nor does it mean or imply that AA agrees with the views expressed herein. Alcoholics Anonymous is a program of recovery from alcoholism only; use of their material in connection with programs and activities which are patterned after AA, but which address other problems, or in any other non-AA context, does not imply otherwise.

Earlier Editions

This book was initially published under two earlier titles— *Addictions and Getting Recovered* (ISBN 1-4120-3131-1), and then *Addictions & Spiritual Transformation* (ISBN1-4120-8398-2). Each new edition was written because of supportive comments from dedicated readers who wanted more information. I am grateful for their avid and positive interest. I must say, though, this is the final rewrite and I'll now get on with finishing the companion volume, *Facets of Personal Transformation*.

Copyright

"God is. That is the primordial fact. It is in order that we may discover this fact for ourselves, by direct experience, that we exist."

Aldous Huxley
Huxley and God, Essays
Edited by Jacqueline Hazard Bridgeman
Harper San Francisco, 1992, p. 17.

"The philosophers of all ages have taught that the visible universe was but a fractional part of the whole, and that by analogy the physical body of man is in reality the least important part of his composite constitution. Most of the medical systems of today almost entirely ignore the super physical man... Paracelsus [1493-1541], noting the same proclivity on the part of physicians during his day, aptly remarked: 'There is a great difference between the power that removes the invisible causes of disease, and which is Magic, and that which causes merely external effects [to] disappear, and which is Physic, Sorcery, and Quackery." (Translated by Franz Hartmann.)

"Disease is unnatural.... Permanent health cannot be regained until harmony is restored. The outstanding virtue of Hermetic medicine was its recognition of spiritual and psychophysical derangements as being largely responsible for the condition which is called physical disease."

Manly P. Hall
The Secret Teachings of All Ages
Tarcher/Penguin Books, 2003, p. 354.

"The world is not a 'prison house,' but a kind of spiritual kindergarten where millions of bewildered infants are trying to spell 'God' with the wrong blocks."

Edwin Arlington Robinson
Edwin Arlington Robinson, Selected Poems
Penguin Classics, 1997, p. xx.

"It is . . . our decided conviction, that to become a genuine spiritual entity . . . [a person] must first create [themselves] anew, so to speak—i.e. thoroughly eliminate from [their] mind and spirit, not only the dominating influence of selfishness and other impurity, but also the infection of superstition and prejudice."

Helene P. Blavatsky
Isis Unveiled
Theosophical University Press, 1988. P. 40.
[Originally published 1877]

5

Acknowledgements

If it weren't for Michael Perry this book would most likely never have been completed. His friendship, support, and editing expertise were crucial in my finally getting twenty years of work between the covers of this book. Ron Jordens and Ryan Angels' support and comments were most helpful in eliminating my oversights. I wish also to thank the pioneers of therapy like Karen Horney, Carl Whittaker, Sheldon Kopp, Leonard Shaw, John Bradshaw, and Thomas Szasz. As for associates, a special note of thanks goes to Rowan Scott, Danny Novak, Holly Jones, Joel Brass, and Leonard Shaw. I'm grateful for the dozens of authors, musicians, social reformers, and artists that have taught me. I remember, with affection and great respect, two monks, one Christian and one Buddhist. Their generosity of spirit, their profound sense of spiritual peace, and their insights that at times bordered on the mystical, have guided me in my own pilgrimage in ways that are beyond words.

I am particularly grateful for the thoughtful contributions of my editor, Gerda Wever. And, most importantly, there are my clients who have contributed the most.

Respect & Dignity

Readers may encounter ideas they disagree with. The intent in writing this book is neither to insult people, nor to persuade them to reject what they believe or cherish. I am putting to words the reality I see around me, and offering alternatives to people who are foundering, confused, or dissatisfied in their pilgrimage out of addictions. The world is large enough for different beliefs, and yet small enough that acceptance and respect are necessary for us to live in harmony.

A Note About Quotations and Citations

I refer to many other authors and to people who are successful or famous in various fields of endeavor. By quoting them, or referring to their ideas, I do not mean to imply that they agree with or endorse the views I offer in this book; and, I may not necessarily agree with everything they say. Regardless of this, I wish to express my gratitude to all of them for provoking and challenging and teaching me. The observations I make throughout this book are entirely my own.

Richard Clark

Table of Contents

Prologue: The Manner of Presentation

This book cannot be read the way people ordinarily read books in this day and age. In some respects, its readers will have to work their way through each page and even each single sentence the hard way. This was done deliberately; it is the only way this book can become what it is intended to be for the reader. Simply reading it through is as good as not reading it at all. The spiritual truths it contains must be experienced; that is the only way they can be of value.

> *Theosophy* (The Introduction)
> Rudolf Steiner, 3rd Edition,
> © 1994, Anthroposophic Press

The foreword, to that edition of *Theosophy*, by Michael Holdrege, is well worth careful study and it applies to this book.

Modern culture appears to be increasingly dysfunctional, and at the same time people are clamoring for some solution. We're sinking fast and trying to swim. The pilot comes over the intercom and says, "Attention all passengers: I've got good news and bad news, folks. The bad news is; we're lost. The good news is; we're flying fast and making good time. We're getting nowhere quickly."

We scramble around searching in therapy, workshops, seminars, healing circles, recovery groups, religions, yoga, and ersatz mystic disciplines (most often led by characters of questionable integrity). We spend thousands of dollars sitting in weird positions, eating vitamins, and reciting phrases in strange languages. We buy self-help books by the dozen and quickly discard them, with minimal affect. Most of the time we don't know what we're searching for, but we look, and are again soon lost in the aftermath of yet another unfulfilling experience. I've witnessed this first hand for 40 years. I did it for ten years. What is recovery? What is spiritual integrity? What's wrong? Where are we going? What's wrong with this picture? What's wrong with us?

Several things, but in brief it is thus: technology, quick-fix solutions, and addictions. Let's face it, our culture—principally North America and the other modern cultures—are magnificently corrupt and riddled with addictions.

When I talk about spiritual transformation I am *not* talking about religion (any of them). They're as corrupt as the cultures that harbor them. When I talk about "God" I am certainly not referring to any of the definitions or concepts that filter into our language through religious dogma. Those definitions are abusive, as are the religions that use them, and they refer to concepts of "God" that are fashioned by insecure people to meet their own selfish ends. To me, a higher power is completely without concepts and images. It's the harmony and balance of the energy of the universe—healthy quantum physics. Even that definition is inaccurate, but that's as simple as I can make it.

The potential to be spiritual exists within everyone. It exists underneath the biological and secular trappings of personality and culture. Becoming spiritual requires unlearning old ideas, clearing away defects, abandoning pride, and having faith that your insecurities are meaningless.

There are ways in which to live that contribute to the harmony of the universe. I believe these are contained in the five spiritual principles (explained in Appendix II). If you choose to live a life governed by these it would necessarily exclude violence, religious dogma, addictions, and other ailments like greed, racism, patriotism, righteousness, and sexism that are a plague in modern culture. Knowing or wanting this is one thing; how we individually get there is another.

This book is written as a careful inquiry into addictions, twelve-step programs, dysfunction "in general," culture, and spiritual transformation. Why from the perspective of addictions?—for three reasons.

1) Addictions (defined as a pathological relationship with a mood altering experience that has life damaging consequences) are the most common, largest, and most destructive problem facing modern culture. This book speaks to socially approved addictions like television, gambling, health, computers, work, money, internet, shopping, spending, consumerism, adrenaline, pornography, dating websites, relationships, food, shiny things, competition, fitness, sports, cosmetic surgery, religion, anger, and righteousness. It also applies to the unapproved addictions like drugs, alcohol, sex, and tobacco. My experience and observation suggests that about 80% of the population is actively involved in an addiction to one type of mood altering experience or another.

2) The original twelve-step program, devised and explained in the book *Alcoholics Anonymous*, presents a path to exit addictions. Since addictions are so abundantly common, it's the best place to start. Granted, the original twelve-step process has been commercialized with disastrous consequences, and it was originally written from a Christian point of view for alcoholics, but it has nonetheless been proven to be a successful and viable path or pilgrimage out of addictions. Those steps are available to anyone who diligently applies themselves.

3) The five spiritual principles are most quickly accessed through a very specific, self-disciplined path. That path is most succinctly explained

through the twelve steps. (It is also available through a certain type of Buddhism, but that's a more complex process and largely misunderstood in the romanticized, dysfunctional religious versions of Buddhism we are usually exposed to.)

After 40 years of research, study, and personal experience, these spiritual principles consistently align me with the energetic harmony of the universe. That's the safest and most fulfilling place for me to me—aligned with the energy of the universe. By living by spiritual principles I contribute to the harmony of the universe and do not disrupt it (human foibles notwithstanding). *Follow the path of least resistance,*

Six Perspectives of Being Recovered

After an examination of addictions, and the recovery process, in Chapter Eight there's an examination of "addiction" and "recovered" from six differing models or perspectives. These are from (1) the World Health Organization; (2) a mental-health model; (3) a medical or psychiatric model; (4) a psycho-social model; (5) a spiritual perspective; and (6), the view of addiction presented within *Alcoholics Anonymous*. Regardless of how it's defined, people can become recovered from addictions.

What I present in this book is not intended to imply that any professional, or layperson, or any organization, that is associated with addictions recovery agrees with me. Neither am I representing that I am a doctor or psychologist. I am an addictions counsellor/therapist. The observations and perspectives presented about being recovered are intended to suggest a more open awareness of the broad scope, and far-reaching possibilities, of the original twelve-step process of getting recovered from addictions.

This book is a difficult read for some people; it's not a "feel-good bed time story". It examines what works, what doesn't work, "why", cultural influences, and (and since most of us are addicts in one form or another) addictions-related personality concerns. I explain how recovering addicts achieve more clarity and success. There may be other proposed avenues to the resolution of addictions, but after 40 years of dedicated inquiry, none that I've found is as effective to resolve them as the original AA twelve steps, meticulously applied to your life. I've included some careful analysis of what happens in the mind of an addict, information about culturally approved and poly addictions, some new perspectives of personal spiritual discipline, and what "should" happen in the mind of a spiritual person.

There are many therapeutic proposals that suggest how to manage addictions or make acceptable substitutions for spirituality in treatment. Those other suggested and varied addictions management tools are not explored in detail here. This book is for people who wish to acquire a deep awareness of personal motives, and accomplish transformation (or self-actualization) from an addicted lifestyle into a life of authentic spiritual discipline; it is a discipline, and it isn't easy.

Addictions and a spiritual lifestyle are at opposite ends of a living spectrum. Spiritual transformation is the path in between. Addictions and a spiritual lifestyle are each multi-dimensional, interrelated, and layered. To say they are complex is a magnificent understatement.

Imagine an intricate, three-dimensional spider's web—a "ball" of sticky connections and fragile threads where every point of intersection of web is somehow directly connected to every other point of intersection. Nothing is linear; everything is connected to everything else, and when something happens anywhere in the ball it affects everywhere. That's the way addictions live in your mind. They are a state of existence.

The active dynamics of addictions, or of getting recovered, exist like a massive spider's web of symptoms and issues that are all connected. You get sick everywhere and throughout your entire personality all at the same time, and you become spiritual everywhere and throughout your entire personality all at the same time. There's no single cause to addictions or dysfunction (by whatever name); there's no specific psychological focus to get out of them. Everything is global, nothing is linear, and it all happens at once. This is why recovery (transformation) is so painstakingly slow. Being addicted, like being spiritual, is an actual state of existence.

Everything in this book, from discussing the many and varied issues that create a firm basis for understanding and exiting addictions, to embracing personal transformation, to becoming spiritual, is important in the overall task at hand; and, it is complex. Please be patient and go through this with me slowly.

I have been asked whether this book is for therapists or for ordinary people getting recovered. First: Counsellors and therapists are ordinary people. Second: There have appeared two closely related and pervasive myths; not even myths exactly, but a malignant ambiance in our attitudes about addicts, alcoholics, and otherwise unhealthy people. These are:

(i) addicts don't really want to get recovered; and,

(ii) they're incapable of comprehending complicated things.

Granted, there are exceptions, but for the most part, remember . . .

- Counsellors and therapists are ordinary people with special skills;
- People with addictions and emotional issues are capable of comprehending complex ideas;
- Many addicts do want to get recovered; and,

- What's required is to offer valid and authentic alternatives, patience, and a dictionary—a determined and focused effort, over a long time, in a very specific direction, that is applicable to them.

"The unfolding of [person's] *spiritual nature is as much an exact science as astronomy* [or] *medicine."*[1] Manly Hall wrote that over 100 years ago. What he tells us is there's a requirement for obedience to a specific and complex approach to becoming a spiritual being. There's a "standard formulae" that cannot be modified. Spiritual transformation and the resolution of addictions cannot be approached through psychology, self-esteem improvement strategies, or religious dogma. Understanding the progressive, ubiquitous, and destructive nature of addictions, and how psychology can assist but only a spiritual lifestyle can resolve them, is incredibly complicated.

Misconceptions about twelve-step programs, addictions, and spirituality are reflected in the media, treatment modalities, self-serving interpretations of religion, and in the carnival-like atmosphere of most twelve-step meetings. This book presents ideas and perspectives that will contradict much of what is presently, commonly thought to be recovery work, treatment, self-help psychology, religious dogma that's passed off as spiritual (it isn't), and most of what is routinely said and done in present-day twelve-step groups.

Respect cannot be offered to people, nor can this broad subject be held in the regard it deserves, when people and addictions are treated in a superficial or trite manner. It may sound silly, but this book is as long as it is because that's how long it has to be.

Your rewards will be commensurate with your efforts. When anyone desires to transform themselves, and they undertake to resolve their addictions, throughout that process they gradually become more graceful in assimilating deeper awareness. The further along they are towards achieving spiritual integrity, the more they can appreciate spiritual nuance.

---

[1] *Secret Teachings of All Ages,* Manly P. Hall, Tarcher/Penguin Books, 2003, p. 120. Procrastination and working grudgingly, which are characteristics of an alcoholic/addict (*Twelve Steps and Twelve Traditions,* p. 49), should not be preemptively interpreted as disinterest. These can be overcome, which is a specific part of the process of getting recovered. *Twelve Steps and Twelve Traditions,* and *Alcoholics Anonymous*, and this book, are an explanation of that process.

Language

Regarding language, I have tried to accomplish three things that are important to me in the use of language.

There are times when the grammar in using the pronoun "they" may not be perfect. "His or hers" and "him or her" may be more grammatically correct but it is cumbersome to read. I have opted for the smoother reading of they or them.

In alternating between nouns (addicts, alcoholics) and pronouns (you, we), my descriptions of the process that relates to spiritual transformation are for convenience and grammatical style. This is not intended to be accusatory, or to include readers where they wish not to be. The anecdotes and examples are true; however, the names and circumstances are generic and do not represent any particular person.

Then, regarding sexist language: I have avoided as best I can patronizing, sexist language and also tried to present "god" and spirituality in gender neutral terms. Sexism in addictions recovery is a problem that requires more attention than it gets. To this end I have altered, in a minor way, some of the quotes.

You have the difficult task of trying to assimilate extremely complicated information that is multi-dimensional, interrelated, and layered—and it all happens at once: the three-dimensional spider's web. *And*, it requires you question every aspect of your life and values, and much of what our culture holds in high regard. Many of you are trying to do this with an ego that will resist much of what's in this book. By reading this slowly and thoughtfully, you will eventually sense how it all fits together.

As Rudolf Steiner wrote:

> *This book cannot be read the way people ordinarily read books in this day and age. In some respects, its readers will have to work their way through each page and even each single sentence the hard way. This was done deliberately; it is the only way this book can become what it is intended to be for the reader. Simply reading it through is as good as not reading it at all. The spiritual* [and psychological/scientific] *truths it contains must be experienced; that is the only way they can be of value.*

That applies here. Be kind and patient with yourself. Be gently determined. From wherever you are right now, at this immediate point in your own transformation, you are a newcomer to the rest of your life.

Chapter 1

Begin at the Beginning

We owe a definite homage to the reality around us, and we are obliged, at certain times, to say what things are and to give them their right names and to lay open our thought about them to the men we live with.

Thomas Merton

Addiction: *a pathological relationship with any mood-altering experience that has life-damaging consequences.*[1]

Twelve-step programs have been proven to be the most (and some might say the only) effective method for addiction recovery. However, in addition to the long, difficult process of comprehending and completing the twelve steps, there are the addict's ego defenses, their suspicious and defiant attitude, puzzling program clichés, confusing jargon, various myths and inaccurate information, and preexisting therapeutic issues. Interventions that support abstinence or the normalizing of addictive behaviour (such as in work or sex addictions) often fail because of this profoundly complex constellation of symptoms and issues. What adds to the addict's struggle is the often heard, fear-based, blaming statement: "Well, addicts who relapse don't really want recovery. They don't try hard enough."

Since about 1984, there has been a huge surge of awareness in North America about twelve-step groups, and a dramatic increase in the number of professionals and institutions catering to the specialized needs of people with addictions. These social shifts, abetted by changes in communication technology, cannot adequately address the needs and awareness's of the treatment explosion around addiction and recovery. The resulting chaos and problems aren't entirely due to the identification of, or probable increase in the numbers of people with addictions. It also certainly isn't because addicts don't want help. It is much broader and more complex than that.

---

[1] Definition by the World Health Organization, cited: *Bradshaw on: The Family*, John Bradshaw, Health Communications Inc., 1988, p 89.

With the advent of an insightful family-systems theory of shame, many therapists have unknowingly acted in concert with the machinations of addictions. Therapists created a decided tendency to shift the responsibility for addictions and getting recovered off the shoulders of the addict and onto community and family. As much as that may be influential in an addiction's origin, it is generally irrelevant in its resolution.

Additionally, the restructuring of psychiatric hospitals, the reductions in funding for the treatment of mental disorders and support programs, and the discharge of many people from these programs, caused another set of problems for twelve-step groups. Through publicity, easy availability, and promises of support and healing, came a wave of new people. With their open-armed welcoming of any and all who were (or might possibly be) afflicted with an addiction, and their self-diagnosing rule of membership, twelve-step groups received a huge influx of people who were formerly being cared for in professionally structured programs and facilities.

With the increase of professionals (many with minimal training, with addictions themselves, or who have serious, unresolved personal issues) who cater to addicts; with the plethora of healing and treatment centres; with the huge influx of new people, some of whom were only marginally appropriate to the mandate of twelve-step programs; with too much publicity and false promises about twelve-step programs being a panacea (they decidedly aren't); and with insightful psychological theories, there came a disastrous blurring of the boundaries between therapy and twelve-step work. This has almost completely obscured the spiritual vision presented in the original twelve-step literature. The efficacy and spiritual integrity of twelve-step programs (especially AA and NA[2]) could not withstand this tidal wave of change. A critical mass was reached and, in the mid 1980s, cultural awareness about twelve-step groups and self-help simply exploded. It became trendy to be in AA or NA, or for that matter, any other twelve-step program (except the ones for sex addictions).

Three important results are:

(i)   a subtle, treacherous trend within "self-help" groups and within society at large to marginalize and demean mainstream therapy;

(ii) a dangerous myth that twelve-step groups are a modern therapeutic panacea; and,

(iii) a loss of spiritual integrity as the goal of recovery.

In concert with these, many therapists and people within twelve-step groups misunderstand addictions, or see twelve-step groups and treatment centres at odds with a traditional therapeutic mandate. For the most part, neither the therapist nor the twelve-step participant clearly understands how to effectively enroll the other discipline as an ally in the healing journey, and neither are clear on the crucial importance of maintaining the independence of each process. The result of this misunderstanding has been to naively force each process together or to belligerently keep them apart. People are lost in this confusion and too often the consequences are relapse or death.

The Origin Of This Book

In 1986 I was working in a treatment centre. On Fridays, a very informal group of clients would convene in my office and we would ruminate about the vagaries of life. Out of this, one day they requested I deliver an impromptu lecture on depression. So, I gathered several reference texts and some old course notes and, over the next couple of hours, gave them what they asked for. Their interest astonished me. A few days later, I was approached by another group of clients who wanted a presentation on something else.

I was, at that time, subtly intimidated by the request for more impromptu lectures. I was anxious about setting a precedent whereby clients could closely examine me. They could possibly, thereby, hold me accountable for my own lack of therapeutic integrity. Months later I realized how I had adopted the belief that client lethargy, perceived lack of ability, or disobedience were the sole problems responsible for high recidivism. I began to see how deeply the clients were foundering in ignorance, myths, contradictions, and the dislocation of ethics within the bureaucratic and coercive care being offered to them (both in their treatment *and* in their twelve-step groups). I admitted all this to them, and with noticeable anticipation, the lectures became a standing-room only, regular event.

When those clients finally understood there was learnable, valid information beyond trite clichés—many became proactive in their own healing. At their insistence, it developed into a regular Friday lecture—for me to offer information, and for them to listen, puzzle over dilemmas, relax, laugh, debate, take notes, and ask questions in an informal setting. They decided the general topics; I'd do the research and lecture. As they acquired knowledge, they demonstrated a new interest in self-care and developed the courage to advocate on their own behalf. They began to discard that which had never been real and to recognize and embrace that which was.

---

[2] AA and NA refer respectively to the groups Alcoholics Anonymous and Narcotics Anonymous.

Those people had been written off as only suitable for therapeutic babysitting. Those men and women, who were referred to as dead-end, low-bottom junkies and drunks, hadn't until then asked for reference books or videos. They began banding together in support of each other and questioning what they didn't understand. Many started using the centre's reference library, which had been largely dormant.

Within a few months the other counsellors and management felt threatened by the clients' new assertiveness and, in true wounded-healer fashion, became defensive and blamed me. Some professionals see demands for information from clients perceived as psychologically blind, no-account failures to be intimidating, confrontational, or representative of defiance— especially professionals and caregivers who well conceal their insecurities and prejudices.

Those clients offered me the opportunity to uncover and examine my own prejudices about addicted people, prejudices that I was also holding against myself. I realized the significant need for caregivers and sponsors to be more than just "knowledgeable" about addictions. They must be *much* more than sober, offer more than rehashed clichés, and have thoroughly resolved their own well-concealed arrogance and prejudice. Caregivers must be insightful and sensitively attuned to the unique and complicated needs of those who seek their help. Sadly, in my experience, most aren't.

Many of us are deceived about the malignant and inexorable power of untreated addictions, including many caregivers. The machinations of addictive self-destruction are subtle and vicious.

I am forever indebted to that first group of clients who trusted that they could push hard against the edge of their treatment (meaning me); for in fact, most often, the counsellor is the therapy, not the books and theories. I am grateful to the thousands of people who have attended my presentations, and to the many hundreds of clients who have shared their lives with me. Ultimately, my responsibility is to demand of myself what I can only encourage in others, and to live by my convictions regardless of the respect or antagonism this generates.

Therapy and Twelve-Step Work

Many, if not most, addictions-treatment service providers and many people in twelve-step programs offer ineffective services. Within twelve-step groups, "carrying the message," sponsoring, posting up a website about your own recovery opinions, or publishing your own interpretations of the steps, is offering a service. The amount of destruction and chaos that results from this is alarming.

For any number of reasons noted throughout this book, including the ease with which a Misalliance of Commitment[3] is established, people getting recovered fail to maintain a proper segregation between the mutually exclusive requirements of well-managed, long-term, formal therapy, and a twelve-step spiritual pilgrimage. In my experience, sadly, most don't know what an authentic spiritual pilgrimage is.

The Sphere of Human Health

There are three general treatment modalities for addressing issues of ill health.

Medical Model (including psychiatry)	Psychological Model	Spiritual Model
Generally organic mental disorders, illness, and injury (physical trauma), treated with medication, surgery, massage, diet, or chiropractic.	Generally mental or emotional dislocations that are addressed with variations of talk, art, music, or other dynamic therapy and adjustments of perception.	Addictions treatment.

Certainly there is a great overlap, especially between the medical and psychological modalities, which is ever more apparent with recent breakthrough treatment strategies like Self Regulation Therapy® and Emotional Freedom Techniques.[4] There are also people with dual- or multi-diagnosis concerns where one of the issues is addiction and others that belong in the other modalities. The issues do interweave themselves.

It's crucial to understand that in relation to derivative medical issues that stem from addictions (like detoxing), and where there are multiple-diagnosis concerns, there is a need to incorporate medical or psychological treatment of those "outside" issues. The addiction itself, however, is treated and resolved with spirituality.[5]

Spirituality treats addictions. That is the foundation of the *original* twelve-step program, and is what is outlined in its reference texts. Separating out the addiction from all other health concerns and treating it independently (spiritually) is certainly delicate, but it is essential because an addiction, in its ubiquitous origin and unique manifestation, stands segregated from all other types of health concerns.

---

[3] A Misalliance of Commitment, explained in detail in Chapter 7, occurs when a person on a path of spiritual transformation is actually committed to, and engaged in, psychological healing, but calls it spiritual healing.

[4] See Appendix III.

[5] This book is primarily concerned with the effective resolution of addictions. There is some reference to their origin and their cause, but only to the extent of helping addicts get recovered.

At the same time, it's essential to understand and enroll the compli-mentary importance of psychology and/or medicine in the treatment of the derivative issues, and to maintain the segregation of spiritual twelve-step work when addressing addictions. This is incredibly delicate when a person is attempting to resolve any abstinence not-available addiction. The differ-ences are explained in the following section.

Abstinence-Available & Abstinence Not-Available Addictions

There are many ways of categorizing addictions. For the purpose of this book, and to more clearly understand addictions, they are divided into two main categories. Which addictions you're addressing (the category they belong to) will significantly affect the early stages of your healing work.

Abstinence Available	Abstinence Not-Available
These are addictions to alcohol, tobacco, drugs, and gambling (which often includes the socially approved forms of lottery and bingo). The addict can clearly establish complete abstinence; hence, an abstinence available addiction.[6] *This category commands virtually all government attention, polic-ing, research, and press coverage. Yet, these are the least common of the addictions. Sex, work, pornography, relationships, religion, television, computers, and violence addictions are much more prevalent and just as de-structive to the human condition.*	These are addictions to anger, vio-lence, adrenaline, work, relationships, sex, food, etc., where complete absti-nence is not available.[7] Addicts desiring recovery must *first* establish an ethical and credible standard of "normal" behaviour at and during Step One before other twelve-step work begins. This means they establish and maintain a standard of behaviour that, if it were not met, would be considered a relapse. The difficulty is, the stan-dard is subjectively interpretive. "Abstinence", here, has to be negoti-ated with and between personal perceptions, instinctual influence, en-vironment, and pre-existing psychological issues, all of which causes all manner of confusion. It eas-ily lends itself to irresponsibility, repeated failures, and constant relapse. (This is explained from another per-spective in Appendix IV.)

---

[6] Here I refer to gambling as wagers and various games of chance. Yes, it's a "gamble" to cross the street, but the generic risks of life are not what we're discussing here.

[7] Relationship addiction is a more accurate representation of what was formerly referred to as codependence. I elaborate on this later.

There are various theories that addictive acting out is self-medication, self-regulation, a reaction to unresolved trauma or abuse, an expression of rebellion, a genetic flaw, or a result of unfulfilled developmental dependency needs and despair. There is research and psychological evidence to lay some claim to all of these; however, none are, independently or collectively, sufficient to encompass a consistent theory of origin. What is common is that a profound spiritual dislocation exists in all addicts, and self-annihilation sits at the core of all acting out. *Addictions are the self-destructive outcome of deep spiritual dislocation.*

The original twelve-step process established a way to access a spiritual lifestyle that resolves addiction. Access to any credible spirituality is completely dependent upon the ability to abstain. This is crucial: The fundamental prerequisite to all bona fide spiritual endeavor is abstinence: not acting out in any addiction.

Achieving this prerequisite, although difficult, is rather straightforward with abstinence available addictions. With abstinence not-available addictions, however, any chaos around establishing bottom-line behaviour—any failure to maintain a spiritually credible standard of abstinence, renders all twelve-step work ineffective. There is no end of abuse and confusion about this in the twelve-step and counselling communities.

With abstinence not-available addictions, cautious and well-conducted cross-over work[8] is essential to establishing and maintaining an ethical, non-addicted standard of bottom-line behaviour. Without this, any medical, therapeutic, or twelve-step work is only temporary crisis management, which in itself sets up another host of problems.

Two crucial requirements early in the process of addictions treatment are: (i) eliminating the self-annihilating quality of behaviour; and (ii), eliminating all self-serving, shallow definitions of bottom-line behaviour.

---

[8] Cross-over work means a combination of therapy and spiritual twelve-step work, which are different, but done simultaneously. It is necessary so as to achieve authentic abstinence from not-available addictions (some of which were noted in the chart above). This is partly to establish ethical, non-addicted bottom-line behaviour. Cross-over work is also necessary when twelve-step participants respond to invasive "Step One Guides" that are discussed in Chapter 3; and it's always required when addressing a religious or sex addiction. There is also a reference to cross-over work in Chapter 4 regarding Step Two and the fifth type of spiritual dislocation.

Cross-over work is delicate and time-consuming, and should only be undertaken with an insightful therapist who: a) is very well versed in spirituality, addictions, and the intricate requirements of twelve-step programs; b) has a well-established relationship with you (longer than several months of regular weekly appointments); c) is patient and generous of spirit without strong religious bias; and d), is someone you intend to continue working with. In cross-over work the focus is always to end up with spiritual integrity more than psychological health, a priority that is mandated by addictions. Cross-over work facilitates access to the truths of psychology, but eventually these become subservient to the principles of spirituality, which are outlined in Appendix II. This process is *very* delicate. The consequences of mismanaged cross-over work are far more onerous than they may seem. The possible rewards are often not worth the risk of undertaking the work where the four criteria are not reasonably well met.

Once ethical "abstinence" (bottom-line behaviour) is established *and maintained*, and there appears to be some element of spiritual curiosity, the twelve steps are only then undertaken and applied to the addict's life exactly as they are laid out in the original twelve-step literature.

With abstinence not-available addictions, which are directly related to instinctual drives, establishing an ethical/spiritual level of meaningful abstinence requires a unique and personalized approach with each individual. A metaphor that I use is that I must discover the addictions fingerprint for each client and then we create a completely new strategy around that.

With the abstinence not-available addictions like sex, relationships, adrenaline, work, righteousness,[9] romance, food, and religion, any kind of heavy-handed approach to establishing bottom-line behaviour, or any generic "group" approach, invariably entrenches the following vicious relapse-cycle in the addict [10]:

(1) **Desire** (to heal): "I want to get recovered. I want to change my life. I'm really going to do it this time. I'm dying. I'm serious."

| (5) **Retreat** from recovery, from therapy and "their issues", and from spirituality. The viciousness of addiction, and a faint hope of recovery, however, soon leads to another…

(4) An **aversion** to self, to treatment, to twelve-step spirituality. This causes the addict to… | (2) **Action**: "I'm going to quit acting out, leave abusive relationships (or whatever), and establish abstinence." This is tremendously difficult because abstinence is intimately personal. Too often, in a twelve-step or therapeutic environment, addicts meet up with generic, impersonal abstinence strategies that can't work. Abstinence fails. This entrenches… |

(3) **Guilt** and a deep sense of personal inadequacy. The abstinence strategy that was generic and political (imposed by peer- or therapeutic pressure) at #2 is rendered meaningless. The subsequent self-doubt, fear, and shame generates…

Because people must contend with food, sex, work, relationships, and spirituality, and cannot eliminate them as someone can eliminate alcohol, drugs, gambling, or tobacco, establishing abstinence (bottom-line behav-

---

[9] Being righteous about religious beliefs is quite common. Righteousness is also readily apparent in politics, capitalism, and many social reform movements.

[10] This cycle is discussed from a different perspective in relation to traditions in Appendix I.

iour) is one very delicate task of well-conducted cross-over work. Once this is established, which may take upwards of one or two years of regular therapy, treating any abstinence not-available addiction is a matter of twelve-step work with ongoing supportive therapy.

The Ubiquitous Nature of Codependence

Codependence *is* relationship addiction. It is important to realize that the nature of addictions, as I discuss throughout the book, will not allow only one addiction to be present. An addiction is "a state of existence" and not limited to participation in any single acting-out ritual or substance. Poly-addictions are a given.

All addicts will have, at the minimum, a relationship addiction[11] that sits near the core of their acting out, and then at least two other associated addictions at the same time. It is therefore important, if you are addressing a substance addiction like alcohol, drugs, or tobacco, to understand that if you intend to get recovered and be truly spiritual, you will eventually have to address the underlying associated relationship addiction.

In short: *All* addicts, in order to become recovered, will have to address at least one abstinence not-available addiction—relationships, wherein they will have to understand, establish, and adhere to bottom-line behaviour.

I am very aware of people's ability, through their ego, to convince themselves that there is nothing wrong within themselves, and that solutions to problems they face belong with someone else: externalizing responsibility.[12] This is often just as true for people offering help as for those seeking it. Yes, addicts/people frequently blame. Caregivers, however, whether sponsor or professional, are ineffective when they consistently blame multiple relapses, or repetitive conflict in the treatment dyad, on the client/newcomer. It is often the case that the caregiver has a shared responsibility.

People, trying to get recovered, will unknowingly rely on misinformation from wounded service providers, where those service providers, especially sponsors, unknowingly live in a Misalliance of Commitment (discussed in Chapter 7). Newcomers often hope for or participate in the

---

[11] Codependence is usually a generic catch-all label for all manner of relationship dysfunction. You'll have more clarity and success in addressing "codependence" if you understand it's likely a relationship addiction. In my view, relationship addiction is the more accurate name for codependence. All alcoholics... *all addicts*, regardless of the style of acting-out behaviour, live with an underlying relationship addiction (which is abstinence not-available).

[12] Externalizing responsibility (blaming someone else—the mindset of accusation) is a crucial aspect of addictions and is discussed throughout this book.

illusion of an expedient or easy process, while enmeshed in a subtle conspiracy theory that someone else is to blame for their addiction and misery. No one is to blame, and there is no expedient process.

Therapy and twelve-step programs complement each other, but must be combined with extremely careful consideration and forethought. Integrating psychology, the five principles of spirituality[13], the medical model of addiction, twelve-step programs, and formal therapy, into a personalized, effective spiritual pilgrimage out of addiction is profoundly complicated.

Many books have been written about twelve-step programs and their wonderful healing powers. The mass of published literature that misrepresents or recasts the original twelve-step spiritual process onto various and sundry problems is overwhelming. There are literally hundreds of different twelve-step programs (and adaptations and variations and mutations of programs) that try to address everything from drinking too much soda pop to being a child survivor of war. I don't question the need for help, but I do question the insecure and greedy misapplication of the original twelve steps.

This book is designed for people who want or need to eliminate confusion, and get recovered from addictions, within the framework of a twelve-step program (which is a process into spirituality). It's for people who would like clarity regarding the spiritual intent of the twelve steps and the role of appropriate therapy.

I have been told that this material is valuable in helping professionals and interested non-addicts gain insight into the workings and intent of the twelve steps and addictions in general. It offers detailed explanations of the nature and symptoms of addictions, the twelve steps, the spiritual philosophy that underlies those steps, and the subtle dynamics of being recovered. It also explains how to effectively incorporate medical, psychological, and therapeutic assistance into a twelve-step journey.

This book details the journey "from addicted to recovered" within the spiritual framework that's outlined in the original twelve-step program. There is a specific view to exit all addictions via spirituality, with encouragement to compliment and enhance personal recovery with well-conducted formal therapy and wise spiritual counsel.

Someone once asked me to sum all of this up. I replied that clamoring for simplicity is one manifestation of addiction that is significant in creating the mess we are in. Demanding expedience is fatal to spirituality; however, for better or worse, and subject to change, this is my answer:

---

[13] These are outlined in Appendix II. Spirituality refers to that type of spirituality that is ethical, has integrity, and is deeply sincere and non-religious — spiritual behaviour that stands the test of very close scrutiny — the type that we "ought" to aspire to.

You are a sexual being, in a physical body, trying to be a spiritual entity, in a human context, within a limited but unknown segment of eternity. Even without dysfunction and abuse, or addictions and a selfishly oriented ego, it's incredibly complicated.

As an addicted person getting recovered, somehow realize within yourself that simply learning and doing will not guarantee your becoming spiritual. Knowledge and action are not the solution—in its broadest sense, God (spiritual harmony) is. Be patient; labor with devotion for many years; live intimately with trusted loved ones. Respect the earth and all living things. Have an intimate long relationship with a mentor or therapist. And, in all of this, hold personal responsibility, truth, respect, humility, kindness, charity, and non-violence as the highest values. Labour with devotion and patience only to this end: through the maintenance steps be forever obedient to the five spiritual principles.

You will eventually cross some ubiquitous line and then sense, but only in hindsight, and only by embracing your ever-present frailties, that you are recovered. Some might then call you wise, many will resent you, and you will smile gently because, for you, it will be sufficient to quietly repose in the safety of knowing that the mysterious machinations of the universe are beautiful.

The Ordinary Alcoholic: Fact or Fiction?

When people stumble into a twelve-step group and begin to address their most obvious addiction, they suffer from terminal uniqueness. "You're not alone," is the resounding and often repeated refrain. It's meant to be reassuring and, to a large extent, it is. As newcomers, they may not be unique within the group of people getting recovered, but they are alone and isolated from their higher power, from themselves, and from others. Isolation from all things is the nature of addictions.

How often have you dimly or secretly sensed how profoundly alone you are in the whole mess called "your life"? Within the camaraderie of groups there's an unnamed isolation. It's too big to handle, and too frightening for the socializing glad-handers to acknowledge.

I recall a wonderful story called *The Loneliness of the Long Distance Runner*.[14] Our lives are a lonely, long distance run, which is, in many aspects, an essential and healthy component of a spiritual life. Fears, myths, and fanatic commitment to superficial social interaction repress the truth of spiritual loneliness. We're born and die alone; we must each look after ourselves as best we can (by our self); we realize we are separate from every-

---

[14] Allan Sillitoe, *The Loneliness of the Long Distance Runner*, Plume/Penguin Books, 1992.

one else, and no amount of self-help or giggling social interaction is going to change this sense of alone-loneliness. This type of authentic loneliness is looked after—we cope with this, by being true to our own, individual natures and passions. When I am truly me, not some extension of cultural or familial expectation, then this sense of alone-loneliness is quite pleasant.

A significant part of *un*healthy loneliness and fear is trying to be something I'm not. Here, I am separated from you (as I described above), and I am also separated from myself. That's painful loneliness. The more I am culturally obedient, or the more I am controlled by the expectations of others, especially family and lovers, the more I am painfully lonely. This is, of course, inculcated and deepened by people explaining, often in a patronizing way, that we don't *have* to be lonely, just smile more and try harder, which means being more obedient to social values and not respecting yourself. They tell us it is our own fault; that we misunderstand, or we're wrongly focused, so when we feel lonely we were at fault for feeling that way.

When I discovered and carefully examined the contradictions I was being fed, sorted out the dilemmas, and puzzled through the paradoxes, I was able to see that very often other people's claim that they weren't lonely was a sham. Being gregarious, telling ribald or racist stories, orchestrating practical jokes, bragging about acting out, talking loud, getting laid a lot, belligerent celibacy, gossiping, teasing, staying in the adrenaline of a chaotic life, constantly regenerating the life of a victim—all of these behaviours merely keep the loneliness at bay. It's difficult to confront the socially imposed, long-believed-in myth that isolation and loneliness are curable. They aren't; they're modifiable.

True Spiritual pilgrims eventually understand and accept the essential isolation and loneliness inherent in a Spiritual life, which is remarkably different from the relationship-addicted loneliness that people "in recovery" experience most of the time. Spiritual loneliness in a life of devotion to a higher power always carries fulfillment and love within it.

It is also difficult to accept and enjoy that life is randomly benign. Calamity is never ever directed at anyone personally. This aspect of life has been identified for thousands of years (by many wiser than I) and cannot be dismissed without the presence of some self-serving agenda. Struggling to see what signs "God" may reveal in the mundane trivia of life, or to understand the spiritual message in random successes or calamities, are ego-driven exercises in vanity. These trivialize both the human spirit and "God". All of life's circumstances are opportunities to demonstrate integrity and responsibility, which takes a spiritual life beyond all temporal coincidence and any definition of God.

In my own struggle to fit in, I had to go through several transitions. Yes, I belonged to a group and I fit in, but secretly I believed I really didn't. I participated and shared until it hurt, and took everybody's advice so I would be liked—and stayed lonely. After years of confusion, and using intellect and arrogance to conceal the fear and doubt, I cut back on my social participation in my support group and began to study the original twelve-step texts, *Alcoholics Anonymous*[15] and *Twelve Steps and Twelve Traditions*.[16] I was determined to find out what was so powerful about the original twelve steps when they were done exactly as suggested. I sensed there were strong and familiar aspects of the perennial spiritual philosophies, but they were hardly visible beneath the social hype and psychobabble within groups.[17]

I think it was M. Scott Peck who said that as future generations look back on the 20th century, it wouldn't be nuclear fission they remark on; it will be Alcoholics Anonymous and what happened to the world because of it. Considering the changes in the politics of twelve-step groups, it won't be the groups so much as the original literature. What is it that makes Mr. Peck's statement true? For better or worse, that's what I set out to discover.

What I eventually learned, among other things, was that I was an ordinary person, with or without my addictions resolved. In the literature I was encouraged to openly establish my own ethical spiritual pilgrimage. At the same time, many people expected me to embrace the hype and drama in meetings, repeat the clichés as if they had substance (they don't), and endorse spiritual irresponsibility. I wanted to *be* ordinary, and not do those things, but most twelve-step people rejected me for it.

Principles Before Personalities (maybe)

In the world of twelve-step programs, thousands of times each day people ask one another: "How long have you been sober?" or "How long have you been clean?" The only answer is "one day," but there's a hierarchy within the meetings that denies this—the status and social reputation that's associated with celebrating dry dates and abstinence anniversaries. Key

---

[15] *Alcoholics Anonymous* refers to the book published by Alcoholics Anonymous World Services, Inc., third edition, seventh printing, 1980. Alcoholics Anonymous in Roman script refers to the groups.

[16] *Twelve Steps and Twelve Traditions*, published by The AA Grapevine, Inc. and Alcoholics Anonymous World Services, Inc., 1983.

[17] There are underlying and recurring themes in authentic spiritual disciplines, and in some religious theology (but obscured by religious dogma). These are variations or interpretations of virtues—compassion, veracity, a universal energy cohesiveness (*"It"*), and humility. These are a perennial and recurring philosophy in what is considered "good" conduct. There is all manner of arrogance and debate about how these themes do or don't apply within religion.

fobs, medallions, marbles, poker chips, parties, cards, and cakes have become more important than spirituality.

Someone will always put you on notice where you fit in the ubiquitous pecking order. A measure of amazement or a tone of awe can be heard in the gossip about the local twelve-step legends. In some meetings special chairs are actually reserved for "sobriety dinosaurs," which is often nothing more than avoiding an old-timer's petulance should they not be treated with reverence.

Most introductory social conversations will include, besides names, information on drug of choice, alcohol of preference, home group (especially if it has any historical status or local legend attached to it), and the infamous sober or clean date. There's often information on who the respective sponsors are (especially if the sponsor is a local "character") or how many people each person is sponsoring—all to establish the recovery pecking order. The theme of personalities before principles is as pervasive as it is real.

Then, there are "The Hunters"—those men and women in twelve-step or self-help groups who peruse and cruise for relationships, people to sponsor, sex, marriage partners, jobs, transportation (anywhere), loans, housing, food, someone to look after them, or someone to look after. These hunters, whose opening conversations exaggerate or minimize status, depending on what they are hunting for, will work either end of the status game to gain advantage.[18] Any of these defeat any hope of being spiritual. I've often commented that in just about any twelve-step group it's easier to find a wife, a husband, or a good deal on a used car than it is people with dependable, sound, spiritual qualities. It's sad. Really.

Another status tactic is creating a spectacular, flamboyant story and telling it *repeatedly*. Tales of violent adventures, extreme suffering-and-degradation, sexual embarrassment, graphic descriptions of insanity and reprehensible behaviour, are all gambits that actually defeat the purpose of sharing. This doesn't promote belonging; it subverts it, creates isolation, and clearly establishes another pecking order. Sensationalism defeats spirituality and creates distance, not intimacy.

Everyone who hears these stories of flamboyant degradation is affected in some unhealthy way. Those who are of a spiritual nature might notice a poignant sadness at the emptiness of it all and the harm it causes. Those who resist flamboyance or have more gentle sensibilities are often offended, and some become decidedly uncomfortable about their own non-

---

[18] The "humble" end of the status game is: "I'm not special, and we are all equal and clean only one day," as the old-timer hits on yet another newcomer for something (usually sex). The arrogant end of the status game is: "Yes, I've been sober much longer than you, so I'm offering my experience and wisdom to help you along, you poor thing."

dramatic story. Others shame themselves: "I didn't have it *that* hard; I should have quit sooner," or they criticize themselves and demean their own feelings: "I didn't have it that bad. What have I got to talk about?" Others confabulate or lie to match the notoriety by aggrandizement, and others say nothing and withhold a simple heartfelt story to avoid looking as if they are whining complainers.

The specific *and* indirect guidelines for sharing at meetings, according to AA, are: (i) we share in a general way what we used to be like, what happened, and what we are like now (not what we did), (ii) we must drop the word *blame* from our speech and thought; and (iii), the message of a spiritual awakening (not the message of our chaotic autobiography and the crazy, mean, nasty people in our lives).[19]

There are many honest, emotionally moving *ordinary* stories of pain in addiction that are, by implication, demeaned by the purveyors of excess. Grand stories of debauchery, conquest, violence, abuse, racism, sexism, trainloads of alcohol, degradation, and escapades of crime, when recast as humor and presented as entertainment, are seriously damaging. Flamboyance defeats spirituality and entrenches cliques and isolation. When you hear this, don't laugh. The tellers are expressing deep insecurity and shame. They need compassion, not applause.

There's another type of subtle, petulant uniqueness that often runs unchallenged. Yes, newcomers belong and are "understood" by those in the group, but they are too often manipulated into believing the quiet rumor that nobody "out there" understands. Twelve-step "insiders" are special, and people outside twelve-step groups didn't care, don't understand, don't want to care, wouldn't help if they could, or can't help. Addicts petulantly lick their collective wounds, and thereby create the "Evil Blue Meanies"[20], labeling various outsiders as stupid, mean, selfish, cruel, and inept.

Many addicts proudly wear an invisible badge of "The Heroic Minority of Recovering Addicts". This attitude is easily reframed into, "I'm a good person for doing this and you're not because you're not doing it," yet another isolation tactic. This self-congratulatory attitude all too often ends with bragging about being dedicated to spirituality and helping others. This is arrogance, camouflaged by false humility and rhetoric about carrying the message.

All of these are variations on a theme: personalities before principles. In this pervasive oppression any chance of sincere spirituality is lost. Groups and members cling to the illusion of moral superiority—they're

---

[19] These three guidelines are found in *Alcoholics Anonymous* (p. 58/59), and in *Twelve Steps and Twelve Traditions,* in that book's chapter on Step 4.

[20] The Evil Blue Meanies is a phrase taken from the AA pamphlet *A Member's Eye View of Alcoholics Anonymous,* Alcoholics Anonymous World Services Inc., 1970.

actively seeking "God," "spirituality," "healing," and everyone else really needs to do this too. This arrogance justifies hiding in recovery groups, avoiding step work and spirituality, and condemning the community at large. It successfully maintains a destructive isolation inside recovery, which is a core issue of all addictions.

The pecking orders of moral superiority and entitlement are rigidly enforced. There is always someone nearby who will compete using their own more ribald or spectacular story, or spiel off slanderous details of the unsympathetic, uncaring "Normies" that reside outside of the twelve-step membership, or subtly put you on notice that abstinence seniority harbors wisdom and carries political privilege. The fact of the matter is that the principles before personalities principle is held in low regard.[21]

What dovetails with this is a sometimes well-concealed arrogance about helping others. In the process of becoming recovered, newcomers are unknowingly duped by people in the program who pretend to "know" but don't (people who spout recovery rhetoric); or people who hope they know but conceal that insecurity (dishonest about their lack of faith and experience); or by still others who know they don't know what they're talking about, but claim they do and just don't care (cruel indifference). The more I learned about all of this, the more I appreciated the fascinatingly unique symptoms of the disease of addictions.

Addicts, with some degree of belligerence, often decide something is untrue for no other reason than they don't like it. At other times they refuse to admit the truth of something to avoid embarrassment, such as when they learn that something they've believed in is false. They're insecure and manipulate others to agree with them so they, themselves, feel more secure. When I first recognized these traits in myself, I expected to encounter similar behaviour from people who, like me, were in the initial stages of their recovery. I didn't expect it from those who had been around for a while, and I was shocked out of my naiveté by many old-timers who claimed to be on a spiritual path but weren't.

An ego is resourceful and tenacious in clinging to old ideas—a non-spiritual exercise in being right. Other people's attempts to avoid their own insecure loneliness by telling me to get involved, to get social, to smile more, to take responsibility for not trying hard enough, used to arouse my suspicions of myself. It now arouses gentle curiosity about them.

As I began to understand and experience what could happen through the process of meticulously following the original twelve-step path, and saw the beauty inherent in the universal principles of spirituality (which are contained within the original twelve-step writing and in the wiser perennial philosophies), I knew there was profoundly more available to me than membership and isolation in a terminally unique subculture. My own dissatisfaction with the changing atmosphere in twelve-step groups, and a rising philosophical conflict, set me on a journey.

When I would discuss some aspect of the original twelve steps that took me out of this addicted, political/spiritual isolationism, and into the greater spiritual community, I would almost always be dismissed, ignored, or argued with. Rarely would anyone listen with any real interest. I assumed that I was being arrogant in how I presented what I believed were profound truths. Later I realized that those who criticized me were envious or insecure, and they circumvented their feelings by making me wrong—just as they did with people outside twelve-step programs.

There is something timeless and profound about the original twelve-step path. Most people, although they have the instructions, miss it almost completely. There is a perennial philosophy at work there, but to me, very sadly, people get abstinent, get popular, get employed, get socially alive, and remain spiritually dead. They, as with almost everyone else in this culture of compliance, get caught up in expedience, clamoring for power, and the "what God-is-or-isn't" debate. The underlying presence of fear and peer pressure in modern culture forces them to become righteous, or remain perpetually vague. Either posture accomplishes nothing spiritual.

By questioning not so much what I was doing, but what I was told to do, and by entering therapy[22], studying the literature, and learning to trust my own intuition (which I had been too afraid to speak openly about to others), I identified myths and misconceptions that were being touted as "program." As I studied the perennial philosophies of "spirituality," I found similar, subtle themes in the original twelve steps. I noticed, beginning immediately in Step One, respect for the body-temple, veracity, and responsibility[23], three of the five spiritual principles. I struggled to become voluntarily obedient to the principles embodied in the twelve steps, and recognized themes from other spiritual disciplines. I realized in the secret

---

[21] *"This odd trait of mind and emotion..."* and *"This subtle and elusive kind of self-righteousness... ,"* *Twelve Steps and Twelve Traditions*, p. 94.

[22] I was fortunate to meet and work with Dr. Rowan Scott who, at that time, although not strongly informed about twelve-step groups, worked in helping me to examine and understand the exclusive and inclusive aspects of his expertise (therapy) and my "expertise" (the twelve steps). That work was invaluable. Thank you, Rowan.

[23] Most people in twelve-step programs avoid obedience and responsibility like the plague, and yet these personal commitments to ourselves form the essence of integrity. Without these two qualities there is no access to spirituality. See Appendix II, Five Spiritual Principles.

dark corner of my heart that I had a place in the world's pilgrimage. I was deeply relieved.

The world, as an entire system, is stronger and more beautiful than the sum of its parts. This is synergy—a synchronistic energy where all parts have a vital function to keep the whole thing operating. A mosquito, an elephant, a person, a tree... everything has a vital role. Synergy: we each contribute to the total effect of this amazing (to humans) planet.

Addicts are a part of that synergy—they contribute to it—but where do they fit? If addicts or people in early recovery buy into the historical, *cultural* perspective of addictions, there's shame and isolation—they lose. If they buy into the current twelve-step myth that they're unique and "outsiders" can't help them, they're arrogant and isolated—they lose.[24] If twelve-step people participate in the social hypocrisy rampant in their groups, they may be popular but won't become spiritual—they lose. Any of these take them out of that universal synergy.

My work and presentations, and this book, are my explanation of how to escape these destructive and isolating traps. It's okay that I had addictions. The world is mine, too. I contribute to the beauty and strength of the universe. My struggle for spiritual integrity is no different than the struggles of billions of other people over thousands of years.

With increasing frequency over the years, people asked for transcripts, for reference handouts, for permission to record my presentations. There have been hundreds of demands for a book. I was at first flattered and embarrassed. When questioned about what stopped me from writing this book, I made excuses about being very busy or that I was fine-tuning the research material. I would patronize or stall; silently wrapping myself in the convenient myth that people like "me" didn't know how to handle success (arrogantly presuming my book would be successful). It wasn't that I couldn't handle success (or failure). I was afraid of being held accountable. I would rationalize that there was no need to write this—if I could figure it out, others could too; they just didn't want to. So...

Why Bother?

There have been books upon books written about counselling and addictions. It would appear there is too much *writing* about it and not enough *doing* about it, and yet here's another book. Why bother?

Over the years, as I became more aware of my life's journey and became more aware as a therapist (the journeys are the same), I've repeatedly

---

[24] There is no such thing as an "outsider". We all have a membership in the Everybody's A People Club, whether your ego likes it or not. Gracefully accepting this is spirituality in action.

encountered a series of problems that manifest in different ways, but can usually be reduced to:

- poor client/newcomer individuation with counsellors, sponsors, and communities too invested in the success or failure of the newcomer's process;
- difficulty in transposing theoretical concepts into cognizant therapeutic interventions and definable spiritual behaviours, which if reduced, would make the process of exiting addictions into spirituality a more tangible reality;
- people unnecessarily complicating, or irresponsibly simplifying, the requirements of the steps of the original twelve-step program. The consequences are more deeply entrenched confusion, failure, and self-perceived repetitive inadequacy, which altogether reflect the hopeless confusion and failure in untreated addictions;
- various myths, illusions, delusions, social success equations, and acquisitions of tenuous sobriety, that are promoted in groups and by sponsors and professionals as "spirituality"; and,
- a debilitating shift of responsibility for addictions and the consequences of an addiction (derivative damage, if you will) away from the addict onto community, family, or life circumstances.

It never fails that some of the pain that needs to be resolved in people who struggle in twelve-step groups isn't related to (historical) emotional or physical trauma *per se*. It's also related to the confusion and sense of failure that arises from contradictory information that is presented, and emotional abuse that is perpetrated by self-styled, self-help gurus, unspiritual sponsors, righteous religious officials, and poorly trained or still-wounded professionals. This is compounded by the client/newcomer's complete inability to confront the subtle contradictions and abuse from people who hold themselves out as caring and capable. It exacerbates and entrenches the newcomer/client's shame at believing they're inadequate. This engenders a pervasive fear of relapse, reinforces mistrust, and perpetuates a self-defeating confusion.

Caregivers, sponsors in self-help groups, therapists, doctors, counsellors, and spiritual advisors—anyone in addictions-treatment—are charged with the paramount responsibility to do no harm. It appears that too many of them haven't done enough work on themselves to enable them to help addicts without abuse and interference.[25]

People with addictions (especially relationship addiction, and all addicts are inherently relationship addicts) have pervasive fear, mistrust, shame, and pain to some serious degree. These are (a) manifested in a need to control, and (b) noticeably worsened by the attempted short-cuts to spirituality embodied in the myths and psychobabble that permeate many twelve-step groups and consulting rooms. Many people, who are caregivers, and twelve-step spiritual pilgrims beyond the stage of newcomer, perpetuate these myths. They evince pervading fears of relapse, recidivist acting-out, obsessive hyper-vigilance, repeated attempts to maintain environmental control (other people are a part of the environment), a noticeable lack of spiritual self-discipline, dishonesty, phasic addiction substitutions to a consistent and unsettling degree, and demand newcomers comply with self-indulgent and arbitrary rules.[26]

For over 20 years I have focused my studies, healing, and spiritual inquiry not so much on the assumption that I didn't get it right or that I didn't try hard enough, which is what I was told often enough, but on the distinct possibility that I may have been misled, both within the twelve-step community and the culture at large. I discovered that I had been offered myths as truths, and had often allowed myself to be manipulated into someone else's spiritual insecurities.

I soon became too impressed by the confidence, clarity, and spiritual truths that I read in *Alcoholics Anonymous* and *Twelve Steps and Twelve Traditions* to believe that the petulance, bitterness, and spiritual shallowness I witnessed in meetings was the best that I could hope for. Being "accepted" by others because I allowed them to manipulate me into agreeing with them was no longer acceptable. Within twelve-step groups, the amount of peer pressure that's exerted through gossip and covert ostracism to ensure cooperation, all the while denied by loud rhetoric about love and tolerance, is staggering.

I know that some people will soundly disapprove of both myself and this book. They may accuse me of telling tales out of school; interpret my observations as harshly judgmental, or express disbelief and angry dis-

---

[25] Regarding addictions treatment: Certainly there is significant pain from addictions, and everyone carries varying degrees of unresolved developmental/family trauma. In the last twenty years these are very often exacerbated by the confusion, conflict, contradictions, and hypocrisy that is more and more prevalent within the healing community in general, and within twelve-step groups in particular.

[26] This is *some*times related to an undiagnosed and subtle anxiety disorder or learning disability. For an insightful and important view of the influence that family of origin, addictions, and stress have, see *Scattered Minds,* by Gabor Mate, Alfred A. Knopf (Canada), 1999.

agreement. I had to develop the courage to contend with patronizing dismissal (by people with more education), condescension (by people with more sober time), overt rejection (by people who are fanatical about some other belief system), and disrespect from insecure people who need to punish me for breaking their rules.

Years ago, in anticipating these responses, I was afraid to share my ideas and beliefs through a book. I delayed responding to the needs of those people who asked for help, by way of my writing this, and who asked out of a genuine interest and desire to learn more and change.

This book puts a name to what is happening, and provides clarity through detailed information about the spiritual intricacies of the original twelve steps. This book is neither an improvement nor a short cut. It explains what monumental work is involved, and offers spiritually oriented alternatives that challenge the ineffective pop-psychology or traditional religious values that permeate twelve-step meetings. I encourage a shift to hold spiritual principles as the highest value. I am living up to my commitment to hundreds of people who asked for this book so they could carry these ideas with them. And, finally, I wrote this book to continue to live within the five spiritual principles myself.

Many times I resisted writing this, and at times I decided not to complete it and hid the manuscript away from view. As much as I sometimes tried to ignore it, I couldn't. It seemed that writing this book was the job that I had been given to do.

Chapter 2

General Information Important to Getting Recovered

In order to apprehend what someone is up against in getting recovered, it is necessary to examine many topics that are directly and indirectly associated with addictions and spiritual transformation. This requires that I explore various topics that are apparently unrelated to Step One. They are grouped into this chapter. Before someone can wisely re-educate (which I will discuss later) and discipline themselves into being recovered, they must first unravel the misinformation and dislocation that pervades twelve-step groups and treatment programs.

Walled Up Consciousness

Expending the energy to beat yourself into an all-encompassing addictive mess takes a sustained effort over a long period of time. Being a successful addict of any kind is very hard work. In telling about a different type of chaos and pain, Matthew Arnold wrote a poem called *Dover Beach*. The last stanza of that poem is:

> *Nor certitude, nor peace, nor help for pain;*
> *And we are here as on a darkling plain*
> *Swept with confused alarms of struggle and flight,*
> *Where ignorant armies clash by night* [1]

I am of the opinion that this about best describes the confusion people face when they set out on a journey to get recovered from addictions.

Life is dark. You don't know where to turn. Nothing is certain. Everything hurts. You're confused. You hear opinions about therapy and twelve-step programs and God and the medical model of addictions and abstinence and spirituality and self-help books and sharing and your ego and your inner child, and it just doesn't seem to stop. You hear opinions about Narcotics Anonymous and Emotions Anonymous and Smokers Anonymous and Alcoholics Anonymous and Overeaters Anonymous and Cocaine Anonymous

---

[1] *The Poems of Matthew Arnold*, Matthew Arnold, Oxford University Press, 1961, p. 212.

and Debtors Anonymous and Gamblers Anonymous, and many others.[2] They're all publishing their own reference/text books and it just doesn't seem to stop. There's Sex Addicts Anonymous (SAA) and Sexaholics Anonymous (SA) and Sex and Love Addicts Anonymous (SLAA). If it's a sex-addiction, which twelve-step group should you belong to? Alternatively, is your problem a relationship addiction (which hides under the label "codependence"), and should you also attend CODA or ACOA or Alanon or Naranon?

At the core of it all, there's this thing called *spirituality*. What about you and your spirituality? Do you have to deal with the low or the high "perspective" of being an Anglican, or is that Episcopalian if you're in the U.S.? Are you the Catholic version of being a Christian, and is that Orthodox or Roman? Don't forget Presbyterian, Alliance, Gospel, Unity, Baptist, the all-faith churches, Unitarians, Jehovah's Witnesses, and the United Church (only in Canada). What *exactly* is Christianity, really? What about Buddhism? Being Sikh? Being Jewish? Being Muslim? Being Wiccan? Shamanism? Hinduism? Jainism? Baha'I? Of course there's God (which is more specific than a Higher Power), and The Goddess, Tao, Allah, Mother Earth, the Atman-Brahmin, YHWH, and many hundreds of other names to choose from.

Is that spirituality with a religious or non-religious focus? Is it spirituality that is apophatic or kataphatic?[3] What about meditation—is it transcendental, mystical, or a meditation on wisdom (Step Eleven)? What *exactly* is Step Eleven meditation, anyway? Is the Step Seven prayer petitionary, as opposed to contemplative? Which style of prayer should you be doing? Does it matter? Are you praying in the style of whichever tradition that you may or may not be temporarily attached to? Maybe you're angry at praying in the tradition you were raised in, or feeling guilty for not praying before you go to bed. Do you have to?

All of this is dark, confusing, and threatening to people in twelve-step programs; it can't not be. It's so threatening and overwhelming that most veterans of twelve-step groups barely scratch the surface of spirituality. People aspire to only the absolute minimum so they can appear "devoted" while they, themselves, remain lost, confused, and preoccupied with forni-

---

[2] These names, and others similar to them, refer to twelve-step groups and organizations.

[3] Kataphatic approaches place a high value on the content and images of spiritual experiences; Apophatic approaches place a high value on the consciousness aspect and argue that content and images are a hindrance. Most popular religions including Hinduism and the religious versions of Buddhism are kataphatic. Zen and many of the truly mystic disciplines are apophatic. For an insightful and detailed exploration of spirituality and psychology read *Will & Spirit, A Contemplative Psychology*, by Gerald G. May, Harper & Row Publishers, 1982.

cation and shiny things. This is dangerous, for the experienced members are the sponsors and role models of spiritual commitment.

The point lost in all of this is that the original twelve-step literature is very specific. The goal is to get recovered and to be sincerely spiritual, eventually living a life that reflects the will of a higher power, and being spiritually disciplined in every area of life, *and* to do this willingly and joyfully. Sadly, this appears to be less and less of what is actually happening.

In spite of the blatant spiritual dislocation within twelve-step programs, I believe what keeps addicts coming back are a glimmer of realization that there's something for them in twelve-step programs, and whatever that may be, they can get it nowhere else. In its broadest sense, a psychic shock happens, and crossing the threshold into "recovery" becomes possible. Regardless of how nebulous, vague, or distant, they sense it and search for it. But, because they don't really know what they're looking for, can't see what they're supposed to be looking for, and don't know how to look; and because there are so few people to turn to for sound twelve-step *spiritual* guidance, they flail away at spirituality and end up with mediocre recovery or socially approved addictions—both unfulfilling at best.

In the late 1930s *Alcoholics Anonymous* developed a method to get recovered from alcoholism. By the early 1940s, AA[4] was only a few years old, and the method it presented for alcoholics to become spiritual was still largely an experiment and not well trusted. Over the next 35 years, the original twelve steps and the "self help" groups that embody them were proven effective and reliable.[5] Now, almost 80 years later, that history, which borders on legend, is an attraction to those who follow.

Regarding counsellors at treatment centres, therapists who offer specialized services, and sponsors—many attempt to take the proven process of the original twelve steps and re-work it into a brand of psychological healing. Unless these people are exceptionally clear on both what the mandate of a twelve-step program is (spirituality), and what the mandate of therapy is (which varies considerably), and are at the same time generally healed themselves (and at the very minimum absent of all addictions), any program

---

[4] AA is the coveted acronym that represents Alcoholics Anonymous (the groups and people). *Alcoholics Anonymous,* in italic script, refers to that group's reference text, cited at an earlier footnote.

[5] Twelve-step programs are not self-help. "Self-help" *groups* don't exist. If you belong to a group that helps and supports you, it's not self-help. There are times when the phrase "self-help" is used to brag about vigorous independence from everyone (which is often a dysfunctional symptom of addiction). More often, self-help is used to mean that lay people are doing something without the aid of a professional, and there's often a prideful and belligerent exclusion of "professionals" when touting their healing endeavors. There is no such thing as self-help. All our successes, in every endeavor, are interdependent to some noticeable degree.

they devise that combines these processes will backfire. The people seeking help from them will be damaged more than they already are.

Despair from repeated, failed efforts to combine and negotiate therapy and twelve-step recovery is far too common. Addicts are being sold a bill of goods that suggests there's a combined, expedient process. There's no expedient process. And, unless the counsellor (or sponsor) is well informed, treasonably healed, and spiritually insightful and adept the newcomer/client gets lost.

To be recovered from addictions—to become spiritually disciplined via the original twelve steps—is long, hard, delicate, painstaking, and (up to Step Seven) painful. Addicts are so unique in their requirements for healing that any heavy-handed, generic intervention is doomed. The individual's special needs are primary. Certainly, recovery-communities and support networks are elemental to success; but more importantly, there must be a significant focus on individual uniqueness in spiritual endeavor. Considering that we are playing with lives here, no less than surgeons do in operating theaters, delicate touch, prudence, and consideration of the individual are paramount in addictions treatment.

I believe that many service providers, and most people in twelve-step programs, deliver ineffective services. They don't understand the mutually exclusive dynamics of "successful" therapy and acquiring spiritual discipline through the original twelve steps. What works in one discipline is often detrimental if applied in another. They complement each other like salt and pepper but cannot be substituted for each other.

When the lecture series that led to this book was in its early stages, I was astonished (and still am today), that the majority of addictions-affected people "in recovery" could articulate nothing substantive about the phenomenon that was killing them—beyond being glib about drinking or drugging. I drew a parallel with the dark ages when people would die of disease and know nothing about it except superstition and myth.[6] Considering how epidemic addictions are, people still know very little about them, about spirituality, or about the difference between the therapy and the twelve-step programs people are expected to facilitate or participate in.

Knowledge dispels ignorance and is one element of awareness, but knowledge isn't awareness and it never substitutes for healing. Clients will often acquire knowledge and then quit therapy, presuming they're healed. Many "sober" addicts become counsellors and abuse their positions by using their education as "proof" of their health and wisdom. Practicing addicts "counsel" addicts, which is very often destructive and at best marginally

---

[6] The damage and destruction from addictions leaves me with no doubt we are facing an addictions-plague of epidemic proportions. Alcohol and drugs are only a very minor part of the problem.

effective, and everyone is left in deepening dislocation. Many professionals who live with secret or visible, socially approved addictions offer treatment that is harmful to those they claim to help. In all these circumstances the abuse is concealed under rhetoric, clichés, education, socially approved addictions, and socially approved dysfunction like greed, cult-like religions, aggression, and irresponsibility.

The poignant aspect is through unexamined stereotyping, addicts are too often viewed as incapable of change or morally weak, or otherwise "bad." Knowledge is withheld. No one informs them, which tends to abet denial (a symptom of the disease), and that works to preclude awareness.

This brings about a complex dynamic between the counsellor/therapist (or sponsor), the addict in recovery, and the bureaucracy of the treatment centre (if there is one), the specific dynamic of any recovery group, and the client's historical family-culture. All of this results in various inappropriate demands (too many or not enough), expectations (too high or too low), and accountability (not parallel with ability). This guarantees more damage and deterioration.

Taken together, this book and its companion volume *Facets of Personal Transformation*[7] are intended to take you from active addiction, through the original twelve steps and the related issues surrounding addictions, to being recovered (spiritual). At the end, you should be informed enough to differentiate clearly between a therapy and a twelve-step issue, to maintain healing integrity, and therefore achieve some notable success in getting recovered. These books should eliminate therapy and recovery-confusion so you'll know where you're [supposed to be] going, and what it approximately looks like when you get there.

As a client, my own first serious course of therapy began around 1982. I'd be talking to my sponsor about something and he'd ask: "Have you got your therapist's card?" I'd answer, "Yes." He'd say: "Phone him, I don't know anything about that." At other times I'd be sitting in my therapist's office and going on about my addictions. He'd push the phone towards me and say, "Phone your sponsor." I'd ask: "What do you mean, phone my sponsor? You're the psychiatrist." And he'd say, "Yeah, but I'm not an addict. Phone your sponsor."

My therapist, my sponsor, and I, with some stumbling about, became clear on each of our roles. Of course, it ended up that my role was to do all the work of healing myself, which, if the truth were known, annoyed me to no end. Those were days of sometimes-petulant struggle—me trying to get those two men to indulge my perception of my own inadequacy. I wasn't

---

[7] *Facets of Personal Transformation* is scheduled for publication in late 2011.

inadequate to the tasks and they didn't indulge me. This was my first (very strange) experience of being in non-codependent relationships (read non-addicted). I began to see both the profound and the subtle distinctions between therapy and spirituality.

Addicts cling desperately to justifications for acting out and have an endless supply of reasons for blaming others. They are brilliant at external-izing responsibility.[8] Irresponsible behaviour manifests itself in countless ways.

Irresponsibility is secretly hoping/praying that love will go right, food will taste good, bills will get paid, or that someone will arrive with a pana-cea for all your ailments. Irresponsibility is waiting for a benevolent hero to hold your hand and tell you it's okay to do whatever you want; or searching for someone who has a magic formula or secret mantra or a magic blue pill to make spiritual discipline easy. Irresponsibility is complaining about any-thing, especially that life hurts, your pain won't go away, people won't stop being mean to you, that it's someone else's fault, or that life isn't fair. These, and ten thousand variations of them, are all irresponsible. With irre-sponsibility, secret, subtle, or blatant, there can never be spiritual peace or true commitment to anything, intimate love will be absent, contentment will be tenuous, fulfilling sex will be unavailable, life will at best be mediocre, and "God" will never be trustworthy. For irresponsible people, the implaca-ble grandeur of life will be forever elusive.[9]

If, after some period of abstinence, people claim to be puzzled about suddenly ending up drunk; or plead they really couldn't help it that they committed adultery, lied, stole, seduced yet another newcomer; or are angry they had to declare bankruptcy because they mysteriously ended up in huge debt; or are particularly belligerent about honesty or spirituality, they are irresponsible. Their claims to have "suddenly" ended up in trouble, and the justifications for their irresponsibility, are not usually challenged in meet-ings. This is twelve-step political deal making at its best. Irresponsibility is spiritual cancer.

Drama & Pain

Addicts love drama—having crises, hardship, pain, love, angst, joy, and successes all larger than life. An ego controlled by addiction is espe-

---

[8] When addicts become curious about the freedom that's inherent in complete responsibility (which curiosity should begin to dimly appear at Step Four, and be marginally clear by Step Seven), they take responsibility and stop blaming others or finding fault elsewhere. Equally important, at the same time they cease feeling non-contractual guilt—they only feel as guilty as they've agreed to.

[9] *"For if there is a sin against life, it consists perhaps not so much in despairing of life as in hoping for another life and in eluding the implacable grandeur of this life."* Albert Camus, *The Myth of Sisyphus And Other Essays*, Vintage Books/Random House, 1991, p. 153.

cially relentless in finding ways to create and justify drama. Related to this is the self-serving arrogance associated with rewriting, editing, or rearranging the original AA steps, which often serves as an escape clause into drama.

Drama is created out of some authentic pain or insecurity, and is often evinced as a distorted sense of entitlement, harsh judgments, or comparisons: "I didn't try hard enough." "They didn't try hard enough." "My penis isn't big enough." "I'm not pretty enough." "My breasts are too small (or too big)." "I'm too tall (or too short)." "I can't run fast enough." "I'm too heavy." "I'm too horny, too often." "I've got bad teeth." "It's not fair..." "My car isn't fast/shiny/new enough." "I'm poor (or rich)." "...*And nobody understands the anguish I endure!*"

Creating drama is a way to add to, and intensify, already existing pain, anger, and shame. Once drama is created and goes unchallenged, there are two "types" or sources of pain within a person. There's the (first) insecurity/pain that became the set up for the drama, which will be buried underneath the (second) pain arising from the drama itself. The despair and pain arising from the drama is no "less painful" than the pain or shame that originally motivated it. All of a person's pain is experienced as real but for many people it arises from two different sources — trauma and drama.

Resolving the emotional (or physical) pain we experience is a priority. Strategies for resolving "authentic" pain are different from those for resolving pain that arises from drama. For pain from an authentic incident, with no drama attached to it, there's compassion, empathy, validation, problem solving, individuation, assertive re-framing, etc. However, when trying to resolve pain that's generated from self-created or imposed drama, there's a long-term crippling effect from using those afore-mentioned, traditional therapeutic pain-relief strategies.

In this context, with poorly trained, naïve, addicted, or still-wounded therapists, or with self-styled self-help gurus, or still-wounded/addicted sponsors (abetted by spiritually unfocused groups), using traditional "pain-relief" strategies for drama will validate the drama as externally authentic. It isn't; it's drama. The vicious complication is that this entrenches and reinforces the drama as real. [10]

Common therapeutic strategies for relieving emotional pain are only effective if the pain they are addressing is not based on drama. Resolving emotional pain where the origin of pain is rooted in drama (i.e. "dramatic" pain) requires a very different healing strategy. This is why so many therapies go on and on and on . . . and remain less than effective—the issue is

---

[10] Pain and shame from shock, emotional, or developmental trauma (see Appendix III) is authentic. Pain arising from drama is experienced as real; however, its origin is only "real" in relation to the self-generated or imposed drama, not to the original pain-causing circumstances.

drama and it's inauthentic. (It feels authentic, and is presented as authentic, but it isn't.) The therapist gets trapped in the drama and everybody goes nowhere.

To relieve pain caused by drama you must eliminate the drama, then that pain goes away. However, there's the horrendously complicated and delicate task of sorting out which pain is rooted in drama and which isn't.

Reducing drama is a very complex process. Drama "junkies" invariably have poor inter-personal boundaries, and often live by consensus. At the minimum, eliminating drama is directly related to taking complete personal responsibility, the explanation of which is part of the theme of this book.

Besides exaggerating for dramatic effect, there is often excessive minimizing for dramatic effect. In the midst of real calamity you hear: "Ah, it's *nothing*! My house burned down after the fire-insurance expired, someone stole my car, my partner left me, I lost my last pair of glasses so I can't read the instructions for my heart medication; and yes, I also lost my job, my wallet, and my dog died, and I can't afford bus fare to the Food Bank, but really, no problem, I'm fine." This ego-style creates drama by making legitimate hardship seem inconsequential.

I do not imply that all pain is dramatic. Pain and hardship are legitimate. However, the suffering arising from the drama; the plaintive wail, "Nothing's My Fault"; the justifications of the relationship-addicted martyr; the magnificent struggle of the twelve-step hero, are drama. And, of course, the bigger the drama, the harder it is to resolve the pain and to get started on organizing your life around abstinence and the five spiritual principles.[11] A client, after months of struggle, finally admitted, with a shy smile, that he was responsible for organizing his own unhappiness, as much as his own happiness, both of which included a responsibility to eliminate his own created drama.

Drama and irresponsibility are always directly or indirectly associated with a belief that Step One is in two parts. Greater complications and more drama are always the consequence.

Another issue that arises from dividing Step One into two halves is you get to marginalize the consequences of drinking or acting out. The speech goes like this: "Well, yes, I couldn't control my drinking [the first half], and of course my life was unmanageable [the second half], but my life is still unmanageable, so I guess unmanageability doesn't have very much to do with drinking. The drinking wasn't the problem it was the unmanageable life. If I learn how to manage my life, I guess I'll be able to drink." This rationalization is *carte blanche* permission to relapse. In any of this, character defects are never resolved, abstinence is never stable, and there's

---

[11] See Appendix II.

constant compensation to stay ahead of the fear. The compensation tactic is to create [more] unmanageability—drama.

When you extend yourself into a spiritual lifestyle, which is done by willingly committing to the requirements of the steps, it is for the most part to eventually become benignly indifferent to the transience of life's circumstances that you experience. Being spiritual is not to transcend them, but to lovingly ignore them in favor of the five spiritual principles. When you create drama, you avoid the reality of your own ordinariness. When drama is perceived as reality and you attempt to be spiritual without *first* eliminating the drama, the resulting "spirituality" becomes an extension of the drama and is either obsessive[12] or sentimental.[13] Your faith and relationship to the divine, usually through religious dogma, are then rooted in drama (delusion or illusion) and of little substantive value.

After any reasonable period of abstinence in a twelve-step group, what precedes any "relapse" is a combination of petulance, blaming, anger, and dishonesty. These are related to Isolation Thinking that is discussed in Chapter 11. This combination covertly guarantees the probability of relapse, but the reasons presented for the relapse are misrepresentations and cover-ups that are rooted in drama.

You wanted to teach someone a lesson (vindictiveness); you wanted to rub some misdemeanor in someone's face (righteous pride); you're not going to be told what to do (defiance); or you resent spirituality (arrogance; insecurity). These expressions of fear and insecurity are witnessed as character defects.

To admit your "drama" doesn't promote sympathetic responses from other drama junkies; however, a plaintive cry that you're trying really, really, *really* hard, and you didn't get the other half of Step One, is good for garnering sympathy. It's awkward to admit that the step is relatively simple, and embarrassing to admit you relapsed into your primary addiction because you were pouting and behaving irresponsibly.

Rights, Freedoms, and Values

The following exposition isn't directly related to the topics at hand. There isn't a smooth segue into it, but it is crucial and related to everything. In the realm of human relations, to achieve true intimacy and fulfillment,

---

[12] Religious devotion that arises out of drama, which includes the charismatic religions, or that is compensation for insecurity and character defects, usually manifests as obsessive, rigid, or arrogant. Intrusive proselytizing, fundamentalists, "born-agains", and fanatic "twelve-steppers" are evidence of this.

[13] Beware of the thwarted sentimentalist. Their viciousness when crossed is only exceeded by their phony benevolence and deeply camouflaged insecurities.

you need, probably more than anything else, to claim and offer your rights and freedoms.[14] You should have been offered them when you were an infant; before you knew you had them; before you even knew you were a person.

In all your relationships, with anyone, and especially in any healing transformation, muddy notions of dignity and ethics detrimentally influence your rights. Too often they are equated with legislated culpability.[15] Here are your rights in intimate, personal relationships:

- You have the right to say "No" without fear of malicious or punitive consequence. If you decline an invitation to participate or limit what you do or say, there should be no other-imposed harmful consequence.
- You have the right to expect confidentiality; what you say or do will be kept appropriately or respectfully private. Gossip is always a betrayal of trust. Confidentiality isn't limited to the legislated sanction of privileged information and it doesn't automatically mean keeping secrets. Confidentiality cannot masquerade as a device to perpetuate abuse, or to conceal reprehensible behaviour. To offer confidentiality is to offer respect.
- You have the right to your dignity and respect: you will not knowingly be shamed or humiliated, maligned, or misrepresented.
- You have the right to question or challenge anything that happens in relation to yourself or to those under your legitimate care. You have the right to ensure that you understand what's going on in relation to you.

Children live with authority figures that wield tremendous power. Hopefully their caregivers are loving and benevolent, since personal rights are only available to a child if they are generously offered by the authority figures that control the child's life. The time to learn to say "No" and to set boundaries is when you're three, not when you're 37 and sitting in a treatment centre.

As an adult, whether or not you have your rights and freedoms in relationships is a function of how you allow yourself to be treated (primarily by yourself).[16] Without them you can only act at being a grown-up.[17]

---

[14] This will be expanded upon in *Facets of Personal Transformation*.
[15] Legislated culpability means, in part, we let lawyers and politicians dictate our morality. Religious officials are politicians.
[16] See Appendix IV.

There are many insightful, pioneering books that are less than specific on definitions of codependence, and many early theories were long and somewhat inconsistent. As we discovered years ago, when trying to understand the many facets of addictions, codependence was a phenomenon that was not easily defined. However, it became clear that if you were an addict, you were codependent.[18] All codependence is some variation or combination of relationship addiction, sex addiction, or romance addiction.[19] If you are in Alanon, Naranon, ACOA, CODA, or some other similar twelve-step group, you're a relationship addict.

What's the connection to your rights? Briefly, and this is oversimplified: having limited or no access to your rights and freedoms; allowing someone to have emotional privilege over yourself, or demanding emotional privilege over others, indicates a relationship addiction.[20]

Attendant to your rights, you have this primary responsibility: *You are responsible to ensure that you offer these rights to others*; to offer them gracefully, as a matter of course. The fact that someone doesn't know their own rights (and freedoms) doesn't mean you have license to withhold them.

Out of your rights, which under ideal developmental conditions would have been offered to you freely and graciously by your caretakers, before you were old enough to know you had caretakers, you would have automatically evinced your freedoms. If you're given your rights, acquiring your freedoms is automatic. The first five of the six freedoms are from *Making Contact*, by Virginia Satir.[21] The sixth is my addition to the list.

(i)   *The freedom to see and hear what is here instead of what should be, was, or will be.*

(ii)   *The freedom to say what one feels and thinks, instead of what one should.*

(iii)   *The freedom to feel what one feels, instead of what one ought.*

(iv)   *The freedom to ask for what one wants, instead of always waiting for permission.*

---

[17] Many adults only mimic what they've seen other adults do and so they "act like grown-ups", whatever that means. They don't really have a clue about what "being" themselves entails, and can only make it up as they go along, which most often ends up with them in awkward and unfulfilling circumstances.

[18] See: *Co-Dependence, Healing the Human Condition*, by Charles L. Whitfield, M.D., Health Communications, Inc., 1991; and *Bradshaw on: The Family*, John Bradshaw, Health Communications Inc., 1988.

[19] *Escape From Intimacy*, Anne Wilson Schaef, Harper Collins, 1990.

[20] I will explore this in greater detail in *Facets of Personal Transformation*.

[21] *Making Contact*, Virginia Satir, Celestial Arts (Press), Berkley, CA, 1976.

(v)   *The freedom to take risks on one's own behalf, instead of choosing to be only "secure" and not rocking the boat.*

(vi)   The freedom to desire and create for one's own benefit, instead of catering to the wishes, demands, or expectations of others.

Rights and freedoms are embodied in the five spiritual principles.[22] Invariably, the people I've discussed rights, freedoms, and spiritual principles with have been vague on what they are, and very confused about how they might apply in relationships. No one I've ever spoken to, including professionals, has spoken of them in a manner that touched on substantively all of them.

A surprising number of people concerned with mentoring others into emotional health are genuinely puzzled and mumble some dismissive comment like, "Don't know, I never thought of it." Usually any discussion of these is vague and borders on legislated culpability or religious dogma. Work at having these perceptible, well defined, and visible in your life. Insist on them for yourself and offer them to others.

This is important: After a person lives with their rights for an extended period, they will naturally accrue their freedoms. The sequence is important: rights first, freedoms second. Only then can you figure out how you are to "be" not what you are supposed to "do".

These rights and freedoms are sometimes not available in politics and commerce. People knowingly surrender them in favor of some perceived gain. In political or contractual situations, or when facing danger and overt power, or with your employer, it may not be wise to demand your full compliment of rights and freedoms. Wisdom and priorities will govern your behaviour. Notwithstanding that, if you don't routinely have these in your intimate or sexual relationships, with your family and friends, you're in trouble. Those who deny you your rights and freedoms are also in trouble, but more importantly, you are for surrendering them.[23]

The only way we realize our potential is by living with our rights and freedoms, regardless of the cost. You may have to forego relationships with family, friends, or spouses, but unless you are willing to insist on your

---

[22] The five spiritual principles are respect for the body, veracity, humility, charity of spirit, and responsibility/obedience. These are explained in detail at Appendix II.

[23] An important addendum to rights and freedoms is values. After you've lived with your rights, and then your freedoms, you will graciously figure out and express what you value. What's important to you, what you value, is actually the true expression of the person you are. If you don't have your own rights and freedoms then what you value isn't something you have chosen, it's something imposed by outside authority figures. The sequence is rights —> freedoms —> values (who "I" am.) Values are explained in more detail in Appendix I.

rights and freedoms for yourself, you will remain unfulfilled. Do this: post your rights, freedoms, and your one responsibility somewhere prominent in your home and read them *out loud* every third day for six months or a year. Examine your relationships with *every*one and notice whether you insist on them for yourself. Who offers you these and who doesn't? Do you offer them freely to others? Estimate the cost of living without them.

What you value is evinced in how you are as a person. Should you have been raised in optimum circumstances, where rights were offered as a matter of course, and freedoms were available for you to claim, you would develop and adopt values that were determined by you. Again, this should have been done as you grew up, not when you're 43 and sitting in therapy. All practicing addicts, and too many abstinent ones, don't know what adopting values means, or how to go about doing that.[24]

When you live gracefully with your rights, are responsible, claim your freedoms, and adhere to your own values, all the while respecting these in others, you will experience a spiritual sense of "being." And, of course, being in *any* addiction makes all of this unavailable.

811 Facts About "Rigorous Honesty"

As a stated rule of conduct, rigorous honesty is so straightforward that it defies definition. However, you can study the AA literature to learn why it was important to those who wrote the books and memorize how many times rigorous honesty is referred. You can hunt for references to "withholding the truth to spare others". You can study dishonesty as a symptomatic aspect of addiction. You can research religious and psychological literature to learn how religious and secular authorities discovered honesty was important. In a couple of years, with all this studying, you would sound like a twelve-step guru, make wonderful speeches, and impress everyone with your 811 facts about rigorous honesty.

Even after all that, *you* are no closer to being rigorously honest yourself. You may have become an expert on the theoretical development and spiritual implications of honesty, but you remain dishonest. You would have the power of knowledge, and could make potent speeches about rigorous honesty, but still be an inveterate liar; no closer to being honest or spiritual yourself.

For the most part, the AA texts (excluding the personal stories) are revealed truths. That's why it's never necessary to rewrite them. After all, what's confusing about "rigorous honesty" or "a self-imposed crisis"? The required understanding is self-evident. The material doesn't need "under-

---

[24] Uncovering and abandoning old values and adopting new ones is a profound exercise unto itself. Changing values is discussed more specifically in Chapter 6 and at Appendix I.

standing", and bragging to anyone who'll listen that you're struggling to understand it is a diversion from the responsibility of doing it. I think of the thousands of times I've heard addicts complain they are not fulfilled within their life, and it's obvious they aren't following the instructions.

The only reason for participating in discussions about the AA textbooks is to figure out what you're doing that's contrary to the instructions. Don't investigate the instructions; investigate your disobedience to the instructions. Getting recovered is simply an exercise in obedience, (the "**O**" word again). A book-study is to understand yourself *vis-à-vis* why you're not willingly doing what you are told. Study the literature to understand why *you* are disobedient to the instructions and your life will take on a completely different texture.

In Step One, you begin to generate some commitment to obedience to the instructions. That small kernel of responsibility allows a belief at Step Two that will eventually transform your life into a sincerely Spiritual one. This is about your apprenticeship to spirituality—committing to the instructions in *Alcoholics Anonymous*, exactly as they're outlined. When listening to the opinions of others about addiction and recovery, regardless of their length of abstinence, education, or reputation to determine how closely their opinions follow *Alcoholics Anonymous* or *Twelve Steps and Twelve Traditions*. If their opinions are not contained within those books, be cautious about adopting their opinions. Your only real safety is in trusting people who willingly follow those instructions in a humble manner.

When you manufacture personal, anecdotal interpretations of spirituality and the steps, you are playing with your life: suicide gambling with a fatal illness. The consequences are devastating. Remember Matthew Arnold's poem:

> *Nor certitude, nor peace, nor help for pain;*
> *And we are here as on a darkling plain*
> *Swept with confused alarms of struggle and flight,*
> *Where ignorant armies clash by night.*

For addicts and alcoholics who are exhausted by the insanity and self annihilation of their illness; tired of the conflict, turmoil, shame, and anger; drained by the struggle to avoid the fear, they are to frequently remind themselves of the sentence on page 45 of *Alcoholics Anonymous*: *"Well, that's exactly what this book is about. Its main object is to enable you find a Power greater than yourself which will solve your problem."*[25]

The importance of obedience to the original twelve-step instructions cannot be overstated. They are designed specifically to resolve whatever it is within you that forces your extreme avoidance of spiritual discipline. Your addiction isn't evidence of how hard your life was or how badly you were mistreated, it's evidence of your separation from the spiritual realms of life.[26] The steps are intended to mentor you from the addictive, darkling plains of self-annihilation to spiritual health, not social success. Granted, some social success and stability accrue from doing the steps, but these are not what is intended, and are of no account in the matter at hand.

I offer an analogy that might show that this general theory of spiritual regeneration isn't new. In doing this, I'm not advocating for Christian hegemony. Saint Benedict (c. 480–547 CE) was the next major Christian spiritual influence after Saint Augustine, and is considered to be the founder of western monasticism. He established The Order of Benedictine Monks and wrote *The Rule of Benedict*, affectionately referred to as The Rule.[27] It is a short and profound manual that instructs how to transform the dislocation of daily life into a serene life via Christian beliefs—ethically practicing "a life in Christ". The Rule is about spiritual faith, love of God, charity, humility, and responsibility, not social accomplishment and popularity. It concerns itself with developing a devotion to God and maintaining a sense of spiritual community. Granted, this is over-simplified, but these are the themes.

In *Alcoholics Anonymous*, the theory is very similar: healing of the inner life of the alcoholic, and then developing a devotion to a higher power (of your own understanding). As evidence of the success of this, three major principles would operate:

(i) a life of abstinence and rigorous honesty (i.e. sincere humility in relationships);
(ii) service to a higher power by demonstrating spiritual principles in all activities; and,
(iii) carrying the message of spiritual transformation out of addiction to those people who are interested.

---

[25] Emphasis added. Notice it doesn't say, "...which will solve your parent's problem, which they passed on to you." Your addiction is always your spiritual problem, no one else's.
[26] Being spiritual does not mean you will have an easy life. At times, in spiritual realms, life is very difficult. The difference is in the underlying serenity with which you approach the "problems" of life, and having a benign indifference to the outcome.
[27] Many books have been written about *The Rule*. Two of my favorites are Esther de Waal's *Seeking God, The Way of St Benedict*, The Liturgical Press, 1984; and Joan Chittister's *The Rule of Benedict - Insights for the Ages*, Crossroad Publishing, 1992.

The original twelve steps are a *very* loose parallel to The Rule of Saint Benedict. [This is only to make a point about the perennial and recurring nature of spiritual transformation presented within the twelve steps. There are equally appropriate non-Christian spiritual alternatives. The steps also have ethical themes and responsibilities that are similar in aspect to The Four Nobel Truths of Buddhism.]

The cofounders did not invent the spiritual principles contained within the *Alcoholics Anonymous* program. The path of *Alcoholics Anonymous* is stylistically unique for a specific spiritual dislocation—addictions— effective and inspired, but the themes are not original, which is good.[28] Spiritual regeneration, the manner and path to spiritual integrity through inner cleansing, truth, responsibility, and humility, is at least 3000 years old. The AA cofounders did, however, tailor it to the specific needs of people with alcoholism (addictions). If you put into your life what *Alcoholics Anonymous* has to offer, you are adopting universal spiritual principles.[29]

Once Upon A Time

Consider that in all of the fairy tales we tell children, the poor person never goes to the rich person to find spiritual peace. It's always the king or queen leaving the castle going to the poor hermit in the cottage to learn of inner peace. There are powerful metaphors in this traditional motif that are reflected in the original twelve steps.

The direction of these "fairy tale" pilgrimages is always away from commerce and wealth (the pilgrim leaves the city or the castle), and towards poverty (to a humble cottage and a poor person). Spiritual pilgrimages are always away from crowds and groups (leaving parties and courtly celebrations), and involve traveling alone, over unused, faint paths, without a map, deeply into a dark forest (through the pilgrims' unknown insecurities and frailties), towards a single wise person (to solitude).

As evidence of this, Siddhartha Gautama, Yeshua, Benedict of Nursia, Gio, Francesco Bernardone (and many others) abandoned wealth or power to pursue spirituality.[30] Regarding spirituality, all of this implies that inner turmoil and non-fulfillment are always associated with *unnecessary* wealth

---

[28] Profound spiritual truths appear when they are needed to address specific issues at some particular time when humans become involved in grand-scale self-annihilation particular to their eras: *The Four Nobel Truths, The Sermon on The Mount, The Rule of Benedict,* The Protestant Reformation, The Twelve Steps, are examples of this. There are others.
[29] See Appendix II.
[30] Respectively, these people are The Buddha, Jesus of Nazareth, St. Benedict, and St. Francis of Assisi.

or political/social power.[31] This is an unalterable truth about lifestyle and spirituality.

The original twelve-step program isn't really concerned with 'social success' like employment and romance. It does stress the importance of personal responsibility, rigorous honesty, generosity, etc., regardless of your social position. The original program is only concerned with teaching you how to create and live a life of spiritual integrity embodied in the maintenance steps.

You start the journey by admitting you were powerless (over self-destructive, acting out behaviour)—that your life had become unmanageable. Step One is for you to admit your powerlessness *when you acted out*, and then by inference from your historical experience, to believe that if you act out again unmanageability will reappear. Out of the particulars of your past, you can reasonably anticipate the consequences of repeating old behaviours.[32]

Seeing and admitting your powerlessness through Step One is the fundamental *pre*condition to Step Two. Being able to understand what is required at Step Two is generally parallel to seeing a spiritual lifestyle (spiritual discipline) as the source of "power" that the addict doesn't have.

When Step One is diverted away from powerlessness towards family of origin and insight psychology, which is the present trend in twelve-step meetings, the fundamental nature of powerlessness remains vague and unrealized. This makes Step Two impossible to accomplish, which renders the remaining steps meaningless. They are all structured to access a higher power, not to enhance insight psychology.

Symptoms

The words in bold print in the next few pages identify attributes that all addicts manifest, in varying degrees, which, for the sake of this examination, might be called symptoms. These are all consistent with the phenomenon of addictions, and when all addictions are resolved, they largely disappear.

Acting out is engaging in any behaviour that is detrimental to yourself or others in any manner—**life-damaging consequences**. There are endless variations of minimizing or explaining away life-damaging consequences so addicts can maintain the illusion that they aren't addicts. One brief example

---

[31] Benevolence and wisdom are never justifications for the accumulation of power. This is an alteration of Alan Watts' general observation about our culture: *"…we feel justified in using dangerous powers when we can establish that there is a relatively low probability of disaster."* From *This Is It,* Alan Watts, Vintage Books, 1973, p. 152.

[32] The saying: "Insanity is repeating old behaviour and expecting different results," is a reflection of this.

is: "I'm not an addict. I know I'm unpredictable and I black out when I drink, but it's only two or three times a year." Infrequency is the *ex*clusionary excuse. Because you infrequently participate in destructive behaviour; because the life-damage is subtle, socially acceptable, or it appears no one is hurt does not exclude you from having an addiction.

Some life-damaging consequences, that are often not viewed as addictions-related, are contained in the failure to achieve common, universal social goals like graduating from high school, holding a job for longer than a year, staying out of jail, paying taxes, or buying a car. Not to achieve any one of these is not necessarily of itself a symptom of addiction; however, if not achieving the usual social accomplishments is the ambience of your life, there's a good chance you're addicted. Other life-damaging consequences and destructive patterns of addictions *might* be:

- divorce (one or many, it doesn't matter);
- contracting HIV/AIDS; other sexually transmitted diseases;
- some pattern of medical treatment regarding injuries from lifestyle;
- admission to psychiatric wards and treatment centres;
- unemployment, marginal or erratic employment, being fired;
- being negligent or irresponsible regarding children and significant others;
- sexual anorexia[33], promiscuity, using pornography, neurotic or belligerent celibacy, adultery, infidelity, erratic or moody sexual life-style, "hunting" relationships or sex through dating clubs, personal ads, internet sites, twelve-step meetings;
- erratic, inconsistent, or repetitively unfulfilling friendships and sexual relationships;
- some eating patterns and food relationships;
- inability to make and maintain commitments—regardless of whether it's in one or many areas of your life;
- violence, ongoing threats of violence, repetitive arguing and fighting, participating in violence in sports (vicariously as a spectator or as a participant), excessive competition;
- gossiping and bingeing on righteousness (self- or other-oriented righteousness, apparent in rigid religious beliefs);

---

[33] In sex and relationship addictions (and less often but sometimes in romance addictions) addicts go into a complex reaction—they react to their acting out addiction and shame by being sexually anorexic: NO SEX EVER! In a subconscious, emotionally violent response to sexual promiscuity that is destructive they do a hard-line 180-degree change and become sexually anorexic to control the sexually acting out destructive behaviour.

- being noticeably, frequently angry, rage binges, road rage;
- having your private life noticeably different from your public life—maintaining significant secrets about private attitudes and behaviour; impression management (fn. in Chapter 2);
- frequent trouble with landlords, creditors, relatives;
- recurring debt, financial instability;
- getting drunk or stoned, having black-outs, smoking;
- any drinking or drug use and driving;
- gambling, crime;
- shopping, buying, excessive working hours;
- compulsive exercise, preoccupation with body image, some cosmetic surgeries;
- isolation via reading, television, videos, computers, internet, etc.; and,
- obsessing and/or fanaticizing. This last one is entirely concealed and difficult to evaluate. Some addicts spend *most* of their waking life in fantasy and accomplish very little because of it.

To experience any one or two of these isn't necessarily indicative that you are an addict. If, however, you experience a few of these to any noticeable recurring degree, you are likely an untreated addict, or destructively compensating for some other serious problem.

Many people in twelve-step programs are abstinent from their obvious acting out (like alcohol and drugs) and still experience many of these destructive behaviours. Maintaining abstinence from only the obvious mood-altering experiences looks good, and often gives them a marvelous defense to avoid addressing the more socially acceptable or secret addictions: "Hey, I quit drinking, so get off my case about the smoking." "Quit complaining about six hours of TV every day; at least I'm not shopping on line every day." "So what if I rent a porn video once in a while; at least I'm not doing drugs anymore."[34] Poly-addictions are a given.

---

[34] Some people will take exception with my suggestion that using pornography "once in a while" is indicative of addiction. In my experience, it is. Since I haven't spoken to everyone who uses porn, I grant that it may not be in some rare occurrences. However, if not an addiction, it is unhealthy. Pornography sets imaginary standards of comparison; teaches objectification of people; and presents unrealistic expectations regarding responsibility and intimacy.

Another possible indicator of addiction is **neurosis**[35], although it isn't usually talked about as a part of an addiction. Neurosis is a mental/emotional disorder, characterized by strong inner conflict, which does not have an organic cause. The routine symptoms of neurosis are insecurity, anxiety, irrational fears, or depression but not to the degree that a person would be generally incapacitated. A neurosis leaves your inner life out of balance in an exaggerated way, although your outer life may appear reasonably normal.

For example: If someone casually observes that the color of your shirt doesn't quite match your jacket, then later, in private, you tear the shirt up and agonize for hours over the comment; or should you worry for an hour, trying on a dozen outfits to look "perfect" for a casual lunch with friends, and these are ongoing, secretly typical behaviours, you would be neurotic. No one would see the unreasonable, anxious behaviour in response to these everyday situations.

The anxiety and inner conflict must be significantly *dis*proportionate to the extant conditions, but a person can still function in community. It's often a limited participation because of the secret conflict and turmoil, and there's often little joy or pleasure in life, despite outward appearances.

Addicts, when they are acting out or in the early stages of recovery, and many people in twelve-step programs with extensive abstinence, are neurotic to some noticeable degree (noticeable in therapy; noticeable if we could view their secret thoughts and emotions, not usually noticeable in public life). Some neuroses are resolved in the normal course of getting recovered and going through proper twelve-step work, but the more serious ones aren't.

Denial, another requirement of addiction, is an unconscious, automatic ego defense mechanism (one of several), that's characterized by an inability to recall and acknowledge painful truths, realities, thoughts, or feelings. Denial is an unconscious, automatic mind-survival technique of "not remembering". All addicts have denial to some degree. [To all addicts: Congratulate each other that you're in denial, it helped you survive your self-imposed crisis so you could enter recovery.]

Repression is also common amongst addicts and is different from denial in that it begins with a more conscious, willful effort. It's not automatic. When reality is repeatedly painful, the memories and emotions that stem from the conflict are consciously thrust aside (like willful forgetting). Over years of repetitive willful forgetting, the incident is repressed out of memory.

---

[35] Carl Jung said that neurosis was a way to avoid legitimate suffering. At another time, when asked if he believed in God, Jung said very calmly, "I don't believe. I know," as reported by Gerald May, *Will and Spirit*, Harper & Row, 1982, p. 135.

Regarding denial and repression: Suppose your life is completely falling apart. Within a short while, your siblings are killed in a train wreck, your house burns down, you get laid off from work, the dog has fleas and bites the neighbor and now you're being sued. Your one-and-only best friend moves away, your partner leaves you, you get a speeding ticket on the way to the doctor's office, and you're told you have cancer. The pain of it all is too big to handle, so you'd naturally (and appropriately) develop these two ego defenses that would allow you to cope.

If calamities befall someone in otherwise optimum circumstances (i.e. over time and not closely impacting one upon the other) this person might experience the pain in a supportive environment, in increments that their psyche could stand. If there was no supportive environment and the trauma was continuous, or more importantly when addicts continuously act out and regenerate crisis and trauma, the denial and repression become "permanent". This sets up a cyclic re-experiencing of crisis and is the source of most, if not all, physical ailments.[36]

For people who have suffered repeated trauma (especially self-inflicted), ego defenses allow them to survive. Developing denial and repression, and to some extent being neurotic, are ways addicts compensate and survive. It is how they avoid legitimate pain because at the time they experienced the pain, with circumstances as they were, they were unable to cope any other way. These conditions are entrenched, and prevent addicts from being proportionately aware of the realities and pain in the circumstances of their life. That's is how people with addictions live.

Try to not use psychiatric words like denial, repression, depersonalization, neuroses, abandonment issues, inner child, or dissociation, unless you're well informed and know exactly what you're talking about; and even then, don't use them too often. Misuse of complicated psychological words hurts people and is sometimes affected by bias and prejudice. Millions of people, for thousands of years, have been spiritual without these scientific words that dissect and analyze another person's character. Unless you are truly compassionate, try not to use them.[37]

Addicts often base their values and beliefs on **assumptions.** They assume (1) various "things" about other peoples' character, which beliefs are rooted in ignorance or supposition; and (2), that most people believe, or if

---

[36] Self Regulation Therapy® and/or Emotional Freedom Technique both address body-energy dislocation that is associated with physical and psychological trauma. (Appendix III)

[37] There's a lot of unexamined power mongering and mean-spirited labeling of character. Certainly many psychiatrists, other doctors, therapists, religious officials, and poorly informed sponsors are guilty of this. Quite often it's elitist and self-serving. The ever-thickening manual of mental disorders (the DSM), and the addictive, common-place lifestyle of legal pills is, to me, disheartening. *The Myth of Mental Illness* by Thomas S Szasz, M.D. ©1961, is worth close examination.

they don't they should believe, as they, themselves, do. Assumptions are created out of fear, ignorance, naiveté, or out of the insecurity that underlies cynicism and arrogance. Assumptions keep people trapped in destructive, limiting thought patterns. This leaves prejudices and stereotypes unchallenged. As Herbert Spenser said, contempt prior to investigation keeps us trapped in ignorance.[38]

Shame[39] is arguably the most powerful emotion and the greatest block to human development. Other emotions are certainly influential, but none carry the power to contaminate personal awareness or defeat personal accomplishment to the degree that shame does. In short: It is the emotion that separates us from ourselves—internal isolation. Shame mandates that we be "human doings" rather than human beings.[40]

The destructive influence of shame sometimes (but not always) begins in early childhood; and in an addict's life, shame is always created, reinforced, expanded, and entrenched further by their acting out and by societal values and mores in relation to addictions. Shame is also a significant factor that helps to keep addicts in a cycle of acting out. It is, however, easy for people to erroneously believe that shame is the cause of addiction, and to therefore hunt for some (possibly nonexistent) severe circumstance in childhood and then blame caregivers.

Some addicts are shamed in childhood significantly less than others, and yet are *not* shamed to the degree that would correlate to the vicious addictions they demonstrate. Not all, and sometimes very little, of an addict's shame came from their family of origin caregivers, and it is irresponsible and abusive to insist otherwise.

Addicts are psychologically **isolated** from themselves (by denial, shame, and repression) and have no dependable sense of self.[41] They are often socially isolated through shame or excessive, **disproportionate fear**. Addicts who present themselves as gregarious are still isolated, regardless of their claims©451 to the contrary.

Being a practicing addict requires that you lie or deceive as a matter of course. **Dishonesty,** and its emotional-cousin **withholding** are to garner power or manipulate and maneuver for selfish advantage. Addicts lie because their addiction requires it, not because they are bad. You cannot be a practicing addict (in *any* addiction) and be completely honest. An "unrecovered" or practicing addict's dishonesty or deceit or withholding may be calculated, spontaneous, deliberate, or unconscious, but it is not optional.

---

[38] *Alcoholics Anonymous*, p. 570.
[39] Shame, fear, and guilt will be discussed at length in *Facets of Personal Transformation*.
[40] The phrase "human doing" carries an edge of satire from over-use. Nonetheless, it is still very appropriate here.
[41] "No dependable sense of self" is explained in more detail in Chapter 12 in Thought, Form, Fascination, Fall.

Selfishness is a facet of being irresponsible and intrinsic to addiction. It shows up in three ways: (1) Selfishness is the manipulation of people and circumstances, or the disregard for the rights and dignity of others, to avoid exposure of your own shame, frailties, fears, and mistakes. (2) Selfishness is any behaviour that avoids personal responsibility or accountability and unjustly (irresponsibly) externalizes responsibility onto someone or something else. (3) Selfishness is avoiding exposing your limitations, defects, errors, or resentments at the expense of others—making them guilty, bad, wrong, or responsible for your own faults and misdemeanors.

Irresponsibility permeates *all* aspects of an addict's life. Here's a short list of behaviours that demonstrate irresponsibility: accusing, admonishing, arguing, attacking, avoiding, blaming, censuring, cheating, condemning, deceiving, defending, defying, demeaning, disregarding, embellishing, evading, exaggerating, finding fault, gossiping, hiding, invading, lying, minimizing, moralizing, pouting/petulance, rebuking, reprimanding, undermining, whining and withholding.

Addicts are masters at irresponsibility. One of the greatest challenges they face is becoming completely responsible for everything in their character, and for the historical, ongoing, or developing circumstances of their addiction and their life.

Cynicism, among other things, embodies a belief that the cynic is superior to whatever they are cynical about. It's often rooted in assumptions about the shortcomings, failings, or hypocrisy of others and implies the cynic's *self*-held conviction about their own superior character attributes and/or superior insight and wisdom. The more cynical someone holds themselves, the more they demean others, and the more they are isolated and out of touch with their emotions. This leaves the cynic living with illusion, delusion, and loneliness.

Arrogance is the demonstration (or secret existence) of a belief in some personally held superior quality. One common understanding of arrogance is that it's the opposite of humility. With arrogance, there is isolation.

Within a recovery program, there are three obvious paradigms of arrogance, and these are very often silent. (1) Believing you are the smartest or most perceptive or most experienced person around and because of that you don't need help. (2) Believing you are (or someone else is) the sickest or the most depraved person around, so nobody can help. (3) Believing you (or someone else) is the most worthless or useless person in the room, and nobody should then waste time giving help. These are arrogant.

The more cynical or arrogant you are, the more distant you are from your feelings, and the more you are isolated from yourself and others. Cynicism and arrogance are emotion-avoidance tactics. If you are openly or silently arrogant or cynical, you cannot be spiritual and you're isolated, afraid and lonely, even if you aren't aware of it.

Fanaticizing and **obsessing** are serious components of addictions. Since having some fantasy is a healthy part of being creative, and obsessing and fantasy are characteristics of other emotional health issues, I mention them here with caution. For addicts these are instant ways of mood altering, which makes them a significant factor in the perpetuation of any addictive cycle. Fantasizing and obsessing are also a significant factor in the generation of drama and the inability to resolve pain.

And finally, these symptoms of addiction, regardless of how obvious or subtle, will be **chronic** and **entrenched**. They will be so pervasive that the addict will be unaware of their all-encompassing nature.

Blindness To The Disease

In The Manner of Presentation, at the beginning of this book, I described the three-dimensional spiders web of symptoms and issues. Addictions are incredibly complicated. I wrote this: "You get sick everywhere and throughout your entire personality all at the same time." Addictions affect *everything* about an addict's life: how they brush their teeth, how they make love, how they drive, how they eat, what they eat, what art and music they like, how they think, how they work, how they celebrate holidays, how they earn a living, how they sleep, how they dress, how they comb their hair... literally *everything* is affected by an addiction.

Other diseases (except possibly some rare mental illnesses) don't have the all-encompassing effect on a person that addiction does. When someone gets some disease *other* than addictions, it affects certain aspects of their life but not *every* aspect of it. With other illnesses, they're noticeable because the illness is experienced in a specific area—the person can "notice and feel" some particular pain or mobility problem. Illnesses affect certain aspects of a person's life, but not their selection of clothes, the type of food they eat, the type of music they like, or the type of person they choose to love. Illnesses, other than addiction, have defined boundaries of influence. An addiction exists globally; it's a state of existence. [Being spiritual is also a state of existence.]

Altogether, addicts manifest acting out and life-damaging consequences, neurosis, denial, disproportionate fear, repression, isolation (from self and others), assumptions, shame, dishonesty, withholding, selfishness, irresponsibility, arrogance, cynicism, and fantasy/obsession—all chronic and entrenched, and they are largely blind to them.[42] This all-pervading in-

---

[42] This blindness remains forever subtly present, unless there is a sincere devotion to the five spiritual principles that inform the maintenance steps. A pervading self-blindness is (cont'd)

ternalization, and the *un*usually inexorable trickle-effect of addictions, makes them invisible to the people who have them. Out of this blindness comes the famous first line of defense when an addict is confronted: "There's nothing wrong with me. What are you talking about? I'm fine."

Some of these symptoms are not usually talked about in terms of addictions, and I'm sure some will disagree that I call them symptoms. However, under close examination these attributes are present in all addicts, and they are significantly reduced or eliminated when they stop *all* acting out and become sincerely obedient to spiritual principles. Note: These are external symptoms of the disease they are not the disease itself. The disease of addictions isn't resolved by making the symptoms go away, but by healing the spiritual dislocation that allows these symptoms to exist.

It's no wonder, then, that The Doctor's Opinion identifies restlessness, irritability, and discontent as hallmarks of an addict.[43] *Restlessness* is an absence of quiet or repose; not being able to relax or be still; being worried, anxious, or uneasy. *Irritability* is being easily irked or annoyed, and sensitive to stimulus. *Discontentment* is being unhappy with circumstances and desiring change—a dissatisfied and impatient longing for different circumstances. These are traits of the addict, and they arise from the symptoms. People cannot continuously use a mood-altering experience (which includes things like shopping, television, or chocolate cake) over an extended period of time, without entrenching restlessness, irritability, and discontentment.

Honest Misrepresentation & Drama

A man once said to me, with very dramatic intensity: "I started drinking as a teenager. I've been clean and sober a while and a lot of times I'm back to acting like a child. I believe the damage caused my addiction. I was *literally destroyed* as a child going through foster homes. Did abuse, denial of my rights and trauma create my addiction?"

As explained earlier, childhood abuse can appear to set the stage for addiction, and it does make addictions more complicated, but addictions aren't a guaranteed result of abuse. To believe they are isn't scientifically accurate, and it isn't spiritually responsible. There are three related points that are examined here: insecurity and sex, seeking approval, and drama.[44]

Regarding sex: When addicts begin recovery, they go through a *long* phase of being anxious, angry, afraid, very confused, and insecure about life. These emotions are often evident in their sexuality. Coincidental to

---

what mandates constant self-examination and wise, ongoing spiritual counsel, throughout the addict's life. It takes *years* for self-examination to become accurate and dependable.
[43] *Alcoholics Anonymous*, p. xxiv.

this, sexual acting out can be an addiction in and of itself, or a component of relationship or romance addiction, and not necessarily symptomatic of overt abuse.

In many cases that I've seen, early-recovery anxiety, fear, or shame around "sex" has been too easily explained as the result of childhood neglect or abuse, when in fact, it was simply an issue of early recovery. Certainly, some addicts were sexually or otherwise overtly abused, but many were not. A general assumption that serious abuse must have happened, otherwise the person wouldn't be so anxious or ashamed of sex is risky at best. This misperception sometimes leads to confabulation in sobriety. It fosters exaggeration, witch-hunts, blame, and drama, and creates serious complications in the already very complex dynamic of sexuality.

Regarding fear and rejection: Clients and newcomers seek approval and avoid rejection. Many will alter their story to fit the pet theories of those who help them. Therapists, counsellors, and sponsors who don't understand the dynamics of the horrendous damage that addicts do to themselves, irrespective of childhood, and who endorse more recent, culturally popular theories about addictions, all too quickly label fear, confusion, irresponsible sexual behaviour, or vague memory, as evidence of childhood abuse. This undermines the aspect of self-imposed crisis and makes early caregivers, or some childhood calamity, responsible for (i) the addict's addiction; and (ii), their recovery experience of pain, confusion, and insecurity. Addicts will easily confabulate stories to match the pet theories of professionals and sponsors that offer recovery help.

Regarding drama: I return to the man's statement: "I was *literally destroyed*". The dramatic intensity and inflection he used, more than its content, will help to begin to sort out the dynamics of what's afoot here. Much was implied by the passion and conviction he had in believing he was literally destroyed; but is that accurate? Through his own perception-filtering mechanism, it may appear honest, but it misrepresents the circumstances. If he were *"literally destroyed"* would he be alive? Would he be sober in a twelve-step group, or at the lecture? Using that phrase with the pretentious, passionate, angry conviction he did has a self-serving advantage related to drama, and various other factors like culturally imposed guilt and shame. So... what does he *do* about it?

First, I would invite him to examine what the ego-payoffs[45] are for being so theatrical and intense in his descriptions of his childhood. I do not intend to demean his (or anyone else's) pain; however, there are times when

---

[44] I make these points here only to examine addicts and addictions, not to pass judgment on the authenticity of someone's life experience. I go into this in more detail later.

[45] All behaviour is purposeful. For a discussion about ego, see Appendix IV.

legitimate pain is exaggerated or minimized to accomplish some subtle, unhealthy, self-serving agenda.

In this, and in similar scenarios, there are three areas to examine that are connected, but at the same time subtly independent of each other. One: How and to what extent they were abused as children and (from that) developed an unhealthy personality? Two: Later, as adult-addicts acting out self-destructively, they caused additional, *serious* damage to themselves: To what extent? Three: What complications arose, and what self-serving advantages were accrued by them (consciously or unconsciously) altering their perceptions of their childhood experiences?[46]

An addict getting recovered must first address abstinence, and then understand it's a self-imposed crisis—what they did to damage themselves by acting out.[47] This is always first. If they are not reasonably willing to accept responsibility for their addiction, and all the crises and damage done to themselves and to others from it, *and* for getting recovered, then that irresponsibility must be addressed before anything else. Without taking full responsibility, any therapy or twelve-step work entrenches the unspiritual ego-posture of addicts being victims. Taking personal responsibility must be reasonably well established and present *before* addicts can successfully negotiate the deeper areas of healing. Yes, perpetrators of abuse should rightly be held responsible for that abuse; however, addicts should rightly be held responsible for their addiction, the consequences of that, and any self-serving exaggeration or drama.

The nature of active recovery (from any addiction) requires that long-held perceptions of themselves and personal history be altered. These shifts in perception are initiated by having the addict stop externalizing responsibility and reduce their romanticizing. When people begin their recovery it's essential they begin to shift from avoiding to taking responsibility.

With addicts, any premature attempt to heal pre-addiction trauma, especially healing that is encouraged by naive caregivers, creates all manner of horrendous complications. At the very minimum, these caregivers will reinforce the victim mentality that's now attendant to addictions, and abet addicts in finding someone (other than themselves), to hold responsible for

---

[46] Perceptions of childhood trauma and life circumstances may be changed in many ways for many reasons. Three more obvious ones are minimizing abuse and thereby rescuing the abusers, or exaggerating it and thereby persecuting them, or exaggerating the pains in drama and thereby attributing accountability for outrageous or egregious behaviour to a cause other than the addicts themselves. Regarding the unconscious nature of this memory manipulation, there is a parallel theme in Thought-Form-Fascination-Fall (Chapter 12). This discussion is not to undermine the sincere representation of trauma. This is to understand more clearly how the mind of an addict works.

[47] *Alcoholics Anonymous*, p. 53.

their life and how it turned out. [From another complicated perspective, this is self-serving for the caregivers.] Extricating the alcoholic/addict from a blaming mentality is an extremely difficult thing to do.[48]

The harm from childhood trauma, and the self-inflicted damage from addictions exacerbate each other. Over years of acting out, as the life damaging consequences become more destructive, an addict creates subtle tactics for justifying the self-destruction. By tweaking memories, they find ways to explain their blatantly self-destructive behaviour, which, at the minimum, includes (1) creating enemies where none exist, (2) minimizing their own culpability; and (3), exaggerating, or at times minimizing, the influence of others. Addicts inflict so much damage specific to their acting out, that if encouraged at all, they will confabulate or modify their memory of historical circumstances to make their addiction more palatable to themselves and "justifiable" in the eyes of society.[49]

One of the subtler and debilitating demonstrations of relationship addiction (codependence) occurs when sponsors, mentors, or professionals (doctors, counsellors, therapists, social workers, priests, ministers, etc.) co-operate in this. Without addicts *painstakingly* and *patiently* separating the actual from the perceived traumatic circumstances, and without eventually accepting addiction as a self-imposed crisis, the degree of responsibility they accept for the state of affairs in their life will always be insufficient and self-serving. Their mythologizing, minimizing, exaggerating, or blaming remains unexamined. The results of this, for everyone concerned (caregivers, communities, professionals, families, loved-ones, and the addicts themselves) are disastrous over the long term.

About half of the people I work with spend a large part of the first two years of therapy overcoming the confusion and pain from mismanaged and ineffective "help" from poorly trained or still wounded sponsors, religious officials, and counsellors. These caregivers don't understand addictions, confuse spiritual fitness with social success, and are themselves often spiritually suspect. This requires they be ineffective at unraveling this Gordian Knot, and therefore vague about promoting responsibility. Easily 75% of the clients I work with, who also attend twelve-step meetings, spend well over a year sorting out the confusion and misdirection they experience in meetings. The misunderstanding and chaos about therapy, spirituality, addictions, twelve-step programs, and responsibility is horrendous.[50]

---

[48] I refer to this again in Chapter 5. Also see *Twelve Steps and Twelve Traditions*, p. 47.
[49] Recall I wrote earlier about the propensity of some addicts to significantly dramatize their addiction in the way they "share" at meetings. This theme applies.
[50] There's a well-considered perspective of responsibility in Nathaniel Branden's book, *Taking Responsibility*, Simon & Schuster, 1996.

The Ripple Effect of Irresponsibility

Consider this scenario: As a child, a priest abused Jack. It's now thirty years later; the offender is old, retired, and moved away (or maybe dead). The church's congregation has changed; there's a new priest; the committee of elders has changed. If the abuser is alive, Jack charges him with abuse and sues him for damages. And, whether or not the offender is alive, Jack sues the church (meaning the registered nonprofit organization, the bishop, etc.). Eventually, Jack "wins" a settlement. Now, the new congregation, the new church, the new priest, the new bishop, or some insurance company (whomever, but *not* the priest), has to come up with the cash. Going to church costs more, everyone who uses that insurance company has their rates go up slightly, and the church's insurance premiums double. Yet the new priest, the new congregation, the insurance company, are innocent. They didn't abuse Jack, but they are made to pay for the crime of the now dead or retired priest.

Jack is demanding reparation from, and making innocent people pay for, something they didn't do. Yes, Jack was completely innocent when he was abused. Historically, the priest, as a child, was also innocent when he was abused. And this now-gone/retired/dead priest, who abused Jack, made Jack pay for something that was done to himself [the priest] long before Jack was born.[51] Moreover, as Jack struggles in the irresponsible activity of suing innocent people, abetted by an addicted system of civil law that enables revenge, Jack will harm the people that are close to him. Jack is perpetuating the cycle of abuse by making innocent people pay.

Holding people accountable for their own behaviour is always appropriate. In all sincerity, every effort should be made to hold offenders accountable. When, for whatever reason, perpetrators escape accountability, that is hard to accept; but making innocent bystanders pay for someone else's crime is much worse.

Children are completely innocent of whatever abuse was done to them. As a child, if you were abused, you are *not* responsible for it. However, it appears from a spiritual point of view, as an adult, only you are responsible to clean up the mess. Waiting for someone else to clean up the mess of *your* life, while you as an adult stay bitterly "sick", demand reparation from innocent people, and hunt up scapegoats, continues to harm everyone… especially yourself.

Indirectly harming innocent people like employers, children, friends, and spouses, because someone was mean to you when you were a child, is mean and irresponsible on your part. You cannot externalize the responsi-

---

[51] All people who were sexually abused do not themselves become abusers. All people who are abusers were themselves abused.

bility for cleaning up your life onto innocent people without seriously harming people who are innocent of responsibility for the harm that was done to you.

Most people in twelve-step programs and in our culture generally, wander aimlessly inside themselves, isolated and lonely, acting out in socially approved addictions. They often pounce like jackals on the weakness of others, seek scapegoats, and are ambivalent about their careers and relationships. Their ethics are situational and opportunistic.

They wonder what they want in life; what's it's about—subtly demanding purpose and meaning from the outside, and punishing innocent bystanders when they don't get their own way. They meet and associate with other opportunistic people and loudly complain when someone "takes advantage". To them, people become disposable. [When Jack sues the innocent church people, they become disposable to Jack's selfish ends.]

"Some of us have tried to hold on to our old ideas and the result was nil until we let go absolutely."[52] Maybe the most potent old idea is that we must be servants and victims to our past; to our heredity. This observation has far-reaching consequences for the spiritual pilgrim as it relates to spiritual integrity and accountability.[53]

Tragedy: To Whom It May Concern

Tragedy was originally a term for fictitious/literary drama. It has become a word that alleges the true nature of some circumstance of life. As much as it may appear that "tragedy" is rampant in modern life—tragic car accidents, tragic illnesses, tragic crimes, that's an illusion.

Life isn't more (or less) tragic now than at any other point in history. In part, what has happened is modern culture has inserted technology in between people and life and thereby created the fantasy that life should be free of misadventure. Technology fosters irresponsibility and the illusion that there should be fewer bad things happening. The truth is technology can neither reduce the frequency of death (it happens once to everyone), nor can it improve the odds of avoiding random calamity; however, victims and

---

[52] *Alcoholics Anonymous*, p. 58.
[53] Norman Allan MacEachern, MA, DD, was a Presbyterian minister. In a speech he wrote and delivered to the graduating class at Presbyterian College (Montreal), he told them that they should be wary of ministers who do not make the laity uncomfortable. A minister's job, according to him, was to challenge and confront various forms of spiritual inactivity, to encourage the hard work of being spiritual, and for ministers to push themselves and their congregations out of their comfort zones—to call everyone to a higher way of living. (This is my précis of what I consider to be an insightful and detailed address.) That is my purpose here. I don't hold myself out to be a minister, but my intent is to invite you to challenge yourself. Dr. MacEachern's address was entitled "The Common Factor in All Great Preaching", from *The Pilgrim Heart*, Thorn Press, Toronto, 1948.

romantic sentimentalists transform random circumstance into a tragic, personal event.

Tragedy and calamity aren't personal. They're always addressed "To Whom It May Concern" and you happened to be standing where the bus crashed. Life is randomly indifferent to everyone and the only meaning it has is the one *you* give to it. Your childhood difficulties weren't targeted at you in particular. Understand that any other child born in your approximate space in the universe, plus or minus a few months, as the result of an act of intercourse between the same two adults, would have more-than-likely ended up with some variation of what you had. Tragedy and calamity are not addressed to you personally.

Some people got slammed pretty hard with addictions, but that isn't about them *personally*. Neither is gray hair. Yet, in the machinations of your addicted personality, with a victim mentality, your ego generates an illusion about life not being fair, and you soon "believe" that life is out to get you personally. Life isn't anybody's fault. Chance exists and misadventure happens. Everyone has a randomly equal opportunity to escape disaster. Pain is required and suffering is optional. Believing otherwise is one of the greatest blocks to spirituality and serenity there is.

Life isn't fair, but also it isn't *un*fair. It just is. If you heal enough to not take it personally, then you don't have to personalize random calamity by blaming whomever you assume was your oppressor. You need to heal from the pain, but beyond that, there isn't anyone to blame and there are no tragedies.

The International Association of Petulant Victims (The I.A.P.V.) was going to have a convention, but they couldn't get any one *else* to take charge so they cancelled it. The complaining was horrendous. Eventually they had to disband because everyone wanted someone else to make a decision. Watch out for members of The International Association of Petulant Victims in twelve-step meetings; they are everywhere and always on the lookout for someone (else) to blame. Members of the I.A.P.V. live with a mindset of accusation. Many people cling tenaciously to their I.A.P.V. membership, but there's no spirituality there. The more you believe you are a valiantly struggling oppressed victim, the less you are recovered.[54]

Only by adopting a doctrine of obedience to spiritual principles, and taking complete responsibility for their life, can an addict can have access to freedom and spirituality. When people are completely responsible, regard-

---

[54] There's common sense required here. I'm not referring to bona fide hostages of crime and terrorism, or to children who are abused. Yes, the perpetrators have to be held accountable; but once children become adults, and once hostages are freed, responsibility for healing becomes theirs alone. It's the law of spiritual healing. Right or wrong, good or bad, that's the way it is.

less of whatever situation they are in, it frees them to respond however they choose. If, however, they see the problems in their life as someone else's fault, then the person they're blaming is in charge because the victim can only wait and complain until the other person does something.

Imagine this: A courier, dressed in elegant, formal evening attire, knocks at your door and delivers a large parchment envelope decorated with flourishes and cherubim. Trumpeters sound a grand chorus to herald the arrival of your beautiful, expensive invitation. With surprise and anticipation, you break open the fancy wax seal. Slowly you pull out a very expensive, gold-embossed card.

Dear You:

You are cordially invited to attend the celebration of Your Life. It will begin tomorrow at 6:00 P.M. at wherever you are tomorrow at 6:00 P.M. Dress in layers and bring an umbrella because it might or might not rain (on anyone). You are advised to pack a lunch, and do what you want to enjoy yourself because life lasts a long time. If, however, you've started celebrating your life without receiving this invitation, you're having a good time already and life won't last long enough.

We would like you to know, that we know, that you're sorry for the delay in our getting this invitation to you, but there are so many people who wait for us to invite them to celebrate life that we're rather behind schedule.

Be advised: You only have this one life to live, and if you won't live your life for yourself, you'll end up living your life for someone else.

Sincerely,
An Unnamed Deity,
Asst.. to the Co-chair of The Invitation-To-Life and Spiritual Oversight Committee.
- RSVP not required –
(Dictated/not read; per AUD/mgp)

No one gets this invitation. Your own invitation to live was actually the ritual of your creation. "You" are in this life by way of *you*, and no one else. Nothing will ever arrive in the mail inviting you to be happy or to make something of yourself. You'll not be getting permission from anyone to do anything with your life. You'll not be getting a certificate of exemption from calamity. Your birth was your invitation to get the life *you* want. Maybe your caregivers didn't tell you that, but that's the fact. No one will ever give you permission; you just jump into life and elbow out your own space. Joseph Campbell, the expert on mythology, once said that life was like a big free-for-all—it isn't a private fight, anyone can join in.[55]

I was giving a lecture once and I expressed a contrary opinion—not rude or mean, just contrary and uncommon. A man became *very* indignant, rose to his feet, and said loudly in front of 200 people: "How dare you say that! What gives you the right to say that?" I answered, "Me." He stalked out of the lecture hall in high dudgeon. He deeply believed that I had no right to espouse a value that, by *his* standards, offended his sensibilities, unless some outside authority (like a priest or the prime minister) had given me permission.

He did not understand that I am the highest authority there is for my life, as is he, for his. I don't need an invitation, nor do I need permission, to be me. I was born and my inherent birthright is to be me. Granted, my responsibility is to clean up the messes in my life (regardless of who created them) but only so that I can get on with the job of being me, because, after all, being me is my job. And while being me, I must take care to not infringe on the rights of others to be them.

If you happen to be standing on the spot marked "X" close to where the plane crashes, you will never get a telegram or an email that reads:

> Dear You:
> We decided it's your turn. Good luck with the plane.
> > Sincerely,
> > The Calamity Gods, Ad-hoc Crisis
> > Distribution Sub-Committee #55/mgp
> > (12 for; 1 against; 2 abstentions.
> > Carried by majority.)

Calamity is random; therefore, since no one is really to blame, the responsibility for your life remains with you. Becoming who you want yourself to be is only available as the result of your choosing to live with loyalty to the code of complete personal responsibility. You cannot be what you want to be if someone else is responsible for the circumstances in your life. Be completely responsible (for yourself) and obedient (to the five spiritual principles) if you wish to be recovered and fulfilled—if you are not both, then you are neither.[56]

Your attitudes and biases, which are simply the events of your life filtered through your ego; and your commitment to (or rejection of) personal

---

[55] *Joseph Campbell & The Power of Myth, with Bill Moyers*, PBS TV, Apostrophe S. Productions, Inc., Public Affairs Television, Inc., 1988.
[56] Being abused is a valid reason for a sad and painful childhood. It's a poor excuse for an unfulfilled life. Also see: *Blues ain't nothing but a good soul feeling bad*. Sheldon Kopp, Simon & Schuster, 1992, the entries for Jan. 12 and July 15.

responsibility, are the magnets that attract or disarm the calamity in your life. That's why trouble gravitates towards you, and this is especially true in personal relationships.[57] I remember this anecdote from a book I enjoyed: A woman was complaining about the men in her life. "There's no nice guys left, they're all irresponsible, poor prospects for long-term, fulfilling relationships, and just generally jerks." Her therapist observed that it appeared that there were some nice, dependable men available, but the woman gave only the poor prospects her phone number.[58]

It isn't that *all* men or *all* women are poor prospects for fulfilling partnerships. It's about people behaving in ways that repeatedly invite only the irresponsible (angry, dishonest, addicted) types of people into their life. This behaviour is always rooted in irresponsibility, a disrespectful self-concept, and fear. It's a matter of long-term therapy and hard work to learn how they set this up themselves, and how they stop it, without blaming their neighbors, their parents, some ex-spouse, or the dog that lives down the lane.

In the mind of a practicing addict, "looking after oneself" means getting away with things and not getting caught. Should addicts enter recovery and continue to believe this, they neglect their true needs and all of their energy goes into maintaining the "game" of hiding and misleading—impression management.

Emotional self-care requires always gently offering and advocating for truth, responsibility, and respect.[59] There's hypocrisy about insisting that others treat you with respect when you keep putting yourself in disrespectful situations, or secretly think disrespectful and abusive things about yourself or others.

What makes you continuously invite dishonest, disrespectful people into your life? The key is to unravel and challenge your own abuse and neglect of yourself and to develop inner integrity. Controlling others so they treat you with respect doesn't accomplish this; it's done by being aware and negotiating yourself out of your own internal, self-abusive, self-neglecting ego-scripts. It's gently "moving on" when people don't care enough about themselves, or others, to respect your commitment to spiritual values. Responsibility *always* begins and ends with you.

Once in a while we are innocent and happen to be standing on the corner exactly where the plane crashes, but the large majority of times, people attract the calamity in their lives into their lives. In this culture, being re-

---

[57] I will discuss this in *Facets of Personal Transformation*.
[58] *A Return To Love*, Marianne Williamson, HarperCollins, 1992.
[59] Some people, under the guise of "working their program", use honesty as an excuse for meanness and belligerence.

sponsible is a lonely prospect. Think carefully about this truth: It is a sign of spiritual health that you consistently and gracefully choose loneliness over conflict and chaos.[60]

Focus your effort on not abusing yourself in your own mind. Don't associate with dangerous, disrespectful, or abusive people. If you do, you're putting yourself in emotionally or physically dangerous situations. Decide that anger won't be a part of your own day-to-day life.[61] You will sometimes feel angry, which is only being the human that you are, but your decision will require that you take complete responsibility for it. [Recognize that the consequences of anger are far-reaching.]

Decide that people who are irresponsible about anger will not be personally close to you. Period. No exceptions. Decide that people who are irresponsible, violent, or dishonest (aggressive sports fans, racists, sexists; people who blame, gossip, or lie and cheat) will not be in your intimate/personal life. They can do those things anywhere other people will let them, but you won't subject yourself to this. Period. No exceptions. Quietly rearrange the circumstances in your life to exclude them and that behaviour. Make no demands on them. Don't gossip.

The more you are *completely* responsible for your feelings and your life — regardless of the circumstance — the less time you will spend in negative emotions.[62] You will experience more and greater joy, and the more graceful your self-care will become. Invariably this is true, but members of the International Association of Petulant Victims don't believe me.

I was once asked: "What happens if it's your roommate who's angry and throws things or kicks holes in the wall?" The person who asked this was obviously upset by their roommate's anger. I asked how long it had been going on and was told that the behaviour had been continuous for over a year. I offered this response:

"What is it inside *you* that believes you must subject yourself to that angry behaviour? You put yourself in that situation. Many people, and right now you, claim to desire a peaceful life. You make splendid speeches that you're sick of conflict, rage, anger, and meanness. You've probably talked with your roommate about this, maybe given meaningless ultimatums,

---

[60] Over the course of several gigs a few years ago, a fellow musician and I discussed lifestyles. I offered that I didn't drink or smoke, was a vegetarian, didn't watch TV, and didn't participate in sports, racist or sexist jokes, etc., *and* that I made an effort to be spiritual. With a wry smile, he admitted he had a similar lifestyle and commented: "No wonder we're single, we've priced ourselves out of the market." Working towards spiritual integrity has a significant price tag attached to it. What are you willing to pay?

[61] Firmly deciding to live without anger, and being willing to pay the price for that, regardless of the cost, *before the fact,* is one fundamental prerequisite to a serene life.

[62] From one perspective: There is no such thing as positive or negative emotion.

complained to friends, and solicited sympathy. Yet you're still living with this person. You're *choosing* to live in conflict and fear, and complaining about it to anyone who'll listen.

"You're making your roommate responsible for the lack of safety in your life, which is irresponsible on your part. You must make your life safe: no one else can. In spite of your pretty spiritual speeches that you desire peace in your life, you really don't because you are allowing anger and abuse to enter it. You (your ego) obviously needs the conflict, which justifies your complaining, and makes you appear innocent and superior. You avoid the fear, criticism, and loneliness that comes with being responsible.

"Think about this: 'It's not acceptable behaviour.' Do I mean your roommate's behaviour of irresponsible anger is not acceptable, or *your* behaviour of passively sitting in the rage and abuse and complaining about it is not acceptable?

"I mean both. But right now, more importantly, I mean it is not acceptable that you voluntarily and willingly subject yourself to aggression, and then do nothing but complain about it. When you [eventually] learn how to properly self-care, and quietly insist on respect from others—even at the cost of being lonely, socially unpopular, poor, criticized for being too demanding, or rejected by your peers because they think you are a snob—then you will immediately leave this roommate and begin to stop attracting calamity and misadventure into your life."

How many times have you thought: "Here I go again—another crazy relationship." So you change meetings, change jobs, and pick new partners with a different body type, different hobbies, different education, and, "Oh my goodness, here I go again!" How do you keep attracting these crazy relationships, one after the other; the same arguments, again and again? It's because you're unaware of, and unwilling to challenge, the subtle *self*-abusing nature of your personality. You are *un*willing to work hard, to face loneliness and pain, to take responsibility. You're unwilling to abandon and *self*-challenge your values, your ideas, your religious views, your family, your peer group, this culture, your prejudices and defects—whatever. Your ego chooses conflict because in being a victim, and being in disharmony and failure, there's always someone (else) to blame.[63]

It's always very rewarding for clients when, after *long* periods of therapy and struggle, they finally announce that life is peaceful, and I ask, "What happened?" Their answer is always some variation of: "I met an angry (dishonest, rude, needy, mean) person and they asked me out and I said no. I may be alone, and now I have to do everything by myself, but I'm happy." There it is—all taken care of by sensing when to say no and firmly

---

[63] I will discuss this at some length in *Facets of Personal Transformation*.

saying it. Become responsible to the spiritual principle of self-care, and obedient to your declared value of inner peace, in spite of solitude, poverty, or being labeled unpopular, unforgiving, arrogant, or a snob.

Oversimplification Never Works

One horrendous problem we have with many self-help and twelve-step groups and counsellors, and with self-appointed spiritual "gurus", is healing from addictions—becoming spiritual—is oversimplified.[64] How many people have read a self-help book and actually done any sincere, noticeable, long-term self-helping? This is exceptionally rare. They read two chapters, skim the rest, and their good intentions fade away. Many people do, however, skim a book and then play junior-therapist by pushing it onto others whom they think it would really help.

One of the disservices people do to themselves is to go through a long history of reading self-help books without the wherewithal to do anything but read them. People spend thousands of dollars hunting for expedient solutions. They have a *long* list of justifications to justify and excuse their self-generated fears, their spending, unhealthy relationships, TV, prescription drugs, in short, anything to avoid admitting they're addicts *and* doing something sincere about it.

The journey of exiting all addictions and becoming Spiritual is the most complicated process that I have ever read about, studied, or participated in. For the most part, in the first decade of spiritual transformation, egos don't self-modify, they self-justify.

What acts in conjunction with Terry Kellog's observation about substituting addictions is too many people in, or associated with, "recovery" reorganize their personality into a better Impression Management scheme. They switch to substitute addictions and appear better or healthier. These are invariably into the socially approved addictions like greed, spending, work, relationships, sex, romance, religion, adrenalin, fitness, anger, TV, twelve-step programs, and righteousness. There's nothing more complicated than trying to restructure your ego and become spiritual—not to slickly reorganize yourself, but to actually change.[65]

---

[64] For an accurate and considered approach to the complicated nature of codependence, read Dr. Charles Whitfield's book *Codependence, Healing the Human Condition*, Health Communications, Inc., 1991; and Anne Wilson Schaef's book, *Escape From Intimacy*, Harper Collins, 1990.

[65] Any therapy or spiritual discipline that attempts to reduce or eliminate your ego may sound good but is generally ineffective. Becoming humble is not an exercise in ego reduction. Humility is *not* an absence of ego. In fact, only someone with a strong definition of self—with strong ego boundaries—can be sincerely humble or spiritual. This is expanded upon in Chapter 9 and Appendix IV.

Alcoholics Anonymous is not a self-help book, and neither is this one. You're on a journey with other people, are encouraged to be with like-minded individuals, encouraged to seek out well-conducted therapy or spiritual guidance, and you're encouraged to assist others. There's nothing "self-help" about it. To be successful, you have to be spiritually motivated, but that's not self-help, either. The thing about authentic personal, spiritual transformation is you can't do it alone. It is untenable for an addict to insist that self-help is the solution.

People with socially approved addictions participate in community in a subtly destructive way. The *Alcoholics Anonymous'* instructions are intended to develop spiritual integrity and to reintegrate addicts and alcoholics into community, but in a spiritual way. Sadly enough, in recent years, twelve-step groups have lost that focus. There's so much talk about treatment centres, and so many self-help books being pushed on everyone (as substitutes for hard work and devotion), that the established success of the original program and spirituality are hardly visible.[66]

Not all, but many, twelve-step groups have lost the focus regarding their primary purpose—encouraging spiritual transformation. They have become social clubs with entrenched pecking orders that focus on dances, anniversary parties, and cake. Any excuse is given for a party—one-day chips, thirty-day chips, sixty days, ninety days, this birthday, that anniversary, Christmas, golf parties, summer parties, barbecues, camping parties, ball games, and bowling. Any excuse for a party—just as it was in their addictions. As much as it is important to celebrate our successes, even the small ones like 'one day at a time', and it's important to develop strong friendship bonds in recovery, when groups lose focus on their spiritual intent, getting recovered becomes impossible and addicts die.

Family histories and detailed recollections of childhood trauma are sometimes, but not always, valuable in a well-conducted therapeutic process. These have very little value in authentic, spiritual twelve-step work. When the original literature advises alcoholics to talk in a general way about *"what we used to be like, what happened, and what we are like now,"*[67] they are referring to:

a) *"what we used to be like"* (not what anyone else was like, and not what *it* was like): meaning during the period of using, drink-

---

[66] The larger the group of people, the less probable is the presence of God. In very large groups, the conscious presence of God almost vanishes. *Huxley and God, Essays,* by Aldous Huxley, edited by Jacqueline Hazard Bridgeman, Harper Collins, 1992, p. 123.
[67] *Alcoholics Anonymous,* p. 58.

ing and other acting out, the insanity, unmanageability, and early abstinence,

b) *"what happened"*: the circumstances that caused a shift out of addictions and to desire a better life, i.e. the transition from acting out to abstinence, and the various recovery experiences that pushed them deeper into spirituality; and,

c) *"what we are like now"* (not what anyone else is like, and not what *it* is like): meaning your relationship with a higher power, any inner transformation struggles, and your successes or failures at responding spiritually to the circumstances of life now.

For a twelve-step spiritual pilgrim to belabour, to mention, or to describe at all the sins and misdemeanors of *any*one, including family of origin, isn't forgiving, charitable, kind, responsible, or spiritual. *Alcoholics Anonymous* advises and teaches you to live humbly in a community of like-minded souls, who are [hopefully] only interested in three things: maintaining abstinence, developing a relationship through the steps with a higher power, and carrying this specific message to interested others.

I am aware of a debate between a newcomer and someone who'd been around for many years. The old-timer would ask: "Did you say your prayers?"

"No," the newcomer would answer.

The old-timer would smile gently and say, "Well, you're probably going to get drunk, and you'll stay miserable."

"Well, I don't want to get drunk," countered the newcomer.

"Then say your prayers," was the old-timer's considered reply.

Days later, the old-timer would ask: "Did you say your prayers?"

"No, not really."

"Well, you're probably going to get drunk."

"I don't want to get drunk," the newcomer would say.

The old-timer would say, "Well, then, say your prayers, " and again, the newcomer would say, "But I don't want to say my prayers."

The old-timer said, "If you don't work at saying your prayers, you're probably going to get drunk. Regardless of this, you're taking an awful chance, and you'll stay miserable, too."

After a couple of weeks of this banter, the newcomer finally said: "You keep telling me I've got to say my prayers or I'm going to get drunk or be miserable. I don't want to pray, and I don't want to be miserable *or* get drunk. Aren't there any other options?"

The old-timer's answer was: "If you're an alcoholic, no, there aren't." He wasn't invested in the success or failure of the newcomer's life. He was only interested in honestly carrying the spiritual message in a gentle way, and then leaving the choice to the newcomer. That's sponsorship.

Becoming spiritual, at the outset of your transformation, is the most challenging work you will ever undertake. Provoke and challenge yourself, not others, into thinking differently, and hopefully you will abandon some of your old ideas and [then] be closer to a spiritual life.

Pity, Self-Pity and Suffering

People are very often told, when feeling sad or hurt, that they are feeling sorry for themselves—it's just self-pity. They're instructed to get over it, or to smarten up and get off the pity pot. These instructions are evidence of disrespect and intolerance, and nothing more than a belligerent demand for them to change.

Anyone in any twelve-step program has "unresolved issues" (whatever that means). It's not a perfect world, and quite probably *every*one has unresolved pain and sadness from the past, but not everyone is an addict. Unmet needs and trauma are not the reasons for your addiction, but they are a complicating factor.

Once addicts have remained abstinent for any noticeable period beyond a few months, they often feel quite sad (or lonely and hurt) at the tremendous losses and damage they inflicted on themselves in their addictions. Years and years of buried sadness and hurt are now available to be felt. Mixed in with this will be confusion and all their unaddressed historical issues. This sadness isn't self-pity.

"Pity" (for someone else) is that feeling of sympathy, combined with sorrow or sadness, which is aroused by the misfortune or dire straits of another, and always contains some element of a belief that the person who is pitied can't help themselves. There's an implication that the person being pitied doesn't know any better (ignorance), and can't escape whatever the "tragedy" is. Pity includes a cynical or patronizing attitude on the part of the beholder: The person being pitied just can't or will never get it right. Feeling pity (sorry) for someone, and telling them often occasions a very strong reaction: "Don't you *dare* pity me!" This is because of these patronizing and demeaning implications inherent in the transaction of expressing pity.

When people hurt, it's natural to try to make the pain go away. The three most common but ineffective tactics that I've seen in my work are to (i) try and control or blame others, (ii) to repeatedly talk about the pain and solicit empathy or sympathy; and (iii), to act out in an addiction (mood alter, which does, temporarily, make the pain go away).

A sense of futility develops when no permanent relief is found over the long term. The two results I've witnessed from this futility are: (i) people develop a mindset that they are helpless and it's hopeless; and (ii), they will offer sympathy to themselves. This turns into the dynamic that is often referred to as self-pity, which evolves from otherwise ineffective efforts to resolve continuous pain.

Self-pity contains the same beliefs as feeling pity for someone else, and your ego has turned these beliefs inward, by you, upon yourself. Self-pity originates out of authentic, original pain; develops from long-term unsuccessful attempts to heal; and is coupled with your own, erroneous view of yourself as being helpless and hopeless. Self-pity rescues yourself out of responsibility; carries an element of aggrandizing the underlying, legitimate pain and subscribes to the belief that you are a tragic victim. [Regardless of whatever participation others may have had in your pain, it is still your responsibility to resolve self-pity without blaming others for your plight.]

In my experience, very few people, including many counsellors, know how to wisely ask where it hurts, and know how to help sort out pain. Is it pain from childhood? Is childhood pain minimized or exaggerated? Is it pain (and shame) from acting out? Is the acting out minimized or exaggerated? What acting-out pain is exacerbated by cross-over pain from childhood? Is it pain and sadness from the realization of lost opportunities in self-destructive behaviour? What acting-out pain is fused by shame to historical issues? How clear can the experience of childhood pain be after years of self-destruction and foggy, overlapping memories? How do you facilitate resolution without codependence, rescuing, or entrenching a victim ego posture? How do you sort out reality from delusion, illusion, and authentic pain from dramas? If there is drama, where is it, and how much is there? Will empathy resolve pain or entrench it? When and how do you offer empathy? Resolving "pain" is incredibly complicated.

All of this can be largely resolved—enough to sincerely enjoy life—but there are different resolution strategies, and it takes a *long* time. Empathy itself doesn't resolve pain. Empathy is only part of some strategies for healing, but it isn't healing. Very often, empathy and sympathy make matters worse. Accusations of being in self-pity, true or not, also make everything worse. Yes, many of us do feel sorry for ourselves part of the time, and, at times, manipulate the world to get sympathy, but self-pity isn't a given when someone is sad and lonely.

Self-pity and suffering are built upon some underlying legitimate pain and sadness. Sorting out what is legitimate sadness, and what is drama and self-pity, is difficult, even for many therapists. How do you sort this out? Carefully. Consider well-conducted, *long*-term professional help. Forge ahead on your own initiative. Examine how you see yourself as a victim and your belief that life isn't fair. Remain abstinent. Go very slow.

You probably often feel hurt and sad, but lack the insight and ability to articulate that clearly and that inability, by itself, can make it sound like you're living in self-pity. Because self-styled do-gooders, and home-made "wanna-be" counsellors in twelve-step programs don't know what to do with their own feelings, and your own sadness provokes something in them they must avoid, they'll tell you: "Smarten up—you're just feeling sorry for yourself." Too many people compensate for their own discomfort and in-adequacy by making someone else's sadness a bad thing.

Some people in twelve-step programs, sponsors, and professionals will dismiss as unnecessary the subtle dynamics and required detailed work that I describe here. These people are actually dismissing complex issues in fa-vor of superficial solutions. They, themselves, are uncomfortable with the somewhat arduous and complex work (which conceals a self-serving agenda on their part, rooted in fear and shame). That attitude in the helper will often leave the client-newcomer in self-pity and confusion because yet another attempt at healing failed.

Here's the key to understanding the connection between self-pity and suffering and how to make them both optional. *Suffering* is a combination of three things: (i) some "legitimate" pain, fear, loss, loneliness, hurt, or distress that cannot be remembered accurately; (ii) aggrandizing that with drama or exaggeration by perceiving yourself as a victim: it's tragic; and (iii), having an attendant perception that you are helpless or the situation is hopeless.

If you're *suffering*, then attendant to some long-ago legitimate pain, you're trapped in, you have a sense of hopelessness that the object of your pity (yourself) is incapable and helpless. You have the belief and the sense that you are doomed to your own pain—self-pity. [These are all issues of perception.]

Here's the viciousness: Because a person trapped in self-pity believes they cannot change, they won't. And, because it's attached to some long-ago experience of pain the associated dramas appears legitimate. When try-ing to recover from long-term recidivist behaviour, because they believe it's hopeless, they will unknowingly sabotage their own recovery or therapy, and are most often successful. This sabotaging behaviour is so subtle that caregivers will mismanage treatment and will set up a subtle termination strategy out of sheer frustration.

Perceiving yourself as a victim automatically makes someone else re-sponsible for the healing journey in your life. If "they" are responsible then you can't do anything about it, only "they" can. With a victim mentality, suffering is guaranteed. "*They* aren't doing anything to help me, and I am helpless. It's not *my* fault! It's hopeless; there's no solution." That's suffering. Stop blaming people for the state your life is in. Take responsibility for yourself and the suffering will immediately stop. You will be left to deal with the underlying original pain, but without suffering.

Heliotropism & Impatient Step Work

Heliotropism is when a plant turns naturally to face sunlight. It does this without the ability to think. Within each step is the potential to access what I refer to as spiritual heliotropism—an effortless turning of yourself towards spirituality. If you're painstaking and thorough in the assigned tasks, patiently complete them in order, and seek wise spiritual counsel, you will unconsciously and gracefully sense when it's time to move to the next task. There's a natural, spiritual heliotropism in the original steps, which requires no decision from you; one that will shift your interest to draw you deeper into yourself and closer to your concept of a higher power.

Whenever you're struggling, delaying, fearful, or impatient with any specific step, you've missed the point. Go back at least two steps and reexamine your work. Impatience or "forced decisions" are evidence of insecurity and a misalliance of commitment (explained in Chapter 6). Being badgered by impatient sponsors or counsellors, or harassed by your own insensitive ego, as in: "Hurry up, you've been around 'X' weeks and you've not finished Step One," or, "You've been here six months and you haven't done Step Three," creates problems. Anxiety, pressure (from *any* source), or impatience, always demonstrates insecurity and intolerance in the person doing the demanding. Whether it's you demanding of yourself, or anyone demanding or you, impatient demanding embodies nothing spiritual.

When you absorb the *intrinsic* nature of the step you're on, the way it's spiritually designed (not psychologically or socially designed), it will inherently draw you onward without pressure or fear, like a flower turning to face the sun. One day you will think, without planning it: "I wonder what the next step has in store for me?"—a simple and peaceful, willing desire to move on to the next step to accomplish what's required. It's very subtle, which is the nature of spirituality. You can't smell the roses if you run through the garden. In your pilgrimage *you are your only enemy*. Spirituality is a patient, friendly discipline of devotion.

You may be concerned that you've forced yourself impatiently through the steps a few times and wonder if there's any sense in going back to Step One and starting over. Yes, there is. If you're struggling with any individual step; if you've completed any of them in a forced, impatient manner; or if you've repeated the steps a few times, and are somehow still anxious about not getting it right, you've missed the point. If you believe you have to repeat the steps over and over, or you think you have to do any of them every year or two, you've missed the point.

What do I mean by "completing" the steps? For this to work, in the manner I'm describing, you must be willing to abandon *all* your addictions and work towards being spiritually self-disciplined. Study *Alcoholics Anonymous* and *Twelve Steps and Twelve Traditions*. When I refer to *Alcoholics Anonymous,* I mean up to page 192 and the appendix entitled Spiritual Experience. The rest are personal stories. Don't take personal stories as "the program", they're just personal points of view which you hear at meetings all the time. The two AA pamphlets to study are *A Member's Eye View of Alcoholics Anonymous* and *The Jack Alexander Article.*

Begin at the beginning of the books. Gently incorporate the specific instructions into your personal life so you can become spiritual, not so you can become socially successful or mold yourself to someone else's view of the world.

The Inappropriate One-Year Rules

Newcomers are often admonished with two instructions that are controlling and destructive, and merit special attention. **The first inappropriate instruction** is that newcomers are told that staying out of sexual relationships for the first year is a good "recovery" thing to do.

The focus of abstinence-available programs[68] is to get clean and sober and maintain it, then through the steps, work diligently towards being spiritual. That's the end of it. For the abstinence not-available addictions, the first priority is to establish a spiritually credible standard of non-addictive behaviour. Adhere to it. Then, through the steps, work diligently towards being Spiritual. That's the end of it.

There are places in the original twelve-step literature where it tells you that anyone's sexual life, newcomer or otherwise, and their intimate relationships, are nobody's business. It advises: *"...where 'boy meets girl on A.A. campus,' and love follows, that difficulties may develop. The prospective partners need to be solid AA's... ."*[69] For people in twelve-step programs, this is a guideline, not a prohibition.

---

[68] Remember the two categories of addictions: abstinence-available addictions (alcohol, drugs, tobacco, gambling), meaning those addictions that allow *complete* abstinence and abstinence... not-available addictions (sex, work, relationships, food, etc.), where complete abstinence is never available and you must establish an acceptable standard of "abstinence", which is interpretive and not legislated. This second category of addiction can severely limit the effectiveness of twelve-step programs because access to spirituality in the original twelve steps is designed around the ability to abstain. Which category you and your addiction fit into will significantly affect your healing work. There is no end of abuse and confusion about this in the twelve-step community.

[69] *Twelve Steps and Twelve Traditions,* p. 119.

If you're interested in getting married, or by implication, dating, because that's what usually happens before marriage (although I know of several marriages, old-timers' included, that didn't noticeably include dating), the AA literature advises caution. It doesn't say not to. In the discussions on Step Four and sexuality, there is this: *"Here we find human opinions running to extremes—absurd extremes, perhaps,"*[70] closely followed by: *"We want to stay out of this controversy. We do not want to be the arbiter of anyone's sex conduct."*[71]

There are advisories throughout the original literature that when carrying the message, you need to strictly adhere to your expertise—becoming abstinent, the steps, and developing a relationship with a higher power. Have no opinions on anything else, including dating or sex. The arrogance in imposing this one-year newcomer's no-sex rule is astonishing. In some circumstances, it may happen that someone (newcomer or otherwise) decides to be sexually abstinent on their own, and on their own behalf. That's well and good, but it's not a sponsor's business what other people do in their private life.[72] A sponsor's 'job' is to role model spiritual behaviour not to make up rules.

One exception for having a sex guideline *might* be in well-conducted therapy where a therapist might make suggestions for sexual behaviour. Hopefully the therapist is well trained and thoroughly aware of the personality dynamics their client. The therapeutic agenda must be very clear, and the client willing to participate. Even with all that, it's advised only after thoughtful and considered discussion.

Regarding newcomers: What's to be done with newcomers who are in long-term partnerships? If they're not supposed to be in a sexual relationship for the first year, do they have to separate? How many times have you heard from someone who has been sober for years: "I never should have got into that crazy relationship." Many people with longer sobriety frequently get in and out of crazy relationships. Harmony in any relationship is dependant on much more than length of sobriety.

The idea of anyone in a twelve-step program instructing anyone else not to be in a relationship or have sex for a year is an opinion running to extremes, and irresponsibly meddling in the lives of others. This is self-righteous interference. Twelve-step people are [supposed to be] experts on abstinence, the steps and spirituality, not sexuality and dating. It's completely outside of the twelve-step mandate.

---

[70] *Alcoholics Anonymous*, p. 68.
[71] Ibid., p. 69.
[72] This refers to sex between consenting adults, not violence or crime.

If many addicts and alcoholics make "poor" relationship decisions after years of abstinence, why have the one-year rule? There's the usual patronizing, sentimental reply that new people might relapse if they have sex because they're so helpless and confused (the poor things), and the sponsor has the new person's best interests at heart. The sponsor who insists on a no-sex rule has an inappropriate investment in the life of the new person. It's intrusive and abusive moralizing. The newcomer, who doesn't know the original literature, can only assume they are being advised ethically. They aren't. This rule takes advantage of the uninformed newcomer and imposes a morality that isn't freely chosen.

What is it about relationships or sex that so threatens sponsors? Who really benefits from the no-sex rule? The exact reasons are particular to each situation, but here are a few general themes:

- In their beginning, sexual relationships introduce some major changes to a person's life. For addicts this is often surrounded with chaos and drama. For addicts, when they get into a sexual relationship there may be lies, secrets, and power struggles, whether they are sober ten months or ten years. There is heartbreak and celebration, which makes life more complicated, which can also make sponsoring more difficult. The sponsor thinks: "I'm sponsoring them and they're in *another* relationship... more phone calls about heartache and conflict." For a sponsor who may be codependent, irritable, celibate, insecure, lazy, jealous, or unhappy in their relationships, the one-year rule makes life more peaceful for the sponsor.
- I know of situations where sponsors developed a desire for a relationship with the person they were sponsoring. They were adamant "their" newcomer stay out of relationships because they secretly wanted a relationship with them for themselves.
- Independent of the previous point, are sponsors jealous because the newcomer is having sex and they're not? I've encountered noticeable envy in many of the advocates of the "no relationship" rule. If the sponsor isn't getting laid, nobody is. Being a petulant spoilsport isn't limited to newcomers.
- There are claims, with this rule there will be less chance of the newcomer's relapse into addiction. That's only biased opinion, and a minor point of passing comment. This is no different than saying that maybe they shouldn't drive, too. Road rage and traffic jams may prompt the newcomer to drink. Since people spend more time fighting traffic than having sex, maybe newcomers should take the bus for a year. When any

twelve-step person, regardless of their sobriety, is in a relationship and relapses into their obvious addiction, someone blames the relationship, and that's *not* where responsibility lies.

The example: Two people in a twelve-step program are dating. They quite like each other; maybe they love each other. They're relaxing one evening. One says: "I'm going to take a hot bubble bath," and goes into the bathroom. Both people are feeling romantic and aroused. A few minutes later the other person walks down the hall and stands in the doorway of the bathroom. The first person has just finished getting undressed, gets in the tub, snuggles back into the bubbles, and says hopefully: "Would you like to scrub my back?" As the partner is getting undressed, they notice it's 7:00 o'clock, and their recovery home groups starts at 7:30.

The question to ask is: What priorities were brought into the relationship? It has little to do with whether or not they're in a relationship, or have sex, or don't have sex, but how easily will either of them place their relationship commitment ahead of their spiritual commitment?

Imposing "no-sex rules" doesn't resolve the problem of not having spirituality as the priority. It's just another rule. If it's imposed from the outside, rather than willingly adopted by the person in recovery, it is of little benefit. Getting recovered has nothing to do with any external circumstance like relationships, employment, or road traffic. After attaining a few weeks of abstinence, any relapse often identifies a problem of priorities more than anything else.

Here's a true story: A man in his early thirties was in AA and was just a year sober. He was single, healthy, had a well-paying job, was living in a high-rise apartment building with a rooftop pool, and drove a new car. He knew his way around the city and enjoyed restaurants, clubs, and dancing. He had a girlfriend. One weekend they had dinner out, went to a concert, then an after hours club. Later, they swam in the rooftop pool, watched the sun come up, had a light breakfast, and went to bed. Two hours later the phone rang.

"Hello?" the man answered in a sleepy voice.

It was his friendly sponsor. "Hello... I'll pick you up in a half an hour."

The man said, "I'm going to pass on the meeting. I was up all night... had this date... " Of course, he briefly told his sponsor the story, expecting his sponsor to understand. His sponsor *did* understand.

"Listen," his sponsor said, "if you don't maintain your priorities, you place your sobriety at risk. Your home group starts in forty-five minutes. Do I pick you up?" They went to the meeting.

His sponsor made no negative comments about the relationship or staying up all night—it was none of his (the sponsor's) business. In fact, the sponsor was curious what the bands were like (they were both musicians). The sponsor's only *brief* comment was that it seemed that the newcomer almost got his priorities backwards.

"We do not want to be the arbiter of anyone's sex conduct."[73] When sponsors invade the private lives of those they sponsor, or struggle for dominance in the relationship, the esteem and credibility of the sponsor and the sponsor's "program" is dependent on the success of those they sponsor. Any newcomer should be told plainly that whether or not they have sex is no one's business but their own. Sex makes for a more interesting life, but their program allows them to have a life, so establish your priorities.

A sponsor should be spiritually stable enough (meaning they should have a strongly defined, spiritually focused agenda) and maintain the relationship based only on abstinence, the steps, and God, but that would mean tremendous work on the sponsor's part. It's far easier to make up rules for newcomers so the sponsor's own insecurities and jealousies aren't prodded awake.

A woman, with a few years of sobriety, was told by her sponsor: "Go ahead, get in a relationship. It won't work and you'll bring yourself lots of grief. So, go ahead, waste your time and break your own heart. Just don't drink." This sponsor's attitude is arrogant and presumptuous. The sponsor was claiming to be so wise and all seeing, and was so confident of her "authority and insight", that she believed she could patronizingly dismiss another woman's life. The sponsor didn't know how it would turn out, and made a mean-spirited assumption that any attempt to create a romantic relationship was doomed, implying that the woman she sponsored was a fool. What does this judgment and harsh criticism say about the sponsor?

Who really knows if any relationship will or won't work? From another point of view, relationships *always* work. Even if you argue a lot and break up, it provided opportunities for love, kindness, and awareness; it gave opportunities to learn about amends, and opportunities for insight. Just because it didn't last, or because it causes pain, doesn't mean it didn't work. Every circumstance embodies the potential for learning, transformation, and love, if you approach it from the right perspective, breakups included.[74]

If someone makes a sincere effort to be abstinent, and to live by the five spiritual principles embodied in the maintenance steps (meaning they're following instructions), that's all a sponsor need be concerned with.

---

[73] *Alcoholics Anonymous*, p. 69.
[74] The actor and author Peter Coyote once said in an interview: "Consistently reach for the most enlightened possibilities in any given situation."

Even if they aren't making a sincere effort, their private life is *still* no one else's business. As a sponsor, offer gentle comments on the overall spiritual nature of their life—their prayer and meditation, rigorous honesty, program-commitments, etc., and have no opinion on whether or not they should be in any relationship. If you, as a sponsor, disagree with their relationship or sexual lifestyle, then quietly excuse yourself from their life. Don't gossip.

Until Step Seven, no amount of cajoling or rule making will change the fact that addicts learn the hard way. Until such time as they appreciate Step Seven, they will always learn the hard way. Struggling to boss new-comers (or clients) around by making rules and demands, with the shallow justification of helping them (which is evidence of relationship addiction) is addiction) is abusive meddling.[75]

Don't forget the early-recovery success stories about love (which never get any press); and don't forget that many people in programs with years of abstinence are still all screwed-up about relationships. Everything depends on the attitudes and priorities you bring into a relationship, and those you leave it with.

In treatment centres there's probably a "no sex" rule, especially sexual relationships with other clients. It's often an automatic discharge offense. There are reasons that range from insurance liability and possible civil suits, to keeping chaos out of the treatment environment as much as possible and to keep clients focused on their therapy. (Notice I did not say focused on their spirituality.)

Residential treatment is usually intense, short-term, and addresses psychology, not spirituality. Preventing distractions like romance and sex helps keep attention focused and reduces chaos for short-term therapy. By entering therapy in a treatment centre, the client would, beforehand, knowingly agree to the guidelines of the treatment program. Therapy, and the professionals who offer it, maintain a very different mandate than any spiritual pilgrimage. This is only right.

Outside of a treatment centre's rules, or in voluntary cooperation with the obvious wise counsel of a well-trained, bona fide therapist, be very cautious of anyone (friend, sponsor, counsellor, religious official, self-appointed guru), who tries to impose sexual-conduct/abstinence rules. If someone you are associated with is conducting their life in a manner that offends your sensibilities, then you should *gently* excuse yourself from their

---

[75] *"If he is not interested in your solution... you may have to drop him until he changes his mind,"* and *"We find it a waste of time to keep chasing a man who cannot or will not work with you." Alcoholics Anonymous*, pp. 95 and 96 respectively.

life. Don't gossip, and especially don't try to control them. Role-model spirituality and mind your own business.[76]

The second inappropriate instruction to newcomers is: Don't make any big decisions for the first year. This might be wonderful if the machinations of life would cooperate with the rule, but life has a tendency to do whatever it wants, regardless of the puny rules people make up to suit their convenience or cater to their insecurities. Granted, stability is important, but people must respond to the vicissitudes of life. Choices are forced upon us. There is a major element of foolishness present when people try to live by a rule of making no big decisions because there is no way that they can trust that life will cooperate.

People who are newly abstinent and insecure about many things are easily influenced into greater insecurity. Trying to avoid big decisions, when they have no control over what circumstances may befall them, generates anxiety. Even if nothing happens, and no big decisions have to be made, the anxiety of hoping that nothing big happens, so as to avoid the possibility of having to make a big decision, makes abstinence more difficult than it needs to be. There is the additional concern of being forced to make a big decision and possibly incurring the disapproval of their sponsor. Besides that, isn't it more appropriate to instill confidence that with faith in a higher power, and commitment to abstinence, you can negotiate through anything?

Assuming that making no big decisions for a year is a rule that you agree to, and some major choice is then thrust upon you by life's circumstances, you will face indecision when responding to the choices that you have to make. In other words, in addition to life forcing you to make a big decision, you now have to contend with whatever guilt accrues from breaking the "no big decisions" rule.

Life forces choices on people. When you are required to make decisions in response to the vicissitudes of life, the decision is immediately more difficult when you aren't supposed to make decisions. You will want to avoid the decision (thereby being irresponsible), because of an arbitrary rule that's impossible to uphold.

Addicts spend much of their addicted life avoiding responsibility. It's hard enough making big decisions without some intrusive, arbitrary rule that complicates an already difficult situation. Besides that, forcing yourself to avoid important decisions to please someone else may cheat you out of fulfilling opportunities in your own life; and *again* besides that: Who de-

---

[76] This is not about sexual abuse, pedophilia, or other conduct that may be illegal. I intend that these observations be about consenting adults in the normal course of their life.

cides what decisions are big? Usually the sponsor (or counsellor), but how qualified are they to decide on your life?

Two "big" decisions, if they can be called that, are staying abstinent and finding a higher power. Abstinence and pursuing spirituality are what enable addicts to make big decisions and wiser choices—about everything. Deciding to be abstinent and spiritual, and to overthrow an entire lifestyle, are huge decisions in themselves and they're made in the first year.

If the role-models and more senior members of twelve-step programs work at being spiritual and responsible in their own lives, rather than meddling in the lives of others, we'd all be the better off for it.

The Relationship Between Abuse and Addictions

To make this easier to investigate and comprehend, I will offer two spectra. One is for Family Dysfunction, where the right end will represent a mild/subtle variety, and the left end will represent severe/blatant family dysfunction. The second spectra (#2) will be for Addictions where the right end represents mild/subtle addictions, and the left end, severe/blatant addictions. This is not intended to minimize or aggrandize anything or insult anyone. It's to make a general observation about families and addictions.

Spectrum of Family Dysfunction

Severe / Blatant	*Mild / Subtle*
overt sexual abuse	*no overt abuse*
repetitive or severe violence	*minimal or no violence*
cruel, shaming atmosphere	*minor emotional manipulation*
isolation, poverty, hunger	*some social life, no deprivation*
crime	*primarily law-abiding*
no support or caregiver attention	*some support and attention*

Spectrum of Addictions

Severe / Blatant	*Mild / Subtle*
crime, unemployment	*generally law-abiding*
sexual promiscuity	*minimal or no sexual acting out*
no family, homeless	*have family and home life*
chronic diseases	*generally healthy, employed*
destitute, poverty	*have lifestyle/disposable income*
significant instability	*reasonably stable*
chronic, visible acting out	*less obvious, subtle acting out*

Now, put these two side by side would leave you with a diagram similar to this:

Family Dysfunction

Severe / Blatant   *Mild / Subtle*

Severe / Blatant   *Mild / Subtle*

Addictions

If you are an addict, or if you know or work with addicts, consider each spectrum *separately* and estimate the overall, general state of your life in terms of (1) your childhood and then (2) your addiction. Mark where your life fits on each spectrum, and then join the dots. Find several other people who are getting recovered and ask them where they would place themselves on each spectrum. Join the dots for their choices. After several people have chosen for themselves, you will end up with a crisscrossing web of lines.

Family Dysfunction

Severe / Blatant   *Mild / Subtle*

Addictions

Some people with mildly dysfunctional families ended up on the severe end of the addictions spectrum, and others with severe family dysfunction ended up with "milder" addictions (or possibly none at all). You will find being severe on one spectrum *does not* guarantee you will be severe on the other.

Within a family, siblings that were exposed to similar parenting will not develop similar personality issues. The appearance or virulence of an addiction cannot be reliably predicted in relation to family issues. Yes, on a balance of possibilities, being from the severe end of "family" may *tend* to put you on the severe end of "addictions", but that is not to be depended upon. Do *not* buy into the myth that because you had a horrible childhood, you must be a severe addict; or that because you had a pretty decent family, you are less entitled to be an addict or to have a virulent addiction.

Multiple Variables and One Phenomenon

Genetics, biology, and related biogenealogical energy are the crucible out of which you were created. As a child, your family crucible, social environment, and education mold your personality further.[77] These set the stage for your own perceptions of whatever happens in your life. Your personality [ego] is created in the crucible of genetics, physiology, energy, infancy, temperament, childhood, and multiple cultural variables, and is then profoundly altered by addictions (a phenomenon). As an *un*spiritual or *un*recovered addict in sobriety, you will continue to choose some particular world-view that is always a subtle variation of the view your genetics, your environment, and your addiction gave you.

Children have caretakers and adults who provide for them: efficient, loving, or otherwise. No origin-story is perfect, but some are better than others. You can go into any book store and find dozens of books on "inner child", addictions, spirituality, healing, and meditating, each with varying degrees of credibility. You'd be very hard-pressed to find one book on ego that is for the layperson and relatively easy to understand. In short: Your personality is your ego in action.[78]

Egos are amazing things. They can make you completely responsible for everything that's gone wrong in your life and, a moment later, blame someone else for exactly the same things. Within the phenomenon of addictions, the real problem is that your ego is brilliant at externalizing responsibility onto everything except itself. To many, this seems an almost mystifying paradox, but it is understandable. You can reorganize your ego to take the heat off of yourself, but more importantly, off of whomever else you happen to be blaming.

Siblings often have remarkably different views of their parents and develop remarkably different worldviews ("issues"). Sometimes people from rather dislocated families develop very few "issues". Family dynamics and personal history are what they are: factual, and subject to personal interpretation, and always have unpredictable consequences.

Your personal worldview, your physiology, your personality, biogenealogical issues, and other factors like culture, educational experiences, and random calamity, will altogether decide where you end up on the addictions spectrum, but these do not put you on the spectrum. Being an addict of any description does not depend on whether you were beaten, abused, neglected, or abandoned. There is, or has been, dysfunction in everybody's life. Your

---

[77] This will be discussed in *Facets of Personal Transformation*. I refer you again to Gabor Mate's book *Scattered Minds*, cited earlier.
[78] See Appendix IV.

acting-out rituals are too easily classified (read: dismissed) as a metaphor for various and unresolved dynamics of rebellion and abuse.

With all the exceptions to the "dysfunctional family so I'm an addict" theory, none of the factors noted previously will explain why any particular individual ends up with an addiction. The factors influence where a person fits on the spectrum of addictions. It *is* possible to achieve some understanding of the relationship between all these factors, but only in long-term, in-depth therapy, with a therapist who authentically understands addictions, therapy, *and* spirituality, and is themselves recovered or not addicted, and meets the other criteria for cross-over work that I described earlier.

It's also unpredictable as to whether addicts can find spirituality and recover, and many transplant themselves into a socially approved addiction and stumble through their lives lost and confused, never really knowing "why". And regardless of the apparent cause, it's always the individual's responsibility to take charge of their life. Regarding addicts, there are no victims in this self-imposed crisis.[79]

Time and again it has been shown that when you attempt to categorize an addiction from some specific sociological or psychological perspective, the result is an externalized hunt for scapegoats, and after all is said and done, the addict will maintain a Victim's perspective of life. If you're an addict, the oftentimes confusing relationship between you and your choice of mood-altering experiences can be unraveled enough to be reasonably understood. The dynamics of that relationship, and those choices, operate within a complex paradigm, and are a metaphor for a corrupt relationship pattern within yourself, related to your spiritual nature.

What appears to be consistent among addicts is some long-standing, deep-seated, spiritual corruption. This manifests as spiritual corruption. This is why religion, new-age workshops, intense awareness groups (and the like), and twelve-step participation are very appealing acting-out rituals. They provide a socially approved avenue to self-righteous behaviour (i.e. sanctioned arrogance), and the illusion of health.

Spirituality is Attractive

You may be wondering, with all the problems there are today in twelve-step groups, how is it that anyone stays abstinent at all? The sad, short answer is, most people stay clean or sober on belligerence and defiance as they act out in some socially acceptable addiction. The original twelve-step program, beyond Step One, isn't about being sober, it's about

---

[79] "*Hurt once, shame on you! Hurt twice, shame on me!*" from *Blues ain't nothing but a good soul feeling bad*. Sheldon Kopp, Fireside/Parkside Recovery Book, Simon & Schuster, 1992, entry for December 12.

how spiritual you're willing to become. In meetings, notice the predominance of bragging about escapades, struggles about sobriety, and the absence of sincere discussion about obedience, humility, or a higher power. You cannot be angry, dishonest, and spiritual; but you can be angry, dishonest and sober. Compared to being spiritual, staying sober is quite easy.

Saint Augustine wrote that spirituality is not efficient.[80] It's awkward, elusive, demanding, and sometimes frightening. At times it seems contradictory. For addicts in particular, it is all of these things—and it's also very attractive. Why?

Spirituality is opposite to anything an addict has ever experienced. The peace, confidence, harmony, composure, and serenity that are dimly perceived as available are a powerful magnet. When newcomers see spiritual principles in others—even only corrupt and faint shadows of them—they are drawn in. But for me, sadly, the metaphor is of moths crashing into bright lights at night—newcomers are drawn in and slam up against hypocrisy, myths, misrepresentations, social success equations, psychobabble, and politics. They crash into relapse and despair because of most people's shallow investment into carrying the message of spirituality.

Newcomers celebrate abstinence, but are dazed and confused about what to do "after" abstinence, and it's not their fault that they aren't getting it. What are they not getting? That Steps One to Five are insight oriented, and not focused on transformation.

In the first five steps you discover things about yourself that are already there. These first five, albeit sometimes embarrassing, are safe. Self-insight is logical and can be influenced by self-will. You deepen your self-knowledge and insight.

Step Six, however, is the cornerstone of your transformation, and is therefore the most difficult. At Step Six (and thereafter) you are required to actually change your personality (transform), which is spiritually influenced and therefore unpredictable. It is threatening for "control oriented" addicts to surrender to transformation beginning at Step Six. It leaves them entirely in a position of "unknowing" at the hands of their higher power. Step Two (the most important) and Step Six (the most difficult) are deftly avoided because they demand so much.

Step Two is actually the cornerstone of a recovered life. It is therefore the most important step beyond abstinence.

---

[80] *The Confessions*, St Augustine.

Chapter 3

Step One and Some Related Details

Myths and Misinformation

Before I get into the details of doing an actual Step One, which is: *"We admitted we were powerless over alcohol—that our lives had become unmanageable,"*[1] [Remember to substitute any addiction for the word alcohol.] I want to talk about a few myths and "rules" that are often touted as being part of healthy recovery. These horrendously confuse or entirely prevent your getting recovered, which is complicated enough already.

The Two-Part Step One

One myth exists in the way that some people represent Step One. They claim, usually as an excuse for relapse, or yet another defense of their irresponsible or insensitive behaviour, that they have only done the first half or the second half of the step. This explanation is usually given in a tone of self-castigation (which often rings hollow), and now that they are back for the seventh or more time, they are determined to focus on whichever half of Step One they had been ignoring. This excuse is flawed: There are not two halves to Step One.

Remind yourself, and it is so obvious that we don't think about it, that one reason we can impart knowledge through writing is grammar. If you took any book and removed the punctuation and the capital letters, the book would make no sense. If you substituted commas for periods, or semicolons for dashes, the writing would take on a different meaning. Editors insist on correct grammar, especially in books of instruction. Grammar is what organizes words so people can transmit ideas in some manner close to what they intend. Those who wrote *Alcoholics Anonymous* were schooled in traditional English and grammar and they were intelligent. It would be reasonable to assume they wrote the words they intended to write and used the grammar they intended to use.

In Step One, the short line between *alcohol* and *that* is a dash. A dash is a specific piece of punctuation—an abrupt interruption, which advises the

---

[1] *Alcoholics Anonymous*, p. 59, and *Twelve Steps and Twelve Traditions*, p. 21.

reader that what follows the dash, is an appositive phrase or summary. Whatever phrase or clause follows a dash, within the same sentence, is an explanation or summary of what preceded the dash. So, *"—that our lives had become unmanageable"* is an explanation or a definition of the phrase *"We admitted that we were powerless over alcohol—."* They are the same ideas, represented by different words, so we can understand the point that the author intended. The phrases immediately before and after a dash do *not* offer ideas independent of each other.

Additionally, note that there is no writing regarding Step One in *Twelve Steps and Twelve Traditions* or *Alcoholics Anonymous* that reads "and now for part two." Nowhere is it written: "Now, for the second half of Step One." There are serious risks in creating the idea that Step One is in two parts. These risks are subtle and the consequences vicious. When people view Step One as being in two parts, they create serious complications that allow them to dramatize the simple idea presented in the step. One result is that they are provided another excuse for irresponsibility.

Step One is in the past tense. One purpose of this is to begin, and then to expand awareness during your abstinence, of the consequences and repercussions of your acting out. "Acting out" happened before or prior to your abstinence. "Acting out" is history. Regarding the original Step One, "life's" unmanageability is directly attached to your former acting out and powerlessness. They are symbiotic.

Should you change the dash to an "and" or a semicolon, or when you ignore the correct grammatical use of a dash, you thereby create two parts to Step One. You now have an opportunity to redefine an unmanageable life as independent of the context of your former acting-out behaviour. This separates the drinking/acting out from the unmanageability. This is subtle and dangerous. Understanding it is tricky.

When you separate unmanageability from acting out, the destructive behaviour stays "in the past" and unmanageability (now erroneously independent from acting out) can be examined by itself in the present. This allows "unmanageability" to be used in the present as an excuse for irresponsibility. Unmanageability can thereby become an independent, preeminent issue: "It wasn't *really* the drinking [acting out], it was the unmanageability, so maybe if/when I get my life manageable I will be fine."

As soon as you separate acting out from "unmanageable"; once unmanageability stands independent unto itself, there's an escape route to avoid responsibility in sobriety. With Step One in two parts, unmanageability in sobriety becomes an easily available excuse for irresponsible behaviour rather than a defining quality of active addiction. Irresponsibility that's justified (concealed) by calling it "unmanageability" cannot be addressed properly because it has become camouflaged as legitimate. Many people classify their irresponsible sober behaviour in abstinence as unmanageability, when, in fact, it's a complicated justification for deliberately spiteful, mean, irresponsible, or petulant behaviour; or they're denying the presence of another addiction.

Is it Really Relapse?

When seen from a more responsible point of view, most relapses aren't "relapses" because the person concerned didn't exit their addictions. The common experience called relapse should be more accurately described as the resumption of an obvious addiction in association with ongoing subtle addictions.

Consider people who are addicted to tobacco, relationships, and alcohol. This is a common combination of addictions. They quit drinking and join AA but continue acting out in other socially acceptable addictions that are perceived as less destructive, like tobacco, relationships, righteousness, spending. After some period of not drinking, all the while still acting out in the other two addictions, they suddenly start drinking again. They then attend their twelve-step meeting and confess their "relapse." Yes, technically, they relapsed into alcoholism, but they didn't relapse into addiction: they never got out of it.

For the most part, people who claim to have relapsed haven't, they've only resumed some blatant addiction they had previously discontinued; an addiction that garners more disapproval and destruction than the subtle ones they had continued to practice that didn't garner disapproval. Should people exit all their addictions, they are so spiritually aligned that they don't relapse at all. Use the word relapse carefully.

The Manageable Truth About Unmanageability

In the original literature, the concept of unmanageability is used in relation to active addiction.

You meet a person. You date, sincerely love them, and desire fidelity in the relationship. You get married. A year later you wake up in bed with somebody else and you're getting divorced; yet when you got married, your love and commitment were sincere. Maybe it's your child's birthday and certainly you love your children. You make a commitment about the birthday, but because you have a couple of drinks on the afternoon of the party, you cause a huge scene and the party's a disaster. Or, you really enjoy your career, but you blow it by getting stoned and missing work just before that one big project is finished. Remember that at the moment you made the commitment, you were sincere.

How many times have you had a sincere intention but were later irresponsible because of your acting out? The unmanageability of your life, that's in concert with your active addiction, makes it appear that you weren't sincere or serious about your marriage, your children, your recovery, or your job. Not following through on a commitment doesn't necessarily mean you were insincere when you made it.

When you are active in your addiction you are irresponsible. An unmanageable life, in this context, is a symptom of, and intended to be a part of, the truth of what active addiction does to a person. You appear to be insincere because you're an addict, not because you're insincere.

Step One is to be read in the past tense by people who are abstinent. It offers clarity on what active addiction encompasses. Step One is in the past tense. That our lives *had become* unmanageable is a reference to the historical chaos attendant to alcoholic drinking or other acting out. Knowing that a dash means what it means, the clause *"—that our lives had become unmanageable"* means you *were* powerless over acting out.

Here's the insight: If your life "in sobriety" is still unpredictable and unmanageable, in some ways vaguely similar to what it was when you were in your obvious addiction, then you're acting out in another addiction, although not the one from which you've been abstinent.

In sobriety, because you don't like your life, because your life is hard, because you don't get your own way, does not mean your life is unmanageable. Notice the number of times "unmanageable" is misused in twelve-step conversation to complain about the state of affairs in someone's life of abstinence. What I'm getting at here is, while you become recovered, your ego will want to define a life you don't like as "unmanageable", and blame your addiction, rather than viewing yourself as petulant and slothful.[2] Labeling the usual slights and misdemeanors of life as unmanageable is fatal to spiritual integrity.

In early abstinence, you probably begin to show up for your appointments on time. Although you don't like visiting the probation officer or the banker or the doctor, you show up on time, which you rarely did when you were drinking or using. You show up for work on time although you don't like your job or your boss. Maybe you don't like living in a recovery house and your life circumstances are unpleasant: you're broke, you have to take the bus because you don't have a car, you've got to stand in line to use the bathroom, the food is too salty, everything's overcooked, and your room-

---

[2] Your ego defines your life in the way it filters and interprets the relationship between the Matrix of Your Soul and the Corporeal Universe; see Appendix IV. And, in Chapter 8, I discuss The Two Step Dance, which is this dynamic in action.

mate snores, but you still show up for meals and appointments. You don't like that you've got to get a minimum-wage job and start paying rent.

Any typical "unpleasant" life situation is your excuse to label your life as unmanageable. But, none of these circumstances mean your life is unmanageable; they just mean your life is difficult and you don't like it.[3] Unpleasant circumstances are *not* a symptom of the disease they are the result of it. Symptoms are not external they're internal. The symptom of addiction is in the irresponsible, cynical, or petulant way you blame life and people, and misuse the term *unmanageable*. External unpleasantness is the result of the disease, not the motivator of it.

Addicted egos cling to an entrenched belief that addicts are somehow, supposed to be exempt from the routine pains and irritations of life. Addicts complain that life isn't fair for them, and by that imply it should be more unfair for others.[4] Lives in early sobriety aren't unmanageable: they are hard work, often unpleasant, and for a long while, painful.

When you're getting recovered and label a difficult life as unmanageable, you're (probably) using "unmanageable" in the wrong context. Unmanageable is symbiotic with acting out in this context. The adjective *unmanageable* is not intended to legitimize whining and complaining; after all, addictions and early recovery from them are self-imposed crises.

Regardless of any of this: At first glance, it would appear that unpleasantness is a condition attendant to life, addicts included. The magic of a truly spiritual life is that all unpleasantness becomes optional.

Step One "Guides"

There are many instruction sheets that are circulated in the recovery community that are referred to as Step One Guides. I've collected quite a few over the years and they have several things in common. I will choose to assume well-intentioned people wrote them all, but who apparently missed the point of the steps, and made getting recovered much more complicated than it needs to be.

Many tell you to write and talk about your parents—describe what kind of people they were emotionally, mentally, spiritually, and physically. In contrast, *Alcoholics Anonymous* suggests that you examine your own drinking behaviour. I cannot find, in either AA text, any direct or indirect suggestion requiring you understand the emotional or mental attitudes of

---

[3] Remember: Most of the work in the world is done by tired people who don't feel very good.
[4] Life is neither fair nor unfair; it is benignly indifferent to everything. There is no meaning to life, except what meaning we each assign to it.

your parents. What kind of family you had is not mentioned as a factor contributing to the difficulty of becoming spiritual.[5]

In a Step One guide from a recovery house, whose stated mandate is to address addictions in a twelve-step model, respondents are asked to analyze their family of origin. Many counsellors can't do this; why demand it from a confused newcomer? It implies some "family-of-origin" responsibility for the addiction. Not only does this misrepresent Step One, it lays the groundwork for a victim mentality and exacerbates anxiety and futility within the newcomer. This is blatantly contrary to the idea presented in the AA literature, that alcoholism/addiction (with all its unsavory ramifications) is a self-imposed crisis.[6]

Similarly: Another treatment centre asks, "How did your parents [in other questions, siblings, and grandparents] express their love and affection toward each other?" Yes, some dysfunction arises out of the inability to express love, or from never having received unconditional positive regard.[7] And yes, relationship patterns are passed on through generations, and sometimes fail to meet developmental dependency needs. These step guides imply, however, that these relationships, if troubled, explain the addiction, which in turn makes it easy for the addict to externalize responsibility for any life damaging consequences. The client/newcomer reasons, with an ego-smile of absolution: "It's not me, it's my parents and grandparents. My siblings didn't properly express their love; that's why I'm an addict. What a relief! I thought for a moment that it was *my* fault." Addicts go to great lengths to avoid responsibility and far too many treatment centres and professionals are complicit in this.

In many Step One "guides", newcomers with minimal insight are asked to puzzle out complicated psychological paradigms. By implication, they are being told that an addiction and the self-annihilation related to it are somehow the responsibility of some classification of caregiver. [As a complicated aside, the counsellor who uses this type of guide goes to great lengths to avoid responsibility, too.] Caregivers may have evinced unsavory behaviour, but they did not cause the addiction. According to *Alcoholics Anonymous* it is a self-imposed crisis.

---

[5] Being aware of the neglect or abuse you experienced may contribute to an understanding of why you are ashamed, neurotic, or racist, etc. Developing that awareness, however, is not the purpose of twelve-step work. Becoming spiritual is the purpose of twelve-step work. Psychological health is noticeably different from spiritual integrity. Cross-over work that I described earlier may be necessary to establish abstinence, but cross-over work is not necessarily focused on historical family dynamics.

[6] *Alcoholics Anonymous*, p. 53.

I have another Step One guide that presents this: "We accepted that we were powerless over the *effects* of our addictions, that our lives had become unmanageable," [emphasis added]. First, there is a notable difference between *admit* and *accept*. A newcomer at Step One is incapable of "accepting" anything—admitting, yes, accepting, no; I explain this elsewhere. This particular Step One guide changes admit to accept (disastrous in itself) and requires more than a new person is capable of.

Being powerless over the *effects* of an addiction (such as the derivative consequences of poverty and ill health) is significantly different from being powerless over the behaviour of acting out. These changes expand the scope of Step One to include acceptance, which because of character defects they are incapable of, and requires they take responsibility for events (the *effects* of their addiction) over which they have no control. This type of hyper-responsibility is a facet of relationship addiction.

Admission of anything more than truth of the basic relationship between acting out, unmanageability, and powerlessness is quite impossible to a newcomer at Step One. In *Alcoholics Anonymous,* Step One is to establish the truth of the clear and definite relationship between unmanageability and acting out, which is the initial major inroad to the truths of powerlessness and irresponsibility, *and* which is the only effective precondition for Step Two. This particular recovery house guide, and many other psychologically reworked Step Ones, dangerously conceals the relationship between acting out and powerlessness, which will subsequently, seriously undermine the efficacy of Step Two.

The original Step One is for you to (a) clarify the obvious and direct relationship between unmanageability and powerlessness during your acting out; (b) to see the unmanageability and attendant consequences that are related to your acting out; and (c), for you to admit the truth of these.

The authors of guides like this rewrite the step to psychologically spoon-feed clients, in an attempt to hasten the process of recovery, or they assume they can make lighter the burden of Step One. They thereby impose an expanded, personal interpretation of the step. They're emotionally invested in the success of clients, which indicates abusive or unreasonable expectations on the counsellor's part. This subtly legitimizes relationship addiction. In the nuance of the underlying issues here, the writers of these guides are very likely untreated relationship addicts.

Another guide states a goal of Step One is to achieve humility, and defines humility as "a clear reckoning of who we really are." In the original

---

[7] Unconditional positive regard is one aspect of Client Centred Therapy, developed by Carl R. Rogers, *The Carl Rogers Reader,* Edited by Howard Kirschenbaum and Valerie Land Henderson, Houghton Mifflin Co., 1989, p. 225.

literature, humility is only vaguely implied in Step One by the required admission of truth—humility is *silently* inferred by the unstated spiritual axiom of humility-via-honesty. Step One has a reference to being humbled by the admission of personal powerlessness, and humbled by the truth of the newcomer's devastating weakness. "Being humbled," in this context, refers to the introduction of reality and the loss of delusion in a newcomer's life; not humility *vis-à-vis* a spiritual principle.

Spiritual humility is *not* described as a specific goal of Step One, and humility is certainly much more complex than "a clear reckoning of who we really are." This guide has taken the complicated concept of humility, offered a very inefficient definition of it, and pushed it visibly into the middle of Step One where it doesn't belong.

People who have been abstinent for years struggle with humility. Priests, ministers, yogis, monks—the experts, never mind the laity—see humility as a life-long quest fraught with pitfalls. Psychologically and spiritually defiant newcomers detoxing from years of insane thoughts and self-annihilation, are not to be given the impossible and unnecessary burden of understanding humility at Step One.

Other guides have Step One as: "We admitted we were powerless over alcohol; that our lives were unmanageable." [changed the dash to a semicolon] Or: "We admitted we were powerless over alcohol and that our lives were unmanageable." [dash changed to and; also changed 'had become' to were] These changes alter the very nature of the step. Unmanageability is here presented as independent of the addiction, and creates unnecessary complications and opportunities to justify irresponsible behaviour.

These guides go on to say specifically in relation to Step One: "Furthermore, here in this treatment centre, which uses the twelve steps, the only real source of unconditional love is God as you understand Him."

There are these serious problems in these guides: (1) Step One is in two separate parts, which creates the problems discussed earlier. (2) Spirituality is presented as an *active* part of Step One; it isn't. (3) The author, who is a counsellor, has interjected and imposed personal, spiritual values into Step One. They declared love as the gift of God as you understand Him. To the newcomer this denies freedom of choice in spiritual matters. (4) By changing "had become" to "were," the guide edits the original scope of Step One, which is supposed to allow an awareness of the progressive nature of untreated addiction and not its singular end result.

Another document is called a Step One Assessment. An assessment is quite different than a guide. This assessment is comprised of 49 questions and instructions regarding Step One. Here are seven of them:

- Briefly describe your memories of your father in your early childhood years.
- Have you or your partner ever had an abortion, miscarriages, or given any children up for adoption?
- Briefly describe any significant sad or happy events that you remember in your childhood.
- Briefly describe your home life as you remember it in the first ten years of your life.
- Which parent are you most like?
- Have you ever been physically, sexually or emotionally abused as a child or as a teenager? By whom? How has this affected you?
- Have you ever had or desired sex with animals? How has this affected your life?

Of the 49 questions, 24 are related to substance abuse and 25 are therapeutically intrusive, related to various and sundry psychological issues. There is no theme or structure to the 25 intrusive questions, six of which are of a prurient sexual nature, and all 25 are overall, a random inquisition, fishing for something dramatic. It presupposes an egregious life.

In a twelve-step meeting or an addictions treatment centre, the Step One issue is the unmanageability from your acting out, not that you were abused or your parents didn't like each other. Parental affection *may* be important as far as being in therapy goes, but within the context of early abstinence, these questions are inappropriate. Acting out must be kept generally separate from family of origin influence so that abstinence is entirely a function of personal responsibility and commitment.

There are two implications with long term, devastating consequences in these various corruptions of Step One. The first is the clear implication that if you ended up in formal treatment for addictions there must be horrible abuse or major trauma; otherwise, you wouldn't be in treatment. The second is that trauma (real or imagined) is the primary cause of your addiction. It decidedly isn't.

Far too many addicts and caregivers fail to appreciate that the degree of self-harm through addictions is rarely proportional to the trauma experienced in childhood. Having an addiction doesn't require there be egregious childhood "issues." This is expanded upon at various places in this book, and specifically on p. 121, The Relationship Between Abuse and Addiction.

Misunderstanding this leads to the dangerous, erroneous supposition that by resolving the trauma, you resolve the addiction. It also sets up a psychological witch-hunt—the addict gets to hunt for someone to blame. Also: In histories where there was no specific violence the newcomer may not feel entitled to participate; will withhold a simple heartfelt story to avoid being teased, or will exaggerate in order to compete and garner attention. These styles of "Step One" make abstinence more difficult than it is, and irresponsibility more difficult to address.

Additionally, some twelve-step/support groups complicate matters when they encourage discussions about how caregivers and early family relationships didn't meet childhood needs, and how this historical (emotional) deficiency is now compensated for by the love or acceptance in the addict's twelve-step group. This is a nice thing to say, but it is, more often than not, political and probably not true. Subtle peer pressure that limits participation to whatever is within the group's comfort zone, the rampant and abusive gossip, the often overt and always covert rules for acceptance, aren't demonstrations of love. Being told you are loved unconditionally when you really aren't is very damaging and often a re-creation of the hypocrisy in many families. And there's the corollary—many addicts were sincerely loved and were so destructive they destroyed the relationship. Whether or not you were (or are) loved has nothing to do with the requirements of Step One.

These are only a few examples of how the seemingly innocuous altering of Step One can cause harm. It identifies a destructive combination of therapy and twelve-step work. From one perspective, these so-called Step One "guides" represent some counsellor or sponsor's attempt to make abstinence easier to attain. At a deeper level, this effort to make it easier is indicative of unresolved issues within the people who rewrite the steps; various caregivers' confusion or insecurity that's being acted out in a form of relationship addiction, which is concealed by altruistic rhetoric.

Now, combine this with a second perspective—staff at treatment centres wrote the aforementioned examples. When viewed as treatment centres needing to generate or maintain funding by creating a psychological version of step one (because "becoming spiritual" won't get government money), these rewritten steps are motivated by commercial enterprise. This is explored in more depth at Appendix I, in the section Self Supporting.

Doing "good" things like rewriting the steps to make them easier for the suffering newcomer is very often a mercenary endeavor so that a treatment centre can generate and maintain funding. It may appear benevolent, but upon close examination, it is very likely not as efficient, honorable, or wise as is claimed. Every newcomer has to pay the full admission price for spiritual integrity—nothing is free, getting recovered is expensive, and you pay in advance.

The original Step One offers that the resolution of addiction and un-manageability begins with abstinence, taking full responsibility for that abstinence, and admitting the truth of powerlessness. The majority of treatment centres' "Step One" guides is rooted in mercenary endeavor and implies that the resolution of addictive crisis and unmanageability is in insight psychology. Insight into developmental trauma and shame will make you less confused, but that won't make you spiritual, and you will invariably end up being only a more insightful practicing addict.

The majority of clients I worked with in the last 15 years are drowning in pop-psychology. Their command of therapeutic jargon would rival many therapists' and invariably, the more they have experienced relapse and recidivist indoctrination in programs and treatment centres, the worse off they are. When they relapse yet again, yet another doctor/therapist/sponsor sends them to yet another program/therapy group, or often the same program, with the admonition to "try harder." These clients *are* trying "harder" otherwise they wouldn't be back in a professional's office or a twelve-step group. The client, or someone else on their behalf, then pays thousands of dollars and the "Recovery Opera in One Act" starts over again. Everyone waits for the repeat ending, which happens 95% of the time.

There is something valid in the colloquial definition of insanity: repeating destructive behaviour and expecting different results; but whom does it apply to? Doctors and counsellors repeatedly send (the same) clients to (the same) treatment centres and get the same results. The same sponsors repeatedly take the same relapsing newcomers through the steps the same way and they relapse (again). The professionals keep their jobs, the sponsors look spiritual because they work *so* hard, and the addicts die. [It's hard to describe this without sounding cynical. I'm not cynical: that's just what's happening.]

Where there are unresolved addictions in caregivers; where unnecessary prying into client's lives are camouflaged as psychological investigation; where a belief exists that addictions treatment is a moral issue or social responsibility; when caregivers push expedience or avoid spirituality for financial considerations; or when people seek to heal themselves by sponsoring or counselling others, there is abuse to the client/newcomer. All of this is a part of the significant mess that most doctors, counsellors, training programs, caregivers, treatment centres, newcomers, and twelve-step programs are in regarding addictions.[8]

---

[8] Yes, I know it sounds cynical or hopeless; possibly overly critical. I know the staff is usually well intentioned; however, empathy and good intentions are insufficient, here. I wish to express my support for some treatment centres; especially detoxification centres. I have occasionally consulted with agencies to smooth out their program and make it more (cont'd)

Sentimental commiserating isn't appropriate in getting recovered, and neither is being socially good. Substitutes for hard work, attempts to replace self-discipline with external obedience, expecting sympathy to resolve suffering, blaming others, creating scapegoats, suppressing spirituality, denying freedom of choice in spiritual matters, and suggesting quick-fix solutions to tremendously complicated problems, are all manifestations of relationship addiction, which used to be called codependence. Wounded caregivers—be they parents, therapists, counsellors, priests, doctors, ministers, friends, spouses, or sponsors—are a recipe for disaster.

Guides that use intrusive psychological questions are inappropriate *vis-à-vis* the intent of the original twelve-step program. Moreover, when the clients' responses are not addressed by an experienced, non-relationship-addicted therapist, who understands the intrusive nature of the questions and the intricate multi-dimensional relationships of the issues; a therapist who can actually do something appropriate and can negotiate effectively between psychology and spirituality—then these self-styled guides always make things worse. *Always.*

This wise counsel from Mary Caroline Richards should be never far from the awareness of caregivers: *"Do not be deluded that knowledge of the path can be substituted for putting one foot in front of the other."*[9] Writing down histories of childhood abuse, reading about spirituality, scanning self-help books, taking courses, knowing things, being a counsellor, or sitting around at meetings sharing (which is usually either gossiping, bragging, or complaining) will accomplish nothing spiritually.

Client selection for addictions treatment is often generic. The fact that you're addicted, claim to desire abstinence, are facing calamity, and can pay the fee, means you meet the admission criteria. Given this, and that all early recovery is about poly-addictions[10] (personality structures that harbor addictions are horrendously complicated), an effective Step One must simply be a recognition of the powerlessness or unmanageability, with a single view to establishing a successful continuation of abstinence. Anything else misrepresents the actual requirements of the step and the spiritual dynamic of the original program. That's why the chapter on Step One in *Twelve Steps and Twelve Traditions* is so short: recognize the direct relationship between unmanageability/self-destruction and drinking/acting out, become and stay abstinent, and wait until the fog clears. In doing anything beyond this,

---

effective (less relationship addicted). This involves working with the staff. If they are willing to self-examine and not blame the clients, it is not as difficult as it may seem.

[9] Mary Caroline Richards has written at least two books that I know of: *Centering*, Wesleyan University Press, 1969, and *Towards Wholeness*, Wesleyan University Press, 1980.

[10] No addict lives with only one addiction. At the outset of all healing journeys, they all have *at least* two and usually three addictions.

within the boundaries of something called a Step One, the caregiver will create additional problems, which must eventually be resolved by the client, not the caregiver.

Twelve-step group members, sponsors, medical doctors, and recovery-house staff aren't (usually) trained to handle the trauma associated with abuse and unmet developmental dependency needs, which do contribute to the viciousness of an addiction but are not responsible for it. And even if these people are trained, they shouldn't necessarily be facilitating that work in early recovery.

To become recovered requires a certain environment; what I refer to as a crucible of safety. The atmosphere that surrounds someone's efforts to heal or recover must have certain qualities that promote it.

(1) Addicts who are healing (in therapy) from developmental, shock, or abuse trauma need abstinence and a safe crucible for that therapy in order for the therapy to be even marginally successful.[11]

(2) The twelve-step group that supports [or is supposed to support] abstinence and encourage a spiritual pilgrimage out of addictions must also offer a safe crucible for spiritual work.

These "crucibles of safety" are quite different and must not be confused with each other. Only very cautiously should these be combined, and more often than not, they shouldn't; but if they must be, it should not be in a group format. Investing Step One with psychologically intrusive material is risky, and for the most part self-defeating because the original twelve steps are not for psychological health, they're for developing and maintaining spiritual integrity.

Addicts may well be the most dysfunctional, quasi-successful group of complicated, self-destructive people on the planet—the sickest of the "functioning" sick. They are often seen as misfits, rebels, trouble makers, and failures one and all. This is not final. The number of socially successful professionals, house-wives or -husbands, students, and otherwise ordinary folk that are destructively practicing addicts is quite staggering.

To me, it's like we are all swimming in an ocean of addictions, but we can't really notice it for what it is. So few people are truly healthy (non-addicted) we tend to label them as "abnormal". It's interesting to me, but also understandable, that we don't spend more time impressing upon people the life or death nature of this reality.

Take a look around any twelve-step meeting room. There's anywhere from a dozen to several hundred people, most knowing nothing substantive about what it is that's killing them. Probably well over half are clean and

---

[11] These three types of trauma are briefly explained in Appendix III.

sober less than two years, more than eighty percent of them will not maintain their abstinence, and someone in that room will very likely be dead from their addiction in the next year. Who will it be? Untreated addicts and early newcomers live on borrowed time. Don't have any illusions about the dangers of addictions.

Every time an addict "in recovery" tells a lie, they're collecting relapse points. Those who smoke, use pornography, are self-perpetuating victims, work addicts, religious addicts, whatever . . . they'll never understand spirituality in its deeper beauty—they're practicing addicts. Every time they avoid responsibility, their abstinence is that much more tenuous. There's a serious price to pay for disobedience to, or deliberate avoidance of, the instructions outlined in the original twelve-step literature. Nothing is free.[12]

If you're an addict, and desirous of the spiritual integrity that is available via twelve-step work, then I want to impress upon you that your journey is a life-or-death matter. Remember, the first rule is people die from addictions, and the second rule is you can't change the first rule.

If you go to a meeting to try to find a girlfriend or a boyfriend, you're in trouble. If you go to a meeting to try to find a job, you're in trouble. If you go to a meeting to find somebody to lend you twenty dollars or take you to the dance, you're in trouble. If you go to a meeting to get and stay sober and thereby enable you to find a higher power, you'll be fine. If God or spirituality scares you, well . . . that's tough; I mean that gently: that is tough. A higher power might scare you; addictions will kill you. Do you want to be scared or do you want to be dead?

Take as much time as you need to make this palatable, but understand, in no uncertain terms, right from the start, that spirituality and some form of a higher power are at the core of twelve-step work. The purpose of participating in a twelve-step program is to (one day at a time) maintain abstinence, get rid of character defects, and participate in a spiritually disciplined life. It's to be of service to your higher power, as you understand this phrase, not to serve yourself a good life. Accordingly, by far the most important step is Step Two, and the most difficult step is Step Six. Over the course of this book, you will read why these statements about Steps Two and Six are true. Yes, social and financial stability often result from abstinence, but these are neither the intended goals, nor are they the real rewards.

Addictions Prohibit Spirituality

Many addicts in recovery presume of themselves that they're spiritual, or "kind of" spiritual, or spiritually on track, or at least making an effort to

---

[12] My favorite proverb is Spanish: "Take what you want," God said, "and pay for it."

be spiritual. In many cases they secretly know they are dishonest or manipulative or otherwise acting out in concealed addictions like pornography or work. This usually means they are making an attempt at the secular notion of being morally good, which is different than actually attempting to be spiritual. Many also believe that they're "spiritual" because they make a sporadic effort at praying, or belong to a support group of one kind or another. Other people attend church services and so label themselves spiritual. Most aren't.

If they're participating in any addiction: adrenaline, aggression, aggressive-sports viewing, alcohol, anger, drugs, food, gambling, compulsive masturbation, moral self-righteousness, pornography, relationships, religion, romance, sex, shopping, spending, sports, television, tobacco, twelve-step meetings, violence, work, workshops, to name a few—*any* addiction—they can't be spiritual. How can people be spiritual when they are actively negligent to their own welfare, are willfully irresponsible, or are degrading and harming themselves and others? How can people be spiritual when they take pleasure from watching people beat up, injure, and dominate other people (which some people call sports)?[13] The conditions that must exist within anyone to enable any addiction preclude absolutely the person being sincerely spiritual and living with their rights and freedoms.

Be aware that, even though abstinent from their primary addiction, people who curse and swear with vehemence and rudeness, who participate in violence through sports, who are sexually irresponsible, righteous about religion; who are racist or sexist, and who *also* claim they're spiritual, aren't. They may believe in a higher power and probably do; however, their spirituality is an illusion and lacks integrity.

An addiction is a disease of self-destruction, impression management, and delusion.[14] It embodies self-annihilation, deceit, arrogance, selfishness, and blame. These conditions of personality are mandated by the addiction itself. To be spiritual there must be a willing posture of deep respect for self and others, veracity, humility, charity without contract, and responsibility and obedience. *Being in any addiction and being spiritual are mutually exclusive.*

---

[13] What follows is one specifically Christian view of violence that has a universal application. Dr. Martin Luther King, Jr. said, *"I am expert in recognition of a simple, eloquent truth. That truth is that it is sinful for any of God's children to brutalize any of God's other children..."* As reported in *Martin Luther King, Jr.* by Marshall Frady, a Lipper®/Viking Book, 2002 Viking/Penguin, p. 188.

[14] Impression Management: investing energy into making oneself appear as one isn't—a devious self-advertising campaign designed to conceal shame, fear, or aspects of personality that might or would meet with disapproval or are inner-personally repressed. This is a significant manipulation strategy and it will be referred to many times.

Despairing, isolated, not participating in life in a meaningful way, enduring loneliness, and self-annihilation are conditions of addictions regardless of how gregarious, healthy, or spiritual you *act*. After you've quit all addictive acting out, you start to find out what's really going on inside you, and what being spiritually disciplined really is. Stop all of your addictions, be responsible, and abandon your devotion to the accumulation of shiny things and influence. Being an active addict and being spiritual are mutually exclusive.

The technological tendency to ignore matters of the spirit is demonstrated in the medical/scientific determination to categorize addiction as a medical concern. Certainly there are derivative medical or psychological consequences of addictions (detoxification, physical damage, shame, etc.) that require expert medical or psychological attention. Also, there may well be contributing psychological factors. Addressing these is crucial, and certainly it's important to do skilled cross-over work for the abstinence not-available addictions. But, doctors and therapists can't heal addictions because the actual addiction *itself* isn't a "medical" illness. Only inner, self-determined, ongoing spiritual integrity resolves it.

Addictions encompass such a wide range of manifestations that they defy any consistent scientific classification. The only perspective that, so far, *is* consistent and effective is that addictions are a manifestation of spiritual corruption, and can appear "everywhere." (Notice, too, that "a higher power" also defies any scientific or cultural classification.)

Elementary Truths For Addicts

The Forward to the Second Edition and The Doctor's Opinion of *Alcoholics Anonymous*[15] report this anecdotal evidence: *"Of alcoholics who came to A.A. and really tried, 50% got sober at once and remained that way; 25% sobered up after some relapses, and among the remainder, those who stayed on with A.A. showed improvement."*[16] They're telling you that if you really try, you've got three-to-one odds of making it. [As a teenager, I was told several times that the odds of me living to 30 were very slim. Years later, when I joined a support group, I was told in no uncertain terms that if I tried hard, and did *exactly* what is outlined in *Alcoholics Anonymous,* I had a 75% chance of making it. Those were the best odds anyone ever gave me, for anything.]

Of course, that success is dependent upon making a real effort. Obedience (the "O" word), and responsibility (the "R" word) are often a curse to addicts, but nothing is free. If you are obedient to the instructions, and re-

---

[15] Pages xiii and xxiii respectively.
[16] *Alcoholics Anonymous*, p. xx.

sponsible for your self-imposed crisis, according to the AA textbooks, you have a 75% chance of becoming recovered.

The two AA reference texts are the source material for all twelve-step programs in the world. Everything effective regarding addictions and spirituality is contained in those two books. They are more dependable than sponsors, meetings, and conventions (but not as entertaining). I'm not cautious about applying the original twelve steps to any addiction; I'm only cautious about rewriting the material. Rewrites always obscure the spiritual integrity of the original material, which is intended to be a program of spiritual transformation not psychological help. Regarding all addictions, once abstinence is established, I suggest that people getting recovered read *Alcoholics Anonymous* and *Twelve Steps and Twelve Traditions,* pencil in their addiction in place of "alcohol", and change nothing else. It may be as nondramatic as TV viewing or shopping. More than anything else, that will guarantee spiritual results. Go to the source.

Alcoholics Anonymous is a textbook and offers instruction like other textbooks do.[17] *Twelve Steps and Twelve Traditions* is its companion volume. What is notably different about them, and crucial to understand, is in all other areas of study you seek knowledge outside of your spiritual nature. This includes studying psychology and religion, which are respectively the study of your personality, and the sociological study of delusion and cultural rituals. All knowledge seeking is a secular pilgrimage external to your deeper spiritual nature, and you will thusly not find the Great Reality, which lies deep within you.[18]

Alcoholics Anonymous and *Twelve Steps and Twelve Traditions* are for spiritual transformation; nothing else. The purpose of studying the AA texts is not to understand them *per se,* and not to acquire external knowledge. You study the AA texts to study yourself, and thereby understand how and why you are not accessing your deeper spiritual nature. They advise how to transform yourself so you can become spiritual—entirely an *internal* process. Excluding the AA texts, all the other twelve-step instruction books that I've examined are recast in such a way as to include some psychology, which dilutes the spiritual intent and renders them less effective.

If you believe that participating in a twelve-step group is a journey to psychological health and social contentment, you will study the original literature as a sociological, external process. The steps will be used as a set of social improvement tools to get ahead in the secular world, and you will use willpower alone to manage your defects. This is fatal to spirituality.

---

[17] *Alcoholics Anonymous,* p. xi.
[18] Modern psychology may be effective as a way to create some social harmony or mental peace, but as the "technology" of spirituality, it's doomed to spiritual inefficiency.

You will then view yourself as the agent of change (which, paradoxically, is partly what got you into trouble in the first place). Studying the original literature to acquire knowledge results in the illusion of recovery. The result will be a spiritual disaster. I discuss this in the section 811 Facts About Rigorous Honesty.

From *Alcoholics Anonymous*: "*. . . that's what this book is about. Its main object is to enable you to find a Power greater than yourself which will solve your problem.*"[19] A few pages earlier, it asks, not rhetorically but specifically: "*But where and how were we to find this Power?*" The answer is "*We found the Great Reality deep down within us. In the last analysis it is only there that* [higher power] *may be found.*"[20] Always, *always*, look inside yourself. Looking outside defeats the process. Finding a good sponsor, a good meeting, doing the steps, or memorizing page numbers and passages, will not solve your addiction problem. It therefore follows that anyone who gets involved in a study of *Alcoholics Anonymous* or *Twelve Steps and Twelve Traditions* should be using those books to study themselves, not studying the content of the book. Don't analyze the words; analyze yourself for compliance or defiance.

The vast majority of people I've encountered act like becoming spiritual is a scavenger hunt: being under pressure, with a time deadline, to discover unique things in strange places; some type of vague competition hoping to win some serenity award or admission to normal. I refer to this again in the section The Addict's Secret Desire in Chapter 11.

I often hear people speak of "finding God" like they're hunters going on a hunting trip. They pack their weapons, food, special clothes, and equipment and go off for a few days to some special place with a compass. If they're fortunate they return "triumphant" with pictures and a trophy: the dead deer, the big fish, some photograph, or dead monument to their success that *proves* they found it.

It's the same in social representations of "spirituality" [sic]. We get tidied up (in our special clothes), clean our fingernails, and go off to a church, a synagogue, a mosque, or a meeting (a special place). We have our tools (a book, a self-appointed religious/political official, crosses and flags and flowers and incense and songs). Or, we go to a remote cave with a cushion to sit on, or eat vegan food in a building on the top of a mountain in a faraway country. And of course, we look for enlightenment or spiritual wisdom in a pithy prayer that runs parallel to our secret prejudices or caters

---

[19] *Alcoholics Anonymous*, p. 45.
[20] Ibid., p. 55.

to our deeply disguised angry reactions to how we see ourselves as op-pressed.

A scavenger hunt to find God never works. Nothing spiritual exists 'out there', not even a higher power, for in the final analysis it is only deep within ourselves that integrity, true harmony with the universe, and the 'great reality' may be found. You never need to go anywhere but in.

Insightful adherents to the original twelve-step program, as rare as they are, understand that social success is not what you're [supposed to be] hunting for. In using the AA textbooks as guides, you're not studying the literature *per se,* you're studying yourself—an internal pilgrimage. Sit still. Use the steps. Look inside. Wander through the dark and hostile territory of your own personality. Examine how you defeat access to your own spiritual nature. Here is an example: The Search for Rigorous Honesty.[21]

Your Pilgrimage Begins

How are you going to save your life beginning with Step One? What does it actually require? Clichés and shallow metaphors are as dangerous as drinking. Someone said that violence is the repartee of the illiterate. I offer that recovery rhetoric is the repartee of the insecure, and clichés are the ha-ven of the confused. By masking your insecurity and confusion with rhetoric and clichés you make impression management your lifestyle. Sin-cerity then becomes political, and successes are illusions. When [if] you ever get through this by demanding rigorous honesty only of yourself, you'll be able to relax and not take it too seriously; after all, it's only life.

In presentations I often ask: "When you plan a journey of any kind, what do you need to know? You're planning a trip, so what information must you have?" The usual replies are about where you're going, the type of transportation, the route, when you'll travel, knowing the cost, the dates of travel, obtaining special clothing or equipment, and who's going. There is an essential piece of information, however, that is very rarely offered as one of the answers. You need to know very specifically where you are leav-ing "from". The travel agent who books your holiday will need to know your point of departure. If you are going to the Caribbean, your point of departure must be more specific than western Canada. I know it may sound silly, but it's symbolically important—if you want to get to someplace where you're not, you've got to leave the place where you're at.

Then I'll ask: "On your pilgrimage out of addictions, what's your point of departure?" I usually get replies like insanity, drinking, drugging,

---

[21] Here are a few references to rigorous honesty: *Alcoholics Anonymous,* pp. 58, 64, 67, 70, and *Twelve Steps and Twelve Traditions,* pp. 59, 60, 72. There are many others.

chaos, alcoholism, or the disease. These are all partially correct but, from a spiritual point of view, the answer that everything depends upon is that you're leaving from *powerlessness*. Admitting and then beginning your pilgrimage from powerlessness precedes everything. In the AA steps this is the very first thing you read: *"We admitted we were powerless...."* Addicts begin their journey from powerlessness, *vis-à-vis* addictions, to get to spiritual peace.[22]

In the all-protecting safety of a sincere spiritual life you find great strength, which allows you to serenely cope with life on life's terms—the courage to govern yourself by the five spiritual principles. Step One is to figure out where you are leaving from. Knowing where you are leaving from is different than leaving. Abstinence, and the remaining steps, allows you to actually leave.[23] You're not leaving your addictions; you're leaving powerlessness. This simple notion is crucial.

Now you know you are leaving a place of powerlessness you must ask: Where am I going? There are many speeches about going to the promises, into community, back to work, to a happy life, to a healthy relationship, to success. In the work that lies ahead of you, these are non-issues. Understand that you are going very deeply *inside yourself,* into the dark, hostile areas of your personality, to embrace your frailties in the *inner* presence of a higher power of your own understanding. A twelve-step pilgrimage, any true spiritual pilgrimage, is always a journey *In,* finding The Source, which is known *a priori,* and boundless, and called by many names.

The original twelve steps are not concerned with whether or not you make lots of money or find a happy love affair. They aren't concerned with whether you make president of the company or get a new car. The original program *is* concerned with taking you from self-destructive powerlessness (evidenced by your addiction) to a place deep inside yourself to your higher power (as you understand this)—the source of courage and power.

---

[22] All authentic relationships with a higher power, regardless of the cultural/ethnic structure that surrounds them, must originate from powerlessness. One principle that humility is based on is abandoning influence—being *voluntarily* absent of power. This applies as much to ecclesiastical/religious power and authority as it does to temporal/secular power. Having any kind of power detracts from humility. Faith is what counteracts the ego-insecurity attendant to powerlessness. "It's easier for a camel to get through the eye of a needle than it is for a rich person to get into heaven." Or, "How can I be saved?" "Give away all of your possessions and follow me," (attributed to Jesus of Nazareth). The subtext is: abandon power, political clout, authority, weapons, possessions, and wealth. Why? This forces an opening for humility, and only in humility can spiritual association with a higher power be realized. There are similar secular themes in Buddhism's "middle way".

[23] This is not a play on words it is true. Addictions are a self-destructive compensation for (or a reaction to) spiritual dislocation and powerlessness.

Powerless, Helpless, Hopeless

I have been asked: Is powerless the same as helpless or hopeless? No, but to understand this, I have to explain it carefully. It is subtle. I ask that you please reflect carefully on what I am about to say. There are two perspectives to consider: spiritual and psychological.

Generally, *psychology* advises that feeling helpless or hopeless are issues of perception—evaluating temporary circumstances through an ego that creates the illusion that there are no options, hence, helpless or hopeless. From a *spiritual* perspective, the AA reference texts, and the observations of various spiritual masters, describe helpless or hopeless as directly or indirectly related to lack of faith or neglect of spiritual commitment. And so psychologically *or* spiritually, the feelings of helplessness or hopelessness are optional. To change them requires responsibility, commitment, self-discipline, wise counsel, abstinence, and very hard work. You may feel hopeless, or believe you are helpless in the face of your addiction or difficult life circumstances, but these are optional. In abstinence, as powerful as the sense of helplessness or hopelessness may be (psychologically *or* spiritually), feeling helpless or hopeless are the result of wrongly oriented beliefs, faulty perceptions, irresponsibility, or spiritual sloth.

Being powerless regarding an addiction is another matter altogether. Powerless, by definition, means lack of ability, or being without sufficient force or resources to accomplish something. Time and again, since 1936, in millions of situations, for millions of people, we have learned that the unaided individual human will is entirely insufficient to resolve an addiction. The issue of individual, secular "powerlessness" against addictive self-destruction has become a substantive fact.

Out of the repetitive emotional disasters in acting out arise a sense of despair and a false, but very powerful belief that hopelessness and helplessness are facts. They're not. These are issues of perception. But, the fact of powerlessness (re: addictions) can be overcome with devoted spiritual discipline. *Alcoholics Anonymous* offers a process (the steps) to acquire the necessary "power" to establish and maintain transformation. You will eliminate your addictions and live serenely in the maintenance steps.

Voluntarily following the spiritual principles won't give you power over life; that you can never have. If we had it, we'd get bored. What you can achieve, however, is a sense of power and personal choice about abstinence and addictions; and a noticeable measure of influence and appreciable serenity as you participate gracefully in the circumstances that the universe presents.[24]

---

[24] It is appropriate at this point to define 'serenity'. It is very rare. There are three aspects to authentic serenity: (i) confidence you are capable to cope with whatever life may yet (cont'd)

This was put to me once: If someone were to swallow rat poison, they'd be powerless over the fact that the rat poison is going to kill them. They thought similarly about powerlessness over alcohol—as an alcoholic, if they drank alcohol it would kill them. It may seem to make sense at first glance.

In these scenarios, this person spoke of rat poison and alcohol as the agent of destruction; they aren't—the addict is. Spiritual integrity requires that addicts not blame alcohol, drugs, rat poison, or anything else, even caregivers, regardless of how they treated them. *Alcoholics Anonymous* advises this is a *self*-imposed crisis. Addiction is active self-annihilation. Acting out doesn't kill you—you kill yourself. The substance or the behaviour of addiction is only a metaphor for you harming yourself. "You" are the agent of destruction.

When addicts are exposed to the alternative of not drinking or acting out (which is a surprising option to many of them), they may start to accumulate hope. The first year of any abstinence is "breathe in, don't drink, breathe out, don't drink". So the new person asks: "Yeah, but what do I *really* have to do?" Well, you breathe in, and you don't act out, you breathe out, and you don't act out. That's all you do. "But how long do I do that?" they ask. Until you don't know you're doing it. You breathe in, you go to a meeting, you breathe out, and you don't act out. You breathe in, you go to a meeting, you breathe out, and you don't act out. Try praying.

If you want to get married, get married and don't drink. If you want to get a divorce, get a divorce and don't drink. If you want to move, move and don't act out. If you want to change jobs, do that, and don't act out. If you need to quit your job, quit, and don't act out. If you want to go to a movie or not go to a movie, then do that, and don't act out. Go to a meeting. *Breathe in, don't drink, breathe out, don't drink, one minute at a time*. Regarding your "program", that's all you do for the first year. And, say your prayers.

Out of the success of not acting out is created a legitimate sense of hope (that was always available but not appreciated). The initial year or two of "breathe in, don't act out, breathe out, don't act out, and pray", coincidental to the sense of success and joy, creates a very powerful dilemma. It's either…

- act out and remain self-destructive/powerless and die; or,

---

inflict upon you; (ii) a sublime or begin indifference to what's going on about you. In the vernacular it's called minding your (cont'd) own business; and (iii), an understandable sense of completion that you have tidied up ALL the misdemeanors and loose ends from your past, more to the benefit of others than yourself.

- maintain abstinence and face the unknown, fearful requirements of abstinence and responsibility. Abstinence, honesty,
  and responsibility are terrifying enough to keep some addicts acting out.

This dilemma is associated with Step One but does subtly recur
throughout the first nine steps. This dilemma's resolution (and it must be
resolved to avoid tenuous abstinence) is brought about by coming to believe
the following two sentences:

- The pain, fear, and self-annihilation in acting out is permanent and always slowly escalates for as long as you act out.
- The fear of abstinence and honesty/responsibility (which are
  always painful and difficult at the outset) may appear to be
  excruciating and insurmountable but, with perseverance, are
  always temporary. Temporary may mean many months, but
  they *are* temporary.

What do you do when you are seeking help from someone—a doctor
or therapist, for example—who doesn't support the twelve-step spiritual
philosophy? If you are convinced that the twelve-step philosophy is intrinsic to your survival, then discuss that with them. Advocate for your beliefs.
Professionals are often insightful and caring people. Consider what they
offer, for they are often well trained and may have much to contribute.

Decide *for yourself* your course of action: the twelve steps, therapy,
medication or not—you decide. The harder part follows: Live responsibly
with the consequences of *your* decision. Do not externalize responsibility:
Don't blame them. You must account only for yourself.

My Group is the Drug

For people in twelve-step programs, there are, at times, healthy, spiritually related reasons for staying away from certain meetings. Terry
Kellogg wrote, a number of years ago, that the most common solution to an
addiction was another addiction.[25] I see this as the motivation for many
people who attend meetings—they're addicted to the hype, chaos, sex or
relationships, and gossip (righteousness). It is difficult to discern, but there
are times when people in recovery are actually addicted to meetings.

An addiction, according to The World Health Organization, is *"a
pathological relationship with any mood-altering experience that has life-*

---

[25] *Broken Toys Broken Dreams*, Terry Kellogg, BRAT Publishing, Revised 1990, p. 72; and,
see the discussion of EFT and SRT at Appendix III, for related information.

damaging consequences."[26] I've seen, hundreds of times in my personal and professional life, the damage that arises from an addiction to recovery groups—irresponsible parenting, perpetual welfare, belligerent arrogance, shaming, divorces, irresponsible expressions of sexuality, social cruelty, racism, sexism, and more, all justified as "healing".

In the case of being addicted to meetings, it has the appearance of respectability, and carries a built-in defense for addicted behaviour—you're "in recovery". Your neglect of responsibility or selfish disregard for others is at least for a "healthy cause". The most common, instant defense to program/workshop addiction is this: "Well it's better than being addicted to cocaine or alcohol." Maybe so, but it's not that simple. Participating in an addiction is inherently self-destructive and damaging to your family and your community. It may be perceived as less damage, but it's damage nonetheless, and you cannot be spiritual while practicing any addiction.

Certainly it is important to attend many meetings in the beginning, and it is important to socialize within your support group. If, after some extended period of time, you find yourself unable to get on with your life, or if 'meetings' have become your life, and you are defensive or righteous about that, there is the possibility that recovery has become a substitute addiction. Look for righteousness and defensiveness within yourself. Another indicator is that if, after a few years of meetings and step work you are defensive about being 'in recovery' and never recovered, recovery as a substitute addiction is a possibility. It takes time to sort this out.

If you believe the original twelve steps are a route to anything other than spirituality there is an ever-present danger you will substitute your program for your drug of choice. Your meetings become the mood-altering experience. The inner turmoil and never-ending despair of unfulfilled recovery creates shame just as any other acting out does. This is often apparent in those who attend multiple twelve-step groups. If you're a person who is perpetually in recovery and cannot fathom eventually being recovered, you are probably in an addictive cycle with your program(s) being the mood-altering experience.[27]

The One-Addiction Myth

A person who requires eyeglasses to function may have prescription sport-goggles, reading glasses, and all-purpose glasses. The permanent, constant nature of the eye condition requires they use eyeglasses all the time. Bad eyesight is a twenty-four hour proposition. Even though you're sleeping and not using them, your eyes are still "bad".

---

[26] *Bradshaw on: The Family*, John Bradshaw, Health Communications Inc., 1988, p 89.
[27] This will be discussed in *Facets of Personal Transformation*.

Like bad eye sight, addiction is an unrelenting condition. Spiritual dislocation is a state of existence, and addiction is the automatic compensation for this. Addiction affects *every* aspect of someone's life, *all* day, *every* day. An addict isn't an addict only when they're acting out; they are an addict *all* the time, and must constantly compensate for their spiritual dislocation. However, at the same time, addicts cannot be destructive (act out) in their primary addiction *all* day *every* day. They may be drunk every evening, or at the track every afternoon, or act out sexually twice a week, or go on eating binges every other day, but the primary addiction, whatever it is, cannot be sustained *all* the time.

Spiritual dislocation is an all day, every day condition. An addict requires secondary and tertiary addictions to compensate for the always-present spiritual dislocation, for those periods when they are not in their most visible, primary addiction. This dynamic is what underlies Mr. Kellogg's statement about substitute addictions (cited in Chapter 2).

Aside from the primary addiction, there will be at least two other addictions operating. One will be a relationship addiction, and then, additionally, other substances, sex, work, shopping, spending, romance, pornography, gambling, television, tobacco, righteousness, religion, adrenaline, anger, or variations and combinations of these, or others.

An active addict must participate in some addiction every waking moment because that is the only way to continuously compensate for the global and constant presence of spiritual dislocation. For the most part, even if you're abstinent from your most obvious addiction, you've a second full-fledged addiction going, and a third one hovering in the background to take up the slack. Poly-addictions are a given. A sincere effort at being spiritual is the antidote to this poly-addicted lifestyle.

The Doctor's Opinion

Historically, up to 1935, the interventions for addictions (primarily alcoholism) had all been spiritually belligerent and caustic in their view of alcoholics. They were also very limited in terms of success.

For its time, The Doctor's Opinion[28] was one of the more profound pieces of writing on addictions. It is essentially a letter of reference. The cofounders of AA wanted to give credibility to their newly written book and their fledgling program. They invited a knowledgeable and respected doctor to write an introduction, so people would treat the book more seriously than seeing it as a couple of drunks singing the praises of being religious teetotalers. Dr. Silkworth wrote that he'd specialized for many years in the treatment of alcoholism; he had seen the cofounders' plan work, and saw

---

[28] The Doctor's Opinion, *Alcoholics Anonymous*, p. xxiii.

the possibility of rapid growth. Dr. Silkworth pointed out that the twelve-step plan was often a successful intervention[29] in working with alcoholics of a kind that he had formerly considered hopeless.

The important diagnostic issue Dr. Silkworth made clear is that the body of an alcoholic is as abnormal as their mind.[30] He, and the AA co-founders, knew that to get recovered there had to be a strategy to address the behaviour of alcohol consumption, and there had to be some sort of mental/spiritual treatment. Beginning with Dr. Silkworth and Dr.'s Jung and Tiebout, and the cofounders of AA, there was evidence that a dual approach (physical and spiritual) was elemental to successful treatment. These two categories *physical* and *spiritual* each have two sub-categories.

Physical Recovery

(1) This is from the behaviour of drinking or acting out. Out of des-peration, addicts, with frequent guidance from fellow pilgrims, consciously and deliberately decide to focus their willpower on behaviour modification: Don't go to the bar, go to a meeting instead. Stop drinking and start reading *Alcoholics Anonymous* or start making phone calls. Stop spending or look-ing at porn and call someone. By the exercise of willpower, they literally force their bodies to go to places where people don't act out rather than places where people do—change their physical behaviour; and,

(2) There must be recovery (or stabilization) from the physical damage that results from acting out, including detoxing. Addictions are not medical diseases in a purist sense, and neither are they psychiatric. Doctors want in on the cash cow, but it isn't a medical concern. Medical care is, however, essential to address any physical damage that is derivative of acting out. Addicts should consider consulting a physician and follow instructions only in regard to illness and injury that stem from addictions.

Spiritual Recovery

(3) There is an entrenched, defiant, sub-conscious mindset that per-petuates long-term, self-destructive behaviour. An active, practicing alcoholic, a tobacco smoker or other drug user, a pornography user, *any* addict, is on a long-term run of self-annihilation.[31] This arises partly out of a vicious ongoing process of isolation. Addicts isolate from others in an un-healthy way, and isolate from themselves.

---

[29] Intervention means a behaviour or action of some sort intended to stop or change a process. Penicillin given to cure an infection is a pharmacological intervention. If someone is drinking incessantly, then treatment centres, therapies of many types, Alcoholics Anonymous (cont'd) meaning the groups, or *Alcoholics Anonymous* (the book) would be intervention strategies intended to stop (or sometimes only modify) the drinking.

[30] *Alcoholics Anonymous*, p. xxiv.

[31] A smoker once said to me, in a reflective tone: "I am committing suicide by cigarette."

"Isolated from themselves" means there's a significant degree of detachment and ignorance about who they are emotionally. Subsequently, whatever self-perceptions practicing addicts have will be inaccurate.

Alienated from themselves, addicts are unable to rely on themselves. This is what guarantees the never-ending painful misadventures of an addict's life. The dynamic of *self*-abandonment and isolation enables the abuse "of self" which then shows up as self-destruction. Because they can't rely on themselves, or be responsible to themselves, addicts do far more damage to themselves than anyone else. Getting recovered requires addicts to commit themselves to the work of self-discovery; and,

(4) Addicts *"have lost their reliance on things human."*[32] This profound observation identifies an unalterable truth—addicts can no longer rely entirely on human willpower, intellect, or psychology for healing. Most importantly, since they themselves are human, *addicts cannot rely on themselves to ensure their recovery or use "themselves" as a reference for wise choices*. It's crucial to understand this unalterable dynamic of alienation that sits at the core of lost reliance on things human. This fourth subcategory, the inability to rely on things human, is one of the two most unique aspects to this disease.[33]

Items 3 and 4 are (partly) what mandates spirituality, or at least the over-riding importance of spiritual principles, as the only effective addictions "treatment". And, in a strange twist, it also precludes all things religious.[34]

Social scientists, doctors, and psychologists can analyze addicts regarding abuse, neglect, shame, loss, natural- or human-made calamity, unmet developmental dependency needs, vitamin deficiency, or diet (make up your own list). They can categorize addicts, prioritize the issues, and write books about addicts until the world runs out of ink. Addicts can cooperate in therapies, be obedient to psychology, read self-help books, find love, be generous, accumulate money, and demonstrate social skills until the cow jumps over the moon, but regarding their addictions: never will they be able to deeply and sincerely rely on things human. This does not mean that in order to become recovered addicts must become religious fanatics or weak-willed religious sheep.

Dr. Silkworth's observations identified and clarified the basis for all successful intervention strategies for addictions. He refers to the required spiritual (psychic) change and the poor success rate of other approaches that

---

[32] *Alcoholics Anonymous*, p. xxvi.
[33] The other unique aspect is it's the only disease that has a built in ego-script that tells addicts that nothing is their fault, it's everyone else's; or that they're not sick, everyone else is.
[34] This will be explained in detail in *Facets of Personal Transformation*.

he was aware of c. 1937.[35] He believed to do less than address all four areas leaves the treatment unbalanced and ineffective.

Only a deeply sincere relationship with some form of higher power, which is shown in a life governed by the five spiritual principles, can compensate for the self-annihilating alienation from "things human". It is what precipitates the necessary psychic change. In other words, only a drastic rearrangement of values and operating principles will work. *"Well, that's exactly what this book is about. Its main object is to enable you to find a Power greater than yourself which will solve your problem."*[36]

Old Ideas and The Disease

Within both addicts and our culture, one of the old ideas to be confronted is the belief that this is not a disease.[37] Recall the symptoms I listed: acting out and life-damaging consequences, neurosis, denial, repression, isolation (from self and others), disproportionate fear, assumptions, shame, dishonesty (and withholding), selfishness, irresponsibility, arrogance, fantasy, and cynicism—all chronic and entrenched.

There have been many debates on whether an addiction is a disease. There are incredibly complex spiritual and psychological issues in play and lives are at stake. What needs to be said, in defense of the use of the term, is any addiction isn't a matter of simple defiance or disobedience. Paranoia isn't a disease in the classic virus-like medical model of interpreting life's problems; but neither is it a matter of willpower or intellectual weakness.

Addicts go through definable phases of being powerless to their mood-altering behaviour. It is long known they are as puzzled as anyone about their self-annihilation and flagrant irresponsibility. Doctors, therapists, treatment centres, and twelve-step programs are all rather busy with addicts wanting, but unable, to achieve recovery. [This book is encouraging a return to a formerly more successful, and now largely ignored, avenue to successful treatment.]

That some professionals or family members call addicts weak-willed, bad, or defiant, in relation to the condition says more about the naiveté or frustration of the person saying it than the addict or the addiction. Because science isn't clear on the *exact* nature/cause of the disease (and may never be) doesn't mean that addicts are to be called names. They, and their health concerns, are entitled to be examined with respect and dignity.

---

[35] *Alcoholics Anonymous*, p. xxvii. This clinical observation was also made by Dr. Harry Tiebout and Dr. Carl Jung, both of whom I refer to later.

[36] *Alcoholics Anonymous*, p. 45.

[37] Medical science is very clear about the treatment of the derivative damage and side effects of alcoholism and addiction. The actual addiction, itself, is not resolved by the elimination of the symptoms or the resolution of its consequences.

As an addict, in one conversation you may declare you have a disease. In other conversations, you condemn yourself for doing something you believe you shouldn't have: "I shouldn't have gotten that divorce," or "I was really stupid to tell that lie." These self-condemnations are contrary to the declaration that your addiction is a disease. If you think that you *should* have done something differently than you did (shouldn't have lied, shouldn't have divorced, shouldn't have... whatever), that implies you believe you had choices regarding your symptoms.

Having a fever is a symptom of pneumonia. After you've recovered from pneumonia it would be foolish to declare: "Oh, that was stupid of me to get that fever; I shouldn't have done that." It's acceptable to have a fever with pneumonia—it's a part of the pneumonia package. Addiction is a disease. Symptoms are not optional.

An addict who harbors self-criticisms of their own addictions-related symptomatic behaviour, or other people who disparage addicts displaying symptomatic behaviour like lying, cannot also hold a simultaneous belief in addictions being a disease. This contradiction arises from deeply ingrained confusion about the nature of addictions, cultural misunderstandings, cooperation with externally imposed guilt, and poorly defined ego boundaries.

Demanding that you (or someone else) should have done or not done something that is contrary to the symptoms of the disease implies that you think there were choices where no choice existed. You declare you have a disease and then criticize yourself for having the symptoms. This denies the truth that symptoms aren't optional. To claim that you believe an addiction is a disease, and then to ridicule yourself or another for having the symptoms, means you don't understand or accept the nature of the illness that is killing you (or them).

My describing destructive or "irresponsible" behaviour as symptomatic, meaning unavoidable, does *not* offer an excuse to avoid accountability for it. Addicts must be held accountable, especially by and for themselves. *Alcoholics Anonymous* advises that this is a self-imposed crisis—addicts are to be held accountable, but they're not to be blamed or called names, especially by themselves.

The Selfish "Program"

Being selfish is manipulating people and circumstances to avoid exposure of your shame, insecurities, fears, and mistakes. You avoid exposure of your humanness or meanness by unjustly (deceitfully) shifting responsibility away from you and onto someone or something else.

"This is a selfish program," is a frequently heard statement that dangerously misrepresents the spiritual intent of the original twelve-step process. The original twelve-step literature isn't selfish. The other twelve-

119

step program outlines that I've reviewed are not intended to be selfish. Regardless of the program's efficacy, each of them, in their own way, suggests a path that wants to stand in opposition to addictions. Yet there is ample evidence of neglect and irresponsibility under the guise of attending meetings. If the programs aren't selfish, how do they become selfish?

What has been verified time and again in my work is that the most common "solution" to an addiction is a substitute addiction.[38] A twelve-step group can easily become a substitute acting-out ritual. Put another way: Recovering addicts become (more) selfish when their twelve-step program becomes a substitute addiction, in which case their program would be inappropriately require selfish behaviour. There are many ways addicts can be selfish under the guise of becoming recovered. Addicts' selfish behaviour is especially destructive when it's camouflaged as a spiritual endeavor. Here's a true story…

A woman owned a company, was an alcoholic, and a relationship and work addict. Her ritual was to get up early and go to work, start drinking at lunch, and work and drink all afternoon. She'd come home in the evening and drink and work, or sometimes stay out and drink and work with employees. Day in, day out, often seven days a week, for years: get up, work and drink, go to bed. She had a spouse and children. Finally her spouse had enough, got some help, and advocated for change. She eventually entered AA. After getting sober her general ritual was to get up early and go to work, meet program-people for breakfast or lunch, and work, and talk with program people whenever possible, all day. She would come home and work, and talk on the phone to program people all evening. Often she'd work late and go to twelve-step meetings. Finally (again) after a few years of this, her spouse had had enough, got some help, and advocated for change. They divorced.

In this case, and many like it, the meetings and groups become a substitute addiction. Participation in recovery becomes the "morally correct" justification for irresponsibility: "Honey, I can't watch the kids, I've got to go to my meeting," (1,713 nights in a row). Or: "I'd love to spend time at home but I'm sponsoring 27 people. I have to meet them and I have to carry the message or I'll relapse. I think I'm free two weeks from next Thursday between 4:30 and 6:00 PM."

As soon as the partner talks about neglect, absence of commitment, or avoiding responsibility the response is an ominous defense of the substitute addiction. "Listen, I know I've been gone seven nights a week and every Saturday morning for four-and-a-half years, but that's better than drinking,

---

[38] Recall the earlier discussion about poly-addictions. And, see Terry Kellogg's book, *Broken Toys Broken Dreams*, BRAT Publishing, Revised 1990, p. 72.

isn't it? At least we didn't get a divorce, right? *Right*? I know I'm never home, but I'm getting help and that's what *you* wanted, right? So would you rather have me drunk?" This is justifying a substitute addiction.

Being busy in recovery is fine, and a significant commitment is necessary at the outset. However, the intent of going to meetings is to become spiritual and to eventually create a spiritual life without addictions—to get back into community and healthy relationships. It's actually a self-less program. However, when the program becomes a substitute addiction, it is used selfishly to avoid responsibility.

People stay on social assistance for years getting someone else to pay for their "recovery". Victims lick their wounds, whining about how hard their life is; how they were so horribly abused by their father, mother, wife, husband, ex-wife, ex-husband, grandparents, children, bank managers, the police, politicians, lawyers, the school system. The list is endless. This is irresponsible, and others in society who get up and go to work every day have to pay. There are no free rides. Social pampering and rescuing people out of personal responsibility is fatal to getting recovered, for both those who are rescued and for those who rescue them.

If you break your leg, it's a ludicrous proposition to accuse you of being selfish when you go to the hospital. You broke your leg and going to the hospital is generally considered intelligent, and yet going to the hospital is an inconvenience. You'll miss work and need special help from your partner or family. Friends might miss a meal or cancel an engagement to help you. Breaking your leg is an inconvenience to other people in your life. But you go to the doctor, get over it, resume your life such as it was, and the inconvenience to others stops.

You were selfish when you were acting out. That's a symptom of the disease. Once you decide to get recovered, you need help. If you have to inconvenience people to get beyond early recovery you're not selfish, you're intelligent.

A twelve-step program or treatment centre, *properly* used, is like an "addictions hospital". Inconveniencing people is necessary; however, remember to only inconvenience others only as much as is necessary for proper self-care to get recovered. As soon as the program becomes a justification for irresponsibility it's become a substitute addiction. This is often the case when participation in twelve-step programs is motivated by a desire to be healthy rather than spiritual. Granted, some are sicker than others, but years and years of excessive participation in twelve-step meetings isn't evidence of spiritual fitness or recovery.

People sometimes see me for an addictions assessment. Since the symptoms of this disease go far beyond "acting out", I don't [really] want to find out *exactly* how much they drank or shopped. Yes, I am interested, but that isn't my primary focus. I want to also assess how much they lie; how isolated they are, even though they claim to be gregarious and have friends; how they try to manipulate people (including me); how they misrepresent themselves and others. I want to assess their fear, loneliness, desperation, and the subtle ways they self-annihilate. I will notice their assumptions and arrogance and cynicism. For a professional to assess for addiction on only the evidence of acting-out behaviours, in any but the most blatant cases, is insufficient.

Step One isn't concerned with whether or not your grandmother loved you, your parents were mean, you were forced to take music lessons, you went to a strict school, or went to school at all. Step One is interested in how you drank or acted out (not how much, but how), and the unmanageability that was generated in your life. Using a broad definition of trouble: how you got *yourself* in trouble. In getting recovered, beginning at Step One, addicts begin to take on ever-more responsibility regarding the truth of their self-imposed crisis; but... as addicts, they have a perspective of life that resists this by creating excuses for acting out: their parents, their brother, their boss, their wife, their husband, the government, the schools, the neighbor's dog, the policeman, traffic lights, bad TV reception, road traffic, and on and on.

Addictions are an issue of corrupt spirituality, which is yours alone to deal with. You're not in control of what's done to you, but you're responsible for cleaning up after it. Out of uncompromising, personal responsibility comes the beauty inherent in spiritual devotion and humility. Spirituality is only truly available in the deeply self-responsible life.

How many times have you heard the plaintive cry of the suffering addict: "It's not fair! I don't deserve this!" That life is supposed to be fair is one illusion that addicts live with.[39] It often shows up like this: "I'm going to be nice (meaning fair) so other people will be nice to me". Unlike TV shows and commercials, life isn't neatly solved in thirty minutes of rudeness, sarcasm, and sympathy, which sadly, passes for entertainment. The number of people who find violence and disrespect entertaining is evidence of the poignantly sad state of affairs in modern culture. Life is not a television show; it rarely resolves itself "fairly" and nothing is free. We're

---

[39] When this illusion goes unchallenged, it ends in all manner of abuse and irresponsibility. One is in situations like "Jack" (from a few pages ago) suing the innocent church people. Jack believes the world wasn't fair to him, and so he doesn't have to be fair either. People justify gossip, crime, meanness, betrayal, lying, harsh judgments, etc., thusly: Life wasn't fair to me (past tense), so I don't have to be nice or fair to you (present and future tense). This is spiritually corrupt and dooms you to an unfulfilled life.

dealing with a terribly dislocated culture, globally addicted lifestyles, and gross personal and cultural irresponsibility.

Denial and Newcomers

Denial: Within the psychobabble of twelve-step groups there is noticeable confusion between being "in denial", and the defiance or belligerence that is routinely present in unspiritual addicts. Denial, the ego-defense mechanism that allows you to not remember, is not the same as belligerence or denying something.

Imagine this: You walk into the kitchen and someone is chewing something and swallowing. You see brown crumbs on their lips, brown crumbs on the counter, a cookie jar with the lid removed, and a few brown cookies in the jar. You ask this person if they are eating cookies. They mumble "No," as they swallow and shake their head vigorously. This person isn't "in denial"; they are denying. To berate them that they are in denial is inaccurate and ineffective.

Refusing to admit the obvious is not being in denial; it is denying something obvious. Being belligerent or stubborn is not psychological denial. And, in the face of demeaning criticism, like being berated for being full of self-pity or in denial, people become belligerent and stubborn, and distrust becomes more deeply entrenched.

Accusing an addict, in recovery or otherwise, of being in denial is like accusing someone of having a nose. If addicts weren't in psychological denial (and they've all got some), they'd be dead or clinically insane from the overwhelming pain. The psychological state of denial is only relieved by being in a very safe environment of acceptance, for a *long* time and with gentle and competent therapeutic technique. It's important to be in denial *and* to come out of it gradually. Accusations of denial, akin to berating others and attacking their character, are always harmful.

Newcomers: With consecutive days of abstinence, and continuous efforts to "follow the suggestions", you're a newcomer in any twelve-step program for at least five years. It doesn't matter how hard you work, how well you do the steps, how diligently you study the book, how devoted you are in prayer, or how much service work you do. The five-year period is due to the subtle, painstaking work that must go into reorganizing how you think and how you perceive the world. Reeducating yourself regarding the incredibly complex issues (the three-dimensional spider's web) is a long, trickle-effect transformation. Here's the catch: If you don't pursue spirituality, you'll always think and act like a newcomer, regardless of how long you've been abstinent.

Having an addiction is a state of existence. If it were purely an issue of intellect you could take a course and resolve it. However, since you're challenging deeply rooted and immaculately justified, self-defeating perceptions; *and* eliminating subtle and entrenched patterns of self-destruction; *and* doing so in the context of overcoming spiritual dislocation in a spiritual pilgrimage (in an unspiritual culture), it takes years to cast off the cloak of "newcomer". You cannot race into recovered, so learn to enjoy the ride. You're a newcomer for at least five years.

Craving

Dr. Silkworth observes that craving may be the manifestation of an allergy,[40] and that a medical perspective of "allergy" may account for the unique relationship between some people and the drastic consequences of their ingesting alcohol. I'm cautious about using the word allergy; however, if you're a substance abuser, you will experience physical craving while you are using and during early abstinence. You'll also mentally obsess about your acting-out behaviour, which then generates a variation of craving. Resisting this is crucial. Emotional Freedom Techniques (EFT) can be significantly beneficial in eliminating cravings.[41]

There are times when the "craving" isn't a craving in the classic sense of having an intense physiological desire for a substance. It may be that you're experiencing emotional pain, or dealing with unpleasant circumstances in your life, and you know from your history you could immediately avoid this unpleasantness by consuming a substance or acting out. You become obsessed with making the pain go away, or making the circumstances disappear, which, after a time, will feel like a craving. This obsessing isn't necessarily a physiological craving.

Epinephrine addicts, whom we casually call adrenaline junkies, are addicted no less than other addicts. Epinephrine is the hormone secreted by the adrenal glands (near your kidneys), which is produced in response to fear or stress. It stimulates bodily changes: increased heart rate, blood pressure, and blood glucose concentration, among others. Withdrawal from a diet high in epinephrine is responsible for the craving sensation in people with excitement, anger, danger, righteousness, religious, or aggression addictions.

Relationship and sex addicts who cruise through bars or twelve-step meetings, gamblers, high-risk financial investors (sanctioned gambling), criminals, high-risk sports participants, people who binge on rage or right-

---

[40] *Alcoholics Anonymous*, p. xxviii.
[41] Emotional Freedom Techniques (EFT) is a self-applied way to heal from trauma and adjust body energy. It is referred to at Appendix III.

eousness are, among other things, generating high levels of epinephrine. Usually they live with an addicted relationship to adrenaline.

People who are addicted to exercise get three rushes. The first is from the ego-created vision of being more "desirable" (slim, muscular, curvaceous)—watch them watch them*selves* in a mirror. The second rush is from the adrenaline produced during the exercise. The third is from the binge of self-talk (either self-righteous or self-castigating), after the exercise, about the perceived success or failure of their effort. People can talk or think themselves into an adrenaline rush. Here, as with anger and religion, nothing is quite so satisfying, and so quick to conceal shame and insecurity, as a good binge of self-righteousness.

Intermittent reinforcement is another significant factor in adrenaline production—the bigger the bet, the greater the odds, the bigger the risk, the more unpredictable or sudden the surprise... the greater the rush. For illegal behaviours, the risk of getting caught is powerfully addicting. Consuming gratuitous violence and sex through films and literature (touted as art or action/drama) generates the rush, too. It's not participation in art: it's addiction. [There is valid purpose in some representations of violence or sex in art, and certainly it's in the eye of the beholder. I am *not* touting censorship. I am advocating for enlightened common sense.]

Competition creates an adrenaline rush. I recall a football advertisement which declared that fans had the opportunity to "watch a war" from the safety of their living room. I often encounter "sports fans" in my work who participate vicariously in abuse by their endorsement of dominance, violence, cruelty, and injury. From boxing, football, rugby, basketball, and hockey, through to sports car racing, tennis, golf, and the Olympics, there is the deliberate infliction of emotional or physical pain on oneself and on one's opponent. For addicts who participate in sports there is often power (dominance) in the sense of winning and shame in the experience of losing. The issue here is competition that's rooted in a dominance model of relationship—an aggressive win-lose mind-set, not physical health.

The determination to win (rather than personally excel) is grasping for the opportunity to feel good (gloat) at someone else's expense. There's excitement, the possibility of grand failure, and the potential for huge success. Winning is the empty bolstering of self-worth arising from the illusion of superiority. Aggressive sports fans, the hard-liners, the fanatics, are compensating for some lack in themselves by endorsing violence. [The fact that it's men who are usually injured and considered "disposable" for the sake of entertainment is entirely another matter. As women are disposable when they are unattractive or old, men are disposable when they are poor or weak. The consequences for all are horrendous.]

It's interesting how this is justified. Someone told me that professional hockey, in between the fights, shaming, insults, violence, aggression, arguing, injuries, and abuse had grace and beauty in it. The physical grace and skill somehow made the violence acceptable. This rationale requires that violence be called "competition". When I asked what he did for leisure, outside of his career, he replied that he watched sports as often as he could.

It's well known that from what's called The Second World War, (1939-45), came many advances in technology, communications, transportation, medicine, surgery, and prosthetics. These advances can never justify the deaths of fifty million people. Physical fitness and grace don't justify violence. In a truly spiritual life, violence is never acceptable. How is it, then, that violence and brutal competition masquerade as entertainment? Through insecurity, addictions and the interpersonal transfer of shame.

Promoting and developing competitive skill to win is training people to perceive weakness in others so they can take advantage for themselves (quite unspiritual). That's the nature of competition—taking advantage of weakness or inability. This creates the temporary illusion of superiority. On the other hand, promoting collaboration, which excludes competition, is promoting skills that perceive strengths and compatibility in others—an advantage for all.

All of the foregoing information regarding myths, inappropriate rules, misinformation, violence, and misapplication of the twelve-step process, may not appear to have too much to do with Step One. However, it is essential to create an awareness of exactly what unnecessarily complicates or prohibits your entry into a spiritual lifestyle. Have no doubt that if you don't get spiritually on track in the first two steps, there are disastrous consequences throughout the journey.

Some Important Reminders

Part of the purpose of Step One is to show you that you have been living in, and are now leaving, a state of powerlessness in order to begin your spiritual pilgrimage. The focus of Step One is to generate an insightful self-awareness about the content and context of your life when you were acting out. At the end of this chapter, the exercises I suggest regarding Step One are designed to expose the self-destruction (primarily in context), and the consequences, of your self-imposed crisis.[42] That's not always obvious with

---

[42] Over and above the Step One concerns I have written about, there is this: A crucial error in the first nine steps is in examining the content and not the context of life that is created by the addict. Realizing the dynamics of context (how context enables calamity before calamity ever happens, i.e. you orchestrate the divorce before you started dating)... has more impact than rehashing the mundane content of an addict's life. It's in examining context, in the first nine steps, that addicts come to appreciate accountability and responsibility. This is (cont'd)

subtle or culturally approved addictions like relationships, work, sex, anger, and religion. It *is* obvious with the culturally disapproved of addictions like crime, illegal drugs, tobacco, and gross alcohol consumption.

Aldous Huxley wrote:

> *In most civilized communities public opinion condemns de-bauchery and drug addiction as being ethically wrong. And to moral disapproval is added fiscal discouragement and legal repression. Alcohol is heavily taxed, the sale of narcotics is everywhere prohibited, and certain sexual practices are treated as crimes.*[43]

The twelve-step journey must begin with you thoroughly understanding the intrinsic unmanageability attendant to your acting out. That unmanageability resides in the context of your life. Step One is to identify your personal powerlessness so you know exactly from where you're starting. Approached with the right perspective, it instills appropriate hope that if you become obedient to "the steps" (and forego your defiance), and work *very hard*, you will change. At Step One you will come to believe in the impossibility of becoming spiritual while you are in any addiction. It is simple and straightforward: *"We admitted we were powerless over alcohol—that our lives had become unmanageable."*[44]

Step One is not in two parts. It requires no information about family history or childhood, and only calls you to account for your addictions. Should someone expect you to provide details of your childhood and family as part of Step One, quietly inquire about the reasons for that. It isn't what's prescribed in the original twelve-step literature; however, question them respectfully because with professionals who are experienced and properly trained, it can be of benefit, and it might well be in your best interest to provide it. Discussing your family history with twelve-step "gurus", lay counsellors, sponsors, or in any twelve-step discussion group is always ill advised.

Admit & Accept

There is a remarkable difference between admit and accept. They are not interchangeable. Beware of people who tell you that in Step One, you're

---

especially true regarding relationships. The regeneration steps, 1 – 9, address the context of life; the maintenance steps, 10- 12, address the content.

[43] *Huxley and God, Essays,* by Aldous Huxley. Edited by Jacqueline Hazard Bridgeman, HarperSanFrancisco, p. 122.

[44] *Alcoholics Anonymous*, p. 59, and *Twelve Steps and Twelve Traditions*, p. 21.

supposed to admit anything other than the fact that you were powerless over your acting out—that your life has become unmanageable.

In *Twelve Steps and Twelve Traditions*, the authors described acceptance of the devastating weakness (p. 21), and admission of personal powerlessness. For Step One, if there was more than that required, they would have written something other than what they did. Because of the raw nature of a newcomer's defects, and the glaring symptoms of addiction, delusion, and denial that conceal painful reality, acceptance of anything else isn't possible until the addict has gone beyond Step Six. Newcomers are only capable of becoming aware enough to admit and accept the reality of their helplessness and devastating self-destructive behaviour. Here's why...

The ability of anyone to "accept" something requires five things: a willingness to be responsible, understanding that life is neither fair nor unfair, authentic self-insight, the ability to be kind, and a noticeable presence of an egalitarian mindset. True acceptance of anything is only possible when these attributes of character are sincerely present; they're inherent in the nature of acceptance.

Newcomers do not have these attributes. They're oppressed by their defects, especially irresponsibility and anger, and they live with delusion.[45] It's beyond a newcomer's ability to accept anything but the blatant, obvious truths of powerlessness and unmanageability. (Acceptance is discussed in the sections Forgiveness and Covenants in Chapter 6.)

Here's another perspective of this: Because of the nature of addictions, addicts require spiritual assistance to address any character defect. However, spirituality isn't available or "detectable" until after Step Two or Three, and can only become somewhat apparent beyond Step Five. When at Step One, there isn't enough spiritual awareness or faith to have any positive impact on character defects. The very nature of acceptance requires graciousness and serenity, and an absence of belligerence. Acceptance is impossible for a newcomer to attain at Step One because spiritual integrity is absent—there is too much interference from their defects of character.

A newcomer is only capable of admitting the fatal progression of the disease—an obvious truth, which is all that's required. For a sponsor or therapist to demand or expect from a new person, acceptance of anything

---

[45] Many twelve-step participants who are beyond "newcomer status" are irresponsible in not more diligently eliminating their anger. Some anger, in a very few shocking situations, may be unavoidable (we are human), but even then, a spiritual person must be willing to be completely responsible for their anger and its consequences, which will be subtle and far-reaching, *and* they must ensure that it doesn't last longer than a few moments. For addicts, anger is always representative of a character defect. Beware the long list of justifications for anger, including being "helpless". Any justification for anger is a justification for abuse and will skew spiritual truths to selfish advantage. This is discussed from another perspective in The Two Step Dance (in Chapter 8).

beyond this, is a set-up for failure. When anyone tries to accomplish too much recovery too fast there is this devastating consequence: there automatically develops a sense of inadequacy in relation to completing the steps. This subtle and never articulated sense of inability to "do" Step One, because of a sponsor's unreasonable expectations, becomes the attitude that undermines all future step work.

At Step One it's okay to be angry that you're an addict or that your life is in a mess. It's acceptable to somewhat grudgingly complete Step One — admit it cleanly, be angry if you have to be. Admit the obvious truth of powerlessness. You'll eventually be able to accept more than this, but not for quite a while.

Re-Education

Here are some words picked at random from *Twelve Steps and Twelve Traditions*: personal powerlessness, complete defeat, no self-sufficiency, bankruptcy, absolute humiliation, utter defeat, devastating weakness, and fatal progression. These describe the state of life that's attendant to acting out. By studying Step One carefully, a newcomer would develop self-knowledge, and reasonably understand and admit how those eight aspects of powerlessness governed their life, when they were in their addiction.

This is important: In Step One, *Twelve Steps and Twelve Traditions* makes no reference to love or the absence of love, or violence or the absence of violence, between your parents. *Alcoholics Anonymous* asks you nothing about sibling rivalries and nothing about the sexuality of anyone in your family of origin. The original literature is entirely concerned with, and specifically focused on, your addictive behaviour and what that self-imposed crisis created in your life. Staying abstinent, and maintaining that focus, gives you a chance to get recovered (spiritual). Your Step One is *your* re-education, not your family's and not your friends'.

There's something interesting about education and re-education. One thing happens in education. Two things happen in *re*-education. In education, you are in a process of adding new information to your mind—putting new facts into your brain. Education is simply acquiring knowledge and learning new things. In re-education, you are doing two things: adding new information and unlearning old information. You cannot be re-educated without giving up old ideas or modifying old beliefs.

Becoming spiritual is always re-education, and often called a letting-go process—letting go of your judgments, letting go of your old ideas, letting go of your prejudices, letting go of your old beliefs; in short, unlearning, and at the same time that you unlearn old information you take in new information.

Many people who have achieved long-term abstinence haven't really changed. They've only learned things which supported their pet theories, and haven't *un*learned much. They cling to old beliefs and coveted prejudices, like racism or religious elitism, even in the face of overwhelming evidence that refutes their old beliefs.

For rather complex reasons, which I will explain in *Facets of Personal Transformation*, it is far more important to unlearn old beliefs than it is to learn new ones. The added dimension of unlearning old beliefs is complicated and takes courage. Notice a sentence in *Alcoholics Anonymous* where one of the cofounders admitted his tendency to do what was convenient, and to disregard what wasn't (p. 11).

In simple terms, the re-education process is to maintain abstinence, read and *study* the appropriate literature, and challenge and abandon your old ways and beliefs. This is the posture of spiritually committed people. How many times, in twelve-step meetings, have you seen people act exactly as they did in the bar: party hard, be dishonest, gossip, curse and swear, argue, force their opinions on others, tell racist or sexist jokes, show off, be irresponsible, be aggressive, hunt for sex, and treat people as if they are disposable? Many new people are told to not go to the bar anymore. Consider telling yourself not to bring "bar" behaviour into meetings. There is a specific reference to *un*learning in *Alcoholics Anonymous*: *"Some of us have tried to hold on to our old ideas and the result was nil until we let go absolutely."*[46]

The process of Step One gets you involved in a community that is supposed to allow you to spiritually re-educate yourself.

Recurring Chaos: Content and Context

Unmanageable, recurring conflict is on the list of life-damaging consequences noted earlier. You can identify unmanageability where you haven't achieved the reasonable, common goals of your culture. Graduating high school or holding a job longer than a year by the time you're twenty-five are reasonable, common achievements, as are: being stable enough to get your name in the phone book, living at the same address for a year, being in a relationship for more than a few weeks, or saving a few thousand dollars before you're in your forties. These are "content".

Underneath content are the deeply held, often unconscious beliefs and values that support any lifestyle—the paradigm of beliefs and perceptions that underlie behaviours is context. *Content* is multiple relationships, adultery, poverty, conflict, going to meetings, what job you have, divorces,

---

[46] *Alcoholics Anonymous*, p. 58.

addictions. *Context* is subconsciously defining life as hard, sex as bad, people as unfair/mean, or "self" not worthy of respect or love. We approach life—where we live, the clothes we wear, who we have sex with (content) through our deeply held subconscious beliefs (context).

Achieving authentic spiritual serenity, which is also being recovered from addictions, requires an important context adjustment. Fundamental values are changed, not just maintaining sobriety and changing behaviours.

"Context adjustment" begins at Step Two and is the purpose of the first nine steps. These first nine steps are to change the most basic and fundamental ways that addicts view their existence (context). The last three are primarily concerned with content.

In Recovery vs. Being Recovered

When contemplating being "in recovery" *vis-à-vis* "being recovered"[47], learn these equations:

- Active addiction = increasing illness and permanent pain.
- "Being in recovery" = repetitive pain without relief.
- Becoming recovered = intense pain and fear at the outset, but gradually leads to true serenity.

What newcomers need to hear; what you need to convince yourself of, is that becoming recovered may be frightening or extremely painful, but the pain eventually subsides. It requires being meticulous in the completion of the first nine steps and a gradually increasing obedience to the five spiritual principles embodied in the maintenance steps. This entails a significant demand for self-discipline and a determination to confront only yourself.[48]

Getting recovered may hurt more intensely at the outset, but the pain eventually goes away if you painstakingly follow the instructions.[49] With willing obedience to the original twelve steps, you will eliminate the al-

---

[47] Being recovered is discussed in detail in Chapter 8.

[48] In 1927, the American blues singer Bessie Smith (1895 - 1937) was performing for her fans in a large tent in the southern U.S. She was warned of the approach of several Ku Klux Klansmen and advised to flee. Ms. Smith left the tent but rather than flee, confronted them with threats and shaking her fist at them. The KKK people fled and she finished her concert. In becoming Spiritual, you must marshal the (cont'd) courage and determination to shake your fist at your own addiction. Don't shake your fist at your parents' addiction or family history of addiction—only at your own. If you are truly committed to emancipation from the slavery of your addictions that's your job and your responsibility. [The anecdote about Ms. Smith is part of a larger commentary from Episode Three of the PBS film series *Jazz*, directed by Ken Burns and narrated by Keith David.]

[49] Staying "in recovery" doesn't seem to hurt because the historical experience of repetitive pain of inadequacy and failure is familiar. The new experience of fear from responsibility and commitment is more frightening, but only because it's *un*familiar.

ways-in-recovery cycle of self-harm (entrenched inadequacy), which is much more damaging than the vicissitudes of life.[50]

In Step One everything "should" begin to shift. Some addicts are emotional and others are intellectual; some are loners and others are gregarious—all are lonely. As newcomers maintain their abstinence, they will (hopefully) gently shift the focus of their personality from isolation to union, from superficiality to sincerity, from gregarious behaviour to an appreciation of solitude, from emotion to intellect, and for these foregoing examples, vice versa. In any event they should shift from irresponsibility to responsibility. Step One is the beginning of all these things.

Multi-programming

People often see me to sort out twelve-step recovery confusion. One person was attending four different twelve-step groups (AA, NA, CODA, & SLAA), had three sponsors (AA, NA, and SLAA), saw them each once a week, saw a psychiatrist (bimonthly), a therapist (monthly), and sought counsel from a medical doctor every so often for some phantom ailment. This person's collection of self-help books numbered over one hundred volumes, and each one was only partly read and discarded. They attended church sporadically, and occasionally sought confession and counsel with that religious official. They wanted to add me to this list of chaos, thinking that I could help them stay focused on church so they could become more spiritual. We eventually sorted it out, but it took over a year.

This type of multi-programming chaos is very common and is an unstructured, addictive cycle that uses "helpers & groups" as the mood-altering experience. This frantic, reactionary recovery is very self-destructive. People must exit the damaging pattern of addicted, erratic, fear-driven healing and stabilize into a coordinated effort. A scattered, multi-program approach is never successful. It entrenches an even deeper sense of shame and failure through repetitive inadequacy.[51]

How many different twelve-step programs you should attend is an individual decision. Remember that there are abstinence available and abstinence not-available addictions. For the first category, decide what your primary substance of addiction is and check out the major substance-abuse twelve-step programs. They're different and will each expect that you speak primarily about the substance that that particular program focuses on. Re-

---

[50] One of the reasons there is so much dislocation and mismanagement in completing the steps is people "read ahead". Reading ahead and trying to understand some step before you are there, or getting caught up in anticipating doing it before you are actually there and ready to do it, is self-defeating. The spiritual discipline that's required for any step is only achievable and non-threatening when you have thoroughly completed all the steps that precede it.

[51] This addictive cycle will be explained in ore detail in *Facets of Personal Transformation*.

spect that request. Decide which one appeals to you, and participate with a view to be spiritual.

As far as actually doing the steps goes, it should be no surprise that my view is that you should use the original material (*Alcoholics Anonymous* and *Twelve Steps and Twelve Traditions*). That will give you the best chance of creating a Spiritual lifestyle. It's always wiser to go to the source material; but that's only my view. This is your quest, so embrace spirituality and not your addictions.

If you are addicted to alcohol, drugs (including prescription drugs), to-bacco, or gambling—the abstinence-available addictions, or if you believe you have just abstinence not-available addictions like sex, work, religion, etc., again, in either situation you will also be a relationship addict. The abstinence not-available addictions are more complicated addictions and formal therapy is a wise option to consider. Sadly however, it has been my experience that it is difficult to find a well-experienced therapist who is well trained and detached from codependence enough to be of valuable service in addictions work. They are "out there" but they are hard to find.

It may be beneficial to attend a twelve-step program for what seems to be the most destructive addiction, always maintaining abstinence. You must decide what ethical abstinence is. Reflect carefully on where you will focus your energy. Don't squander or scatter your efforts. If you're locked into recovery chaos like four twelve-step programs, workshops, therapy, church, psychiatrists, doctors, three sponsors etc., that *in itself* is an addicted pat-tern. With proper balance and focus, no one ever needs to attend more than two twelve-step programs and have one good therapist.

All addicts inherently embody corrupt and broken relationships with people. What sometimes offends people in Alanon, CODA, ACOA, and other similar programs, is that they are, in fact, relationship addicts, work-ing on an addiction to people and martyr-like destructive relationships. Their drug of choice is the mood-altering experience of being in a relation-ship with an addict. Here's a way of looking at it that may make it simpler to understand. The metaphor may sound a little outrageous, but bear with me.

You go to a doctor and report a horrible pain in your left thumb. The doctor thinks it's a very rare disease—the mysterious Left-thumb Luxation, but isn't sure. The doctor advises that there's a unique blue pill that is the *only* pill capable of curing the painful Left-thumb Luxation. The blue pill has no side effects and cures nothing else. The doctor isn't really positive that you have this rare disease, but since this blue pill is only effective for Left-thumb Luxation, and there are no side effects, it's worth trying. And if you take the pill and your thumb gets better, then you'll know what disease you had. You take the pill and your left thumb gets better.

We know that twelve-step programs are successful in treating addictions. It's the only thing they can treat. They resolve nothing else. The blue pill for addictions is a twelve-step program. If you go to Alanon or CODA (twelve-step programs, which can only treat an addiction), and get better by doing the steps, you've proven you're an addict.[52]

We're dealing with a life-threatening disease. Remember the two rules about addictions: The first rule is that people die from addictions; the second rule is that you can't change the first rule. If you don't understand these rules, your addiction may kill you, and it will seriously harm you and people who care about you.

Years ago, I was working at a treatment centre and received a call from a police constable who thought I might be able to identify a body. I went to the local morgue. The body had on only a pair of torn, ragged, dirty jeans. He had no money, no identification, no socks, no underwear, no shirt, no shoes, and no jewelry. They found him in the stairwell of a sleazy hotel, with a syringe stuck in one arm and a treatment centre "graduation medallion" clenched in his fist. Four weeks earlier, the man had completed the treatment centre's program, smiling and happy like everyone else.

Step One

Doing a Step One is that process of taking the general information about addictions, described in Step One, and personalizing it so it has intimate meaning for *you* and you alone. Step One is actually coming to believe what is written is true for you, without exception, and that can only be done by personalizing it. The personalized version of Step One might be: I see and admit my unmanageable, uncontrollable acting-out—how "my behaviour" showed up in me and my life and was destroying me.

Learn exactly how addictions showed up in you (not how they showed up in your family). Step One teaches you how your addiction made your life unmanageable—what you did to yourself to make your life more difficult (*not* what was done to you by others). The disease has to be personalized in a way that is specific to you so that you can own it. After all, it is a *self-*imposed crisis.

---

[52] Enabling behaviour, which is commonly discussed in these programs, is indicative of relationship addiction. *Any person who enables an addict is also an addict*. The general themes of these programs is to disengage from the person with the addiction—not rescuing and not taking responsibility for their problems. This is actually the struggle of establishing bottom-line behaviour in an abstinence not-available addiction.

Challenge these misperceptions and myths: (1) It's a selfish program; (2) Don't make any big decisions for the first year; (3) Being criticized and badgered eliminates denial; (4) Step One is in two parts; (5) Staying out of sexual relationships for the first year is an important recovery thing to do; (6) You're just feeling sorry for yourself; it's self-pity—get over it.

- Don't confuse an unmanageable life with a life you don't like. Not being happy, or not getting your own way are not evidence of an unmanageable life. Once you achieve regular abstinence and some measure of support (secular and spiritual), your life becomes generally manageable. It may be painful, and you may not like it, but it is manageable. If your life is still unmanageable, there's another blatant addiction to abstain from.
- It's a disease of isolation—from others and from yourself, because of the shame, fear, pain, denial, and repression you carry within yourself.
- Step One only requires "admitting". Demanding that newcomers accept anything at Step One is a set-up to undermine confidence and will further entrench a sense of inadequacy.
- *"We admitted we were powerless... "*[53] is in the past tense and it means exactly that. Once you achieve regular abstinence, and some measure of spiritual support in the process of getting recovered, you are no longer powerless. Do not justify petulance, sloth, or irresponsibility underneath claims of being powerless.
- In a twelve-step group, people who are desirous of being spiritual, and who diligently work towards that by being obedient to the approved literature, are the safest to seek help from.
- Notice, and remind yourself: *"We of Alcoholics Anonymous, are more than one hundred men and women who have recovered..."*[54]. It's about getting recovered, not perpetual recovery.
- Active addiction equals permanent, increasing pain. Being forever in recovery equals repetitive pain. Getting recovered equals intense temporary pain.
- Getting recovered from any addiction is unconditionally dependent upon complete abstinence *or* sincerely adhering to

---

[53] *Alcoholics Anonymous*, p. 59, and Twelve Steps and Twelve Traditions, p. 21.

[54] *Alcoholics Anonymous,* p. xiii; see also pp. 17, 20, 29.

bottom-line abstinence that's representative of health (no compromises). Be abstinent.

What You Actually Do

In Step One, many things are accomplished at the same time. Start with this: Get a copy of *Twelve Steps and Twelve Traditions* and go to the beginning of Step One. It's the shortest of all the step chapters, which might at least indicate it's the most straightforward. On lined paper, write out in long-hand, verbatim, the entire Step One chapter from *Twelve Steps and Twelve Traditions*. Leave at least three blank lines between each of your own hand-written lines.

Now, closely following the theme and meaning of the original text, write out your own version of Step One (in a different color of ink) in your words. Carefully follow the meaning in the original text. Put another way: personalize the original Step One by writing your own experience, so that your words are different but the story is identical. What you are doing is "translating" the English used by the author(s) into English used by you.

In the example that follows, the bold italic text quotes the first lines of Step One from *Twelve Steps and Twelve Traditions* (p. 21). The plain italic text underneath uses different words someone might use to personalize Step One into their own words. It follows the same theme, but has a specific personal meaning.

The Book: ***"Who cares to admit complete defeat? Practically no one, of course. Every natural instinct cries out against the idea...***
Your Words: *"Who wants to say truthfully they're beaten and licked? Not me! Everything I ever believed in, every thought and idea, was to fight...*

The Book: ***of personal powerlessness. It is truly awful to admit that, glass in hand, we have warped our minds... "***
Your Words: *against being whipped and losing. I hated the truth when I admitted that with liquor and sex, I screwed up my entire life and my mind..."*

When you read both stories, they will compare in theme, but the second one will be your personal version of the original Step One chapter. When you're done, you'll have your story in your words, in sync with the theme of the original. Your story (your words) will embody *both* the theme of addictions in your life, and the theme of Step One in the original AA literature (context).

Read and discuss your Step One story privately with a few trusted people in your group, individually. Invite them to ask you questions about it. From this discussion, add information to your version that deepens your awareness of *your* disease. As you personalize Step One (without showing off), you will experience insights and nuances of your self-imposed crisis.

Here are two more exercises that will keep you in line with what the original program requires. Again, these are about the context of your addictions and life…

- Here are five general areas of life: i) Personal, ii) Family, iii) Work-Education, iv) Community, v) Leisure or Recreation. Identify and write out five (try for ten) examples for each area to show how you structured your life to make drinking or using or acting out, easier.[55]
- List 30 people you associated with during your acting out and then, in relation to each person, identify at least five (try for ten) lies you told, and secrets you kept, about your acting out.

When you're done, you will have identified at least 25 ways you organized your life to make acting out easier, and over 150 lies and secrets so you could act out with impunity. You can also work at accomplishing these:

- Maintain your abstinence. Absolutely.
- Demand only of yourself ever-increasing honesty in *all* circumstances with *all* people.
- Don't gossip. *Ever*. Stop telling "stories" about other people.
- Begin the letting-go process: Stop doing it your way and start doing what *Alcoholics Anonymous* advises. Work hard at doing what you're told to do in the original literature. It's obedience to, and compliance with, the instructions that gets you recovered.
- Be thorough and painstaking and patient in all aspects of your step work. Your life depends on it.
- Take complete responsibility for your addiction; it's yours and no one else's.
- Don't blame anyone for anything about your addiction. *Ever*.

---

[55] Here's an example from Work-Education to show "structuring your life" to facilitate addictions: You may hate your job as Area Sales Manager—there's a lot of business travel, *but* drinking or having affairs are easier to conceal. You are offered a promotion to head office, which is a good career move, and find excuses to refuse it. The promotion interferes with your addictions.

The purpose of these exercises is for you to "force yourself" to become honest with yourself. As it says in Chapter 5 of *Alcoholics Anonymous*, those who do not recover are those who cannot or will not become honest with themselves.

The authors of *Alcoholics Anonymous* offered the world a program that is universal beyond any secular or religious boundary. The original, written program incorporates no classes or hierarchy within its membership. Gender and orientation are non-issues. All ages, religions, colors, cultures, and creeds are welcome. It challenges hypocrisy, misunderstandings, and harsh judgments about addicts and addictions and spirituality that have permeated human affairs for all time. It does all of this unobtrusively and gracefully.

With your determined cooperation, *Alcoholics Anonymous* is powerful enough to break through your addictions and offer you an opportunity that's available to few, and that still fewer take meaningful advantage of. Your dues were paid, and your initiation was completed, prior to joining. Once you join you can't be denied membership. Of their own accord, without advertising or proselytizing, twelve-step programs have become international and are thriving and expanding. Alcoholics and addicts have the opportunity to leave behind what is possibly the most puzzling, devastating, and insidious illness known to humans, and it offers us all an equal chance to be Spiritual. Remember...

> You are a sexual being, in a physical body, trying to be a spiritual entity, in a human context, within a limited but unknown segment of eternity. Even without dysfunction and abuse, or addictions and a selfishly oriented ego, it's incredibly complicated.

> As an addicted person getting recovered, somehow realize within yourself that simply learning and doing will not guarantee your becoming Spiritual. Knowledge and action are not the solution — in its *broadest* sense, "God" is.

> Be patient and labor with devotion for many years. Live intimately with trusted loved ones. Respect the earth and all living things. Have an intimate, long relationship with a mentor or therapist. And, in all of this, hold personal responsibility, truth, respect, humility, kindness, charity, and non-violence as the highest values. Labor with devotion and patience only to this end: through the maintenance steps be forever obedient to the five spiritual principles.

> You will eventually cross some ubiquitous line and then sense, but only in hindsight, and only by embracing your ever-present frailties, that you are recovered. Some might then call you

wise, many will resent you, and you will smile gently because, for you, it will be sufficient to quietly repose in the safety of knowing that the mysterious machinations of Providence are beautiful.

In a Zen way, remember your addiction fondly. You have been led to an opportunity that's so rarely available to addicts or alcoholics—the opportunity to influence your destiny, which was absolutely unavailable until the exact moment you forced yourself to study... Step Two.

Chapter 4

Step Two and Step Three: The Specific Direction

I have been asked if becoming a good person, without actually being spiritual, is sufficient to recover from addictions. Is aspiring to being spiritual essential to being recovered?[1] In my view the answer is yes, but the explanation is complex. It's much more about having a clear understanding of spiritual principles than a clearly defined view of "god". Actually, being spiritual has very little to do with god.

First: There are people who are psychologically healthy, moral, who live a principled life, and who are atheists or agnostics. There's a notable distinction between atheist and agnostic, but regardless of that, there are non-God believing people who are ethically principled. Excluding addictions issues and the claims of religious zealots, it is possible to be a good person and deny or be disinterested in god—a morally committed atheist or agnostic.

Following that, in a general way, a morally committed non-spiritual person would demonstrate attributes similar to these: (1) respectful self-care, (2) veracity, (3) secular humility[2]; and (4), some manner of sincere concern for community/humanity. These four, acting in concert, might be called a morally-based system of inner-personal ethics. I'm going to repeat this another way; it's important.

Should a person *not* believe in "God", and live with (1) respect and consideration in their general attitude towards health and life, (2) honesty at all levels of interaction with others (meaning no manipulation or deceit), (3) universal equality as a governing principle; and, (4) considerate or responsible participation in community, then they would generally qualify as a non-spiritual "good" person. [Note that these are some, but not all, of the

---

[1] Recall the distinction between spiritual and Spiritual described in a footnote, pg. 24.
[2] Secular humility is the recognition of our human limitations and the honoring of the inherent value of all people—being sincerely egalitarian, and offering and receiving support in the celebrations and calamities of life. (See the first requirement of Humility at Appendix II.)

attributes that a recovered addict/alcoholic or a spiritual person would have.[3]]

And, finally, before I leave you with a general "yes" to the question: Is being spiritual essential to being recovered? We must consider...

The Phenomenon

A phenomenon is an occurrence or an observable event that arises and is perceptible by the senses, which is unusual, significant, and unaccountable regarding its origin, *vis-à-vis* scientific insight. A phenomenon is something that appears real to the mind, regardless of whether its underlying existence can be proved, or its nature understood.

Research has offered various hypotheses about genetics that are interesting, but these are always inconclusive and insufficient. And, as discussed earlier, trauma or family issues as predictors are unreliable. The vagaries in the appearance of an addiction; the varying degrees of its virulence; its duration and phasic nature; the myriad manifestations, substances, and behaviours; and, the inconsistent pattern of its onset indicate it is unusual, significant, and unaccountable regarding its origin, vis-à-vis scientific insight (therefore a phenomenon). As regards addictions, there is a phenomenon component to their manifestation.

Addictions have become the province of medicine. Yes, there are consequences that must be treated by doctors and therapists, but the resolution of the addiction itself isn't in the sphere of medicine, and it certainly isn't an issue of willpower or insight-psychology. Considering the increasing cultural problems with pornography, greed (debt), and violence, and a parallel increase of alienation and instability in modern culture, *and* an apparent corresponding rise in people manifesting addictions (especially to sex, spending, some drugs, and gambling) the last thirty years of psychological and medical attention to addictions have done little to curb this trend. As regards twelve-step programs, it's decidedly made things more complex. An addiction is entirely independent of medicine or psychology, and purely and strongly indicative of corrupt spirituality (which is only my reframing of what's in the original twelve-step literature).

As millions can attest: An addict may be given wise and generous secular help, but it will be insufficient for recovery to prevail. Depending on science or psychology to get recovered is temporary at best. When you consider the tenacious, self-annihilating, all-pervading nature of addictions, their often mysterious appearance, the ubiquitous influence of their myriad

---

[3] A religion that has Spiritual integrity would have to embody and advocate for these virtues. I will expand on this in *Facets of Personal Transformation* in the chapters on religion and spirituality.

symptoms, and the paltry influence of "willpower" or "medicine/psychology" in their resolution then living by spiritual principles and maintaining an authentic relationship with a higher power (of your understanding) is the only paradigm that addresses all facets of addictions. A spiritual lifestyle facilitates a non-harmful response to all vicissitudes of life, and does so without contradiction. Addictions are a phenomenon related to unexplainable, deep spiritual corruption.[4] This is crucial so it bears repeating in another way.

The strategy to resolve addiction must be so universal that it is the antithesis to all of these: their ubiquitous nature, their lack of predictability, the phenomenon component, all the symptoms discussed earlier, the addict's self-annihilation, the defiance to socio-cultural influence, and the *in*ability of the addict to rely on things human. Their resolution must be effective in such a way that cooperates with and allows harmony in all secular/worldly circumstances, and enhances life in all its aspects (because addiction affects *all* of life's aspects).

This requires significantly more than the limited capabilities of science and psychology, thus, psychology and medicine or just being good, are insufficient to resolve an addiction. When all aspects are considered, it appears only authentic spiritual endeavor confronts and resolves everything that an addiction entails. So, the answer to the question is yes, sincere spirituality is crucial to getting recovered, but that doesn't mean an associated and traditional belief in "God".

Surviving Calamity

Many people, including addicts, wonder if surviving egregious trauma or calamity is evidence of a spiritual awakening, and they often interpret this as divine preference. According to Appendix II of *Alcoholics Anonymous*, surviving danger and escaping death are not a spiritual experience, only a personality change is.

How you perceive the historical events of your life, before, during, or after any event is a function of your ego. The theory of "divine preference" (meaning "God" has some special purpose for you, and you were kept alive to fulfill that purpose) is a very risky belief for an addict and is fatal to humility and getting recovered. A traumatic event may be a catalyst for personal change, but simply surviving calamity is not evidence of anything but surviving calamity.

In my own life I've been in many violent and life-threatening situations. Considering my history of illness, injury, and violence, had I lived

---

[4] In the sphere of addictions, in the process of actually getting rid of them, try as some of us might, it is difficult to deny the machinations of Providence.

prior to 1900, I would have been long ago dead, well before reaching thirty, simply because medicine was not sophisticated enough to save me, and so it is for millions of others. Does this mean that those who now survive grievous injury are divinely chosen, or simply born after 1900? Notice that as medicine becomes more sophisticated, more people survive serious illness and injury. That doesn't mean that "God" favors people in this century more than in centuries past.

If I allow my spiritual insecurity to recast the role of efficient ambulance drivers, competent doctors, and modern medicine as divine preference, my ego views me as having special spiritual status. If I believe that I escape trauma or death because God is doing something especially on my behalf, it's easy to believe this is because God has some special purpose for me: I am "specially chosen" over anyone who has an ordinary story, or who doesn't survive calamity.

When I respect that calamity is random (which in itself is scary enough), and that I was born in the era of "modern" medicine, I force myself to eliminate the arrogance inherent in believing I'm especially chosen. Addicts getting recovered cannot afford to participate in any belief that offers them special status with God. They may have sobriety, but they don't have divine privilege.

Recall that two of the symptoms of addiction are arrogance and isolation. As much as addicts may humbly claim otherwise, as soon as they believe they have divine preference, they justify a subtle arrogance. There's also isolation in believing they're closer to God than anyone who lacks a hair-raising survival story. It certainly implies a divine preference over those who don't survive, and that the "chosen" addict has privileged spiritual status — slippery ground for any mere mortal.

These beliefs are enmeshed with the arrogance of self-aggrandizement and the need to isolate from shame, which arise out of a severely skewed concept of "self". Any time addicts set themselves up for that degree of uniqueness, they end up in serious social and spiritual trouble.

To make it a bit confusing, there's a different perspective to this I sometimes ponder. In any twelve-step program it's [supposed to be] a given that no one is more special than anyone else. This policy of equal ordinariness, although not often followed, must extend itself into the community-at-large. No one is more entitled than anyone else. No one is closer to a higher power than anyone else. It follows that because someone survives egregious trauma, he or she is not entitled to more respect or consideration than someone who hasn't. However, I sometimes do meditate against this conundrum: What is it about twelve-step pilgrims *collectively* that allows them the opportunity to pursue spirituality and influence their destiny, when many millions of addicts don't? I don't know what providence may intend regarding the entire twelve-step pilgrimage as a whole, *and* at the same time, I don't believe anything spiritually special accrues to the individual.

As an aside, as we are told through legend, the prophets "God" has apparently directly influenced—Jesus, Mohammed, Moses, and the other chosen few, had a very hard time with that privilege. The spiritual responsibilities that accrue to people to whom God has apparently spoken certainly appear to be more than a recovered addict can handle. Let's face it: Addicts can hardly handle being honest, so how can they handle being especially chosen by God? Avoid believing that you are especially chosen by, or spiritually closer to, God. Be watchful for arrogance and a need to feel special at the expense of others, and especially a need to believe that your path to God, or your own perception of God, is somehow more special than others'.

Misadventure and bounty are really quite random. All of us are no more or less safe from calamity than anyone else. This fact is very hard to appreciate, and insecure people will generate all manner of divine theory and superstition to avoid the truth of our vulnerability and helplessness. We live by geological consent. Being spiritual is a continuing exercise in humility. As much as anyone may fall short of the goal to achieve humility in both its manifestations, it is wise to adopt beliefs that keep you away from the doctrine of privilege with the almighty.

A Standard of Conduct

When people are recovered from addictions, as a general guide, they would not allow themselves to participate in any relationship, or subscribe to any belief, that is morally squalid or ethically questionable in order to gain the very tenuous security of being popular or socially successful. They would not voluntarily be in any relationship that embodies deliberately unspiritual behaviour. Recovered addicts would not be willing to abandon the pursuit of spirituality (their commitment to the five spiritual principles as they appear within the maintenance steps) for a confined and suffocating "membership" in socially popular organizations and rituals.[5] They would respectfully address insensitive behaviour directed at themselves, and when made aware of their own, make an effort to challenge themselves.

As best they can, they make spiritual principles (or the maintenance steps) the basis of their relationships, and if there isn't a desire from the other person to reciprocate, they would quietly move on. These standards of conduct very often generate insecurity in others and those others, rather than examine themselves, usually criticize. (Remember the Bessie Smith

---

[5] This also includes my adherence to the rights and freedoms, which I discussed in Chapter 2.

anecdote and ask: "At whom must I shake my fist?" In all inner- *and* inter-personal conflict, the answer is *yourself.*)

Being Recovered

"*We... are more than one hundred men and women who have recov-ered from a seemingly hopeless state of mind and body. To show other alcoholics <u>precisely how we have recovered</u> is the main purpose of this book.*"[6] This statement was made in 1938 to a world that was disbelieving and suspicious about any treatment for alcoholism. At that time, it must have seemed outrageous. Considering all the debates, the psychobabble, and the ineffective treatment programs that exist today, this is still a very coura-geous statement, let alone in 1938 when it was first made.

People often tell me that when they speak about being recovered at twelve-step meetings it generates insecurity in others—so much so, in fact, that at times they have been openly warned by many against trying to achieve it. This is one example of how insecure people groom newcomers so the newcomers will not challenge the insecurities of older members.

My deliberately chosen beliefs about getting recovered—and I am re-covered—arise from my commitment to spirituality as it is presented in the original AA literature, not from some arrogant idea I've manufactured on my own. This endears me to a few, offends many, and frequently makes me unpopular. If you examine this material closely, and begin to subscribe to the ideas that I am telling you about (which, for the most part, derive from the original twelve-step literature), you will become recovered. If you painstakingly follow the instructions in *Alcoholics Anonymous* and *Twelve Steps and Twelve Traditions*, you can't *not* become recovered.

In the AA literature, being recovered is specifically referred to or im-plied in several places. That being the case, why would anyone argue with it, or caution someone against it? My answer is they are trying to conceal their own lack of faith and commitment, and to camouflage their own irre-sponsibility. I once remarked on something from the AA text, and a man disagreed with me rather intensely. I offered I was only trying to point out the instructions in the literature, and that his disagreement with me was akin to killing the messenger.

If you are participating in a twelve-step program, do exactly as you are told according to the instructions in the books *Alcoholics Anonymous* and *Twelve Steps and Twelve Traditions*. Don't add suggestions that simplify the requirements or be swayed by myth or opinion. Don't modify any re-

---

[6] *Alcoholics Anonymous*, p. xiii, emphasis theirs.

quirements. When you're in turmoil, examine yourself for disobedience to the instructions, and *never* blame anyone for any feeling you have or circumstance in your life. Study and be obedient to the instructions in the AA reference texts so you can [eventually] enjoy the serenity of a spiritual life, which is called being recovered.

Being "recovered" is in the literature and it *is* possible. In Chapter 7, I discuss being recovered in detail, and argue that if you painstakingly follow instructions you can't help but be recovered when you get to the maintenance steps, or stay recovered if you painstakingly follow those instructions.

Relapse and Obedience

In order to add depth to the discussion of the dilemmas (which is next), I will offer this bit of information about abstinence and "relapse". In the beginning, anyone who attends a twelve-step group has at least two addictions operating, and probably three. Newcomers usually only address the most destructive, and most obvious addiction. For example: a person smokes tobacco, is a relationship and sex addict, and is an alcoholic. They attend AA, address the obvious alcohol addiction and become sober, and act like that's all there is to it. They're still practicing addicts: tobacco and addicted to relationships and sex, and there's a very destructive atmosphere to their life, which they ignore and gloss over. Assume things "don't go well" and they start drinking again. The discussion is then about them "relapsing" but since they never got out of their other addictions, they aren't relapsing, they're simply expanding the range of their ongoing addictive behaviour. Relapse—in the usual twelve-step meaning—misrepresents the actual dynamic of what was happening during the previous period of "abstinence".[7]

Most therapists, to my knowledge, agree that our personalities like our families (and on a large scale our culture) have to have a certain balance. We are like a mobile that hangs from a ceiling—it seeks out balance and stability as it hangs, and if you bump it, it soon returns to stillness. People are like that; we consciously and sub-consciously seek to balance ourselves. This is called compensation.

Addictions are a self-annihilating compensation (a balancing act) for severe problems and spiritual dislocation (imbalance). Newly found abstinence creates a horrendous inner imbalance, which is very obvious and temporarily extremely painful. Without: (a) an *internal* resource, i.e. "a

---

[7] Once addicts are recovered (meaning *completely* free of addictions), they don't relapse because they are reasonably spiritually fit, which is the only way you can be free of addictions and safe from relapse.

higher power", as understood by the individual, to provide the courage to persist in recovery and confront the dislocation; (b) an all-encompassing, non-belligerent paradigm that addresses all the dynamics of addiction (a spiritual lifestyle within the maintenance steps/five spiritual principles); and (c), right association with some reasonable representation of spiritual endeavor, it's impossible to transform oneself out of addictions.

When suddenly abstinent from any blatant addiction, like alcohol or drugs, other attendant, balancing addictions like relationships, sex, romance, anger, tobacco, or work, may not be enough to compensate for the new inner pain and imbalance (it's abstinence-induced dislocation). When support from recovery caregivers is wrongly focused, and spiritual effort is inadequate, what happens is a socially approved addiction and gossip/self-righteousness reestablishes some manner of ersatz inner harmony.

Relapse into the former, blatant addiction indicates the associated or secondary addictions were insufficient to compensate for the newly created and unaddressed imbalance through sobriety. Only concerted spiritual effort will compensate for this in a healthy way. Without spiritual effort, and properly focused secular support, relapsing is inevitable.[8]

Considering how technology and cultural arrogance (fear) have so drastically changed the human condition, it's extremely difficult to establish and maintain an authentic spiritual lifestyle. Technological, modern culture is actually designed and structured to encourage greed, irresponsibility, a quick-fix mentality, and the classification of people as disposable. This perverse and vicious cultural ambiance makes it astonishingly easy for groups and sponsors to quote psychology, send people to treatment, lecture rather than role-model, and evade the all-encompassing demands of spiritual integrity. Not only must twelve-step pilgrims stand against their addictions, but to be truly spiritual, they invariably have to stand against this culture. It takes tremendous courage and perseverance to actually be obedient to the instructions and to spiritual principles.

Don't delude yourself into believing that non-compliance with the original program is wise or viable. Clinging to self-reliance, and being disobedient to its spiritual mandate allows only insecure, conditional abstinence. This entails grave risk and always leaves you potentially at the mercy of any twelve-step guru/charlatan who presents a good story, including sponsors who modify the original program. Without spirituality, there's always the possibility of relapse, and abstinence depends on nothing "too big" happening to you. Since you are forever unaware of what circumstances life may present, your abstinence is conditional.

---

[8] Properly focused secular support would be that which is addictions-insightful, spiritually oriented, absent of expectations, non-relationship addicted, non-belligerent, and consistently dependable.

The Three Dilemmas

The essence of a dilemma is experiencing pain or anxiety when being forced to choose between alternatives with apparently equal consequences. Being forced to choose between equally wonderful alternatives is a dilemma, just a much as alternatives that are perceived as equally painful. If you don't understand the following recovery dilemmas, and how to address them, you will always be in danger of relapsing or remaining in a conflicted spiritual condition.

Once an addict initiates the process of going from active addiction through the steps to being recovered, they must resolve three major dilemmas along the way. If any of these are not resolved in favor of a deepening of spirituality, regardless of the social cost, the addict immediately intensifies his or her confusion and will either regress from spirituality and remain in turmoil or relapse. Living in painful dilemmas is the sad lot of those addicts who refuse to pursue spiritual integrity.

Active addiction means generating permanent, increasing pain. Abstinence and honesty will also generate pain, but it's temporary and lasts during the transition from addiction to recovered, and eventually disappears.

The non-resolution of this dilemma is often evident in the short-term relapses: in for a year, out for a year; in for a month, out for a month. If you are not told clearly, by people whom you sense have spiritual integrity, that pain from abstinence and honesty is temporary, you will continue in some "relapse pattern" of addiction. You exit this pattern by reorganizing your 'life of abstinence' from social to spiritual (new context), and learning that when you follow the instructions of getting recovered the pain is always temporary. It may last a few years, but it is temporary.

People resolve dilemmas by challenging their assumptions and acquiring new information. Newcomers trapped in dilemmas must be gently offered information on the consequence of inaction—increasing frustration/confusion that leads to substitute addictions or a renewal of their prominent addiction. When offered honest, credible information, and properly focused support, addicts most often choose to exit their dilemma towards spirituality (the 75% success rate described in *Alcoholics Anonymous* and mentioned earlier).

In Step One, you face the painful dilemma of living with an addiction, which is terrifying at the best of times, or living with abstinence and rudimentary honesty, which also is terrifying. Talk to anyone who has been in AA anywhere between six days and six months, and you will hear (maybe not articulated clearly), this is probably one of the more painful choices they have had to face.

Dilemma One — The Early Stages of Step One

either (a): continued acting out, addictions, drinking, drugs, death; continuing irresponsibility, conflict, pain and insanity etc. ...	or (b): continued and increasing commitment to abstinence and honesty, and "going through" the pain.

The resolution strategy for this is three-fold: (i) to acquire additional information; (ii) to self-challenge; and (iii), to unlearn old beliefs about helpless/hopeless (issues of perception) and powerless (the absence of a higher power). Choosing to resolve this first dilemma and forge ahead will soon present a second dilemma. This is created by the requirements of Step Two: *"Came to believe that a power greater than ourselves could restore us to sanity."*[9]

Dilemma Two — Near the End of Step One and Step Two

either (a): stay sober, insane, angry, lonely, and in danger of "relapse" into the primary addiction...	or (b): continue abstinence, incorporate increased honesty, and develop beliefs about a higher power and spirituality.

The added dimension of spirituality and surrender increases the degree of anxiety, the depth of self-examination, and the level of commitment. The resolution strategy is to acquire additional information, to self-challenge, and to re-educate yourself about your higher power and spirituality, which is the essence of Step Two. This will soon present...

The In-Recovery — Recovered Dilemma

In the third dilemma, people who choose to be always "in recovery" have chosen to live at 3(a) and avoid the hard work of spiritual commitment.

Dilemma Three—Near the End of Step Two Recurring to Step Seven

either (a): stay abstinent and be "in recovery"—live with repetitive inadequacy; recycle the steps; re-experience recurring doubt and failure; sentence yourself to perpetual, repetitive anxiety and work...	or (b): commit to becoming recovered; increase significantly spiritual faith: be *completely* responsible and *obedient* to Spiritual principles.

---

[9] *Alcoholics Anonymous*, p. 59, and *Twelve Steps and Twelve Traditions*, p. 25.

I repeatedly witness an innate and almost unconscious awareness in addicts in recovery that they can't manage recovery without spiritual assistance. They may not admit it, but they're aware of it. They also faintly know of their grossly irresponsible behaviour *and* they alone are somehow responsible for the chaos in their lives.

Getting recovered entails bringing these faintly perceived truths to the forefront, which is an anathema to the unregenerate addict. It's so threatening the majority of addicts in recovery address only their obvious addiction by belligerent abstinence and remain noticeably irresponsible, choosing to live at 3(a) rather than 3(b), in Dilemma Three. [A parallel metaphor to Dilemma 3[a] is The Myth of Sisyphus.]

These dilemmas force huge choices on addicts. Choosing the "a" side of the dilemmas always results in personal stagnation or regression into relapse. The pain of insanity and addictions will remain, and the struggle to become spiritual through the steps will seem insurmountable. The result is being perpetually "in recovery" and a life built on clichés and rhetoric.

Recycling through the steps generates this insidious cycle of addictive behaviour: You will repeatedly re-experience acting out through rhetoric and fantasy (or relapse) at Step One; revisit insecurity and distrust at Step Two; re-experience the fear of spiritual commitment at Step Three; justify insecurity and irresponsibility at Step Four; re-experience guilt and shame at Step Five; declare willingness at Step Six when in fact you're not, and be dishonest and participate in hypocrisy and politics. This fosters shallow faith and impression management rather than humility at Step Seven, which leads to another exercise of guilt and blaming at Step Eight, and guilt and apology at Step Nine. The promises remain unavailable.[10] Serenity (inherent in the maintenance steps), and the potential to be spiritual, aren't available to the perpetually in-recovery addict. Facing this cycle repeatedly, for as long as you are sober, is the consequence of being always in recovery.

Repeating the steps in the way just outlined is thematically similar to the cycle of addiction. Being forever "in recovery" is simply another example of repetitive inadequacy and failure, two of the hallmarks of an addict who is acting out. It's the posture of someone who is secretly or subconsciously unwilling to resolve his or her spiritual belligerence. (This means they changed only content, not context.)

Living in the unappealing cycle I described two paragraphs above unconsciously generates and entrenches the belief that you never get anywhere. It guarantees you'll never experience the beatitudes of spirituality or acquire enduring faith in a higher power. Living like this is painful, but the always-in-recovery addict becomes quickly inured to it because it is

---

[10] 'The Promises', *Alcoholics Anonymous*, pp. 83-84, and discussed here in Chapter 7.

very similar to the dynamic of being in addiction, and without strong spiritual grounding, addicts always choose the familiar pain.

The Perpetual Excuse

Irresponsibility and willfulness are ever-present in people who are always "in recovery". For every incident where they insult or abuse; for every situation that shows a character defect, they always have a defense: "I'm in recovery—I'm working on it." Commitment becomes a euphemism for convenience. Being "spiritual" is rooted in impression management and depends on the prevailing social climate. As soon as the five spiritual principles (which are universally embodied in the maintenance steps) require the addict to be socially unpopular, make a significant effort, or jeopardize some coveted belief or prejudice, they will abandon spirituality and blame their disease, blame someone else, personalize some random calamity and pout, or hide behind dogma.[11] Do not underestimate the insidious and ubiquitous nature of self-destructive irresponsibility in the unregenerate addict.

Being recovered does not include being cured. Because you become *"...recovered from a seemingly hopeless state of mind and body"*[12] doesn't give you license to drink or act out. You are recovered, but your recovery/spirituality depends absolutely on continued abstinence. The insane thinking, the craving, the dishonesty, the need for acting out, the manipulation is gone in that they won't exist within you anymore. But... only your sincere and continued obedience to abstinence and the maintenance steps will keep you that way.

If being recovered means having spiritual serenity in the maintenance steps, which sounds desirable, why do so many in-recovery addicts avoid it? Avoidance comes from the addict's innate knowing what being recovered implies: a global respect for self and others, an active seeking of humility, unconditional gentle honesty, willing prayer and meditation, unqualified responsibility, and very hard work. They're afraid life won't work out in their favor if they're truly spiritual.

If you choose to view the program from the position of getting recovered—and this always depends upon obedience to the AA texts, not your sponsor or the personal stories—you will do Steps One to Nine once, slowly and painstakingly, and then incorporate Steps Ten, Eleven, and Twelve regularly, consistently, and sincerely in all ways, in all circumstances, with all people, regardless of the cost to yourself, and regardless of the effort

---

[11] Hiding abuse behind dogma is what religious officials and many doctors, psychiatrists, therapists, and sponsors do.

[12] *Alcoholics Anonymous*, p. xiii.

required. Being responsible, in addition to the obvious spiritual connotations, would mean that:

- your anger, rage, depression, moodiness, unhappiness, frustration, selfishness, greed, petulance, dishonesty, and arrogance about *anything* are completely *your* responsibility;
- your unemployment, under-employed, or poverty, is always *your* problem;
- all conflict with everyone; all your addictions both past and present; and all your failed relationships and romances, are completely *your* responsibility;[13]
- as an adult, if you see yourself as being abused or taken advantage of in any way, it is always completely *your* problem; and,
- there would be three cornerstones to your life: (i) prayer and meditation; (ii) obedience to the five spiritual principles (which are embodied in the maintenance steps); and (iii), always holding a willingness to let go of old ideas.[14]

Subscribing to these requirements gives you a limitless potential to experience joy and to continuously transform and enhance your secular and spiritual life. If, as an addict, you choose to become recovered, you must abide by these. The vast majority of addicts will do anything to avoid diligent spiritual work.[15] There are few truly spiritually disciplined people. It is very difficult to convince newcomers at Step Two that, although terrifying at the outset, and certainly emotionally demanding, making these commitments eventually becomes a pleasure.

---

[13] This doesn't mean everyone else is innocent, it means: Regardless of how blameless, innocent, or only partially responsible you think you are, you cannot allow yourself to "investigate" the other person's share of the conflict, or to figure out what they did wrong. You must ignore "their share", even if it's obvious. You are completely responsible for the conflict because you participated. Another relationship "fact", that is sometimes hard to grasp, is each person in any committed or long-term relationship has the same capacity or incapacity, or the same ability or inability, to bring love and commitment or conflict and tension to the relationship. Regardless of all your "evidence" that one person is emotionally healthier, it isn't true. Neither person is healthier (or unhealthier) than the other person.

[14] *Alcoholics Anonymous,* How It Works, p. 58.

[15] The reason there are so few saints is that it is such hard work. *Huxley and God, The Essays,* Aldous Huxley, edited by Jacqueline Hazard Bridgeman, HarperSanFrancisco, 1992.

Pain-Induced Willingness

I have often been asked about the value of, or necessity for, pain-induced willingness as the motivator for personal change. Is it healthy?

Addicts initially enter a twelve-step program because of pain. They are (or feel like they are) dying, falling apart, or going insane. The addict often harbours an unstated belief other people should make the addict's pain go away by those others changing some behaviour and, other than pain relief, the addict won't need to change much.

- "How do I buy prostitutes and not hurt myself?"
- "How do I use porn or drink or shoot junk and be healthy, too?"
- "How do I spend $300 a week on things I don't need and feel good?"
- "I want to commit adultery and have a fulfilling marriage."
- "How do I watch TV for forty hours a week and have a life?"
- "How do I refill five prescriptions a month for uppers and downers and mood altering drugs, and still have emotional insight?"

Addicts generally arrive in twelve-step programs as pain-filled, self-destructive neurotics (or worse), and hope that without any concerted effort on their part, they will end up pain-free. Attending a twelve-step group and being always "in recovery" (i.e. sober with shallow spirituality) is often evidence that the addict has only learned how to be a more effective neurotic.

Personally, I didn't attend my first support group because I wanted the glories of spirituality. I attended because *at that time* I believed my wife was crazy, my boss was a jerk, and nobody liked me. I also had constant nightmares, regular migraines, would frequently break out in cold sweats, was twenty pounds underweight, and hardly ate. I was in huge debt, owned nothing, drank every day, believed the world was generally evil and notoriously unsympathetic to my plight, and if someone *else* didn't do something, I was going to die; hence pain-induced willingness.

Pain-induced willingness is "good" as the motivator of your initial participation; however, "no pain no gain", the usual *cliché*, is only applicable to the spiritual newcomer.[16] At a specific time later in your spiritual

---

[16] If someone stays sober/abstinent, but with minimal spiritual effort, "no pain no gain" will forever be the theme of personal change—an unappealing prospect at best. However, once a person goes beyond being a *spiritual* newcomer (which is very different than a program newcomer), change happens without pain. A *twelve-step* program newcomer is just that—a newcomer—for at least five years. A *spiritual* newcomer (a beginner at spiritual devotion and transformation) remains a spiritual newcomer until such time as they are *well* practiced at Step Eleven, and have at least ten years of *sincerely and continuously* living in the all (cont'd)

growth, at a point that I'll identify clearly later on, pain-induced willingness is completely unnecessary. In fact, pain-induced willingness as the motivator for change eventually becomes evidence of spiritual neglect.

It is easier to be a sober social success living *in*sincerely than it is to be spiritual. Bill Wilson wrote that he discarded those parts of spirituality he found less than convenient.[17] How far away you are from spirituality, or the less diligent you are about constant self-examination and spiritual responsibility, is exactly how far away you are from being recovered and how close you are to relapse.

Thoroughly re-address Step Two and change your perception of the program. This will force you to exiting the in-recovery cycle that was described earlier. When you re-design your life as instructed — painstakingly towards spirituality, a higher power, and spiritual principles — the pain and fear of responsibility, honesty, etc., regardless of its intensity, is always temporary. When you don't follow the instructions, the result is lack of faith, permanent pain and stagnation, dishonesty (which is fatal to spirituality), and shallow manipulative behaviour. These consequences are not optional — the disease dictates this.

My assertion that doing Steps One to Nine once (and thereafter remain in the maintenance steps) does not imply that you must do those steps perfectly. Doing them by following the specific instructions in great detail, to the best of your ability, is entirely sufficient.[18] Repeating the steps in a shallow manner demonstrates repetitive disbelief (no faith), repetitive inadequacy (I'm not smart/good enough to do them only once), and repetitive failure (I'll get them right next time). When you recycle the steps, you diminish their impact, remain subtly petulant, and have little faith. Faith is the key, but it has two aspects:

- faith in the program and its instructions, that they are accurate, sufficient and need not be adjusted, *and* that the results promised are not an illusion and are attainable; and,
- faith in the unseen influence and benevolence of a higher power, and the related belief of being supported both in abstinence and the vicissitudes and random calamities of life.

---

maintenance steps, and have regularly sought and followed wise, bona fide spiritual guidance. It is no mean feat to go beyond the level of spiritual novice, but it is certainly worth it. At that point, change will actually embody the sense of joy — regardless of what the change is.
[17] *Alcoholics Anonymous*, p. 11.
[18] Four references to thoroughness from *Alcoholics Anonymous* are: "*thoroughly followed our path*," p. 58; "*if we have been thorough*," p. 70; "*painstaking*," p. 83; and "*carefully followed directions*," p. 85. There are many others.

These faiths develop simultaneously and your certitude of them is directly related to (a) whether or not your sponsor demonstrates them; and (b), your hard work. Most people don't get that being sober is not evidence of a spiritual life; being sober only means you're sober. Being "sober" doesn't mean a higher power is acting in your life, it could only mean you're stubborn.

Now that you've read this far, you may see the possibility of getting recovered, but you may also be somewhat overwhelming and intimidated. Approach each step—approach getting recovered— *"with willingness, patience, and labor."*[19] When you approach the steps in this manner, there is an intrinsic sense of when you are done any one step and ready for the next one. (We're back to spiritual heliotropism.) However, this is not revealed until you complete the step in the manner demanded by its spiritual content. You must undermine your anxiety, and ignore social peer pressure, which will demand you be only as spiritual as the group can tolerate.

Please Stop Jumping Around

Chapters in a book are in a certain sequence for a reason. Knowledge must be presented so that it builds on itself; otherwise, it's chaos. Nobody can do differential equations before they understand addition. A novel has a structure. The author had some dramatic intent in mind. You don't generally read Chapter 11 for ten minutes, read the end of Chapter 5, read Chapter 2, and then check out the first page. You read from beginning to end, which allows the novel to deliver its dramatic impact. In school, how often were you told not to read ahead in the textbook?

Spiritual transformation happens in a ubiquitous but subtly rigid, structured manner. I refer to this in Chapter 4, in the section There Are Laws Here. People cannot change the steps with impunity.

I offered this solution to someone who was struggling with the steps. Buy *Twelve Steps and Twelve Traditions* and separate it into twelve "packages" so that each package is the writing on each individual step. Put all these packages in a drawer someplace, and then start with Chapter 1 (Step One). Study it all by itself, for many weeks. Look up words in a dictionary. Be thorough in completing the Step One exercises I suggest in this book. Understand them. Do not go chasing off into any other step. This prevents intellectual and spiritual chaos. More importantly: (1) it stops you from looking for an easier, softer way by jumping ahead; and (2), it prevents your avoiding an awkward/difficult step (like Step Two) by plunging into the

---

[19] *Alcoholics Anonymous*, p. 163.

drama of Step Four. Command the philosophy and truth of each step in a focused and deliberate manner.[20]

With the help of what insights you've acquired in the steps previous to the one you're on, and the self-discipline you've established, the problems you encounter within each step are resolvable from within the step itself. Stay where you are until you are finished. Then, when you sense spiritual heliotropism (which takes a long time), read the next chapter, which would be the next step, and work at that one.

Once you have completed a step in this manner, there should be no reason to repeat it or refer back. The philosophy, the problems encountered within the step, and their resolution, and the related spiritual tasks are integrated as a part of you.

There are not enough people in twelve-step programs who see this as a spiritual apprenticeship, which is what it is. In any apprenticeship, you can't do fourth year work in the first six months. Apprentices are not allowed to attempt tasks beyond their training. We need more of this in twelve-step programs. A frequent request from me to those I assist is to slow down and back up. This is an apprenticeship—you are attending spirituality school and you should not attempt tasks that are beyond your training and faith.

People recovering from addictions increase their confusion and spiritual dislocation when they encounter a problem in any one step and hope to seek the solution by leaping ahead in ascending sequence to steps they have not completed. This manifestation of fear and impatience is fatal to abiding spiritual faith. It inculcates shallow understanding, spiritual and intellectual sloth, and impatience into an already insecure lifestyle. The fact that they jump around means they are insecure and didn't do the steps as required.

You also demonstrate insecurity when you jump backwards for spiritual discipline that you "should have" already incorporated into your lifestyle. The fact you're jumping backwards indicates you didn't *really* get it. "Jumping around" problem solving indicates willingness, patience, and labor were not applied in the earlier steps. It is debilitating in the extreme.

Problem solving, in relation to life and addictions recovery is simple: Apply each of the five spiritual principles to every situation and every relationship in your life; if there is a "problem" you didn't. When you encounter a "problem", apply the spiritual principles to the problem that you didn't in the first place and the problem will go away.

---

[20] It is worthy to note here, the different purposes of the two AA reference texts. At their essence, *Alcoholics Anonymous* is "what to do" and *Twelve Steps and Twelve Traditions* is "why to do it". The later steps, and especially the maintenance steps, are significantly more spiritually complex. If you don't understand the "whys" of the early steps—their spiritual (cont'd) intent—or haven't done that work, should you read ahead you will undermine your confidence and faith and confuse yourself.

There is No Group Experience

The original literature is written using plural pronouns, which is simply a grammatical structure for describing what each member of a group did individually. The pronouns do not imply that people sat in a group and did the steps together. It is a grammatical representation of individual journeys.

The instructions, as outlined in the first 192 pages of *Alcoholics Anonymous,* and all of *Twelve Steps and Twelve Traditions,* are a spiritually revealed truth that enables addicts to become spiritual and get recovered from addictions.[21] The purpose for attending a group that studies the literature is not to understand the literature it is to understand you. Studying the literature is (also) to identify the specific instructions, and to figure out which fears prevent you from doing exactly what you are told, exactly as you are told to do it. Book study groups are dangerous if you're simply accumulating knowledge, debating the wisdom of the step, looking for ways to improve or simplify it, or forcing yourself (or someone else) to attempt a step before you (or they) are ready.

Addiction is representative of an inner spiritual dislocation and has similar emotional themes for everyone. As a social, external structure, it shows up differently. My own story is rather flamboyant. I ran around a lot, got in fights, played with guns, and drove places at a hundred miles an hour. I drank hard, played hard, and lived with danger. Other people's addictions showed up differently. They drank less (or more), got in less (or more) trouble—but felt just as horrible about the whole thing. They viewed their addiction just as seriously life-threatening as I did mine, regardless of the fact that, at the social level, we were remarkably different.

The steps are highly personal. Doing them as an individual is important. Doing the steps, as a group exercise, is ill advised. The purpose of Step One is to figure out how *your* addiction showed up in *you*. It is a personal statement. That's why, when you share your experience, strength, and hope, it's important that you share a minimum of social content and expose your self-destruction at an emotional level. Understand your feelings and the context of your life. Share those quietly, at an emotional level, and you can potentially reach everybody. When you aggrandize and show off, you reach no one; and I mean no one.

---

[21] In my view, the text *Alcoholics Anonymous* is essentially limited to the first 192 pages, this being the Introduction through to page 164 and the first personal story (being Dr. Bob's) which ends at page 192, plus pp. 563-569. The other material is personal stories and anecdotal information that has little to do with the task at hand (spiritual transformation).

What You Do and Where You Go

If you develop a terrible, persistent stomachache, somebody will probably tell you to go to a doctor. If you break your leg, you'll go to a hospital. When you have an illness, there are places for you to go. That's part of the social structure in our culture.

You realize you have addictions. Many members of a twelve-step group will tell you where to go: Step One, where you learn and believe that you are sick and not crazy and that abstinence is essential. People will then suggest solutions: go to meetings, go get a sponsor, go do service work, go read the literature. It all seems to make sense, *except*... those are what you do but they're not where you *go*.

Step Two does *not* read, "Came to believe that having a good sponsor could restore us to sanity," or "...that doing service work could restore us to sanity." And, more importantly, is does not say "Came to believe that completing the steps could restore us to sanity."

These may keep you sober, and it is what you do, but you are to go to a higher power (as you understand this). Where you go is to a spiritual lifestyle; what you do is the steps, which teach you how to gracefully abide by spiritual principles. If you confuse "what you do" with "where you go" the results are disastrous—for you and for everyone else in your life.

Every time anyone recasts the original AA instructions they dilute the spiritual integrity of that message. The various myths that you are led to believe, and the deification of psychology (which is only an inadequate technology of spirituality), imply that something other than spirituality will restore you to sanity: going to meetings, sponsorship, service work, literature, and therapy. They won't. The greatest source of program chaos and misalliance arises at Step Two. If you don't get Step Two, you don't get anything except maybe abstinence/sobriety based on willpower, and a social life rooted in peer pressure, politics, and impression management.

I have never yet met anyone who sincerely worked towards being spiritual who relapsed. I have seen many people get drunk because they didn't go to meetings, or they went to too many meetings, or they were sponsoring too many people, or they didn't have a sponsor, or they lied, or they... well, there are thousands of "excuses" for relapse. Over the long term, if you want guaranteed abstinence and sincere peace of mind, become sincerely spiritual. Dependence upon a higher power, *vis-à-vis* the five spiritual principles, is the only solution. Believing this is the essence of Step Two. Addicts either work at becoming spiritual or they stay sick to some noticeable degree.

This is dictated by the phenomenon of addiction and can be threatening. Some addicts will do anything to avoid getting spiritual—even relapse and die. They'll get three sponsors; they'll sponsor seventeen people; they'll go to sixteen meetings a week; they'll donate until it hurts; they'll have seven good reasons for one "harmless" lie; they'll answer the phones five nights a week until four in the morning (and not complain or brag about it very much). They'll serve on committees, buy the coffee, and drive people around until their car runs out of gas. They'll do almost anything to stay sober and *appear* spiritual rather than *be* spiritual.

Disease, Clarity, Health

Self-awareness about their own disease is not readily available to addicts. That's because, as I described earlier, it's an internal, universal state of existence. Except possibly for some mental illnesses, addiction is the only disease that has an entrenched "self-blindness" that specifically tells the addict they're not sick.

This mind-set (of self-blindness and blame) is often suddenly fractured by a transformative moment. That moment, a type of unitive experience of clarity, informs addicts that something is terribly wrong with *them* and there is [possibly] another option, both of which they were previously unaware. The trenchant and entrenched phenomenon of self-blindness is cracked enough so that clarity or awareness (sometimes, later attributed to divine intervention) pierces the blindness of the addicted condition.

This sudden clarity (#2, below) has very decided spiritual tones to it, and is never people-induced. People, especially in treatment centres, therapists, and caregivers, try to arrange and manipulate secular circumstances so that breaking through this self-blindness (going from #1 to #2) may happen. The purpose of twelve-step work is to act on the clarity at #2 and promote recovery and spiritual health. However, the breakthrough from blindness to awareness (from #1 to #2) is never guaranteed. It might look like this:

#1 Blindness (Disease)	The presence of an addiction: blindness to the conditions of self-annihilation, deceit, arrogance, greed, defects, selfishness, irresponsibility, disobedience and defiance.
#2 Clarity (Awareness)	An opportunity is created from, or out of, a spontaneous, insightful moment that fractures "self-blindness" and allows some insight that something is terribly wrong. A new option becomes available that previously didn't exist.
#3 Recovery (Health)	With diligent step-work, perseverance, and mentoring the lifestyle of self-destruction transforms itself into a commitment to spiritual health; i.e. devotion to recovery and spiritual principles.

Consider: (1) the varied and inconsistent etiology, virulence, and duration of addictions; (2) The Universe (or Providence) somehow provides an initial transformative moment; (3) the demonstrated success that the tenets of spirituality have in eliminating addictions; and (4), the generally con-flicted and erratically unsuccessful attempts of medicine or psychology to resolve addictions. These should altogether provide enough convincing evi-dence that addiction recovery is an issue of spiritual discipline, not science.

Alcoholics Anonymous advises that it is deep within us that the great reality is found.[22] This philosophy, in one form or another, has been around for about three thousand years. If your physical body and mind are cor-rupted, in this case by addictions, you cannot get deep within yourself to find that great reality. In other words, your character defects and addictions are a barrier between "you" and your "inner spiritual nature". The steps and spiritual principles are how you remove that barrier.

By definition, the attributes you need to be spiritual are the exact op-posite of the symptoms that comprise active addiction. To be spiritual in the fullest sense of the word, you have to properly care for your body and live by spiritual principles. This commitment must be in *all* of your affairs: sexuality, parenting, leisure, relationships, education, recreation, employ-ment, career; with people you love, like, and don't like; with people you have authority over; with people who are being mean, insensitive or dishon-est—literally everywhere and with everyone.

Sponsors, abstinence, sponsoring, speaking at conventions, studying the texts, service work, attending meetings, sharing—these are only what you do (the avenues to the solution); they are not the solution. The solution is a relationship with a higher power. Believing this truth is what is required at Step Two.

Beliefs, Experiences, Awakenings

This section may seem like semantics, or it may read like a shallow ef-fort to appear erudite. It is neither. Having clarity in the nuance of spiritual issues is critical to the development of an abiding faith and for the acquisi-tion of sincere humility. I cannot overstate the importance of thoroughness in Step Two.

As regards to "getting recovered", a phrase was needed to describe this unique process—the changes that occur as an alcoholic/addict endeavors to become spiritual. This positive change is healing (but not exactly), and it increases awareness (but it's more than that), and there is a personality change (but it's much deeper than psychology). The phrases used in *Alco-holics Anonymous* are spiritual experience, spiritual awakening, and religious experience. In that book they are used interchangeably and refer to

---

[22] *Alcoholics Anonymous*, p. 55.

a personality change sufficient to bring about recovery. This takes the twelve-step pilgrim away from complicated definitions and esoteric meanings, which lightens the burden of transformation.

You may wonder about the difference between a spiritual experience, a religious experience, and a spiritual awakening. According to the literature, there isn't any difference, but there are certainly misunderstandings about them.

There are misunderstandings about the relationship between the [often] alternating sequence of having a spiritual belief and having a spiritual experience. Beliefs and experiences are different. You might have a religious or spiritual experience without believing in anything spiritual; and you can believe in spiritual things without having a spiritual experience.

Many people think they've got to find God first and then accumulate faith—it doesn't usually work this way. Having a spiritual awakening, or a personality change, without believing in a higher power is very often how spiritual transformation begins. A spiritual experience or a spiritual awakening is what usually happens before you believe in a higher power, not after.

Many readers got a false impression from the first edition of *Alcoholics Anonymous* and that was the reason for writing the appendix Spiritual Experience.[23] From one perspective, that appendix is an amend for being less than clear when the book was first published. The first paragraph asserts a spiritual experience, or awakening, or religious experience *"shows that the personality change sufficient to bring about recovery from alcoholism has manifested itself among us in many different forms."* This information is intended to make the spiritual journey easier in two ways.

The first has to do with language. In all specialized fields of endeavor, there is a lexicon of words that have special meanings because of the nature of the subject. Medicine, philosophy, mathematics, computing have their own unique jargon. Spiritual endeavor is no exception. However, *Alcoholics Anonymous* advises that you use everyday language when discussing spiritual matters so there is less possibility of misunderstandings.[24] Using uncommon words, where the definition more clearly articulates a point, isn't creating jargon.

The second way the appendix Spiritual Experience lightens your burden is by lowering your expectations. Many people become trapped in the expectation that they'll experience some extraordinary phenomenon, which will instantly become the basis for having faith in a higher power (which would require less hard work on their own part). Some people wonder why they've been around a program for a while, and haven't seen burning

---

[23] *Alcoholics Anonymous*, p. 569.
[24] Ibid., p. 93. It is important to recognize that "everyday language" isn't restricted to one-syllable words, and that spiritual language is absent of cursing and swearing.

bushes or divine visions attendant to their prayers. Is God overlooking them? Are they not doing this right?

Spiritual Experience advises that many alcoholics concluded from the first printing of the book "*in order to recover they must acquire an immediate and overwhelming God-consciousness...*". [Notice, it's not to be in recovery.] People wait for some divine flash of transformation and if none happens they assume they are doing something wrong or "God" isn't noticing them.

If they sit around long enough (they secretly hope) a divine flash of transformation will eventually occur, and they won't have to do any real work. While they wait for an easier, softer way addicts generate drama. After months or years of waiting, with no divine revelations, many spiritual complications are created. If addicts proclaim they've prayed and nothing happens, they become insecure. This can generate so much anxiety they'll withdraw from their support group. Insecurity requires they create delusions or illusions about themselves and spiritual uniqueness, which requires a supporting drama (which they'll relentlessly reinvent). I expand on this later in the section on Prayer.

Defect-laden personalities inject all manner of self-serving meanings into coincidence. Some people perceive an uncommon circumstance as validation that God exists. They interpret dreams and coincidence in some context of divine message. I've known people to claim God "spoke" to them because there was a powerful gust of wind at a particular moment of prayer. Others entreat a higher power to provide parking spots so they won't be late for appointments, and still others characterize the Atman-Brahmin as a trickster, a social secretary, or an omniscient Santa Claus. Curious coincidence, anxiety-induced visions, and dreams do not prove God is paying particular attention to someone, nor do they prove the existence of God. To believe that they are, is only proof that our minds and neurotic insecurities are powerful in creating distractions from humility and hard work.

Most people completely overlook or ignore any subtle personality change that is a valid manifestation of a spiritual experience as defined in the appendix to *Alcoholics Anonymous*. For example: In the middle of an argument with your partner you suddenly realize you are wrong, so you spontaneously and humbly make an amend. That is a spiritual awakening that arises from deep within you, but it doesn't look like one because you only feel regret and take responsibility for hurting someone you love. You're just making an amend. If your sponsor understands spirituality, and you told them what happened, they might comment on the lovely spiritual experience: a moment of personality change that was sufficient to bring about recovery from the selfishness of addiction. That type of behaviour is a spiritual awakening and the world is a safer place for it. However, it didn't occur with a celestial-trumpet fanfare. Realize these small personality changes are satisfying the definition given in spiritual experience. Celebrate the fact that spiritual awakenings require very hard work, which enables you to treasure the experiences, and develop a stronger faith in a spiritual lifestyle. Humble, honest effort in obedience to rights, freedoms, and five spiritual principles is the order of the day, *every* day.

Most people will have slow, gradual spiritual awakenings—the educational variety. If you look for burning bushes, you will become disillusioned and disappointed. You may wonder: "What's the point? I'm going to meetings and nothing's happened. Why am I hanging around?"

A spiritual experience (or awakening or religious experience) appears in different ways. If you are participating in a twelve-step program, and are willing to be more honest today than a few months ago, you've had a spiritual experience. You're probably noticing, in the same period, you may be slightly more interested in kindness. The fact that you can't pinpoint exactly when, or exactly what happened to motivate you to be more kind or honest (and certainly no person "caused" these changes), indicates the change is of a spiritual nature. This in no way undermines its authenticity. Suspicious egos have a tendency to cast about frantically looking for some secular reason, when in fact, it's spiritually oriented.

It's interesting that there is little or no talk about having a religious experience. I wonder how popular you'd be at your next twelve-step meeting if you spoke eloquently and passionately about a *religious* experience. Many people in twelve-step groups are vehemently opposed to religion. It's interesting these are most often the people who misrepresent the philosophy of the twelve steps, and thereby create social prejudice against twelve-step groups (just as other fanatics have misrepresented the invisible beauty of their religions and so helped to create prejudice and opposition to religion).

What Makes An Addict Honest?

Trying to understand these personality changes as a function of psychology, rather than viewing them as spiritual experiences, as described in the appendix of *Alcoholics Anonymous,* obfuscates the evidence you need to develop spiritual faith for the yet larger trials ahead. If you attribute an increase in honesty to your own willpower, your ego takes the credit. If you attribute it to your sponsor, your therapist, your therapy, your ego takes the credit for picking that sponsor: What a good person I am; see how hard I'm working?

In addictions, you had countless opportunities to be honest, even when there was no risk to being honest. Still, you weren't. If you believe your own willpower gets you honest, you may well be honest, but no farther ahead since one defect (arrogance about yourself) is as bad as the other defect (being dishonest). For the addict getting recovered, any sincere increase in honesty, however slight, is a spiritual experience. When you define these changes as the mysterious derivative of praying and spiritual commitment, developing faith is inevitable.

In a twelve-step program, there's no sanctioned punishment for being dishonest. People continue to be dishonest in many areas and there appears to be no overt consequences (except spiritual corruption and on-going socially approved addictions). Really, then, why get honest? There are three reasons. **First**: Honesty requires less energy than deceit, so you'll have more energy and pleasure in life. **Second**: Honesty always feels better than dishonesty over the long term—looking at yourself in the mirror is easier. **Third**: The more honest you are, the farther away you are from relapse.

Self-challenging vigilance is always the order of the day. Here are two declarations to consider. In order to become recovered, they are not negotiable.

Declaration I
(approximately the first five years of spiritual/step work)
If I drink, use drugs, act out, or lie, in any circumstance of my life, my destiny is in the hands of those around me.

Declaration II
(after five years)
If I manipulate anyone to disadvantage or participate directly or indirectly in anything morally squalid; if I am overt or covert in disregarding any of the five spiritual principles; if I blame anyone for any condition in my life, then my spiritual condition is tenuous and my destiny is in the hands of those around me.[25]

These declarations are hard to live up to; they're all encompassing. I wrote them that way. I am in charge of so little in the universe. Life's benign indifference to *me* motivates me to keep as much influence over my own life as I can, without controlling or imposing on others. The only position that consistently allows this is to live up to these declarations. Being spiritual is a very difficult thing to achieve. That's why few people seriously attempt it, and why its rewards are so sincerely and wholly blissful.

Steps One to Nine allow you to accomplish everything you need to become recovered and then to embrace Declaration II. Many people "in

---

[25] These declarations are related to two types of that are discussed in Chapter 12.

recovery" are only as honest as they need to be to get by. They are still liars (but not very often), and on any occasion when someone points that out, they become defensive and present some self-serving interpretation of rigorous honesty. For them, honesty is a matter of convenience and lying is a solution to awkward circumstances. At the minimum, the error is in equating sobriety and spirituality—they mistakenly believe that long-term abstinence indicates some degree of spiritual integrity.

The spiritual authority and beauty of the original twelve-step program, as revealed in the first 192 pages and Appendix II of *Alcoholics Anonymous,* and in *Twelve Steps and Twelve Traditions,* is two-fold. Firstly, it never contradicts itself. There are very few "guide" books on spirituality that don't somehow contradict themselves.[26] Secondly, it is its own training ground. If taken as presented, it's a completely self-contained program for achieving regular, deep, and sincere association with a higher power, without attacking any other religious doctrine.

The original twelve-step instructions are so humbly confident about what they offer, that they don't allow for any troubling circumstance to be too difficult for them to resolve. They deny any spiritual problem as too sophisticated to be beyond the scope of what *Alcoholics Anonymous* and *Twelve Steps and Twelve Traditions* have to offer. There are no philosophical or spiritual contradictions within them (excluding the personal stories, for after all, they are only personal stories). These books are probably the most profound writings on spirituality and the human condition written in the last 1,500 years—since *The Rule of Benedict* (c. 520 CE). For people with addictions, the precision and clarity of the AA texts' spiritual intent, that path's proven effectiveness, cannot be overstated.

In the first few years of becoming recovered, you will have spiritual experiences without really believing there's a higher power. For example: You may subscribe to any number of reasons by which you explain any increase in your honesty—your willingness, your determination, you're working your program, or because you believe it's worth it. These reasons will appear valid at the time, so your increase in honesty, which brings about recovery from addiction, won't be interpreted as a spiritual awakening but as an ego exercise of willpower. And, during that spiritual experience, you may not believe in the worth or value of a higher power.

---

[26] Very often, the authors of spiritual books, or the defenders of formal religious doctrine, will allow a contradiction in their doctrine, or the doctrine will embody some glaring injustice in its program of salvation. They will then explain this away by blaming God, some long-dead prophet, the mysterious machinations of Providence, or their own inability to explain Divine Prerogative (which is blaming God). There are no contradictions, paradoxes, or injustices in a sincerely spiritual life.

At the early stages of getting recovered, or if you're forever in recovery, you will tend to credit yourself for these personality changes (i.e. I'm working *my* program), and conveniently forget the historical fact that while acting out, or in unspiritual sobriety, good intentions, determination, and willpower never changed anything.

When getting recovered, any consistent devotion to *sincere* spiritual effort brings about a spiritual experience, regardless of where *you* place the credit. Personality changes like honesty or being more responsible for your abuses and misdemeanors will creep into your personality. You'll be in the middle of these various spiritual experiences/awakenings that bring about recovery *before* you have a strong faith in a higher power (of your own understanding). It's very common to have a spiritual awakening prior to having strong faith.

Don't confuse spiritual experiences with spiritual beliefs. You do not have to believe in a higher power to begin this journey. All you have to do is follow the instructions in the original texts.[27] It can also work the other way where people may have spiritual beliefs without spiritual experiences: i.e. There are people who believe in a higher power of some description who are also mean, dishonest, or selfish, and who don't have spiritual experiences. There are still others who believe fervently that their system of spiritual belief is superior to all others, and who are silently or openly racist or mean on behalf of "their God"; spiritual elitism. [Insecurity motivates these types of beliefs, and abuse always results from representing any spiritual doctrine as superlative. The spiritual path presented in *Alcoholics Anonymous* is the most effective for addicts seeking recovery, but it isn't necessarily "the best" for everyone.]

In this book, I'm explaining that the original twelve steps, as a route out of active addiction and into spirituality, guarantees the best results. They are quite "perfect" the way they are written, and require no modification or amendment. They do, however, require hard work and commitment. The spiritual masters throughout history have consistently told us the way to a higher power and a sincerely spiritual lifestyle is the most difficult personal journey there is. The original steps are very particular in their demand for commitment and detail; you are well advised to do exactly as instructed if you intend to become recovered.

---

[27] If you're being advised to do anything regarding your "recovery" by apparently well-intentioned friends or sponsors, ask them where their advice to you is found in the approved literature. If it isn't in *Alcoholics Anonymous* or *Twelve Steps and Twelve Traditions* (and watch they don't take something out of context to win a useless argument), be cautious about following it. The advice will be more for their benefit than yours. If you do as the literature instructs, you will start to have spiritual experiences, regardless of whether you believe in a higher power of your own understanding.

For addictions, experience has proven that the original twelve steps work. Other addiction/recovery programs and modifications may or may not work; however, in order to find out if they do or not, you may have to pay with your life. Is it worth the risk?[28]

The point of this book is to offer some clarity on the original instructions, along with an awareness of how therapy and psychology might assist, and what the risks are for disobedience to spiritual principles. Be cautious when the AA textbooks are used as general guides. Be cautious about following the advice of people who did any of the steps "their own way". You are putting your life in the hands of people who think they are wiser than *Alcoholics Anonymous* or *Twelve Steps and Twelve Traditions*. I don't know of too many people who are that wise.

At this point, I assume you understand that when you drank or acted out (past tense) you were powerless over alcohol or acting out, meaning inherently that your life *was* unmanageable. You believe there aren't two halves to Step One. You've carefully examined your life and have figured out how you structured it and were dishonest to facilitate drinking or acting out. You're convinced that continuing abstinence is crucial. Once you establish abstinence and are convinced of these truths, and admit that you are powerless, you are ready for Step Two—not before.

Step Two

In Step Two, you first come up against the phrase "*Came to believe....*"[29] At face value, and do take it at face value, it means that, over a period of time, you judged something as accurate and truthful. Because of what it is you must come to believe, accomplishing Step Two is time-consuming. I am never surprised or concerned when people take six months, or a year (or longer), to complete Step Two. What you have to accomplish is subtle and there's a lot to it. What you came to believe must be clear. You must also be confident; otherwise, everything you attempt there after is undermined by ambivalence, and *ambivalence is spiritual can* (Ambivalence is relationship cancer also, but more about that in the book.)

Everything in your recovery and in your life that transpires ʹ One is dependent upon how you addressed Step Two. After absti Two is by far the most important step.[30] The ease of everythi

---

[28] People without addictions (as few as there are) can attempt a spiritual lifesty number of reasons, decide to abandon their quest. For them, there are no dire ᴄ For addicts who abandon the spiritual path, the consequences are disastrous.

[29] *Alcoholics Anonymous*, p. 59, and *Twelve Steps and Twelve Traditions*, p. 2�5

[30] Regardless of any topic under discussion, always understand that everything upon complete abstinence from acting out behaviour. Clean, sober, abstinent, a

predicated on your relationship to a higher power. Step Two is where you begin that relationship. It's the foundation for how you reorganize your values and perceptions. The basis for your spiritual journey, which, according to Step Three is your life, begins here. Spirituality must take an ubiquitous and dominant position in your life. As an addict getting recovered, *how* you come to believe that spirituality is the solution, and *what* you believe about that, will affect every decision you make for the rest of your life.

Believing encompasses a specific attitude. People believe $2 + 2 = 4$. It isn't negotiable. If you believe something, you don't "kind of" believe it. When you believe a thing, you accept it as true and allow that it's not open to debate. You assume an intellectual position of conviction and confidence: no substitutions, vagaries, or equivocations. You either believe something or you don't. Notice one of the AA co-founder's declarations on page 11 of *Alcoholics Anonymous*—how he once accepted moral teachings he liked and disregarded those that were inconvenient. A sincere belief requires that something be true, even when it may be inconvenient.[31]

Beliefs of "convenience" are treacherous, and the exact thing to avoid in Step Two. Should you believe as you are advised, you will soon reorganize all of your old ideas, eliminate previously destructive behaviours, and voluntarily impose *on yourself* new values and attitudes. Should you believe, with conviction, what the original literature counsels (and of what use is believing something if there is no conviction behind the belief?), and if you adhere to the five principles of spirituality with quiet determination, I can assure you that you will be viewed as suspicious and face disapproval from many people—even within your twelve-step group. But, your life will become your own and change in wonderful ways you cannot imagine.

What "Came To Believe" Encompasses

There is significant work involved prior to believing *"that a Power greater than ourselves could restore us to sanity."*[32] You must select the concept of god that you believe in: Spiritual essence, a universal consciousness, a higher power, the great reality, Allah, YHWH, Atman-Brahmin, Jesus: there are hundreds of names and points of view for this conception. You *start* to get clarity on your point of view concerning the name and concept of god. This is very personal.

---

bottom-line behaviour—it doesn't matter what you call it, everything Spiritual depends on tinence from all acting out behaviour.

t the beginning, for probably the first ten or so years, becoming spiritual will be the most nvenient thing you'll ever do; but take heart, after ten years of diligent application and work, spiritual transformation does become graceful.

oholics Anonymous, p. 59, and *Twelve Steps and Twelve Traditions*, p. 25.

Although this next point is not discussed in the AA literature, it is my experience and I offer it for your consideration. Your concept of a higher power (by whatever name) is *not* for discussion in large groups or at casual coffee table conversations. This is quite intimate and "should" be for quiet, reflective conversation with non-judgmental people you trust. Avoid contentious debates about this.

What isn't personal is what this higher power will help addicts accomplish. Picking a personal conception of a higher power is important, but each individual higher power does the same thing for all addicts getting recovered: it restores them to sanity. The following four processes will all be happening during Step Two:

- deciding upon which concept of God is right for them to start their pilgrimage;
- working to eliminate their spiritual belligerence (which I discuss later in Spiritual Dislocations);
- slowly understanding the "theory" and content of Step Two; and,
- coming to believe (being convinced) that How It Works is true, and that a higher power will restore them to sanity.

No Substitutions

It is especially important to not substitute anything in place of the phrase, *"a power greater than ourselves"*. Step Two does *not* read: Came to believe that going to lots of meetings could restore us to sanity. It also does not read that getting a job, or being a circuit speaker, or getting someone to love us, or sponsoring lots of people, or attending lots of twelve-step social occasions, or studying the books, or doing service work could restore us to sanity. More particularly, Step Two does not say that doing the steps could restore you to sanity. Substitute nothing for the phrase, *"a Power greater than ourselves."*

Yes, the AA textbooks and sponsors advise you to be at meetings, be at a time and place where other people can share their problems, be charitable, carry the message, pay your own way, be honest. These, and many other instructions, are to facilitate your becoming spiritual. These are not the solution; they are the avenues to the solution. The substitutions I listed (above) may allow you sobriety, but you will remain not spiritual, and therefore at risk. Being always "in recovery" is proof that substitutions have been made, and getting recovered does not allow for substitutions.

If you don't believe that getting recovered depends upon your relationship with a higher power, and sincerely act upon this, then you believe that

169

recovery rests on some combination of willpower, therapy, getting in touch with feelings, social success, fulfilling sex, meetings, and sponsors. Of course, if all you want is sobriety, then these may well be sufficient—you'll be in the social loop, and popular, but living on the edge of insanity and relapse. Relying on anything other than a higher power to resolve your addictions is relapse gambling with your life as the stakes.[33]

What newcomers use for their higher power during the initial stages of getting recovered is very often a survival/grasping-at-straws reaction to the fear of acting out and failure. That's fine. There is much encouragement to use the group or anything else that's neutral or has psychological safety. Believe in what you have to at the beginning. If this rudimentary concept persists beyond the newcomer phase, however, it is risky for several reasons.

Over an extended period of time, if you use the group as a higher power, you are allowing yourself to be dependent on something that is loosely organized and subject to the ego-pressure of charismatic members. Groups and meetings are untenable as a "higher power" because the traditions and steps are not scrupulously adhered to. If you use the group as your higher power, you limit your ability to participate in the community at large. A higher power that is defined secularly, that does not extend beyond some arbitrary intellectual concept, is thereby limited in scope and will not allow you to participate beyond that narrow limit—the intellect.

Using anything finite, be it a cat, the memory of your nice grandmother, "a group", or nature, as your higher power places limits on your spiritual resources. It will eventually restrict you to whatever the limits are of whatever you choose. I cannot find any respected treatise or major ethical writing on God or spirituality, including the original AA texts, that suggest you pray to your dog, the sunset, or any group. The spiritual masters teach this would be idolatry and defeat any sincere spiritual endeavor. From a Western perspective, yes, I grant that God may talk through people, but this is usually a trite euphemism for something pithy, but "God" is not people or the groups they form. *Twelve Steps and Twelve Traditions* discusses different attitudes of spiritual newcomers and what you have to do to go beyond

---

[33] In recent years, "getting in touch with your feelings" has become possibly the most popular (and most ineffective) strategy to resolve addictions. Addictions are not an issue of misplaced emotion. If you're resolving an abstinence-available addiction, then belligerence, social networking, and entrenching yourself in thirty meetings a week may be enough to keep you clean and sober. This is because of the hard line you can draw between abstinence and acting out. For any abstinence not-available addiction (like anger, sex, or relationships), sobriety based on meetings, sober-networking, and willpower will not allow sobriety for any length of time because a hard line cannot be drawn between abstinence and any addictions that generate directly out of instinctual needs.

this narrow and limiting spiritual perspective. (See Spiritual Dislocations, Chapter 3)

Step Two advises that a power greater than yourself *could* restore you to sanity, which implies that this restoration is dependent on something. It depends on your continued abstinence, appropriate prayer and meditation, and your continued devotion to sound spiritual endeavor. This is what is implied by the word could. *Restoration to sanity and sincere spiritual endeavor are intrinsically interdependent.*

It is crucial, so I will briefly repeat this: Just because you don't cheat or lie, and do go to meetings, have a sponsor, and answer your phone late at night, doesn't mean that you are going to stay sober; nor does it mean you are spiritual. In fact, people go to meetings, sponsor others, go to the round-ups, and still relapse. What happened? They didn't come to believe that living by sound spiritual principles and devotion to a higher power (which can only arise out of "believing" at Step Two) is the solution.

Restore

Notice this: *"When dealing with such a person, you had better use everyday language to describe spiritual principles."*[34] Restore means to bring back, or return something to an original, former condition or position. These are straightforward definitions found in any dictionary, which have far-reaching implications for the addict getting recovered.

Creating a unique jargon to discuss addictions or spirituality defeats the intent, which is to reach everyone. Pious or insecure people try to compensate for their perceived "inadequacy" when describing the indescribable, such as a higher power, by creating obtuse or abstract words and meanings: jargon. This doesn't mean people shouldn't use uncommon words, nor does it mean that we have to use one-syllable words. It means jargon and slang words with unique meanings are to be avoided. These create cliques and allow clique members to exclude others and avoid truths. Getting recovered is somewhat complicated; it is arduous; it is not beyond ordinary language, and neither is a higher power. The AA textbooks use ordinary definitions to present the ideas and describe the process.[35]

At one point in time, you were okay. Then you became not-okay (by virtue of an addiction). With proper application, you are going to become okay again. Restore means exactly what it means. It doesn't say create—it says restore, and yet you will hear both old-timers and newcomers say:

---

[34] *Alcoholics Anonymous*, p. 93.
[35] With the massive presence of television, videos, movies, computers, etc., we are becoming more and more linguistically lazy. Buy a dictionary. Nothing is free.

"I've been broken and defective from the moment I was born." What arrogance and drama is in that claim?

Some addicts expend a lot of energy trying to convince others they were the meanest, wildest person in town, which in a very few cases and in very small towns, might have been true. There is drama and insecurity in their claim to have been sick *all* of their life—addicts from the moment they were conceived. It's pretty hard to top that story. If they can convince you they were sick from the moment they were born, and by age three were killing and pillaging the countryside (or at least swearing and stealing cars), they have status and notoriety. They are now more special by virtue of being the sickest person in the meeting.[36]

When you are deciding to *"thoroughly follow our path"*[37] then *restore* implies at some time in the past you were not insane. You can't go beyond Step Two if you believe you were "created" insane. What degree of self-abuse or grandiosity pushes you to that degree of self-rejection? What ego pay-off is there for convincing anyone, especially convincing yourself, that you were an addict from conception? Is it to put responsibility on your family? Is it to avoid the pain of being ordinary? Is it to justify or excuse your gross irresponsibility as an adult? Is it to maintain special status and impress people? Is it to frighten people away? All claims to uniqueness defeat spirituality, create isolation (especially from yourself), and maintain your own unheeded loneliness.

Balance what follows with common sense. Fetal-alcohol and fetal-drug syndrome are serious medical concerns. There are other seriously damaging congenital conditions. I'm not talking about these, nor am I denying there may be valid genetic links that influence a predisposition to addictions. The next time you're around an infant, notice it's not a psychologically debilitated, dysfunctional, mean-spirited, deceitful, corrupt addict. It's an infant—an innocent, beautiful child, and so were you. Respect that about yourself. I am referring to drama and exaggeration. Evading the implication of *restore* contains a justification for bragging and irresponsibility. Granted, for some of you, you can't remember when you weren't "crazy" so you may have to act on faith regarding *restore*; so, act on faith.

Blank Spots

Addicts often feel a need to explain away, justify, or compensate for a memory blank-spot, especially big ones. They do this by deliberate dishon-

---

[36] While acting out, such people go to unusual lengths to be extravagant or outrageous— deliberately generating calamity to command attention. They do the same thing "in recovery"—command attention by flamboyance and drama.

[37] This is part of the opening sentence of How It Works, *Alcoholics Anonymous*, p. 58.

esty, or by assumption and confabulation, which aren't necessarily dishonest.[38]

Addicts sometimes have very few memories of their early life, and all addicts have memory blank-spots from their childhood and during times of acting out. With a propensity to blame, and a tendency to label themselves as bad, and often enabled by poorly informed therapists and helpers, they easily assume that memory lapses mean they were doing something horrible, or something horrible was being done to them. Couple this with an insecure need to be seen as unique, and a need to absolve themselves for their destructive behaviour, they will try to fill in these memory lapses in a way that compensates without responsibility and keeps fear and shame at a distance by blaming.

If addicts repeat to themselves, for years, that some memory lapse means something horrible happened, that memory lapse will eventually become something horrible—as much from any legitimate trauma or abuse that *may* have occurred, as from the self-inculcated idea of "very horrible". Addicts can convince themselves of just about anything.[39] The truth here is, addicts will need therapy to resolve the self-harm that results from living with self-inculcated, imagined, horrible memories just as much as they would for real trauma that did exist.

If you look at a blank piece of paper, it's blank. There isn't pornography on it, there isn't an abstract painting on it, there isn't a poem written on it; it's just blank. Many people (themselves wounded) assign intrusive therapeutic labels and make risky assumptions about memory blank-spots with only two pieces of evidence: (a) someone is complaining they can't remember; and (b), he or she is an addict.

Some of you will have memory blank spots because of serious abuse (given or received), and others because life was repetitive and mundane.

---

[38] Memory blank-spots themselves are caused for different reasons, possibly for as mundane a reason as extended, repetitious boredom; or alcohol/drug use and acting out; or as important a reason as the concealment of historical trauma. From one point of view: Confabulation is a compensatory defense against insecurity or shame and fear, where memory blank-spots are filled in, or unsatisfactory memories are replaced with some more acceptable fantasy that, over time, becomes a "truth".

Confabulation is sometimes ego-deliberate, in that a fantasy scenario is created and replaces reality, where the historical reality is unacceptable to a later specific ego agenda like needing to justify behaviour. Over the course of years, the memory manipulation is subsequently suppressed, and the created memory is held to be true since the ego-generated manipulation is forgotten. This does *not* imply that all memory is false. "Memory" is very complicated. It can only be resolved in well-managed, *long-term* therapy, and if there is any organic damage it may never be resolved. Competent therapeutic counsel is essential if this seems to be of concern for the recovering addict.

[39] Prisoners in wartime are brainwashed. They are kept tired, hungry, in pain, cold, confused, disoriented, lonely, and frightened, and are repeatedly told some story. Addicts treat themselves like prisoners of war, and they repeatedly tell themselves stories.

Not having memories is not in and of itself evidence of trauma or abuse. Be very careful about making assumptions about memory blank spots and trauma; it is exceptionally dangerous without accurate, qualified, thorough, cautious, "un-biased", in-depth clinical support in addictions-related symptom recognition and diagnosis.

Twelve-step programs are not treatment modalities for psychological problems, *per se*. They do not address childhood-onset psychiatric disorders (or any other psychiatric disorder for that matter). They only address spiritual dislocation, which is Addiction. Inasmuch as it is true that you will, throughout your spiritual life, challenge all of your old ideas, it's nonetheless tremendously important to accept this as true: *"To believe that the alcoholic who approaches A.A. is an unprincipled, untaught barbarian, suddenly transformed by the previously unavailable spiritual illumination of the Twelve Steps, is, to me, utter foolishness."*[40]

Addicts are ordinary people and innocent when they were infants and children. Through a process of spiritual dislocation, they manifested an addiction. The good parts became hidden through their addictions and yes, sometimes through abuse inflicted by others. Addicts are now charged with the responsibility of resolving their addictions by slow, painstaking spiritual transformation.

The essence of Step Two is that over some period of time, you become convinced that some version of a higher power could restore you to sanity. Substituting meetings or the steps, or anything else for a higher power, or skimping on the requirement of *being convinced,* will corrupt the outcome and prohibit you from realizing the freedom and beauty of being recovered (and all that implies). In getting recovered, your soul isn't recreated; spirituality is restored.

It's impossible to realize spiritual integrity (meaning much more than "sober and happy") without firmly entrenching these two fundamental preconditions: abstinence (from Step One) and belief (from Step Two). Lacking these will show up as reversion into primary addictions, the intensification of subtle addictions, a failure to exit all addictions, a shallow commitment to honesty and responsibility (you'll be honest and responsible providing it's not too inconvenient), recycled step completion, or as a reorganization of, or an attempt to camouflage your character defects (impression management). Not *being convinced* results in your having shallow faith in the program (regardless of how loudly you proclaim otherwise),

---

[40] From the pamphlet A Member's Eye View of Alcoholics Anonymous, Alcoholics Anonymous World Services, Inc., 1970.

being suspicious and fearful of those who are sincere and honest, and never achieving an abiding sense of safety in intimate relationships.

People in this painful quandary often work hard, but they work hard in the wrong direction.[41] Twelve-step spiritual misalignment is discussed in Misalliance of Commitment in Chapter 6.

Spiritual Dislocations

There are five types of spiritual problems, more aptly called dislocations that newcomers face at Step Two. At the minimum, this means that although the newcomer desires transformation and has a belief that spirituality is good, something is subtly wrong and persists in interfering with their pilgrimage. The spiritual novice (the newcomer) has to appreciate the nuances of these dislocations to resolve them so they can stay on track spiritually.[42]

The first type of spiritual dislocation is defiance—the person who won't believe. This defiance can be well concealed underneath many apparently well justified, stalling tactics like studying religions and checking out alternatives. Be aware of the consequences of continued defiance to spiritual principles—relapse, continuing humiliation, self-destruction, anger, chaos, and possibly death. Review the top of page 26 in *Twelve Steps and Twelve Traditions,* where you will find paragraphs that describe what the spiritually belligerent person has to do.

If you fit into this category, *Twelve Steps and Twelve Traditions* advises the hoop you have to jump through is bigger than you think. You don't have to believe everything all at once. Take your time. With continued effort, you only need a little honesty, open-mindedness, and willingness. A spiritual experience has already happened and your belligerence will lessen.

There are two important side issues to this first type of spiritual defiance that need to be examined in detail—HOW and WPL.

HOW — Honesty, Open-mindedness, Willingness

These three attributes, hereafter referred to as HOW, allow addicts to work on the specific problem of spiritual belligerence at Step Two. Step Two is a perception and faith step, as are Steps Six and Seven. The other

---

[41] Many people work hard at completing the steps. I mean that in all sincerity. They are diligent and painstaking; however, sincerely working hard in the wrong way is just as ineffective as making a half-hearted effort in the right way.

[42] One of the more applicable and lucid explanations of dislocation is found in *The World's Religions,* Huston Smith, Harper Collins, 1991, p. 101.

steps (One, Three, Four, Five, Eight, and Nine) are "action" steps. The maintenance steps are in a separate category altogether and are exempt from this discussion.

When addicts or alcoholics take the problem-solving paradigm of HOW out of Step Two (a perception and faith step), and apply it to any of the action-oriented steps, they usually fall into a destructive trap. In doing this, they take HOW out of context, and end up unknowingly using it as a justification for sloth (see fn. p. 324).

Addicts must abandon their victim attitude that the messy state of affairs in their life isn't their fault, and begin to take personal responsibility. If a victim mentality goes unchallenged, addicts will whine and commiserate with other victims while they wait for someone or some*thing* else to "take charge" of their transformation. Not addressing this victim posture allows them to misapply HOW and it camouflages spiritual inactivity (sloth).

Example One: I knew a person who had been planning on doing a Step Four (an action step) since their second year of abstinence, and had been "planning" it for about eight years. For all the years I knew him, he had been proclaiming: "I'm honest, open-minded, and willing to do my Step Four. I really am. I'm serious." And, they were serious, and they sat there. Five years later, this individual was still making sincere speeches about Step Four and honesty, open-mindedness, and willingness. He had taken HOW out of Step Two (perception and faith) and applied it to Step Four (action), therefore, out of context.

Example Two: People who are controlled by an addiction like sex or rage, or a character defect like sarcasm, anger, or jealousy, will claim, over the course of years of sobriety, to be honest, open-minded and willing to address their defects or other addictions, but will never actually do anything about them. They have taken the problem-solving attribute of HOW out of a perception and faith step, and (inappropriately) applied it to a problem that requires action. They've taken HOW out of context. The speech about HOW *sounds* good, but carries no weight.

When HOW is applied out of context to any problem within an action step, *and* the person also has a victim mentality, they won't "act" within the action step. They'll wait—again, for someone else to take charge or some*thing* to happen. They will make passionate speeches about HOW, but their victim-attitude keeps them inactive. Other than the fact they'll make speeches about HOW, nothing will happen.

The misapplication of HOW results from not relying on a higher power for the courage to transform. Relying on a higher power is essential to effect any change, and praying, for the addict, is *always* the first step in problem solving and transformation. Passionate speeches about HOW are usually evidence of taking honesty, open-mindedness, and willingness out of context (meaning out of a perception and faith step), and using speeches about commitment as a way to conceal their fear and spiritual inactivity. It is irresponsibility and fear cleverly hidden underneath political speeches about devotion and effort.

If you apply honesty, open-mindedness, and willingness *by themselves* to problems other than those regarding perception and faith (Steps Two, Six, and Seven), you apply the theory out of context. You will actually create more problems than you are trying to solve. HOW is designed for spiritual defiance at Step Two (or similar issues within Steps Six and Seven). For all other problems, you may be honest, open-minded, and willing, and that *is* all well and good, yet these are entirely insufficient without two additional attributes: patience and labor, which must be added to the application of HOW, to make the resolution of problems effective.

WPL—Willingness, Patience, and Labor [43]

Be aware: The underlying essential requirement for *all* spiritual endeavor (including HOW) is identified in this sentence: *"To duplicate, with such backing, what we* [the AA pioneers] *have accomplished is only a matter of willingness, patience and labor."*[44] So being "honest, open-minded, and willing" is, by itself, always insufficient. Without labour (meaning action and effort) and patience, all claims to spiritual devotion through honesty, open-mindedness, and willingness are rhetoric (and therefore Impression Management).[45]

"Faith without works is dead."[46] "Works" is labor and consists of the following: Pray and meditate regularly. Shut off the TV, go to a stationery store, and buy pads of paper, pencils, and a dictionary. Study the AA textbooks. If it appeals to you, study this book. (Reread the quote of Mr. Steiner, p. 9.) Search for meanings; look for themes; cross-reference the information; examine your own defiance, doubt, and evasiveness. *Study* the texts with an intent to discover how you may be more obedient to spiritual principles as a life-discipline. If you struggle with dictionaries and "book

---

[43] Patience and labor, as presented in *Alcoholics Anonymous,* are two aspects of Right Effort, which is one tenet of The Eight-Fold Noble Path of Buddhism. How you focus your energy (willpower) is a theme of Right Effort and something that all spiritual pilgrims must examine, regardless of the religious path they choose. For an insightful view that has a universal application, see *The World's Religions,* by Huston Smith, p. 108. On the large scale, *Alcoholics Anonymous* is the "what to do" and *Twelve Steps and Twelve Traditions* is the "why to do it" of Right Effort for addicts getting recovered.

[44] *Alcoholics Anonymous,* p. 163.

[45] Impression Management: see footnote in Addictions Prohibit Spirituality, Chapter 3.

[46] This is one of the observations from *Alcoholics Anonymous* (p. 88) that has an unqualified universal application in all spiritual endeavor.

studying", then spend a lot of time talking about this with someone who can and does study the original material.

"Work(s)" may mean taking a course on the history of religions, or making effort to persevere in the face of others' disapproval when you quietly distance yourself from their unspiritual behaviour. It may mean meeting regularly with a therapist or a spiritual advisor, and working extra to pay for that yourself. Labor always means challenging only yourself to achieve greater levels of responsibility in every area of your life, and not challenging others. "Work" very hard at minding your own business, which calls for a lot of silence on your part.

In Japanese, written in Roman letters, there is a word *mokusatsu,* which means, "to remain in wise silence". Talking doesn't destroy serenity. It's destroyed by the desire to be heard or the need to conceal insecurity. Serenity often resides in *mokusatsu*. Work towards never showing off at a meeting, and *never* impose your will on others—even if you "know" you're right, or are a group's founder, an old-timer in sobriety, or in a responsible service position.

Meetings are not supposed to be social gatherings *per se,* they should be safe and pleasant places where people can search for truth and establish integrity by carrying the message of a spiritual awakening. Keep this in context—I am not saying that you can't or aren't supposed to enjoy yourself, but "fellowship" is not the first priority of meeting attendance. Fellowship is fourth on the list behind learning about spirituality for yourself, helping others to establish a spiritual life, and providing a place where people can bring their spiritual problems. Twelve-step meetings [are supposed to] contribute to people's restoration to sanity (not to their sex life), and are for establishing and maintaining a commitment to a higher power, as you understand this.

If you're belligerent and argumentative about spirituality, review page 26 of *Twelve Steps and Twelve Traditions*. Do what is suggested, for a long time.

The second type of spiritual problem encountered at Step Two is that of the person who does believe in God, a higher power, etc., but has no faith. One way this shows up is believing you have been too bad. God has a book of celestial coupons and you're only allowed nine major transgressions (or eleven, or some vague number you can't pinpoint). Every time you did a big one, God tore out a coupon, and by the time you were old enough to vote you used up all your celestial coupons. Now you couldn't get into heaven for love nor money. These spiritual newcomers believe in God, but have no faith that God will act on their behalf.

Confusing God with Santa Claus results in weak faith. People believe in "God" and pray for optimal parking spots, nice weather, and deliverance from illness and trying circumstances. When God doesn't give them what they want, they may continue to believe in God, but their faith becomes tenuous. Or, not having their "morally good" prayer requests answered leads to self-condemnation: If I were good enough, God would have answered my prayers. God didn't, so I mustn't be good enough or trying hard enough.

In reference to this person, page 28 of *Twelve Steps and Twelve Traditions* discusses the roadblocks of indifference, fancied self-sufficiency, prejudice, and defiance. There's often arrogance about their "sinning ways" [sic]. These are the usual attitudes of people who believe but have no faith. The book talks about these attitudes prohibiting a well-grounded approach to spirituality, and what to do to resolve them. If you are not willing to read and follow these instructions, you will believe, but live with a weak faith. Your abstinence will therefore be tenuous.

The third type of spiritual problem is found in the intellectually self-sufficient person: "You can't prove God exists. I can't accept this spirituality stuff." This results from arrogance and cynicism, often rooted in the theory that the presence of selfish or cruel behaviour, or natural disaster and war, is proof of the non-existence of God: God does not exist because there are earth quakes and mean, nasty people in the world. This logic about God and mean people has elements of racism in it.

As soon as everyone's perfect (read: there's no crime or poverty and all of us are wonderful and kind), this person will believe, i.e. it is possible that God exists because there is no pain and suffering. If you live with this type of spiritual dislocation, the instructions on pages 29 and 30 of *Twelve Steps and Twelve Traditions* tell you what the route is for you to begin challenging your old beliefs.

The fourth type of person that has difficulty coming to believe in God is the one who is devout and religiously perfect: self-righteous. *Twelve Steps and Twelve Traditions* advises that this person is so arrogant that they have come to suspect that God doesn't believe in them. This person's view of themselves and of faith is related to wallowing in self-aggrandizement and emotionalism: "I'm praying perfectly. I'm devout. I'm spiritually pure. The fault is that God doesn't see this. God doesn't recognize my righteousness and my unwavering fabulous devotion. It's God's fault, not mine."

There's often an analytical-elitist approach towards religious communities (superlative comparisons and belaboring the faults of other paths). The melodrama of immaculate faith and superb devotion, quantity rather

179

than quality, is the barrier. The transformation guidelines for this problem are on page 31 and 32 of *Twelve Steps and Twelve Traditions*.

There is a fifth type of spiritual problem that isn't discussed in the AA texts. When these books were written, this specific spiritual problem wasn't commonly identified. It is today, and is worthy of special attention. There are those addicts and alcoholics who want to, but are terrified of, abandoning an entrenched and painful system of religion—cults and ex- tremely orthodox religious systems.[47]

This is usually present when people leave a rigid point of view that was imposed on them. Or, being psychologically damaged, they join and are indoctrinated into a tyrannical belief system (cults, etc.) and then, for whatever reason, choose to leave. Often, God, or the cult leader, is repre- sented as omnipotent and vengeful. While they know what they believe is unfulfilling and unhealthy, they cannot, through fear of retribution, let their old beliefs go for something new and fulfilling.

This is, essentially, a struggle to change the indoctrination that hap- pens in a closed-loop, bigoted, elitist religious structure. Besides cults, this indoctrination can be present in any religious or social/political structure where there are rigid or extreme orthodox beliefs.[48] Getting out of this is a complex process.

If you are frightened about abandoning beliefs that you were indoctri- nated with, wish to heal from the abuse you endured in a fundamentalist religion, or wish to get recovered from a religious addiction (which is far more common than can be safely discussed here), there are some things you can do. This (as with all abstinence not-available addictions) requires going beyond a twelve-step program.

- Go "counsellor shopping" for a therapist who is gentle, sin- cerely open-minded, and patient. Make an appointment with a few therapists and ask them questions about their style, training, and religious beliefs. *You interview them as much as they interview you.* If the therapist is defensive about be- ing interviewed, what does that tell you? Bring a tape recorder and record the session, and then listen to it later.

---

[47] This discussion is for people who wish to voluntarily change the views they have been in- doctrinated with—they recognize the importance of that fact on their own, and decide to voluntarily adopt different religious values. Conducting formal interventions to rescue people who are trapped in cults and who will resist leaving them is another matter entirely. In either case find competent professional help.

[48] Keep this in context. I'm referring to religious extremism, not well-intentioned, respectful personal conviction.

- The therapist should be well versed in addictions, especially abstinence not-available addictions, and religions and their traditions (or cults, if that is applicable). Their having a reasonable working knowledge of Buddhism or Unitarianism (or some other ethics-based, middle-way philosophy) can facilitate a safe avenue to begin exploring non-dogmatic alternatives.
- If other addictions are a concern, achieve and maintain your abstinence.
- Take a Contemporary Religions or History of Religions course at a non-religious university. Read books by authors like Huston Smith and Joseph Campbell. Avoid books that promote a one-option or superlative religious point of view.

Then *slowly*, over a *long*, gentle course of therapy, and if applicable participating in your twelve-step group, you will acquire accurate knowledge about alternatives. The fear, shame, and guilt will gently abate and, *by your own initiative*, you will acquire the ability to choose a safe spiritual path. There will be some traumatic dysregulation that will need to be addressed. (See Appendix III)

It is important to make choices that are not a reaction to the tyranny you are escaping from.[49] Choosing without reacting is crucial in order to create your own spiritual value system, which will eventually allow you to emotionally exit an oppressive system with dignity and confidence.[50]

While you are learning about other religious traditions, you may experience a desire to pray. This will probably be frightening. At those times of fear and image-confusion in your prayers, adopt a "neutral" stance. Try this: Assume a comfortable position—at a minimum, have your eyes closed or almost closed, and sit quietly. Arrange it so you're comfortably warm. In your mind, picture or imagine a limitless, empty panorama of blue-black nothingness. Clear your mind of all images and concentrate on a space of emptiness. If some traditional or threatening image appears, quietly refocus your attention and concentrate on some other section of the limitless blue-black emptiness.

---

[49] In this situation, a reactionary choice isn't limited to choosing another oppressive religious system. It can also be to enter abusive/oppressive relationships with lovers, employers, sponsors, and friends.

[50] Spiritual endeavor is needed to resolve any addiction. At the same time, the inappropriate fusion of "spirituality" to cults, extremely fundamentalist religious structures, and religious addictions creates very unique problems, which are coupled with issues related to personality and trauma. Leaving a tyrannical religious structure and at the same time exploring addictions and spirituality is a very delicate, very slow, process. This is incredibly complicated.

In your mind, don't "fight" the intrusive image, just quietly ignore it and look beyond or away from it. Focus on another area of the limitless, empty panorama of blue-black nothingness. After some period of practice you will be able to maintain your concentration on that space or blue-black "nothingness". As you concentrate on this lack of image think or say your prayers to space. Several brief attempts of only fifteen seconds throughout the day will generate better results than one or two long attempts.

In all of this, if you persevere, you will be rewarded with a new relig-ious or spiritual worldview that is a comfortable extension of you, rather than some subtle aspect of the tyranny you're escaping. Be patient. Re-member; spiritual experiences are personality changes. Trust your personality changes, and you will learn that a higher power is working in-side of you in spite of the fear and oppression you experienced in the past.[51]

Healthy spirituality transcends all alienation and all elitist groups. How you transcend alienation is delicate. However, with perseverance and wise counsel, it is inevitable. When newcomers are unsure of how to focus their attention, they often just give up too soon.[52] If you're presently too scared to challenge your old views, go slowly, seek out some authentic sup-port, and trust Step Two in *Twelve Steps and Twelve Traditions*.

Desire only a personality change that will bring about recovery, not an experience of divine revelation. Spirituality will grow in you like a flower; maybe a flower that takes years to bloom, but it will grow. There are effec-tive approaches to the resolution of religious addiction or the tyranny of cults. The way described here is the most effective I've found for address-ing the specific concerns of prayer within the framework of realigning spiritual self-discipline.

When people are ready to attempt meditation as it is described in Step Eleven, and they seek my counsel, I sometimes suggest that they spend a few months meditating in the style of Step Eleven, but on the content of Step Two.[53] When I work with people who want to escape religious oppres-

---

[51] George Santayana wrote: *"My atheism is true piety towards the universe and denies only gods fashioned by men in their own image, to be servants of their human interests."* Having a similar perspective is said of William Blake by Thomas Merton in *A Thomas Merton Reader*, Edited by Thomas P. McDonnell, Doubleday, 1996, beginning at, *"How incapable I was of understanding..."* p. 228.

[52] The reason there are so few truly spiritual people is because it is such hard work. *Huxley and God, The Essays*, cited at earlier footnotes.

[53] This is not to re-do Step Two. It is to expand awareness about on-going, subtle variations of spiritual resistance. An examination of Step Eleven meditation is in Chapter 10.

sion into a healthy form of spirituality, I draw heavily on the material contained in Step Two.[54]

It is crucial you come to believe that acquiring spirituality is the solution. If you repeat the steps over and over you've missed this, and will be living a life that is governed by subtly "tolerable" or not very noticeable dishonesty, insincerity, manipulation, meanness, and irresponsibility.

According to *Twelve Steps and Twelve Traditions,* there are four types of spiritual newcomers. I have added a fifth. There are specific ways of getting past spiritual dislocation. Each technique is a little different. They work if you spend time carefully figuring out which type of spiritual newcomer you are and eliminate your dislocation according to the instructions. You may overlap between two types, or go through phases of having variations of all of them. Be aware of the resolution-strategies and then realign yourself as suggested.

Notice: *"There was a feeling of awe and wonder, but it was fleeting and soon lost."*[55] *Alcoholics Anonymous* reports, in its own way, that we each have some experience of mystery and awe in appreciating a higher power. It is, however, fleeting and soon lost because it is covered up with all manner of dislocation.

Many people are frightened of pursuing spirituality—(a) it's so at-odds with technology, (b) we're afraid if we're truly spiritual things won't work out in our favor; and (c), and as soon as we find a way to achieve it that's minimally sufficient, we tend to take a dogmatic stance and give it limits. Then, if we can convince someone else to do it our way (proselytize) we feel reassured for three reasons: (i) because this is perceived as saving a soul, and "we" take credit, (ii) because we're no longer "alone" in our quest; and (iii), we have (before the fact) prevented another person from going beyond the place we're at in spiritual awareness. If they did, we'd feel guilt or embarrassment at recognizing our own lack of commitment. Very often, when we experience a sincere breakthrough into a true awareness of something divine—a unitive experience—it is so ego-threatening that we abandon it for the suffocating reality of socially approved rituals (living by consensus).

In *Facets of Personal Transformation,* I will discuss a unitive experience, which is that fleeting and rare sense of profound union with the universe. Absolute unity (actually: atonement [at-one moment]) is present and the person, as an individual, ceases to exist. In a few moments it's gone. A unitive experience, which is so threatening to our egos and our sense of

---

[54] Re: Religious addiction, etc.... A few pages ago I briefly described praying to a space of blue-black nothingness, and I also state that I draw heavily on the content of Step Two. There is much more that has to go into resolving extreme spiritual dislocation.

[55] *Alcoholics Anonymous*, p. 46.

individuality, is one of the rewards we seek in living a spiritual lifestyle. The mystics know it well.[56]

When spirituality becomes meaningful for you, you may find yourself uplifted, relieved, and eager to share that. You may feel impatient and annoyed that others don't get it or they don't marvel at your revelation. Be patient and accepting of yourself and others. It is important not to impose your ideas, values, or spiritual experiences on others. Encourage only yourself to labor diligently according to the instructions.

The instructions in Step Two, in the original twelve-step program, are to help you access a higher power. They're not guidelines on how you can convince others to live as you do. Never offer advice unless it's invited, and even then, be very cautious. Never offer advice unless you are confident you can respectfully negotiate out of any ensuing debate. Never offer advice if you cannot be gracious when it is rejected. A gracious person never argues about anything unless it might save a life.

Your opinions on relationships, careers, love affairs, parenting, recreation, lifestyles, diet, sexuality, exercise, prayer, God, and religion are all a result of how you look at the world. Any advice is *your* solution to their predicament, not theirs. When you encounter people who have different values and lifestyle and, if your association with them leaves you judgmental, angry, disapproving, unable to be free and safe, then quietly shift your priorities. Examine yourself for religious or moral arrogance, *never* gossip, mind your own business, and quietly move on in your own life. Right association is essential.[57]

What is 'How It Works'?

The two-and-one-half page summary, colloquially referred to in AA as 'How It Works',[58] extends from the beginning of Chapter 5: *"Rarely have we seen a person fail... ,"* through to *"...God could and would if He were sought."*[59] This is read at the start of most AA meetings. Besides the fact that it begins Chapter 5 in *Alcoholics Anonymous*, what is it? What's the

---

[56] Gerald May explains a unitive experience, in *Will and Spirit*, HarperCollins, 1987.

[57] In addition to abstinence for addicts; for anyone endeavoring to transform into a spiritual lifestyle, Right Association is the next most important ongoing requirement. This is implied in *Alcoholics Anonymous* regarding carrying the message: *"...don't waste time trying to persuade him,"* p. 90; and *"We find it a waste of time to keep chasing... ,"* p. 96. Both of these statements imply addicts are to associate with others who "want what we have"—a spiritual solution, which is referred to several times in the chapter Working With Others. For more on Right Association, I refer you to Huston Smith's book *The World's Religions,* p. 104.

[58] How It Works is the title of Chapter 5 of *Alcoholics Anonymous*, and colloquially, 'How It Works' also refers to the passage from the beginning of p. 58 through to the middle of p. 60, ending with *"...if He were sought."* 'How It Works' contains, in those two and one-half pages, the essence of the entire transformation process outlined in *Alcoholics Anonymous*.

[59] *Alcoholics Anonymous*, pp. 58-60

point of it being *exactly* there? Why are only those two-and-one-half pages read at the start of most AA meetings? The author(s) didn't write these specific words and then stick them where they did because it seemed a nice thing with which to start a chapter.

When you finish Step Four or Eight, which are the only writing-required steps, you know you are done because you put a period after the last word on the last page. That period signals completion. But Step Two is one of the perception-and-faith steps. How do you know when you have finished Step Two?

In meetings and discussions there is a slurring of the boundary between Steps Two and Three. Do people sort-of-come-to-believe and say the prayer, or do they check out Step Two for a while before some "authority figure" arbitrarily tells them to get on with Step Three? How do they *know* when they're finished Step Two? What event signals that it's time to move from Two to Three? There is a very clear indicator of when that is, but first you have to know exactly what 'How It Works' is (the two-and-one-half pages, not the chapter).

A successful journey from active addiction through to being recovered in a spiritual lifestyle is described in 'How It Works'. These two-and-one-half pages contain probably the most succinct version of the whole process—the shortest complete description of becoming spiritual. *"Well, that's exactly what this book is about. Its main object is to enable you to find a Power greater than yourself which will solve your problem."*[60] All the writing in *Alcoholics Anonymous* and the step chapters of *Twelve Steps and Twelve Traditions* are explanations that expand on what is written in 'How It Works' (the two-and-one-half pages).

This is immediately followed by a paragraph that begins, *"Being convinced, we were at Step Three."*[61] A comma follows the phrase *"Being convinced,"* and *"we were at Step Three"* is stressed by italics. That grammar means that the phrase *"Being convinced"* refers back to the preceding information called 'How It Works', and to the three pertinent ideas (noted as [a], [b], [c]) that immediately precede it.

Read 'How It Works' through to *"Being convinced,"* and at that point stop and ask yourself: "Being convinced of what? What am I to have convinced myself of?" The answer is: You are to be convinced that 'How It Works', the two-and-one-half pages, including the three pertinent ideas [(a), (b), and (c)] are true for you. You must be convinced of the absolute truth of the preceding two-and-one-half pages; that what they describe applies to *you*, specifically.

---

[60] *Alcoholics Anonymous*, p. 45.
[61] Ibid., p. 60, emphasis theirs. This emphasis is very important. It has grammatical as much as spiritual meaning.

To make this point more clear, I'm going to insert some words into the middle of the sentence *"Being convinced, we were at step three."* Try it this way: *"Being convinced,* [that 'How It Works' and the three pertinent ideas are true and apply completely to me—that spirituality is the solution— then I was...] *at Step Three."*

When people aren't willing to put serious effort into understanding the nuances and subtle meanings of the words—exactly as they are written; when they rely instead on loose interpretations of others, and substitute anything for "a power greater than ourselves", they cheat themselves out of a meaningful, spiritually rewarding life. They won't get recovered. You must hunt for the instructions within the instructions and be obedient to them. (This is "working the program".) The degree of your willingness to do this is directly related to how convinced you are that 'How It Works' is true.[62]

Completing Step Two is that process, over considerable time, of overcoming your defiance and doubt so you develop a conviction that the program, exactly as it's described in 'How It Works' is true *for you.* Or: When you contemplate 'How It Works', and are deeply comforted by the truth of those two-and-one-half pages—convinced they contain *all* the answers regarding getting recovered that you'll need, you've completed Step Two. Or: When you have a deep and abiding inner belief that being spiritual, as outlined in 'How It Works', is exactly what *you* need to do—that is completing Step Two.

'How It Works' is the substance of Step Two, but why is it read at the beginning of most AA meetings? Reading this symbolizes in words the path everyone follows, and reminds all members *"...Step Two* ['How It Works'] *is the rallying point for all of us. Whether agnostic, atheist, or former believer, we can stand together on this step."*[63] Step Two is what unites *everyone* in AA, *every*where in the world. Step Two is [supposed to be] the common starting point; the foundation of everyone's recovery, and the guide for *everyone's* conduct. Members are to be reminded of their singular purpose and universal unity every time 'How It Works' is read.

Leading Into Step Three

"Being convinced, <u>we were at Step Three</u>."[64] And Step Three is: *"Made a decision to turn our will and our lives over to the care of God <u>as we understood Him</u>."*[65] What exactly does Step Three imply?

---

[62] Twelve-step people are unable to minimize spirituality in any way, with impunity. They are only human and cannot stand with only other humans against addiction.

[63] *Twelve Steps and Twelve Traditions*, pp. 34, 35.

[64] *Alcoholics Anonymous*, p. 60, emphasis theirs.

The speeches often go like this: "I want to turn my will over, but I don't know what that really means or know when I've done it." "I get in this struggle with God about who's in charge." "This is making me crazy — turn it over, take it back, turn it over, take it back." The confusion and struggle around Step Three is unnecessary when you understand it in relation to the philosophy of spiritual transformation, and especially in relation to Step Two. First, here's a story:

In November 1989, I was living in Edmonton. Outside there was a foot of snow on the ground. I decided two things: I was fed up with winter and I would move to Vancouver (you don't have to shovel rain). Every Sunday morning, for ten months, I drove to an Edmonton newsstand and bought a Vancouver newspaper. I checked the apartment and employment ads and I sent out dozens of resumes. I went back to school to enhance my qualifications to make it easier to find employment. The next November I got a job.

Moving to another city is not a simple thing. Literally, there was a ton of books, never mind bookshelves, guitars, CDs, stereo equipment, and other less important things like furniture and dishes. A mover was hired, property was packed, and on December 24, 1990, I arrived in Vancouver.

From the time I decided to move, until I actually arrived in Vancouver, thirteen months had passed. The *decision* to move to Vancouver didn't mean I was there. There were months of work and preparation prior to the decision becoming a reality. You may have decided what you are going to do next Saturday. That doesn't mean that you're doing it — it's not yet next Saturday. Because you *made a decision* to turn your will and life over to the care of God, as you understand God, doesn't mean that you can "turn it over", and it doesn't mean that you are "turning it over". It only means you have decided to do that.

Back to the story of my move: Yes, I decided to move, but that decision meant nothing without action. For five years prior to that, every November I would decide to move away from the snow, as my Edmonton friends could attest to. It was always good for a laugh at first snowfall — me deciding to move to Vancouver (again). However, my decision in November 1989 was different. How did others know it was different? I followed the decision up with the action required, regardless of the difficulty or inconvenience.

A decision by itself is only a passive "thinking action". It's meaningless without behaviours that are a commitment to whatever the decision is. There's deciding, then there's acting on the decision, which eventually re-

---

[65] *Alcoholics Anonymous*, p. 59, and *Twelve Steps and Twelve Traditions*, p. 34, emphasis theirs.

sults in the original decision in your mind becoming a reality in time and space.

Let's assume, only for the sake of this discussion, that a person reading this book is a counsellor and has decided to change their counselling style because of things they have read here. They've thought about it, read this book a few times, and have firmly committed themselves to changing their style of work. After making the decision they must do whatever behaviour is required to make their decision real. At the minimum, they would have to study this book more closely, possibly go back to school, and maybe go to therapy themselves. They would study the books I cite in the footnotes. They may even decide to track me down and work with me for a while (they made "a decision", so whatever it takes, right?). They would have to actually do these things or the decision by itself is meaningless.

All of this applies to Step Three: *"Made a decision to turn our will and our lives over to the care of God"*[66] as you understand this. Assume, right now, in this moment, you are completely and absolutely convinced that 'How It Works' is true, and you *decide* to turn your will and life over to the care of a higher power. That precise moment often contains a subtle and crucial error of expectation that many addicts have regarding Step Three.[67]

Spiritual newcomers at Step Three cannot turn their will and life over, and "leave it over". They haven't learned how or acquired the skills yet. Simply making a decision does not spontaneously create the ability to be spiritual.

Should you decide that you want to be a doctor, a therapist, more spiritual, a musician, a baker, or anything else, doesn't mean you are that something—you've only decided and not taken the steps or completed the training. Commitment, self-discipline, willingness, labor, and training are necessary. It is no different here. Once you've made the decision to "turn it over" the remaining steps, from Four to Nine, are the apprenticeship that teaches you how to "leave it turned over".

At Step Three you are still struggling with fear, character defects, irresponsibility, guilt, shame, etc.—you can neither turn your life over nor be sincerely spiritual; you don't know how. With proper research at Step Two, before you make the decision, you will trust that 'How It Works' and the

---

[66] *Alcoholics Anonymous*, p. 59, and *Twelve Steps and Twelve Traditions*, p. 34.

[67] An interesting aside is that I don't hear people talk about how hard Step Two was, and I hear many people talking about how hard Step Three *is*. Yet, in the actual requirements of the steps, Step (cont'd) Two is the hard one—coming to trust the program, coming to believe that God is the solution, coming to trust with no reservations that being Spiritual and a higher power will restore you to sanity. This is the hard part, and once you have ample faith, making the decision is relatively easy. Most addicts in recovery slide past Step Two because it really calls them to task.

following steps are the itinerary for learning "how" to turn it over and leave it turned over. You're an untrained beginner at being spiritual.

If you make the decision at Step Three, and at the same time think you can do it (and berate yourself when you can't or don't), it will entrench a vicious sense of spiritual inadequacy. You hear people in meetings all the time: "I made a decision to turn my will over and I took it back, and I turned it over and I took it back." The frustration, confusion, and the often-growing despair, is obvious.

When you have completed your training i.e. the steps, and are eventually comfortable with Step Eleven—have years of experience at prayer and meditation, you will only *then* be somewhat trained in the very *basics* of spirituality. You won't be good at it, still largely a novice, but you will have some basic training. You will then also notice some regular, but limited, success at "leaving your will turned over", but only because, and if, you've been obedient to *all* the instructions. Step Three is making a decision to live a life governed by spiritual principles. Only long after that decision is made—after living in the maintenance steps with spiritual integrity for many years—will you realize the reality of that decision, not before.

Turning Over My Life, Too?

Addicts complain and lament about turning or not turning their will over to the care of God. The discussions that revolve around the intellectual struggles of "willpower" seem never-ending. Challenging your more easily identifiable behaviour is avoided by constantly debating the abstract notion of willpower. I have never heard addicts debating turning or not turning their "life" over to the care of God.

How often do alcoholics and addicts who claim to be "in recovery" participate in unspiritual behaviour, i.e. adultery, aggression, blaming, cheating, harsh criticism, defiance to the principles, dishonesty, gossip, greed, insensitive jokes, cruel judgments, manipulation, pornography, prejudice, racism, rudeness, righteous anger, irresponsible sex, petulance, sexism, slander, violence, etc.? Addicts turning their *lives* over require a very dedicated commitment to doing the opposite behaviours of those I just listed.

Turning your will over and taking it back (whatever that might mean) is a dissembling and meaningless intellectual debate. It easily sounds sincere, but demands nothing of the addict but a good speech. As we all know, addicts are great at speeches. Addicts are significantly less accountable when they concentrate on theories and words like "willpower". It's a smoke-and-mirrors distraction from behaving (or *living*) "God's" will, which is entirely another matter.

Turning your *will* over is a specific reference to your thoughts and emotional energy. In turning your *will* over, work at focusing your mental energy on ideas of honesty rather than deceit or manipulation; on having kind thoughts, not angry, mean thoughts; on ideas of sharing and equality, not on manipulating privileges for yourself. Focus your willpower (intellectual energy) on challenging yourself, not others, on not showing off, not being demanding, not gossiping, not arguing, not being petty. Deliberately focus your thoughts and energy—your will—on taking responsibility and not blaming. This requires constant vigilance. Altogether, these are the exercises of turning *your* will (or mental energy) towards the will of God, as you understand this. For the first several years it is exhausting.

Turning your *life* over to the care of a higher power means acting and behaving in a manner that demonstrates respect for the body, veracity, humility, charity, and responsibility—obedience to spiritual principles. It means promote peace in *all* the relationships in your life, *always* behave graciously, offer courtesy, respect, and consideration towards all others (especially towards people you're mad at or that are mad at you). No gossiping, aggression, name-calling, petulance, lying, deceit, sexism, racism, dirty jokes, cheating, lying, malingering, etc. Not doing these real-time behaviours demands incomparably more effort than the spurious, spiritual debates about the ego-construct of willpower and who's got how much focused in what direction.

When was the last time you discussed someone else's character defects and justified this cruel gossip by not telling who they were? This is feeling intellectually or spiritually smug because you can smear their character and conceal their identity, justifying it by explaining you were trying to help, trying to share your struggles, or "working your program". Remember the last time you were in the company of others who were racist or sexist in their "humor". Did you participate or did you quietly excuse yourself and not socialize with them any more?

How have you tacitly justified your own meanness, disrespect, dishonesty, blaming, or irresponsibility? When was the last time you told a "funny" story at someone else's expense and people laughed and you were the entertainer? What about driving badly? What about knowing you're guilty and still fighting over parking and speeding tickets? Being rude to store clerks? Littering? Ignoring the common-courtesy rules about owning pets? All of this is how you respect the people in your community. These are the questions to ask about living a spiritual *life*.

An authentic Step Three decision requires a huge commitment to spiritual behaviour: turning your life over, too. It would include praying often, regularly, and sincerely. A spiritual *life* is: put money in the meters; stop giving people "the finger"; stop at yellow lights; don't complain because the sale price expired yesterday; pick up after your dog; if the sign says don't (whatever)... then don't; put your shopping cart back where you're supposed to; pay your parking tickets; don't litter; return the items you borrow; buy the pet license; don't talk during the movie; don't be impatient in the checkout line at the store. In addition to the obvious praying and meditating, a spiritual person extends courtesy and respect into their community and never excuses their own mean or irresponsible behaviour.

Turning your life over also means you complete the Step Three prayer, which is the first behaviour that demonstrates the sincerity of your decision, and then complete the rest of the steps, as instructed, in a deliberate and thorough manner, without complaining. The fact it may be inconvenient and require you drastically change your lifestyle doesn't matter—your decision was voluntary. Once you've *decided* to turn your will and life over, if the decision has any credibility, unspiritual behaviour must stop.

Step Two is the investigation that leads you to choose a spiritual lifestyle. Your Step Three decision is only firm and unshakable *if* you have been thorough at Step Two. The following actions determine whether you'll remain in recovery or become recovered. The first nine steps are your Spiritual apprenticeship: how you learn to live doing "God's" will. Keeping spiritual principles visible in your life, approaching the work with anticipation and interest, and being honest in all of your relationships, are what prove your decision was sincere. In order for the decision to be genuine, the research before and the follow-up action after must be thorough, regardless of the "cost" to you. Spirituality is never a matter of convenience.

Your willingness to do exactly as you are told will prove how sincere your decision was.[68] Your decision to live spiritually can only be trusted by others if you consistently behave spiritually; regardless of how difficult that is for you.

Think About It

I'm spiritual.	I cheat on my taxes.
I'm spiritual.	I ignore the parking meter and "take a chance" and then complain and pout when I get a ticket.
I'm spiritual.	I tell lies; I'm dishonest (but only sometimes).
I'm spiritual.	I pad my expense account at work. I leave work early and don't tell.
I'm spiritual.	I have affairs or flirt behind my partner's back.
I'm spiritual.	I go to recovery meetings to borrow money.
I'm spiritual.	I steal copyright songs and films off the internet.

---

[68] This is subtle: Willing obedience to the instructions is the solution; being grudgingly obedient solves nothing.

I'm spiritual.	I manipulate newcomers for sex or attention. I use sex/beauty to get things for free.
I'm spiritual.	I yell at my kids. I'm angry a lot of the time.
I'm spiritual.	I pout/get mad when I don't get my own way.
I'm spiritual.	Sometimes I fake being sick because I'm lazy.
I'm spiritual.	I could get a job but I'm staying on welfare because it's easier than working and I need lots of meetings.
I'm spiritual.	I make commitments and then "forget" them.
I'm spiritual.	I make speeches about believing in the steps but then ignore the instructions and do them my way.

Your conduct proves or disproves your desire to live up to the commitment you made. You must consistently recommit yourself to spiritual *behaviour*, which allows you to become what you've decided you want.

I was once asked: "In Step Three, aren't we asked to become powerful instruments of God's love on earth?" Because of the interpretive license in the way this person reframed Step Three, my answer was, "No." I point this out here, partly because of its bearing on Step Three, but also because it shows how easily recovering addicts reinterpret the original program to the detriment of spiritual principles. There are three main observations on that person's question.

One: "God" as an entity, which is limiting in itself and therefore not effective, but more about that later, doesn't "ask" anyone in a twelve-step program to do anything. Addicts are in pain (acting out), they discover (unitive moment), they choose abstinence and volunteer for spirituality. In the vernacular, "God" asks for nothing, and waits for the pilgrim to volunteer. *It's all voluntary*. There's a difference between being asked to do something, and voluntarily understanding the value of something and being quietly devoted to it, without being asked.[69] We volunteer to be examples of the life that is available when we live spiritually. [No one asked you to love or care for your partner. You volunteered; quit complaining.]

The concept of responsibility is subtle. Think about these two statements: (a) I'm on this spiritual-devotion trip because God asked me to; or (b), I'm on this spiritual-devotion trip because I see it's inherently good for me and I want to. Consider the motivation and responsibility that underlies both statements and notice the differences. Regardless of how close you believed you were to your own insanity or death, at the moment you made that decision, it was voluntary, so there's never any reason to complain.

Two: Being "an instrument" has a tone of intrusiveness. I was asked the question with a quality that implied people getting recovered are on a

---

[69] "Surprise" your higher power with a generous gift: devote yourself to spirituality. *You* are the gift.

mission to do God's work. The "mission" is not to do "God's work", it's to only work on ourselves, to stop hurting others, and *never* proselytize.

Three: Describing this twelve-step pilgrimage as some aspect of God's "love" imposes a specific and highly personal view of God on those you would help. Pushing the belief that "God is love" onto others is against the crucial freedom-guaranteeing injunction 'as you understand God'.

Step Two (Revisited)

If you don't develop a very firm belief that some version of a higher power is the only thing that can restore you to sanity, then your recovery will be politically motivated.[70] Too many people in twelve-step programs don't understand that Step Two is the hard one and Step Three is the easier one. They skip lightly over Step Two on their way to the sober dance, wrongly believing that service work, committees, round-ups, sharing, and doing the steps, will restore them to sanity.[71]

Certainly these people will be honest—most of the time. They'll knock around in the program, stay sober and get a job—that'll be good enough. So what if they gossip or fight to win a useless argument, that's not a big deal. They won't lie to their sponsor or to the important people in their life... very often. This political focus to step work is one reason why people carry a nagging sense that the steps are always unfinished. The promises remain elusive, and being recovered will never be available.

Getting recovered arises out of a consistent devotion to embrace the five spiritual principles as they are embodied in the regeneration steps (Steps One to Nine). If you don't acquire belief and begin commitment to a higher power in Step Two, the decision at Step Three is meaningless as far as getting recovered goes. Spend a year on Step Two, then a week on Step Three, and you'll be fine.

If you're struggling with Step Three, tired of repeating the steps, or unsure of your higher power or the program, go back to Step Two and stay there for a *long* time. If you're convinced that you are an addict and you can't act out, yet you keep on relapsing, you missed the crucial spiritual import of Step Two. If you're generally discontented or angry with recovery; if your abstinence is tenuous; if you're subtly confused about where

---

[70] Recovery that is politically motivated happens when people seek "healing" in any of it's forms, because of outside pressure from spouses, children, employers, the courts, etc., but it is not what they, themselves, want. Yes, it may be wise and the pressure may be applied from the best intentions, but the person is only making an effort 'to change' because someone else wants them to.

[71] Without spirituality as the essential foundation of everything you do, not even doing the steps will restore you to sanity. Doing the steps without sincere spirituality is an exercise in Impression Management.

you are in your program; if it vaguely doesn't make sense; if spirituality is confusing or frightening; if the twelve-step process is burdensome or repetitious, go back to Step Two and stay there for a *long* time.

Anyone who sincerely understands Step Two has no serious difficulty after that. Resolve your spiritual belligerence as suggested, and *then* do Step Three. Include both your will and life, and know that intellectual debates about willpower are actually evidence of willfulness.

This is hard work. In Step Two you're refocusing your entire existence. If you're properly oriented, you'll see things you've never seen before. Your transformation has implacable grandeur, and is solely to the credit of your higher power and not to the credit of anything else.

Step Three

The first paragraph of Step Three in *Twelve Steps and Twelve Traditions* begins: *"Practicing Step Three is like the opening of a door, which to all appearances is closed and locked."*[72]

It goes on to say that willingness opens a door, and through the door you will see a path leading to a faith that works. The metaphor also advises that through the door you will see a sign: *"This is the way to a faith that works."*[73] It means that beyond Step Two the steps are the route to an ever-deepening faith. Whatever depth of conviction you achieve in Step Two will be deepened into a faith that works (for the more difficult spiritual trials that lay ahead).

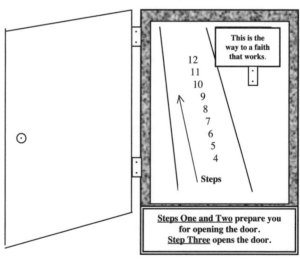

This is
the metaphor
used to show
what happens
at Step Three.

---

[72] *Twelve Steps and Twelve Traditions*, p. 34.
[73] Ibid.

How willing you are to do this isn't a matter of magic or luck; it's a matter of hard work. The harder you work at removing delusion, desire, and anger (at Steps One and Two) the more willing you will be. It's this simple: Everyone is willing to invest where they are guaranteed to gain. If there is no doubt about the outcome, people are willing to work for something they want. So, if there's poor research before the decision, there's less willingness when it's time to make the decision. With significant effort at Step Two, you will come to believe that obedience to spiritual principles guarantees success. You'll then have no doubt and that makes the decision easy; you know, from your own effort, the results are guaranteed. It all depends on *your* hard work.

The Step Three Prayer

"God, I offer myself to Thee—"[74] Here is the offering of yourself (both will *and* life) to your higher power. If you decide to do this, it means completing the steps, following the instructions, and forcing yourself to learn how to think, live, and behave according to spiritual principles. And, of course, it's in all endeavors from planting your garden and doing laundry to... well, everywhere.

"—to build with me and do with me as Thou wilt." Remember, a dash indicates that what follows the dash explains what's before it. When you offer yourself it must be motivated by a desire and willingness to become what "God" wants and in the way of spiritual principles, not what your peer group, insecurities, or culture wants.

The steps are the actual process of building—the process of restoration. You allow God to re-build you by you doing the steps yourself. Too many people speak as though they are waiting for their higher power to actually do something in their life. God "building" you is only a metaphor. God mysteriously supports you as *you* do all the work.

"Relieve me of the bondage of self, that I may better do Thy will." This is a supplication to God that your selfishness (which is nothing more than irresponsibility via the usual character defects) be removed so you can better do God's will, not so you can have a leisurely, peaceful life.

"Take away my difficulties, that victory over them may bear witness to those I would help of Thy Power, Thy Love, and Thy Way of life." The intent of asking your higher power to remove your difficulties is only so other people can see that living a Spiritual life is good. Your difficulties are not removed so that you have a good life, but so that others will be attracted to a

---

[74] *Alcoholics Anonymous,* p. 63.

similar way of life. This hard work is in service to your higher power, not in service to yourself.

"May I do Thy will always." This implies a voluntary and deeply unselfish desire that regardless of how difficult it may be, this will be a permanent way of life, without exception.

And, almost finally, regarding Step Three, consider: *"We found it very desirable to take this spiritual step with an understanding person... ."*[75] In Step Three, which is one of the six action steps, there must be a demonstration of your sincere commitment to a higher power. In doing your Step Three prayer with someone, you're making a public declaration of your sincerity. The books offer that the decision and prayer is vital, but has little lasting effect unless:

- it is preceded by an exceptionally thorough reorganization of your spiritual views in Step Two; and,
- it is followed by vigorous effort,[76] which is Step Four, and then the remaining steps.

In this book, *Spiritual Transformation,* the writing and descriptions that relate to Steps Two and Three are divided at approximately 90% of the material addressing Step Two and about 10% addressing Step Three. That represents the relative effort and importance. As I said earlier: Spend a year on Step Two, then a week on Step Three, and you'll be fine. Really, that's all there is to it.

---

[75] *Alcoholics Anonymous,* p. 63.
[76] Ibid., pp. 63-64, and *Twelve Steps and Twelve Traditions,* p. 42.

Chapter 5

Step Four: How "I" Have Become Me

"Ride your horse along the edge of the sword.
Hide yourself in the middle of the flames.
Blossoms of the fruit tree will bloom in the fire.
The sun rises in the evening."[1]

This poem describes a life of individual self-determination. Some people might interpret it in relation to things external; others may see in it the dynamic of being yourself and challenging your own demons. Challenging your own demons is at the core of all spiritual work; challenging anyone else's demons is a significant aspect of relationship addiction.

Ride your horse along the edge of the sword. Develop a sense of yourself underneath imposed societal attitudes and rituals. Step out from under the mantle of Victim, ignore peer pressure, and put yourself on the edge of your own personality. If you manage to do this without imposing on others, you will appreciate your own freedom. Take risks that are appropriate to accomplish your aspirations, all the while reining in your ego's need to control or criticize others. This accomplishment involves achieving independence, claiming individuation, and taking responsibility.[2]

Hide yourself in the middle of the flames. To remain in tune with a *spiritual* pilgrimage, the place of struggle is within your own contradictions and inner dislocation rather than in external controversy. All transformation is an "inside job". You are the flame. Hide in the middle of who you are.

---

[1] This is from the I Ching. I cannot verify the specific translation, but I'm quite sure it's from *The I Ching or Book of Changes* by Cary F. Baynes, trans., Princeton University Press, 1950, (my copy of which has gone missing).

[2] There are social risks for being assertive and strongly self-motivated. As a general rule, although there are variations, the range of human conduct is on the spectrum of passive to assertive to aggressive. Each one of these types of personality has a certain view of the other two types. Decidedly aggressive people often think that passive people are wimps and hold them in disdain, and view assertive people as "being okay". Passive people are often insecure around, or envious of, assertive people and quite afraid of aggressive people (who, according to them, are mean, pushy, and demanding). Assertive people often view passive people as simply "okay" and aggressive people as only an annoyance, but no real threat (because they, themselves, are assertive). It's all relative.

Don't abandon yourself or "leave" from whoever you are. The more arduous struggle is deep within yourself.

Blossoms of the fruit tree will bloom in the fire. As you wrestle with your dislocation, and develop your own spiritual personality, you will be able to more quietly say, "I am truly *Me* in my relationship with the universe." This accomplishment that you sense, as you pursue who you are without imposing on others, is magnificent (blossoms blooming). You appreciate the fragrance of the universe in the midst of your struggle with yourself.

The sun rises in the evening. You won't know the joy or beauty (sun rising) of any of this until after you've accomplished it (in the evening). Your life is a symphony being conducted by you. There are a hundred and twelve instruments being played, all at the same time, with different tempos, volumes, and tones. *Your* symphony is composed of your career and relationships and vows and beliefs and recreation and leisure and sexuality and values and likes and dislikes and preferences and calamities and successes. You are the symphony; you are the conductor.

Because a note was missed in the 152nd bar doesn't mean it's a bad symphony. It means that there was one note missed in two hours of music. No one knows it's a beautiful symphony until the last note is played. Even then, whether or not the symphony is good or bad is only an opinion. Play your own symphony as if there's no audience.[3] That's the only way you'll know about *you*. You won't know it was a glorious life until the last note is played.[4] You won't know the value of riding your horse along the edge of the sword, or hiding yourself in the middle of the flames, until your life is well along its course. That's the beauty of it.

When I'm old I'll not likely be saying to someone: "Remember that time I played it safe?" And, I wouldn't want to remember very many times when I had a chance to be Me and didn't take it. The purpose of your life is to be you. That's all. I suppose that's one purpose of this book—to show you how, by deliberately (or properly) using the original twelve steps, you discover yourself in healthy spirituality, and reap the rewards of your own personality. It's far too easy to abandon yourself to the dysfunctional community of twelve-step programs or culture, just as you abandoned yourself to illness or your addictions. Abandoning yourself to "consensus recovery"

---

[3] Moments before going on stage in front of several thousand people at a jazz festival in Europe, Miles Davis was reported to have said to a nervous member of his quintet: "There's no need to be nervous, it's just practice."

[4] Musicians, other live performers, and teachers often experience a decided shift partway through a presentation and notice that the last half of a set of songs or presentation was an improvement over the first half. It's always possible to feel the mood and improve as the performance progresses. You can always improve the quality of your own life as it progresses; it's not over yet.

is much easier than being spiritual and living honorably with your own values, but it's not fulfilling.

I was aware of the import of this as I was writing this book, and contemplating how different readers (be they victims, or passive, or assertive, or independent, or aggressive, etc.) might react to what I write. I would occasionally resist being political when I found myself hedging my words when writing something that went strongly against popular opinion. At other times, I was too assertive and needed to recast a sentence into a softer tone. I live with respectful disregard for the opinions of others about *my* life. I also work at having no opinions about theirs. For as much as you agree or disagree with what I write, I certainly wouldn't have written it unless I agreed with the message of the poem.

Here's an interesting perspective and subtle application of the poem: You may casually remark that you are a member of a group or a member of a program. "I belong to this religion," or "I'm a member of SLAA." That may be true; however, it's more intimate, and it subtly changes your perceptions of responsibility, if you say that you are not "a member" of a group, but that you *are* the group.

I'm told in some Aboriginal languages, when people talk about themselves they can't say, "I'm *from* such-and-such community." The literal translation is: "I *am* the community." The syntax and nuance of the language is that they *are* their community. [I refer to this from a different perspective of being rather than doing regarding the maintenance steps later in the book.)

This is an awkward view for people to accept because it puts greater accountability on them for how they act, knowing they actually *are* what they are members of. You are what you do. Your behaviour is purposeful and is always an advertisement for the integrity of your spirituality.[5] You are your group, and to present yourself otherwise easily fosters superficial or artificial associations.[6]

When your ego has you believe that you are from AA, or NA, or the PTA, "from" implies that there's a separation between you and the group. Should the group be unsavory you can distance yourself "from" them; likewise, the group can distance itself from you and your unsavory behaviour. You (or they) get to opt out of responsibility. Your ego has it set up that AA, or NA, or your church, or union, or friends are all somehow no reflection of you i.e. I am me; the group is them. As much as this perspective may

---

[5] This is readily apparent in the way the traditions of AA are presented, which are so easily disregarded in favor of politics.

[6] *"There's no use for artificial discipline, / For, move as I will, I manifest the ancient Tao."* Hsiang-yen, as quoted in *This Is It,* Alan Watts, Vintage Books, 1973, p. 88.

be appealing, it is spiritually untenable. You *are* your behaviour and your associations.

How many times have you heard some variation of "I did a mean (or a dishonest) thing, but that's not *really* who I am." Nonsense. Behaviour is purposeful. You are what you do. Twelve-step groups are the animated reflection of the people who comprise them. When people are absent, the group doesn't exist. You are the animated demonstration of your character. As the members behave, so *is* the group; as you behave, so you are.

By the time you get to Step Four, which is the first of the two major preparations for a visible declaration of your spiritual devotion, you've ridden along this "sword" long enough to understand that one purpose of the program is to assume ever-increasing responsibility for yourself and the state of affairs in your life. It demands that you be completely accountable. You are your associations. Your twelve-step group, your religion, your profession—these don't live in a book or some building; they live in you. You are the way you behave and think, and it's not spiritually tenable to ignore the unalterable fact that you're *It*.[7]

You, as an individual, are the focus of the first seven steps; these are yours, personally. Everyone else gets the last five; they're for others. [Ultimately, all of the steps are done on behalf of a spiritual lifestyle.] At Step Four there's a *much* greater demand for you to be accountable, both to yourself and to your higher power. It isn't about having a good time or a good life; it's about being spiritually accountable. You're learning self-discipline, accountability, and commitment, in order to become a person who demonstrates a sincere and unassuming spiritual life. This is far more onerous than being socially successful.

Disciple, Discipline, Obedience

A disciple is an adherent to a movement or a philosophy. Being disciplined is being consistent in living up to commitments, values, or rules: regularly holding yourself to specific standards of behaviour. The roots are

---

[7] Notice that prior to 1985 twelve-step groups were mentioned in movies and books with a tone of respect. Today they are as much the brunt of sarcasm and racy humor as anything else. The members of twelve-step groups, by not taking themselves more seriously, contribute significantly to this cheapening of recovery and spirituality. Nothing is free.

As an important aside: Therapists, ministers, sponsors, priests, yogis, counsellors, etc., are only capable of bringing someone to whatever level they, themselves, are at. If the helper is neurotic, honest, fearful, serene, mean, carries subtle addictions—whatever—the best that can be hoped for is the people they help will be as (dys)functional or (non)spiritual as the helpers are. For the newcomer/client that *may* be an improvement, but it says little for the integrity of the helper when they refuse to address the dislocation within themselves. Whatever the helper "is" is the best the client/newcomer can hope for.

from Latin—*discipulus* (a pupil) and *discere* (to learn). Only discipline allows you to accomplish anything, and only being a disciple of the original twelve-step philosophy (not the psychology jargon) allows you to become recovered. Being spiritual requires discipline and determination.

At face value, it sounds logical and straightforward, but the number of ways an addict's ego can slip justified irresponsibility into a spiritual pilgrimage is amazing. You're up against a disease that will kill you if you let it, and a culture that pays lip service to integrity. Becoming spiritual is an uphill battle to say the least (but the effort required eases noticeably beyond Step Seven). Spiritual freedom, among other things, is freedom from the annihilating bondage of addictions and an exercise in self-discipline and obedience. It's no mean feat if you accomplish it.

Near the beginning of getting recovered, obedience is felt as a confining thing. In some ways, compared to the erratic, flamboyant behaviours in active addiction, it is. However, when you are recovered, obedience isn't a confining thing at all. When you're living in the maintenance steps, obedience to the maintenance steps is actually the only guarantee of freedom you have. Obedience to the principles identified in the original literature (not to opinions about the literature) allows you to access the program's spiritual intent. Obedience is what creates safety.

It's interesting that proselytizing is strongly discouraged in the two most effective transformation processes in the world's history, Buddhism and the original twelve-step program.[8] If you're obedient to the principles, your success is guaranteed. You don't have to figure out Step Four: you have to do it. But that, of course, requires self-discipline, which addicts often lack.

The instructions in *Alcoholics Anonymous* and *Twelve Steps and Twelve Traditions* are written in a somewhat confusing style. [Usually, anything that challenges the dislocated and self-serving perceptions of an unregenerate ego is labeled as confusing and heard with skepticism.] The

---

[8] Buddhism wasn't always the overt, stylized rituals, in ornate temples that we see today. It was originally, via the wisdom of Siddhartha, without icons, statues, or formal places of worship. What is considered "Buddhism" today bears little and probably no resemblance to the original. Certainly, there was no proselytizing. The intent of original Buddhist discipline was to acquire contemplative peace by taking complete personal responsibility for the entire state of your own life, without recourse to anything external, and without dependence on "God" or anything spiritual. It was not a religion. The original teachings, through the adoption of new values by personal insight, via The Eight-Fold Noble Path, required an *inner*-personal system of ethical conduct that allowed complete respect, in thought and action, for *all* other living things. The Eight-Fold Noble Path and understanding the three poisons provide a method to detach from the dislocation of life. It had nothing to do with "suffering" or "Gods", which is a popular and entrenched misconception about "Buddhism". That misconception began around 250 BCE and was entrenched c. 1870, and related to British colonial endeavor and Anglican proselytizing in India. Original Buddhism (pre-250 BCE) was not a religion, and is probably the only authentic self-help discipline known to civilization.

AA reference texts are hard to read as books of psychological instruction because that's not their intent. What with the long metaphors, which some-times seem incomplete, the symbolism, and the apparently poorly defined structure, they make little sense psychologically. They're not supposed to make psychological sense. However, when you study them as spiritual ref-erence texts they make complete sense, even in their incompleteness.[9] *Alcoholics Anonymous* and *Twelve Steps and Twelve Traditions* make you work for the insights. Nothing is free, especially spiritual peace.

As much as you may hope otherwise, this book won't make your ac-tual transformation easier. It may make the path a little less frustrations, but only because you'll not waste time in "wrong direction" efforts. Your own insights, wherever they lie within you, won't be easier to find because in-sights aren't universal; they are particular to you. Understanding of *your* path cannot be found while walking on someone else's. What I offer here may help to keep you "on track", or prevent you from wandering off into unfruitful endeavor, but your own transformation won't be any easier.

I have no slick tricks, shortcuts, or rules that will ease your burden. Without doing *all* the work yourself, you cannot openly demonstrate the commitment you made at Step Three, and you cheat yourself out of the op-portunity to develop faith and self-confidence, which are the sensed, subtle rewards of diligent effort. Faith isn't free for the asking. When you're work-ing hard, and insight finally clicks, there's an indescribable, comforting little jolt of true peace and relief. But you've got to sit in meditation, in prayer, by yourself, *and* in quiet discussion with a spiritually trustworthy mentor—with the books and a dictionary, *one sentence at a time*, for long contemplative hours, weeks, months, and then years, to get successively deeper insights.[10]

Properly focused, disciplined effort is what creates humility and spiri-tual confidence. Filling in the blanks of someone else's Step Four quiz creates a prison—you become some version of whoever wrote it. The authors are creating followers. It's often patronizing, and certainly indica-tive of relationship addiction on the part of whomever writes them, and fear and unhealthy compliance (again, relationship addiction) on the part of whomever completes them.

---

[9] All of the insightful treatises on spiritual transformation, i.e. paths to "divine peace", like *The Bhagavad-Gita, The Upanishads*, some of the Buddhist sutras, *The Rule of Benedict, The Kabalah, The Sermon On The Mount,* the poetry of Rumi, *and* the AA reference texts (there are others) are found lacking or contradictory when they are examined in a scientific or psycho-logical manner. That's because the writings are most often poetry and complicated symbolic metaphors but are read as scientific, literal prose.

[10] "Take what you want," said God, "and pay for it." A Spanish proverb quoted from *Taking Responsibility*, by Nathaniel Branden, Simon & Schuster, 1996.

I cautiously add there are exceptions. When you're involved in formal treatment, there are psychological agendas and limitations of time. This structured approach to early intervention requires some generic forms, accelerated cross-over work, and forced disclosure. Outside of these time-limited professional settings, for addicts in the course of spiritual transformation, avoid generic guides and remain with personal exploration through the original literature.

Think about this: Someone writes a one hundred question Step One guide. You don't have to read the approved literature—just fill in the blanks on some photocopied handout. It's symbolic of your filling out a job application: You're applying for the job of being just like whoever wrote the guide. That may be fine provided their history, their issues, their addiction, their defects, their sexuality, their emotional perceptions, their physical issues, their values, are *exactly* the same as yours. This is unlikely.

Doing the much harder work of being an unassuming, quiet disciple of the original material, and absorbing its revealed wisdom *directly* into your own life, is where real faith and insights come from. This will guarantee you never become an extension of someone else. (Being an extension of someone else is one aspect of the addictions issues that got you here in the first place.) Yes, it's much easier to go to a bookstore or some treatment centre and buy a step guide and follow someone else's path. This easier, softer way cheats you out of the exercise of self-discipline, which is essential for spiritual integrity, and cheats you out of being yourself. Ask: Do I want to become them or do I want to become me?

The metaphor of a butterfly leaving a cocoon applies here. Yes, it's a time worn metaphor, but it's very true in spirituality. If you force open the cocoon and help the butterfly, it dies because its wings don't become strong enough through the exercise of breaking out to fly. It needs the struggle. *You need the struggle.* You can buy step guides, answer questions, and search for gimmicks that promise success with less investment of energy and emotion. That's a fool's game. To achieve the intimate relationships or the serenity you declare you want, but complain you don't have, there is no easy solution and no easier path. Your propensity to pander to your own sloth, or cater to another person's arrogance is killing you, as well as them.

Faith and Tradition

There are essentially three ways that people acquire faith:

The first way people acquire faith is to assume the faith of the authority figures in their life (which begins in childhood). Here, traditions and beliefs are imposed and sometimes the indoctrination of the young person is absolute and all encompassing. "Outside" knowledge, other perspectives, and personal/alternative experience are rigorously excluded. When people live with imposed traditions, their safety and peace of mind is dependent on obedience to that which was imposed.[11] As the child becomes older, their faith (or trust) in the imposed values becomes intellectually and emotionally "easy". There's little risk because there's no personal responsibility: "I have faith because I was told this is true."

This paradigm fosters a faith with little enduring strength. When the tyrant/authority figure dies, the underling's faith is undermined. If the underling encounters a different life experience, and they always do, dilemmas and questions arise. Or, should they encounter a stronger authority with great charisma and a different experience, or should some startlingly new truth arise that's at odds with what they've been taught, their faith is shaken. Faith that hinges on indoctrination and obedience often becomes untenable. With this scenario, indoctrinated people often grow into adulthood imposing a similar tyranny on themselves, and on those they can control. These dictatorships are only "successful" as long as all new experiences and knowledge are denied to the indoctrinated.

A stringent imposition of tradition indicates deep insecurity and the need to control others. It does not foster healthy psychological or spiritual development within the people on whom the tradition is imposed. "Faith" is protected by dogma and defensiveness. In order to avoid acknowledging any doubt, the defense becomes more inflexible. Whenever there is self-doubt and insecurity, it can only be repressed by an ever-increasing adherence to dogma. This type of faith is not dependent on sincere spiritual investigation and informed commitment but on dogma and the success of political indoctrination.

The second way to acquire faith is to overtly reject *all* imposed tradition through general rebellion, and create your own traditions through your singular experience. This ends with faith only in yourself and trusting no one.

I'm not talking about rebellion as violent insurrection and revolt, although it sometimes ends up that way. Rebellion here means exaggerated rejection and defiance to anything inherited. The proper transition from early developmental dependence to a non-addicted, adult independence, with a clear and stable identity of self (which, sadly enough, is very rare), is thwarted by a need for rebellion. This person struggles to establish beliefs

[11] There's a very fine line here that I am mindful of. Most imposition of religious values and tradition is by tyrants and is blatantly abusive—imposed so that the tyrants can remain secure with various illusions about truth and validation. There is also the imposition of values and tradition by parents who are trying to do well by their children: kind and judicious parenting. In the areas of religion and sexuality, in my experience, there is far too much of the former being disguised as the latter. As regards to sponsorship within twelve-step programs, sponsorship should never involve the imposition of values or assume the dynamics of parenting.

and acquire faith out of a combination of their own defiance, experience, and the belaboring of the flaws in the system or in the person they've rejected. The result is: Faith only in *me*.

Rebellion that rejects a tradition isn't necessarily a revolt against tradition *per se*, although it's usually described that way. It's often a revolt against the authority figures and the manner in which the tradition was imposed—retaliation for the disrespectful and aggressive imposition of tradition by tyrants. Out of rejection, which is often undisciplined or chaotic, people develop an angry, independent belief system, largely based on defiance to authority. As with the tyrants they reject, their beliefs and "faith" are often vociferously defended. This is a weak basis for faith. It doesn't have any historical experience to support it when intellect and defiance fail, when personal perceptions are limited, or when life circumstances change drastically.

The third way to acquire faith is by balancing the wisdom of tradition and the convictions that arise from individual investigation and experience. When you incorporate a clear declaration of "self" with a considered inclusion of established tradition, you create unshakeable faith. Over the long term, you would then be able to conduct yourself with discipline and determination (which is an appropriate situational spiritual response). You participate in life and influence your destiny in such a way that spiritual principles, tradition, and personality, form the basis of faith. This type of faith allows you to get recovered.

Within the twelve steps, and especially Step Two, there is a significant respect for your personality. Your pilgrimage is noticeably molded by who you are as an individual. This is crucial in developing a strong faith in your own conception of a higher power. Your faith must reflect who you are because your faith is what will allow you to address the trials that lay ahead—not because the trials are so arduous, but because they are particular to you and the nuance of your addiction.

Personality is Important

In organized religions there's an overbearing suppression of personality. This is fatal to an appreciation of any higher power because any suppression of personality requires an abandoning of "self". The suppression of anyone's inner self requires they seek external validation. That external validation is then centered on the religious dogma. "God" and "self" are now removed from the equation and replaced by dogma and politics.[12]

---

[12] Spiritual disciplines that embrace and pursue an authentic experience of mysticism, beyond dogma and culturally popular meditation practices, are generally exempt from this observation.

This creates a need to depend completely on the religious organization and religious dogma, rather than on "my inner-self" and my relationship with whatever deity the organization represents. Any image of "God" must be filtered through the dogma and is self-serving to the organization. This foments spiritual and emotional disaster. When people deny or suppress themselves on behalf of external dogma (an overbearing religious structure), and since it is deep within us The Great Reality is found, then people cannot access "God" because they cannot access themselves. Suppression of personality in favor of impersonal religious structures is fatal to sincere spirituality.

Outside of the consideration of "addict", the original twelve-step literature has four factors that make it significantly more effective than many other spiritual pilgrimages that require faith. These four are:

- a clear and authoritative influence of tradition, that is not suffocating, which arises from the specific experience of the early twelve-step members (as detailed in the AA reference texts). The traditions address the flaws found in the historical experience of earlier, similar organizations. What is crucial is the traditions are particular to the needs of addictions recovery and *not* the needs of the organization;
- an egalitarian philosophy and the exclusion of politics;
- an inclusion of personal experience and personality through the work of completing the steps, with the clear proviso that personality is important but gently subservient to principles, not subservient to seniority or the organization; and,
- an underlying and stabilizing presence of the themes of the perennial philosophies (within the five spiritual principles). These, altogether, represent the wisdom of the mystics and the *invisible* beauty of spiritual discipline, which is present in the maintenance steps.

These four factors are inextricably connected and balanced. The way they weave themselves together creates the necessary "unshakable" foundation for faith, upon which your transformation must be built. Whenever the original material is rewritten or transposed for psychological health, the relationship between these four is altered, and the result is noticeably less effective. Addictions are then not resolved. Altogether, this makes four things available to those seeking spiritual transformation that weren't available before. These are:

- a previously inaccessible self-insight regarding their addictions, irresponsible behaviour, and personal belligerence that blocks access to spirituality;
- with discipline and obedience, an eventual recovery from addictions;
- the acquisition of unshakable faith; and,
- the *primary* and established life condition of being in sincere relationship with their own version of a higher power.

Recovered alcoholics/addicts remain within the safety of revealed "truth" (the perennial philosophies); they address the specifics of their addiction (the etiology of the disease and its anamnesis related to them) and become recovered[13]; *and* they incorporate their own personality into their spiritual pilgrimage. This is done without insulting any authority figure (because there are none; or there aren't supposed to be any), and without infringing on anyone else's right to do the same. Through obedience, adherents foster individuation within an effective spiritual philosophy.

As far as I'm aware, this unique combination exists nowhere else. Certainly none of the cultural religions have it. They were formed out of the folk myths and social-cultural needs and the power-brokering needs of the religious dogma particular to the eras they were born in. [As opposed to the original twelve-step program which, although presented in Christian terminology, was formed in response to a spiritual, *universal* cultural problem: death by alcoholism.] Twelve-step spiritual philosophy integrates its principles within any personal relationship with any higher power.

Cultural religious dogma demands an overpowering, vigorous molding of personality, rather than taking the wiser position of fostering a relationship between personality and deity.[14] The wiser position would make formal religious structure secondary to the primary need of a personal relationship with a higher power. Also Note: None of the typical psychological disciplines are capable of allowing for spirituality as the ultimate goal of healing. Modern personality technologies (meaning therapies) are not universal enough in their focus to address the varied needs of addiction, dislocation, trauma, culture and spirituality, which are profoundly unique and complex.[15]

---

[13] Being recovered doesn't imply clinical psychological health. It does imply an absence of addictions and a lifestyle that demonstrates sound spiritual principles.

[14] This is a re-working of the dynamic described by Thomas S. Szasz (*The Myth of Mental Illness*). Mental health institutions and bureaucracies must, by definition, place the needs of the institution ahead of the needs of the patient. It is the same in religion: the spiritual needs of the individual are *always* secondary to the needs of the dogma and the institution.

[15] Dislocation and trauma aren't the same thing. Trauma (meaning a wound), in its varied presentations, is anything from being battered or assaulted, to being yelled at or ignored. (cont'd)

Alcoholics Anonymous presents the only method of spiritual transformation I'm aware of that encourages an individuation of self, combined with a wise and insistent invitation to be obedient to tradition and principle, that's strongly respectful of the perennial philosophies, *and* where politics and authority are seen as dangerous.[16] This is remarkably different than the offerings of any available cultural religion.

Your perceptions of the world and your existence (life filtered through your ego) are amazingly unique. This requires that you create and establish a subtly unique and very personal spiritual ambience in your relationship with each of the five spiritual principles. The principles are universal (context); their manifestation within you is unique (content). What's personal is how you inculcate yourself within them. That is the purpose of the steps and achieving this requires a delicate, patient touch.

In the first two decades of the original twelve-step program, the mean age of members was significantly older than today. Being significantly older, and it being in the 1930s and '40s, the members would have grown up with different traditions in their personal lives, and would have been quite differently established in relationships, religion, friendships, and ca-

---

There is developmental trauma (emotional wounds from childhood) and shock trauma (pain from incidents, illness, and events), which have both common and unique requirements for resolution. And, whatever circumstance initiated the trauma, that incident itself generates different reactions and symptoms depending on any number of variables. I had once audio recorded group counselling while someone was weeping deeply because of the trauma of having been sexually abused. In another segment someone else wept because a parent wouldn't pick them up after a social engagement (which was in the recognition of emotional neglect). When I later played the tape for a class of counsellors in training, they couldn't identify which person was more deeply wounded; the weeping was equally intense. That's trauma.

Dislocation is that ubiquitous sense that, regardless of your efforts and presentation, the machinations of life are capricious and indifferent, and nothing seems to fit or make sense. Life is confusing, random, and hard: bad people win; good people die young; other people work hard and finish last. There's joy and sadness, pleasure and pain, bounty and poverty, it's all capricious and suffering is optional. There is a *huge* misunderstanding about "suffering" in relation to the First Noble Truth of Buddhism. The First Noble Truth has been translated as "life is suffering," which translation was for a religious, political agenda and not philosophical accuracy. It isn't that life is suffering, it's that life is dislocated. Without strong ethical grounding and non-attachment (meaning non-codependence), everyone suffers the struggle of trying to make sense out of life. Whether you continue to suffer is a personal choice. There is some related discussion of this in the chapter Buddhism in Huston Smith's book, *The World's Religions*, HarperSanFrancisco, 1991.

[16] In the last fifteen years, many religious organizations have implemented various so-called modernizations like jazz music at worship services, or folk music sing-alongs at mass, or renting their "sacred" space out to artistic endeavor. This has included having congregation members undertake administrative and service positions called "Personal Ministries" which may suit their individual interest or temperament. This is for the survival of a rigid religious structure responding to drastic cultural change and greatly reduced membership. It may appear that services are being personalized but only to the degree of that religious doctrine remains unchallenged. These modernizations are not for the incorporation of a wise relationship between personality and deity.

reers. Also, the groups were smaller. I was told in the early 1980s, by the then very-old old-timers, that there was no focus on family of origin, and significantly more introspective discussion about the application and mis-application of "self" to spirituality. It follows that the steps were approached and interpreted differently.

Since about 1980, with all the drastic cultural changes, a huge increase in the number of members, with their mean age being considerably younger, and the overwhelming deluge of self-help psychology, the groups have fo-cused themselves on psychological health, intimate relationships, careers, and extended social circles. That doesn't mean that career advantages and romance didn't happen in groups sixty years ago, and it doesn't mean that the newer people are to blame. It means that demographics, culture, and psychological technology have drastically changed the spiritual efficacy of twelve-step groups.[17]

As I've described elsewhere, as regards spirituality, twelve-step groups are foundering badly. This is the result of the members' refusal to maintain a spiritual interpretation of the original instructions and traditions, now supplanted by "attractive", but ineffective psychological/social solu-tions. These are manifestations of the cultural malaise embodied in righteousness, greed, disposability, and illusions about psychology—a poor technology of spirituality. Within the sphere of addictions recovery, nobody is guilty and everyone is responsible.

All of this prohibits the development of an adequate faith that must combine insight from personal experience and adherence to wise tradition. Addictions recovery is dependent upon (i) commitment to a "higher author-ity"; and (ii), obedience to principle, not to psychological astuteness. For the purposes of this discussion, the higher authority is both spiritual princi-ples and the AA reference textbooks. Without this focus there is no spiritual faith, and without spiritual faith, you cannot get recovered.

I cannot overstate the importance of gently applying your personal life experience to the original steps and traditions, with this ever-present caveat: (spiritual) principles before personalities. In this way, when you get to the maintenance steps, your faith is strong, your inner vision is clear, and spiri-tual principles are quiet demonstrations of behaviour rather than entertaining rhetoric and political maneuvering.[18]

Spiritual ineffectiveness results from modifying the steps towards psy-chology and loss of your individuality in favor of a political agenda

---

[17] Where two or three are gathered together on behalf of God, spiritual grace may well be pre-sent. As the size of the crowd increases, the presence of God decreases. *Huxley and God, Essays,* cited at an earlier footnote.
[18] When I suggest you personalize the five spiritual principles by the judicious influence of personality and life experience, I do not imply that personality should prevail.

(religious, psychological, or social). Because of cultural changes, this is happening in all twelve-step groups, and rewriting the original literature accelerates this fragmentation. Regardless of the secular reasons that instigated the rewriting, and although well intended, rewriting subtly refocuses the intent away from spiritual integrity towards psychological health.

Technology, politics, and psychology, acting in concert with addictive irresponsibility, have increased this fragmentation. I've noticed for years, and I make the observation sadly, that in a twelve-step group it's easier to find a new wife or husband, or a good deal on a used car, than it is a wise spiritual sponsor. The spiritual mandate of twelve-step programs is vanishing, and in spite of their being more popular, available, and visible, they are less effective, which is reflected in the individuals that comprise the group.

All of this is repairable, but certainly not easy. Rigorously apply yourself to the original literature and ignore popular opinion. Vigorously stress individual study and strong personal devotion to the original steps and traditions, as they embody spiritual principles. Your spiritual life, and often your physical life, depends on it.

The steps, in their application, aren't group activities. They are not spiritually effective when done as collective experience. Yes, they are written, "we did this" and "we did that", but that's a function of grammar, not an instruction for a group of people to do a step collectively. For example: *"Made a searching and fearless moral inventory of ourselves"*[19] is simply a grammatical way of representing what each person did individually.

In order to provide a different sense of the steps, I'm going to offer a shift in perception so you might see more clearly how the specifics of the steps apply to you individually. For the purpose of clarity, and not to make your work easier, I'm going to "personalize" the first four steps by taking them out of their collective representation, and put them into a singular, personal perspective. I am not suggesting that you should rewrite the steps; I am trying to offer insight on how they apply to *you*.

>   Step 1: My life had become unmanageable—I admitted I was
>   powerless over __(acting out)__. I'm sick not crazy.
>   Step 2: I learned and now believe that only a higher power
>   could restore me to sanity.
>   Step 3: I decided, above all else, I was going to behave and
>   think spiritually—I decided to think and live a life of
>   spiritual integrity.

---

[19] *Alcoholics Anonymous*, p. 59, *Twelve Steps and Twelve Traditions*, p. 42.

Step 4: My self-imposed crisis started at an instinctual level. I wrote out, in detail, what was specifically wrong in my instincts, fears, and sexual behaviour—how I got myself into trouble.

Some Relevant Side Issues

The nature of addictions presents dilemmas and apparent paradoxes. These exist because of an unspiritual mindset. However, once you learn enough truth about yourself, and apply that to the five spiritual principles embodied in the maintenance steps, dilemmas and paradoxes cease to exist. When dilemmas arise, all that is required is to study "yourself" and uncover your belligerence, dishonesty, or irresponsibility. In a life of impeccable honesty that is governed by the five spiritual principles, there are no dilemmas or difficult decisions, ever.

The original twelve-step program is a revealed truth and needs no explanation. Upon close examination, its integrity becomes self-evident. The questions and complexity are generated by the addiction, so the resolution of dilemmas and problems lie within the addict and not the original program. Study the original literature, identify what instruction you are not following, and then follow it. Go deeper within yourself, and don't read ahead looking for answers to problems; you'll only frighten and confuse yourself.

Alcoholics Anonymous and *Twelve Steps and Twelve Traditions,* are two books on spiritual transformation that don't contradict themselves. This is one strength that allows this process to have such success in resolving addictions.

Addicts often believe they are uniquely sick, and very complicated, and harbor secret beliefs they will need much more that just "the program". They're trapped in extreme terminal uniqueness and can't believe that two "simple" books like *Alcoholics Anonymous* and *Twelve Steps and Twelve Traditions* have all the answers to their addictions problems.[20] Lack of faith forces them to rush off in all directions, looking for something that keeps them terminally unique, all the while hoping they'll find an expedient, painless solution and beat the odds.

At the outset, completing the original twelve steps is neither expedient nor painless. As time passes, transformation gets much simpler, and eventually becomes graceful. There are no difficult decisions in a life governed by

---

[20] Another extreme form of terminal uniqueness is that addicts assume they are smart enough for their own good: "I'm creatively insightful and need little or no help at all." Their addictions and arrogance keep them unaware of how much harm they are causing themselves and others.

the maintenance steps; there are difficult decisions in a religious life; don't confuse the two.

With continuous abstinence and diligent step work, you're a newcomer for five years. It doesn't matter if you have a Ph.D., if you're a bus driver, or a priest, or are coming off welfare—you're a newcomer for five years. It's the mandate of the disease and not an insult to your ability or devotion. If you're patient and diligent, demand much of yourself, expect little from others, regularly pray and meditate, and are willing to self-examine more than blame, you will find all of the answers within yourself. However, the answers are only available in conjunction with a rigorous application of yourself to the regeneration steps (Steps One to Nine).

Steps Ten, Eleven, and Twelve are the maintenance steps. It stands to reason if you were forever "in recovery", you wouldn't need maintenance steps because you wouldn't have acquired anything that required maintaining. When you painstakingly appreciate and accomplish, in detail, what's required in each of the first nine steps, you can't *not* become spiritual.[21]

Nine Steps, Three Columns

Each of the steps has a complex spiritual purpose. They aren't sequenced haphazardly. In their aspect, composition, structure, and nuance, they each address specific facets of addiction, spiritual belligerence, and transformation in a non-interchangeable, non-exchangeable, ascending order.[22] They lead directly to a life governed by the maintenance steps and spiritual principles. There are non-negotiable spiritual reasons for them being *exactly* as they are. Yes, there is some derivative psychological healing, but that is not their substantive intent. When the steps are rewritten for other "issues", to make healing "easier", or are altered for personal convenience, the new versions become ineffective for resolving addictions. They cannot be altered with impunity.

---

[21] I have been asked whether getting recovered is available to a newcomer who is spirituality very defiant. Yes. All addicts are defiant to some degree. For however anonymously Providence moved on their behalf, people who are successful in reducing their defiance enough to achieve abstinence have all they need to begin. In the realm of addictions, there is no situation too corrupt or sophisticated that the original twelve steps cannot address spiritually, *providing* the mendicant maintains abstinence and slowly embraces willingness, patience, and labor. Continuous abstinence is evidence of some willingness. Within the original twelve-step literature, the process of becoming willing is gradual. The intricacies of each successive step reduce defiance and draw you closer to the Atman-Brahmin. A spiritual life is available when you begin with abstinence and persevere at Step Two. It's what the steps are designed to do. It's inevitable.

[22] *"The unfolding of* [person's] *spiritual nature is as much an exact science as astronomy* [or] *medicine." The Secret Teachings of All Ages,* Reader's Edition, Manly P. Hall, Tarcher/Penguin Books, 2003, p. 120.

Here's an awareness and integration exercise that will take some time, but is worth the effort. At the beginning of your work on a step, at the top of a sheet of paper, write out the step and draw three columns underneath. In the first column, list the symptoms of the disease (noted in Chapter 2), and in the third column, list the five spiritual principles (noted in Appendix II). In the middle column, note some aspect of the step that would counteract a symptom and, at the same time, would incorporate a spiritual principle. Learn how each step reduces and eliminates the symptoms *and at the same time* engenders spirituality. Here's what the Step One sheet might look like:

1)   *"We admitted we were powerless over alcohol—*
       that our lives had become unmanageable."

Symptoms	Which symptoms are counteracted and which spiritual principles are incorporated.	Five Spiritual Principles
excessive fear assumptions shame dishonesty selfishness irresponsibility arrogance and cynicism being isolated acting out arrogance selfishness/greed	Stops major self harm and annihilation. Incorporates some veracity. Begins to reduce irresponsibility and increase responsibility and obedience. Reduces and addresses isolation and begins self-care. Stops acting out and begins the practice of obedience.	(1) Respect for the body-temple; Respectful Self-care (2) Veracity (3) Humility (4) Charity (5) Responsibility and Obedience

This exercise will facilitate insight into the spiritual intent of each step and the reasons for meticulously following the instructions. If you do this exercise, keep your work. I'll be referring you back to this later.

How you approach the maintenance steps is different than approaching the regeneration steps.[23] The first nine steps are applied *to* your life; the maintenance steps *are* your life (a parallel theme to what I wrote earlier: you are not a member of a group; you are the group). Steps Ten, Eleven,

---

[23] You complete the first nine steps, and they "take" you someplace. The maintenance steps have a completely different function. The maintenance steps are never "completed". You never *leave* the maintenance steps, but you leave each of the other steps up to nine. This isn't semantics; it's the tenor of first *becoming* spiritual and later *being* spiritual. Applying yourself to the maintenance steps is remarkably different than applying yourself to the others.

and Twelve become a part of your persona, rather than exercises to be performed, but you won't appreciate the importance of this distinction unless you study the original textbooks regularly, for years; regularly pray and meditate as instructed; frequently seek well-defined, wise spiritual counsel, and constantly examine your motives and level of honesty.

As I've said: Changes in demographics, new social and psychological perspectives, scrutiny of the process by professionals (who often have unresolved prejudices, are not spiritual themselves, or are twelve-step participants at various levels of spiritual integrity), informed consumers, and media-hype about famous people being in-program, are reflected in the changes in twelve-step groups. Members are now largely focused on anything but spirituality. The twelve steps are subsequently less effective, and are losing credibility. They weren't designed for anything but exiting addictions and becoming Spiritual.[24]

I suppose you could weld large wings onto a car and try to make an airplane/glider, but it wouldn't be an efficient airplane and it wouldn't be an effective car. This doesn't mean the car itself was poorly designed or that airplanes aren't efficient. It means they aren't being utilized as originally designed. This new contraption may fly a little bit, but the car-plane will garner a reputation as being ineffective. So it is with psychology that's injected into the original (spiritually intended) twelve steps.

When twelve-step programs were restructured or rewritten as mandates for recovery agencies, formulas for creative success, avenues to psychological health, or routes to relationship happiness (and some have tried to rewrite them to include all of these), they became ineffective. They were designed for something much more profound and beautiful than mere social efficiency.[25]

If you, as a member of a twelve-step group, or as a professional enrolling the aid of these groups, wish to have them as effective and powerful as they were originally, then use them only for what they were designed—the transformation out of addictions and into a spiritual lifestyle. They aren't a panacea for any illness that is similar to an addiction. They aren't a substitute solution for people who can't afford, or refuse to pay for, therapy.

---

[24] For abstinence not-available addictions, the twelve steps do work, provided there is a sensitive and determined effort to understand and maintain bottom-line behaviour and abstinence. The need for delicately interweaving psychology and spirituality for these addictions makes this incredibly complicated.

[25] Addictions are vicious. Achieving relationship bliss or financial security are completely insufficient for the task of eliminating your addictions.

You've Got A Broken Ankle

One day while out walking, you trip and fall stepping off a curb. Of course, if you're an addict, you immediately look to see who pushed you. You may secretly know that you tripped, but for any number of reasons, you look for someone to blame. You're disoriented from pain and aren't exactly sure how it happened. Finally, you ask someone for help. They help you sit on the curb and gently point out that you tripped—no one pushed you—and you apparently have a broken ankle. They tell you out of kindness that they have done similar things themselves. You finally realize that you do have a badly broken ankle and that no one pushed you.

The person who is helping you now advises that you could resolve this problem by going to a hospital. They quietly explain that was what worked for them. Certainly, you don't *have* to go to a hospital. You could limp off to a bar, go home, or go to the S.P.C.A., and not go to the hospital. You can go wherever you want, but they kindly point out that the most effective thing to do would be to go to a hospital. You admit that a hospital makes sense, and you decide to go there.

How *exactly* do you get to the hospital? You can crawl, ride a bicycle, be carried, call a taxi, or call an ambulance. After some discussion you agree to call an ambulance. It would be the fastest and safest way to get to the hospital. People who knew what they were doing would support you *en route* to the hospital—you would have a guaranteed result: efficiently getting to where you needed to go.

You've Got An Addiction

You're destitute and defeated from your addiction, and "wake up" in a meeting. You think you were "pushed" into your insanity and, in the midst of your pain and disorientation; Step One is learning you weren't pushed at all. You're going to [hopefully] be helped to learn that you hurt yourself. You eventually believe that you have an addiction, and that you're sick from your *self*-imposed crisis. No one is to blame. (You tripped and broke your ankle, all by yourself.)

After you admit you're an addict, the process of getting yourself pointed in the right direction begins. From guidance, reading, and studying *yourself*, you understand and believe that a higher power could restore you to sanity—spirituality is the solution. You can't resolve anything yet, only now you know where to go. This signals the end of Step Two. Next is you decide to live spiritually: Step Three.

You accomplish this "healing" by following the most efficient method for addicts: completing the steps with a view to becoming spiritual.[26] You can try to get better by being social, popular, professionally successful, generous, happily married, kind, or physically fit. Over the long term, however, these don't work. Obedience to the steps is the most efficient way for getting where you need to go; and hopefully someone who knows what they're doing will support you along the way by. (The parallel was going to the hospital by ambulance.) You create a spiritual lifestyle and gain access to a higher power via the steps.

Years ago I spent a week with an old friend from college. We had long conversations about twelve-step programs and he was happy because I wasn't destroying myself any more. Regarding the steps, he said: "Well, those don't seem too hard." He commented that he'd been doing similar things throughout his life. I said to him something like: "Don't you see how hard these steps are?" He thought for a moment and said, "Well, no I don't." Later he added: "I'm glad this program is as important to you as it isn't to me." We laughed. He understood the precepts as a matter of his everyday life: they weren't hard for him—he wasn't an alcoholic.

Being a successful addict requires that you live your life opposite to the maintenance steps. The more you're reluctant to do the steps, the harder they are for you, the more this indicates you have an addiction. If you are confused over whether or not you are an addict, try the steps. If they're difficult, you probably are.

Throughout this I would encourage you to remember: *"When we became* [addicts] *crushed by a self-imposed crisis we could not postpone or evade… ."*[27] Your addiction is a disease. Even though it may appear otherwise, no one is to blame. The original literature is clear that your crises are self-imposed. It's important to heal from the effects of any abuse and violence—for these things there is therapy—but you're not an addict because of them. Drop the word "blame" from your vocabulary.[28]

Alcoholics Anonymous offers this: *"…we believe that early in our drinking careers most of us could have stopped drinking;"*[29] and, *"…we feel we had gone on drinking many years beyond the point where we could quit on our willpower."*[30] Should you complete Step Four (and Step Eight when

---

[26] I imagine that people with*out* addictions may pursue spirituality in any number of ways: they don't need these steps. However, for the addict, *getting recovered* and *being spiritual* (cont'd) are identical. To achieve this requires significant devotion to the exact instructions in the original twelve steps. The existence of an addiction prohibits other options.
[27] *Alcoholics Anonymous,* p. 53.
[28] *Twelve Steps and Twelve Traditions*, p. 47.
[29] *Alcoholics Anonymous,* p. 32.
[30] Ibid., p. 34.

you get there) exactly as it's outlined, you will, among other things, begin to sense when your acting-out went out of control and you crossed that unknown-before-hand invisible line into addictions. And if you do your Step Four exactly the way it's outlined, you will learn how you motivated your self-imposed crisis.

The original twelve-step program is amazingly rich with potential, but you've got to work for it. Nothing is free. At the prospect of spiritual (or the related psychological) work, unfortunately, most addicts stay lazy.[31]

I've been asked many times if there's a difference between a drug addict and an alcoholic, or between, say, an alcoholic and a relationship or sex addict. Some say there is, I imagine so they can lay claim to some spiritually defeating uniqueness. Underneath the preferred mood-altering experience there really isn't any difference.

Your addiction of preference is a ritual of self-annihilation, which often changed with circumstances. Emotional compensation strategies, your particular generation, social pressures, technology, and subculture indoctrination will influence your choice of mood-altering behaviour. And, of course, the medical requirements of detoxing will vary from substance to substance. The consequences of your acting out—the damage done and amends required—may vary somewhat. These are external differences. Underneath it all, after detoxing and moving beyond Step One, there's very little difference (which is the import of 'How It Works'—the rallying point I discussed earlier).

Four Big Topics

Spiritual Integrity and Psychological Health are remarkably different. Both of these disciplines are quite fascinating because of their intimate application to life. They're particularly fascinating and especially important to alcoholics and addicts. Psychological Health carries the hope of personal competence and integration, and Spiritual Integrity carries promise of salvation and deliverance. There aren't enough warnings, however, that these two disciplines and the routes to achieving them are not interchangeable.

In relation to this, twelve-step people precipitate all manner of neverending discussions and debates about the (apparently) critical nature of these Four Big Topics:

(i)   addiction of preference;
(ii)   destructive behaviours and self-damage;

---

[31] *"...at the prospect of work... we procrastinate or at best work grudgingly and under half steam." Twelve Steps and Twelve Traditions*, p. 49.

(iii)   detoxing or withdrawal; and,

(iv)   the struggles of abstinence or sobriety.

It's important to understand (and remember) that any of these four topics can be discussed from either a psychological *or* a spiritual point of view. Psychological health and spiritual integrity are remarkably different. It follows that discussions about any of these four topics would have remarkably different tones to the conversation, depending on which discipline— spirituality or psychology—the discussion pertained to.

Appropriately enough, The Four Big Topics are important to a newcomer. However, to anyone beyond the status of newcomer, debates about these are usually by people who desire to be viewed as erudite addictions gurus (which is spiritually inappropriate). Egos, pushed by character defects, create contentious debates, apologies, comparisons, and analyses of these four topics.

Do not lose sight of this important fact: In any *spiritual* pilgrimage, the farther along you are in the steps (i.e. the more spiritual you are), the less important these four subjects are. However, from a *psychological* perspective, because of the nature of psychology, these four topics must always be important, and carry a noticeable priority over spirituality. Here's why:

In Spiritual Transformation, the relationship between "importance of self" and "a higher power" increasingly changes thusly: a decrease of "self importance" in favor of an enhanced and soulful awareness of spiritual principles. "Me and my struggles" (i.e. the Four Big Topics) become increasingly *less* important. Your higher power is viewed and applauded as the primary agent of change.

By comparison, in psychological integration, the notions of self and willpower are the primary agents of change. A psychological recovery process is always steeped in willpower, self-awareness, and self-determination (all secular attributes of character). In psychology, the grand "I", me-and-my-ego, take the credit and a higher power becomes a minor agent in the process. Regardless of length of abstinence, a psychological bias to the twelve steps requires that "me and my struggles" (the four big topics) always be held in high regard.

Within the realms of spirituality, the four topics of addiction of preference, acting-out and harm caused, detoxing, and abstinence struggles are only a very minor part of what needs to be addressed. When people with years of abstinence still wallow in these debates, they have missed the spiritual point of the exercise. Those who sincerely pursue spiritual integrity speak less and less of any of them. (This is directly related to the Misalliance of Commitment, discussed in Chapter 7.)

Two Views of "Potential"

When the first few groups of AA started, the initial members were described as very desperate cases. They faced imminent insanity or death. Because of that, and because of the limited understanding of the disease, the original members' definition of an alcoholic was largely a simple association test. They knew what they, themselves, were like—extremely desperate—and so, if you were like them, then you were an alcoholic. Over time, despite that narrow definition, people who weren't so desperate were self-diagnosing themselves as alcoholics. The original members, formerly desperate but now sober, referred to these newer, *apparently* not-so-desperate members as "potential" alcoholics. This only meant that, in the opinion of those formerly desperate original members, the new people had a ways to go before they were as desperate as the original members were. Since membership is always self-diagnosing, the original, colloquial definition of extreme desperation used by the program founders had to change.

Another view of "potential" is in the process of addiction. Usually people start out with sporadic levels of substance use or mood altering experiences, which, over time, become more intense or frequent. Eventually, because of damaging consequences, this becomes categorized as "addicted". Early in their acting out, there may have been a time when these people were "potentially" addicts; a time when, had they been more informed, they might have been able to alter their behaviour and not evince an addiction. (Recall Blindness To The Disease, Chapter 2)

Some people say something like: "Oh, I used to drink a lot, but it was getting out of hand, so I quit," or "I did a lot of drugs when I was a kid, and I was getting into trouble, so I stopped." These people perceived, in time to make the choice, that they had a choice, and made it. The original AA literature comments that should alcoholics have been able to recognize that "choice point" before the disease entombed them they might still have been able to avoid addiction. That may be true. As pleasing as that insight is to your ego, in a fashion similar to what I mentioned earlier about the four big topics important to newcomers, it's only an intellectual observation that, over the long term, has no spiritual import.

By painstakingly following the original Step Four instructions you have an opportunity to determine, in hindsight, approximately when you might have been a potential alcoholic or addict. In the first few years of recovery, this awareness is important because when you see, in hindsight, that you may have had a choice and for whatever reason didn't make it, it helps you adopt a more sincere posture of responsibility.

Step Four takes a lot of effort (as I will soon outline), without which people never attain the level of responsibility that's needed to become recovered. People memorize clichés, impress others with how soon or fast they did their steps, argue about opinions, create racy, self-condemning autobiographies, and end up knowing very little about what's offered in the miracle of spiritual choice.

Resentments

There are three parts to Step Four, the first of which is specifically about instincts gone awry and exceeding their function.[32] Listing resentments is only important as an exercise to lead you to understand why you imposed your gone-awry instincts on others; to learn what caused you to demand too much control, protection, or affection.[33] How do you get from "resentment is the number one offender" (a frequently misapplied quote[34]) to instincts gone awry?

What precipitates making unreasonable demands upon, and generating revulsion in, the people who love and care about you? Understanding the motivations underneath resentments is far more important than categorizing and itemizing them. Resentments are only a minor part of Step Four, and yet discussions belabor them to the exclusion of all else. What this means is, because of this exaggerated bias, popular discussions about Step Four are, for the most part, empty rhetoric.

"Creation gave us instincts for a purpose."[35]—self-preservation (avoiding pain, seeking food, shelter), reproduction (sex), and a social instinct. What's written in the literature is that virtually every emotional problem for the addict can be traced to an instinct exceeding its function. These misdirected instincts are liabilities and cause great trouble, but there is no suggestion that they cause our addictions. Be mindful of this important distinction: Your addiction manifests at a behavioural/psychological level, but it exists at a spiritual level.[36]

---

[32] *"Yet these instincts... ," Twelve Steps and Twelve Traditions,* p. 42.

[33] *Twelve Steps and Twelve Traditions,* p. 44.

[34] Addicts or alcoholics getting recovered frequently attach themselves to one or two appealing sentences or phrases out of a chapter, and then reduce their interest in, and give less attention to, the other information. One example is the preponderance of discussion about resentments. Resentment permeates an addict's existence, which makes anger and resentments the most commonly visible, but not necessarily the worst, "shortcoming". Similarly, parking offences may be the most common illegal activity, but they are not the most serious one. As an addict getting recovered, resist clinging to tidbits of recovery jargon. Study each particular point, but not to the exclusion of anything else.

[35] *Twelve Steps and Twelve Traditions,* p. 42.

[36] Remember that psychological issues from your childhood didn't cause your addiction. Some *un*definable spiritual corruption did, and that's debatable, too. That's why psychology cannot resolve your addictions. Bear in mind, as you trudge through all the detail of Step (cont'd) Four, that its *primary* purpose is to draw you closer to a higher power, not to resolve developmental dependency issues or enhance your human relationships.

Ultimately, Step Four is not about being bad or about your resentments at all. Many Step Fours are a wrongly focused list that tries to prove that their authors were the sickest person in town—they did 532 very horrible things, 768 medium horrible things, and lied to 1,943 people. By page twenty-nine of this style of inventory, they're depressed or smugly proud. Some become resentful of the program, God, and Step Four because this style of inventory resolves nothing and adds no insight. Step Four is never a litany of what a disgusting miscreant you were. When the founders wrote that addicts were to understand the *nature* of their wrongs, "nature" refers to the instinctual conflict beneath the resentment, not the behaviour or the resentment.

Throughout this exercise, what will become obvious is, it's impossible to be resentful or angry without having some associated fear. Yes, you've got to start with the resentments to get to where you're supposed to end up, but resentments are only the starting point and of minor consideration in the larger scheme of things.

"We want to find exactly how, when, and where our natural desires have warped us."[37] This means instinctually, not geographically.

How: by your blaming and frustrated efforts to control others; *not* how, by others doing something to you.

When: when you were irresponsible and when you saw yourself as a misunderstood, insecure victim; *not* when they wouldn't do what you wanted.

Where: Where in one of your instincts; *not* where, in Toronto or in the bathroom.

The original twelve-step literature talks about being warped by our natural desires, and what harm this caused others and ourselves.[38] Step Four's focus of examining your behaviour and no one else's is one requirement of spirituality. *"We wish to look squarely at the unhappiness this has caused others and ourselves."*[39] You will not be looking at what you did or what others did to you, but your instincts, fears, and selfishness.

Notice: *"...by discovering what our emotional deformities are."* It doesn't read that you're to discover what your resentments are. It's easy to figure out whom you're mad at; you've probably been telling that to anyone who'll listen for years. However, knowing your emotional deformities is another matter entirely. The requirements of spirituality demand a deeper

---

[37] *Twelve Steps and Twelve Traditions*, p. 43.
[38] Ibid.
[39] Ibid.

investigation of responsibility and truth than any superficial discussion of resentments can ever allow.

In addition to abstinence, Steps One (action) and Two (insight) are "thought and awareness processes". They are by and large an initial, fundamental rearranging of your inner emotional and intellectual relationship with yourself. They reorganize your perceptions, deepen your awareness, and facilitate the possibility if a commitment to spiritual values. (Context.) This is the set up that enables a proper effort at Step Four.

Here's an analogy to make another point: You bring your car to a garage for repairs. Suppose you just say: "My car's broken, please fix it," and leave. That won't be enough. The mechanic will expect some description of what's wrong. Doesn't it start? Is it the exhaust system? The point being that it probably isn't necessary to fix the door handles, the seat belts, or any of a thousand other things. You don't have to fix the entire car.

The purpose of Step Four is to figure out what's wrong in relation to your instincts. You have to fix only your emotional deformities. That may be a lot, but you don't have to fix everything about your entire personality.[40] Even knowing that, in Step Four you don't fix it, you simply identify it. You are not, and I repeat, you are *not* to go marching through your personality attacking everything about yourself. There are very specific, limited things you're supposed to do; it's a clearly defined exercise.

In *Facets of Personal Transformation* I will explore the dynamic of a "real you" that is disowned, denied, and kept hidden.[41] The point of a spiritual pilgrimage is to experience yourself at levels more profound than shame resolution. Underneath this is a poignant loneliness. People go through life compensating for spiritual dislocation by being overbearing, cynical, angry, dependent, promiscuous, celibate, drunk, stoned, bitter, shy, over-achieving, helpless, arrogant, and so on. These self-administered compensations are traceable to psychology and resolving them at that level is, in my view, certainly satisfactory — for non-addicts.

For addicts and those who pursue spiritual integrity, there are levels of integration that people can attain which are much deeper than effective psychological/social "harmony". Yes achieving this much deeper awareness is socially, financially, and emotionally expensive. It's worth it. There's more

---

[40] *"To believe that the alcoholic who approaches AA is an unprincipled, untaught barbarian, suddenly transformed by the previously unavailable spiritual illumination of the Twelve Steps, is, to me,* (cont'd) *utter foolishness."* From the AA pamphlet *A Member's Eye View of Alcoholics Anonymous,* cited earlier. Should you decide to vigorously pursue spirituality and humility, over the course of your life you may certainly end up changing "everything" about your personality. However, that's not the point of Step Four.

[41] This is described in John Bradshaw's book *Healing The Shame That Binds You,* Health Communications Inc., 1988. For a related view of our critical nature oppressing ourselves, read *Embracing Your Inner Critic,* Hal Stone & Sidra Stone HarperSanFrancisco, 1993.

serenity and joy than can be imagined or described, if people pursue sincere spiritual integrity.

Step Four identifies resentments as one entrance point to an awareness of your deeper nature. As with the entrance to a mine, there may be only one entrance to the mine, but there will be miles of tunnels underground. Resentments are one of the entrance points to the underground tunnels of your nature. (Regarding Step Four, the other two entrances are fears and sexual selfishness.)

In order to hide their fears and insecurities, or to conceal that they know absolutely nothing about "why" they are so self-destructive, addicts have an array of tactics to keep everyone, including themselves, out of their own underground tunnels. Alcoholics try to convince everyone, especially themselves, that they aren't hiding, when in fact they are hiding, and regardless of how they explain it away, can't understand their own destructive behaviour at all.

If you're an unregenerate addict, regardless of whether it's your sex partner, your boss, a relative, or a friend, as soon as they speak or behave in some way that causes you to look at the real you, you'll blame, get angry, leave, get sick—do anything to keep yourself and others from knowing about your shame, loneliness, and pain. It's a terrible emotional push-pull. People are drawn, by instinct, into relationships and we desire intimacy, but addicts are terrified of this and sabotage their own best intentions with blaming and destructive irresponsibility.

The belief and conviction developed at Step Two, and a determined decision at Step Three, are crucial prerequisites for addicts to successfully self-examine at Step Four. They can only discover what needs to be changed by going inside, and that's *exactly* what they don't want to do. Without properly aligning themselves at Steps Two and Three, addicts doing Step Four can only list their resentments and examine other people. Until addicts get deeply inside themselves, all of their relationships, especially with a higher power, will be power struggles for control, and end up mediocre at best.

People embark on inner child work (which is an oversimplified, largely misused metaphor for a complex therapeutic strategy) and 'resolve' their shame issues.[42] That work takes a long time, and then they'll eventu-

---

[42] Regarding the resolution of shame, I've heard all manner of psychobabble, like "transforming my shame into guilt and resolving the guilt because I stop disesteeming myself," and "distancing myself from shame through positive thinking and service work," and "my shame left because I did the steps and my higher power only wants good things for me." These are not resolution strategies, but appear so, only because of the tightly bound and limited lifestyles, and the intellectual defensiveness and strong character armor that accompanies them. To make the speech look like it's true, there's a tremendous investment in rigidly controlling their environment, and shame is only held at bay and not resolved at all. Resolving inculcated (cont'd)

ally become aware of how lonely they are. Many people are amazed at the depth of loneliness that exists within them. That's when they appreciate a new aspect of becoming recovered, and only then is a wise perspective of spirituality available to them. Resolve the shame, embrace the loneliness, and learn to rely on spiritual principles. It's always a sign of spiritual integrity and emotional health when addicts, or anyone for that matter, voluntarily and quietly chooses loneliness over conflict.

Shame is one of the more painful things people experience, but for spiritual pilgrims, once the shame is largely resolved, they touch that deep sense of how alone they really are. This awareness isn't available to people who are religious or those of little faith, which is why so very few people appreciate that on the *other* side of this loneliness is where the profound relationship with a higher power lies.

I've worked with addicts who are diligent and arrive at the cusp between insight and authentic transformation. They stand on the brink of addressing their loneliness and isolation and then quit therapy. They know some things, and sound insightful, but choose Impression Management rather than spirituality—looking good and playing politics; taking the larger share of control and attention for themselves, while they convince you they're not—selfishness at its best.

Finger-Pointing by Numbers

Step Four is the exercise that takes alcoholics and addicts inside themselves and away from the historical game of externalizing responsibility (blaming and condemning). Addicts are brilliantly schooled in the fine art of Finger-Pointing, which is vicious at the best of times.

Practice Finger-Pointing by Numbers: First, make your selections at 1(A) or 1(B) and enter this selection at line 7. Then, go back to #1 and read through the exercise, making your preferred selections at 2 through 6.

1 (A) My life is...		1 (B) I am feeling...	
( ) hard	( ) unfulfilled	( ) hurt	( ) annoyed
( ) empty	( ) lonely	( ) angry	( ) lonely
( ) painful	( ) chaotic	( ) sad	( ) depressed
( ) intolerable		( ) empty	( ) miserable

---

shame is a delicate process, and at its deeper levels, always requires a balanced relationship between unconditional positive regard in talk therapy, an enhanced self-regard through understanding the dynamic of the interpersonal transfer of shame, placing and taking responsibility, and some dynamic of physiological healing like SRT or EFT. (See Appendix III).

(2) because...   ( ) you   ( ) he   ( ) she   ( ) everyone
                       ( ) they   ( ) it   ( ) no one

(3)...   ( ) did   ( ) didn't   ( ) couldn't   ( ) won't
             ( ) can't   ( ) refused to   ( ) should have   ( ) shouldn't have

(4) _____.
            (insert description of their bad behaviour)

(5) And besides, don't you know that...
      ( ) no one   ( ) he doesn't   ( ) she doesn't
      ( ) they don't   ( ) you don't   ( ) it doesn't

(6)   ( ) really appreciate me.   ( ) care enough about me.
            ( ) like me.   ( ) really love me.
            ( ) ever help me.   ( ) support me.
            ( ) understand me.

(7) And so it's ( ) your ( ) his   ( ) her ( ) their fault, that
        (A) My life is _____, or
        (B) I am feeling _____.
                    [insert selection from 1(A) or 1(B)]

Step Four is the first of two major exercises you must complete in order to gently negotiate yourself past this vicious mindset.[43]

Conditions Didn't Do Anything

There is crucial information in the paragraph that begins: *"We thought
'conditions' drove us to drink... "*.[44] As the frequency and intensity of your
resentments increased it meant that you were trying harder to correct conditions. You were trying to get people to give you what you wanted; trying to
get people to let you get away with things; or demanding people live their
lives on your terms. This will become self-evident if you complete the Step
Four List chronologically.

In *Alcoholics Anonymous,* the point made is that anger is invariably
reduced to some perspective of addicts not getting their own way: As "we"
tried to manipulate others to do what we wanted, *"and found that we could-
n't to our entire satisfaction, our drinking* [acting out] *went out of hand and
we became* [self-destructive addicts] *alcoholics."*[45] Your drinking, drug

---

[43] There is always some element of righteousness or envy in gossip. One of the most important
reasons to stop gossiping is that it forces you to look at yourself more than you look at others.
[44] *Twelve Steps and Twelve Traditions*, p. 47.
[45] Ibid.

abuse, violence, shopping, sexual behaviour, rage, religious righteousness, gambling, work, physical exercise, etc., went out of control when you tried to manipulate the world to suit yourself and the world wouldn't cooperate.

Your boss didn't understand you, your spouse was mean, the kids were too loud, you were underpaid and overworked, or overpaid and under worked, or they preempted your favorite TV show. You believed conditions and circumstances caused your acting out. Things and people drove you to it.[46] This world-view is directly related to the way your instincts are filtered through your ego. Your ego is the operating agent between the external world and your inner soul-nature and instincts.[47] *"It never occurred to us that we needed to change ourselves."*[48]

How many times have you heard something like this: Two people are arguing. Kim says to Jan: "Every time we disagree, you start throwing things and screaming and shouting." Jan, who screams and shouts and throws things, immediately becomes super-reasonable and makes a speech: "Well, look Kim, I *tried* saying please. I *tried* being nice. I *tried* negotiating. I *tried* asking. I *tried* talking about this. Nothing works! The only time you listen is when I yell and throw things." This really means Jan believes that Kim is "listening" when Kim does what Jan wants—the issue isn't "listening", it's obedience. This is classic behaviour in addicted relationships.

Jan's speech: "I *tried* saying please. I *tried* being nice. I *tried*..." is an itemized list of the control tactics used to try and manipulate obedience or compliance from Kim. When Kim says "No," Jan's insecurity interprets "No" as not listening or being argumentative, when, in fact, Kim is listening and disagreeing. When nothing else works, Jan becomes dangerous.

Alternately, passive-aggressive "helplessness" is also punishing who isn't giving the alcoholic/addict what they want. This is another version of trying to *"correct conditions to our entire satisfaction."*

Resentments are a character defect and only one small facet of your personality. They indicate where you're supposed to start looking for the problem, but they aren't the problem.

Watch for people who avoid responsibility by staying focused on re-sentments. They won't talk about sex addiction as they buy a pornographic magazine or a beefcake pin-up calendar, or watch a stripper at a stag(ette). Listen to the complaining: Step Four! Resentments! They won't talk about tobacco, that they're irresponsible and committing suicide—those resent-

---

[46] This attitude of blaming is outrageously obvious in most people. "You made me mad," "I'm upset because you..." "I'm unhappy because they..." and so on. This is all irresponsible.
[47] See Appendix IV.
[48] *Twelve Steps and Twelve Traditions,* p. 47.

ments, aren't they something? They won't talk about greed and cheating on their income tax—everyone cheats, right? My, my, those resentments are powerful things.

They gossip and spread rumors, which is evidence of righteousness and envy and very harmful to others, but that's minor compared to resentments; resentments can kill you! They avoid their racism, sexism, offensive humor, and crude language because resentments; well… those resentments are something, aren't they? Certainly the lies they tell are only *small* ones, and their boss or children or friends or partner won't find out—they'll worry about lying later; right now they have to focus on resentments. This is a massive campaign to look good while being irresponsible.

At Step Four, you painstakingly look at the patterns of conflicts and irresponsibility in relation to your acting out. If you are fortunate and determined enough to be in well-conducted therapy, you will more easily see that your ego, often referred to as "the addict in me", not only tried to control conditions, but actually orchestrated the difficult circumstances in the first place so you had something to complain about.

Whatever conditions people believe drove them to drink, act out sexually, binge, rage, gamble, steal, spend… whatever, were actually orchestrated by them in the first place. They blame external conditions for their problems, and try to change these conditions by arguing, fighting, punishing others, harming themselves, spending, quitting, lying, leaving relationships, moving, playing dumb, drinking, getting stoned, being sexually irresponsible, gossiping, etc. There are no "external" reasons for addictions or alcoholism. It's never been life. It's perceptions and energy trauma within dislocation, which is demonstrated in how they, themselves, orchestrated the circumstances in their life in such a way that their irresponsible self-annihilation appeared to be someone else's fault.

People come to see me for various addictions and dislocation-related problems. We talk for a *long* time and eventually and finally, everything gets sorted out. They realize that, after all that work, the world hasn't changed very much. They've become much less focused on controlling external events and blaming. What has changed is their perception of themselves and their relationship with "life". They've become internally responsible and are self-disciplined regardless of the extant conditions of their life.

In *Facets of Personal Transformation*, there will be a chapter on Ego, and a detailed discussion of how your ego is created, and how it establishes and maintains relationships and perceptions (here, covered briefly in Appendix IV). You recreate patterns in external relationships, and maintain themes of chaos and conflict, that are a complex metaphor for what's going on inside you. There's nothing haphazard about it. It isn't conditions. It's you. Your life and your world are your perceptions of circumstances selectively filtered through your ego.

Addicts live inside a massive campaign that externalizes responsibility. *"But in AA we slowly learned that something had to be done about our vengeful resentments, self pity, and unwarranted pride."*[49] The AA literature refers to alcoholics [addicts] being victimized by their own erratic emotions. I cannot overstate the importance of this absolutely crucial observation: *"We had to drop the word 'blame' from our speech and thought."*[50] As far as spirituality and getting recovered go, there is never a justification for complaining about anything. No exceptions.

The Buried Treasure

Recall children's stories about pirates. Black Bart and Evil Erma, the nasty pirates, have hidden treasure. There's a map of a deserted coastline on The Dark Continent, and on the map is a trail of dots. They park their ship in a lagoon (surrounded by sharks!) and the dots go from the beach, along the river, through the jungle (with snakes!), past Pointy Peak, over the dangerous rapids, around Lost Lagoon, past the crocodiles, under the waterfall, thirteen paces into the cave, against the east wall, under the big rock, and "X" marks the spot! The treasure, at last! Of course it's a big rock and Black Bart and Evil Erma have to work hard, dig deep, and fight off other pirates to get their treasure.

Resentment is one "X" on your map that marks an emotional spot showing you where you dig into yourself. You also want to look "under" the big rocks of jealousy, envy, pride, sloth, greed, and the rest of your character defects. You have to fight off justifications, blaming, and excuses for not digging. Character defects are emotional clues that, with hard work, effort, lead you to the treasures of insight, faith, compassion, and serenity.

Listing resentments is to start looking at patterns, but *not* patterns of resentments. Establishing the pattern of resentments is easy: Addicts resent

---

[49] *Twelve Steps and Twelve Traditions*, p. 48.

[50] Ibid. p. 49. This all-encompassing requirement eliminates *all* complaining about *every*thing: family of origin, lovers, ex- or present spouses, the government, children, friends, employers, co-workers, the program, newcomers, in-laws, out laws, relationships, the weather, the police, sponsors, sponsors who act like the police, authors of books, politicians, television, money, movie stars—any "thing" that an alcoholic or addict is disappointed, frustrated, scared, sad, unhappy, angry, envious, lonely, upset, confused, or displeased about. What addicts complain about and blame for the state of affairs in their life that they, themselves, have orchestrated, is literally endless. I repeatedly encounter the subtle penchant for complaining and blaming in clients, who are at times, themselves, driven to distraction by the whining and complaining that passes for sharing and carrying the message. All blame must be eliminated from your speech and thought. No exceptions. If people in twelve-step programs stopped blaming, complaining, and gossiping, most of their conversations would screech to a halt.

anything that prevents them from doing or getting exactly what they want, when they want it, or losing anything they want to keep. That's the pattern, but that's not the problem.

Examining the instinctual insecurities underlying resentments, which also operate in patterns, is the task. Should you identify only your patterns of resentment, without addressing the underlying instinctual motivators of all your defects, you will precipitate another self-defeating pattern (like repeating Step Four every year for the rest of your life). You will also further entrench the already established posture of being victimized and blaming others, and insisting that life isn't fair.

Earlier I mentioned that emotions commonly classified as "negative", especially anger and jealousy, are experienced attendant to some experience of fear.[51] This is clearly pointed out regarding pride: *"For pride, leading to self-justification, and always spurred by conscious or unconscious fears, is the basic breeder of most human difficulties, the chief block to true progress."*[52]

It's sad how many people in twelve-step programs stay spiritually corrupt and fear-driven. They constantly and selectively interpret the written material in a self-serving manner to avoid challenging their secret or subtle addictions and character defects—especially arrogance and prejudice. There are any number of justifications that cause someone to adjust or alter the original twelve-step program to suit their own, personal insecurities and prejudices. Each alteration is evidence of unchallenged spiritual sloth. Every time anyone justifies disobedience to spiritual principles they demonstrate fear and defeat the true intent of the steps.

This relates to the concept of the seven deadly sins. "Sin" was used in times long past as an archery term that meant, "to miss the mark". In the struggle to be perfect, when character defects control your personality,[53] people often miss the mark, and are therefore "sinners". If you want an interesting exercise, put a sign on your fridge noting the seven sins (pride, greed, lust, anger, gluttony, envy, sloth) and beside each one write a day of the week. Do some research on the meaning of each sin. Give them a liberal definition. Reflect on them individually, daily. It'll make for interesting dinner conversation with friends. Start talking about important things.

Notice that anger (resentment) is only one of seven "sins". People who talk about their defects primarily in terms of anger are missing the point.

---

[51] Another ego gambit to establish grounds for complaint and struggle is to label some emotions as more desirable than others. There are no "negative" emotions, but there are no positive ones either.

[52] *Twelve Steps and Twelve Traditions*, pp. 48, 49.

[53] Ibid. p. 48.

That would be an unbalanced representation of both themselves and the task at Step Four. I encourage you to take a careful look at what you're being told by people who've modified or ignored the instructions in the original twelve-step literature.

There is a clear and succinct description of the entrenchment-process of fear and character defects. It begins: *"All these failings generate fear..."*[54] I've set this up graphically, and at point #2, included an alphabetical list of "defects" that represent controlling behaviour. The cycle is:

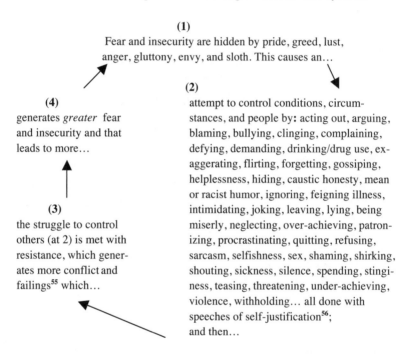

(1)
Fear and insecurity are hidden by pride, greed, lust, anger, gluttony, envy, and sloth. This causes an...

(2)
attempt to control conditions, circumstances, and people by: acting out, arguing, blaming, bullying, clinging, complaining, defying, demanding, drinking/drug use, exaggerating, flirting, forgetting, gossiping, helplessness, hiding, caustic honesty, mean or racist humor, ignoring, feigning illness, intimidating, joking, leaving, lying, being miserly, neglecting, over-achieving, patronizing, procrastinating, quitting, refusing, sarcasm, selfishness, sex, shaming, shirking, shouting, sickness, silence, spending, stinginess, teasing, threatening, under-achieving, violence, withholding... all done with speeches of self-justification[56]; and then...

(3)
the struggle to control others (at 2) is met with resistance, which generates more conflict and failings[55] which...

(4)
generates *greater* fear and insecurity and that leads to more...

Here's another exercise: Set a timer for five minutes and repeatedly read through the cycle for the five minutes. Think about the behaviours listed at position #2. Reflect on some conflict where you tried to control someone or punish them by acting in a way that is listed. Do this exercise once every three days for three months. Drive the point home, within yourself, that this cycle is the state of affairs in an unspiritual person's life.

"...with genuine alarm at the prospect of work, we stay lazy" and *"...work grudgingly and under half steam."*[57] People work "their" program,

---

[54] *Twelve Steps and Twelve Traditions*, p. 49.

[55] *"...the more we fought and tried to have our own way, the worse matters got."* *Alcoholics Anonymous*, p. 66.

[56] This list represents *"self manifested in various ways* [that] *had defeated us."* Ibid., p. 64.

[57] *Twelve Steps and Twelve Traditions* p. 49.

but too often that means their effort goes into recasting and selectively interpreting the steps and traditions. From another perspective, they really are working hard at their own program, but not working the program as it's laid out. Editing and recasting the AA literature is evidence of character defects controlling your effort, and a lack of effective investigation at Step Two.

Everyone is insecure about some things, and addicts are very insecure about many things. If you're an addict (practicing, in early recovery, or one who has manipulated or ignored the instructions), there are these two givens: you have a noticeably unspiritual mindset, and *all* of your relationships are dysfunctional because of your character defects. Demands on others, like on your boss for a raise, your partner for more (or less) sex, your parents for more love, your children for more obedience, your friends for more phone calls, people you sponsor for more gratitude, or your employer for more recognition, are all fear-based and unspiritual. Any effort to control others will generate tension and fear.

Fear is an emotion that people experience as a result of chemicals naturally generated within their bodies when they are in a situation that is perceived as dangerous or unsafe. "Dangerous" could be because of someone chasing them with a knife or because someone may discover their insecurities or mistakes. Fear is the emotion that causes you to want to flee, freeze, or fight (in addict's terms: leave, go silent and sulk, or argue).

The perception of danger, regardless of the type, occasions the experience of fear. In addicts, fear motivates all character defects.[58] Fear in people with generally balanced or non-addicted personalities, or in recovered alcoholic/addicts, is significantly less than fear in unregenerate addicts. Step Four is the process of beginning to make your fears, which show up as character defects, optional.

In order to do this, you have to do exactly what is suggested in the original twelve steps, and possibly go into long-term, well-conducted therapy. Shortcuts always defeat spiritual fulfillment. Consider that doing what you are told is the real shortcut: work very hard for several years and experience authentic spiritual peace, *or* stay in untreated addictions, hold onto your old ideas, and work painfully and repetitively through the steps for the rest of your life.

Immediately after the Step Three prayer, it reads: *"Next we launched out on a course of vigorous action* [a general reference to Steps Four to

---

[58] At the moment you feel afraid, the fear is authentic. Whether or not the extant circumstances might "objectively" be considered dangerous is a matter for well-conducted therapy and sincere meditation and prayer.

Nine], *the first step of which is a personal housecleaning* [a specific reference to Step Four]...".[59]

The Step Three decision requires vigorous follow-up action for it to be
meaningful. I suggest this means doing it the detailed way, and not to fill-
in-the-blanks of someone else's interpretation. Choosing the detailed way
would be a demonstration of your sincerity regarding the decision you made
in Step Three. Nowhere does it recommend that you take a shortcut and do
someone else's interpretation of Step Four. Neither does it advise (or ever
imply) that while doing Step Four you are to worry about Step Five. Be
mindful of your ego's determination to subvert the ever-deepening commitment to spiritual integrity.

With all character defects there is an associated fear. Resentment may
head the list because it is the most common, but pride is apparently the
more dangerous because it heads the procession.[60] Pride heads the list because it is diametrically opposed to humility. Fear is the universal common
denominator in all character defects and underlies all the harm done to others. However, be mindful that *"Instincts on rampage balk at investigation.*
The minute we make a serious attempt to probe them, we are liable to suffer
severe reactions."[61]

Depressed or Self Righteous

These two types of general temperament are described as having
unique needs in addressing Step Four. *"If temperamentally we are on the*
depressive side, we are apt to be swamped with guilt and self loathing."[62]
Within this melancholic group are people who tend to blame themselves for
everything, or view any situation as hopeless. *"Comforting the melan-*
choly..."[63] refers to this group that, secretly or not, often feels so badly, all
they see about themselves are character defects. From their point of view,
there's no need to self-examine because of the foregone conclusion that
everything's their own fault, and they'd probably fail at the task anyway.

The next paragraph describes the second type: *"If, however, our natu-*
ral disposition is inclined to self-righteousness or grandiosity...". And, the
next following paragraph offers another perspective of this same self-
righteousness: *"...another wonderful excuse... [to avoid Step Four because]*
our present anxieties and troubles are caused by the behaviour of other

---

[59] *Alcoholics Anonymous*, p. 63.
[60] *"Pride, leading to self-justification... spurred by conscious or unconscious fears, is the basic*
breeder of most human difficulties, the chief block to true progress." Twelve Steps and Twelve
Traditions, p. 48.
[61] *Twelve Steps and Twelve Traditions*, p. 44.
[62] Ibid. This, and the uncited quotations following it, are from p. 45.
[63] *Twelve Steps and Twelve Traditions*, p. 46.

people." [Blaming] The members of this group are generally blind to their liabilities, and think they need no inventory, or at best, have a very short list of defects.

The nature of self-righteousness and blame requires a belief in personal superiority and/or innocence. Whether they admit it or not, self-righteous types cling desperately to their (always exaggerated) good qualities, and avoid any sincere examination or admission of the ubiquitous nature of their own defects. From their point of view, there's no need for detailed self-examination—everything wrong is, for the most part, someone else's fault.

The metaphor used at Step Four is "a business inventory", one object of which is *"to disclose damaged or unsalable goods, to get rid of them promptly and without regret."*[64] If you interpret this from a psychological perspective, rather than a spiritual one, it's then easy to view the metaphor as incomplete or unbalanced. A "pop-psychology and self-esteem" protocol would require a person to recast the instructions and reasonably justify the addition of an inventory of character assets—even though "assets" are noticeably *not* mentioned. A list of character assets has no spiritually authentic reason for righteous types at Step Four.[65]

Psychologically, the metaphor of a business inventory is easily seen as incomplete; but the AA book isn't intended to have a psychological perspective. The step is to facilitate being closer to a higher power, as you understand this, not for psychological integration. When the business inventory metaphor is contemplated from a *spiritual* perspective, nothing needs to be added. A Spiritual life isn't concerned with fairness or psychological recovery.

Generally, people who advocate listing assets in Step Four, without regard for the qualifier of temperament, are in the grandiose or righteous category described earlier. That's why they insist on including them. Challenging their own arrogance by *not* listing their assets is the related exercise in humility and that brings them in line with spiritual principles.

However, should you be generally melancholy and depressive, a list of your assets would be advisable; but here too, listing assets won't bring you closer to God. It does, however, create some relief of the ongoing despair of being temperamentally depressed. The assets list offers a balance in self-perception, but only for the melancholy types. That balance allows for energy and interest to examine their defects, and *that* brings them in line with spiritual principles.

---

[64] *Alcoholics Anonymous*, p. 64.
[65] Step Eleven does refer to addicts being mindful of their successes (but some restrictions apply). The reasons for assets being included at Step Eleven are notably different than at Step Four.

So, the two general types are "melancholy" (everything is my fault), or "self-righteous" (everything is someone else's fault). Each temperament is offered different counsel to get out of their inaccurate perceptions, at which point they can then address Step Four with the thoroughness required. Notice which type usually applies to you, and study the strategy the book describes to overcome your inability to be thorough in completing Step Four. The business inventory metaphor is from a spiritual perspective and needs nothing added to it.

Recall that in Step Two, honesty, open-mindedness, and willingness were for a specific type of spiritual newcomer; and that HOW, used outside of Step Two, contains a built-in opportunity to procrastinate. The same theme of using something out of context, and the subsequent danger of misapplying it, applies to the list of assets. For those who tend to be grandiose or self-righteous, listing assets in Step Four is taking an instruction out of context. [Step Eleven mentions noting assets at the end of the day. Psychology and self-esteem groups promote being aware of assets and strengths. These are valuable in their place, but their place is not Step Four .

Some addicts are phasic—they'll switch between self-righteous and depressive for long periods, and others will be in so much chaos they'll be in either mode at any given moment. If you are in this category of alternating/erratic focus between melancholy and self-righteous, it will help to go back to Step Two. Reflect on your attitude towards spirituality, and again disarm your spiritual misgivings. Enhance your faith, which may take months. Be patient.[66] Over time, with thoughtful self-examination at Step Two, you will notice more stability in your spiritual devotion. Then, when a new spiritual heliotropism brings you back to Step Four, you will be less erratic and have more success in attending to the tasks at hand.

A Change in Focus

In all the years you acted out, as a general rule, you talked about how good (or innocent) you were and complained about everybody else—with an exception for whomever your present company was. At the same time, you managed to mention your good qualities, proclaim the other person's guilt, or remind whomever would listen that you were certainly a Victim in the whole mess of Your Life. You were too short, or too tall; you were not rich, or so rich people only loved you for your money; you had too much hair, or it was too straight, or too wavy, or the wrong color; or you had

---

[66] Addicts act in very complex and individually unique patterns—their addictions fingerprint. Because of this, being patient with yourself is imperative. Impatience never allows for contemplation, which is essential to unravel the subtle ways you cheat on your commitment to spirituality and a higher power. Spirituality suffers at the hands of impatience, however slight.

mean parents. You complained you had big feet, were born into a minority group (or into a majority group and complained about the backlash against you for that), or you complained that someone else was complaining about something that they really shouldn't be complaining about. It was always something.

Sadly, that sounds a lot like twelve-step programs today—the gossip, the blaming, and complaining about everything imaginable are not only vicious, but decidedly unspiritual. In Step Four this focus is changed. You cannot properly complete Step Four and remain a Victim at the same time. You must write specifically about your instincts and your responsibility, and what eventually will need to be fixed in you (by you).

Earlier I mentioned the metaphor of a business inventory. *"We did exactly the same thing with our lives. We took stock honestly. First, we searched out the flaws in our make-up which caused our failure. Being convinced that self, manifested in various ways, was what had defeated us, we considered its common manifestations."*[67] "Flaws in our make-up" implies much more than resentments. It's described in the next sentence as *"self, manifested in various ways"*, meaning selfishness: having your ego put you first in a way that's dishonest, self-serving, or harmful to others. This wears many masks,[68] but the common manifestations are generally classified as seven deadly sins.[69] Each character defect is a demonstration of selfishness—behaviours and beliefs that are motivated by fear and instincts gone awry. Your instincts gone awry have become your character defects.

Step Four is done after you have become abstinent, and it necessarily requires that the list be about instincts and fears when you were acting out. It would also include defects that interfere with your relationship with a higher power in that period from when you became abstinent up to the point where you complete Step Four. [An important shift in perspective here is: Character defects are commonly thought of as causing yourself or other people problems. More importantly, they are what separate you from a sincere relationship with your higher power.]

Notice that there are no grounds for the exclusion of any resentment. The AA textbooks do not suggest that because you may have been resentful at someone, but aren't now, you have a reason to exclude it. Often people in twelve-step programs will stop being mad when those whom they perceive have hurt them make an amend. Or, if the addict is the person hurt, and never receives an amend, they may magnanimously announce that they have let the resentment go—they've "forgiven" the offender. Of course,

---

[67] *Alcoholics Anonymous*, p. 64.
[68] For a definition of harmful, refer to *Twelve Steps and Twelve Traditions*, p. 80.
[69] Ibid., p. 48.

they mention to several people how so-and-so hurt them (gossiping), and that they've let go of their resentment (bragging).

Part one of your Step Four is to examine your instincts gone awry, that exist underneath resentments and character defects (past or present). Because you believe you're "over" a resentment is not a reason to exclude it from the list. There is still a wealth of self-awareness available from that. Avoiding insight by shirking thoroughness is expensive.

The author(s) used ordinary words to describe spiritual principles,[70] and so the words should be taken at face value. Resentment is defined as being *"angry, sore, burned up,"* and having a grudge *("grudge list")*.[71] Resentment is given a broad definition. Don't create a self-serving definition of resentment that allows you to avoid work and responsibility. I've heard many confusing and narrow definitions of resentment; here's four of them:

- Resentments are feelings like anger that last a long time. If they don't last a long time, then they're not resentments (followed by the debate over what "a long time" means).
- Resentments are angry-type feelings that are "bigger" than angry feelings.
- Resentments are emotions that are more than being mad and recur over the same things; and,
- Resentments are the "more important" angry feelings.

This esoteric babble is rooted in insecurity and fear and represents shallow spiritual commitment. It's modifying the original program to avoid self-examination and hard work because the more exotic the definition, the shorter the list. The book advises that generally, resentment, whether present or past, is feeling angry, sore, burned up, or having a grudge. That's going to make for a *long* list. (There's great spiritual opportunity in thoroughness.)

You have the instructions for Step Four, but at what point in your life do you start? This work is in relation to your addiction, not childhood trauma. It would seem obvious, then, that you would start your list at about the time you started to drink or act out.

One of the more "endearing" traits addicts have is they're notoriously brilliant at selective remembering. One significant reason for doing what I'm going to suggest, which may seem like tedious nonsense (but is compliant with the instructions) is it counteracts selective remembering. Only you can call yourself to task on your spiritual journey, so enjoy your Step Four-

---

[70] *Alcoholics Anonymous,* p. 93.
[71] Ibid., pp. 64, 65.

stroll down memory lane and have fun with this. Be willing, patient, and thorough. It will pay off.

To begin: Let's assume you were born in 1960, your primary addiction is alcohol, and you started drinking when you were thirteen. At the top of the first page write "13/1973"; on the next, "14/1974"; on the next, "15/1975"; and so on, until you are as old as you presently are. Allow yourself at least one page per year. Maintaining chronological order offers advantages and insights that aren't available otherwise.

Next: Write a list of everything and everyone in your life, from each particular year of your life, on the page that represents that year. What I mean is, you would write a list on page "13/1973" of *everyone* you can remember from that year, even if you liked them and weren't mad. Put them on the list. I'm not changing the instructions in the original literature, I'm showing you how to be painstaking and thorough; which means honest. We'll get to your resentments soon enough.

So, at the top of the page noted "13/1973," write the names of *everyone* you can remember who was in your life at that time: friends, enemies, teachers, family members, relatives, neighbors, classmates, bosses, coworkers, cops, lawyers, pets (yours or other people's)—literally *every* person. If you can't remember their names, write "the girl with the blue dress" or "the boy with the green shoes". Write down literally *everyone* you can remember, whether you were mad at them or not, when you were thirteen.

Include places and institutions that were a part of your life in that year such as cities, neighborhoods, houses, apartments, camps, cottages, hospitals, social clubs, restaurants, vehicles, jobs, churches, schools (reform or otherwise), government agencies, courthouses, the police, and the legal profession. And finally, include principles—the ideas, traditions, and rules that influenced your life at that time, like honesty, Christmas, capital punishment, immigration policies, income tax, traffic laws, being polite, bus schedules, insurance, religion, birthdays, fidelity, monogamy, divorce, adoption, probation, parole, seat belt and helmet laws, curfews, child-support payments, alimony, smoking by-laws, school grading policies, homework, the age of majority, and voting.

Do this list in detail for each year (one page per year) of your life. It isn't necessary to duplicate people from year to year, like family members. For each successive age, add new items that weren't listed previously. When you've finished one age, go to the next age. The same person or item will recur at different ages. There's no need to duplicate entries unless there's some notable change in circumstance, such as someone who was in your life when you were seventeen and disappeared for years, then showed up again when you were thirty-one; or you may have been angry with child-support payments as a teenager because one parent wasn't paying them, and then again at thirty-eight because as an adult you had to pay them. Principles and people will affect us differently at different ages.

This part of the exercise is about creating a complete autobiographical list. You might write two hundred names for one year and only twenty-seven for the next year. Don't omit anyone, any place, or any principle. If you can't remember names, write a brief description to identify who they are. Don't be concerned with not remembering everything; just painstakingly note whatever you do remember. Be very thorough and for now don't be concerned with resentments. It's important to take your time. Be patient. This is a voluntary labor of love, which is true spiritual devotion.

Avoid pressure, impatience, and competition with some imaginary standard of performance, or with what someone else has told you about their work. You will trigger memories and have to go back and add names. Challenge your selective remembering. From one (p)age to another, if there's some special change in circumstance, enter a name on the list again. *Thoroughness and great detail is imperative.* At this stage this is a simple exercise of making a *long* autobiographical list.

If you think I'm suggesting tedious nonsense, challenge yourself on that spiritually limiting thought. This does not have to be painful. If you're angry for having feelings—sadness, love, loneliness, sexual feelings—they go on the resentment list too; so does being mad at me for suggesting this degree of detail.

Continue in this manner up to the present, ending with the people, places, and principles of your life today. When you've finished your autobiographical list, you may have well over a thousand entries. Now what? Consider writing the list out neater, keeping it in general chronological order, and leaving three empty lines between each entry. You will then have a neat, very *long* list of your whole life. Make a copy and keep it in a safe place; you'll need it later.

Now, from the beginning, go slowly through the list, reflecting on each entry, and cross off those entries that you weren't (or aren't) mad at or resentful towards, or that you didn't (don't) have a grudge against. If you once had, or still have, any resentment or grudge at all, old or new, big or little, past or present, don't cross them off. The reason for writing down everyone/everything is so you reduce the chance of selective remembering.

Be rigorously honest. If you do this sincerely, it can be very emotionally rewarding to see how many entries you crossed off. Your resentments and character defects were selective. You very carefully choose who and what to resent. Later, when you realize how and why you resented some and not others, you will put that insight to good spiritual use. Remind yourself this is about honoring your decision at Step Three.

You may have resented someone, but since the incident, believe you have forgiven them. This, most often, means you haven't really forgiven them, but the grudge is dim because of time past. The former resentment is often easily triggered awake, and therefore, more sincere spiritual work is required. Regardless of this, if you had a resentment and now don't, the person or principle remains on your list. There are no exclusions for "former" resentments.

If you follow the process I've outlined, you will notice that for the early phase of your acting out, you probably crossed off more than you left on. Then later, as your addiction worsened, you probably had more resentments and grudges. Later still, in abstinence, you started crossing off more names than you left on.

The frequency and intensity of resentments (of defects) is a reflection of your struggle to control situations and people. If you easily participate in resentment, gossip, anger, bitterness, dishonesty, petulance, sadness, etc. that means you're still acting out in addictions; and/or you're very insecure and trying to dominate your environment. You will notice when your addiction went out of hand, not by the amount you drank, which is relatively unimportant, but by insight into your character. *Your addiction isn't in your acting out it's in your flawed spiritual character.*

Step Four requires you change your perceptions of life *from* a preoccupation with what you did—hurt yourself, proclaim your innocence, blame others, take their inventory, and justify, *to* a reflection of who you are—your insecurities, and instincts gone awry. (This relates to the information in the earlier section, Conditions Didn't Do Anything.)

This is where people must realign their fundamental operating principles from blame and dishonesty to responsibility and truth—the second of three major value shifts. This transition begins in earnest here, and it's the genesis of the awareness of an addict's self-imposed crisis. This is not a weekend exercise. Do *not* do your grudge list during the advertisements in a movie. Your commitment to spirituality is [ideally] to work patiently and diligently for as long as it takes. Any impatience or pressure to hurry, lack of thoroughness, or changing this in any way is fatal to the process.

Many addicts ask about including resentments regarding their addiction. Yes, these could go on the list, but there are some important cautions. After having the flu, you may be regretful you missed a party because of your illness—having an illness can be inconvenient—but you don't necessarily *resent* yourself for being sick. It's reasonable to briefly regret the fact you missed a party, but that doesn't mean feeling guilty and resentful. (If you do, find a therapist.)

It's crucial that addicts "get it" they have an illness that shows up externally as irresponsibility, self-destruction, and blame. The symptoms are very often what they resent—they were dishonest, angry, afraid, or made "bad" decisions. Symptoms aren't optional, so why should addicts be resentful of themselves when these symptoms are part of the disease? Here's where the importance of getting Step One "right" becomes more obvious.

The pressure of socially imposed guilt is significantly reduced once addicts understand it's an issue of disease, not morality. Dishonesty, or any other symptom, wasn't a conscious, intellectual choice. When addicts take this to heart, no guilt or resentment will accrue from symptomatic behaviour. Once people getting recovered sincerely understand that they had a disease, that it wasn't their "fault" (nor was it anyone else's), they feel sad and have regrets, but the guilt disappears and they don't resent themselves. If you feel noticeably resentful or guilty about your addiction, you very likely misperceive the nature of "illness".

So, regarding Step Four, should you resent yourself, list these specific resentments separately and reflect on them carefully. Review the list of symptoms in Chapter 2 in this book, read Step One in *Twelve Steps and Twelve Traditions*, and read More About Alcoholism in *Alcoholics Anonymous*. Reflect on the spiritual nature of the disease. Realize that the behaviours that you resent are more than likely derivative of the symptoms, and not something that you "chose" to do.[72]

Another tactic that must be considered is evasiveness by exaggerating or minimizing your defects, resentments, and progress. If you convince yourself that you used to kill people and pillage the countryside, and now only beat someone up every few months, it makes for a remarkable improvement-story: "I'm so much better than I used to be, so I don't really need to look at myself *that* thoroughly."

Watch you don't exaggerate in glorious detail how much you've improved, or minimize to triviality your defects and fears. You may impress yourself, but these tactics are used as justifications for shallow self-examination and intermittent abusive behaviour. When reflecting on your list, watch for embellishment or minimizing. Rigorous honesty is also a euphemism for accuracy.

Let's assume that the first list I recommended—remembering everything and everyone year by year—has 1,987 entries. After crossing off all the people, places, and principles where you had no resentments or grudges, you're left with 456 entries. This means there are 456 people and principles

---

[72] Certainly there are times when addicts or alcoholics deliberately/consciously lied, and they must always hold themselves accountable; but underneath this, the addiction requires dishonesty, no differently than malaria requires a fever.

you are angry about or have a grudge against. If you're overwhelmed by this apparently huge number, remind yourself it's just information about how resentful you were. Notice how many you crossed off. But, if on the other hand, you've crossed off 1,976 and end up with only 11 entries remaining on your list, there's something amiss. In this case, find a wise, spiritual mentor. Reflect carefully on your emotional past, and you'll (probably) need some professional help as you work through this.

You must end up with an accurate list of resentments and grudges. If it's cluttered, you're probably going to balk at this, but, keeping them in approximate chronological order, write a neater grudge list with four or five lines between each entry. This becomes column one, as shown in *Alcoholics Anonymous*.[73] Examine each entry carefully and for each one, ask why you were mad: What did they do that you resented? Itemize and note what you believed the external cause of your grudge was. This will become column two of your list. Don't use ditto marks. Be honest, brief, and thorough.

And finally, *Alcoholics Anonymous* refers to five instincts: self-esteem, personal security, ambitions, personal relations, and sex relations.[74] Think about these instincts and reflect on them in relation to your anger and character defects in general. Your fears and insecurities relating to these instincts, and how those fears interfered with their natural expression, is the root cause of resentments and grudges.[75] Your task is to identify your fears and insecurities in relation to these instincts, *for every entry on the list*. This information becomes the third column. Be very specific about how your instincts were threatened. Every entry gets the same devoted attention. If you're not willing to work in the detail *Alcoholics Anonymous* suggests, evidently you didn't really come to believe (at Step Two), or you didn't understand the nature of your commitment (at Step Three).

Here, for the first time in this process, you begin to intimately understand how you created the crises in your life. You began with whom and what you were mad at, then noted what was "done" to you, and ended by paying detailed attention to how *your* instincts had gone awry through *your* fears and insecurities. Character defects are only the "entrance points" that allow you to delve deep inside your personality. Resentments themselves play a pretty minor part in all of it.

Invest a lot of time in this; be diligent and at the same time be patient. Don't be obsessed and fanatical. Do a half-an-hour a day, or an hour every other day, until it's finished; take breaks and continue to live your life while you do this.

---

[73] *Alcoholics Anonymous,* p. 65.
[74] Remember, the authors were spiritual, not scientific, in their use of the word instinct. Don't quibble about this. This is a process in getting recovered, not a lecture on genetics or biology.
[75] *Alcoholics Anonymous,* p. 65.

In all times of punishing others, trying to get your own way, or argu-ing—which are the behaviours of coveting resentments and defects, the victor only appears to win. Needing to win; being pleased that someone else has beat another person; or being pleased that someone you don't like has lost, must all be abandoned. Triumph is always short-lived and empty be-cause the need to dominate is always motivated by fear and insecurity.[76] Winning doesn't make the insecurity go away, it only camouflages it. This is a truth about a Spiritual life, but eliminating the underlying insecurity is only available if the work is done as outlined. Struggling to control anyone is a fool's game, regardless of its disguise.[77]

This part of your Step Four points out your irresponsibility, which is related to your instincts gone awry. When contemplated spiritually, you expose the insecurity that lies underneath your efforts to dominate and blame.[78] Any other model of a Step Four won't dovetail with the intended, long-term spiritual result. Remember: *"We went back through our lives. Nothing counted but thoroughness and honesty."*[79]

There Are Laws Here

The laws of physics and the mechanics of material determine how things are made. If people want planes to fly, or water to freeze, there are rules. The laws of nature determine these processes, which are not negotia-ble. "Nature" isn't concerned with convenience. The properties of material, the truths about mathematics, and the laws of physics and chemistry are unyielding. People obey these laws, or planes don't fly and water doesn't freeze. If we want any mechanical endeavor to be successful, we must fig-ure out the rules of physics (nature), and follow them.

Regarding spiritual regeneration, this is admirably stated by Manly P. Hall: *"The unfolding of* [a person's] *spiritual nature is as much an exact science as astronomy, medicine or jurisprudence. To accomplish this end religions were primarily established; and out of religion have come science,*

---

[76] Proselytizing is the intellectual contest of trying to convert someone into another value sys-tem or doctrine. It's insecurity and arrogance disguised under the illusion of religious or moral or intellectual superiority.

[77] Keep this in context. I'm referring to adults in the spiritual and judicious course of their lives.

[78] Winning, dominating others and arguing all have damaging consequences. A spiritual being considers actions and their consequences far beyond the immediate result. There are Primary, Secondary, and Tertiary consequences to be considered. A person [an addict] does something: (1) What are the consequences to themselves? (Primary); (2) What are the directly related consequences to people close to them? (Secondary); and, (3) What are the consequences to the community, their careers, to the world/the environment? (Tertiary). The Doctrine of Competi-tion (or of selfish self-interest) continues to exist when people consider the consequences only at the primary level, which by definition, is selfish.

[79] *Alcoholics Anonymous,* p. 65.

philosophy, and logic as methods whereby this divine purpose might be realized."[80]

All spiritual transformation, whether it begins from within an unfulfilling, psychological outlook on life, or within the dislocated/self-annihilating position of addictions, has a required sequence of tasks, and a *non-modifiable* process and structure. The entire process of regenerating yourself into a more spiritual person is resolutely mandated by the inherent requirements of spirituality. There are laws here.

If I were to personify spirituality and nature, I would say, "Nature" doesn't care that making planes fly is complicated and expensive. If people want planes to fly and want to travel quickly, they have to follow the rules and pay the price. Likewise, Nature doesn't care that transformation or regeneration is arduous and time consuming. If people want to experience the bliss of a truly spiritual life, or if addicts want to save their life, they must pay the price of following these guidelines exactly.

How to be obedient to the laws of spiritual transformation—how to effect that change—is brilliantly presented and explained in *Alcoholics Anonymous* and *Twelve Steps and Twelve Traditions*. That process can not be altered in its content or sequence without dire consequences.

Two-At-A-Time Programming

People getting recovered often use expressions like: "When I was doing Steps Two and Three," or "I'm worried about Steps Eight and Nine." This pairing usually happens with "two and three", "four and five", "six and seven", and "eight and nine". When any of the first nine steps are perceived as yoked together—seeing any two steps as somehow joined in execution—problems are created. These pairings are pervasive, and based on the perception that these steps are somehow more connected to each other, than as say, three is to six, or five is to eight.

There is a crucial relationship between the innate paradigm for spiritual transformation and the order of the first nine steps. In this paradigm, any step is just as intrinsically connected to any of the other eight steps, as it is to one that appears adjacent to it. There are no preferential pairings, and creating these pairings causes serious problems. Steps One to Nine should not be viewed in pairs (they are independent of each other) or done out of sequence. If they are "paired up" (like 4 n' 5), or done out of sequence, you'll be working at odds with the paradigm of spiritual transformation. For the addict getting recovered, the results are disastrous.

---

[80] *The Secret Teachings of All Ages*, Manly P. Hall, Tarcher/Penguin, 2003, p. 120. Also: See the quote from *Isis Unveiled*, H.P. Blavatsky, cited at p. 5.

No one can effectively appreciate the nuances, or negotiate through the requirements, or absorb the spiritual tone of any step while carrying the intellectual or emotional burden of anticipating any other step. Each regeneration step (the first nine) can only be accomplished and absorbed within you, as it is spiritually intended, when it's addressed individually, in sequence, and independent of *all* the others. Getting recovered is not possible if, during any one step, you puzzle over the intricacies of any future step, or have failed to acquire the faith, insight, and spiritual grounding that accrues from doing the previous step(s) painstakingly and independently.

It's spiritually untenable to anticipate, plan for, discuss, review, analyze, attempt, puzzle over, meditate on, or contemplate any of the first nine steps in pairs or "together". [Steps Ten, Eleven, and Twelve are remarkably different—they're steps of spiritual maintenance, and therefore inseparable from each other; done simultaneously, but more about that later.]

So, the first part of Step Four was about the relationship between resentments (character defects) and fears in relation to your instincts gone awry. There's a paragraph that is the segue into the second part of your Step Four. It begins: *"Notice that the word fear…"*.[81] This paragraph takes your new-found awareness of the fear and insecurity inherent in resentments and expands your focus to identify *all* your fears. Fears must be thoroughly reviewed by *"putting them on paper, even though we had no resentment in connection with them."*[82] On a new sheet start listing all of your fears, whether or not you had resentments in connection with them. Begin at the time or shortly before you started acting out.

Are or were you afraid of being poor? Are or were you afraid of Spiders? Afraid of… self-awareness, responsibility, honesty, kindness, fire, flying? Dying (suddenly *or* slowly)? Being old? Being alone? Eating different food? Beautiful women? Handsome men? Anger? Assertive people? Rich people? God? Sex? Intimacy? Commitment? Teachers? Snakes? Drowning? Dancing? Doctors? The police? Afraid of water? The dark? Bugs? Elevators? Make a list of *all* your fears, which includes "being intimidated by…". Include a brief reference to the instinctual fears you listed in column three of the previous exercise.

If you're too embarrassed to admit them all, or annoyed at the thoroughness required, you've missed the point that this is a labour of devotion. Go back to Step Two and review your commitment to spirituality, and then reconsider your decision at Step Three. The solution is in spiritual obedience.

---

[81] *Alcoholics Anonymous*, p. 67.
[82] Ibid., p. 68.

Twelve-step recovery programs are *not* therapy and should not be used as such. Be very cautious about probing into fears from infancy and childhood without professional support; and avoid discussing childhood or abuse issues, or relationship issues in your recovery group or with your sponsor. They're not trained, it's not a part of their job description, and it isn't necessary for spiritual exploration. For these, seek out an experienced counsellor who is wisely empathetic to your participation in a twelve-step program. If you've gotten over some of your fears, include them anyway. Old fears are worthy of examination and can often offer substantial insight.

And now for more patience and self-discipline, from *Alcoholics Anonymous*: *"We asked ourselves why we had them. Wasn't it because self-reliance failed us?"*[83] Contemplate this, and then write something down beside each fear.

Notice that in this section of the AA text, which applies to fears and Step Four, there is no guarantee or implied expectation that by this process, all your fears will go away. They *may* be reduced, or they *may* go away, but escaping your fears is not the specific goal—there are two more important goals. The first is to be completely honest about your entire inner experience. There is relief in microscopic honesty.[84] The second is to gracefully and gratefully depend on a higher power; to enroll prayer and meditation as ways to embrace your fears and still have a fulfilling life. This exercise has a spiritual, not psychological, focus.

Getting recovered is a huge undertaking. Carefully reflecting on your fears is an essential, on-going spiritual discipline. Be patient.

Nine Sex Questions

The third and final part of Step Four is *"…about sex. Many of us needed an overhauling there. But above all, we tried to be sensible… ."*[85] It says that with opinions running to extremes *"We want to stay out of this controversy,"* that: *"We do not want to be the arbiter of anyone's sex conduct."*[86] In essence, twelve-step participants are told to mind their own business about other people's sex lives. You are to closely examine your own sexual behaviour and not the behaviour of others.

Make a complete list of *all* the people you have had sex relations with. You can refer back to the extensive autobiographical list you kept a copy of;

---

[83] *Alcoholics Anonymous*, p. 68.
[84] *Conscious Loving*, Gay Hendricks, Ph.D., & Kathlyn Hendricks, Ph.D., Bantam Books, 1992, p. 111.
[85] *Alcoholics Anonymous*, p. 68, 69.
[86] Ibid. p. 69. This peremptorily eliminates any rules about newcomers in relationships. Note the item on p. 111 of *Twelve Steps and Twelve Traditions* about giving advice that addicts aren't competent to give.

your sex partners' names will be there. If you've ever masturbated, put yourself on your sex-list.[87] This doesn't mean masturbation is wrong, it means it's a part of following the instructions and it's being examined. Some people will have a long list and others will have a short list.

There are two general categories of sexual relationships. These are:

- those people you knew: wives, husbands, longer-term partners, boyfriends, and girlfriends. You may have only been with them for a short while, but you knew them. List these individually; and,
- the group of nameless strangers you "woke up" with. You don't know personally the one-night stands and mystery partners. Make an honest estimate of how many mystery partners there were and write at the bottom of your list: Mystery Partners – 142, or 6, or whatever number you come up with.

Don't take the easy way out by lumping as many as you can from the first group into the second group. Don't underestimate the number of Mystery Partners to conceal shame, or overestimate the number to impress anyone (especially yourself). If any particular Mystery Partner stands out as startlingly different from the others in the mystery group, list that one separately. The fact that this person stands out, for whatever reason, affords them special consideration.

Some addicts will be ashamed they have only a very few names, and some will be ashamed they have hundreds. Nothing counts but thoroughness and honesty. Leave at least five or six empty lines between each name on your list.

What I'm about to suggest is in line with thoroughness, responsibility, and spiritual principles. There are two types of "sex partner" that are frequently overlooked. (1) There are people who've lived with obsessive fantasies about others. They've invested significant emotional and sexual energy in fantasizing and masturbating about someone: a movie star, a

---

[87] If, as an addict, you acted out with animals, children, or were involved in incest, pornography, prostitution, or maybe adultery, these must be included in your Step Four. REMEMBER the qualifying guideline (p. 74 *Alcoholics Anonymous*) when approaching Step Five: be mindful of *"Perhaps our doctor or psychologist..."* and review the paragraph on page 79 of *Alcoholics Anonymous* that begins, *"Although these reparations take innumerable forms..."*. It is wise to hire a therapist for these parts of your Step 5. It is within the guidelines. Take responsible action; don't evade. This is essential so you can complete later spiritual tasks within yourself, within the steps, and as a recovered person helping others. I know this may seem tremendously difficult, possibly beyond your comprehension; however, you are capable of doing this if you approach the instructions with patience, *professional support*, faith, abstinence, and a relationship with a higher power.

neighbor's spouse, one of their co-workers. Or, (2) they may have come dangerously close to having sex with someone and the result would have been particularly disastrous: *almost* having sex with a relative, a boss, or the spouse of a close friend. It would be wise to include these sex-relationships for two reasons: (i) there is much to be learned from these demonstrations of sexual insecurity; and (ii), it will help to prevent a recurrence of this.

When your list of names is complete, begin reviewing your sexual conduct. *"Where had we been selfish, dishonest, or inconsiderate? Whom had we hurt? Did we unjustifiably arouse jealousy, suspicion, or bitterness? Where were we at fault, what should we have done instead? We got this all down on paper and looked at it."*[88] This requires that you ask, and answer, nine questions about every sexual relationship you were in—for every person in the Ones-You-Know section (which would include the obsessive fantasies and dangerous close-calls), and one general answer for the group of Mystery Partners. Here are the questions again:

1. Where was I selfish?
2. Where was I dishonest?
3. Where was I inconsiderate?
4. Whom did I hurt?
5. Did I unjustifiably arouse jealousy?
6. Did I unjustifiably arouse suspicion?
7. Did I unjustifiably arouse bitterness?
8. Where was I at fault?; and,
9. What should I have done instead?

It is crucial that you answer these questions about every sexual relationship in your life, in relation to your addiction. If you've been selfish, dishonest, or inconsiderate; or aroused jealousy, suspicion, or bitterness, in a sexual relationship, somebody has been hurt. Carefully examine each one, write a brief answer, and don't use ditto marks. If sexual abuse or rape is a part of your history, or if you struggle with your sexual preference or orientation, or S & M, or fetishes, then your sponsor, meetings, and the steps, are *not* the venues to resolve this. Include them on your Step Four, but share these concerns with competent, professional help.

Consider that the people you harmed through sexual irresponsibility may not have been just the people you had sex with. You may have emotionally, indirectly harmed the children of your sex partner (or your own children), friends, co-workers, or relatives. Did your sexual acting out harm a business or a group?[89] This is an exercise in awareness about harm you have caused. It's fine to be brief, but be thorough.

---

[88] *Alcoholics Anonymous*, p. 69.
[89] In this book, in the section A Change In Focus there is a footnote about Primary, Secondary, and Tertiary consequences. The ripple effect of irresponsible sex is considerable.

For this final part of Step Four, you may want to list yourself as some-one you hurt by irresponsible sexuality—contracting a disease, ending up in jail, being divorced. Should this be the case, at the end, note the harm your sexual behaviour did to you. This isn't to itemize your resentments and fears about sex (which should be already noted in the first two parts of this step). Listing the harmful consequences to yourself from your sexual irre-sponsibility, which is the result of your character defects controlling your sexuality, and then deciding what you might have done instead, contributes to creating values regarding a spiritual expression of sexuality.[90]

Without including everyone *and* answering the first eight questions you cannot intelligently and thoroughly answer question nine. The answer to #9 is where you start to create new values about your sexuality (governed by the five spiritual principles that are embodied in the maintenance steps).

This is a huge undertaking, much of it repetitious, and for some, em-barrassing. However, notice in the way outlined here, which is an explanation of the original twelve steps, it becomes a moral inventory (not a list of bad things), and is fear-less (done largely without fear). Nothing counts but thoroughness and honesty. Take your time, get it all down on paper, and keep a record of what you should have done instead, because *"In this way we tried to shape a sane and sound ideal for our future sex life. We subjected each relation to this test—was it selfish or not?"*[91]

Morality

You're creating new values and incorporating spiritual principles that will govern your future sexual conduct. Neither of the AA texts subscribes to any religiously oriented moral position. They do, however, subscribe to spiritual principles that are to become foremost in *all* areas of your life.

We each have different desires and preferences for how we express our sexuality. Some people like oral sex, and some don't. Some people pre-fer missionary position sex; others don't. Some people like to have sex only in the bedroom and others enjoy different places; some like tickling and giggling; some don't. When you answer the first eight questions, you iden-

---

[90] Because of "modern" culture's notions of sexuality (repression, orientation, prejudice, gen-der stereotyping, etc.), and the powerful dogma of sexually repressive and righteous religions, some readers may believe that there's no such thing as spiritually based sexual expression. Other people may believe that spiritually based sex must be boring, or occurs only in the mis-sionary position, or exclude homosexuality—or any number of other repressions and prohibitions. This is definitely not the case regarding Step Four in the original twelve steps, and not the case regarding sexuality in general. Spirituality only requires responsibility and adherence to spiritual principles as ongoing parts of your sexual expression. There's an impor-tant commentary on sex and religion in John Shelby Spong's book *Rescuing the Bible from Fundamentalism*, HarperCollins, 1992, beginning at page 1.

[91] *Alcoholics Anonymous*, p. 69.

tify the problems that arose in the way you conducted yourself sexually (not necessarily in your sexuality, but in your conduct). Question nine identifies what you should have done instead. This creates your own standards for a spiritually based sexual relationship.[92]

For example: Jane really likes and enjoys tease-and-tickle sex, and is sexually assertive. In her Step Four, she identified the many misunderstandings and conflicts about this from her past. She learned, by detailed self-examination, how to incorporate spiritual principles in her conduct to avoid conflict. John sees himself and his personal taste as not "adventurous". This is equally wonderful and acceptable. He learned this from his Step Four and knows how to conduct himself to avoid sexual conflict with partners who have different tastes and values. Two other people, Jack and Betty, have learned similar things in their own Step Fours. If these four people meet at a party, they can, with devotion to spiritual principles and what they've discovered in their Step Fours, and regardless of their orientation, pair off (or not) in a respectful way and avoid sexual conflict.

Within the original twelve steps, there is no imposition of opinion about "acceptable" sexual values.[93] People develop their own standards of sexual expression. There are no guidelines regarding heterosexual or homosexual sex, length of sobriety, frequency, body oil, chocolate syrup, celibacy, masturbation, lights on or off, or kitchen table or not. There *are* guidelines about the commitment to abstinence, and the adoption and adherence to spiritual principles in the expression of your sexuality, but only so you are responsible, and you stop hurting yourself and others. Step Four is brilliant in the way it achieves this for each individual. There's no imposition of "morality". From page 69 of *Alcoholics Anonymous*: *"We do not want to be the arbiter of anyone's sex conduct."*[94]

---

[92] Too often, problems in sexual conduct are incorrectly coupled to problems in sexuality. The elemental, instinctual nature of sexuality, which is similar to the elemental nature of spirituality, requires that it (and spirituality) embody a quality of attracting problems into them which are unrelated and don't belong there. For example: You may think you have a "sex problem" but really, the problem has to do with something else and it's being expressed in the dynamic of sex. This often renders Step Four (or therapy) ineffective when problems with sexual conduct (anger, shame, competition, greed, betrayal), aren't effectively disengaged from issues of sexuality (orientation chaos, incest, fetishes). And: In as much as Step Four is about conduct, ethics, and spirituality, there is the related and horrendously complicated phenomenon of sex addiction. Sex addiction immediately tangles into an almost Gordian Knot, the already complex issues of conduct, sexuality, culture, and spirituality. After establishing abstinence, it takes a minimum of two years of on-going regular cross-over work in therapy, with *continued* abstinence, to extricate a recovering sex addict from the self-annihilating mess of sex addiction into a comfortable awareness of respectful, self-defining choice.

[93] Bear in mind this is about consenting adults in the normal course of their life. None of this implies the approval, tacit or otherwise, of abusive, incestuous, or violent behaviour.

[94] If people conduct their lives in a way that you disapprove of; if you notice you are envious, insulted, or offended by their sexual behaviour or their lifestyle in general, do not try to control them. Mind your own business, *don't* gossip or criticize, and quietly move on in your (cont'd)

If you and your present (or any future) partner don't have similar sexual values, don't fight about this. Just say thank you very much, but no thank you. Mind your own business, *don't* gossip, *don't* criticize, and quietly move on in your own life. You may be annoyed you didn't have sex, but that's of no consequence; being angry and mean is.

Spiritual principles, and your sane and sound sexual ideal (meaning the answers to question #9 that was discussed earlier), will now arbitrate your sexual expression before the fact, not after the fact. You will end up with a clear view of your sexuality within the larger context of spiritual principles. This affords a better chance of spiritual harmony as you express the deepest part of your physical existence: your sexuality. Without answering all the questions for each person on your Step Four sex-list, including the ones you swore you'd never tell about, you won't be able to figure out how to avoid conflict and harming others in the future.

One thing that many alcoholics and addicts believe, especially overt relationship and sex addicts, is that as soon as they're aroused physically attracted to someone, they've *got* to do something about it. Know that because you are physically attracted to someone, or just horny, doesn't mean you have to do anything about it. A physical attraction may be only a signal to consider investigating the other person's personality as far as being a potential partner goes (meaning dating). The vast majority of "horny attractions" are notoriously unsuitable for healthy intimacy because of different values, expectations, and life circumstances. One of the interesting things about addicts in general is that they will date someone, break up, and afterwards wonder why they dated the person at all—they didn't even like them. This is one indicator of sex or relationship addiction.

If you're in a long-term committed sexual relationship, and find yourself almost (or actually) acting upon a physical attraction for someone other than your partner, that indicates problems that are probably outside the scope of Step Four. Committing adultery and then leaving your old partner to marry or take up residence with the person you committed adultery with, never legitimizes the adultery. Also, being the unmarried sexual partner of an adulterer is equally irresponsible. Should you believe you must act on sexual impulses, or that you are always turned on/horny, or that flirting and romance with others while you're in a committed relationship is harmless, or that adultery is largely inevitable for you, it would be wise to undertake therapy.

You don't often hear people at twelve-step meetings talking about making their list of fears; it's too embarrassing and not as dramatic as re-

---

own life. If your disagreements and judgments are mean or persistent, that indicates something amiss in you.

sentments. You also don't hear anybody talking about sex in the manner required by Step Four. If they were *that* spiritual about their sexuality, the chances of getting laid would be greatly reduced. A clear understanding of your sexual selfishness, and demanding only of yourself that you express sexuality within the context of the five spiritual principles, is crucial for attaining a self-defined and sincere lifestyle.

These statements are in *Alcoholics Anonymous*: *"When we were finished we considered* [the list] *carefully." "We turned back to the list... ," "Referring to our list again... we resolutely looked... ," "We reviewed our fears... ,"* and *"We reviewed our own conduct... ."*[95] This suggests and makes it obvious this is to be a patient and reflective endeavor. There's a wealth of important self-awareness to be gleaned here. Don't burden yourself with impatience or pressure from *any* source; work steadily and slowly. Don't create anxiety with visions of Step Five.[96]

From *Alcoholics Anonymous*: *"In meditation, we ask God what we should do about each specific matter. The right answer will come, if we want it." "We avoid hysterical thinking or advice."* And further on: *"We earnestly pray for the right ideal, for guidance in each questionable situation... and for the strength to do the right thing."*[97] These three general injunctions apply specifically to sex. Interestingly enough, and sadly, it seems that most addicts aren't willing to pray before they have sex or go on a date. It's very often the furthest thing from their mind. It shouldn't be.

Now you know what they meant by: *"If we have been thorough about our personal inventory, we have written down a lot."* [98] That paragraph outlines what you are now learning—you can begin to comprehend the futility and corruption, and the terrible destructiveness, of your old lifestyle. At this point you are very much a spiritual novice, and only a beginner at self-examination, but at least you're (finally) finished Step Four. Seal all of it in an envelope and give yourself a present; you've worked hard.

---

[95] *Alcoholics Anonymous,* pp. 65, 66, 67, 68, 69, respectively.
[96] There may be conflict with the time restrictions of treatment centres. The mandate of a treatment centre requires restrictions on time, and there are deadlines. I see these institutions as valuable. They do (a) help addicts stabilize, somewhat, in their new lifestyle, (b) initiate a formal course of treatment and education that may create the opportunity for permanent change; and (c), expose the addict to the first few steps at an entry/training level. This is important. It is also important to bear in mind most of these programs are psychologically oriented, and some have a decided religious focus. For the addict getting recovered, treatment centres are only an initial and very brief exposure to the detailed spiritual transformation work that lies ahead. The time restrictions of treatment centres require the initial work be incomplete. Once formal treatment is finished, time limitations regarding the steps are gone. Maintain abstinence *at all costs*, and then begin again at Step One (if necessary), or begin at Step Two, and complete the steps as thoroughly as the original twelve-step program requires.
[97] *Alcoholics Anonymous,* pp. 69, 70, respectively.
[98] Ibid., p. 70.

No One is Disgusting

Notice, the original literature *never* instructs you to write how many disgusting things you did, or how horrible you were. Step Four, and in fact, no part of any of these steps, is about your being disgusting or being bad and these cultural perceptions of addictive behaviour have only a detrimental contribution to make to getting recovered. Step Four has everything to do with instincts gone awry, fears, and sexual selfishness, which are all reasonably routine and not spectacular. This is entirely about how you got yourself into trouble and your self-imposed crisis. [As an aside: If you are not required to write down how horrible, bad, disgusting, or mean you were, then there must be no requirement to talk or brag about these perceptions of your behaviour at meetings.[99]]

This all may seem boring and tedious, which usually means you're annoyed and impatient. Step Four is a labor of spiritual devotion, not an exercise of psychological integration. What is it that makes you bored and impatient? Give yourself a few months for Step Four. You've got nothing to do but be sober for the rest of your life anyway, so you might as well do yourself a favor and take your time.

Redoing a Step Four every year or two, forever, is indicative of being insecure, and always associated with weak faith and substitutes for spirituality. To get out of this cycle, go back to Step Two and unravel the nature of your spiritual defiance. Understand the spiritual intent of getting recovered. There is no psychological intent here. *Believe* that 'How It Works' is true and is personally applicable to you. *Decide* that spiritual endeavor will be the superseding aim of your life. In *Alcoholics Anonymous* and *Twelve Steps and Twelve Traditions* you read again and again that faith did for you what you could not do for yourself.

Sex, God, and Death

Some people subscribe to the belief that there are only three subjects worthy of serious discussion: Sex, God, and Death. People passionately pursue or neurotically avoid sex throughout their lives. People talk, write, and make movies about relationships, sex, and intimacy *ad nauseam*. Regarding God and spirituality: People covet beliefs, kill each other, and debate endlessly all manner of notions and theories. The emotional and

---

[99] Overall, you have written fifteen "columns" of information about yourself: (1) resentments, (2) what the other person did, (3) instincts gone awry, (4) fears, (5) handling fears differently, (6) sex partners, (7) to (14) answering the first eight questions about sexual selfishness, and (15) what you should have done instead. Notice you have devoted only one column of fifteen to resentments (less than 7% of your writing), yet it appears that resentments occupy (cont'd)

physical violence that people inflict on each other and on the earth, justifying this brutality on behalf of "God", is as insane as it is horrific, and *every*one in the world lives with the shame of this. Then there's Death—how near, how far, how sudden, with or without agony, deliberate or accidental, and what (if anything) follows it? There's the self-vilification often experienced when people perceive their death is near and believe their life has been meaningless or wasted. Sex, God, and Death—that's all folks.

I see within the complex simplicity of the original twelve steps, recovered alcoholics and addicts might experience peace and spiritual grace at a very deep level in the expression of their sexuality. They can experience an abiding faith in their relationship with a higher power—in facing any circumstance of life; and they can live with a benign indifference to the appearance of death. This is all available to those twelve-step pilgrims who are willing to work for it, and yet, so few are willing to work.

I have been asked many times: "How often do you do a Step Four?" In addition to my prayers, I make a point to read or study some specific aspect of the original literature, or spirituality and ethics, every day. I quietly reflect on how this does or doesn't apply to me personally. About every two years I take a few days to enjoy carefully rereading *Alcoholics Anonymous* (to page 192), and all of *Twelve Steps and Twelve Traditions*. This reading is to reflect on any new insights or nuances, as I contemplate my own humanness and the amazing grace and harmony of the maintenance steps, where I attempt to live daily. This is a gentle review—I don't repeat any of the first nine steps. In doing this, it has so far never failed to allow me to again experience a deep appreciation for the single most profound blessing I have ever received—the ability to choose spiritual principles and harmony over addictions and death.

Throughout any given day, I notice how I do (or don't) live governed by the maintenance steps and the five spiritual principles. When I fall away from these, I don't castigate myself, or rush back to the beginning and start over. I sharpen the focus of my energy into being completely responsible, make amends where necessary, and quietly mind my own business. Then, such as it is, I get on with the business of my own life. I thoroughly studied Step Four, and painstakingly followed the instructions once—that's enough.

95% of the conversations about Step Four. This exemplifies the quirk of addicts to focus on the theatrical aspect of their life (resentments), to the virtual exclusion of all else.

Chapter 6

Steps Five, Six, and Seven: What I Do With Me

Several Reminders

Thus far, some of what you are reading may well provoke anger or discomfort. This is certainly true when I offer this information through lectures. Keep in mind that challenging yourself, not others, is at the core of all spiritual work, and in the early stages of the process, being upset is the admission price you pay for transformation.

One of the many things you have to accomplish in healing and being spiritual, is to be always cognizant of your rights and, while retaining them for yourself, offer them to others.[1] I've tried to offer them to you in the way I have written this book, and I ask that you offer them to me as you read it. (Respect & Dignity, p. 6.)

As I suggested earlier, when people conduct themselves in a way that offends your sensibilities, or in a way that you "disapprove" of, then mind your own business, don't gossip or criticize, and quietly move on in your own life. Regardless of the degree of joy or horror you experience, your task, as a spiritual pilgrim, is to continuously reach for the most enlightened possibilities in any given situation.[2]

Regardless of any topic under discussion, addicts becoming spiritual are locked into this unalterable fact: Abstinence and sobriety are essential and never negotiable. Everything spiritual created in the recovering addict's life is dependent on complete abstinence from addictions. If you're acting out in any way, in any addiction, you cannot be sincerely spiritual.

In becoming recovered, addicts do not become cured. They cannot return to any acting out behaviour without disastrous consequence. In being recovered, they are only being spiritual as outlined in the five spiritual principles, which are themselves, embodied in the maintenance steps.

Remind yourself that being sincerely spiritual does not necessarily imply the achievement of "mental health", or vice versa. In fact, being

---

[1] Rights, Freedoms, and Values were discussed in Chapter 2.
[2] This view of behaviour and life's circumstances was a comment made by the actor Peter Coyote during a television interview.

sincerely spiritual in a modern culture of technology would have many people doubting your sanity.

When you're confused, slow down. (Go slow anyway.) The relationship between these issues is very subtle and complex. Challenge and question only yourself about your spiritual defiance, impatience, lack of veracity, or reluctance to be obedient to the principles. Notice your reluctance to challenge either your character defects or old, coveted beliefs.

Reread the Manner of Presentation.[3]

Addiction shows up in each of us differently. In some, it shows up as heroin and crime; in others, it's cocaine and prostitution; in others, it's wine and divorces; and in still others, it may be chronic poverty and beer, or tobacco and pornography, cocaine and violence, shopping and sex, or marijuana and television... the list is long. Addictions always show up in at least two blatant ways and one subtle way, and at least one of those three will be a relationship addiction. The purpose of your doing Step One is to figure this out. Identify *your* symptoms, which will be slightly different from the symptoms of others.

The process of exiting your addictions into healthy (and complete) abstinence, completing the steps, and then creating, thinking, and living a sincere expression of responsible spirituality, is a monumental undertaking. Sharing the circumstances within your transformation rather than the stories about your acting out, without bragging or complaining about the content of your addiction, in the context of becoming spiritual, is carrying the message. This creates insight and unity in yourself, is significant in getting you out of isolation, and helps you to learn that you are spiritually sick and not crazy.

The program teaches you to live your life spiritually, meaning without addictions, and without the desire for unnecessary affluence and social authority. The purpose of recovery is *not* to get you beautiful, handsome, laid, happy, married, or rich; it's to allow you to become spiritually sound. The original steps, and obedience to them, are intended to replace your addictions with spiritual attributes and spiritual grace—nothing else.

For addicts, abstinence and spirituality are always good. When your ego perceives life as troubling, it isn't; it's your perceptions. Should you be annoyed, frustrated, or angry for longer than a few seconds when there's a minor inconvenience, or for a few minutes in bigger calamities, you're in precarious spiritual condition. Notice I referred to angry and not to feeling sad, afraid, or lonely. These last three may or may not indicate other spiritually limiting values.

---

[3] The Manner of Presentation is at page 9.

Attend meetings with a spiritual agenda. If you're taking penicillin for an infection, you create stress and guaranteed disappointment if you expect the penicillin to also correct poor eyesight. Penicillin has a very specific task and has its limitations. So it is with the twelve steps. If you expect happiness, hot sex, love, social success, acceptance, employment, or absence of calamity, in addition to spirituality; or attempt to impose psychological agendas on the steps, you'll be perpetually disappointed. Eventually you'll become disillusioned. This is a tough one because our culture confuses social altruism (whether corrupt or not) with spirituality.[4] This is disastrous for addicts.

Service work and twelve-step work are not, by themselves, evidence of being spiritual; neither is serving food to the homeless or volunteering at a crisis centre. Most often, and sadly enough, these are evidence of not being spiritual. Social responsibility is important, generosity is nice, happiness is pleasant, and financial success is comforting, but these should not be interpreted as evidence of success at spirituality. These never substitute for the difficult inner searching for some brief glimpse of your spiritual nature (and it may take years of committed devotion to get one brief glimpse).

Many addicts in recovery do all of the approved "twelve-step" things: attend meetings, work on service committees, chair meetings, drive newcomers around, and get a sponsor. To their amazement, they still relapse, or they're secretly afraid and lonely. Others recite a litany of social responsibility, declare offerings of friendship, and perform countless acts of service work; they're well liked and approved of (by the other social do-gooders), yet they often appear insecure, scattered, angry and petty, and forever on the edge of chaos. There's often an edge of belligerence or arrogance to their life.

Altruism and service work are not evidence of spirituality.[5] People are very loyal to the secular belief that being morally good, kind, and generous are sufficient to qualify as spiritual. Logic has it (and being spiritual has little to do with logic) that we are good or should feel good because we do good things; hence, we are therefore "spiritual". People then hope for the ancillary benefits of an amazing love relationship and a sizeable investment portfolio. Not so. The original twelve steps are designed to create a value system that stands in opposition to both addiction and culture.[6]

---

[4] *"He who would do good to another must do it in minute particulars: General Good is the plea of the scoundrel, hypocrite, and flatterer."* William Blake, from *Complete Writings,* ed. by Geoffrey Keynes, 1957.

[5] *Peace of Mind,* by Joshua Loth Liebman, Simon & Schuster, 1946. The chapter Love Thyself Properly presents an explanation of how being spiritually based and spiritually ethical within yourself, is fundamental to healthy charity.

[6] With the changes in technology and culture, and the demands made on any individual in a technologically advanced society, to be socially successful, affluent, powerful, (cont'd)

Addicts getting recovered often unknowingly make our incredibly *un-spiritual* cultural value system their higher power: get abstinent (but only from the disapproved-of addictions), get a job, get money, get sex, get successful—be good, be loved, be influential, be happy. Being spiritual has little to do with any of these accomplishments, and, in fact, often places limits on many of them.

An addict getting recovered has to undermine and replace the modern values of disposable consumerism and greed. The myths around power, beauty, and affluence "should" be replaced with adherence to the five spiritual principles as they are embodied in the maintenance steps. Modern culture and spirituality are diametrically opposed, which makes Step Two (the cornerstone on which all spirituality rests) more difficult than in times past. Taking a year, or longer, to solidify a new belief system at Step Two isn't unreasonable. Reorganizing your personality from "addicted and culturally obedient" to "recovered with spiritual integrity" is the most difficult thing you will do, and that's exactly what's required of you.

When recovering addicts finally understand this, they take the pressure off of themselves and everything about the twelve steps comes into focus. What's to be done isn't confusing at all. The first nine steps, which are a regeneration of your personality, are the process out of addiction and into a value system and lifestyle that is contained within the three maintenance steps.

I am long convinced that the *original* Buddhist teachings, largely limited to The Four Noble Truths and the dislocation attached to the three poisons (desire, anger, and delusion), and what is offered in *Alcoholics Anonymous,* are the only paths of pilgrimage that embody an unrelenting focus on being egalitarian and personally responsible. They have an attractive aura, and appeal to many because of their (valid) promises of inner peace. However, and most often, when people are presented with the actual depth of work and self-discipline required for either discipline, they recast the philosophy into a self-serving political or religious context, pollute the teachings with personal interpretations, and manipulate the tenets to some personal advantage—pretty speeches, with delusion and without substance.[7]

---

intellectually astute, precocious, famous, slim, or muscular, it is often necessary to generate an obsessive or addictive lifestyle to achieve that kind of success. Being sincerely spiritual leaves you at odds with addiction *and* culture.

[7] The spiritual issues around honesty and sincerity are beautifully described in Part Two, Section Seven: Sincerity, *A Thomas Merton Reader,* Thomas Merton, edited by Thomas P. McDonnell, Image Books, Doubleday, 1996. The entire section is applicable here, but the immediate reference begins *"But the fact that men spend so much... ,"* p. 121.

Petulance and greed are subtle, deeply rooted, and more a way of life than addicts or alcoholics realize.[8] Very often, declarations of love, commitment, and spirituality are tainted by convenience—albeit well hidden, immaculately justified, and easily deniable. Cultural perceptions about success (largely arrogant materialism) and what constitutes authentic "spiritual" endeavor are at odds with each other—the offerings of the original program ignore the former and embrace the latter.

Getting recovered requires addicts to actually dismantle the blaming and selfishness they are permeated with. At Step Four, the struggle to replace these with honesty and responsibility begins in earnest. That's one reason the original program's instructions suggest you meditate carefully on your completed Step Four *before* moving on to Step Five.

Changing Values

From my own perspective, my life is always good, and when it isn't, that's only my perception—a perception "I" have created to give me something to complain about, or to justify my irresponsibility. Yet, going back in time to my 1975 beliefs—that pursuing wealth or power was good and life was monumentally unfair towards me—my life today is a complete failure: I'm not wealthy and I have no power over anything (except my attitude and my adherence to my values, which are today noticeably different). So therefore, I have "failed" at life according to my 1975 values.

The values that I embrace today are vastly different from the ones I had in 1975. They are also different from the ones I had in the early 1980s (early abstinence). And my present-day values are different from the ones that, in early abstinence, I imagined I wanted (or would have) when I envisioned reaching the point I am at today. My life today is more in line with the tenets of spirituality—I'm very ordinary—but my life forever unfolds in remarkable ways that I never could have imagined. That is the beauty of a spiritually oriented life.

Yes, I have the disease of addictions, from which I have recovered, and I'm sometimes a little scared or depressed or insecure (I'm human). However, I respond differently to these, and to the vicissitudes of life, be-

---

[8] From birth we are imbued with disposable consumerism, including the reprehensible attitudes that people are disposable, power is good, and that everything "wrong" must be fixed quickly or it isn't worth saving—the self-denigrating, vicious, quick-fix mentality. Alice Miller, in her book *The Untouched Key,* Anchor Books, Doubleday, pp. 10-11, points out the earlier a child learns something, the more entrenched it becomes. If this be positive, the more consistent the successes; if it be negative, and the harder it will be to unlearn. This is discussed in another of her books: *For Your Own Good: Hidden Cruelty in Child-Rearing and the Roots of Violence,* Farrar, Straus & Giroux, 1985.

cause I am able to perceive everything differently.[9] When I ponder this change in myself carefully, it's beyond anything I'd ever imagined.

Authentic spiritual self-discipline will keep you confused — as soon as you get to where you thought you wanted to get to, you realize it's only approximately what you thought you wanted. You are there, but not exactly, so you refocus onto some newly envisioned spiritual goal, and off you go again. True spirituality only allows you to get closer, and when you're closer it's never exactly what you imagined or desired what you previously wanted or needed. Yes, you get recovered, but that only enables you to enhance and deepen your commitment to spiritual principles.

In Chinese, the symbol for "crisis" is made up of two characters; one, "danger," and the other, "opportunity". Out of the danger and spiritual crisis of your addiction, in Step Four, you learned about the danger of blaming others and expecting them to clean up your mess. This created the opportunity to view your life as a self-imposed crisis. Recall in Step Four the tasks were very specific and you couldn't write whatever you wanted. In a convoluted way, you forced yourself to appreciate, in a responsible manner, this idea: *"To believe that the alcoholic who approaches AA is an unprincipled, untaught barbarian, suddenly transformed by the previously unavailable spiritual illumination of the twelve steps is, to me, utter foolishness."*[10]

Aside from how Step Four undermines culturally imposed guilt and offers spiritual opportunity, it is also important to deflate the addicts' untrue, pervading view that they're completely corrupt. The steps are a finely tuned, *very specific* procedure that allows for a clean delineation between (1) what is wrong; (2) what isn't wrong; and (3), what you think is wrong (which, until you are well into being recovered, is usually incorrect). The distinctions are crucial and, with rigorous honesty, will come into sharper focus throughout the remaining steps.

What I explained earlier regarding Step One "guides" applies here: Be cautious around any Step Four guide that includes invasive questions about pre-addiction, childhood, and early family-of-origin issues. These guides can't (and don't) clearly separate what is wrong, from what isn't wrong, from what the author of the guide thinks is wrong, from what you think is wrong. In truth, these are psychological questionnaires, not Step Four.[11]

---

[9] Changing perceptions is working with your ego — Appendix IV. Changing perceptions is also presented as a fundamental tenet of *A Course In Miracles*, The Foundation For Inner Peace, 1985/92.

[10] *A Member's Eye View of Alcoholics Anonymous* © AA World Services Inc., p.16.

[11] Intrusive or insight psychology has much value, but not necessarily in relation to Step Four. And, oftentimes, cross-over work is necessary and wise because of the globalization of addictions and the possible influence of pre-existing psychological concerns. This is delicate, and should only be undertaken with a therapist who meets the four criteria that I described (cont'd)

Your Step Four is an exercise that identifies what needs fixing in relation to your addiction and your personality so there is less interference in your relationship with a higher power (of your own understanding). What's obvious, but not talked about, is that when you arrive at Step Five, telling someone what needs fixing isn't fixing it.

The Disease and Guilt

From a cultural point of view, for most diseases, most people offer and receive compassion and are allowed some consideration for being sick. The following story is true: A patron at a movie theater had a serious epileptic seizure. An ambulance was called, the movie was interrupted by the disturbance for a few minutes, and the woman was taken to the hospital. With some courtesy, the theater manager offered free movie passes to her partner so the couple could view the film at another time. All ended well.

The following story is fiction: Imagine another couple who are alcoholic/addicts and relationship-addicted. They go to a movie. Shortly after the film begins, they argue loudly and accuse each other of various relationship misdemeanors and betrayals that are addictions related. The manager stops the film because of the disturbance. The police are called (not an ambulance). There are no free passes back to the movie, and minimal courtesy. The addicts go to jail.

Both situations involved minor inconvenience to the other patrons, yet one situation is socially acceptable and the other isn't. One person is sick; the other people are seen as disruptive (or bad). Epilepsy and addictions are treatable illnesses. Generally, if you have an addiction, there is very little cultural empathy. Notice your own instant response, and imagine the general response of people, to these two statements:

"I found out Lee's got cancer and will probably die from it."

"I found out Lee's a drug addict and will probably die from it."

We (*you*) live in a culture where addictions are not seen as a real disease, which is because they are the disease of our culture.[12] As an addict getting recovered, like it or not, you carry that attitude within you. Deny it if you must, but it's there and this paradigm manifests itself as subtle self-criticism, self-condemnation, and self-rejection. In the medical model of

---

in a footnote in Chapter 1. The consequences of mismanaged cross-over work, and wrongly established abstinence, are far more onerous than they may seem. Where the four criteria are not reasonably met, whatever harm arises from poorly conducted counselling will eventually have to be cleaned up... by the client.

[12] This will be explained more in *Facets of Personal Transformation*. For an important, and presently undervalued perspective see *Peaceful Measures*, Bruce K. Alexander, University of Toronto Press, 1990.

disease, there's no reason for you to feel guilty about being sick, so you needn't necessarily feel guilty for having an addiction—but you do.

Often, out of your Step Four comes an awareness of an overwhelming sense of culturally induced guilt that you continue to own. In spite of all the new-age rhetoric to the contrary, having an addiction still amounts to having done a bad thing. The original twelve-step program allows addicts to regain their integrity and dignity while believing that an addiction is a sickness—but only when they take responsibility for it.[13]

Most addicts and alcoholics probably feel guilty about things they did when they were acting out—not sad or ashamed, but guilty. Personally, after a few years of reflection on this[14], I feel guilty about nothing I did while in my addiction. I didn't have any choice; the disease dictated the behaviour and it was *not* a matter of willpower. This does not excuse me from responsibility. I have felt sad, afraid, hurt, etc. (all resolved), and I am responsible, but I don't feel guilty.

Guilt is about breaking rules. Notwithstanding the influence of fear and shame, if a person feels guilty, they believe they broke a rule.[15] The "rules" of addiction—the mandated behaviours, are the symptoms: acting out and life-damaging consequences, denial, disproportionate fear, repression, isolation (from self and others), assumptions, shame, dishonesty, withholding, selfishness, irresponsibility, arrogance, a noticeable degree of fantasy, and cynicism; all chronic and entrenched, and addicts are largely blind to them. The disease demands these, even though our culture (you probably included) believes you had a choice. There was no choice; hence there's no psychologically "authentic" reason to feel guilty.[16]

---

[13] Guilt and its cultural imposition, in relation to the disease of addiction, is to be [eventually] eliminated. Guilt is to not to be confused with regret or sadness, nor is this in any way an avenue to avoid responsibility. In fact, subscribing to this view, and achieving a guilt-free perspective of yourself and your addiction, actually increases your responsibility. See: *Twelve Steps and Twelve Traditions*, p. 62.

[14] Insight can only come through reflection or meditation. It cannot come through only belief. You cannot, as a willful act, make yourself realize an insight. Insights can only arise through contemplating and pondering truths; through your mind being open and receptive to teaching. Blind belief is not advised, but neither is belligerence or arguing. The mind should be willing to be receptive through pondering and quietly meditating. *The Four Noble Truths,* Venerable Ajhan Sumedho, Amaravati (Buddhist Centre) Publications, Hertfordshire, England, 1992, p. 39. Also: *"When there's something you don't understand, you have to go humbly to it. You don't go to school and sit down and say 'I know what you are going to teach me.' You sit there and you learn. You open your mind. You absorb. But you have to be quiet, you have to be still."* John Coltrane, jazz musician.

[15] I discuss this from a related perspective in Appendix I, and will examine it at length in *Facets of Personal Transformation*.

[16] The entitlement to "no guilt" only stands with integrity for that period while you are in your addiction, and in your abstinence up to that transformative moment when you realized you have a choice. Once you can choose, guilt will accrue if you choose wrongly because now there *is* a choice, and guilt is about breaking "rules" and knowingly choosing "wrongly". Should you willfully break some law, you must be responsible. However, should some (cont'd)

Freedom from the guilt associated with addiction is only available when you contemplate your discoveries for a long time, through the specifics of the steps, the nature of disease, the symptoms, and spiritual principles. There's a great benefit to the freedom and relief from guilt when you accept that your addiction is a disease, but there is a price to pay for this. Once you realize freedom from guilt, you take on the mantle of complete personal responsibility, and that obligates you to do something more than whatever is just good enough. Nothing is free.

Other themes that will begin to be more clearly understood at this point are the notion of willpower and spiritual self-determination. It follows, but I've not heard it discussed as such, that since an addiction is a self-imposed crisis[17], there must be a self-imposed solution not an other-imposed solution. An other-imposed solution would be addicts expecting to get better when someone other than themselves accepts (some) responsibility for the addicts addictions.

In other words, addicts wrongfully focused "willpower" or spiritual dislocation got them into their predicaments. When (if) they refocus their willpower from blame and self-annihilation to responsibility and spirituality, spirituality becomes an issue of self-determination. Circumstances may have moved to put them *in* a twelve-step program, but they must act to stay in it. Colloquially: Providence may present some addicts with the opportunity to change (at and during Step One), and no one knows why. Hopefully these addicts will then assess the opportunity and come to believe in the plan that's outlined at Step Two. Finally, addicts decide to choose spirituality and "God" at Step Three, which makes them responsibly self-determined. There is nothing accidental about a fulfilling spiritual lifestyle — it's entirely deliberate.

The insidious cultural view of addictions is that addicts are "bad" because they somehow choose to do what they do, and could expediently change if they made up their minds to try harder.[18] Therefore, the major reprehensible "social crime" that addicts and alcoholics must atone for is being willfully bad (deliberately irresponsible), and destroying themselves to be mean or spiteful. The *cultural* position we are saddled with is that

---

former behaviour like lying be symptomatic of your addiction, the presence of "guilt" for that is optional. Ponder this carefully: You are still and always responsible to cooperate with the sanctions of your community *and* to take yourself to task for harm caused, but feeling guilt for symptomatic behaviour is optional.

[17] *Alcoholics Anonymous*, p. 53.

[18] Do not be lured into the cultural deifying of expediency (the quick-fix) and disposable consumerism, where people are disposable objects. That is the underlying truth of "quick fix", "harm reduction", and "substance-use management" programs. The best solution (spirituality) isn't expedient, and therefore addicts become disposable to the quick fix. Many caregivers view addicts, and addicts view themselves (and other addicts), as not worthy of a considerable and determined investment of time, effort, or money.

addicts are simply irresponsible, and if they somehow just smartened up and tried harder... well, you know how it goes.

Addicts I've spoken with or counselled, to any noticeable degree, have experienced sadness about the fact that their life has been devastated. Without exception, they regret the pain they've caused and deeply desire it were otherwise. This is sincere and painful but seldom admitted because they're rarely believed. In the midst of acting out, they don't feel that way, but addictive acting out isn't representative of the morality of the addict—it's the reality of the disease.

Step Five

When addicts in recovery complete their Step Five it will (or should) cause a deep shift in inner perception that addicts aren't bad and will reduce culturally imposed guilt. Step Five further expands the awareness that they aren't alone in their wretchedness. These new perceptions, that weren't available before, are dependent upon their obedience to the original program.[19] The person who shares their Step Five with them, who is willing to listen with unconditional positive [spiritual] regard[20], is in a position to lighten their burden of loneliness and isolation—one theme of Step Five.

At meetings, you tell your story in a general way, and probably throw in some exciting, exaggerated, or embarrassing details. In the ears of trusted friends or a sponsor, you allude to more shameful details, which in itself is often attention getting. The original Step Four works to prevent exaggeration and flamboyance by demanding accurate detail about very specific parts of your personality.

Step Five is the first time that you are required, by a mandate of the steps, to tell completely accurate truths about yourself, to be specific about your *instinctual* excesses, to not blame anyone, to not condemn yourself, and to trust you will not be shamed or judged. If you're inaccurate or insincere; if you attempt to bypass Step Five with a generally painless admission that you were sometimes a bad actor[21], or imbue it with exaggerated (or minimized) descriptions of your behaviour—all of which is only "sober" acting out—you will not initiate the process of guilt-reduction, and will live, to some extent, distrusting of the steps. That is fatal to spiritual awareness.

---

[19] Meaning *Alcoholics Anonymous* (not the personal stories) and *Twelve Steps and Twelve Traditions*. I also recommend the pamphlet, *A Member's Eye View of Alcoholics Anonymous*.
[20] "Unconditional positive regard" is a phrase used to describe one significant aspect of the therapist's attitude in client-centred therapy, developed by Carl Rogers. *The Carl Rogers Reader*, edited by Howard Kirschenbaum and Valerie Land Henderson, Houghton Mifflin Company, 1989, p. 225.
[21] *Twelve Steps and Twelve Traditions*, p. 55.

Bearing all of this in mind, notice: *"get rid of that terrible sense of isolation"*[22] and *"emerging from isolation"*[23]. If your Step Five is primarily a list of bad things, the isolation and loneliness will remain. Beginning to end your isolation from yourself and from "God" is dependent upon pushing through all types impression management and being accurate and specific in a quiet, sincere way.

Addicts, too often immediately after the writing of Step Four, make an appointment for their Step Five. I've often discussed this with them and ask have they admitted it [their Step Four] to God or to themselves? They're usually puzzled and mumble something vague about God watching over their shoulder as they wrote Step Four. I point out that the sequence of instructions in the step is: admitted to God, then to ourselves, and (finally) to another human being.

Reflect on the first sentence of 'How It Works': *"Rarely have we seen a person fail who has thoroughly followed our path."* Then immediately read Step Five: *"Admitted to God, to ourselves, and to another human being the exact nature of our wrongs."*[24] Accordingly then, by specific instruction, it is not sufficient to tell only another person.

Each step is a spiritually self-contained unit. This means that whatever work transpired prior to Step Five has no influence over the detail or effort you put into Step Five. The fact that you wrote Step Four doesn't diminish the attention you must pay to the instructions in Step Five, which is to be read independently of the work in the previous steps. Before any admitting can take place, however, it is important to remind yourself what exactly you are to admit. Notice these:

- *"The objective look at ourselves we achieved in Step Four..."*[25]
- *"We have written an inventory and we are prepared for a long talk."*[26]

Step Four is the list of the exact nature of your fears, etc., so this means in Step Five you only admit exactly what's in your Step Four. Just as there were limits on what you wrote, there are equally specific limits on what you are to admit. There are also equally specific limits on who you can admit all this to.

---

[22] *Twelve Steps and Twelve Traditions*, p. 57.
[23] Ibid., p. 62.
[24] *Alcoholics Anonymous*, pp. 58 and 59, respectively.
[25] *Twelve Steps and Twelve Traditions*, p. 58.
[26] *Alcoholics Anonymous*, p. 75.

In taking the instructions at face value, and using everyday language to describe spiritual principles, addicts would first admit the exact nature of their wrongs "to God". Consider sitting in a meditative mood in prayer and offer your entire Step Four, item by item, to your higher power. This prayer is a specific task of Step Five, not to replace any daily prayer routine. In this prayerful reflection get more honest, with a view to relying more on your higher power for courage in these matters. As you pray reflectively about the exact nature of your insecurities, fears, and sexual selfishness notice where you may have glossed over a few minor details—just "tiny" omissions—so you wouldn't look too bad. This is the second time (of three), in the first nine steps, where you commend yourself directly to your higher power.

The next phrase is: *"...admitted to yourself..."*. Consider actually making eye contact with yourself in a mirror, and at the same time, ask these questions of yourself about each Step Four entry: "Was I *completely* accurate and thorough in my self-examination about this?" And: "Have I avoided any responsibility by *secretly* blaming others for this trouble?" Determine if you have admitted the *entire* truth about your insecurity, fear, and sexual selfishness.[27]

As you ask yourself these while looking *at* yourself, pay especial attention to any hint of blaming. You may notice little glitches of guilt if you've been evasive. Amend your Step Four where you have to. You (and everyone else in your life) will pay dearly for any inattention to detail here.

These two reviews may seem excessive. After all, you've spent weeks writing Step Four, you've read it, you've reviewed it, you've reflected on it. Isn't that enough? Again, notice the exact wording of Step Five.

As you begin to develop new values governed by spiritual principles, and understand the importance of truth and commitment, these first two admissions of Step Five are neither difficult nor foolish. Only you know when you're lying and withholding. Only you are responsible to force yourself to stop weaseling out of responsibility. This is a labour of love, and a deep and moving experience.

One fact about honesty is: As long as you deceive yourself, to *any* degree, you will deceive others. The moment you achieve the willingness to be absolutely honest with yourself and see this as a spiritual virtue, you will not perpetuate deceit outside of yourself. Honesty is an inside job; so is recovery. Only you can look into your soul. Only you can see the edge of the abyss beyond which faith carries you into a life of spiritual principle. The final arbiter of your spiritual conduct is you.

---

[27] Recovering addicts often speak of being unable to make eye-contact with themselves in a mirror. Thinking about doing this may provoke anxiety, or some criticism of my being too particular about detail. What might that indicate about you?

When you do the steps and meditations as instructed you occasionally, and then increasingly, get a glimpse of *you*—the you that's connected to a higher power in a deep experience of unitive truth. Only this can cause a permanent, unpremeditated correction in your previously addictions-twisted structure of values.

"I am personally convinced that the basic search of every human being, from the cradle to the grave, is to find at least one other human being before whom [they] *can stand completely naked, stripped of all pretense or defense, and trust that person not to hurt* [them], *because that other person has stripped* [themselves] *naked, too. This lifelong search can begin to end with the first AA encounter."*[28] Among the many important things that are contained in this quote, two points stand out in relation to Step Five. The first is that truth and trust are essential to the search. The second is that the search only begins to end—it doesn't end.

You must first develop accuracy in all aspects of self-knowledge so that you are capable of standing stripped of pretense or defense in front of yourself.[29] Without this vulnerability you can never be loved for who you are and will always be loved for your pretensions. The exercise of doing Step Five, in the manner prescribed, is the only way that you begin any in-depth, accurate self-disclosure. The task here is not to expose historical data, it's to initiate accurate self-disclosure and eliminate the subtle self-deception that you practice. This self-disclosure will help keep you spiritual, honest, and soulful in times of turmoil and temptation.

Tom Waits sings in one of his songs: *"How do the angels get to sleep when the devil leaves the porch light on?"*[30] It's a wonderful metaphor for the addict's struggle to be spiritual while noticing temptations. What beliefs prevent you from accepting that *you* are in charge of leaving your own porch light on? You're responsible for your temptations and how you respond to them. Your view of yourself and the world creates your temptations. Accurate self-awareness and responsibility are essential keys to turning your porch light off. More importantly, to keep temptation turned off, you must develop insight about how tenaciously you cling to your ability to deceive, to avoid, and to conveniently misrepresent yourself.

You finished writing your Step Four a while ago. You have now meditated through it three times: once as a part of Step Four—reflecting on the

---

[28] From the AA pamphlet *A Member's Eye View of Alcoholics Anonymous*.
[29] At a concert, jazz musician Bill Evans was asked where he was going with his music. The question was framed in a musical context. He answered, *"In."* He answered in a soulful context. *Inside* is where all truly creative and spiritual journeys go; never "out", always in.
[30] From *Mr. Siegal,* written by Tom Waits; the album: *Heartattack and Vine*, Fifth Floor Music Inc., ASCAP, 1980.

source of your insecurities and searching for responsibility; and twice more as parts of Step Five: once with God in prayer, and once by making eye contact with yourself, all the while making necessary amendments to further entrench honesty, accuracy, and responsibility. You are now ready to tell someone else; but whom do you tell?

Making The Selection: The Four Conditions

If, in the past, you have done a Step Five and suspect that it didn't work as well as described, yes, it may be because you were not thorough enough in completing the earlier steps, or didn't understand this as a process of spiritual transformation, not psychological adjustment. However, you may also have been negligent in choosing a confidant who didn't meet the four conditions.[31]

As with so many other things, this is subtle. Within the human relationship you create in Step Five, it's safe to presume that one of you is (apparently) the wiser of the two. The person hearing it is supposed to be farther along in their own pilgrimage than the person offering it, and should therefore know more about what's supposed to transpire. Certainly the accuracy of the content is the complete responsibility of the person sharing. However, the greater share of responsibility for spiritual effectiveness rests on the person hearing the disclosure. That effectiveness is related to the four conditions noted in *Alcoholics Anonymous*, and is primarily the responsibility of whoever hears it.

If you belong *"...to a religious denomination which requires confession* [you] *must, and of course, will want to go to the properly appointed authority whose duty it is to receive it."*[32] However, those who cannot, or would rather not, do this can look for someone else—a psychologist, doctor, therapist, religious professional, or understanding mentor. And, whomever you choose to tell *"must understand, yet be unaffected."*[33] Certainly you should trust them to some degree, but considering you may know this person only by reputation or recommendation, how does it come about that they can be trusted?

First: Make yourself thoroughly aware of these requisite four conditions that the person you choose must satisfy.

---

[31] *Alcoholics Anonymous,* pp. 74-75.

[32] Ibid., p. 74.

[33] If the person you choose is socially or personally involved in your life—a friend, sponsor/friend, co-worker, twelve-step comrade, coffee companion, sponsor/golf-buddy, work-out partner, spouse... they will be affected, and should therefore *not* be chosen. Also, if the person you choose sometimes shares at meetings they hear Step Fives; if you've ever heard them speak about hearing others' Step Fives—even if they guarantee your anonymity—they have been affected. Hence, they should *not* be chosen.

- This person must be able to keep confidence. You have to rely on their ability to be *absolutely silent* regarding you and your disclosure.
- The person you choose must fully understand what you are doing. *Alcoholics Anonymous* doesn't advise that they only "partially understand" or "have a general idea". Your confidant must fully understand, which implies a lot.
- This person must approve of what you are doing. Since (and because) you're being obedient to the instructions, you will not add, change, or delete any requirement. Your confidant should likewise change nothing. So, it's not enough for this person to fully understand; they must also approve.
- They must not try to change your plan. According to Steps Two and Three, your plan should be to simply follow the instructions.[34] Attempts to change your plan are usually very subtle and indicate they do not approve of what you are doing.

Second: Do not rest on the recommendations of others. Get a few names and conduct pre-Step Five interviews. Your first meeting with them is to discuss their view of Step Five, and to enable you to satisfy yourself that this individual meets the four conditions. Do not bring your Step Four writing to this pre-Step Five interview. Bring *Alcoholics Anonymous* and *Twelve Steps and Twelve Traditions* with a few things highlighted that you want to talk about.

Ask about confidentiality. If it's a professional, do they keep a record? How would they maintain confidentiality if someone asked them about you? What is their understanding of twelve-step programs? Do they ever talk about or mention to others that they hear Step Fives? What is their understanding of Step Five? Will they discuss the applicable paragraphs from the reference texts to ensure there's no misunderstanding? What do they think you are to accomplish? Do they approve of what you're doing? Will they try to change your plan by adding anything? How do they end a Step Five? Do they expect you will say a prayer or do Steps Six and Seven with them?

These questions ensure there'll be no surprises later on when you are into your Step Five disclosure. This pre-Step Five interview is not an attack on their character, it's you being self-responsible. What if they are annoyed, argue, or are defensive about your thoroughness? What does that tell you

---

[34] Philosophical analysis of the tenets of *Alcoholics Anonymous* or *Twelve Steps and Twelve Traditions,* and esoteric discussions about any facet of the five spiritual principles, may be interesting and important, but are always only an adjunct to doing what the literature tells you.

about them? Be prepared to discuss anything they don't understand, and make clear your intent to follow the instructions in the approved literature.

In a spiritual sense, all of these precautions should be redundant since both you and your confidant "should" desire to enter into this wanting to follow the instructions. Your plans should be the same. However, the only guarantee of your success in getting recovered is your own thoroughness in following instructions. You must invest effort into ensuring that the person you choose meets the four stated conditions. You need the practice in spiritual assertiveness and self-care.

Be wary of the person who agrees, but kindly suggests some small amendment. They may say they understand, and proclaim Step Five is quite wonderful, but if they suggest some change, they're suggesting you follow "their" program, not *the* program. Here are common suggestions made by people who don't fully understand or accept what is required in Step Five:

- "You don't really need to refer to your Step Four since you know it all anyway. It's all about your fears, so you can just refer to it from memory. Put it away, and we'll just talk."
- "Listen, your fears, and all that sex-stuff, it's all pretty similar, so you can just lump them together. There's no need for repetition. Hit the highlights and we'll save some time."
- "If everything goes well, we can do Steps Six and Seven right after. You'll get all three steps out of the way."
- "I've heard a lot of Step Fives, and it helps people if they come around to my step group. I get to help you out if it gets rough, and you get to expand your spiritual resources."
- "We'll spend a bit of time talking about your childhood family troubles. That often helps. We'll set some time aside for that— but of course only if you want to."
- "When we're done we can say a prayer together."

If any of these or similar suggestions are made to you, do not choose this person. What any of these suggestions really indicate is the person doesn't fully understand or approve of Step Five as it is written. Are you willing to put your life in the care of someone who thinks they are wiser than *Alcoholics Anonymous* or *Twelve Steps and Twelve Traditions*?

If you suspect they can't be trusted to follow the original literature guidelines, or you aren't sure of their integrity, or something in their demeanor doesn't meet the conditions, there are two options. (a) You might respectfully discuss your concerns with them and ask they follow the specific instructions. If they are in the least bit defensive or autocratic, then they are not respectful of your concerns. Will you do your Step Five with someone who doesn't respect you? (b) The other choice is to respectfully say thank you, but no thank you, and quietly move on, without gossiping or complaining. Interview someone else.

Should you push ahead and do your Step Five without clearing up your concerns, then, during your Step Five, you'll cut corners and evade. When you're not rigorously honest, you're dishonest. Dishonesty and ignoring any "danger signs" are symptoms of your addiction. By ignoring your concerns and going ahead with this person, you're being disrespectful of yourself and willfully choosing to withhold and isolate. You will end up participating in addictive behaviour during your Step Five (and how weird is that?). Addictions are insidious—follow the instructions.

Many people grew up with the illusion that somehow, someday, a savior would come along and make their lives safe and happy. Not so, and even if you can lure someone into looking after you, it will eventually backfire. If you don't stick up for yourself, no one else will. You must learn to care for yourself. Take responsibility for your life by taking responsibility for your spiritual transformation.

Remember the two rules—Rule #1 is people die from addictions (and others are determined to stay sick). Rule #2 is *you* can't change Rule #1. I offer this next point gently; keep it in context: Make your confidant earn the right to hear your Step Five. You are playing with your life here—they aren't playing with theirs. Make every effort to ensure your success.

At Step Five you are allowing someone to significantly influence your spiritual transformation. Think carefully: If it doesn't work, you will soon feel empty and unfulfilled; you might relapse, act out, or otherwise destroy your sense of wellbeing. The person who heard your Step Five might then say, in all sincerity, "Gee, that's too bad," but they haven't relapsed—you have.

Receiving a Step Four

Should you be asked to hear someone's Step Four, and they don't suggest a pre-Step Five interview, then you, as the more experienced twelve-step person, should ask for one. You must verify that the newer person is on track spiritually. In the event they aren't, refocus the interaction, and with gentle consideration, start an education process on what a Step Five is.

Supposedly you're the more responsible spiritual person so you must turn the event into a sponsorship process of carrying the message. Using your AA reference texts, initiate a discussion on what's required. This is never about what anyone did wrong, it is only about how it might be made more effective. Reach for the most spiritually enlightened possibility.

For those who hold themselves out to be capable and willing to act as mentors, hearing someone's Step Four requires significant insight about the steps and long-term *spiritual* sobriety. What is required is subtle. They may enter into it well intentioned, but good intentions aren't good enough when dealing with things as vicious as addictions and as subtle as spirituality.

If you're invited to hear someone's Step Five, you're being offered a very special gift. It's an honour to be thusly respected. Veracity, humility, and obedience to the principles and instructions are crucial. To have the opportunity to contribute to the healing of the world; to help resolve addictions in another's life so they may carry on to find spiritual peace, carries a profound responsibility.

It would appear from the literature that the only time Step Five can legitimately be postponed is when you cannot find someone suitable.[35] This implies you have searched, done pre-Step Five interviews, and not found anyone. Keep looking.

In Step Four, you admitted certain defects, ascertained what the trouble was (fear), and identified weak items (related to fear, shame, and guilt) in your personal inventory.[36] You have not inventoried your sins or catalogued your exploits and debauchery. Once you feel generally content about what you've accomplished thus far, including your pre-Step Five interview, only then do you make the appointment for your Step Five. If you make the appointment before you've completed *all* the preliminary work in a thorough and patient manner, there'll be pressure to "get it done". Impatience and deadlines are fatal to contemplative spiritual thoroughness.

Some questions that are asked by people who are sharing their Step Five, about it: What if I relapse? What if they relapse? What if they can't handle what I have to tell them? What if they gossip? What if I see them at a meeting later on? What if I trigger their stuff? What if they start to cry? What if I start to cry? Do they have to be in a twelve-step program?

My replies are fairly standard: *"Rightly and naturally, we think well before we choose the person or persons...."*[37] Notice *"or persons,"* implying you may decide to share your Step Four with more than one person. For example, you may discuss your instinctual insecurities and fears with one person, and your sexual selfishness with someone else.[38] This may be wise

---

[35] *Alcoholics Anonymous,* p. 74.

[36] Ibid., p. 72.

[37] Ibid., p. 74.

[38] Should you decide you must disclose behaviour that carries legal sanction, it need <u>and should</u> only be told to the legal professional authorities that are qualified and duly responsible to receive this information. It may also wise to tell a *bona fide* spiritual mentor and a qualified therapist for trustworthy counsel, but this decision is yours alone to make. It is never for general conversation in meetings.

or it may be evasive. Carefully examine your motives with a spiritual advisor or sponsor.

Look towards those people who have an emotionally peaceful demeanor. No, they don't have to be in "the program"; they only must satisfy the four conditions.

As you enter your Step Five, if you have followed the directions carefully, the result will be a peaceful confidence and closeness to your higher power. Talk about your Step Four in a sincere and straightforward manner. You're on a life-or-death errand. Your purpose is to illuminate every dark cranny of your personality, which is thoroughly outlined in your writing. As you go along, thoroughness and honesty may jog your memory and provoke more awareness and greater detail. During your Step Five, you may remember subtle things that aren't in your notes. Include these.

Spiritual comfort and inner serenity, which are perceived in thought-logic as the nearness of your higher power, cannot arise from a grandiose disclosure of misdemeanors and transgressions. They flow out of a humble sharing of your instinctual conflict, a quiet examination of your fears, and taking responsibility for your sexual selfishness. It is repeatedly experienced that out of these actions, providing they are done with spiritual integrity, will come perceptible relief from loneliness and isolation. You'll now begin to appreciate a sense of belonging—that you have a right to your relationship with your higher power and are entitled to earn a spiritual, peaceful life.

The Two Big Ones

When you commence a twelve-step program of recovery, and in order to get recovered, the two "big" general problems that must be resolved are the obsession to drink or act out (which is the obsession to self destruct), and the insane thinking. Both of these are enhanced and entrenched by blaming (being a victim) and mylenated energy patterns. Notice at Step Five: *"The feeling that the drink problem has disappeared will often come strongly."*[39] Accordingly then, you've resolved the first of these two general problems. During your Step Five, or shortly after it, you may well be aware that you are *in* a spiritual experience.[40] [The second "big" general problem, insane thinking, is generally resolved at or in Step Nine.]

---

[39] *Alcoholics Anonymous*, p. 75.
[40] Ibid. *"We… are delighted* [and] *begin to feel the nearness of our Creator.* [We] *have a spiritual experience."* Being able to appreciate being *in* a spiritual awakening as it happens rather than recalling the experience after the fact, indicates much progress in being spiritually sensitive. The main advantage to this difference is that in the former circumstance there is a more consistent sense of gratitude and serenity.

The pamphlet *A Member's Eye View of Alcoholics Anonymous* offers information about "terminal uniqueness". Step Five contributes to eliminating this spiritually fatal self-perception which then permits the experience of an increased sense of being ordinary. Never malign your ordinariness — it's the substance of saints. Being sincerely ordinary allows you to experience spiritual sensibility.[41]

In your life you've experienced trauma, had difficult decisions thrust upon you, and endured life, but so have billions of others. You are an ordinary alcoholic or addict; an ordinary person with the ordinary wants and needs and desires of everyone else on the planet. You belong *to* the world and *in* the world, no more and no less than anyone else. You are ordinary *and* you have now finished Step Five.

Honesty

Any spiritual transformation process demands and is overtly concerned with rigorous honesty. This is discussed in *Alcoholics Anonymous'* 'How It Works' and in Appendix II of this book. One of the hardest things addicts have to do in their lives (which becomes less arduous as devotion to spirituality increases) is to understand that dishonesty or withholding is *never* the answer. It doesn't matter what you've got to tell, or to whom you've got to tell it. Withholding information about gifts or because of a legal obligation are, of course, accepted social standards of behaviour. Outside of these, and excluding the one *rare* exception identified in Step Nine, rigorous honesty is always the answer.[42]

Taken together, veracity and not withholding comprise one of the only two types of behaviour that prohibit guilt; the other is responsibility. Veracity and responsibility (or their opposites) are the masters of your conscience. When you're indecisive about whether to be honest, you're entangled in anticipating the consequences of honesty based on your perceptions of hardship, discomfort, or loss of personal advantage. These consequences may be accurate or exaggerated; but regardless of this, the fact that you being honest may be tough on *you* is of no consequence, since your dishonesty (or some other character defect) is what got you into feeling awkward in the first place. Honesty may create discomfort; dishonesty may create death.

---

[41] There's an interesting aspect to the notion of "sensible" in relation to being spiritual. Once you're on the other side of the chaos of addictions, and well into being recovered, all of the significant travail, inner struggle, pain, and social calamity, amount, in the final analysis, to very little. Being spiritual, even with the years of monumental effort you put into it, is simply the sensible thing to do.

[42] I go into this in greater detail regarding amends in the next chapter.

In order to maintain a soulful union with your higher power, or another person, or to appreciate any abiding spiritual peace, you must strive for veracity. This is fundamental to all spiritual transformation (but so are the other four spiritual principles). Honesty may well be more painful over the short term, but the pain of deceit lasts as long as the deceit does. If a lie is permanent, the guilt and pain are permanent.

> Only honesty makes your world less painful.
> Only responsibility makes your world safer.

The Honesty Police

If you believe someone is being dishonest, is it your place to say something? Each circumstance is different. If a person's dishonesty affects you directly, then yes; if not, you have a decision to make. It's not your job to be running around challenging or reporting everyone you perceive as being dishonest. It may be important to say something, but... it may be more important to quietly excuse yourself from someone's life, and move on, saying nothing. You are not the honesty police.

Be advised: The way you say something is as important as what you say. Attacking people through your "morally superior honesty" is always ineffective. It's your job to create a safe environment for your life, and a respectful environment for others around you, not to save the world or to save lost souls. Being kind, not attempting to impose your morality, being responsible for how you put yourself in some awkward position, not being angry, not demanding behaviour change from others, are intrinsic to spiritual problem solving.

If someone emotionally close to you is dishonest in some way, the focus isn't on that person's dishonesty. What are you doing in an intimate relationship with a dishonest person? It is wise to feel *un*safe when you are with people who are willing to lie, commit crimes, be mean, or defend their racism or sexism. Be wary of people who will condone their own or another's irresponsibility. If they're willing to condone or do those things, it's a fool's delusion to believe you are forever exempt—eventually it will be your turn because their honesty and integrity are only a matter of convenience to circumstance. Regardless of how sincerely they promise otherwise, it will eventually be your turn (if it isn't already). Examine the insecurity within you that motivates you to continue to be around people like this.

If you know, or suspect that some person you associate with is untrustworthy, and subsequently they lie or cheat on you, it's entirely your fault. You were victimized because you ignored your suspicions and the evidence that gave you the suspicion. If you ignore your suspicions, when you get left, burnt, ripped off, betrayed, slapped, ignored, or cheated you have nothing to complain about; you volunteered to be there. If you are concerned about their unethical/unspiritual behaviour, what are you doing there?

You may find it necessary to distance yourself from whatever people you believe are of "suspicious character" or that treat you badly. You may even decide to report illegal or dishonest behaviour to whichever civil authorities would respond to that information. These are decisions *you* have to wrestle with. Don't gossip.

Regarding awkward circumstances and troubled relationships: The first time you are betrayed or otherwise taken advantage of, it certainly may not be your fault. If it's the second time, or third or fifth time... you're in that awkward situation because of your own questionable integrity. You alone are responsible for your discomfort because you "knew better" and decided to ignore your better judgment.

You must decide how much energy you will invest into reorganizing your life and personality around spiritual principles. Integrity, and its emotional cousin serenity are more expensive than most people are willing to pay.

As an addict getting recovered you were granted, by whatever grace that providence allows, some window of opportunity to see that your addictions were optional, but only with very hard work and huge commitment. You may well become recovered and achieve the promises, but with the unalterable requirement that you pay for them. Uncompromising commitment to the five spiritual principles, as they appear throughout the steps, and continuing to demand more personal integrity from yourself with ever fewer demands on life and others, is the price.

The stated fact is that a higher power could restore you to sanity, and here that means acquiring the insight and courage to act in a way that honors the five spiritual principles. Back at Step Three, your decision required that you forever acknowledge: *"Well, that's exactly what [Alcoholics Anonymous] is about. Its main object is to enable you to find a Power greater than yourself which will solve your problem."*[43]

Being recovered requires the maintenance steps to govern all of your affairs—voluntarily and willingly continue to rededicate yourself to a spiritual way of life. You might not keep your job, you may have to move or divorce, you will lose all superficial relationships, but you'll achieve spiritual integrity—serenity and a relationship with a higher power. You cannot

---

[43] *Alcoholics Anonymous*, p. 45. Note this is present tense. At any given moment "life" distributes another set of problems to "whomever", from broken shoelaces to bankruptcy and illness. Since problems reappear relentlessly, *Alcoholics Anonymous* continuously takes the recovered addict back to "a higher power" that will solve these problems.

evade your commitment to the tasks of the original maintenance steps, or ignore any principle of spirituality, without the immediate consequence of losing whatever spiritual harmony you've earned.

After Step Five, and before Step Six, you are in this position: *"Step Four was, after all, only a look..."* and *"...it didn't necessarily mean that we had yet acquired much actual humility." "Though now recognized, our defects were still there. Something had to be done about them." "[We] could not wish or will them away by ourselves."*[44]

The Review

There's a significant piece of work that's done before you move to Step Six. It's outlined in the paragraph that begins *"Returning home we find..."*, which sits immediately before the instructions for Step Six.[45] It advises you to go home, be quiet for a while, and review your work thus far (the first five steps) to determine if you have omitted anything. This necessitates reviewing (yet again) your Step Four and the interaction and content of Step Five. In this review you are to be mindful of your gratitude and express this to your higher power. Your willingness to carefully review everything is evidence of your commitment.

The metaphor offered is that you are building an arch through which you shall walk, *"a free [person] at last."*[46]

You are being told to examine how you have built your arch thus far. There are nine steps in the completed arch; you've now finished the first five. The obvious implication of "free" is you will eventually be recovered. So, *"...be quiet for an hour, carefully reviewing..."* those proposals.[47] The book asks is your work solid so far? Are these first five stones [steps] prop-

---

[44] All from *Twelve Steps and Twelve Traditions*, p. 58.
[45] *Alcoholics Anonymous*, p. 75.
[46] Ibid.
[47] Ibid.

erly in place? Did you skimp on the cement in the foundation? Should you find something you were lax on or overlooked, call your spiritual advisor or sponsor, possibly speak again with your step-five person, and repair it.

The metaphor suggests if your work is not thorough, the arch will collapse, meaning you will not become recovered; you will not become free; you will not properly experience the promises or the maintenance steps. If it does collapse, you'll have to rebuild the arch (re-do the steps) over and over—I suppose until you get it right or you die, whichever comes first.

This review is similar to school where you review your work before any big test. It's important to notice this is the only place in the original twelve-step literature where you are advised to review all of your spiritual work before proceeding further. This pre-Step Six review precedes the toughest "test" you'll face in the process of getting recovered. Something big is about to be asked of you.

"If we can answer to our satisfaction, we then look at Step Six."[48]

Step Six

The first sentence of Step Six is: *"This is the step that separates the men from the boys."*[49] I am not enamored of the metaphor itself—it's shaming to men and boys, and it excludes and is insulting to women; certainly it's sexist. *Twelve Steps and Twelve Traditions*, the book the quote is taken from, was published in 1952 and we are more sensitive to issues of equality today. The intent of the original passage was to point out the serious difficulty of the work involved. I would offer this alternative expression: Step Six is where we separate the dilettantes from people that are sincerely committed to spiritual transformation.

The point I wish to make here is Step Six is the only step that opens with such a warning of importance and difficulty. No other step requires an entire program review prior to attempting it. This speaks to the import of Step Six.[50]

The underlying philosophy, and the tasks you are required to complete at this point, are harder to assimilate and accomplish than what's required at any of the other steps. I don't assert this only through personal opinion (although that is my experience), but through the writing in the original twelve-step program. It is also a valid observation because the complex

---

[48] *Alcoholics Anonymous*, p. 76.
[49] *Twelve Steps and Twelve Traditions*, p. 63.
[50] Throughout this book I've made a serious effort to stay away from personal pronouns of his and/or hers. They are cumbersome reading. I've also, I hope successfully, avoided sexist language and presented "God" and spirituality in gender-neutral terms. Sexism is detrimental to recovery and spirituality.

issues of active addiction and exactly opposite to the requirements of healthy spirituality.

In brief it is this: At Step Six you become *willing* to permanently and completely change the fundamental operating system of your personality. [At Step Two you came to believe that this difficult job could be done.] Step Six is your becoming willing to do it. This sets up two serious, subconscious fears: who will you become, and how can you survive (or succeed) in the new spiritual value system you are to adopt?

The paragraph *"When men and women…"*[51] likens the self-destruction that addicts are bent upon—alcohol, drugs, smoking, gambling, sex, spending, whatever—to suicide. Notice the opening sentence of the paragraph following: *"But most of our other difficulties don't fall under such a category at all."*[52] Most difficulties are in the sphere of ordinary, everyday life: flat tires, forgotten appointments, money mismanagement, hurt feelings, setting boundaries, and the usual disappointments and resentments.

It's interesting that the most difficult step has only one short paragraph of instruction in *Alcoholics Anonymous*. Granted, it's a straightforward outline of the work you are to do, but its simplicity belies the monumental inner-personal realignment and reorganization that's required. Step Six permeates every facet of your life. It's interesting that Steps Two, Six and Seven are the steps that very few people give any insightful discourse on. This mass-avoidance is a reflection of the spiritual depth and power of these steps.

Willingness

"We have emphasized willingness as being indispensable."[53] Willing, in various dictionaries, is defined as consenting without begrudging or pleasantly inclined. A willing worker completes a task with cheerful readiness. Being "willing" means to go along agreeably; to cheerfully or eagerly consent to a commitment; to be pleasantly inclined to do something—without feeling irked, begrudging, or annoyed. All of this is *willing*.

Willingness is used frequently in relation to getting recovered. *Alcoholics Anonymous* (the recovery instructions manual) is written for isolated, defensive, dishonest, often depressed, suspicious, selfish, insecure, and especially begrudging people (people with addictions). For them to become willing to change the traditional way they participate in life—to change the fundamental operating principles of their personality, are monumental undertakings.

---

[51] *Twelve Steps and Twelve Traditions*, p. 64.
[52] Ibid.
[53] *Alcoholics Anonymous*, p. 76.

People in recovery are brilliantly schooled in adding, "Yes, but..." to anything they're doing, and still convince themselves they are willing. It looks like this: "I'm willing to be spiritual, except that sometimes... ," "Of course I'm willing to be honest in all areas of my life, but... ," "Certainly I'm willing to make amends, as long as it's not... ," "Yes, I'm willing to go to therapy, but...." Adding an exception (openly or silently) to your claim of willingness, as far as addictions recovery goes, means you're not.

The actor Nicole Kidman wonderfully illustrated similar ideas about passion and caring, which are important to life and transformation. She was talking about her perspectives of, and great respect for, the film director Stanley Kubrick (1928-1999). Here are Nicole Kidman's observations of Stanley Kubrick:

> *"His* [Stanley Kubrick's] *understanding of humans was that we are very bittersweet, but he admired... passion, commitment, and loyalty.... The whole process of the film* [Eyes Wide Shut] *was a discovery. It was never about the result. It was never about... 'Well, we have a week to shoot this thing so quick, quick, quick, we have to do it; let's see, we may not fully explore it, but we'll get something good.'*
>
> *"Stanley wanted to explore every avenue and then make his decisions based on that. Stanley was not restricted by time. He refused to be, and that is a great luxury. Do you want to know what's gold with filmmaking? Time is gold. Not having to walk away from a scene before you feel like you've really perfected it.*
>
> *"The other thing Stanley hated doing was ever explaining himself... 'So what's the film about, Stanley?' He'd look down, look away, and not answer. And the same thing applied to a scene: 'So what do you really want this scene to be?' He would never answer that.*
>
> *"Part of Stanley's legacy on my life is that... well, you believe in something. You passionately believe in something, so devote yourself to it—completely, utterly, and don't apologize for doing it."*
>
> Nicole Kidman[54]

Other people in the documentary referred to Stanley Kubrick's view that either you care or you don't. You can't really "partly care", either you

---

[54] This is taken from *Stanley Kubrick, A Life In Pictures,* Warner Bros. Pictures, Time Warner Ent., Co., 2001. In the documentary, Ms. Kidman's comments were offered in excerpts to fit with the style of that documentary. They are reprinted here as one commentary to fit with the requirements of this book.

do or you don't. In your own bitter-sweet existence, people are not dispos-able. Care about what you do or don't do it. Be passionate.[55] Don't apologize for passion. I'm sure other people share similar views, but none I've found have been stated quite as articulately as Ms. Kidman's. It is en-tirely applicable to how we do, or don't, live our lives, and is particularly applicable to any struggle to move through the steps, get recovered, and become spiritual.

You are asked to become willing to be governed by spiritual principles and thereby, eventually, remove your defects of character: *"...any person capable of enough willingness and honesty to try repeatedly Step Six on all* [their] *faults* — without any reservations whatever — *has indeed come a long way spiritually...".*[56]

Here are examples: Are you looking forward to, pleased and agreeable, cheerfully compliant, or graciously consenting, to be gently honest *all* the time, in *all* situations, with *all* people, regardless of the consequences to yourself? Are you willing to be honest all the time, no matter to whom you're speaking? Are you willing to be charitable and kind, all the time, regardless of what the other person has done, or is doing, to you? I imagine some people may wonder: "Can't I be willing and complain a little bit sometimes?" No. Either you are or you aren't. Either you care or you don't. When that clergyman wrote, *"This is the step the separates the men from the boys,"* he meant that this step is spiritually the most difficult because of the requirement of willingness.

Survival Skills

All families have some degree of dysfunction — dishonesty, greed, ava-rice, sloth, manipulation, aggression, codependence (relationship addiction), oppression, sexual problems, envy, shame, etc. These are very often subtle and covert. Regardless of their visibility, they required each of us to de-velop a "compensation strategy" for whatever the dislocated power alliances are (or were) in your environment. You adapted as required (com-pensated) and survived.

Depending on any number of variables, and the power alliances in your family, and to varying degrees, you survived by being overtly sexual or sexually repressed; hiding your emotions or overtly displaying them; being invisible or showing off; being aggressive or subversive; being over-

---

[55] As an aside that is indirectly related: *"Of all forms of caution, caution in love is perhaps most fatal to true happiness."* [Bertrand Russell] *The Blues ain't nothing but a good soul feel-ing bad,* Sheldon Kopp, Fireside Books, Simon & Schuster, 1992, entry for Sep. 17.
[56] *Twelve Steps and Twelve Traditions,* p. 63, emphasis theirs.

achieving or underachieving. Perhaps you were prone to rages, deceitful, greedy, a comedian, bad, disobedient, sick, obsessive, political, manipulative, brave, slim, or overweight. Perhaps you took the role of caretaker in your family, or were prone to self-harm or aggression. You may have engaged in dozens of other strategies and combinations of strategies, all "unhealthy" [sic] to some degree, and became a master at whichever of these you chose. These compensating survival skills, often very subtle, are done as a matter of course. You became so good at them they eventually became who you thought you were and who you think you are.

For however (*dys*)functional a group of people are, especially families, as developing humans we must compensate for our unmet needs. The ways in which we compensate are usually quite unconscious and only rarely seen as maladaptive. In our culture's clamoring for convenience, hunting for scapegoats, obsession with shiny things and technology, and our separation from our souls, human ordinariness has become a defect. The genesis of the animal called "human" now has no room for error. However, character defects are inevitable, as are compensation strategies—both functions of our ordinariness, and they exacerbate the spiritual condition called addiction.

Having character defects or a dysfunctional family—now overly used and trite phrases—doesn't make you an addict. Those sometimes quite ordinary defects and your "dysfunctional family" demanded the evolution of destructive survival skills, which are exactly what you must be willing to abandon.

Regardless of the degree of dysfunction, families are so psychologically rooted in their misalliances, that any maladaptive survival strategies are experienced as absolutely normal. Children oftentimes experience a psychic jolt—a sudden, blunt shock of realization that their family isn't like others. The way they have been compensating has been ruptured.

At some point, usually at or after six or seven years old, whatever is or was seen as "normal" suddenly becomes flawed or fractured. This awareness is dependant on two conditions: a certain intellectual development, and exposure to a strange social environment. There can be a host of conflict and awareness problems that result from this rupture of perceived normalcy. Be that as it may, this only aggravates an addiction that may develop later, but it doesn't cause it.

Addicts develop new self-annihilation strategies and further entrench any old ones from childhood. Addictions create new personality problems, which become fused to the old ones, thereby making the old ones worse. Should these pre-addiction, often quite routine compensatory behaviours from childhood (after all, some addicts did come from pretty decent families) be altered by the phenomenon of addictions, it is easy to perceive that your "childhood" caused your addiction. It didn't.

Your childhood (all "childhoods") required certain survival skills. As destructive as these skills may have been, you needed them to get through your childhood. As a teenager, or older, these behaviours may have endorsed or contributed *to* your addiction, but they didn't cause it. The traits and behaviours of being a self-destructive addict have a subtly different origin and purpose. To the addict, however, this self-destruction feels like it's their nature to be this way; that these behaviours are essential for survival.

Step Six requires that you be willing to abandon the very behaviours that allowed you to be a successful addict. Being spiritual requires you *willingly* quit doing the things that made you brilliantly successful at destroying yourself. Consider that addicts approach this step with only a few months or one or two years of sobriety, and come from years or decades of self-annihilation. It is monumentally difficult, even with good role modeling, strong faith, and long-term abstinence, to become completely willing to abandon your addictions-based survival or avoidance skills.

Psychologically violent behaviours like shaming, teasing, verbal abuse, arguing, moral superiority, pity, intrusive questions, and threats have no place in a spiritual lifestyle. Tough, hard-line, angry, insensitive "recovery" is about dominating, shaming, or pushing people into obedience — doing what the sponsor (or, in many cases, the counsellor, the church, the recovery house) wants. This is entirely inappropriate and has no place in any process of *spiritual* transformation.

This is why your mentor, sponsor, therapist, or doctor (whomever you seek counsel from) should be someone who is *well* conversant with, or obedient to, the principles of an ethical, non-violent life.[57] Anyone who covets any underlying anger, prejudice, moral superiority, righteousness, or contempt will have no persuasive power to attract another person into a spiritual, non-addicted lifestyle.[58] Gentle self-discipline, and sincere commitment to the maintenance steps (spiritual principles), and a sincerely ethical life, is the order of the day, *every* day. Seeing this in others is a prime ingredient and an essential motivator towards willingness at Step Six.

You have to take into your heart the truth that becoming the exact opposite of every character defect, of every symptom of the disease, is where you willingly go. You volunteer for it. Eventually you would pursue this with pleasant anticipation. Step Six requires that you become willing to be

---

[57] Addictions, self-neglect, punishing, self-annihilation, psychological abuse, competition, shame, disrespect, anger, rage, deceit, etc., are violent. These, directly or indirectly, have no place in any spiritual endeavor.

[58] My belief, and this comment, is my adaptation of this: *"You have no morally persuasive power when you possess any underlying contempt,"* said by Dr. Martin Luther King, Jr., which is found in *Martin Luther King, Jr.*, by Marshall Frady, a Lipper®/Viking Book, 2002.

respectful, honest, humble, generous of spirit, and considerate and responsible in all situations, in all circumstances, and with all people, regardless of the consequences to yourself and regardless of how people behave towards you.[59]

If you don't have an abiding conviction (which you established at Step Two) that establishing a spiritual life is the goal, it is impossible to do Step Six, which is the third of the three major demands for a complete realignment of your perceptions. You are required here, to prove that your decision at Step Three was sincere.

"Are we now ready to let God remove from us all the things which we have admitted are objectionable?"[60] This refers to your insecurities, fears, and sexual selfishness uncovered and discussed at Steps Four and Five. The defect-removal process must, and can only begin with willingness. If Step Four or Five is in any way a catalogue of behaviour, rather than a disclosure of instincts gone awry, fears, sexual selfishness, then you're in trouble.

The intent of Step Six is to establish a willingness to remove your defects. You can remove defects because they're still present; but you can't "remove" historical events. You don't "have" these old actions; they're gone. You cannot be successful when praying for the willingness to remove something that you don't have. Past *behaviours* are not removable. Character defects, on the other hand, are removable; they aren't gone; they're still present. If a Step Four or Five identifies a list of "bad behaviours" there's nothing you can do at Step Six because spiritual willingness can't resolve past behaviours. However, what is still present and objectionable are the instincts gone awry, fears, and sexual selfishness. You have the ability to remove or modify these. If Steps Four or Five were about behaviour, completing Step Six is impossible.

"We have emphasized willingness as being indispensable."[61] Getting recovered depends on it. With minimal faith in a higher power, you have no resource for the courage it takes to be willing. *"If we still cling to something we cannot let go, we ask God to help us be willing."*[62] Become willing to abandon your defects (addictions-related survival skills) and adopt a spiritual way of life.

---

[59] Keep this in context. These are to be modified in emergent situations of violence or danger; however, even then, do not abandon spiritual principles.
[60] *Alcoholics Anonymous*, p. 76.
[61] Ibid.
[62] Ibid.

The Objective

Twelve Steps and Twelve Traditions advises you to work towards an objective defined by "God", not defined by you (meaning defined by spiritual principles and not by your defects and insecurities).[63] I suppose each of us has a certain level where some arbitrary degree of honesty is good enough: "I've got a good life now. I'm honest (enough)." Having a strong attachment to a peer group means your life is only as spiritual as the group's, which is an objective defined by the group and not by God: honest enough to get by, but not honest enough to risk social disapproval.

Whatever degree of spirituality you have attained has allowed you to achieve a certain comfortable lifestyle, and you often judge that level as "good enough". You're tired of the hard work; you'll just relax and maybe not be as vigilant. Overcoming your own complacency to deepen your spirituality, which flies in the face of everything cultural, is what makes Step Six the most difficult of the steps.[64]

I wonder what "God" might think of receiving a prayer like this:

Dear God:
I've been trying this spirituality—getting recovered thing for a while. My friends think I'm too demanding of myself about honesty. They're uncomfortable, and there's all this humility stuff. Well... this spiritual work is really hard. Like, it's really hard! So I'm going to take a break. Besides... well... my sponsor's life is okay. I know they sometimes tell little lies and complain and gossip, but they've got a job and a nicer car than me. God, I don't want to have to make all new friends just because I'm honest. Geez! I mean, finding people who are really trying to live by spiritual principles might take forever and... well, if I'm that honest maybe I'll never get laid. Anyway, I don't want to be working at spirituality all that hard all the time. Life's pretty good now. I'm going to take some time off from spirituality and praying.
Sincerely,
Me

P.S.: God, can I please keep my abstinence and maybe a little serenity while I'm ignoring you? Thanks.

---

[63] *"...between striving for a self-determined objective and for the perfect objective which is of God." Twelve Steps and Twelve Traditions*, p. 68, and *"Reminding ourselves that we have decided to go to any lengths to find a spiritual experience...," Alcoholics Anonymous*, p. 79.
[64] Remember the proverb: *'Take what you want,' said God, 'and pay for it.'* The long transition from deceit and manipulation to rigorous honesty is always awkward. Making this transition is both wise *and* difficult, but once you reasonably achieve it, it's a pleasure to maintain.

Once recovered, there's never a vacation from the maintenance steps and the spiritual principles they embody. And, if the truth be known, eventually the five spiritual principles become the vacation that you've always wanted but were too cheap to pay for.

The majority of twelve-step people are honest enough to get by and grumble about how hard honesty is (because they're just trying to get by, like trying to swim without getting too wet). To constantly be responsible, to struggle for deeper levels of willingness, and to adopt completely the spiritual principles in the maintenance steps is to aspire to a standard set by "God". It's principles that govern behaviour, not convenience.

Honesty eventually becomes graceful, but in the meantime, remind yourself that you voluntarily chose a spiritual lifestyle. When you are noticeably willing to live, *all of the time*, by a spiritually defined objective, and are reasonably consistently determined to get back on track when you find that you're not, you are done with Step Six.

Read the single paragraph in *Alcoholics Anonymous* about Step Six. Meditate on how simple and complete it is. It may take several months to understand its all-encompassing nature and to become truly willing. Thoroughness is how you demonstrate your commitment to live a spiritual life. Step Six is acquiring a willing devotion to abandon all of your "addict survival skills"—actually *being* a spiritual pilgrim. Are you completely willing to change completely?

I get variations of two general reactions from people who have a stubborn mindset prior to reading or hearing this. They often strongly disagree, and become angry or defensive (they've been jarred out of their comfort zones). Or if they're foundering or confused, they experience a sense of relief that it does make sense and there is hope. In either situation, there is anxiety (fear) at all of the work involved.

Old Ideas

As I mentioned earlier, I was once offering a seminar on "Christianity and spirituality" at a treatment centre. A man got up in the middle of the lecture, pointed at me, and proclaimed loudly: "How dare you say that!" He went up to his room, packed his bags, and quit treatment. He decided two things: I was wrong and he was offended. When you think you're right, you can't learn anything, and even if you are "right" there's disadvantages to being arrogant about it.

"Some of us have tried to hold on to our old ideas and the result was nil until we let go absolutely."[65] It's easy to interpret this sentence as referring to old ideas from drinking and acting out. That's only part of it. In their first year of abstinence, people getting recovered have to let go of old ideas from when they were acting out; in their second year, they must abandon some old ideas from their first year; and in their fifth year, they must let go of old ideas from the third or fourth years of getting recovered.

An old idea is an old idea—ideas from an hour ago and thirty years ago qualify as old ideas. If you're not willing to let go of old ideas you're in serious spiritual trouble. It isn't that old ideas are automatically wrong because they're old; it's your willingness or unwillingness to self-examine and change that's at issue.[66]

The more you have invested in an old idea—the more passionately you believe in it, the more you brag about it, the longer you have cherished it, the more difficult it will be to challenge it.[67] Your willingness to let go of old ideas, old "truths", old perspectives, old behaviours, is related to humility (i.e. being spiritually teachable), an attitude you are to maintain for the rest of your life. Forcing yourself to shift out of your ego's willful blindness[68] and into willingness is always a significant ingredient in re-education.

When do you let go of an old idea, an old value, an old behaviour? When you realize it operates contrary to any part of any of the five spiritual principles within the maintenance steps. When an insight illuminates some very subtle corrupt motive, or when a more recently felt experience has a more sincere spiritual perspective then the old idea goes.

Become convinced that spirituality is essential (Step Two); commit yourself to achieving this in your own life (Step Three); be responsible and view yourself properly (Step Four); be transparent and honest about yourself (Step Five); desire to be willing (Step Six). And that brings us to...

---

[65] *Alcoholics Anonymous*, p. 58.

[66] "Willingness" will now become a mindset that is essential to all transformation work.

[67] As you read this you may wonder that in how I discuss the older, earlier view of *Alcoholics Anonymous*, I am clinging to an old idea. As I explain elsewhere, it isn't that old ideas are wrong. Many old ideas are worthy of being upheld. As regards the AA philosophy, experience has shown that the earlier (pre-1980) spiritual perspective of recovery is substantially more effective that the more recent psychological interpretations.

[68] Willful Blindness is a principle of jurisprudence. A stranger on the street offers you an obviously new, expensive sports car for $500.00. You buy it and are later charged with some crime related to possession of stolen property. At trial you claim you didn't know it was stolen. You willfully chose to be blind to the obvious, hence "willful blindness", and you may well be found guilty of a crime. In a similar manner, forcing yourself to be blind to obvious unspiritual/abusive behaviour (your own or someone else's) is a transparent, irresponsible ego-tactic of addicts. See again the quote of Thomas Merton at the beginning of Chapter 1.

Prerequisites and Observations Regarding Step Seven

Very soon now, two things will be possible that weren't before. You will be capable of acceptance, and you will not require pain to be the motivator of change.

The demands of Step Six are so subtle and overwhelming that it seldom gets the attention that it deserves. Achieving willingness, as difficult as that may be, is a fundamental quality of character that must be present for humility to exist. *"Since [Step Seven] so specifically concerns itself with humility, we should pause here to consider what humility is and what the practice of it can mean to us."*[69]

Humility

Humility is not the intellectually passive adoption of a philosophical concept. You cannot think yourself into a relationship with a deity. Humility is misunderstood; it's tricky. Humility, as with the other four spiritual principles, goes against every trait of any addiction. Spiritual endeavour requires that you adopt both aspects of humility (see Appendix II) so that, eventually, Grace can operate more freely within you.[70] Humility is the primary underlying theme that operates in concert with all spiritual attributes, without exception.

Humility is active. It's an actual physical set of behaviours, accompanied by a contemplative, willing mindset, where you surrender gracefully to, and put yourself in the position of, rendering service to a higher power. That may manifest, as service to people but "serving others", by itself is only being socially charitable. Humility is rooted in service to, and love of, a higher power of your understanding—an outgrowth of the spiritual principles that form the context for an egalitarian mindset. That, in practical terms, is a life that's voluntarily compliant with the five spiritual principles.

---

[69] *Twelve Steps and Twelve Traditions*, p. 70.

[70] What is "Grace"? First I offer this quote from J. Goethe: *"Until one is committed, there is hesitancy, the chance to draw back, always ineffectiveness, concerning all acts of initiative and creation. There is one elementary truth the ignorance of which kills countless ideas and splendid plans: that the moment one definitely commits oneself, then Providence moves too. All sorts of things occur to help one that would never otherwise have occurred. A whole stream of events issues from the decision, raising on one's favor all manner of unforeseen incidents and meetings and material assistance which no person could have dreamed would have come their way. Whatever you can do or dream you can, begin it. Boldness has genius, power, and magic in it. Begin it now."* Grace is what happens when you are sincerely committed to an ethical course of action, *and* are in-line with the energy of the universe. To those cynics who read this, it may sound hokey or too airy-fairy to believe, but it's true.

I have heard people subtly complain after a twelve-step call, or after some other endeavor, about the ingratitude they encountered. How many "spiritual" people secretly expect gratitude? What's it really like in the shadows of your heart when no one says: "Thanks for your effort."? Being spiritual requires that your effort be in the humble service of a higher power (harmony), not in the service of your ego's notions of *quid pro quo* and social reward.

A story: Once upon a time, a monk (or a sponsor or a therapist) had an acolyte (substitute a newcomer or a client) who was absolutely devoted to her. The monk thought her spiritual student dull-witted and inept, but was pleased she had such a devoted follower. One day the monk heard rumors that her acolyte had walked on water. The monk questioned the young acolyte, who immediately prostrated himself and humbly said, "Yes, Master, they told me that I did that, but I was in walking meditation at the time, contemplating my reverence for you, Master, chanting your name in meditative bliss when this happened. I was unaware of it." The monk marveled at this. In an effort to demonstrate her own spiritual prowess, she walked into the river chanting, "Me, Me, Me," and sank.

When living in dislocation, humility is most often viewed as dangerous. Many people, especially addicts, perceive that being humble is boring, or that when they are humble, they're weak and they run the risk of being humiliated.[71] These are two of the more subtle dynamics of spiritual misinformation that have to be challenged. These perceptions automatically set up a very subtle resistance to humility, and then spirituality becomes that much more distant. The further along you are in the steps, the more responsible you must become. The more responsible you must become, the more you need humility. You've got to sincerely want to be the acolyte and not the monk.

Here's another perspective of humility: You think, "pick up the pen," so you pick up the pen. Or you intuit that a smile is appropriate and so you smile a pleasant, friendly smile. You never notice the process of doing either of these, and have no real comprehension of how these incredibly complicated things happen—brain cells, synapses, nerves, muscles, memory, coordination. Millions of tiny energy impulses all "did something", and you picked up the pen or you smiled. It was unconscious and graceful. Humility has to act that way otherwise it's impression management.

Work hard at not noticing your humility. However, at the outset of your transformation, there is a necessary and concerted intellectual effort required to *be* humble. You have to force yourself into it. Initially, it isn't

---

[71] The truth is that when you are sincerely, spiritually humble, you cannot be humiliated.

graceful or voluntary at all. When you talk about how humble you are try-ing to be, or force yourself to be humble, you aren't. It's forced, but it still has to start with you acting "as if".

All spiritual transformation begins with your acting as if you are what you cannot yet be. Force yourself to do it. Diligently belabour the action within yourself, and embrace your incompetence as natural. The desire to become humble is sufficient to begin. Humility grows out of an unassuming devotion to achieving the spiritual principles within the maintenance steps. Force yourself to surrender gracefully, and be silent about that. When you do this, without want of reward, without knowing it is happening, you are in a humble moment.[72]

I've offered a brief description of "humility" in Appendix II, but it's rather philosophical and not too specific. The definitions are legion. Two things they all have in common are that the definitions are quickly reduced to clichés, and they are always incomplete (words themselves are inade-quate). Additionally, any concerted, energetic effort to define humility fails because of the underlying and camouflaged arrogance of trying to write the "perfect" definition of humility (or likewise, of a higher power).

Humility is also present in authentic love. Or, from another view, nei-ther love nor humility can exist without some noticeable presence of the other. Within this thing we call our mind, where did some abstract concept like humility come from? Where *exactly* does Love reside? These two are inextricably linked and impossible to define. Love and humility appear to be the two human attributes that are innately present at birth and never need to be taught.[73] They cannot be taught and exist somewhere underneath our physical existence and the trappings of culture.

The potential to be spiritual exists within everyone. It exists under-neath the biological and secular constructs of personality and culture. Becoming spiritual requires unlearning old ideas, clearing away defects, abandoning pride, and having faith that your insecurities are meaningless. Humility will be present as you endeavor to experience veracity inside yourself. All of the spiritual principles exist inherently within us. The three maintenance steps are the rituals that demonstrate those pre-existing five principles. Willingly surrendering to this truth is the task at hand.

---

[72] *The World's Religions*, by Huston Smith, HarperSanFrancisco, 1991, The Way to God through Work, is an articulate explanation of "work" through karma yoga, as one path to God. Any work in service to God, and without a personal investment in the outcome, is an aspect of humility.
[73] People never need to be taught how to love. *The Blues ain't nothing but a good soul feeling bad,* Sheldon Kopp, Fireside Books, Simon & Schuster, 1992, entry for March 11.

The Gift is the Opportunity

In studying the writings of the spiritual masters, and from my own experience, it seems the gifts people receive, which appear to arrive from "divine" sources, are of this specific nature: If the gifts are to be appreciated, they cannot be withheld from general distribution. What you must give away; what you have to share freely or lose, are understanding, charity of spirit, serenity, compassion, love, and joy. Once you have these, which are the after-effects of a spiritual lifestyle, they are available to anyone who comes into contact with you by virtue of the fact that you have them. When these spiritual gifts are husbanded or withheld they wither and disappear; they are destroyed by selfishness. With some irony, you keep them for yourself through giving them away—generosity is how those attributes are retained. The spiritual attributes of respect, charity of spirit, serenity, compassion, love, and joy are always retained by egalitarian distribution.

Conversely: People who accumulate or receive secular "gifts" like property, money, influence, and temporal power must withhold them from others in order to keep them for themselves. Withholding them— selfishness—is how these are retained.

Now consider the circumstance of recovery. Many addicts, prior to their first experience with twelve-step programs, or those concerned with healing in general, don't understand that being recovered is an option. There is so much misinformation "out there" about healing and recovery that many of us think we're doomed to a life of depression, anger, or addictions.

Suddenly they are presented with the awareness that they do have a choice, and are then given the opportunity to choose. There are many viable options available for healing that are, or at least showing themselves to be, more effective than pills or psychiatry or traditional (endless) talk therapy).

This new opportunity to choose is often described in terms of "gifts from providence", or grace, and is variously referred to as a spiritual experience or awakening, or a religious experience. Doctors Jung, Silkworth, and Tiebout refer to this as a psychic shift. And so, it would appear that sobriety extends out of the opportunity to choose, and that awareness-opportunity is provided by providence. There is no actual "labour" involved when a person is suddenly presented with that first uninvited *opportunity* to become spiritual.

Spiritual transformation isn't free, the opportunity is. Transformation is earned by working hard to take advantage of the opportunity to choose. In the vernacular: the universe's gift to you is the *opportunity* to choose sobriety. Then, you work *very* hard in a specific way (the original steps) to take advantage of that opportunity. Spiritual virtues subsequently appreciate in you, and your gift to "the universe" is to embody those virtues in such a way that spirituality becomes attractive to others. You do the work; a higher power, as you understand this, gets the credit.

If you want to be a great therapist, you have to study great therapists and (to some degree) act as they acted. Students of painting and music study the great painters and musicians. Study the teachings of Buddha, Lao Tzu, Gandhi, Da Mo, whomever—work to understand what they understood, all the while embracing your resistance and incompetence as natural. Your ego will fight it. Approach this with the idea you're always a newcomer to the rest of your life.

Force yourself inside the steps and principles; force them inside you. This effort is the spiritual use of willpower and the effective use of a strong ego. If you want to have humility as a graceful part of your life, study the people who live humble, spiritually courageous lives. You don't need sit on the top of a mountain in the wilderness. You need to do this *exactly* where you're standing at any given moment of any given day. Now is when it starts and inside you is where it's found.

The Monumental Shift

Humility, partly because of the cultural disparagement of spirituality, and the deifying of greed and power, is routinely discouraged as a desirable attribute. Initially, entering a recovery program or therapy is always moti-vated by fear, shame, or humiliation—the consequences of your addiction or your unhappy life (the consequences of your former choices). At Step One you were forced into your first rudimentary exposure to "humility" which, at that point, closely resembled humiliation only because you are beaten into it. Nobody comes to humility easily, not even the saints. The process I am about to describe is crucial to spiritual success, and takes you directly into the last, and the most important, of the three major value-shifts in getting recovered.[74]

At the outset, acting out beat you into "recovery", which is only the external tip of the problem. The acquisition of humility is initially evi-denced by a subtle and constantly increasing inner motivation to complete the steps while you are in fact doing them. However, if you haven't fol-lowed the instructions thus far, you cannot establish the foundation required for the monumental shift that I am about to describe.

The initial motivation to become abstinent is from shame and fear of insanity, death, punishment, or shame (exposure). At Step Two you believe that spirituality is the solution. That initial motivation of "all fear" changes slightly to include some small portion of a desire for spirituality. Through

---

[74] The first values shift was at Step Two (valuing a spiritually governed life), and the second at Step Four (a non-blaming, responsible lifestyle).

Steps Three to Five, fear as the motivator is further reduced, and their "should be" a correlated increase in a desire to be spiritual. At Step Six, where the task is to acquire willingness to lose your defects, you're now (or are supposed to be) primarily motivated by a desire for spirituality. You're now beginning to believe that spirituality is inherently good for its own sake, which is remarkably different from the Step Two perception that spirituality is good because it's going to save your life.

Your view of spirituality is changing from something imposed by fear and shame to something desired. This shift in motivation is *the* essential prerequisite to Step Seven.

Should you have done *these* original steps meticulously, there's an underlying fundamental shift happening in your world-view—humility and honesty are becoming intrinsically good unto themselves, and are willingly pursued personal attributes. Loyalty and allegiance to spiritual principles are increasingly inner imperatives. By Step Seven, the work has thus far set up a foundation for a life based on spiritual principles (the maintenance steps, even though you aren't there yet)—they eventually become cherished, internalized foundations of non-negotiable conduct. If, at Step Seven, this isn't becoming more obvious to you, then an important teaching has been missed *en route* to this point.

If you believe you've done the steps but are always "in recovery", if you're sometimes political rather than honest, if you avoid awkward truths for your own sake, if you talk about someone rather than to them, if you're interested in being honest, generous, kind, etc., because it's what's expected, you've missed the shift from begrudging spirituality to willing spirituality. Your motivation for recovery is still rooted in addictions-based fear and shame. In these situations, go back to Step Two and reexamine your commitment to spirituality.

It's impossible to be spiritual and at the same time harm yourself or others. It's impossible to be spiritual if you are irresponsible.[75] It's impossible to be humble if you disrespect yourself or others by abuse, neglect, withholding, or lying. Humility and truth are an integral part of self-respect.

---

[75] What follows will be explained in detail in *Facets of Personal Transformation*. I have described people in therapy who get to the cusp between knowledge and insight and then quit. If you are in therapy and it seems to have worked for you for some period of time, laborious or expensive as it may be, don't quit when you get the urge to take a break. The stronger the urge, the more important it is that you stay. You will dredge up several rationalizations that justify quitting: "The therapist didn't.... My friends say.... Keeping the appointments is hard because.... I'm doing fine...." Work through your resistance. If the therapeutic alliance has worked up to that point, and the therapist has been generally effective, then persevere. *Don't quit*. It's exactly at that point that something important is happening for you and insight is on your horizon. In fact, ask for extra sessions. If these circumstances apply, challenge yourself not the therapy or the therapist.

Begrudging participation and shallow commitments are the breeding ground for dilemmas and confusion. When spiritual principles are understood and adhered to, dilemmas and confusion evaporate. *"We saw that we needn't always be bludgeoned and beaten into humility. It could come quite as much from our voluntarily reaching for it as it could from unremitting suffering. A great turning point in our lives came when we sought for humility as something we really wanted, rather than something we must have."* [76]

As soon as you experience in your heart that humility, both spiritual and secular (living an authentic, egalitarian lifestyle), is desirable for you, that moment is a sunrise to the rest of your life. You stay committed to responsibility and truth, and integrity is consistently available. You'll no longer be motivated by pain and shame. While you're being humble, fear of being humiliated will disappear. There won't be any confusion about how you conduct yourself. And, there's this fine point about "voluntary" participation: arriving as a newcomer, and through the first six steps, your participation is motivated by crisis, fear, and pain. Yes, you voluntarily participate, but you volunteered only to get rid of pain and chaos. That's how everyone starts. However, when these steps are done meticulously, and spiritual heliotropism carries you through Step Seven, your voluntary participation becomes motivated by the attractiveness of humility, i.e. *"...we needn't always be bludgeoned and beaten into humility."*

Being an addict, and the tasks that facilitate transformation in the first six steps, require the cliché "no pain, no gain" to be true. With the continuing absence of willingness in spiritual commitment, "no pain, no gain" is the prerequisite to everything you accomplish. However, when you really "get" Steps Two and Six the struggle for transformation is over, and when you desire humility as a good thing, veracity is automatic and painless.

These are permanent benefits of changing your perspective of humility, and it's here that living without suffering becomes possible. If you claim to be beyond Step Seven, and are still generally motivated by pain and turmoil, or if there's recurring conflict and struggle in your life, your spirituality is political; you've missed the point.

"The chief activator of our defects has been self-centered fear— primarily fear that we would lose something we already possessed or would fail to get something we demanded." [77] You have character defects because you're scared. Do you want to know why you lie; what motivates betrayal; why you manipulate people? You're scared. Why are you greedy? Why are you slothful? Why are you mean? Why are you spiteful? You're afraid. You

---

[76] *Twelve Steps and Twelve Traditions*, p. 75, emphasis added.

[77] Ibid., p. 76.

are angry because you're afraid. The chief activator of your defects has been self-centred fear.

When you find yourself displaying a character defect ignore the defect itself and examine yourself for fear. The skill of identifying your fears was developed at Step Four. Getting honest and avoiding theatrics about your fears and sexual selfishness was practiced in Step Five. Because of this training, bypassing the actual character defect to expose the underlying fear should be a fairly straightforward task of self-reflection, and should occur without the need to blame anyone. If it isn't, you've missed something along the way.

Step Seven

> *"I hope you like the wedding gift I bought*
> *you. It's a broken toaster oven."*

The instructions regarding Step Seven are contained entirely within one paragraph. And, of course, they presume you've done what you were told to do to up to this point. The Step Seven prayer is profound and rather straightforward.

> *When ready, we say something like this: My Creator* [My higher power], *I am now willing that you should have all of me, good and bad. I pray that you now remove from me every single defect of character, which stands in the way of my usefulness to you and my fellows. Grant me strength, as I go out from here, to do your bidding. Amen.*[78]

"When ready..." means when you have done *all* the prerequisite work, and have achieved the (reasonably consistent) willingness described in Step Six, regarding each of your character defects. That's when you'll be ready.

"My Creator, I am now willing that you should have all of me, good and bad," has a subtle catch to it. Addicts live with shame, and deep inside believe they are flawed and unworthy. The first sentence is the offering of yourself as a gift to your higher power, but nobody likes to give or receive defective gifts. Did you ever go into a store to buy a gift and say: "I'd like to buy my partner a watch. Have you got one that's scratched and doesn't work right?" There's a social stigma attached to offering broken gifts: "I hope you like the wedding gift I bought you. It's a broken toaster oven." We don't do that.

---

[78] *Alcoholics Anonymous*, p. 76.

People usually give gifts that are pristine and shiny and work right. In Step Seven, you are giving yourself to God. *You* are the gift. If you believe there's something broken in the gift (yourself) there will be reluctance in the offering. You've been ashamed of yourself for so long, so how could *anyone* want you?[79]

Part of your step work has been to eliminate self-condemnation, which began back at the "I'm not crazy, I have a disease," realization at Step One. If you haven't unequivocally resolved the "I'm bad - I'm sick" debate, you can't offer yourself sincerely at Step Seven, and the shift to desiring humility won't happen. You'll remain stuck in the "no pain, no gain" mindset, which clearly doesn't exist in a spiritual life.

At Step Two you learned that social success was *not* the order of the day. At Step Seven, you're not offering only your goodness or social accomplishments, but also your love and spiritual devotion, *and* your defects and misdemeanors. Your devotion to spirituality is the actual gift of "yourself" to your higher power.[80] Your willing commitment to spiritual principles is the gift and what allows the offering of flawed gifts to God. Without sincere willingness, the Step Seven prayer is only Impression Management.

"*I pray that you now remove from me every single defect of character which stands in the way of my usefulness to you and my fellows.*" The prayer is basically petitionary, but not for personal advantage. The purpose of your gift of "you" to your higher power is service to "the harmony of the universe" and to others. It does not read: Please remove my character defects so that I have a serene personal life. The prayer contains no aspect of selfishness and nothing about personal success or popularity. Your defects are to be removed because they limit your usefulness to the people in your life and your higher power.

Ask of your higher power that your character defects be removed *only* so that others can see that praying is good. Ask that regardless of whatever life circumstances befall you, you remain steadfast in your commitment to spiritual principles, so that others will see (by observing you) that this is a worthy lifestyle. When next you say your prayers, plead to remain anonymous and in the background of *all* your good deeds, so that "God" will get more credit than you do. Pray because it's a worthy activity.

---

[79] Outside of spirituality, in the dynamics of love and relationship, one perspective of a long-term sincere commitment to another person is the notion of giving yourself to them: (cont'd) the metaphor of gift-giving in love—I offer myself to thee. If you believe (especially subconsciously) you're broken and defective, you'll withhold on your commitment in the relationship; or you'll generate a complex Impression Management scheme; or you'll give yourself to someone who will agree, with you, that you're flawed, and they'll treat you disrespectfully—or all three.

[80] This theme is expanded upon in the section on prayer in Chapter 9.

Traditional petitionary prayer almost invariably reduces itself to the petitioner trying to control the agenda of life, based on some comparative or superlative analysis of moral values: trying to advise God that the world should be run according to their plan; trying to impose their will on whomever or whatever it is they are praying about; trying to avoid loss, inconvenience, pain, responsibility, or calamity. Most often, petitionary prayer has little to do with a spiritually principled life, and is motivated by the selfish agenda of whoever's praying. Outside of praying only for things that are to the advantage of a universal deity, petitionary prayer is the attempt to impose some personal agenda on life, on God, on others. (Which agenda is what addicts begin to eliminate at Step Three.)

The steps, and this prayer, are intended to reduce the dominating presence of character defects and insecurities, and eliminate an addict's never-ending struggle to get their own way. Confusing God with Santa Claus, under the guise of altruism or moral or religious righteousness is a potent error in prayer. There's an identifiable arrogance—an obvious flaw of hubris, in trying to dictate the terms of life, advising God on how things should be run. From various religious points of view, this is ethically suspect, because "God" is supposed to know much better than we how to run the universe. What arrogance is there in suggesting how God run things?

Selfishness, camouflaged under altruism, righteous proselytizing, and charity, is the refuge of an insecure person who believes they know what is good for everybody; in some cases, even God. Altruism or charity that isn't rooted in reasonably sincere, non-controlling, egalitarian values; that doesn't emanate from someone who is, precedent to the charitable act, reasonably spiritually humble and self-responsible, is to some degree corrupt. Altruism that conceals moral superiority, or presents some selfish agenda as the will of God, is the rationale for righteousness—imposing your will on others, and is decidedly unspiritual.[81]

The prayer ends: *"Grant me strength, as I go out from here, to do your bidding."* Notice it doesn't say: Grant me the strength... to find a lover (or) get the promotion. In twelve-step programs, religious circles, and some other "spiritual" healing endeavors, there are many debates about God's will. These debates are often intellectual stalling tactic while searching for an easier, softer way, i.e. trying to discover some recovery shell game to justify fear and selfishness while claiming spiritual commitment, and

---

[81] Some may argue that when charity is offered with corrupt motives, it's still to be endorsed because it fills an immediate need, and the immediate need is seen as a greater good than the need to withhold the charity until spiritual integrity is established. It isn't that simple when you expose the consistently unexamined secondary consequences of corrupt charity: shame, dishonesty, rescuing, arrogance, implied obligation and debt, pity; and the unexamined, tertiary consequence of perpetuating the social cycle of shame on both the part of the giver and the receiver. As a spiritual endeavor, charity is oftentimes-risky business.

charming everyone into thinking you are what you're not. There are times when claiming to be confused about "God's will" justifies delays in making meaningful commitments and enables continued unspiritual behaviour. It avoids the unaddressed fear, dishonesty and irresponsibility underneath the debates.[82]

The twelve steps allow you to become spiritual and to maintain that. Page 15 in *Alcoholics Anonymous* advises that your job is to work and sacrifice yourself for others; page 19, your job is to have respect for others' opinions; page 77, your real purpose is to be of maximum service to others and to God; and on page 128, that giving rather than getting is the principle of your existence. These are what God's "will" is—from the literature.[83] People who are confused about God's will haven't done the requisite work to clearly understand the focus and spiritual nature of the original twelve steps. If they had done the work, there would be no confusion.

The Principles Aren't the Steps

Within twelve-step groups there is much talk about whether people are or aren't following "the principles", and what those principles are. I've referred many times to the spiritual principles inherent in the regeneration steps and embodied in the maintenance steps.

A spiritual principle is a universal truth against which we evaluate our behaviour and attitude. Huston Smith writes, near the end of *The World's Religions,* that the three universal principles of the wisdom traditions are veracity, humility, and charity. These three don't necessarily have anything to do with "God", but it's usually assumed they do.

Because of the inherent qualities of addictions, and how I understand the perennial philosophies regarding spiritual wisdom, I have added two more—respect for the body and responsibility/obedience. And, again, these two don't necessarily have anything to do with "God". Altogether, these five are what would be aspired to in the acquisition and demonstration of spiritual integrity. (See Appendix II)

The steps themselves are not principles. Each step is an instruction for a task you are to complete. Principles, which would apply to all of the steps, are the foundation upon which the steps are built. Principles form the guidelines for how you do them. For example, veracity is a principle—an

---

[82] For an in-depth explanation of responsibility, see *Taking Responsibility* by Nathaniel Branden, cited at an earlier footnote. Gerald May's book *Will and Spirit* has important observations about God's "will".

[83] Remember your self-assigned task is to make real your decision at Step Three—to turn your will and life over to the care of your higher power, as you understand this. It isn't "My will for God," it's "God's will for me." There's a remarkable difference.

essential theme upon which all the steps are constructed, which also guides the nature of your behaviour while doing the steps.

Earlier, I discussed that there is an external difference in types of addictive behaviour and detoxification, but underneath the behaviour, addicts are generally the same.[84] The symptoms of addiction, listed in Chapter 2, are present to varying degrees in all addicts. The self-destructive acting out behaviours are different, but the symptoms are the same. I also pointed out that the first nine steps are individual tasks to be completed, and the three maintenance steps aren't ever completed—they're ongoing and interrelated. You *do* the first nine; you *are* the last three.

The principles of spirituality lie underneath each individual step. The content of the step (the addictions fingerprint) will vary from one addict to another, but the principles won't vary, which is what makes them principles.

One of the more profound things about the twelve steps is related to Huston Smith's observation about the three universal spiritual principles from the wisdom traditions: veracity, humility, and charity. The maintenance steps, by spiritual design, are virtually perfect representations of those three principles: Step Ten—Veracity; Step Eleven—Humility; Step Twelve—Charity.

In any twelve-step program, the first fundamental spiritual requirement, crucial to your ability to carry the message and eventually be recovered, is to heal yourself first. This is why the first seven steps belong to you. These have little or nothing to do with anybody or anything else. You get the first seven steps; everyone else gets the last five.

Your only guarantee of "success", because of the nature of the disease of addictions, is to negotiate yourself through the original twelve-step steps, exactly as they're written. Up to step nine, each step is intended to do three things: (i) eliminate various facets of the disease, (ii) incorporate aspects of the maintenance steps; and (iii), expose you to a life that is governed by the five spiritual principles. Recall earlier I explained that each step, up to Step Nine, counteracts some combination of the symptoms and incorporates spiritual principles. I also suggested a three-column exercise for each step. Review that exercise now: it will help with your willingness (or lack of it).

Step Six is the third major turning point after you achieve abstinence. Overall, it's crucial that you change your worldview, and Step Six (willingness) creates the foundation for that fundamental change. The generosity

---

[84] This does not contradict the truth that any therapeutic and spiritual strategy in establishing abstinence must be very particular to each addict (identifying and responding to a person's addictions fingerprint). Each addict harbors a unique interaction of personality and addiction.

and sincerity in your Step Seven prayer is a reflection of your personal devotion and determination to focus your willpower towards willing humility.

The President and the Janitor

Once upon a time, there was an exceptionally huge, multi-national corporation that employed 675,000 people. This mega-corporation had investments and controlling shares in 811 smaller companies. The corporation had huge offices and warehouses in 74 countries around the world, and had gross production and sales in the tens of billions of dollars. Overall, this massive, global business conglomerate directly or indirectly governed the livelihood of over four million people and the economy of small countries. (This company was *really* big.) The CEO/President worked out of the very largest office, on the highest floor, at the very top of the tallest business tower, at the very centre of the biggest city in the world.

There was a janitor who had one lunchroom to clean in a small subsidiary company, away around on the opposite side of the world. This janitor couldn't balance a chequebook and would often grumble about other workers being untidy. The janitor certainly knew nothing about running the big international mega-corporation.

One day, however, the janitor sent a note to The President on the other side of the world. The janitor politely insisted that a company policy be changed—a policy that the janitor didn't know too much about, but didn't like. The janitor implied in the note that The President didn't know how to run the corporation, and things would be improved if The President did what the janitor wanted.

In personifying God, which is what I have done here, a risky venture at the best of times, "God" somehow operates the universe and I keep my life clean. I have come to enjoy sending notes to The President (by way of prayer), reporting that my lunchroom is clean and I'm grateful I have a job.

Completing Step Seven properly demands tremendous faith and devotion. It's no place for the faint of heart.

Chapter 7

Social Re-entry: Steps Eight, Nine & The Promises

The paragraph immediately after the Step Seven prayer begins, _"Now we need more action, without which we find that 'Faith without works is dead.'"_[1] Two obviously important points in this sentence are that without effort your faith is rendered meaningless, and that you are urged directly into the next step.

I wrote earlier about the profound psychological shifts required within Steps Two, Four, and Six. [There's yet a fourth major shift within Step Eight, but more about that when you get there.] These paradigm shifts, of what addicts value, and how they view the world, and the difficulty in accomplishing them, make these steps taboo subjects for _sincere_ spiritual discussion.

People in twelve-step programs talk about Steps One, Three, Four, and Twelve the most. These are the easiest about which addicts can declare their "struggles"; the easiest to be dramatic about; the easiest to "act like" they've done them without having really modified anything deep inside themselves. These are the steps that fall most easily into the category of Impression Management.[2] By comparison, it's rare that you'll hear anyone say anything at all substantive or spiritually insightful about Steps Two, Four, Six, or Eight. Be observant for this.

Step Eight is _not_ about what harms were done to you and not about what harms you did to yourself. It is specifically about identifying the harm you've done to others. Regardless of how deeply ensconced you are in your twelve-step subculture, you are here taken back from whence you came and forced into the community at large: social re-entry.

Lingering Obsessions

In its essence, _Alcoholics Anonymous_ advises that you will eventually accomplish two main things. The first is relief from the obsession to self-destruct [act out] and the second is the elimination of insane thinking. Every

---

[1] _Alcoholics Anonymous_, p. 76.
[2] I suspect that if the effort expended on Impression Management (any self-advertising campaign) was diverted to spiritual endeavor there'd be saints all over the place.

addict getting recovered has these two fundamental issues to address. The successful elimination of these over the long term, indicates you're recovered.

It's written that by the time you get to Step Five, you will often have the feeling that the drink problem has been removed (if that hasn't already happened). So, if you follow instructions and are continuously abstinent, the first of the two major problems is more than likely gone by the time you get to Step Five. If an addict is still noticeably preoccupied with destructive behaviour, or otherwise acting out, or has disturbing and lingering obsessions *after* Step Five, this is more than likely because of the presence of one, or a combination of, the following four circumstances.

<u>One</u>: Lingering obsessions, often attached to anger and righteousness, may be the result of an unidentified and/or undisclosed major error in step-work. Repetitive anger frequently arises from a victim mentality, and is often directed at someone who is being blamed for the addiction or for other problems. It is a similar dynamic for righteousness and indignation. Anger will allow obsessions and preoccupation about acting out to persist.

This will occur regardless of whether or not the person being blamed is taking some responsibility (which is always ill advised) for the addict's addiction. Global anger directed at life has the same result. Regarding step work, at the minimum this means the error was impatience, a lack of thoroughness, and improper focus at Step Four. Lingering obsessions can result from irresponsibility and anger. Resolving irresponsibility and stopping blaming can't be accomplished without a painstaking and patient re-addressing of Steps One, Two, and Four.

<u>Two</u>: Preoccupation with acting out may also be a result of unresolved guilt and self-condemnation about the insecurities, fears, and sexual selfishness that were identified in Step Four. This sometimes occurs because of misunderstandings and unresolved conflict regarding the "I'm Sick vs. I'm Bad" debate, and the resulting confusion or ambivalence about "disease" and moral choice.

This can persist because of the negative influence of someone to whom the addict has given control over their life; or, they've not sufficiently reduced the historical, cultural/family imposition of guilt, which is demonstrated in a deeply entrenched, and subtly concealed, self-shaming or self-castigating mindset. Disengaging from the relationship with the abusive authority figure, and/or defeating the self-destructive messages about moral turpitude, are the resolution strategy.

[These two previous situations are related to a Misalliance of Commitment, which I discuss in some detail later in this chapter.]

Three: A third reason for a lingering obsession is that the addict is still acting out in another unaddressed or not-acknowledged addiction. This is very common. Acting out in secondary or secret addictions (tobacco, work, food, pornography, violence, sex, shopping, spending, gambling, relationships, *especially* relationships, etc.) *always* destabilizes the primary abstinence. If you're preoccupied with acting out and you believe you've carefully followed the instructions, maintain your abstinence and examine yourself for other addictions that you're ignoring. For other addictions, which are often abstinence not available[3], go back to Step One and establish abstinence in these unaddressed addictions.

Four: Lingering obsessions are, on occasion, indicative of an undiagnosed mental health concern, of untreated trauma disorders, or of some notable, pre-addiction problem that is unaddressed. The desire to act out, in these situations, *may* be an indication of the need to temporarily medicate or stabilize the mental health issues, or address the trauma-induced dysregulation. (See Appendix III) Maintain your abstinence as best you can and seek some well-qualified therapeutic help.

Resolving lingering obsessions and preoccupation with acting out is incredibly complex. From the addict themselves, it requires a willingness to be responsible and abstinent from substances and destructive behaviour. It will also require a well-grounded, authentic spiritual mentor and, very probably, a well trained and insightful therapist or counsellor.

The second of the two main problems, cited in *Alcoholics Anonymous,* the insane thinking, is beginning to be addressed, and is probably greatly reduced. This should be largely resolved by the end of Step Nine. If the insane thinking is still noticeably present, the reasons will be related to the four situations I just described, and resolved similarly.

When the obsession and insane thinking are gone, your addiction becomes a non-issue. In the next chapter I discuss, from various perspectives, the philosophy and state of being recovered *"from a seemingly hopeless state of mind and body."*[4] It doesn't matter how you define the disease, with right effort and right concentration[5], the original twelve-step program enables you to become recovered.

Why Don't I Belong Here?

I see that most people in our culture, and certainly most addicts and al-

---

[3] Abstinence not-available addictions are discussed in Chapter 1.

[4] *Alcoholics Anonymous*, p. xiii.

[5] These are two self-imposed disciplines from The Eight-Fold Noble Path of Buddhism.

coholics, wander without direction all their life, looking for some place to belong. Maybe, at some time in their past, they did feel they belonged in a social group like a family or a club, but lost it because of their addiction, and now carry a sense of aimless wandering.

If you are presently in a recovery program, there was probably some point early in your participation when you sat in a meeting and "figured out" that you were sitting in *your* chair. You felt as if you finally belonged, and some of that sense of aimless wandering disappeared. Be that as it may, it is often short-lived, and there are a number of factors that contribute to losing it.

Whatever motivates you to attend a recovery meeting, some self-improvement group, or therapy, the attitude that you carry at the meeting, and what you encounter when you're there will all affect your sense of belonging—just attending it isn't enough. There are these four considerations about "belonging". Regarding recovery:

The first one is your personal agenda for attending the meeting. Is it to: (1) Find your higher power and get recovered? (2) Socialize because you're lonely? (3) Find a sex partner? (4) Find a job? (5) Tell jokes? (6) Look for the person who owes you money? (7) Looking for someone to rescue you?

The second one is the group's agenda—the group's conscience that's embodied in the meeting ambiance. Is it the group's intention to: (1) Promote being spiritual and get recovered? (2) Arrange social events? (3) Create a dating club? (4) Provide a venue to network for jobs? (5) Organize an amateur entertainment club? (7) The leaders want to collect admirers?

Of course everyone would like to believe of themselves, and to have others believe that they, or their group, are both in the "# 1" category. However, it is rare that people, and so subsequently the groups they form, are spiritually motivated. Regardless of what the real motivation actually is, should your personal agenda not match with the group's or the leader's agenda, you will neither belong, nor feel safe.

This dynamic is equally applicable, and more complex, when you're completing any of the steps. People often describe a sense of dissatisfaction with step work. Yes, they follow the instructions but it just doesn't seem to work.

The third is what's the reason for your step-work? Is it because: (1) You wish to be spiritual, (2) Your sponsor told you to, (3) You're confused and don't know what else to do so you'll try the steps, (4) You want to get these steps over with, (5) They're cheaper than therapy, (6) Because that's where the step group is, (7) Because your counsellor said...? Usually people claim it's #1, but again, this is rarely the case. Mix the first three with the last consideration.

The fourth: If you have someone helping you (your sponsor or spiritual advisor)—what's the reason for them helping you? Is it because: (1) They are themselves sincerely spiritual and wish to help? (2) They are supposed to? (3) If they're telling someone else what to do (you) they'll feel less confused? (4) They fancy themselves as a guru-lay counsellor and you're a sponsee-client? (5) With lots of people to help they get status and bragging rights? [Have *no doubt* reasons #2 - #5 are much more common than anyone cares to admit.]

And of course, throughout all of this, the books *Alcoholics Anonymous*, *Twelve Steps and Twelve Traditions*, and hopefully this book, are specifically concerned with achieving a spiritual lifestyle.

If you go to a grocery store with the intent to renew your drivers' license, it won't work. The grocery store, and its employees have a purpose that doesn't include the renewal of drivers' licenses. If you're blind to any contradiction between your motives and your behaviour (to get a license renewed at a grocery store) you'll leave disappointed and won't fit in.

If you approach the steps or meetings motivated by social success and relationship bliss, you'll be disappointed and relapse. However, if you approach each step as an extension of what you came to believe at Step Two, that seeking a higher power is the solution, the steps then make sense. Your purpose for doing them is consistent with the reason for the step's existence, and you'll feel like you belong "in" the steps. If your reason is anything other than #1, you're at odds with the original intent of the step.

In theory, meetings are to carry the message of a spiritual awakening, to enable people to recommit themselves to spiritual principles, to show other people how to access a higher power so they can recover from their addictions and attain peace of mind. Spirituality is the path out of addictions. Considering the major realignment of priorities within twelve-step meetings in the last twenty-five years, the more determined you are to be truly spiritual the fewer are the places where you will sense you belong.

At Step Eight, when the harm you caused is identified within spiritual context (rather than social atonement), there's often a peaceful loneliness, and a sense of quiet satisfaction without any need to exonerate yourself. This arises from the loss of chaos, some reflective sadness, and the subtle separation from people who are not of a truly spiritual intent, which is sometimes described as a sense of poignancy.[6]

So, in Step Six you got over the significant hurdle of clinging to your old survival skills (character defects) and in Step Seven you saw humility as

---

[6] This is partly representative of the quiet sensibility present in truly spiritual people who, although they conduct affairs in the secular community, oftentimes sense they don't belong. It's a poignant and simple consequence of being Spiritual. It's rare.

a virtue of the highest order. These two changes allow you to transform yourself without pain, and you can now actually examine the harms you caused in a non-selfish way. *In theory*, you now possess the resources to do the work of caring generously for the welfare of others (called making amends) regardless of what they may have done to you, and with little attention to the advantage for yourself.

The Return

As you became more destructive in addictions, you withdrew more and more from your community, family, and friends. You then joined a twelve-step group and became a member of an organization that was, by definition, quite separate from the community at large. Initially, the process from Steps One to Seven indirectly reinforced and required a new isolation from the community-at-large, in an anonymous, small community, where the focus of the first seven steps was entirely on you.

At Step One you discovered that your addictions showed up in at least three ways: two obvious and one subtle, and one of these was a relationship addiction. You understood that unmanageability and acting out were synonymous, and the reality of this was self-annihilation. You learned you were sick and continued abstinence was crucial for any continued success, *and* you did all of this without going outside the confines of your meetings. You might have also found a counsellor to help you with that early work and still never went outside of your twelve-step community.

At Step Two, through your experience and investigation of Steps One and Two, you came to believe that a higher power (of your own understanding) could restore your sanity. You became involved in a social life within your fellowship. Step Three was also about you: *your* decision and *your* higher power. Once you decided to turn your will and life over to the care of your higher power, and did the prayer with someone else (probably within the program), you were ready for Step Four. As you figured out who you were, and not what you did, you probably decided which twelve-step member you would do Step Five with.

You likely completed your Step Five with someone in "the program", and felt safe in that world. Step Six was certainly the most difficult of them all—you became completely willing, without reservation, to leave behind your survival skills. But, notwithstanding that, it too, was done inside your twelve-step world, and was about you. At Step Seven you adopted a spiritual view of humility, and you made a sincere offering of yourself to your higher power.

Thus far, up to and including Step Seven, everything has been about you, and you never had to go outside your group. You develop friendships in your twelve-step program, expand your social skills, find employment, find sex partners, find a real-estate agent, buy a car, complete the steps to Seven, and learn to dance, all within the social club of recovery meetings. You never have to do anything but think about yourself, *and* you can exist completely inside "the fellowship".

From the drastic isolation of addictions, you recreate yourself inside a closely-knit, small, self-protective, quasi-underground community. Now, combine this isolated social sub-structure with these addictions-related personality attributes: suspicion, fear, insecurity, anger, envy, cynicism, and defensiveness. These two sets of attributes become spiritually defeating when combined with a decided tendency to blame others for any self-generated crises. Altogether, this allows addicts to create the "Evil Blue Meanies"[7] — people outside of a twelve-step program. A nasty variation of this is calling people "Normies" — people who haven't faced the grand calamities, suffering, chaos, or hard times that addicts in recovery have faced. The addict's resulting elitist, self-serving theory that "Normies don't get it" is always unspiritual. To become spiritual, addicts must force themselves to abandon these self-limiting perceptions.

Altogether, this creates a spiritual ghetto of twelve-step programs. It recreates yet another self-serving, impoverished view of people, which cheats addicts out of the prospect of getting recovered. Twelve-step groups, being an isolated sub-culture, and the isolating/blaming personality attributes of addicts, create the subtle and dangerous spiritual problem of being walled off from the community at large. The larger community is where you find those people you harmed. But it's impossible to complete the steps beyond seven while you are isolated from the larger community by arrogance and harsh judgments. *Step Eight, and those steps that follow, require community participation — going "out" to the larger community.*

All addicts getting recovered in a twelve-step program have hurt people who aren't involved in those programs. Neither Step Eight, nor any of the steps following it, can be completed without confronting the demons that belittle and judge harshly those people who live their lives outside of meetings. If you have subtly created the Evil Blue Meanies (unsympathetic outsiders), you have manipulated your perceptions to justify avoiding the community at large.

If you create this subtle and subtly vicious mindset, when you address Step Eight, there will be an underlying resistance to self-examination. You

---

[7] This phrase comes from the AA pamphlet *A Member's Eye View of Alcoholics Anonymous*. I imagine that if members of twelve-step programs spent less time blaming and accusing others of not caring, and stopped using derogatory terms like "Normies", then those other people who are being blamed might be somewhat more understanding and caring.

will therefore make only a minimum effort to amend harms outside of your "program" relationships. That's stultifying and defeats the point of the process. This is certainly contrary to spiritual principles, and is one of the main reasons that so many Step Eight lists are done half-heartedly (which makes any subsequent amends self-serving).

Another resistance to thoroughness stems from the refusal to accept addictions as a self-imposed crisis. If you believe it's an "other-imposed" crisis (parents, caregivers, police, mean relatives, teachers, priests, bullies), it's easy to avoid examining what harms you did to others. If your struggles are their fault they don't deserve an amend. Irresponsibility is insidious.

Many people who weren't alcoholics were instrumental in helping the cofounders of the original twelve-step group. *Alcoholics Anonymous* might never have been written, and AA might not exist, if it wasn't for the dedicated efforts of non-alcoholics: millionaires, priests, doctors, ministers, therapists, friends, and spouses. People who will help, or are willing to help, are out there by the millions. These "outsiders" are, for the most part, potential allies. It's up to you to find the kind ones, and regardless of how anyone treats you, respond to *every*one with consideration. When addicts make spiritual ghettos of twelve-step programs, everyone gets hurt. [The same dynamic exists in religion and most, if not all "members only" clubs.]

When it comes to making a list of people you have harmed, whether they are still alive, or using, or drunk, or empathetic, or remember, or care, or don't care, or don't like you, is immaterial. Whether they understand is irrelevant. Whether they support you is irrelevant. Blaming others, being suspicious, denigrating their character, casting aspersions on their integrity, withholding compassion, are manifestations of your lack of spiritual commitment. Harboring these attitudes makes all program work beyond Step Seven ineffective.

Identifying the harms, eventually making amends, and maintaining a spiritual attitude doesn't imply you have to be friends with everyone. You voluntarily obligated yourself to abide by spiritual principles. Creating stereotypes that "they" can't, won't, or don't care defeats the purpose of the steps, and makes for a narrow, self-righteous version of spirituality, and a self-serving vision of God, by whatever name.

If you're having trouble starting Step Eight, review four things: (i) the thoroughness of how you came to believe at Step Two; (ii) your decision to commit to a spiritual *life* at Step Three; (iii) your willingness and humility from Steps Six and Seven; and (iv), the way you view other people— especially those outside your twelve-step program. If you find yourself less than willing to create a detailed list of harms you have caused, you've somewhere missed the spiritual point and may erroneously think Step Eight is an exercise in social atonement.

Passion

If you're passionate about something, and it doesn't matter what it is—painting a picture, cooking, wind surfing—you will probably go off and do it. It won't really matter at the beginning that you make mistakes or that you're not very good, because your passion will push you to overcome the errors of the novice. Whether you're good at it is secondary to the desire to do it.[8]

In Step Seven... *"A great turning point in our lives came when we sought for humility as something we really wanted, rather than something we* must *have."*[9] Pursuing humility, and the desire to take responsibility, are attributes that you should be attracted to at this point. Willingness to care for the well-being of others (a part of Step Eight), and a desire for humility, are both associated with passion and love, and are at the core of spiritual heliotropism between Steps Seven and Eight.

If an activity like playing the guitar, or an attribute like humility, is attractive and perceived as valuable, it's easy to become committed to it. Seeing willingness and humility as valuable will allow you to be eager and interested in making amends, regardless of the inconvenience or cost. However, when humility is absent or imposed out of fear and pain, as in the first few steps, you'll do Step Eight grudgingly. That means you missed the point of humble service to a higher power in caring for others (not rescuing, caring). When you're quietly passionate about spirituality, and if humility is good, then making the list of harms you caused will be a pleasure.[10]

None of us are perfect and people flail away at life, temporarily forgetting the beauty of what they've learned within the twelve steps. When this happens, it's only a matter of gently nudging yourself back to a spiritually principled life. Too many people fumble around unnecessarily in the steps, interpreting spirituality as a matter of inconvenience. They miss the celebration of a spiritual life in heartfelt amends.

---

[8] Don't confuse soulfully motivated passion with overachieving, anger, obsession, or a desire to impress others. These latter scenarios are rooted in insecurity and shame.

[9] *Twelve Steps and Twelve Traditions*, p. 75.

[10] As with all virtues that manifest attendant to passion, caution is advised. Thomas Merton points to the disruptive danger of passion arising in a soul given over to human violence. *A Thomas Merton Reader*, Revised Edition, Edited by Thomas P. McDonnell, Image Books, 1996, p. 124. The relevant passage begins: *"The delicate sincerity...."* The section of the book entitled Sincerity is worth careful examination. The introduction to that book, written by M. Scott Peck, ©1996, contains many succinct observations about contemplative people which, by analogy, would be also worthy of contemplation by any person who is sincere about a spiritual life. Passion that arises out of anger, arrogance, self-righteousness, or viewing a twelve-step path as superlative to other spiritual endeavors, always harms people, prohibits sincerity, and denies a life governed by spiritual principles.

Any time there's a struggle in any step-related work after Step Seven; if it's hard to write the list, make the amends or pray; or you're afraid, reluctant, or bitter, these are evidence that humility has become *un*attractive. Humility is to be willingly sought. That's the essential, crucial, fundamental, basic, remarkable, unavoidable, and unalterable premise for the rest of the program. Being quietly passionate about humility makes *every*thing easier.

Misalliance of Commitment

Many people view the steps as "tools" to get through onerous and trying times—an acquired skill-set that facilitates a successful life. This misperception arises when the greater focus is placed on psychology rather than spirituality. What follows is based on the many references in *Alcoholics Anonymous* and *Twelve Steps and Twelve Traditions* that clearly indicate that the solution to addictions [alcoholism] is spirituality, that serenity is dependent on a relationship with a higher power, and that no human power (intellect, willpower, science, psychology) is adequate for recovery.

None of the steps are designed to allow you to resolve psychological deficits. The steps, such as they are, are for the creation of a spiritual life, not for the reorganization of your secular life. It's far too easy to get sidetracked off of spirituality onto psychology because as you complete the steps, there's obvious derivative social improvement and some psychological benefit, which are easier to see and appreciate than the spiritual benefits. The disastrous result of completing the steps psychologically rather than spiritually is a misalliance of commitment. An unregenerate ego always chooses the easier, softer way (psychology).

What follows is a rather long aside to Step Eight, but it is appropriate here because of the deceptively easy misinterpretation of the purpose of this step. Precedent to abstinence and the steps—within any active addiction— addicts, for the most part, live with the illusion of unity and competence because while they are acting out, the sense of estrangement-from-self disappears. The purpose of acting out is to achieve unity, but in a destructive way. In acting out, the unity is an illusion and the actual result is self-annihilation. [Bear in mind, too, there is the other equally devastating illusion that spirituality and unity are present when suffering is absent.]

Remember the five spiritual principles: respectful self-care—respect for the body (yours and others'), veracity, secular and spiritual humility, charity, and responsibility and obedience (to these principles). And, recall the purpose of *Alcoholics Anonymous*, cited on page 45—to help you find a power greater than yourself that will solve your problem. The primary intent is spiritual, but there are also psychological/social benefits, which, although not the primary goal, are easier to sense and appreciate. This means that each step has one purpose—to promote "spirituality", but has two results: improved spirituality *and* some psychological integration. This is where the misalliance of commitment is born.

Step One

Purpose: To begin to establish the first, second, and fifth spiritual principles.

Spiritual Result: Establish some respectful self-care (the reduction of blatant self-destruction), and the laying of the foundation for the second and third spiritual principles. Together these are the beginning of responsibility and obedience.

Psychological Result: Through and in abstinence, the obvious reduction of mental chaos, self-destruction, and conflict.

Step Two

Purpose: To completely reorganize (and lay the groundwork for future reorganizations of) your perceptions regarding the disease, spiritual corruption and its resolution, and to establish a new basis for life: the commitment to spirituality.

Spiritual Result: The recognition that willpower directed towards recovery is ineffective; an increased interest in pursuing a spiritual life; a clear perception that the steps are the structure for the addict's spiritual transformation. These results altogether lay the groundwork for the third, fourth, and fifth spiritual principles.

Psychological Result: Experiencing success through social stability in "the fellowship"; the reduction of social alienation, and the development of the illusion that "the program" is the solution.

Step Three

Purpose: To commit oneself to, and to marshal and focus personal willpower towards, an all-encompassing "higher-power" oriented lifestyle, in terms of both will and life.

Spiritual Result: The development of the second, third, and fifth spiritual principles.

Psychological Result: The experience of life organized around a twelve-step social structure, which creates regular social interaction. Life becomes gradually less chaotic. The association between "sobriety" and "hanging around in the program" is an easily drawn conclusion.

Step Four

Purpose: To create an awareness and belief that misaligned and out-of-control instincts are exacerbated and never resolved by blame, resentment, or controlling others; to understand that addictions and the related crises are all *self*-imposed.

Spiritual Result: The ever-deepening awareness of the second, third, and fifth spiritual principles, and an increasing desire to experience spiritual grace (which solves problems). This lays additional groundwork for the fourth and fifth spiritual principles.

Psychological Result: New "self-insight and awareness" creates a determination to focus personal willpower on secular concerns. This misdirected effort encourages the addict to strive to "control" their own character defects through a determined effort to get along better with others.[11]

Step Five

Purpose: To take complete responsibility during accurate self-disclosure for the self-imposed crisis and defects of character; *and* to establish a style of self-disclosure that exonerates others and assumes personal responsibility at the public level.

Spiritual Result: A deeper awareness of humility and more practice of the second, fourth, and fifth spiritual principles. A very subtle aside is the proper context for petitionary prayer is established within this step.

Psychological Result: The experience of "acceptance" at a social level, through the interaction with the person chosen, which creates an experience of less guilt and shame. This is often described as "feeling stronger and more determined" (the illusion of psychological integration).

Step Six

Purpose: To create an internal spiritual atmosphere of personal willingness to remove character defects and to abandon old survival skills, which have been blocking the action of Grace in the pursuit of spiritual humility.

Spiritual Result: An actual shift in the perception of a higher power, and a deeper entrenchment of spiritual principles two,

---

[11] In Step Four, the problem *appears* to be that you resent others and don't get along with people, but that isn't the problem. The addiction underneath the conflict is the problem, but that isn't really the problem, either. It's spiritual corruption and alienation through the absence of spiritual principles—that's the problem.

three, and five. Additional groundwork is laid for the fourth spiritual principle.

Psychological Result: Superficial psychological integration: "I feel better and feel less guilty," (primarily from Step Five), which creates the illusion of spiritual commitment. This generates deal making as the primary basis for recovery efforts—I'll continue because life "conditions" are improving. This entrenches the idea that recovery is a social reward process and the steps are an acquired skill-set of tools for improving secular relationships.

Step Seven

Purpose: To commit to realigning personal values, and especially to enhance devotion to a higher power through a willing search for humility, and beginning to see this search as the highest human good.

Spiritual Result: Sensing a power greater than yourself as an evermore present and reliable source for the courage to transform; and expanding the principle of humility to include serving a higher power *in the context of human relationships*. There's a dramatic increase in selflessness (which is intrinsic to the third and fifth spiritual principles) and more groundwork is laid for the fourth spiritual principle.

Psychological Result: Addicts "in recovery" appear to get along better with each other. This illusion of humility exists because they have become more selective about whom they associate with, and thusly appear to have fewer defects—it's easy to appear spiritual when everyone agrees with you. This is Impression Management and not authentic humility, and entrenches further the illusion that step-work makes them happier.

Step Eight

Purpose: To identify harms done (and amends required) to all others; *and* to take complete responsibility for these harms. This is a clear demonstration of spiritual generosity and devotion to the spiritual principle of Responsibility.

Spiritual Result: A deeper intuition around the spiritual benefits of, and freedom inherent in, taking complete responsibility, regardless of the personal cost. There's much more acceptance of the spiritual principles, especially the second, fourth, and fifth.

Psychological Result: The anticipation of less social and inner-personal tension and less guilt through social atonement. This is often accompanied by a subtle motivation related to expectations of being forgiven. [This plays on the often-unresolved confusing debate of "I'm bad" vs. "I'm sick", which is particularly more difficult to resolve for Christians.]

Step Nine

Purpose: To repair the harms done and damage caused, and to sincerely facilitate peace in the lives of other people; to demonstrate spiritual responsibility through social responsibility.

Spiritual Result: A deep and direct experience of the five spiritual principles, and a substantially different sense of freedom, in such a way that The Promises are now appreciated as the direct result of spiritual self-discipline.

Psychological Result: A sense of getting along better with other people; feeling more confident in personal/social situations, with a sense of self-congratulation for your own hard work: "*I'm* working *my* program." "*I'm* getting along better with people."

Someone using these steps as a psychological process is successful only as long as their socially approved, secondary addictions remain somewhat manageable, or fate doesn't present calamity in too many big or successive doses, meaning one or several big things happening they don't like or can't control. [With an addict's propensity to drama, any misadventure can be turned into a calamity of magnificent proportion.]

A non-spiritual approach to these steps is evident when people say things like: "I'm mad/scared/worried about __(insert circumstance)__ , so I'll do another Step Four." Or, "I just broke up with __(insert name)__ so I'll go to more meetings. Or, "I'm fighting with __(insert circumstance or name)__ so I'll do another Step Eight-and-Nine." All of these, and similar statements, are social control tactics and the result of a misalliance of commitment. These indicate the steps are used as situational problem-solving techniques, which is not what they are designed for.

It is also a misalliance of commitment when an addict, working through the steps, decides they have to "repair" everything about their personality. An addict believing they are *completely defective* and must repair everything about themselves is a misalliance of commitment. As an example: You're driving your vehicle and get a flat tire. You don't get an engineering degree and a calculator and redesign the construction of tires and the wheel assembly. Fixing the problem is changing the tire. Fix what's wrong and get on with the trip. In addictions recovery, getting recovered means you fix what's wrong, appreciate what isn't, and get on with the trip.

The steps (up to Nine) are the mechanics of transformation, which aren't "problem solving", they're to redesign your personality. Altogether, they create the foundation for a new you. The maintenance steps are different. They're the intrinsically interdependent themes of an ongoing spiritual lifestyle: coping with life spiritually (maintenance steps or spiritual principles = spiritual problem solving).

Steps Ten, Eleven, and Twelve are not separate tasks that an addict completes independently of each other. They reflect the on-going ambiance of a Spiritual life—problem solving and problem prevention. As regards a misalliance of commitment, they are here examined together.

Steps Ten, Eleven, and Twelve

Purpose: To maintain being recovered; to solve problems spiritually, and to enhance and deepen a sincerely spiritual lifestyle. This enriches spiritual integrity. These steps involve exerting your will on behalf of "your higher power", as you understand this, meaning through the maintenance steps, you live a life which embodies the five spiritual principles.

Spiritual Result: A continuing and deeper awareness of spiritual grace (aligning yourself with the energy of the universe), and a gradually increasing devotion to the five spiritual principles. This results in: (a) more consistent serenity, regardless of what events occur, (b) Life ceasing to have a personal/secular agenda, and taking on a spiritual agenda (the difference is profound), (c) a greater devotion to spiritual principles; and (d), noticeably less meddling in the affairs of others. There's a certain benign indifference to what's going on around you. The adage of attraction rather than promotion will have a definable presence.

Psychological Result: Addicts claim to get along better with people, usually and primarily inside the program and establish a network of friends they turn to more than their higher power. Life is experienced as less chaotic. When it's chaotic, they avoid responsibility and blame "life". Providing that Fate cooperates, they establish a lifestyle that embraces their character defects and rationalize various subtle harms and disrespect to others.

Many of these psychological benefits have some value because we do live "in" the world, but psychological benefits are ancillary to the spiritual intent of the twelve steps. It is easy to see in this age of technology and self-help how psychology can easily supplant spirituality. More traditional psychology and organized religions are more visible, socially easier to access, easier to get compliments on, and don't "oppose" culture. Cooperation with, or success in, these social endeavours is easier to accomplish.[12]

The risk for addicts, however, in not choosing the more difficult spiritual orientation to life, leaves your abstinence at risk and your integrity dependent on the cooperation of fate. A misalliance of commitment is often demonstrated in unresolved moodiness, recurring bouts of depression, complaining, gossiping, anger, general discontent, disregard for the emotional rights of others, belligerent or caustic behaviour, justified deceitful behaviour; and the ongoing presence of character defects or socially approved addictions.

Step Eight brings into focus the nature and degree of all the harm you did to others. When humility is a desired virtue, cataloguing the damage you did to everyone is an exercise in generosity, not an attempt to accomplish personal atonement. This is especially important when examining the very serious harms where the amends may place you in poverty or at legal risk. You may balk at including these in any detail on your Step Eight list, in which case I refer you to the paragraph that begins: *"Although these reparations...."*[13]

The natural outcomes of devotion are willingness, love of spirituality, and a desire for humility. Only these can resolve the insecurity and reluctance about making amends where you are at risk of social sanction, financial hardship, or long-term inconvenience.

Historical arguments notwithstanding, rumour has it that Yeshua of Nazareth taught primarily two things: people should love "God" above all others (a process that begins in Step Two and comes to fruition in Step Eleven); and people should do unto others as they would have done unto themselves. How to "do unto others" (responsible, kind, charitable, etc.) is what's learned in the first nine steps and practiced and strengthened in Steps Ten, Eleven, and Twelve. In theory, realizing these two spiritual axioms is one end result of the transformation you experience in doing the steps.[14] This includes accepting responsibility and making amends for the harms you have done, with little consideration for the consequences to yourself, without keeping a secret scorecard of the wrongs done to you by others.

---

[12] Obedience to the five spiritual principles, which usually invites social suspicion, is hard to justify in our culture. People will wonder why you work so diligently to live by spiritual principles. Other people wonder: "All that effort and for what? You can't afford a world cruise and your car's ten years old. Why bother?" The rewards of a spiritual lifestyle are held in low regard in this culture, especially in view of what those rewards cost.

[13] *Alcoholics Anonymous*, p. 79.

[14] As I've said before, I'm not advocating for Christian hegemony. The invisible spiritual philosophies; the underlying mysticism that informs many of the cultural religions, even (cont'd)

Humility is the premier prerequisite to being able to clearly and accurately identify what harm you've done. Without humility being attractive, you'll be caught up in various kinds of selfish justification that permits a half-hearted or begrudging effort here. Without humility as the primary, underlying principle at Step Eight, you'll not be able to see clearly what harm you've done. You will not, therefore, be able to clear up the wreckage of your past.[15]

The New Mandate

Here is the twelve-step spiritual pilgrim's new life mandate: *"Learning how to live in the greatest peace, partnership, and brotherhood with* all *men and women, of whatever description, is a moving and fascinating adventure."*[16] This sentence outlines the task at hand, and defines the new focus for your behaviour in all relationships—getting along graciously with *every*one. This is required because *"...defective relations with other human beings have nearly always been the immediate cause of our woes, including our alcoholism,* [and] *no field of investigation could yield more satisfying and valuable rewards than this one."*[17] Defective relations with others are self-generated, and are a significant justification to act out (through blaming and complaining), and a significant contributor to the entrenchment of addictions.

If, in the maintenance steps, you are to become responsible and charitable (Steps Ten and Twelve), it follows that you must learn to be forever considerate of others. This means to resolve your relationship addiction. It is here, with your ever-deepening commitment to being responsible, that you begin to create that *"moving and fascinating adventure"* with others.

The twelve steps are presented in the only effective sequence that would enable an addict to reduce alienation from a spiritual lifestyle. The

---

though often corrupt in their present form, have equally subtle and beautiful applications within these steps.

[15] Without humility in Step Eight, the amends required will be inaccurate or inadequate and insincere. To step for a moment into Step Nine, that will leave the amends themselves in spiritual misalliance, and a subtle sense of unfinished discomfort will remain after the amend. This contributes greatly to the need to repeat all the steps again, and again, and again...

[16] *Twelve Steps and Twelve Traditions*, p. 77, emphasis added.

[17] Ibid., p. 80. This may appear to be at odds with several previous assertions that addictions aren't caused by abuse. This passage refers specifically to "defective relations with others" causing addictions. This is an indirect reference to the relationship addiction that underlies all other addictions. At Step Four it was clearly identified that alcoholics are responsible for their own conflict and resentments. In all defective relations, the addict is responsible. If, then, defective relations cause alcoholism, and addicts are responsible for the defective relations, then "addicts" are causing their own alcoholism because they are never innocent of responsibility. The addict always contributes to defective relations, and therein lies the place of (cont'd) complete personal responsibility—for the defective relations *and* all subsequent consequences. This is a self-imposed crisis.

316

first steps begin with creating new perceptions and altering the addict's interior life. This is an inner integration of disparate elements of awareness, and the resolution of dilemmas and distress. Whatever is corrupt in the interior life of an addict (or in anyone for that matter) manifests itself metaphorically in social distress and conflict. After establishing some inner harmony in the early steps, through the inculcation of spiritual principles, the later steps shift to resolving the disharmony in external life with spiritual behaviour. Without first largely resolving inner conflict, all attempts to resolve outer conflict are efforts in impression management, and layered over unaddressed inner corruption.

That's the "why" of working on yourself and your commitment to a higher power first. Any reorganization or re-sequencing of the steps, or combining them in a way other than they are exactly laid out, or recasting their content, or forcing a relationship with a higher power through pious behaviour or dramatic devotion, may look good, but will eventually prove ineffective.[18] These are the underlying causes of much of the recidivist, relapse behaviour in "early" recovery, *and* why so many people with longer-term sobriety talk and act like newcomers.

Prior to Step Eight you are (supposed to) have largely resolved your inner bewilderment, and have come to rely on your higher power. Only then are you ready to go away from "you" towards "others". Should you have created the Evil Blue Meanies (as discussed earlier), and done nothing to resolve that abusive stereotyping, it will be impossible for you to sincerely approach Step Eight—after all, if all those outsiders are mean and don't care, why should you make a sincere effort?

The primary goal of all twelve-step work is to establish an authentic and meaningful relationship with a higher power, and subsequent to that, a spiritual relationship with *every*one else. Addicts are clearly told that henceforth, the general purpose is *"...that we may develop the best possible relations with every human being we know."*[19] Obviously *"every human being"* is all-inclusive. There is no exception for people whom you believe have hurt you badly (or other scoundrels) that have thereby meritoriously earned your resentment or disapproval.

The significant disregard of this requirement is demonstrated in racist and sexist jokes, gossiping, breaking anonymity, being dismayed at the

---

[18] Re: Dramatic Devotion... For alcoholics and addicts, this is why short-term conflict-resolution strategies (like anger management courses and weekend-long conflict-reduction workshops) never offer more than very temporary relief, and do more harm than good: they entrench a need for a dramatic catharsis. The drama and adrenaline of the intensive workshop is addictive and falsely reassuring. Their popularity is evidence of their addictive nature and the quick-fix, disposable mindset of our culture. Have no doubt about the workshop junkies' vicious, vehemently denied, deep sense of failure.

[19] *Twelve Steps and Twelve Traditions*, p. 77.

good fortune of others, being pleased at the misfortune of people you don't like, practical jokes, teasing, and patronizing character assassination.

How am I doing? I'm not sure.

Addiction is an illness of isolation and self-destruction. Addicts isolate from others and especially from themselves. Because of fear and shame, they don't have any insightful way of judging how well they're doing. Having minimal and largely inaccurate insight about the truth of what is actually going on in their life results in significantly skewed self-perceptions. They're generally afraid of the truth, confused, and bewildered. Until they're abstinent from *all* addictions, and are comfortable with sincere spirituality, they have no reliable system of self-evaluation.

Defective relations with others always run parallel to their inability to get along with themselves. As a person goes through their life, whatever overt or covert conflict they experience—loneliness, turmoil, suffering, complaining, demonstrated racism or sexism, etc.—to whatever degree that is, whether declared or held secret, is an accurate reflection of their own largely unconscious inner turmoil within themselves about themselves.

Because of our instinctual needs, and the social infrastructure of our communities, *and* the subtle demands of addictions, all of this requires an addict to seek relationships physically for the mood-altering experiences of romance, sex, chaos, conflict, some form of love, or receiving affection and dispensing all manner of self-righteous advice or abuse. And, at the same time, to also stay emotionally "out" of those same relationships by withholding compassion, emotion, generosity, and responsibility, and oftentimes being dishonest. The relationship must eventually fail, or remain in habitual tension and reciprocal abuse—deal making (keeping score).

The lonely result is that no one ever really gets to know addicts, and they fail to know themselves. When anyone asks them how they are doing at a meaningful level, it's generally a guessing game. Until a person lives without addictions for years; at the minimum has several years of solid abstinence and are well along in spiritual self-discipline, they are a very poor judge of how well they're doing.

While sorting all this out, it doesn't mean that you can't create a new life, or you can't have a relationship or be happy. It means you're a newcomer for a very long time. The disease requires it. Do not think that a few years of sobriety and hanging around meetings leaves you capable of accurate self-evaluation. [And of course, this also means you can only guess about the character and motivations of others.]

For an addict to achieve reasonable psychological-emotional health—the ability to be respectfully assertive, and to become established in a re-

sponsible and ethical lifestyle, takes *at least* five years of continuous abstinence, *including* at least three years of well-conducted, weekly therapy, all
the while working at understanding and completing the steps.[20] For people
with additional, more complicated non-addictions issues, having ten or fifteen years of abstinence and spiritual work and eight or ten years of devoted
work in therapy is not uncommon.

Independent of psychological health, to attain true *spiritual* integrity
beyond some arbitrary, self-defined standard of "good enough" requires ten
years of abstinence after completing the first nine steps, and *regular*, *ongoing*, devoted spiritual prayer and meditation, including regular counsel from
a bona fide spiritual advisor. This means someone far more insightful about
spiritual defiance than the run-of-the-mill sponsor. At the outset it's daunting, but it's worth it. Really.

Amends To Yourself?

Some people defend the idea it's acceptable to put yourself on your
Step Eight list. From a spiritual perspective, if you do, you've missed the
point of spiritual transformation. As I mentioned earlier, between Steps
Seven and Eight there's a major reorientation—the focus shifts from assertive self-care to compassionate generosity.

When you look at the steps from a global perspective, you got the first
seven. They're yours. It was during these steps you were to have made
whatever "amends" to yourself you needed to make. The first seven steps
allow you to fix whatever harm you did to yourself through these following
actions: quitting your addictions, becoming abstinent, ceasing to hurt yourself through acting out, caring for yourself by developing self-respect,
attaining gentle self-insight rather than caustic self-judgment, recovering
physical health, ceasing to blame yourself for being stupid or weak-willed,
developing and maintaining a relationship with a higher power, distancing
yourself from people who hurt you, and associating with those who are respectful towards you. All of this is "making amends" to yourself, and
should have been done by the time you get to Step Eight. Whatever amends
you owed to yourself should have been attended to by this time.

After Step Seven, you are no longer the primary focus of step work;
other people are. Humility becomes active and now shows itself as behaviours of kindness, respect, caring, charity of spirit, and responsibility *to
others*. The direction of transformation changes from proper self-care and

---

[20] Charles Whitfield, in his book *Co-dependence, Healing the Human Condition,* Health Communications Inc., 1991, indicates that five years, and sometimes as much as eight years, of
work is required to recreate yourself out of codependence and addictions. "Work" (cont'd)

self-love (Steps One to Seven) to proper spiritual love for others and a willing compliance with spiritual principles: compassionate generosity (Steps Eight to Twelve).

Including yourself on the Step Eight list implies that (a) you missed some aspect of self-care in the first seven steps; or (b), you're working with a misalliance of commitment. Any misalliance of commitment will act directly against the required shift away from self towards others and a spiritually principled life. Because the last five steps are other-oriented, putting yourself on your Step Eight list is clear evidence of misunderstanding what's to have transpired before you got to Step Eight, and would turn a selfless program into a selfish program.[21]

Some amends require that addicts put themselves into hardship: paying large bills, owning up to some crime, etc. Putting yourself on the list will create a conflict with the instructions contained in the paragraph that begins, *"Although these reparations..."* which includes this phrase: *"...no matter what the personal consequences may be."*[22] If you believe you are to put yourself on your Step Eight list, it naturally follows that you can't make amends "to yourself" if you harm yourself by putting yourself into hardship when making amends to others. By putting yourself on the list, you create conflict, what might be referred to as a contradiction of intent:

- Step Eight *intends* that you identify what amends to others are required, regardless of the possible consequences to yourself, which necessarily requires that you may have to cause hardship to yourself; but,
- If you include yourself at Step Eight, you won't make amends to others where those amends will detract from your personal "comforts" (cause yourself hardship).

If you create this contradiction of intent by placing yourself on the Step Eight list, whenever an amend causes yourself hardship, you'll always renege on the side of selfishness and your amends to others will be inadequate or entirely avoided.

There is much to gain from reflection about yourself—which is the focus of all that you have been doing up to Step Seven. The literature

---

implies much more than twelve-step participation, and any therapy has to be with a non-addicted therapist who understands addictions.

[21] By doing Steps Eight to Twelve in an other-oriented manner, the way they are intended, you indirectly make amends to yourself by working spiritually to reintegrate yourself into the community. This secondary benefit counter-acts the harm of isolation and eliminates social dislocation.

[22] *Alcoholics Anonymous*, p. 79.

recognizes the *"...emotional harm we have done ourselves"*[23] might be great, but that *"making restitution to others is paramount* [of overriding importance]."[24] It is authentic spirituality when someone is capable of depriving themselves of comfort and shiny things, and *willing* to place themselves in awkward circumstances in order to care for the wellbeing of others by making amends. This is especially true for others they may not know well, or care for, or when there is decidedly no social advantage for themselves to making the amend. Being truly spiritual requires that occasionally you may have to you put yourself into awkward circumstances to make amends.

In the chapter on Step Eight, there's no instruction or inference that you are to put your name on this list. You're already well on the way to developing the best possible relationship with yourself that you can. The goal here is to develop the best possible relations with every *other* human being. *"We are there to sweep off our side of the street..."* "[Their] *faults are not discussed. We stick to our own."*[25]

Reflect on the depth and the breadth of *"...the best possible relation with every human being that you know."* It's all encompassing, and it can be frightening. It's an exercise in patience, determination, and thoroughness, and it's impossible to be spiritual while ignoring this instruction. And (almost finally), to be spiritually successful in negotiating through Step Eight three things are essential: (1) time—be patient with your own painstaking effort; (2) have a spiritual advisor who is very firmly grounded in spiritual responsibility; and (3), have a higher power—be well-established in your relationship with one.

You learned and accepted that humility is good (Step Seven) and your character defects of sloth[26] and fear have been regularly challenged by prayer, so the task of making a detailed list is, in fact, something you by now [should] enjoy. You're now *willingly* pursuing spirituality. If this is not a labour of love, it's of questionable benefit to anyone. Being cheerfully compliant is essential to this task. Should you become discouraged, review Steps Six and Seven.

While making the list of harms done, addicts and alcoholics are crafty at hanging on to grievances. *"To escape looking at the wrongs we have*

---

[23] *Alcoholics Anonymous*, p. 79.

[24] Ibid., p 80.

[25] *Alcoholics Anonymous*, p.77, 78.

[26] When undertaking such demanding spiritual endeavor as the original twelve steps, it's worthy to note an important definition of sloth. Sloth [*acedia*] means much more than generic laziness. *"For Dante, acedia was a central spiritual failure. It was the failure to be sufficiently active in the pursuit of The Recognized Good. It was to acknowledge Good, but without fervor."* From How To Read Dante, by John Ciardi, *The Divine Comedy*, by Dante Alighieri, translated by John Ciardi, New American Library, 2003, p. xiii.

done another, we resentfully focus on the wrong [they have] *done to us.*"[27]
Your ego will remind you of the presumed transgressions of others as often
as it can. Lingering over the harms you perceive that others did to you,
whether real or imagined, results in:

- withholding thoroughness in identifying what harm you did
  to others. Step Eight will then be incomplete (which will
  render Step Nine ineffective); and,
- being irresponsible, where you avoid examining your own
  conduct and won't admit truths about yourself. This keeps
  your inner life in turmoil, and perpetuates external conflict.

Only through humility can you focus on personal responsibility, and
only that allows you to abandon grievances with others. Doing this is completely unselfish behaviour. Your fellow human beings benefit, and being
completely responsible is evidence of your devotion to your higher power.
Anything less than a willing generosity of spirit towards those you have
harmed results in superficial amends, which are probably worse than none
at all—they add insult to injury.

Contracts & Reciprocity, Forgiveness & Covenants

Contracts, reciprocity, forgiveness, and covenants are the governing
dynamic principles that inform the paradigms of relationships. These four
concepts contain, within them, the rules that dictate how we create and
maintain relationships. Altogether, they carry a very subtle spider's web of
meanings and obligations, which need to be closely examined in order to
bring integrity and clarity to relationships. This is intricate, so go slow.

When a person forgives someone, apparently sincerely, people usually
view this as evidence of spiritual soundness, i.e. forgiving for some crime or
misdemeanor is "good". Forgiveness, in itself, is commonly understood to
be the spiritual last step in conflict resolution, and certainly with a mindset
of righteous judgment, it is. However, should the transgressor reappear after
some absence, or should anyone discuss it or some other similar offense, it
often follows that the memories are dragged out, the pain dredged up, the
grievance aired yet again, and the moral high-ground claimed once more.
This is contrary to the aggrieved person's claim of having forgiven the offender. In reliving the offense, the person who carries the grudge goes
through the cycle again: offense, victimization, accusation, blaming, debt-
obligation, benevolence, forgiveness, and righteous indifference.

---

[27] *Twelve Steps and Twelve Traditions*, p. 78.

Outside of socially legislated culpability or contracted mercenary endeavor, the politics and impression management around forgiveness, the misunderstanding of its application, and the self-serving shortsightedness in viewing it as an ultimate good, are evidence of how unwilling people are to be truly compassionate and responsible.

Forgiveness may be viewed as the saving grace in relationships with a higher power where the concept of a higher power is the more traditional "God" interpretation. However, in secular terms, it does nothing to address the underlying arrogance in people who find it necessary to offer or seek forgiveness.

In other words: Forgiveness is an important concept where there's conflict in relationships with a traditional religious god, but it's destructive in resolving conflict between people. If you become well-established in spiritual integrity (meaning *authentic* compassion and responsibility), it's possible to render forgiveness unnecessary. What I'm about to offer is a perception of acceptance that allows for compassion in the face of egregious personal calamity.

I am proposing that forgiveness is a second-best solution to human conflict—it actually perpetuates shame and generates more conflict. There's a more fulfilling alternative to aspire to. For this to make any sense it is dependent upon understanding that:

- Addiction is a self-imposed crisis.
- Acceptance of our humanness (our fallibility) is something to strive for, which would then prohibit mean-spirited judgments.
- Whenever there's conflict, you are completely responsible for your participation in it. If you're involved, to *any* degree, you are completely responsible for the conflict.
- An objective governed by spiritual principles is preferred to an objective defined by you or your peer group. (life by consensus is always self-defeating.)
- The five spiritual principles are beyond personalities and preferences. They are to be striven for, and are only of value if you adhere to them when it's inconvenient.
- Because something is difficult to understand, hard to achieve, or stands contrary to popular opinion, does not detract from its truth or worth. *"Some of us tried to hold on to our old ideas..."*

How involved anyone is in spiritual pursuits—their level of devotion, is always a matter of choice. Regardless of your position on the spectrum from theism to atheism, you assign your own position, *and* it's not something you can exempt yourself from. That's the ubiquitous and unique nature of spirituality—everyone believes something about it. Even atheism might be seen as participation in spirituality, in that an atheist must work at maintaining proof of the non-existence of deity, probably as much as the theist works at belief. Not everyone believes *in* God, but everyone believes something *about* God.

This indicates some type of connection exists, *a priori,* between a person and the broad concept of a spiritual energy in the universe. There's no exemption from having some belief about spirituality. It's the same with sexuality and love. On the spectrum from sex is dirty/evil to sex is wonderful/spiritual, or that love is or isn't worth it, everyone has values and opinions.[28] Human nature requires that people have some opinion about God, love, and sex. The relationship between people and a deity, demonstrated in spiritual principles, mandates that very unique dynamic be a covenant. And, it's within the nature of "covenant" that lays the dynamic of forgiveness. Between people, however, their interactions are...

Relationship Contracts

All relationships between people, even the "strangers" you pass on the street or sit beside on the bus, are agreed-to deals of one sort or another. Every human relationship has a set of expectations attached to it: they are contracts, *not* covenants. Generally, the more significant the relationship, the greater are the overt and covert expectations, which expectations are the fine print of the contract.

In human adult relationships, it's fairly assumed because a person participates voluntarily, each person knows and is capable of doing what they imply they can do because they are participating. Take the traditional western view of marriage: fidelity, honesty, compassion, one person at a time, affection, care, support, etc.—that's "the deal". Your relationship with your best friend has many different expectations attached to it because of the designation "best friend". In a restaurant, you reasonably expect the other patrons, all of whom are strangers, to follow the restaurant-patron rules: don't take your clothes off; don't scream socialist slogans; don't smear the desert on the windows; don't blow your nose on the table cloth; don't throw water at the people next to you; don't set the table on fire. There are "restaurant rules", right?

---

[28] This is partly why most problems related to relationships and life manifest in expressions of sexuality and "religion". That's not where the problems originate, but that's where they show up and are played out.

There are expectations in *all* human relationships. Generally, each person expects the other person to deliver what's declared *or implied* in the relationship agreement. What arises when a person doesn't voluntarily follow the "best friend rules", the "marriage rules", the "student-teacher rules", the "house-guest rules", "the restaurant rules", is conflict regarding a breach of the contract—someone is not living up to their end of the deal.

When one person doesn't live up to, or fails to maintain, the conditions of the agreement, the aggrieved party thinks: "Hey, that's not right! Girlfriends or boyfriends, or commuter-train passengers, or whomever, aren't supposed to __(insert transgression)__." The aggrieved person in the relationship has convicted the "offender" of breaching the contract.

Here is the subsequent trap: This is immediately followed by a sense of entitlement. A debt has been created in the mind of the person who has decided they've been hurt or insulted. There's some subtle expectation of amends, restitution, apologies, or contriteness from the offender for the breach of the rules. *It's the nature of all unregenerate human relationships that, declared or implied, expectations and rules are in play, and when the rules are broken, someone owes.*

To make it more confusing, there are two crucial variables—(a) everyone has subtly different rules; and (b), the size of the debt owed "depends". Someone named A. promises to do something. They forget (creating a level of debt), *or* they deliberately change their mind without telling the other person (an increased level of debt: people owe more for rudeness than forgetfulness). Person A. didn't live up to the rules.

Partner B. now expects one "I'm Sorry" and an act of contrition—A. has to do the dishes, or give them sex, or buy lunch. For the same offense, a different partner, C., might say, "Okay, we'll forget about it this time, but don't let it happen again." This is conditional forgiveness; a veiled threat and a suspended sentence that depends upon future good conduct (romantic probation!). And another different partner, D., might expect a very sincere promise from A. that they'll *never, never, never ever* do it again, cross their heart, and A. will have to also pay a token financial penalty—flowers, or theater tickets and dinner, or a summer home in the Caribbean.

This is the courtroom relationship. I know of situations where people kept written diaries of their partner's offenses, like a judge's notebook. A relationship in these circumstances isn't graceful or kind. It's about keeping score—reward and punishment, and whoever has the best memory (or takes detailed notes) wins. These are contracts and have little to do with love.[29]

---

[29] I will explore this in more detail in *Facets of Personal Transformation*.

Expectations of Perfection

Relationship rules, declared or implied, cause no end of problems; especially because of the way they lend themselves to the expectation of perfect behaviour. Perfection in this context doesn't mean being a perfect person, it means doing *exactly* what the other thinks you agreed to do and the operative word here is *agree*. We all have these silent evaluations of error; it's okay to make these mistakes, but never *that* one.

Whether the rules are particular to an individual or implied by social custom, you can tell when one person isn't following them, meaning abiding by the contract they said (or implied) they would. The person who did not breach the contract (the rules and expectations), announces the infraction in a morally superior tone:

"You didn't phone. When you're late you're *supposed* to phone."

"*You* left the lid off the toothpaste."

"You're masturbating! When *I'm* in a committed relationship…"

These condemnations are about infractions of the clauses of the contract, i.e. Page three, paragraph F, subparagraph (ii): Changing Plans and Notification Thereof: We the undersigned, agree to telephone…. Or: Page four, paragraph J, subparagraph (iv): Parameters of Residential Etiquette and Moral Turpitude; Sub-sub paragraph (e), Toothpaste Lids. Be it understood…. Or, Page two, paragraph C, subparagraph (viii), Miscellaneous Expressions of Sexuality….

Of course the defensive responses from the offender are variously: "Oh, ya? Nobody told me." Or, "Who said so?" Or, "I didn't agree to that." The arguments that ensue are about the offender not adhering to "the rules" of the relationship contract for which they volunteered; rules which are contained in the expectations of the aggrieved party.

One person reasonably expected (trusted) the contract would go ahead according to their rules, and when it didn't, they presumed they were *owed* something. In business, when someone breaks a contract, they owe. In romantic/sexual relationships, friendships, etc., the same paradigm of debt and obligation is activated—when a rule gets broken, someone owes.[30]

All human relationships are styled on the basic premise of contracts: "I agree to do __this__ and you agree to do __that__."[31] However, these rules

---

[30] In relationships of coercion (prisoners, hostages, sometimes spouses and children), the nature of coercion establishes that ordinary rules of respect-commitment-reciprocity don't apply. Regarding war, the Geneva Convention naively and foolishly tried to add a veneer of legitimacy and sophistication to the vicious brutality of war by assigning rules to murder and violence. Since prisoners and hostages aren't voluntary relationships in the usual sense, the usual rules don't apply, but there are still rules there, too.

[31] As regards an unregenerate ego: Poor relationship choices and willful blindness are always self-serving. Out of fear-driven reaction, or desperate attempts to avoid loneliness, or acting out in relationship addictions, or a need to recreate conflict, people are irresponsible (cont'd)

aren't always clear, or one person assumes other person understands the unwritten rules, or no one knows what the rules are until they get broken (naïveté), and of course the rules change over time.

Reciprocity

In addition to a human relationship being voluntary *and* contractual, people carry expectations of reciprocity. They may not contribute equal property, but within the contract, and especially in romantic, committed relationships, they expect, oftentimes foolishly expect, reciprocity of effort. There's no end to the arguing that goes on about this.

You can tell right away when reciprocity doesn't happen. One half of the agreement says to the other half of the agreement, and always with a tone of indignation or moral superiority: "You're not trying as hard as I am." Two obvious examples are: "I work all day, and I do the __*insert extra effort*__ and you don't even __*insert examples of laziness*__." And: "I'm going to therapy to save this relationship and you're not. I'm trying harder than you!" These identify the grievance of not following the rule of Reciprocity of Effort.

To sum up relationships thus far, there are these considerations:

- All human relationships are voluntary.
- Relationships carry declared, implied, and silent, "rules" of conduct *with* expectations. This makes them contracts.
- The rules and expectations vary from person to person; especially in romantic relationships.
- Failing to abide by the expectations/rules activates the notion of debt and obligation.
- The level of debt and obligation varies from person to person.
- Reciprocity of effort is expected and always open to biased interpretation.
- The Conflict Responsibility Factor is silently calculated and expressed. "Yes, I know it's *partly* my fault, but only 49%." This is a source of chronic complaint.

---

about what they expect from whomever they get into relationships with, and are often willfully blind to the obvious. People are never innocent in the consequences of poor choices.

Forgiveness

Forgive: verb 1. To excuse for a fault or an offense; pardon. 2. To renounce anger or resentment against. 3. To absolve from payment (of a debt, for example).[32]

Certainly all the definitions are pertinent, but note especially #3. To forgive someone means to give up some entitlement to personal compensation—grant others relief by abandoning any claim to recompense for some grievance/injury; to give up a debt that's owed to you. In any transaction between people that's commonly called forgiveness, there are unspiritual preconditions that exist that are seldom, if ever, examined.

Guess Who's Late For Dinner?

You're invited to a dinner party. Of the dozen people there, you're acquainted with the host, and couple of the people are your friends. The others are strangers. You're noticeably late. The group delays dinner, waiting for you. When you arrive, there's some teasing about your being late. After dinner, the host, whom you've met only once before, approaches you and says quietly and seriously: "I know you said you had to work later than usual and were caught in traffic. I feel hurt that you didn't arrive on time or maybe didn't give my dinner party more of a priority. You could have at least phoned. I feel hurt by what you did, but I want you to know I forgive you."

You would probably have some reaction of indignation or affront for being formally forgiven for being late to a dinner party. Yet you were late, you didn't phone, the host did feel hurt, some people felt inconvenienced/annoyed (which was evident in the teasing), and the host forgave you. According to a strict definition of forgiveness, you being forgiven by the host was appropriate to the circumstances, but it didn't feel right. Why is it so many people defend forgiveness and applaud its use in conflict resolution when, upon closer examination, they are often insulted by the temerity of anyone who forgives them?

The Forgiveness Transaction

To forgive someone indicates that in between the infraction and the act of forgiveness, the offended person (the host in the dinner party example) assumed they were entitled to claim a debt because the offender (you, being late) didn't try as hard as they should have; they broke a rule, etc. The in-

---

[32] Edited excerpt from *The American Heritage® Dictionary of the English Language, Third Edition,* © 1996, Houghton Mifflin Company. Electronic version.

jured person (the host) had a right, therefore, to blame the transgressor (you) for their own unhappiness.

That period of time between the commission of the offense and the act of forgiving, be it minutes, days, or years was occupied with spiritual sloth and irresponsible blaming: "You were late... had an affair... kicked the dog... spent all the money... didn't return my call... didn't take your shoes off... and therefore I now feel insulted, hurt, sad, angry, lonely, (or) scared. You caused me... pain, hardship, trouble, more work. Now I'm _entitled_ to get a gift, receive an apology, be offered contriteness, because you did that bad thing to me. But it's okay, I'm a good/spiritual/wonderful person so I forgive you." The subtext is: I forgive your debt (to me) for doing that bad thing (to me).

The magnitude of the crime has no bearing on this. Someone tells vicious lies and you're fired from your job or someone steals the carrots from your garden: there was a transgression, an offender, an injured party, and the creation of a debt owed to you. You forgive the debt. The theme is identical to being late for the party.

Forgiveness is usually only thought of in relation to big transgressions, but if it's a principle of good conduct, it "should" apply to all offenses regardless of the circumstances. For the most part, people think it's spiritually sophisticated to forgive for big offenses, but almost invariably become indignant when forgiven for the little ones. In the big calamity people think forgiveness is nice, and in the small annoyance, people think it's pretentious. Apparently, we're not supposed to accept big offenses as a matter of course, we have to forgive for those; yet we're supposed to accept the tiny offenses, and be "above" forgiveness for them.

Who decides which crimes require, or which are exempt from, forgiveness? Our parents? The police constable? The minister? The bank manager? The therapist? The priest?... who decides? Of course, it's the aggrieved person who decides what's forgivable and what isn't. Therein lies one major corruption when forgiveness is seen as the "spiritual" final step in conflict resolution. It's not uncommon to hear: "I'll never forgive them. Never!" And, neither is it uncommon to hear: "Oh, that's fine; don't worry, I'll get over it. But don't let it happen again." Both responses are entirely self-serving, based on the perceptions of the forgiver. (And never forget that receiving some token of regret from the offender like sex or movie tickets are always appreciated.)

If forgiveness is a principle, it can't be a convenience. For spiritual integrity, people must choose to either forgive for every wrong, regardless of how slight (and appear pretentious), or give up forgiving anyone, regardless of how horrific the offense. This is no small challenge—when considering this, you are in the deep end of the spiritual pool.

Regarding the five spiritual principles, the maintenance steps, and life in general: People are spiritually handicapped in that life can never be lived, and love can never be offered, perfectly. Knowing this full well, many people still choose to deny our limitations and humanness when they condemn people for mistakes.

For you to forgive someone it implies that some thing happened *you* judged bad or wrong; that *you* have decided it should not have happened (at least not to you); that you are now owed something because of this reprehensible conduct, and rather than collect the "debt" (whatever it is that you have decided you are owed), you will not demand they pay (you), hence you forgive them. There is a very definite thread of self-defined, pretentious arrogance that permeates this. Being human requires bad things happen. If we know this, why would we condemn someone and expect they owe us something for being human?

As I offer this information, I know that it's risky to personify "God". Sages throughout the centuries have observed that as soon as we create icons or personify God, regardless of the image we've created, it isn't "God". Truly, God is beyond anything we can conceive. However, being the mere humans that we are, it's necessary to speak about God in recognizable, human terms. Look at the moon, but do not mistake the image for the thing. Feel love in your heart, but know that it isn't love—it is the sensation-image of love.

Mystics, some monks, a very few writers and poets, and wiser spiritual pilgrims, know we can never tell of love *or* God. There is only metaphor and felt experience. Symbols are confusing and barely adequate; signs are dead-end roads of insecurity, and all words can offer are inadequate metaphors to tell of the transformation out of the spider's web of addictions into spirituality. Do not mistake my "picture" of spirituality for the real thing.[33]

Covenants

As I mentioned earlier, what requires a relationship between a person and the concept of deity (of whatever description) be completely different from *all* relationships between humans is the relationship is not voluntary. The relationship is mandated by the nature of our existence and no one's exempt. The mystery of the nature of life, to our inquiring minds, is drawn to the puzzle of there is a god or their isn't. Whether people affirm or refute the existence of an ever-present energy that informs the universe; whether they call *It* God, call *It* something else, or insist nothing is God—however they arrive at whatever their beliefs are, the intrinsic nature of people re-

---

[33] I expand upon signs and symbols later.

quires they have some style of relationship relative to a belief about *That Which Art*.

Atheism, in its argument, also resting on faith, for the proof of the non-existence of *That Which Art*, is still a relationship relative to the belief. Theism is an argument, equally based on faith, for the existence of a god. Every one has, in some context, a belief related to their perceptions of *Its* nature or non-nature and if so, *Its* degree of influence. Similarly, everyone has a belief or an opinion about sex. People must have an opinion because of the intrinsic nature of sex. The relationship with *That Which Art* is not voluntary, and so the usual rules of human relationships—expectations and reciprocity—don't apply. Human relationships are "voluntary" and that requires they be contracts. Any relationship that isn't voluntary, like the one with "God" if you chose to believe in a god, can never be a contract; it's a covenant.

In what might be called old-fashioned, arranged marriages (i.e. not voluntary), it was common for the officiating authority to say something like: "In this covenant of marriage between this man and this woman, entered into before God…". Marriages, then, were considered more as covenants (not voluntary) than contracts (voluntary). As marriages made the transition from local-custom, pre-arranged public declarations in small communities, to religious rituals where self-appointed religious officials wanted to generate revenue and legislate sexual conduct, to free-choice agreements in politically complex industrial cultures, our view of them shifted from covenants to contracts.

The rules and expectations for contracts are very different than for covenants, and the rules for one cannot be successfully applied to the other. These distinctions are important.

When the rules for contracts (human relationships) are applied to covenants (relationships with a higher power), or vice versa, regardless of the social structure out of which the conception of God arises, they are doomed to inefficiency. A covenant with a higher power requires a completely different style of commitment and obligation than contract relationships between people. People enter into covenants with God and contracts with each other. (There are only two exceptions to the contracts-rule, which I'll mention in the next section.)

In a spiritual covenant with "God", your responsibility is to be the person you are and you're required to do nothing but be human (which requires making mistakes). From a quite limited, western/Christian perspective, if you think god's "love" is the closest word to describe the action of a deity towards people, your higher power loves you *because* of your shortcomings and humanness, whereas the opposite is true for people: we love each other *despite* our shortcomings. This is because "God" embraces our humanness, and people for the most part reject their humanness by expecting perfection. In relationships with a higher power, the unalterable and required *in*equality makes reciprocity impossible. Forgiveness is crucial in covenants and dangerous in contracts.

The Idea of Debt

In human relationships, if you don't harm others, invade their life to their detriment, or take anything from them, or if you live up to your end of whatever the deal is, you don't owe them anything. In the spiritual realm, it's different. In the traditional idea of religious gods, people can't harm "God", or ever take anything from God. People also can't *not* live up to their end of the deal because their end of the deal is to be human. And, in the truth of common definitions, "God" being what God is, people cannot cast aspersions on God, but can (and do) cast aspersions on other people and their beliefs about God. In the vernacular, God isn't offended by different beliefs; people are. So, because people can't hurt or harm "God", they're never indebted to God in the usual manner of human relationships.

Self-appointed religious leaders imbue god with human qualities— pleasure (god is happy because you __*insert good deed*__) and disappointment or resentment and vindictiveness (god is upset because you __*insert transgression*__). These are human qualities. The debate continues among religious types about whether god will be offended, but we know the religious leaders are. "God" may not be offended you missed your church meeting your religious leader will be.

Regarding people: We are what we are. People are their "good" parts and their "bad" parts. Everything that "I" am is me. In a general, symbolic interpretation, in the Eastern traditions, everything *is* God. In the western traditions, everything *belongs* to God, and some version of god is everywhere or *in* everything. In either perspective, since everything belongs to God or everything is God, then (from within the context of human interpretation), human shortcomings and harms caused are a part of God just as much as love or compassion are.

Calamity and misadventure are random. Mistakes are mandatory. Pain is required. Suffering is optional. Death is inevitable. God cannot be held accountable or indebted to people for their suffering and misfortune (like illness) because people are the authors of their own misfortune. "God" never "owes". And, people cannot harm God, so people can never be indebted to God. There can never be indebtedness, either way, in true covenants.[34]

---

[34] For those of us who claim a more traditional notion of god, expressing gratitude in prayer is for the existing covenant. If the spiritual relationship were a contract, rather than a (cont'd)

A general, intellectual perception of "God" holds the belief that gods are ubiquitous and beyond comprehension, with the common implication being that God is beyond imperfection (but that would also make God beyond perfection, too). However, as regards people, because of the human limitations inherent in our being, imperfections are a given. This requires that the best we can conceive of is that god (by whatever name) must be beneficent and forgiving. Otherwise, all people would be forever condemned because we are forever making mistakes. This, and the unequal and non-voluntary relationship with God, requires it be a covenant.

An inadequate metaphor might be: An infant is attempting to drink juice from a glass. The infant spills the juice, drops the glass, and it breaks. The child has completely "failed" at the complicated task of drinking from a glass: juice spilled, glass broke, and the child never tasted any of it. Here, being inept is a condition of existence, not a moral deficit. A loving parent accepts this lack of perfection as a matter of course, is beneficent, and doesn't even think about "forgiving" the infant. The parent isn't hurt. The infant doesn't owe anything.

In an uncommon perspective of this, forgiveness is the exact nature of the covenant. From the parent's perspective, forgiveness is the context that embodies the entire relationship. [As an aside, this will be explored in *Facets of Personal Transformation*. Part of the maturation process that therapists call healthy individuation is that relationships between parents and children (are supposed to) evolve from covenants into contracts.]

Consider the circumstance where you enter into an association with someone who is obviously developmentally disabled. Whatever the relationship is, the usual expectations of relationships are automatically suspended. The mentally challenged person is incapable of meeting the usual standards of relationship. Many tasks will be beyond their capabilities to do well, or even to do at all, so there's a charity of spirit in participating in their life, in taking pleasure in the fact that whatever they do is perfect and wonderful. That they can't do something well, or because they don't reciprocate with the correct amount of effort, is of no account.

These two examples of human relationships (with infants and developmentally disabled people) are thematic examples of the two exceptions to the contracts rule. Automatically forgiving *is* the "one way" transaction. In temporal terms (which are inadequate), humans fail miserably at being spiritual, but are perfect at being spiritual infants.[35] Forgiveness from God

---

covenant, we'd all be dead or fired for not living up to our end of the deal. Prayer is to express gratitude for the state of forgiveness and grace, which allows for the appreciation of the implacable grandeur of the experience of our humanness through spiritual failure—not for the relief from the guilt of transgressions. I discuss this in more detail later.

[35] Reflect on the quote at the front of the book by Edwin Arlington Robinson.

isn't a considered action that God does (like in a contract); it *is* what God *is* in the covenant.

In the spiritual realm, a higher power holds no IOUs. Forgiveness *is* the relationship, not a part of it. In secular terms, you cannot separate forgiveness from a higher power because that's what *It* is. Try it this way: You think; you can't "not think". You may think about important things or trivia, you may think about thinking about nothing, but you are always thinking. Your mind hasn't stopped thinking (asleep or awake) from the instant it started. Thinking *is* you. You can't separate or suspend thinking from humanness. A higher power *is* Forgiveness.[36] No degree of obedience, misbehaviour, or groveling can ever change that.

If spiritual forgiveness is the action of God in our covenant with God, regardless of our conduct, why bother with the five spiritual principles at all? Colloquially: If "God" automatically forgives the sinner, regardless of the transgression, why bother being good? God doesn't need anyone to act spiritual to(wards) *It*, and god doesn't require that people act spiritual towards each other. However, in order to appreciate the implacable grandeur of life exactly as we have been given it, we need to at least be obedient to spiritual principles. These principles, emanating out "from people", are what allow people to create heaven on earth.

At the human level, in emotional or social contracts, in order to forgive someone, in between the "transgression" and the "forgiveness", you first must hold a belief that you are owed something. In a subtle model of entitlement, you have judged that because they were bad or somehow negligent, they owe you an apology, reparation, some money, a favor, or contriteness: you're *entitled*.

In the example of being late for the dinner party, the host viewed you as rude, insensitive, or irresponsible (some degree of condemnation). The host then decided they were "entitled" to feel hurt. You, therefore, "owed" them something for the transgression of being late. The host, therefore, had the authority to decide between: (i) insisting or manipulating you into guilt and getting an amend of some sort; (ii) if they never receive whatever payment they believe the debt they created demands, they get to feel righteous and resentful; or (iii), forgiving the debt, which they, themselves, created by condemning you, and then magnanimously forego "collecting" it. [In this last scenario they, then, get to secretly feel righteous and charitable and collect good-Samaritan points from all their pals for being so "spiritual".]

---

[36] From Alan Watts: People don't say: "I am beating my heart." Your beating heart is not a considered action of will; from *This Is It*, Vintage Books, 1973, p. 91. Similarly, people will say "I am thinking," as if thinking as a function of will. It isn't. And God's forgiveness isn't a considered action, either. It just *is*.

The host lives by relationship rules that allow them to condemn you for being the human that you are. For the host to presume they're entitled to forgive you, or they're even capable of it, is arrogant and presumptuous. You're a person (it's what people do) and being condemned is tantamount to being condemned for being human, and therein lays the first major corruption when forgiveness is seen as the final step in conflict resolution.

Being human requires that mistakes, hurts, errors, harm, and transgressions *will* happen, caused by you and done to you. Attaching condemnation and forgiveness to these mandatory, usually random foibles is one source of dislocation that exemplifies and enables the wheel of suffering as described in Buddhism.[37]

In the context of human forgiveness, preceding the belief that you can forgive someone for hurting you is your belief that that person shouldn't have "hurt" you. When you're offended, it isn't their offense that causes your offendedness, but your interpretation of their behaviour, and your presumption they should have somehow been above their humanness. You've decided they owe you something for being human. Therein lies the second major corruption when forgiveness is seen as the spiritual final step in conflict resolution.

The condemnation of humanness leaves people perpetually prepared to feel hurt before anything happens: Victims in Waiting. The traditional stance of the victim is: "I have been hurt and the offender owes me." (This is the Two-Step Dance.[38]) When forgiveness is the transaction between people, at its core, one person is being condemned for being human and the other person is (at least temporarily) holding themselves above being human. This unexamined arrogance is the third major corruption in the dynamic of human forgiveness.

The Forgiven

When (if) people subscribe to the idea that forgiveness is the final, best step in conflict resolution, and then they, themselves, commit some offense, any subsequent amend they offer requires, at least in part, some contriteness for being human. Within the forgiveness transaction, the offender who is apologizing for the misdemeanour must include some apology for being human because that's what they are being condemned for. How damaging is that?[39]

---

[37] Regarding Buddhism and attachment, in the scenario of forgiveness it's attachment to entitlement, debt and obligation. Attachment, in any context, is always self-serving. The resolution of this is not to be perfect, but to change your attitude towards the fallible nature of people.

[38] The Two-Step Dance is described in Chapter 9.

[39] This is one theme at the core of the Christian parable "Let those without sin cast the first stone," which speaks to hypocrisy. Since we are all "sinners" [sic] to some degree, the (cont'd)

This doesn't absolve addicts or alcoholics (or people in general) of the responsibility to be reasonably determined to not hurt others. All efforts must be made to take responsibility and amend any damage done; but at the same time, identifying the harm you caused in Step Eight does not carry any obligation to apologize for having shortcomings, or to defend the fact that you have an illness, or to be contrite about being human.

Because human relationships are contracts, they carry an expectation of reciprocity. Many people assume that when they're hurt, the ultimate spiritual response on their part—the reciprocity required of the aggrieved party—is to offer forgiveness.[40] Additionally, when addicts are caught up in cultural and religious confusion regarding relationship contracts, they often expect to be forgiven by the person they have hurt after they make an amend. These are evidence of a serious misalliance of commitment within a spiritual lifestyle and defeat the task at hand.

Forgiveness is spiritually *in*efficient in secular relationships. It implies condemnation for being human; is evidence of the Two-Step Dance; and assumes a debt is owed by the transgressor to the aggrieved person, when all that happened was someone was being human. It implies psychological superiority on the part of the forgiver, and moral turpitude on the part of the forgiven. It implies *in*equality between the parties in the transaction and embodies hypocrisy. There are seriously unspiritual aspects to believing that forgiveness is the highest spiritual solution to human problems.[41]

However, in a relationship between a deity and a human, the secular notions of reciprocity and equality don't apply. Forgiveness on the part of "God", and prayer and meditation (worship) on the part of people to(wards) a higher power are what honor the inherent inequality of the relationship. Forgiveness for being human is God's covenant with people. Responsibility/acceptance for our human failings is your contract with people. Confusing contracts with covenants is disastrous to either relationship.

---

moment anyone condemns another for any human failing, regardless of its magnitude, there is hypocrisy. In addition to the hypocrisy, at a deeper level than the original offense, the "offender" is being condemned for being human. None of us are above being human.

[40] Should a person think it's spiritually sound at the human level to forgive someone, then if they can forgive them, it implies they can also withhold forgiveness. People who believe in forgiveness will often withhold it until the offender is contrite enough to satisfy their wounded dignity. How spiritual is that?

[41] Wherever condemnation is present in any human relationship, in terms of the transaction of forgiveness, three of the five spiritual principles are subtly absent (respect for the body-temple, veracity, and responsibility and obedience), and two are flagrantly absent (humility and charity). Being in a relationship where one person has political advantage or legislated authority doesn't automatically mean there is inequality.

Getting Beyond Forgiveness

Before alcoholics, addicts, or people in general, can get beyond forgiveness to a more peaceful and fulfilling mindset these beliefs are required:

- addictions, unmanageability, and related "life" problems are self-imposed;
- complete personal responsibility, and consistent self examination, not other-examination, is the order of the day— every day;
- for spiritual pilgrims, regular, frequent, and properly focused prayer and meditation with an adoption of non-angry moral responsibility; and for morally-committed atheists, an adoption of non-angry moral responsibility, are crucial; and,
- for those getting recovered, diligent adherence to the original instructions throughout the steps (without editing or rewriting), and eventually living "in" the maintenance steps which embody the five spiritual principles, is the primary task at hand.

No one of these is any more important than the others. Any commitment to one of them is rendered meaningless without an equal commitment to the others. Alternately, an absence of commitment to one of them makes any commitment to the others political. Integrity requires equally sincere devotion to all of them.

For the self-proclaimed aggrieved party, consider that in between being hurt by someone and offering forgiveness to them, there is that period where they believe they are an entitled victim. As has been discussed elsewhere, being a victim is about insecurity and blaming.

Recall earlier discussions that self-examination and commitment to uncompromising personal responsibility are what takes a person out of being a victim and frees them from self-pity. As discussed earlier, self-pity is a self-managed perception of helpless inadequacy.

The four beliefs noted above are also the fundamental conditions that allow people to go beyond forgiveness. When people reeducate themselves through personal responsibility into a very deep level of self-acceptance regarding their own limitations, they achieve a wonderful sense of inner peace through compassion and gentleness towards themselves regarding their humanness. They (eventually) stop condemning themselves for anything. As soon as you assume uncompromising personal responsibility and attain self-acceptance, you stop condemning others.

When people accept their own humanness; when addicts and alcoholics accept their disease and themselves, without apology or guilt, exactly as they are, especially their imperfections, they are capable of offering that acceptance of "self" out to others. Others see this as true respect and egalitarianism—even when others grievously hurt them.

What the truly spiritual people accomplish by microscopic self-examination and complete responsibility is insightful *self*-acceptance, regarding their own frailties. They are then able to eliminate all condemnation and offer out love and acceptance. That sets other people free from being blamed and condemned, regardless of the transgression; free from your judgments they owe you anything, and renders forgiveness unnecessary.

From a slightly different perspective: When you understand the necessity for accepting your own shortcomings, which is the accepting of your humanness, the truth is that your own ever-present frailties and misdemeanors make a mockery of you ever forgiving anyone for anything. In this mindset you find authentic self-love and peace. Then it's natural to love others because and in spite of their frailties, regardless of how grievously you are wounded or inconvenienced by them. This is only available with you believing in consistent, uncompromising devotion to veracity and personal responsibility. This is the key for going beyond the spiritually limiting place of forgiveness, to true acceptance (which again), then renders forgiveness unnecessary.

Character defects are demonstrations of insecurity and fear. They allow you to avoid personal responsibility—that's what you've designed them for. More directly: Every time you find it necessary to either offer or seek forgiveness, that in itself is motivated by a character defect. In other words, forgiveness is your Character Defect Concealment Strategy—it conceals your own hypocrisy, arrogance and harsh judgments about others. Going beyond forgiveness is dependent upon your ability to take complete responsibility for your character defects.

When you become truly *willing* at Step Six you gently reduce your insecurities. Without willingness, you sentence yourself to forever secretly managing your insecurities as the top priority of your inner existence. But, whatever goes on inside, goes on outside. If you're managing your insecurities, that requires you to constantly, secretly, manage your human relationships. If you're stuck in managing yourself, you're stuck in managing others.

With this, the cycle of forgiveness: offense, hurt, fault finding, condemnation, recrimination, contrition, benevolence, forgiveness, and righteous indifference is all that's available to you. All of this work "managing" things leaves no time to appreciate that life is monumentally spectacular and overflowing with beauty—exactly as it exists.

Character defects are always self-serving. They magically magnify those circumstances where it appears you are "more right" than the other person. How many times have you thought you forgave someone and then found yourself, days or years later, in another fit of pique about the circumstance you had forgiven them for? Reliving the event occurs because character defects, like anger and righteousness, which conceal insecurity, are themselves concealed under the transaction of forgiveness. Forgiving someone (yet again) allows you to reclaim the moral high ground. At the human level, when forgiveness is the ultimate good, that justifies condemnation of another, and leaves the arrogance and absence of humility underneath the forgiveness unchallenged.

Without accurate, sincere realizations about your selfish, self-destructive character (gained through to Step Seven), *and* a commitment to complete personal responsibility, *and* a willingness to become humble, forgiveness remains the necessary game of relationship politics. Self-absolution through forgiveness of others is an amazing vehicle through which you conceal hypocrisy, perpetuate guilt, and foster your own spiritual irresponsibility.

Addicts get to rush about, recreating their offenses. It does nothing at the human level to further the responsible pursuit of sincere spirituality. There's no serenity in a life-posture of victim in waiting—the repetitious cycle of offense, hurt, fault-finding, concealing defects, condemnation, recrimination, contrition, benevolence, forgiveness, and righteous indifference.

Embrace both aspects of humility (Appendix II) and embrace a deep acceptance of your own humanness. You will then sidestep the need to judge, condemn and forgive others. This is truly, serenity at its best.

The Foundation for Step Eight

To sort out all these subtleties, it's important that you have laid the proper foundation for Step Eight in the preceding steps. If you've not done them exactly as instructed, you will be incapable of emotional balance and responsibility when itemizing the harm you caused. Here is the foundation you have laid thus far, and its specific relation to Step Eight:

Step One: A significant reduction in culturally imposed guilt, along with a solid conviction that you are resolving a disease. Your soul doesn't need fixing; the phenomenon of addictions needs resolution. At Step Eight, this realization allows you to admit the harm and be responsible without being controlled by guilt and shame. You may still feel a little of them, but they won't control you, and they won't undermine the integrity of your investigation into the harm you caused.

Step Two: The recognition that the solution to your self-destruction and the related insanity rests in your sincere alliance with spiritual principles and devotion to something bigger than selfish self-interest. At Step Eight you will then be focused on spiritual integrity and service to those principles, rather than social atonement and service to yourself. This permits charity and thoroughness when identifying the harm done.

Step Three: The decision to turn your will and life over to the care of a higher power (as you understand this) allows you to always be clear about your purpose: *being governed by spiritual principles*. That decision, when you arrive at Step Eight, allows you to remain consistent in your devotion. Inconsistent devotion in making amends is hard to uncover. It's your secretly pandering to any political advantage by amending one harm more thoroughly than another harm. The decision at Step Three entitles every incident of harm to equally thorough examination.

Step Four: The examination of your insecurities, fears, and sexual selfishness allowed you to be aware of the subtle ways you tried to control life, and thereby blame and harm others. Step Four trained you to examine your responsibility and ignore the behaviour of others. This is training for Step Eight, and allows you to see the harm you caused, and ignore the other person's participation.

Step Five: The honest admission of your insecurities, fears, and sexual selfishness facilitates two things at Step Eight. (1) It alleviates cultural guilt that will arise when you identify harms caused, and allows you to retain your integrity when you itemize harm. (2) Step Five is the crucial training experience for talking about your responsibility without blaming others. Honestly calling only yourself to account at Step Eight is only possible because of the exercise at Step Five.

Honestly identifying the harm you caused others at Step Eight is a natural extension of your Steps Four Five, but only if you very specifically followed the instructions. Additionally, what sometimes comes up during Step Nine is people you harmed may be curious about why it happened. Should the need to discuss your motivations for causing harm arise, practicing self-responsible, non-blaming disclosure at Step Five makes that discussion at Step Nine a non-threatening experience for the person receiving the amend.

Step Six: Here you became willing to make a necessary, fundamental change: giving up your survival skills and abandoning your character defects on behalf of spiritual principles, not for personal contentment. This makes it possible to eliminate the need to seek social atonement in later step-work that is, itself, crucial for transforming your perspective of life from social success to spiritual integrity. At Step Eight, this willingness counteracts any selfishness, which will otherwise detrimentally influence the patience and thoroughness that's required.

Step Seven: You learned that humility is a desired virtue and it's to be sought because it's inherently good. You're now able to transform without being motivated by fear, shame, pain, or guilt. After Step Seven, spirituality isn't self-serving, which means examining the harms you caused isn't done to escape pain or guilt. "No pain, no gain", which was true up to Step Five, becomes unnecessary. Step Eight becomes charity of spirit in the form of spiritual responsibility and has nothing to do with you.

Without devotion to humility and responsibility, Step Eight will be onerous and superficial. If your effort is without a sense of willingness and joy for the task at hand, go back to Step Two and reexamine your belief that a higher power through obedience to the five spiritual principles is the solution. Then, review Steps Six and Seven until such time as you notice you're willing. That will clear up any begrudging attitude towards the huge amount of work that is necessary at Step Eight.[42]

In the final analysis, you cannot for long seek a spiritual life that's motivated by guilt or shame, otherwise, the resulting relationship with your higher power is self-serving. This renders spirituality selfish. When you were in your addiction there was no end of shame, pain, and self-destruction. These were what initially motivated your pursuit of transformation. After Step Seven, when humility is a desired virtue, you "should" be eagerly motivated by the inherent joys of responsibility. This makes microscopic honesty and everything you do thereafter, a labour of love. In other words, by Step Eight, you should not be awkward or reluctant to be honest with anyone about anything. If you are, you've missed the spiritual point.

The Administration of Step Eight

Patience, thoroughness, and honesty are paramount to the task at hand: *"Made a list of all persons we had harmed, and became willing to make amends to them all."*[43] Certainly, it's direct and to the point.

Retrieve the copy of the autobiographical list of everyone/everything in your life that I suggested you make at Step Four. Since this would have been months ago, reflect on your life since then and, if necessary, add to the list those new people you have met since you finished Step Four.

The guiding phrases are: *"...and really makes an accurate and un-*

---

[42] Oftentimes, when spiritual self-discipline becomes difficult, pilgrims forget that they volunteered for it and can always choose to return to their old pains and behaviour. There are always choices.

[43] *Alcoholics Anonymous*, p. 59, and *Twelve Steps and Twelve Traditions*, p. 77.

sparing survey... , " "...[we] *ought to redouble* [our] *efforts to see how many people* [we have] *hurt... ," "Calm, thoughtful reflection... ," "ransack* [your] *memory...".*[44] There is no guideline about how this should actually be laid out on paper. My suggestion is to use a layout of three columns, similar to Step Four.

The instruction is: "*as year by year we walk back through our lives as far as memory will reach, we shall be bound to construct a long list of people who have, to some extent or other, been affected,*"[45] (meaning harmed). The wording implies the list is chronological—you would begin in the present and work back into the past; the list is thorough and long; the harm is either minor or major; and, the tone of the sentence, along with the phrase "*walking back,*" implies patience and thoughtfulness in the effort.[46]

The author(s) of *Twelve Steps and Twelve Traditions* were well aware of an alcoholic's [anyone's] tendency to minimize the harm done by creating self-serving definitions of "harm", and thereby evading responsibility. They eliminate that loophole by defining harm as "*...the result of instincts in collision, which cause physical, mental, emotional, or spiritual damage to people.*"[47]

The next paragraphs in the AA text outline the obvious forms of harm that addicts do, and provide a detailed list of the subtler forms of harm that you are to look for. Addicts may "*...lie and cheat* [and thereby] *deprive others;* [or be] *...miserly, irresponsible, callous, ...cold, irritable, critical, impatient, and humorless;* [or they may] *...lavish attention on one and neglect others; ...dominate the whole family by rule of iron or constant outpouring of minute directions;* [or] *...wallow in depression, self pity oozing from every pore. Such a roster of harms done others... ".*[48] This identifies the fifteen ways that addicts and alcoholics cause harm in relation to Step Eight. Yes, it may end up with you having to make some type of amend, large or small, to quite a few people. Remember, you have volunteered to go to any length for a spiritual experience, and you have acquired the willingness and humility to do that. Examine your behaviour in relation to every person on your autobiographical list. Ask yourself the following questions:

---

[44] Phrases from Step Eight in *Twelve Steps and Twelve Traditions*, pp. 77, 80, 81.

[45] Ibid., p. 81.

[46] Be cautious with the phrase, "*as far as memory will reach.*" This is about your addictions. If you insist on examining your pre-addictions life for incidents where you harmed others, do this under the protective umbrella of well-conducted therapy. The propensity of addicts to oscillate between justifying their offences and debilitating self-blame for everything imaginable is to be kept in mind.

[47] *Twelve Steps and Twelve Traditions*, p. 80.

[48] Ibid. p. 81.

- Did I harm this person physically? Did I harm this person mentally? Did I harm this person emotionally? Did I harm this person spiritually?
- Was I miserly, irresponsible, callous, cold, irritable, critical, impatient, or humorless with this person?
- Did I lavish attention on one and neglect another? Did I dominate the whole family, or attempt to dominate people, constantly issuing minute directions?
- Did I wallow in depression or self-pity?

The more you are thorough and responsible here, the greater your eventual sense of spiritual peace will be. Nothing is free and in recovery you pay in advance.[49] If you want deep and lasting contentment, be meticulous and responsible in defining what harm you have caused. Be patient. Pray for willingness to do this as a part of a spiritual lifestyle. Seek wise spiritual counsel. This *"is the beginning of the end of isolation from our fellows and from God."*[50]

After thoughtful reflection regarding each person on your list, as regards the very broad definition of "harm", given in the AA literature (noted above), if you have not harmed them cross them off the list. Once you identify that you did harm them, write briefly what the harm was beside their name. Don't use ditto marks. When you have noted the harm you caused, which actually creates a second column, beside that, note in a third column what amend is appropriate. This can range from sending cards and letters, making a phone call, arranging a personal visit (plan what you will say), reporting your self to the authorities (plan ahead), and/or paying off debts. Whenever you are in doubt, err on the side of responsibility, avoid blame, and seek wise spiritual counsel.[51]

This is a seldom-discussed, crucial exercise that you must participate in for any lasting change—the long, gently repeated exposure *of* yourself, *by* yourself, *to* yourself. There are several things about patient, responsible self-discipline that are *un*attractive to addicts getting recovered: it isn't dramatic, it isn't quick, it can be expensive, it requires concentration, it can be embarrassing, there's no one to blame, *and* it exposes you for exactly

---

[49] Recovery, or spiritual integrity, is not like your favorite restaurant where you get the good food first and pay after. In recovery, you pay first and get the good life after.

[50] *Twelve Steps and Twelve Traditions*, p. 82.

[51] Seeking wise spiritual counsel doesn't include jogging partners, the consensus of the people in your group, workmates, your spouse, or your sponsor if your sponsor is someone you call your friend and with whom you loiter about in coffee shops. The awkward truths, intimate details, and objectiveness required for wise counsel excludes all people who have a vested interest in the politics of your relationship with them; demand of yourself to go outside (cont'd)

what you were (or are)—a selfish, inconsiderate addict (ouch!). This is awkward and difficult, which is why this aspect of spiritual transformation is presented after you have developed the willingness to see humility as desirable, *and* after you have the personal courage and insight to complete the task without blaming anyone, including yourself.

It takes a *long* time to become spiritual. While *en route* to "spiritual bliss" [sic], fall in love, change jobs, go to a movie, paint a picture, go back to school, make love, learn to play the trombone, sail a boat, do the tango (whatever)—continue living your life while you do your step work. Keep abstinence and spiritual principles as the higher priorities, and live.

Sensitivity and Awareness

Many addicts end up with inordinately short lists of harms caused. Often times this is because of a self-serving definition of harm and an arbitrary classification of which harms are important enough to pay attention to. This self-serving, selfish behaviour isn't always deliberate. There are understandable reasons for alcoholics and addicts minimizing the harm caused, which are related to self-awareness and sensitivity.

When anyone is significantly out of touch with feelings (when subtle emotions are unknown to them), they're only aware of their own blatant feelings. They're legitimately unaware of the small hurts and insults that might be experienced by people who are more sensitive to emotion. [Yet, some others are *so* sensitive that all emotional experience is traumatic.]

Accuracy and thoroughness in evaluating harms at Step Eight are influenced by your own sensitivity. You may well be sincere and mean well, but not sensitive. Should you be noticeably unaware of emotional nuance within yourself, or have a limited view of a person's rights and freedoms, you'll be unable to accurately appreciate the nuance of emotional harm you caused.

Notice these two conversations between A. and B. regarding the same conversation. In the first call, A. is the more sensitive.

> **A.:** "Yesterday, on the phone, I was impatient with you. I regret the abrupt tone I used and how I ended the call. I'm going to make a sincere effort to not do that again. I'd understand if you felt hurt."
> **B.:** "What? Rude? What're you talking about? It was fine."

Next is a conversation about the same phone call where B. is the more sensitive person.

---

of this comfort zone. Seek authentic counsel that seriously calls you to task regarding responsibility and spiritual principles. *"Hard on ourselves..."*, p. 74, *Alcoholics Anonymous*.

B.: "Yesterday, on the phone, I felt a little rushed and, I guess, a little hurt that you seemed so abrupt. You sounded impatient and almost hung up on me. Are you upset with me?"

A.: "What do you mean, abrupt? I didn't think I was. Really?"

Sometimes people are insensitive because they are deliberately unwilling to be responsible. They're afraid. Other people appear insensitive because they really are out of touch with their emotions and unable to understand emotional nuance in themselves, which necessarily means they are unable to appreciate emotional nuance in others.

From a psychological perspective, a person's response to being dismissed by a deliberately rude or mean person would be quite different from their response to dismissal by someone who is sincere but insensitive to emotional nuance. Sometimes it's very difficult to tell which is which. In Step Eight, be sensitive. If you identify what harm you've caused with a "hard heart", or if you are still entrenched at all in blaming others, you'll have only seven people on your list.

Reflect carefully on the broad definition of "harm" in the AA literature. Narrow definitions of "harm" are irresponsible. [The theme here is similar to an issue discussed at Step Four: avoiding responsibility by creating a narrow definition of resentments.]

Watch for indirect harm. For example: B. is making a list of harms. When in active addiction, B. would often manipulate K. into irresponsible, drunken behaviour by intimidating, bragging, shaming, teasing, and flashing money. If B. had left K. alone, there would have been much less conflict in K.'s family. [Yes, K. might have said "No," but that's not the point. This is about B.] B. contributed to K.'s family conflict, even though B. didn't know K.'s family, and didn't harm them directly. In this spiritual endeavor, an amend *may* be in order from B. to K.'s family.[52]

Earlier, I pointed out the regeneration steps must be viewed independently of each other. Thinking about any one step, while completing another, always contaminates the outcome. Here's one area where that's obvious...

At Step Nine, the original twelve-step literature identifies an exception to making amends when the amend would cause further harm. That's wise, but that applies to Step Nine, not Eight. While in the midst of Step Eight, if you debate whether or not you should make the amend because that may cause more harm, you will evade thoroughness in identifying what harm you actually did cause. In the midst of Step Eight, if you ruminate about

---

[52] *Twelve Steps and Twelve Traditions*, p. 79. Begin: *"There were cases, too, where..."*

Step Nine because you may not make an amend, you'll shirk the responsi-bility of a detailed examination of the harm you caused.

It's too easy to decide in Step Eight that dredging up old wounds "that are better left forgotten", or reminding people of their hurt and anger at *your* past behaviour, is causing harm. People being reminded of painful, histori-cal events that you are responsible for, does not automatically qualify as them being harmed, and it never exempts you from examining the circum-stance in detail (Step Eight).

There are different ways of evading honesty and thoroughness. You can make your list shorter than it needs to be due to unmanageable shame, fear, guilt, blame, or anger. You can make it too long by taking on too much responsibility and blaming yourself for all the conflict and harm every-where. And, whether real or fancied, you may edit your examination by deciding no amend should be made because you'll be harming others by dredging up the past.

Step Eight has nothing whatever to do with actually making the amend, it's only identifying in detail exactly the harm you caused. Be very thorough in examining your harmful behaviour, no matter how slight or egregious. You need the exercise in veracity, responsibility, and obedience in self-examination. Whether you make an amend later is entirely separate from identifying the particular harm you caused.

Earlier, I talked about newcomers being unable to judge how well they're doing. This "insight-shortsightedness" is applicable in the process of closely examining your relationships for harm you have caused. It's crucial to have the counsel of a trusted sponsor, *bona fide* spiritual advisor, or therapist who is well versed in the spiritual aspects of twelve-step programs, *and* has no investment in the politics of your life. They are "supposed to" gently, and firmly, and persistently encourage a high standard of responsi-bility and spiritual commitment.

Don't Apologize or Be Sorry

It's a given that practicing addicts, and many other people, are irre-sponsible. This is also true for unregenerate addicts in recovery who have invested only a superficial effort in spirituality. Nowhere is this as obvious as in their self-serving attempts to manipulate others by penitent declara-tions of "I'm sorry" and "I apologize". When deciding what must be done to amend the harm, do not apologize. Do not say, "I'm sorry."

Here are two definitions of apology: (1) a formal defense or vindica-tion against an accusation; and (2), a justification, an explanation, an excuse.[53] Certainly there are other interpretations of "apologize" that include an expression of regret or an acknowledgement of fault. However you define it, making an apology (i) carries some direct reference to extenuating circumstances: a defense, (ii) implies an expectation you'll be forgiven or that you're less accountable because of those extenuating circumstances; and (iii), carries an implicit expectation that the aggrieved party should cooperate with the offender's effort at self-exoneration.

Any time you defend a harm you have caused by tendering reasons and justifications, it follows, as an accepted principle of jurisprudence, if the reasons are good enough, you will be exonerated from accountability (meaning not held responsible). It's called self-defense. And, if you're held "less" responsible because you can justify the nefarious deed, you may be quite guilty but only minor accountability accrues to you. So, if you can justify it, you really don't have to change at all and, the icing on the cake you have baked is, you get to do it over again.

Apologies are not amends and they make any amends patently self-serving and disrespectful to the aggrieved party. The offender is (yet again) trying to control the aggrieved person and the situation. We'll go through this in detail. It is crucial.

Apologize By Numbers

The three instructions are: (a) Read through the options; (b) Using a pencil, check off/select one sentence-stem from each section, (1) through (6); and (c), Read through your selections from the beginning, following the suggested inflections.

(1) **The Set Up**: (be very sincere) ( ) I'm *very* sorry that I... *or*
( ) I *apologize* that I...

(2) **The Confession**: (contrite, minimized, and/or dramatic)

( ) had an affair.	( ) didn't put gas in the car.
( ) slapped you.	( ) was... ( ) one, ( ) two,
( ) wrecked the car.	( ) eleven... ( ) hours,
( ) took the car.	( ) days, ( ) months,
( ) lied to you.	( ) years, late.
( ) didn't call.	( ) drank, ( ) used drugs.
( ) did call.	( ) ate the ice cream.
( ) left.	( ) spilled the milk.

---

[53] *The New Shorter Oxford English Dictionary,* Clarendon Press, Oxford, 1993.

( ) spent the money.
( ) called you names.
( ) hit the dog.

( ) didn't __(oversight)__ .
( ) did __(misdemeanor)__ .

(3) **The Exaggerated Self-Attack**: This is to elicit sympathetic disagreement from the person you hurt and bolster the planned defense (for best results be dramatically and sincerely contrite).

( ) I know I'm *terrible*.
( ) I'm such a *jerk*.
( ) How can you *stand* being with me?

( ) I'm so... ( ) *horrible*,
( ) *disgusting*,
( ) *stupid*.

(4) **The Defense**: But, you see... ( ) **Dear**, ( ) **Sweetheart**, ( ) **Honey**,
(Pick two; it's much more effective when trying to side-step responsibility.)

( ) I'm in recovery.
( ) I'm under a lot of pressure...
( ) My foot was sore.
( ) I didn't mean to.
( ) I got carried away.
( ) The meeting was...
( ) I thought that...
( ) The bus was late.
( ) I missed the bus.
( ) I got hit by the bus.
( ) I had a headache.
( ) I couldn't find a taxi...
( ) I didn't think that...
( ) The guys insisted.
( ) I'm a drug addict and you knew that...
( ) The courier didn't...
( ) I'm an alcoholic and you knew that...
( ) The girls wanted me to...
( ) I was... ( ) horny, ( ) lonely,
( ) angry, ( ) hungry,
( ) tired, ( ) sad.

( ) It was ( ) snowing, ( ) raining,
( ) windy, ( ) hot, ( ) dark.

( ) My   ( ) mother, ( ) father,
( ) priest, ( ) therapist.
( ) sister, ( ) uncle,
did (or didn't) ___?___.

( ) You *knew* I was like this when we met.
( ) When I was...
( ) in college...
( ) a child...
( ) at summer camp...
( ) away in Europe...
___insert sorrowful details____.

( ) My boss...
( ) didn't ( ) couldn't
( ) wouldn't..._____??____.
( ) You're *not* going to believe this, but... __(insert unique excuse)__.

(5) **The Obsequious (Exception) Factor**: (this must be said with *very* sincere conviction)

        ( ) but I *really* didn't mean it.
        ( ) but I *won't* do it again.
        ( ) but I'll *try* not to do it again.
        ( ) but it's really *not* as bad as it used to be. Right?
        ( ) ah, come on, I haven't done it for a *really* long time.

(6) **Shifting Responsibility**: (with a *dramatic* gesture sad eyes):

        ( ) I'm *so* sorry, but *you've* got to understand.
        ( ) I'm *really* trying, and I hope *you'll* understand.
        ( ) I'm very, *very* sorry. *Please* forgive me.
        ( ) I apologize, so can I *please* get another chance?
        ( ) I promise, I really, really promise… !

(Now read through your selections following the acting instructions.)

By beginning the apology with a penitent declaration of how sorry you are, you attempt to shift the transaction away from the other person's hurt and onto your excuse. If you've enough good reasons (justifications) for your irresponsible or mean behaviour (at #3 & #4) you won't have to change. *And,* if you can make your sorrow/regret (at #1 & #5) and your self-serving compassionate plea (at #6) "bigger" than their hurt, you get the empathy spotlight.

The end results are that you have minimized your own culpability, the "wrong" isn't fixed and, by shifting the focus at #6, the aggrieved person is made responsible for the outcome. Now the "amend" is completely self-serving and the person you hurt is responsible, not you. (Neat, eh?)

If the aggrieved person doesn't "understand" or give you another chance (at #6), you get to think with self-absolution: "Well, this conflict is their fault because I apologized and they didn't accept it. I *told* them how bad I felt—I was sincere what do they want, blood?" This is a controlling set-up for additional irresponsibility—the intricacy of blame. You blame other circumstances for the misdemeanor and blame the person you hurt for not understanding.

The primary purpose of Step Eight is to identify where you were wrong (did harm) and decide exactly what you need to do to fix it. Throughout the Apologize by Numbers exercise, none of it addressed the harm that was done, and there was no action to actually repair the damage. In making amends, whatever you think may be a probable defense (at 4) is irrelevant. Amends must begin with sincere willingness and humility otherwise, the exercise is motivated by selfishness and you'll portion out responsibility and offer excuses. Focus on what needs to be done to actually repair the damage you caused; nothing else matters.

Don't be sorry or obsequious in responding to the circumstances of life. If you have an addiction, that's a *bona fide* reason for symptomatic behaviour. People with narcolepsy fall asleep. It's not an excuse and it doesn't mitigate responsibility, it's just the reason for falling asleep. The disease dictates addictive behaviour, not your evil soul. Yes, there's a need to be completely responsible and, in identifying the harms, you may feel sad or regretful, however these are noticeably different from being sorry or obsequious, which are an attempt to elicit sympathy and minimize responsibility.[54]

There's no reference within the original twelve-step literature (personal stories excluded) that advises an apology or being sorry are amends. The implicit task is to decide what harm you caused and, as you do this, not to justify your irresponsibility or meanness. From a spiritual perspective, an amend is to repair the damage and re-establish some harmony in the life of the person you harmed.[55]

Inappropriate Compensation — Make Anyone Pay

The spiritual responsibility that I am about to describe can carry a difficult demand that is laid on the conscience of those who were harmed by others. Being harmed by the misfortunes of life or others, in our blame-oriented culture, has created a victim's game called Make Anyone Pay.

As a child, if you were abused, you were completely innocent. That childhood innocence does *not* carry itself over into adulthood as a justification for mean or irresponsible behaviour. Only by irresponsible anger and other defects can you justify demanding reparation from people who didn't cause the harm. If you demand innocent people pay, you're taking the role of persecutor—harming innocent people—an exact parallel to how, as a child, you were harmed. The victim becomes a persecutor. (I explored this earlier in The Ripple Effect of Irresponsibility, p. 91.) It bears repeating because of its insidious nature.

Whoever hurt you as a child tore a hole in the spiritual fabric of the universe. True. However, punishing innocent people because of that is never warranted, no matter how badly you were hurt. In a spiritual lifestyle

---

[54] *"We should be sensible, tactful... ,"* Alcoholics Anonymous, p. 83.
[55] *"Our real purpose is to fit ourselves..."* and *"...having the other one's happiness uppermost in mind."* Alcoholics Anonymous, p. 77 and p. 82, respectively.

nothing justifies violence or revenge. Making innocent people pay is both violent and vengeful. Morally self-righteous victims, and the professionals, TV talk shows, judges, lawyers, therapists, doctors, politicians, etc., and righteous religious who aid and abet this behaviour, crash through our culture suing anybody they can, making anyone pay.

Greed and vengeance masquerade as justice—clothed in social respectability. It frequently happens in intimate relationships. Partners inflict revenge on their spouse, their children, and friends for harms done to them by others.

The people who make anyone pay are as harmful to others as were those who hurt them in the first place. It is complex and insidious in our personalities. "I was hurt by... a Jew, an African American, a white person, a cop, a woman, a man, an Asian, a teenager... (pick your own)... and now I can despise all of them. Someone will pay!" The recreational pastime for many victims is: someone hurt me so I'll hurt anyone. This is irresponsible and the cycle of abuse continues.

Should you be a person who was hurt and at that time you were innocent, be cautious about how you attend to your healing. If "it's not fair" is the ambience of your motivation, it will turn into a grievance with the universe, and through vengeance ("make anyone pay") you'll initiate another cycle of abuse.

Spiritual Reasonableness

At Step Eight, you're going through the process of examining the harm you did to others to take *full* responsibility for this without expecting any cooperation or support from the aggrieved person. Disregard whatever they might have done. This is being spiritually responsible. However, as you examine your behaviour, that examination has to have some balance.

As you decide what amends are required, it must have a tone of what I call spiritual reasonableness. Enjoy frequent guidance from a mentor or sponsor who is spiritually principled, who is uncompromising in responsibility and fairness, and with whom you can discuss the details of each situation. This person must be cognizant of the requirements of the original twelve-step program and cooperate with them. You need sage counsel that is uncompromising and accurate for you, and easy on others.[56]

The last phrase of Step Eight is: *"and became willing to make amends*

---

[56] From *Alcoholics Anonymous*: *"...we resolutely looked for our own mistakes"* and *"tried to disregard the other person involved entirely,"* both p. 67; and this: *"...hard on ourselves but always considerate of others,"* p. 74. Then, from *Twelve Steps and Twelve Traditions*: *"...we had to drop the word 'blame' from our speech and thought."* p. 47.

to them all."[57] Recall that willingness was the primary teaching of Step Six. If you haven't commanded Step Six, then you will be unwilling at Step Eight and begrudge the amends. If Step Eight is difficult, go back to Six, and if Step Six is difficult, go back to Step Two.

Regeneration

All things generate from something. Plants originate from seeds, animals and people from parents; everything from the earth. Personalities also have a crucible of origin, which is made up of genetics, physiology, and environment (culture, education). And, of course, within every personality are willpower and character defects. For most people, willpower and character defects are of a garden variety, and people aren't particularly noticed for how they create their life.

However, some people stand out because of their character, including its defects, and their strong willful energy focused intensely on a specific thing. They are noticeably different and garner attention for this, which is witnessed at both a social and psychological level. Some peoples' characters, including their defects and willful energy, are organized around committing crimes—serious career criminals. Other peoples' characters (again including its defects) are organized around the relentless pursuit of wealth or fame, music, other artistic endeavor, or writing. An addicted person's character embodies character defects and willful energy, but their character, and all that energy is organized around self-annihilation.[58]

It is long known that a problem can't be resolved on the same level that it manifests. We can't eliminate war with guns, or sexism with anger and privilege. Neither can we resolve addictions with psychology because an addiction shows itself as the psychology of self-destruction. An addicted personality must therefore regenerate at a level underneath psychology. It must regenerate within the crucible of a much deeper level of ethics which some people call "spirituality".

The original twelve steps and five spiritual principles are the method of self-introspection that facilitate or allow an addict to go underneath "personality and psychology" where they can then experience transformation. The self-annihilation begins to stop at Step One; but abstinence and completing Step One aren't a change in personality: they're a change in behaviour. Regeneration really begins at Step Two.[59]

---

[57] *Twelve Steps and Twelve Traditions*, p. 77.
[58] How this condition originates is the subject of much debate, and is not what's under discussion here. The resolution of addiction is the matter at hand.
[59] Regardless of how long someone has been abstinent, if they still act like a sober drunk— angry, rude, insensitive, sexist, manipulate for attention, dishonest, blame, gossip, are racist, etc.—they have not completed any of the other steps, even though they claim (cont'd)

The "...*Greater Mysteries discussed the principles of spiritual regeneration and revealed to initiates not only the simplest but also the most direct and complete method of liberating their higher natures from the bondage of material ignorance.*"[60] Material ignorance, in this case, is bondage to self-annihilation. Unregenerate means living as a practicing addict, or as a "sober" but unspiritual addict where nothing has changed, or where the change is only political. Regenerate means to resolve dislocation by regrowing and reorganizing your personality within a sound spiritual paradigm (read: practical application of the five spiritual principles).

What I see, and what thousands of people have told me about their addictions recovery is this: Many people in twelve-step programs do just enough to get by. They're only as charitable as their guilt requires; only as kind as the social image requires; only as industrious as they need to be, and are honest only so long as it's convenient. Honesty as a default behaviour because of ineffective lying skills isn't spiritual in any sense.

Many people smoke, curse and swear; are sexist, irresponsible, racist, mean in relationships, lie, and cut corners on everything from downloading pirated software and stealing copyright-protected music to completing Step Eight. They appear to be acting differently but other than abstinence, nothing has really changed.

In order to be recovered, the requirements of spirituality and the tenacity of addictions won't allow for cutting corners, substitutions, or half-hearted efforts. There are two reasons for this: one is because of the spiritually corrupt and incredibly complicated nature of addicted personalities. Addictions are rigidly constructed and unyielding. The other is because: *"The unfolding of man's spiritual nature is as much an exact science as medicine* [or] *astronomy...."*[61] Surgeons or auto mechanics can't change the rules of their craft because they don't like them, and neither can addicts or people wanting to get recovered. Addicted personalities can only successfully regenerate within a firmly structured paradigm. An all-encompassing demand for obedience, detail, and commitment are what makes solid that place out of which your self-destructive personality will transform.

By following the instructions thus far, you should be fairly aware of the rudiments of spirituality. However, if you find yourself at Step Eight and are confused about the role of a higher power in your life; if your praying is sporadic; if you're in conscious ethical turmoil about anything in your

---

otherwise. Step One requires a specific change in behaviour (sobriety); all the others require a change in personality.

[60] *The Secret Teachings of All Ages,* by Manly P. Hall, Reader's Edition, Tarcher/Penguin, 2003, p. 71. Also: See the quote from *Isis Unveiled,* H.P. Blavatsky, cited at p. 5.

[61] *The Secret Teachings of All Ages,* by Manly P. Hall, Reader's Edition, Jeremy P. Tarcher/Penguin, 2003, p. 120.

life; if you're consciously neglectful of your health in emotional or physical matters; if you're willfully lying to anyone about anything; if you're awkward about honesty or responsibility, these behaviours are evidence of either (a) the presence of unaddressed addictions, or (b) a commitment to spirituality that is misaligned and rooted in convenience. There has been no significant regeneration in your personality.

Alcoholics Anonymous advises that in the final analysis, it is deep down within us that we find the Great Reality.[62] That means they believe some subtle nature of "a higher power" exists in each of us politics and personality notwithstanding. In order to regenerate yourself, you must be completely aware and convinced of what is required at Step Two (the common starting point for everyone). Otherwise, you will be at loose ends and cutting corners, wandering haphazardly or repetitively through the steps. If you are like this at Step Eight, you've worked outside of the crucible of transformation.

Addicts act out at the expense of other people. They must not get recovered at the expense of other people. They have to pay for their own recovery. Step Eight is about being willing to be called to account for your former irresponsible behaviour: "I did this harmful thing and I'll make it right." Regeneration into spiritual peace is expensive.

It's too convenient and superficial to dismiss an addict's lack of accomplishment as a fear of success. It's much more complicated. It often bears out that addicts are more afraid of accountability and the responsibility that goes with success, than the success itself.[63] They may be petulant about the hard work that goes into being successful; or unable to be a success because of the all-encompassing demands of unaddressed addictions; or avoid success because of an uncanny ability to avoid the resentment of others.[64] The most likely time for addicts to avoid success by relapsing, quitting therapy, or quitting a support group (or a job) is when they sense the impending arrival of responsibility or truth.

With a self-imposed crisis (addiction), only a self-imposed solution (spirituality) will work. Self-responsibility, individuation, and assertiveness are crucial to ethical spiritual endeavor. Self-help jargon includes the phrase "back doors". A back door is a subtle way to avoid accountability or responsibility. Some "back doors" to avoid conflict are television, exercise, reading, sports, the kids, shopping, eating, friendships, chaos, eating, work-

---

[62] *Alcoholics Anonymous*, p. 55.
[63] To be generally successful usually requires individuation and self-defined assertiveness, which many addicts [people] lack.
[64] Aspects of this are discussed at length in *Resentment Against Achievement*, by Robert Sheaffer, Prometheus Books, 1988.

ing, affairs, fantasy, and recovery.

The focus of Step Eight is figuring out exactly what you did that was damaging and harmful to others and being willing to fix it, *after* having slammed shut all the back doors that permit irresponsibility. Some back doors that avoid responsibility at Step Eight are:

- No one will ever know.
- I was stealing from criminals.
- They did bad things, too.
- They hurt me more than I hurt them.
- They don't remember.

- There's no point, they won't understand.
- They were too little to understand.
- I kind-of already made an amend by getting sober, clean or abstinent.
- Everyone else was doing it.

Here are four quotations regarding Step Eight that I refer you to: *"This is a very large order,"* and *"We should avoid extreme judgments, both of ourselves and of others."*[65] *"We are there to sweep off our side of the street,"* and *"[Their] faults are not discussed,"*[66] These are "why" you need wise and compassionate spiritual counsel that is hard on you and easy on others, ample time, and much willingness and humility through your relationship with a higher power, to accomplish Step Eight.

For those of you who have been around "recovery" for a while, you've no doubt attended meetings, feel like you belong, and everybody knows your first name (many people know your last name, too). You've attended the summer barbecue, the Christmas party, all the "cakes", and the round-up. You're generally well liked. You've been the group secretary and chaired meetings. But when you're in bed at night, in those quiet moments when you're all alone with your very-secret thoughts, there's a tiny, noticeable loneliness that you avoid. You wonder if they knew the *real* truth, would they still like you? *"Whenever our pencil falters, we can fortify and cheer ourselves by remembering what AA experience in this Step has meant for others. It is the beginning of the end of isolation from our fellows and from God."*[67]

In spite of all the work you've done to this point, you won't begin to lose that deep sense of isolation until you become completely responsible for the harm you've caused. It's this heretofore-unexamined core of irresponsibility and harm caused that perpetuates that subtle, painful isolation that sneaks up on you when you least expect it. It's always present in those

---

[65] *Twelve Steps and Twelve Traditions*, pp. 77 and 82, respectively.
[66] *Alcoholics Anonymous*, pp. 77 and 78, respectively.
[67] *Twelve Steps and Twelve Traditions*, p. 82.

quiet moments—if you look for it.

Irresponsibility manifests in many different ways. Greediness, small manipulations, subtle exaggeration, tiny dishonesty, withholding, silent blaming or anger, subtle or silent racism or sexism, petulance, and envy are examples. Out of character-defect driven irresponsibility comes isolation. If you're irresponsible, and conceal this, you're lonely and not loved for who you are—you're loved for the image you project; impression management (to conceal the corruption). Therein lies the loneliness.

"Learning how to live in the greatest peace, partnership, and brother-hood with all men and women, of whatever description, is a moving and fascinating adventure."[68] First, it's worthy of note that this effort is de-scribed as a moving and fascinating adventure; not something arduous or painful. If this isn't a moving and fascinating adventure, go back to Steps Six and Seven and figure out where your willingness and humility went.

Second, at this point, learning how to make your life a moving and fascinating adventure has nothing to do with learning about other people. It's always about learning about yourself and deepening your relationship with your higher power, *vis-à-vis* the maintenance steps.

When you become microscopically responsible[69] in all aspects of your life, you will noticeably and gradually lose your isolation from the universe. If you don't do Step Eight in this manner, you will forever cover up the loneliness with politics. Why do people with five and fifteen and thirty years abstinence step up to the podium, tell ribald drunk-a-logue stories, curse and swear like they're still in a bar, break anonymity, or brag about their program and the people they sponsor? They're scared, lonely, irre-sponsible, and hiding it. This is what breeds a carnival-like atmosphere in many meetings; none of it is spiritual.

"Since defective relations with other human beings have nearly al-ways been the immediate cause of our woes, including our alcoholism, no field of investigation could yield more satisfying and valuable rewards than [repairing harms caused]."[70] Intimacy and fulfillment cannot coexist with exaggeration, deceit, withholding (even a little bit), manipulation, or shirk-ing responsibility. Backtrack and make an accurate and unsparing survey of the wreckage of your past.[71] Redouble your efforts to identify those you have hurt.[72]

---

[68] *Twelve Steps and Twelve Traditions,* p. 77.
[69] Being microscopically responsible can only happen with microscopic truth telling. Being honest with yourself is paramount. This perspective of honesty, which is crucial to recovery from addictions, is found in *Conscious Loving,* Gay Hendricks, Ph.D., & Kathlyn Hendricks, Ph.D., Bantam Books, 1992.
[70] *Twelve Steps and Twelve Traditions,* p. 80.
[71] Ibid. p. 77.
[72] Ibid.

Step Nine

"Made direct amends to such people wherever possible, except when to do so would injure them or others."[73] The actual wording of Step Nine, and the chapter regarding Step Nine in *Twelve Steps and Twelve Traditions* don't contain the word "sorry". In *Alcoholics Anonymous* we find the word "sorry" used twice. On page 78: *"Arranging the best deal we can we let these people know we are sorry."* This passage refers to debts of money. Within that paragraph it very clearly implies that arranging the best deal for repayment is the way we demonstrate that we are sorry. There is no reference to saying the word, it's demonstrating being sorry by arranging the best deal we can. The other is on page 83: *"A remorseful mumbling that we are sorry won't fill the bill at all."* This needs no explanation.

It's worthwhile to closely examine why people, in the routine of everyday failings, in most discussions regarding amends include some notable reference to the transgressor being sorry or apologizing. To amend anything is to repair it, to change it for the better, or to improve it. That's the focus of the work required—to change the situation for the better and to repair the damage. There are *un*spiritual reasons why people say they are sorry within the context of Step Nine.

As described in Apologize by Numbers (p. 351), to say, "I'm sorry," when making an amend, blurs the transaction by shifting the focus away from the person you hurt onto you. How could anyone be mad at you, or not forgive you, or wish to do anything but understand, because you feel *so sorry* about the mess you created? Your feeling sorry is exactly where the focus should not be.

You are not the harmed person. The amend isn't supposed to be about you, so don't make it about you. The spiritual truth of the matter is that your feeling sorry really doesn't matter at this point. Feeling sorry doesn't fix anything. At some much later point, after the amend is complete, and you have acknowledged the harm you did, *and* have taken complete responsibility for it, only then, (maybe) make a sincere and simple statement of your regret. Nothing more.

Please-Sorry-Thank You

If you practice chanting, there's an insightful experience within the mantra: "please-sorry-thank you".[74] As westerners, in our insecure passion for wealth and power—they're the same, and an insecure need to win (which bolsters our self image through shame and dominance), we're so

---

[73] *Twelve Steps and Twelve Traditions*, p. 83.
[74] *The Only Dance There Is,* by Ram Dass, Anchor Books, 1973, pp. 92, 93.

inculcated with guilt, servility, envy, and irresponsibility that we've become jesters in the court of spiritual integrity. Many of us wander through our entire lives offering a polite and continuous apology for the effrontery of our own existence. This is hard to escape since it's inculcated in our culture. It takes years of work to understand that *"As God's people we stand on our feet; we don't crawl before anyone."*[75]

At Step Nine, getting recovered is about generously undertaking the adventure of creating the best possible relations you can with everyone, willingly admitting where you have harmed people, and then repairing that damage regardless of the cost to yourself. You being sorry, or you being offered forgiveness from people for the harm you caused, are very distant, unrelated concerns to actually making amends. Step Nine is the training ground for charity of spirit.

Being spiritual and recovered is not some sober retrenchment or reorganization of inculcated religious and cultural guilt. The steps are intended to achieve the opposite—authentic freedom. When making amends, servile invitations to please understand; abject or grandiose declarations of being sorry; a droning, mumbled thank you to avoid imprecation; and struggling to absolve yourself of your own human condition, have no place in a life governed by spiritual principles.

When you admit that you were wrong, without giving a detailed explanation about the extenuating circumstances, and you repair the damage, the aggrieved party will be left to feel about you, as they will. Don't underestimate your ability to disguise an irresponsible agenda under some apparently benevolent behaviour (like apologizing). This is self-serving in the extreme. There are literally millions of examples of this and many of them are quite complicated. Here's one example:

The Story of Kim and Terry

Kim and Terry are going away for the weekend. Kim, who has to work on the day they leave, promises to leave work early, be home by 4:00, and help Terry with preparations so they can be gone by 5:00. Kim tells Terry to depend on it. Kim goes to work, doesn't call, and doesn't get home until 6:30.

Terry is quite upset and says so. Kim replies sincerely: "I'm really sorry I'm late. I apologize, but my boss wouldn't let me leave early." Kim's sorrow and the reason given, both of which are true, should, according to Kim, end the matter. Kim expects, by implication that Terry should understand and not be mad.

---

[75] *Alcoholics Anonymous*, p. 83.

Kim's declaration of penitent sorrow and the reason for being late are intended to exonerate Kim from accountability. Terry's feelings are (technically) no longer a part of the transaction.

Terry is hurt and frustrated, and after the apology from Kim, Terry somehow senses being insulted but can't pinpoint what happened. If Terry responds with anything other than: "I understand, it's okay," Terry will appear unsympathetic and selfish. Kim would then say some variation of: "But I had to work! Don't you understand? Do you want me to quit my job? My boss said no at the last minute. I couldn't phone. Hey, I'm *really* sorry! I apologize. I'm *really* sorry. What more do you want?"

After this exchange, if Terry is still dissatisfied or hurt, according to Kim the conflict is now Terry's fault for being unreasonable and unsympathetic. Kim explained it away by professing great sorrow and presenting "good" reasons (and thereby shifted the responsibility onto Terry). Kim has made a defense, not an amend, and has taken no responsibility. Terry, still somehow insulted, decides to say nothing.

The apology addresses nothing substantive, and if Kim's irresponsible blaming of the boss, and Terry's passive behaviour, go unchallenged, their lives and relationship will remain in turmoil. But in the face of Kim's "good reasons" and "deep sorrow", it's hard for Terry to challenge Kim's irresponsibility without appearing unsympathetic or argumentative.[76]

The underlying issue—the error, if you will—is Kim's sincere promise that Kim could not guarantee with reasonable certainty, and yet declared that Terry could depend on the promise. Terry did depend on the promise, which was appropriate to the manner it was made. The contract went sour when Kim took no responsibility for having made an unreliable promise. Kim immediately defended that irresponsibility by blaming the boss, and work, and focusing on being sorry rather than on what Terry was feeling. Terry's subtle sense of insult is related to the disrespect shown by Kim for Terry's feelings and sensibilities. To fix it, Kim is (i) required to be responsible for commitments and promises, (ii) must stop blaming the boss and Terry for being unsympathetic, (iii) should accept and honor whatever it is that Terry feels; and (iv), must make every attempt to not repeat the behaviour or making unreliable commitments.

---

[76] The emotional manipulation is the offender making their "sorrow" bigger than the offense, or bigger than how badly the other person feels. In this way the person hurt or (cont'd) "wronged" is manipulated into compassion for the offender, and then the hurt person feels guilty for expecting compensation or being angry at what was done to themselves. If the person who is hurt allows the offender to "get away" with this manipulation, they are relationship addicts (codependent), and are putting the offender's selfish manipulation ahead of their own dignity and self-respect.

This will seem pedantic on paper, but Kim's amend should be similar to this: "You're right, and I understand that you feel angry and hurt. I made a commitment that I didn't live up to and I didn't call you. You depended on me because I told you you could. I'll have to be more clear and responsible about the commitments I make. I was wrong."

Kim must recognize and accept Terry's feelings exactly as they are. In this circumstance, the measure of sincerity is in respecting Terry and not repeating making unreliable commitments. Sincerity, like honesty, isn't a matter of convenience. Being recovered means bringing a measure of wisdom to commitments—people make decisions based on what they're told.

To argue on behalf of popular opinion—that apologizing and saying sorry is acceptable—is to argue on behalf of irresponsibility and selfishness. It's irresponsible to make excuses, and selfish to shift the emotional content away from the person you harmed onto yourself.

Regarding the accurate meaning of apology, I'm someone who defends, by considered reflection, a twelve-step perspective that would not include saying sorry or apologizing. I'm an apologist on behalf of not apologizing for harm done.

What follows is an edited and compressed version of a true story. A person had been saying unkind and untrue things about Lee. Some time later they admitted this to Lee: "I realized I've been slandering you to some people and I'm really sorry about that." Lee said, "I don't care that you're sorry." They said, "What? Lee, I'm making an amend to you." Lee said, "No, you're not, and I don't care that you're sorry. There are people wandering around with misinformation that's harmful to me. You slandered my character and your being sorry doesn't fix it." The person asked, "What can I do to fix it?" Lee said, "Examine carefully what fear and insecurity caused you to say these unkind and untrue things about me. If you are sincere about making amends, speak personally with *every*one to whom you lied about me. Tell each of them your fear, and that you lied, and that you were wrong in what you said. Pass along a sincere compliment about me and, if possible, do this also in a public forum." The person did just that.

Attending to Step Nine with glib and self-serving interpretations of amends is, from one perspective, worse than making no amends—it adds insult to injury. Be cheerfully disposed (willing), and completely devoted (sincere), and interested in the adventure of establishing the best possible relations with *everyone* that you know. Here are a few indications of what's required:

- *"We must lose our fear of creditors no matter how far we*

have to go,"
- *"Reminding ourselves that we have decided to go to any lengths..."*
- *"...[we must] do the right thing, no matter what the personal consequences may be,"*
- *"We must not shrink at anything,"*
- *"[if a] drastic step is indicated we must not shrink,"*
- *"A remorseful mumbling... we are sorry won't fill the bill at all..."*
- *"The spiritual life is not a theory. We have to live it,"*[77]
- *"...[we must] take the full consequences of our past acts, and... take responsibility for the well-being of others."* [78]

None of these statements leave any doubt about the detail, the level of commitment, or the thoroughness required.

When making amends, it's important to set yourself up for success. Here's another compressed, true story: D. lived on the west coast and had unresolved legal issues on the east coast. It was serious and appeared that jail time would be a certainty. D. was determined to follow the program guidelines. In the west, D. had become well-established in sobriety, had started seeing a therapist regularly, was involved in his community, and after two years of weekly therapy, hired a lawyer in the west, who on behalf of D. hired a lawyer in the east. Seeing that D. had *factual* evidence to prove his sincerity, and had extensive professional support, the lawyers worked with the authorities. D. went back east and dealt with his past.

D. achieved extended sobriety, worked at prayer and meditation, became established in a career and in the community, had references, enlisted the aid of therapists and lawyers, paid for it all without complaining, and followed the rules (of our culture and of the original twelve-step program). There was no relapse, amends were made, and the obligations inherent in a spiritual life were met. If you work diligently, use common sense, get help from professionals, plan carefully, be responsible, and trust in "God" meaning spiritual principles, you can clean house.

Yes, some addicts have done some pretty nefarious things they are reluctant to address. Only you can decide how much responsibility (and irresponsibility and secrecy) you're prepared to live with. It's a personal choice. If you think you can live a comfortable, safe life and not make some particular amend, or can conceal some particular harm you caused, then live with that. Even though *Alcoholics Anonymous* is rather clear that people

---

[77] These appear in *Alcoholics Anonymous*, pp. 78, 79, 80, 83.
[78] *Twelve Steps and Twelve Traditions*, p. 87.

must be willing to go to any lengths to make amends, we all live at some personally chosen level of spiritual responsibility.

Sponsors, spiritual advisors, therapists, can only interpret *Alcoholics Anonymous* and encourage you as they think best. Regardless of any advice given, it will always reduce itself to your having to decide for yourself. You are responsible for the quality of your life. There is never anyone to blame.

Living by Consensus

A man approached me for professional counsel. He was in a chaotic, conflicted relationship with almost constant arguing, betrayals, and lies. He explained it all and concluded his tale with this (which I relate almost verbatim): "Before you tell me what I should do, I want you to know that I've spoken to several other people and the consensus is I should leave my relationship. What do you think I should do?"

Examples this blatant aren't common, but examples of living by consensus (popular opinion) are legion. Living by consensus evades hard work, avoids criticism or rejection of you by others, and guarantees you'll always have something missing from your life. It may not be as physically destructive as acting out, but it's emotionally destructive and just as unfulfilling. Far too many otherwise capable people live their lives out of a ballot box — obedient to popular opinion, just good enough to get by, and always with something to complain about.

D., in the preceding example of amends, willingly returned to the east coast to deal with the crime. This met with a great deal of criticism and some derision from many of his twelve-step peers. D. was called a fanatic, a perfectionist, arrogant, and foolish. Those that criticized him lived "good enough" lives. Good enough wasn't good enough for D., who wanted a spiritual life. *Nothing is free.*

Get a few years of abstinence; get a good sponsor — spiritual, gently assertive, and responsible; get into well-conducted, long-term, weekly therapy; get a spiritual advisor; get a lawyer if you need one, and get a job. Force yourself to live by the five spiritual principles — do whatever it takes — and deal with your past. Your freedom and serenity depend on it.[79]

Judgment & Discernment

The first sentence in the Step Nine chapter is: *"Good judgment, a careful sense of timing, courage, and prudence — these are the qualities we*

---

[79] By doing these things, and adhering to this lifestyle, you will remove the sense of dislocation and alienation you experienced in your addiction. Only this allows you to create a soulful lifestyle and live with a sense of belonging and purpose.

shall need when we take Step Nine."[80] The first sentence of Step Nine requires you should make judgments. What about the all too-common admonition, from so many people, instructing others to not make judgments?

Why did you pick this book to read? Why do you choose this person rather than that person for a sponsor? You made a judgment. Life is a judgment call. You made a judgment to attend this movie over that one. You picked a brown jacket over a blue jacket. You joined this group rather than that group. You chose this therapist rather than that therapist. You picked this sexual partner over some other one, and this person for a close friend rather than another one. These are all judgments, and judgments reflect values. Outside of obviously cruel judgments, there is nothing wrong with judgments *per se* — it's more how they're arrived at and what you do after you've made them that needs examination.

You must develop the ability to evaluate circumstances from a spiritual rather than a racist, sexist, angry, addicted perspective; from a humanitarian-humble rather than arrogant/victim point of view. Examine carefully how you spend your life and make respectful, prudent judgments because you are trying to both save *and* recreate, your life. An addict's history of self-abuse proves, beyond any doubt whatsoever, what addictions and poor judgments can do. Establish ethical criteria, make judgments, don't advertise them, and live with the consequences.

Once you have judged that you would rather do this than that, or be with this person rather than that person, do not announce your criteria: "I dated A. rather than B. because B. is a jerk. Let me tell you why B. is a jerk…." In relation to judgments, what you're required to do is: act on the circumstances you deem more acceptable to you, and say nothing about whatever you decided against.

I recall an adamant and angry person who insisted loudly that no one had the right to be the arbiter of anyone's sex conduct. It was an accurate, but self-righteous quoting of p. 69 of *Alcoholics Anonymous*. In the next breath they loudly condemned someone for asking a newcomer on a date. The hypocrisy escaped them completely.

It is your task to make discerning choices — your decisions reflect your preferences (i.e. your judgments). Investigate wisely, decide accordingly, act quietly, never condemn, malign, gossip about, or slander anyone. As you get on with your own life, kindly mind your own business.

It is possible to ignore truths, but with a guarantee of harmful consequences. The truth is, it is not possible to not make judgments. Trying to force yourself to make no judgments, at the insistence of someone else, is

---

[80] *Twelve Steps and Twelve Traditions*, p. 83.

judging that you should live by someone else's judgments. Living your life by others' judgments will most often lead to an unfulfilling life, yet a common twelve-step admonition seems to be to not make judgments (which is, in itself, a judgment judging that judgments are bad). Or, refusing to make judgments leaves you unfulfilled and a victim at the mercy of others. Without judgment there's no discernment. Without discernment, life becomes inordinately dangerous.

Where will you learn about good judgment, a careful sense of timing, courage and prudence—the necessary attributes for completing Step Nine? You will learn these by being with people who graciously demonstrate these as natural parts of their lives. You learn about courage, prudence, good judgment, and timing by associating with, and paying attention to, spiritual people—people who aren't mean or sarcastic; people who are responsible and live spiritually disciplined lives that evince spiritual principles.[81]

You cannot learn about spirituality from tough, crude sponsors who "kick your butt". Emotionally abusive, dictatorial sponsorship reinforces alienation. There is no place for that type of behaviour in spiritual transformation. Spiritual people don't shame or emotionally knock others around. They treat people gently, with dignity, regardless of the other person's beliefs or behaviour. Sponsors must remember their commitment to spiritual principles. The only way that you can learn the four attributes essential to Step Nine is by associating with kind, gentle people who are wise about the spiritual philosophy and intent of the original twelve-step program.

Once you've completed Step Eight, and have a fair grasp of these qualities, begin attending to Step Nine. You've probably made some amends throughout your recovery thus far, but this is where you formally begin. You'll now have clarity and direction—knowing exactly what you have to do, and with whom.

As an aside: Since you've achieved abstinence, you've probably become more considerate by not forgetting birthdays, showing up for Christmas, and making an effort to remember and respond to the important events in the lives of people you care about. Etiquette and courtesy go a long way towards establishing trust and respect, but being considerate of others is something that happens *now* and making an amend is repairing the harm from past inconsiderate behaviour.

There are four categories of amends. **The first** category addresses situations of harm where there are no mitigating circumstances: You hurt someone; you fix it. By the time you get to Step Nine, you may have been abstinent for two or three years and you will already have made amends to

---

[81] Recall the quote attributed to A. Einstein, "Role modeling isn't a good way to influence people, it's the only way."

various people along the way. It is certainly wise to review these with the clearer eyes of longer abstinence, but it isn't necessary to repeat the amends if nothing has been overlooked.

The second category is making partial amends, or in *rare* circumstances, no amend, to avoid harming others. Here's a story to illustrate this potential scenario:

The Story of Jack & Jill and Miss Muffett

Heading home drunk from an after-hours club at the top of the hill, Jack falls down and breaks his crown and Jill comes tumbling after. They spend some time as in-patients at the hospital and a few weeks later, all is well. Jack and Jill have a notorious party to celebrate their discharge from hospital. It's near dawn. Jack has passed out. Jill's pretty stoned, and Miss Muffett entices her into a brief sexual encounter. Then Miss Muffett takes Jack's car (without permission), and drives over to her ex-boyfriend's, Jack, The Giant Killer. They argue and Miss Muffett drives off in a fury in the first Jack's car, crashes through the garden into her ex-boyfriend, Jack the Giant Killer's beanstalk, abandons the car, and leaves town on the midnight bus. Only Miss Muffett remembers what happened.

Five years later, Miss Muffett has made it to *12 Steps for Fairy Tale Creatures* (a very closed group—it's hard to find). Everyone's older and wiser and settled down. There's a new edition of nursery rhymes out—hard cover, glossy pages, and full-color artwork—and everyone's prosperous off the royalties. Jack and Jill have straightened out their lives, moved to the flats, and installed indoor running water. They're making a go of their relationship. Out on the coast, Miss Muffett isn't frightened of arachnids now (from good therapy and a few years of abstinence), and she's at Step Nine. Imagine that one day Jack and Jill, who remember nothing, get an unexpected letter:

Dear Jack and Jill:
Surprise! Remember the big bash five years ago after Jack's crown got better? Well, Jill, I was wrong for pressuring you into having sex with me. At the time I was jealous because my boyfriend Jack the Giant Killer was flirting with The Green Fairy, so I had sex with you, Jill, stole (your) Jack's car, and then bragged about it to (my ex-boyfriend) Jack the Giant Killer.

365

We got in a fight, and I took out his beanstalk with your car, Jack. I abandoned it in a ditch, and hence the damage.

Jill, I don't think you remember having sex with me, and (your) Jack doesn't know I'm the one who wrecked his car. I really feel sorry about the whole thing. Here's some money (cheque enclosed). Hope you're both doing well.

Do you know if Jack the Giant Killer still lives with his mother at the old cottage? Apparently I took out her flowerbed before I ploughed into his beanstalk. I owe an amend for gardening expenses. You know, I had to replace the beanstalk and that cost a tuffett full of money... magic beans are expensive. I'm doing well on the coast and feel much better since I got sober and went vegan.

Sincerely,
Miss Muffett

P.S. Did I mention I had herpes? I'm happy it's been in remission the last two years. Do you know where The Old Woman Who Lives in A Shoe is? Is she still in the shoe? God I hated that boot... and all those squalling kids. I've got to find her and sort out something about my family of origin. Apparently Peter Peter Pumpkin Eater is involved. Ugh! Drop me a note if you can help.

Thanks.
M. M.

How Miss Muffett should conduct herself, within these circumstances, is not with this irresponsible disclosure. Other fairy-tale creatures will be hurt. Alcoholics and addicts must not get recovered at the expense of others.

To negotiate yourself into being recovered, and maintaining that spiritual perception of life, requires a sponsor, a spiritual advisor, and very likely a therapist, all of whom understand the nuance of authentic twelve-step work and the tremendous commitment and responsibility required of spiritual people. If it's wise to make no amend, or a partial one, and your advisors concur, you may have to carry some guilt within yourself and be responsible silently. Seek wise counsel.

The third category is amends you may postpone if there's a good reason. Your own fear or awkwardness isn't a good reason. If you have noticeable fear in making amends, you've missed the point of willingness — go back to Step Six and sort that out.

Let's assume you need to make an amend to someone who lives in another city. You're planning a trip there next year. Possibly it's an amend that should be made in person but you want to write a letter because you are afraid. Do you wait until you get there to make the amend in person? Maybe a letter or a phone call is sufficient. Is it? If you wish to delay the amend, discuss the matter with your advisor and examine your motives.

The fourth category are those amends that cannot be made—to people you don't know, or to people who are dead. This includes a subcategory where you have to make an amend, but the harm you caused is so grievous and irrevocable that any amend seems entirely insufficient.

What do you do when the amend is to someone who's dead or untraceable? I've heard many suggested solutions: write a letter, pray, visit the grave, never repeat the behaviour that caused the harm, make a donation to some charity. These are all rituals may not be an acceptable substitute for the amend. Any substitution: prayers, letters, visits to the grave, etc., are a minor consideration in the process.

It's easy to write a letter of amends to someone who's dead or untraceable—there's no emotional risk, potential loss, or impending inconvenience. It's easy to fulfill the requirements of Step Nine by writing a letter to a nameless stranger—there's no risk. Ask yourself, if you knew who or where they were, if they were alive, how willing would you be?

Imagine you have a major amend to make to someone who's dead. You claim to be willing. If that person walked in the door right now, would you be eagerly and pleasantly disposed to be completely responsible, and to create the best possible relations with them if they were standing in front of you right now?

Imagine having to make an amend to someone who, years earlier, you had seriously injured and they've been physically handicapped ever since because of something you did. This amend begins when they hear in the tone of your voice, and see in your demeanor, complete willingness and sincerity. This doesn't mean anything stupid or grandiose, like: "Oh, I'd cut off my arm if only...". That's theatrical nonsense. The key is the sincerity and willingness underneath the words. In this category, as with all amends, that is the vital test: whether or not you're sincerely willing. The key to any amend is always rooted in your willingness to be responsible, which is directly related to being humble on behalf of your higher power.

Think about this very carefully: How often have people said, "I'm sorry," or made some apology to you, or made an amend [grudgingly], and by the time they got to the third word, you knew their "amend" was meaningless? The insincerity was obvious, and even though they said the correct words, it was for their benefit, not yours. If you've got to make amends to someone and they're dead, you can't find them, or it's for some irreparable harm that you caused, the underlying spiritual attitude is what makes the amend sincere.

In some complicated situations, or with people you haven't spoken to for a long time, there are ways to proceed through the actual making of an amend. First, very *briefly* describe the incident and the harm you caused. State your responsibility to fix the damage, and then offer what you propose to do. In some situations it may be appropriate to ask what they think you might do to fix the harm. If the aggrieved person expresses emotions, or offers any comment, spend time listening to how the harm affected them. Make a sincere effort to understand what they say, from their point of view, without defending yourself. Don't justify or excuse away your behaviour. "Ah, geeze, I'm really sorry but I'm an addict. I come from a broken home and the dog bit me and my classmates teased me and I'm in recovery so I have to make this amend." Don't do this. Fix the damage you caused. Be emotionally responsible and spiritually generous.

Only if they ask, and only if it seems appropriate, briefly and quietly explain what happened. The reason you harmed them will be some aspect of your fears and instincts gone awry. You learned this in your Step Four. You didn't do the harm because of anything this person did to you, or because of anything that anyone else did. You did it because you wrongly handled your insecurities by hurting them.

You may occasionally offer an amend where the other person is completely surprised. You believe you did cause them harm, but the other person asks: "Whatever are you talking about?" They're truly surprised and don't remember the incident as harmful. Some may not even remember the incident at all. People have different values and assess life's vicissitudes differently. They may sincerely believe no harm was done, or that circumstances were *quid pro quo,* and therefore finished.

Discuss this with the person, but don't force your point of view on them. If they appear to be sincerely satisfied that no harm was done, your argument that your assessment of the incident is more accurate than theirs can be insulting (and you'll have to make an amend for that). Thank them sincerely for their time, and then seek wise counsel. It may well be that there was no harm done, and your ego is blaming you for some imagined wrong (which could be over-coupling, fusion, globalization of affect, or an introjected family of origin script). Very often, this can only be modified through therapy.[82] It's complicated.

The presence of guilt in you; the fact that you feel guilty or ashamed, is not necessarily evidence of wrongdoing. People, depending on the "outside issues" they have to deal with, and because of the possibility of unresolved trauma, can feel guilty in circumstances where none need exist. This is through an over-coupling or fusion of emotional experiences and traumatic circumstances, or the globalization of an emotion into unrelated

---

[82] I will explore this in some detail in *Facets of Personal Transformation.*

facets of your personality. This is very complicated psychology. [Now that I've said this, don't use this to avoid responsibility. Your sense of guilt and the obvious harm will, for the vast majority of cases, require an amend. Feeling guilty or ashamed is always reason to examine the circumstances, but it is not a guaranteed indicator of harm done. Seek wise counsel.]

Some people will be curious and interested; others won't. Each situation will be different. Remember that sorry and thank you are worn out, misused words in our culture. Avoid self-serving interest in others like trying to get them to forgive you or to give you a break. Limit yourself to making the amend and go beyond that only if the tone of the conversation invites it. At the end thank them for hearing you—*be gracious regardless of their attitude*—and if it seems appropriate, sincerely (briefly) offer that you regret the pain (or hardship or extra work) you caused them.

Compassion and Self-Awareness

By the time you get this far in your pilgrimage, you should be somewhat in touch with your own emotions and appreciative of your fears and insecurities. This is important: It's only when you are in touch with your own emotions that you can hear clearly how you hurt someone else (since you can now appreciate both the feelings you have and the damage you caused yourself within yourself).

People who are violent or mean, and those who lack compassion, are significantly out of touch with their own humanity and emotions. They can't appreciate the consequences of what they do because they can't experience their own frailty and pain. When they (hopefully, eventually) sincerely appreciate and experience their own pain and loneliness, especially the unresolved ancient pain they've been carrying for years, they stop hurting others.[83]

At Step Nine, if you appreciate your own pain, and are truly aware of your humanity and feelings, you will be able to sincerely listen to and appreciate what others tell you about the pain they experienced as a result of your behaviour. Your appreciation, of your own pain, is the emotional insurance policy that goes a long way towards your not repeating the harm again. You'll be left with a clear sense of how harmful you were in interpersonal relationships.

The inherent value and subtle wisdom of any step is only clearly seen in hindsight. This is another reason why it's so important to do exactly what is suggested in the original literature. You won't understand the power and the beauty of any one step until you've gone beyond it. As you move into

---

[83] Again, use common sense. This is in the realm of general human conduct and not in the twilight zone of sociopathology.

Step Nine, reflect on the close relationship between willingness and humility when making amends.

Be diligent and persevering. Resist the impulse to rush. If you've to make an amend that is particularly sensitive, have your sponsor meet you immediately afterwards. Set yourself up for success. Practice prudence rather than evasion. Don't avoid amends—any of them, ever.

The Promises

The promises are not gifts purely "from God". In getting recovered, you don't get the promises because you did a good Step Three, or because you chair meetings and make coffee. You do not start to experience what the promises offer because you're staying abstinent. You may get glimmers of them as you complete the first few steps; however, they only arise substantively because of an exceptional effort at Step Nine.

They may be described as spiritual "gifts" but they are behaviourist-oriented. Yes, a higher power and providence may participate in the uncanny manifestation of courage and strength required to be humble and honest; and yes, faith marshals the energy for you to be sincere and willing, but it's from thoroughly attending to the details of Step Nine that the promises are created. [And, it is only by rigorously adhering to the requirements of the maintenance steps that they remain.]

"If we are painstaking about this phase of our development, we will be amazed before we are halfway through."[84] Some people ask: "Halfway through what?" This question arises because of the decided tendency of addicts to take things out of context. You will be amazed before you are halfway through Step Nine; however, the qualifying precondition is *painstaking*. If you aren't painstaking, you won't be amazed. I imagine anyone could find several dozen references to painstaking, thorough, detailed, or rigorous if they made a careful search of *Alcoholics Anonymous* and *Twelve Steps and Twelve Traditions*.

Personifying God, even as much as calling *It* "energy"; claiming divine influence in the trivia of life; confusing a decision with an accomplishment or an intent with an action, are fatal to realizing The Promises. Here they are, explained as the result of detailed amends and hard work.

"We are going to know a new freedom and a new happiness."[85] Before addicts make amends, they hide from, and avoid, some people, situations, and places. They'll be subtly cautious as they go through life,

---

[84] *Alcoholics Anonymous,* p. 83.
[85] This, and the following quotations, are "The Promises," *Alcoholics Anonymous,* pp.83-84.

consciously or subconsciously anxious about the possibility of meeting some person that they owe something to because of a harm or debt. Addicts' social and emotional freedom is restricted because of that anxiety, and their anxiety is managed by (1) avoiding people, places and circumstances; or (2) by controlling others, like friends or lovers, to prevent those others from doing things that they, themselves, are discomfited by.

Once they understand exactly who they owe what to, and address it, or carry the Spiritual willingness to address it at the first opportunity, they know a new freedom. This creates the liberty to go where they want, and to encounter anyone, without anxiety. A new freedom and a new happiness come from the absence of anxiety that results from addicts making amends responsibly.

"We will not regret the past nor wish to shut the door on it." To regret is to feel disappointed or distressed about something, and to remember it with a feeling of loss and sadness. There's regret and shame at the harm addicts have caused others. This regret persists because of "hiding" the past by avoiding people, places, and memories. They avoid because they don't know how to resolve it. When there's regret about the past, joy about the present is not available. When addicts responsibly and willingly make amends, i.e. learn how to effectively deal with the past, regret disappears.

"We will comprehend the word serenity and we will know peace." Serenity isn't the absence of conflict it's that abiding sense of confidence and trust that you can handle the vicissitudes of life. Through making amends, which is the solving of your own previously, repeatedly ignored, repetitive problems, you develop confidence that you know how to handle awkward situations that arise in your life.

Invariably, solving problems (making conflict evaporate) entails being honest, unselfish, and responsible. When you have faith in spiritual principles, and feel confident in your own ability to respond to life, the more competent you will feel about handling any situation. The result is you'll comprehend serenity.

Here, "comprehending" has four perspectives: (i) understanding the process of how you created conflict and harmed others, rooted in your blaming, deceit, and irresponsibility, (ii) understanding the method to resolve conflict and harm you generated; (iii) understanding that you make others lives easier by you taking responsibility; and (iv), to appreciate the experience of serenity.

One of the things addicts seeking spiritual transformation usually don't get told is that sincere spiritual serenity is accompanied by a gentle and lovely loneliness. That loneliness is not a problem to be solved; it's a beauty to be appreciated. When they achieve that in their recovery, life ceases to be difficult. Life is no longer difficult in the common complaints about hardship: traffic jams, taxes, illness, or broken hearts in love. For the spiritually *un*regenerate person (people who live ungoverned by the five spiritual principles), life is hard and the usual complaints remain because it is dislocated from its spiritual potential. Once that spiritual potential is realized those common hardships evaporate and are replaced by a pleasant and serene peace.

When you learn at Step Nine, by making (often repetitive) amends, how all-encompassing was the harm you did to others, and remain determined to be humble through spiritual self-discipline, you acquire an ability to rein in your character defects. Few things, if any, will remain more important than not hurting others. This fosters serenity and peace, and allows insights into the loneliness of the human condition. In the final analysis, we're alone in our spiritual transformation, which isn't bad in and of itself.

"No matter how far down the scale we have gone, we will see how our experience can benefit others." The "experience" referred to in this promise isn't primarily the experience of the harms caused; it's the experience of making amends. There are four parts to benefiting others.

Imagine someone owes you $375.00. This has gone on for several years. You've mentioned it casually a few times, but they've been evasive and vague or rude about paying it back. Your telephone rings right now. It's them. The instant you recognize their voice, something unpleasant hits you: They owe! They say, "I'd like to come over and pay what I owe you." Your annoyance and resentment immediately switches to hope and suspicion: "Oh, really? Yeah, that'd be nice." It's been years, but maybe it's true.

You wait hopefully. They arrive and pay you the money. They admit their irresponsibility, and graciously include an extra $50.00 so you can have lunch on them—a token condolence for the trouble they caused. They don't demand any favors, ask for any special consideration, or expect gratitude. They leave. You feel happy. *You* have certainly benefited by the experience of that person making an amend to you.

Now switch roles. You're the person who's just paid the debt. By your making amends—the way they're outlined in *Alcoholics Anonymous*—your experience has benefited the person you paid back, but it will also benefit people in your life and twelve-step program in two ways. One is from your deepening serenity and quiet, responsible nature. This is powerful role modeling for everyone. You can now guide others in how to make amends, and wisely encourage them to make amends exactly as the original literature describes. It doesn't matter how far down the scale of "destruction and harm caused" you've gone you'll see how your experience of making amends will benefit others.

Four benefits are: (i) The people you hurt get some peace; (ii) people in the program get a good role model; (iii) you may become a wiser spiritual mentor; and (iv), you bring serenity to people in your private life. Your higher power gets all the credit. Everyone benefits.

While you're making amends, the subject of "why" may come up. Don't blame your addiction. A quiet, simple explanation regarding the mishandling of your fear and insecurity, and your new spiritual responsibility, is all that's required. Without advertising, or forcing your opinion on anyone, you present spirituality as an attractive lifestyle.

"That feeling of uselessness and self pity will disappear." Useless means, "having no value". By seeing what you are now contributing to the world—the benefits to everyone noted above, you acquire an increased sense of authentic personal value. You're now able to contribute to life in new, very useful ways. When you benefit others, you no longer feel useless.

Self-pity, as I wrote earlier, always contains an element of feeling so flawed and defective that you really can't help yourself, or help others for that matter. Thoroughly addressing each amend demonstrates you are changing. You aren't hopeless or doomed to perpetual guilt and misery. You're realizing various positive changes in yourself. Self-pity disappears.

"We will lose interest in selfish things and gain interest in our fellows." Understanding this is closely related to the next promise: *"Self seeking will slip away."* Here's an example: Kim has been in a program for a while and has not yet made any amends. Kim was born and raised in the west end of a large city, drank and used in the west end, and knows hundreds of people there. Kim hides from the past, and controls the anxiety from *un*made amends by altogether avoiding the west end.

Kim meets Terry. Terry is interested in spending an evening with Kim so Terry invites Kim to dinner and a movie in the west end. There's a great restaurant there, and the west end is the only place that some particular movie is showing. Now Kim has a problem: Kim is very interested in spending time with Terry, but Kim has to be evasive about going to the west end. In order to deal with the anxiety, and because amends haven't been made yet, the west end is unsafe for Kim.

Kim hides this insecurity and anxiety by manipulating Terry: "Oh, it's hard to find parking, and the west end is so crowded, and we both live way out here in the east end, and we have to drive *all* that way. Maybe the movie's on video. There are good restaurants in the east end, too." This is Kim's selfish self-interest and manipulation. Kim can't be generous with Terry. If Terry is persistent, Kim may go, hoping not to meet anyone, but the subtle anxiety during the date will detract from the joy and pleasure they might otherwise have had. Terry will probably sense the discomfort in Kim and silently wonder what's wrong.

Change the scenario. Kim has made dozens of amends to people in the west end. Debts are being paid and Kim is completely willing to make amends whenever and wherever that's required. When Terry suggests a date in the west end, Kim can gracefully agree. There's no selfish self-interest on Kim's part, and Kim can easily gain interest in what Terry would like do and not have to manipulate Terry away from the west end. Kim is graceful and generous because there's no hiding. Self-seeking has slipped away.

This scenario applies in all areas of the unregenerate addict's life: at work, where they socialize, where they live, what meetings they attend, their recreation and leisure, where they go on vacations, and where, when, and which family members they visit. The avoiding of emotions, places, or people by manipulating others is rampant in the personalities of addicts. Self-deceit and manipulation are standard operating procedures.

A sincere and detailed application of the twelve steps may be sufficient to eliminate controlling behaviours. However, some addicts were entrenched in destructive manipulation as a survival skill in their childhoods. Therapy, in addition to the original twelve steps, is often required for any significant resolution of this isolating behaviour.[86]

"Our whole attitude and outlook upon life will change." For addicts, a good life, in a spiritual sense, is dependent upon adhering to the five spiritual principles. To the extent that they amend the harms that they caused, they (with authentic integrity) gradually view themselves as capable of repairing damage, being of benefit to others, and no longer feeling useless or selfish (as explained above). Altogether, they experience significantly less anxiety in life. People, especially in interpersonal relationships, are easier to be around, and the addict begins to experience spiritual competence at a social level. As the result of their hard work in making amends their whole attitude and outlook upon life changes.

"Fear of people and of economic insecurity will leave us." There are two types of fear. (1) Fears are generally existential or "spiritual" in nature, i.e. fear of death or of having no human value. Ever deepening spirituality *and* your upcoming work at Step Eleven will address these anxieties. Or (2), fears are cultural or social in nature: afraid you're not good looking enough, tall enough, wealthy enough, or that the line-up will be too long, the plane will be late, or there won't be enough mashed potatoes. These are all ego-

---

[86] This will be explored in *Facets of Personal Transformation*.

constructed/cultural fears. What follows is subtle and complex...

Perseverance in making thorough amends initiates a chain reaction. When you are *consistently* responsible, over a *long* period of time, people begin to trust you. As people begin to trust you, they will help and support you. People will enjoy being around you, and they'll believe what you say about yourself. People will offer you opportunities to participate in their life. Having other people, over a long period of time, sincerely participate in your life allows you to slowly create a different self-concept, a different concept of others, and a different concept of relationships.

Several things will happen. As you feel more confident about being able to respond to misunderstandings in personal relationships; as you gracefully assume complete personal responsibility; as others become more trusting of you because of your non-blaming, responsible nature, you will be less afraid of people. This will allow you to interact with people in a way that you hadn't been able to before. Through making detailed, sincere amends your relationships will eventually embody respect and integrity rather than manipulation and power struggles. Relationships become a resource for celebrating joys and managing hard times.

Thus far you will have established a true and sincere relationship with a higher power (spiritual trust and commitment), and should have relationships with people that are governed by the five spiritual principles. At a spiritual level, you finally "get it" that experiencing joy, celebrating life, and coping with hardship aren't about successful economic strategies. You *know* that life is really about love, spirituality, and companionship. All else becomes less important, and you will not be afraid of people.

Fear of economic insecurity doesn't mean you will be financially secure. It means you won't be afraid of financial insecurity which arises from an erroneous and entrenched belief that fulfillment is based on wealth and the accumulation of shiny things. *"Wealth only closes a man's reputation and determines it as good or bad."*[87] Otherwise, and without wealth, a person's character is determined by behaviour and merit.

The associated illusion is that money (power) ensures happiness. Having a fear of economic insecurity, therefore, is rooted in the cultural illusion that money is the prime source of happiness and abundance. When you lose your fear of people, through responsible and meticulous amends, *and* you establish an authentic relationship with your higher power through spiritual principles, you appreciate the non-importance of money in the attainment of peace and joy. You will have then removed "economics" from the recipe for fulfillment. It soon follows that there won't be fear of economic insecurity.

---

[87] This quote is taken from the film *Easy Rider*, cited at another footnote. Within the film, the quote appears as a plaque on a wall in a bordello.

"We will intuitively know how to handle situations which used to baffle us." If, over the course of one or two years, you make 357 amends, and understand and resolve the problems from your past, you will learn how to handle situations which used to baffle you. You'll learn how to confidently address problems that you previously avoided. Problem-solving "intuition" doesn't come from God, it comes from solving 357 problems from your past. Now, in the present, when faced with a situation that is potentially a problem, you will know how to handle it—probably in some manner approximating the 81 other, similar problems from your past you've solved.

What's equally important to having solved all your old problems is you have now become skilled at preventing new ones. If you've been reflecting on the fears and selfish behaviour which continuously pushed you into conflict, and have thereby hurt others, and have conscientiously made detailed amends, all that hard work is intuition in the making. Trust this: The five spiritual principles, used repeatedly and sincerely in your life, will solve every problem you could ever encounter.[88]

"We will suddenly realize that God is doing for us what we could not do for ourselves." Usually what dawns on you, in mid-Step Nine, is you're accomplishing things you only heretofore dreamed about. Through your effort and devotion to the work and spiritual principles, the realization is, you have received two things. The first is the attributes of courage, willingness, prudence, perseverance, and faith. The second is: In as much as you may have thought you and "your program" (sponsor, steps, meetings, etc.) were the substantive force of change, you appreciate at a deeper level that in getting recovered, your higher power, as you understand this, and obedience to spiritual principles, are the source and resource for transformation.

The spiritual attributes of faith and humility (which allow people to depend on "God"), allow an addict to find a spiritual solution to human problems.[89] The perseverance and courage to embrace transformation comes from seeing success in others and from diligence and commitment to spiritual principles. There is a deeper appreciation for the sentence in *Alcoholics Anonymous* (p. 45)—the purpose of that book being to find a higher power. That is realized in a human context by "obedience" to spiritual principles.

"Are these extravagant promises? We think not. They are being fulfilled among us— sometimes quickly, sometimes slowly," which leads into the most important and final promise: *"They will __always__ materialize if we work for them."*[90] That's a guarantee. The work referred to is the labor of

---

[88] *Alcoholics Anonymous,* p. 42.
[89] I often remind myself of the ancient Arabian proverb: Trust in Allah, but tie your camel.
[90] *Alcoholics Anonymous,* p. 84, emphasis added.

prayer and meditation (this being the proper use of willpower) directed towards being meticulous and responsible in doing Step Nine.[91] The rewards embodied in The Promises are only as profound as you are responsible and "other directed" in a humble manner. If The Promises are fleeting, intermittent, or vague, then so is your commitment to the five spiritual principles.

The closing paragraph of Step Nine clearly identifies two themes.[92] The first is being personally and completely responsible, and willing to take the full consequences for your past behaviour. The second is to take responsibility for the well being of others. That's a hard, bitter pill to swallow for those who haven't properly done the prerequisite work. The prerequisite work is, of course, the preceding steps.

Through willingness and humility you take full responsibility for yourself, your behaviour, and the harm you've caused, and fix it. There are no exceptions to the instruction to *"develop the best possible relations with every human being we know."*[93] Being humble and responsible for the well being of others, in the context of spiritually based relationships, is the underlying philosophy of Step Nine, and one of the dominant themes of relapse prevention.

What started as travail has ended as an adventure. You are now recovered—not cured, but recovered. Now what?

---

[91] An interesting parallel is on page 163 of *Alcoholics Anonymous. "To duplicate, with such backing, what we have accomplished is only a matter of willingness, patience, and labor."* Nowhere else have I ever found such a global guarantee about healing from addictions.
[92] *Twelve Steps and Twelve Traditions*, p. 85.
[93] Ibid., p. 77.

Chapter 8

Being Recovered: The Spiritual Life (Where This Ends Up)

The state of being recovered is referred to many times in the original twelve-step literature. Here are two instances:

- *"We... are more than one hundred men and women who have recovered... "*
- *"...clear-cut directions are given showing how we recovered."*[1]

These two quotations, and many others like them in the original literature, clearly point out that people don't have to stay sick or in recovery. This implies that the object of being in a twelve-step program is to get recovered (which means to be spiritual)—they're the same thing. It is viable, and from the outset, it is the point of the exercise. Appreciating the complexity of what happens in getting recovered requires the coalescence of ideas from apparently unrelated disciplines, but it really does all fit together.

When people do the original steps as they are outlined, they can't help but become recovered. This appears to be threatening to many people. It would appear this fear exists because they lack spiritual commitment, or are probably still acting out in some other addiction, and afraid of the social responsibility and social isolation that may go with a life governed by spiritual principles.

Should you have meticulously followed the instructions thus far, and be absent of socially approved addictions, you are recovered. You are, at a basic level, living by spiritual principles. The task now is to enhance them, which is the function of the maintenance steps—for the rest of your life. Chapter 8 will focus on the importance of ongoing self-monitoring and responsibility (admitting wrongs); Chapter 9 on prayer (don't confuse God with Santa Claus), and meditation (spiritual humility through open-mindedness); and, Chapter 10 on the art of discussing spiritual transformation, which is authentic twelve-step work (humility in carrying the message).

Lao Tse (c. 580-500 BCE) advised that to venerate without understanding or to worship without inner vision would be blasphemous and vain. Regarding veneration, which is a heartfelt deference for someone or something, the observation implies for twelve-step participants that to hold their "program" in authentic reverence, they must understand it to a significant degree. According to him, anything less would be blasphemous vanity.[2] What I will be addressing in the following discussion is the apparent, general lack of understanding of how all encompassing being recovered is, from the perspective of completing the original twelve-steps.

There's a subtle parallel in M.C. Richards' observation cited earlier: *"Let no one be deluded that knowledge of the path can be substituted for putting one foot in front of the other."* Intellectual astuteness, precocious or otherwise, does not imply understanding, which was explained by example in the section 811 Facts About Rigorous Honesty in Chapter 2. Nothing can substitute for the discipline and hard work of actual spiritual transformation. By completing these steps in the manner described here, you put one foot in front of the other. That eventually gives you an experience of "the path" that integrates emotional, physical, and spiritual awareness. From within this integrity, there can be authentic veneration.

Twelve-step meetings are full of politics and glib *clichés*; meaningless spiritual words. People start "sharing" and the switch flips on, and out comes the spiritual rhetoric. At home they yell at their kids, lie to their partners, tell racist/sexist jokes "for fun", smoke, cheat on their taxes, pirate software and music and movies off the internet, slander and gossip, complain (about anything), and still, at meetings, talk about honesty and spirituality.

Living without authentic awareness, constantly recreating petty conflict (samsara for the Buddhist[3]), they live a dislocated and defiant existence, but without the blatant self-destruction of gross addiction. The harm is now subtler. They've done little beyond learning how not to drink or use, and continue their self-annihilation in well-concealed, quiet desperation.[4]

From what I understand about spirituality, addicts seeking recovery would make every effort to avoid circumstances or relationships that are

---

[1] *Alcoholics Anonymous*, pp. xiii and 29, respectively.

[2] The other clause from Lao Tse, *"...to worship without inner vision... "* is explored in Chapter 9 at Meditations on Wisdom.

[3] *Samsara* is sometimes translated as "perpetual wandering", which results in the experience of dislocation and misery.

[4] In *Huxley and God, Essays*, by Aldous Huxley, edited by Jacqueline Hazard Bridgeman, HarperSanFrancisco, 1992, the chapter Knowledge and Understanding is well worth extensive meditation.

morally or ethically squalid (unspiritual) for the suffocating and dangerous "advantage" of popularity, sex, convenience, or financial reward. In those relationships with others who declare a desire to live by spiritual principles, and who appear to be doing so, but later those others willfully, repeatedly ignore spiritual principles or don't challenge their own defects of character, they are demonstrating that integrity and spirituality are only a matter of convenience. Addicts in recovery would be wise to distance themselves from them because that unspiritual behaviour will eventually be turned onto them. Nothing is free.

Yes, it may be necessary to end relationships because the other person continued to deliberately ignore some principle of spirituality. Misdemeanors of ignorance or naiveté are entirely different from deliberate non-spiritual conduct. Relationships are important and, whether spiritual or un-spiritual, always contribute to the quality of life. Other people's *deliberate* participation in some behaviour that is spiritually untenable will be, by as-sociation, spiritually costly. Addicts seeking recovery cannot afford to evade their commitment to the honesty or the other spiritual principles by ignoring someone else's non-compliance. This is a standard that, although difficult, is a long-known truth, especially in Buddhism, regarding Right Association.[5]

Spiritual integrity requires that you attain a clear understanding of the inherent importance of the five spiritual principles, *and* that with observable success, you direct your will towards adhering to them within the mainte-nance steps. After following the specific instructions, and finding yourself at Step Ten, it implies you will have acquired some integrity. This means you think, feel, and act spiritually in your behaviours. In falling short of that, your effort was at least well intended: you amend any harm, and you adjust future efforts to become as you proclaim you desire to be—spiritual.

Being Recovered: The Preliminaries

Throughout this process I assume:

* You are willing to accept, at face value, the statement that:
  "*...you had better use everyday language to describe spiri-*

---

[5] Huston Smith in *The World's Religions*, HarperSanFrancisco, 1991, pp. 104-105, discusses Right Association. Although not stated specifically as part of The Four Noble Truths of Bud-dhism, Right Association is a cornerstone of all spiritual action, and a given in all forms of human endeavor. People naturally understand, without explanation or instruction, that to aspire to anything contains within it the necessary requirement to reorganize their conduct to associ-ate with people who evince similar aspirations, and/or to distance themselves from people who have a strong contradictory intent. Right Association is imperative in spiritual transformation, and especially so in a twelve-step pilgrimage.

tual principles."[6] There is nothing convoluted or particularly esoteric about spirituality. Be cautious of people who apply self-serving definitions and interpretations to words. Do not allow yourself to do this.

- You have followed the instructions in both *Twelve Steps and Twelve Traditions,* and *Alcoholics Anonymous*, from the beginning of the book to the end of Step Nine (p. 84), as well as Appendix II, Spiritual Experience. You did not use step guides from other sources.[7]

- You've completed each step, up to and including Step Nine, in sequence, slowly and thoroughly, while being dedicated to understanding the nuance of each instruction in the original literature. You stayed on each particular step until you realized the spiritual principles inherent within it, and understood the spiritual connection to the step before it.[8] You've not done any step in a pressured, impatient manner (which is evidence of fear and results in having more complications than you started with).

For addicts seeking to be recovered it may be helpful to review the definitions of the words *recover, precise*, and *solution*. It will have relevance to how some passages of the AA literature are understood.

Some References to "Recovered"

These following quotations are from *Alcoholics Anonymous*:

- *"We, of Alcoholics Anonymous, are more than one hundred men and women who have recovered from a seemingly hopeless state of mind and body. To show other alcoholics precisely how we have recovered is the main purpose of this book."* (emphasis theirs, p. xiii).

---

[6] *Alcoholics Anonymous*, p. 93. "Everyday language" does not limit people to using words of only one or two syllables. Use a dictionary.

[7] No one needs to write personalized step guides: the best one has already been written.

[8] Earlier, I advised you to keep each step independent of all the others, and here I advise that you must understand their connection. As an exercise that you complete, each step is entirely independent of any other step. However, each step has a spiritual content that directly or indirectly relates to each of the five spiritual principles, and each step is connected to all the other steps through these principles. Note that although unstated, the first, second, and fifth spiritual principles are implied at Step One. There is a spiritual connection between Step One and your earlier, addicted, destructive life. The connection is the glaring relationship between relentless suffering/self-annihilation and the complete absence of spirituality. Through the continued abstinence you initiate in Step One, you develop an awareness of the complete absence of spiritual content in your life.

- *"...we work out our solution on the spiritual as well as an altruistic plane... "* (p. xxiv).
- *"Nearly all have recovered."* And: *"The tremendous fact for every one of us is that we have discovered a common solution."* (p. 17).
- *"There is a solution." "When, therefore, we were approached by those in whom the problem had been solved..."* (p. 25).
- *"Further on, clear cut directions are given showing how we recovered."* (p. 29).
- Regarding the book *Alcoholics Anonymous*: *"Its main object is to enable you to find a Power greater than yourself which will solve your problem."* (p. 45).
- *"...the problem has been removed. It does not exist for us."* (p. 85).
- *"...others, who have since recovered... "* (p. 96).

Notice, also, there is an entire chapter entitled There Is A Solution (p. 17). There is an undeniable confidence in these quotations—no half measures. The author(s) of *Alcoholics Anonymous* were very sure (were convinced) that these steps allowed alcoholics to become recovered.

There's a qualifying requirement that relates to the effort you invest in all of the work you do. This requirement is found in 'How It Works' on page 59 of *Alcoholics Anonymous*: *"Half measures availed us nothing."* This relates directly back to the state of being recovered. It would appear that being forever "in recovery" is a half-measure.

"In Recovery": The Mediocre Solution

Addicts and alcoholics are told that they can get recovered, and these are people who don't like to do what they're told. Unregenerate alcoholics, victims, and addicts don't want responsibility put on them, and being responsible is a mandatory part of getting recovered. When an addict or an alcoholic argues that they can only be forever in recovery, they're trying to justify their own fearful half-measures.

People who live in desperate mediocrity, or continue to fail away at life, are too easily, glibly labeled as being afraid of success. The reasons for "failure" are much more complicated. In addition to those I mentioned earlier, here are eight other possibilities: (1) People underachieve because they're angry, and underachieving is one way to punish and keep disappointed those people who love them—people at whom they, the underachievers, are mad at. (2) Failure is possibly an expression of self-loathing. (3) Being a failure prevents caregivers who were mean to them (that the underachiever may subconsciously wish to punish) from taking some credit for, or taking pride in, any success. (4) If they become noticeably successful, their own introjected, self-critical scripts will have nothing to berate them for. (5) They'll be resented by other underachievers, and so fail to avoid being resented. (6) They'll be held accountable—no more hiding. (7) If they become a success they'll have to leave their underachieving comfort zone and create a new social circle. (8) Being spiritually successful is complex, difficult work. It could be they sincerely want to change but don't know where to go for guidance.

The spiritual principles described in Appendix II are the antithesis of the five main symptom-constellations of the disease of addictions, which are: (i) self- or other-destructive behaviour, (ii) deceit and dishonesty, (iii) arrogance, self-righteousness and pride, (iv) greed and selfish behaviour; and (iv), irresponsibility and defiance.

Being "in recovery" allows you to be mean or irresponsible and to justify it. You present the big, final excuse and demand compassion for your never-ending struggle of continuous healing: "So I told a lie. What'd you expect? I'm in recovery. I'm *trying*."[9] Being "in recovery" doesn't sound like a solution; it sounds like petulant purgatory.

Regardless of how long you've been sober—three years or three decades—if you're always "in recovery", after you claim to have done all of the steps (several times) you still get to act like an addict: harm yourself, hurt others, lie, be arrogant, selfish, rude, disobedient, and irresponsible, and when challenged on any unspiritual behaviour, you're able to invoke the defensive In-recovery irresponsibility clause, "I'm in recovery. I'm *trying*." Instant exoneration, and who can argue with that? Remember the perfect in-recovery prayer: "Please God, let me be honest and humble (but not yet)."[10] Being recovered is threatening to the spiritually unfit because it requires an ongoing posture of no excuses.

Being recovered doesn't mean that life will become a conflict-free, love-zone of bliss. When recovered, there are still times when life is demanding, and probably more so for the truly spiritually minded. This may cause you to wonder if spirituality is so difficult to attain, and if there's going to be hardship anyway, why bother going through the struggle to be

---

[9] Take some small object and set it on the floor in front of you. Now try to pick it up. Don't pick it up, just *try*. In definable (absolute) areas like honesty, you either are or you aren't. You care or you don't. "Trying" is very often a petulant excuse for irresponsibility and a plea for unearned leniency.

[10] This is a variation of an observation made by St. Augustine.

spiritual? Why not give up, settle for mediocrity, and take it easy? There are three reasons.

The first reason is the addict who's abstinent but forever "in recovery" endures perpetual pain, loneliness, and isolation, and it never gets better. **The second** is because the steps are constantly repeated, the fear and anxiety during step work is constantly re-experienced and cannot be resolved. **The third** reason is all that's available in social situations is commiseration, and a gossiping interaction of comparison and one-upmanship. Authentic intimacy and love are forever absent.

However, for the recovered person who is spiritually determined, the pains of life are never carried alone; they aren't re-created, and they can be resolved. Life always gets better. Only the truly spiritual person can celebrate the implacable grandeur of life in the midst of calamity and misadventure.

Too many people, regardless of abstinence seniority, hide in twelve-step meetings making enemies of people unlike themselves. They refuse to believe, or haven't been shown, what's available through the original steps. Many twelve-step participants fail to (first) closely examine the original literature, and (then) therefore, cannot explore spirituality at a depth sufficient enough to permit the detailed self-examination that is required. They are unable and unwilling to call themselves to task. Defending against being recovered is one manifestation of a fear of being responsible, and is evidence of a lack of spiritual commitment.

"We... have recovered from a seemingly hopeless state of mind and body."[11] If you don't believe this is possible, you are disbelieving of *Alcoholics Anonymous* and lacking in faith. It appears too self-evident to require articulation, but there is a direct correlation between being spiritual (recovered) and the effort you invest in spirituality. When the author(s) entitle a chapter There Is a Solution[12], who is it, within twelve-step programs, that thinks there isn't one? It doesn't say that there is an almost-solution. It says: *"...we have discovered a common solution."*[13] And, *"...clear-cut directions are given showing how we recovered."*[14] What is it, exactly, that's unclear?

If a person has cancer, the flu, or a broken leg, the goal is to get recovered, not to almost get better and stay in recovery. Being "in recovery" implies you are in the process of getting out of a disease, not that you are out of it. From the moment a person becomes abstinent, the goal should be to get recovered from any addiction, not to stay "in recovery". Believing

---

[11] *Alcoholics Anonymous,* p. xiii.
[12] Ibid, p. 17.
[13] Ibid.
[14] Ibid., p. 29.

that an addict cannot get recovered is an issue of investigation, commitment, and faith, not representative of fact.

To be recovered must mean you are no longer *in* recovery and have finished recovering. However, this does not mean that you are cured, can "act out" safely, or that you are spiritually perfect. It means you are living within the five spiritual principles, in the maintenance steps, without addictions, and are consistently accountable for your behaviour—responsible with no excuses.

Without a sincere spiritual purpose, all step-work is only an exercise in Impression Management. That is sufficient for remaining in recovery, but insufficient for those who actually intend to become recovered and experience spiritual joy.

Understand how the spiritual principles are embodied in each step and how these principles connect the steps together. Understand how obedience to spiritual principles will eliminate the symptoms and eliminate addictions. This will inform your inner vision of a higher power and establish its relationship to your life. Be determined, patient, and obedient, and you'll become recovered.

Recovered and Step Two

The potential to eventually be recovered is born in Step Two. *"Came to believe that a power greater than ourselves could restore us to sanity."*[15] If addicts believe that being in recovery is the best that's available, they lack faith in the program and in a higher power, and have missed the point of Step Two.

For addicts seeking to be recovered it may be helpful to review the definitions of the words *believe*, *restore*, and *sanity*. It will have relevance to how some passages of the AA literature are understood.

Step Two doesn't read: "Came to believe that a power greater than ourselves could keep us in recovery." Step Two is a whole-measure, not a half-measure. Don't settle for mediocre commitment and partial responsibility, which are all that's available when you create a psychological orientation within a spiritually structured process. Remember to avoid the Misalliance of Commitment (p. 314).

One Item of Twelve-Step Jargon

In twelve-step programs, no one refers to the first nine steps as Maintenance Steps. That bit of jargon is reserved for Steps Ten through Twelve.

---

[15] *Alcoholics Anonymous*, p. 59.

The implication is that the first nine steps enable you to attain some-thing, and the last three allow you to maintain it. At Step Nine you attained the state of being recovered. If the best end result is to remain in recovery, the last three steps wouldn't be called maintenance steps. In fact, they'd be redundant. Through willingness, patience, and labour,[16] you achieve the same level of confidence that is evident in the original twelve-step litera-ture — guarantees the cofounders discovered through spiritual devotion.[17]

Six Perspectives of Being Recovered

What follows is an examination of "addiction" and "recovered" from six differing models or perspectives.[18] These general perspectives are from (1) the World Health Organization; (2) a mental-health model; (3) a medical or psychiatric model; (4) a psycho-social model; (5) a spiritual perspective; and (6), the view of addiction presented within *Alcoholics Anonymous*. But

---

[16] *Alcoholics Anonymous*, p. 163.

[17] There is a particular discontent in some quarters of some twelve-step groups and recovery programs. Demeaning comments and observations are made about the personalities and possi-ble unspiritual behaviour of a few of the original members and co-founders of AA.
Professionals or twelve-step participants who appear to be seeking status, justification, or credibility for some unspiritual agenda express these disapproving views at the expense of the people whom they gossip about. This undermines the ability of newcomers to trust the integrity of the original written program, and it slanders and undermines the sincerity of the program founders. The comments and writings by others this author has been privy to, whether accurate or not, were unnecessary in context, and unspiritual in principle.
   Regarding these unkind criticisms, these *Alcoholics Anonymous* passages are relevant here: *"play the big shot..."*; *"all people, including ourselves, are to some extent emotionally ill..."*; *"our ancient enemy, rationalization..."*; *"We 'constructively criticized' someone* [to] *hide a bad motive underneath a good one..."*; all from *Twelve Steps and Twelve Traditions*, pp. 92 -94. There are other relevant passages.
   I have described elsewhere in this book that the original AA texts are in that very small group of spiritual teachings that changed the world. They are arguably the most profound writ-ings on spiritual transformation in 1500 years and what may be referred to as a revealed truth. They grew out of a very specific need to address the horrendous spiritual dislocation in addic-tions, and the related alienation in modern culture; which culture promotes and enables addiction and these unkind comments. The AA program texts stand independent of their author(s). The people who conceived of AA and authored the books were just "people" with the foibles common to humanity. That neither detracts from the integrity of what was written, nor detracts from their personal sincerity.
   It is this simple: The co-founders were not perfect. So, what's that got to do with anything besides the fact that they were people? They were devoted and sincere. What they wrote is true. It is spiritually profound *and,* it works. For these teachings, millions of addicts are grate-ful. That the original few people, themselves, didn't achieve spiritual perfection is of no account in the matter. The comments that demean their private lives speak more to the insecu-rities and fears of the purveyors of the gossip, and the malicious ambience of this culture, than anything else.

[18] What I present here is not intended to imply that any professional, or layperson, or any orga-nization, that is associated with addictions recovery agrees with me. Neither am I representing that I am a doctor or psychologist. I am an addictions counsellor/therapist. The observations and perspectives presented here are intended only to suggest a more open awareness (cont'd)

first, I will present a problem, the discussion of which will establish the structure for what follows.

Imagine you see an old woman slouched up against the wall of a run-down tenement building. She's obviously very poor, in tattered clothes, emaciated, somewhat disoriented, in ill health, disheveled, dirty, and drunk. A committee is formed to address "the problem". Imagine these people on that committee: social worker, medical doctor, addictions counsellor, psychologist, sociologist, feminist, minorities advocate, someone from a twelve-step program, and a minister or priest.

If you were a social worker, you might focus on finding adequate housing, getting medical attention, and accessing seniors' services. If you were a medical doctor, your resolution strategy might stress medication, hospital care, and diseases unique to gerontology. If you were a psychologist, you might tend to define the old woman's problems in terms of family systems, a psychological crisis of aging, and long-term de-compensation arising from any number of factors. A sociologist may find legitimate cause for the woman's problems in the midst of a highly mobile culture and the disintegration of the extended family. If you were a feminist, you might view the woman's problems in relation to culture and the apparent social and political advantages available to men. If the old woman were a member of a visible minority, and you were a social activist, you might create a resolution strategy that identified racism or prejudice as a core issue. If you were an addictions counsellor, or a member of a twelve-step program, you might classify the woman as an alcoholic and argue that if she could get sober, many of her problems would be solved. A religious professional might categorize the old woman's problems in terms of an ineffective relationship with God, and point to evidence of lack of religious charity in a secular culture.

Whomever on the committee is given the authority to prioritize the problems determines the focus of the solution: different perspectives, different truths. All of these people are well intentioned and quite possibly right from their own particular point of view.[19]

---

of the broad scope, and far-reaching possibilities, of the original twelve-step process of getting recovered from addiction

[19] Should anyone whom you seek guidance from be spiritually unregenerate, noticeably struggling themselves, or be a good friend, relative, or lover, their insights to your problems will be particular to their needs and not necessarily in your best interests. Should your sponsor or mentor be one of your friends; someone you socialize and loiter about the neighborhood with, their counsel will be self-serving to their needs within the politics of their relationship with you. If you, personally, have a recurring problem, create a new view of the problem and abandon the previously ineffective resolution strategy. Don't try harder, try different.

There are many views of addictions—different philosophies if you will—and each covets definitions that dovetail with that particular view. They're all well intentioned. Each of the six addiction-perspectives I listed at the beginning of this section is slightly different from the others, and each would necessarily have their own view of what it means to be recovered.

The "getting recovered" process outlined in the original twelve-step literature is so all encompassing in its resolution of alcoholism [addiction], that achieving the promises, being recovered, and being spiritual, not only address all the concerns of the other five perspectives, but also goes far beyond anything offered anywhere else.

(1) The World Health Organization

The definition of addiction that seems to have the most universal credibility, and is most concise and universally applicable, is from the World Health Organization. An addiction is *"...a pathological relationship with a mood-altering experience that has life-damaging consequences."*[20]

A pathological relationship would be a destructive and unhealthy condition. i.e. life damaging where the person cannot "stop" (which is what makes it pathological) like the ingestion of a substance, or some other behaviour, that is mood altering (changes one's state of mind or emotion), where the behaviour or consequences create damage or harm.

This compasses all the symptom constellations and dynamics evident in this self-annihilating behaviour. It's easily applicable to the abstinence not-available addictions (food, sex, anger, religion, spending, relationships, righteousness, etc.), the distraction/behaviour addictions (television, work, exercise, shopping, gambling, etc.), and the substance addictions (alcohol, tobacco, adrenaline, and drugs).

Within the original twelve-step program, a loss of the obsession or compulsion occurs through continued abstinence and sincere self-application to the twelve-steps. There is no mood altering through acting out, and the pathological relationship ceases to exist. With continued twelve-step work and abstinence, life-damaging consequences cease. Making amends addresses the consequences and harm done to others. Taken altogether, abstinence and authentic step-work resolves each component of the World Health Organization's definition. Within this particular perspective, an addict could become recovered through the original twelve steps.

---

[20] This definition is cited in an earlier footnote (John Bradshaw; *John Bradshaw on the Family*). Life-damaging consequences are discussed in detail in Chapter 2, under Symptoms.

(2) Mental Health

A mental health worker might define alcoholism or addiction as a mental obsession that causes a person to repeatedly engage in a self-destructive lifestyle, with attendant emotional problems and social isolation. When addicts arrive at the threshold of Step One these problems are evident. Accordingly, then, to be recovered an addict would have to address these four constellations of issues: mental obsession, destructive lifestyle, emotional problems, and social isolation.

Alcoholics Anonymous advises: *"The feeling that the drink problem* [obsession] *has disappeared will often come strongly,"* (p. 75); *"We are not fighting it, neither are we avoiding..."* and, *"...the problem has been removed,"* (both p. 85); *"For by this time sanity will have returned,"* (p. 84). The obsession to act out, with the related insane thinking and destructive behaviour are resolved.

Additionally, within a twelve-step program lifestyle, social isolation is eliminated and, though there may be emotional problems, these are modified or reduced in the majority of cases to manageable or treatable levels. Even in the situation of dual-diagnosis, the mental-health issue that is attendant to the addiction *isn't* an issue of addiction. Life may not be a text book version of peace and harmony, but should the non-addiction part of the diagnosis remain evident, that wouldn't negate the resolution of the addiction itself. Through the twelve steps the addict would qualify as recovered.

(3) Medical / Psychiatric

The following criteria for the categories of Dependence and Abuse are edited here, and found in the DSM-IV.[21] My intent is to capture the themes of the issues to enable some observations about being recovered, not to provide medical advice. Distraction and behaviour addictions can be substituted for "substance" to provide insight into assessing other addictive behaviour. The DSM-IV requires a one-year period for the presence of symptoms for either classification to be valid. In order to err on the side of caution, I have arbitrarily chosen a two-year period of abstinence as a baseline for the consideration of being recovered.

Criteria for Substance Dependence[22]

Clinically significant impairment or distress from a maladaptive pattern of substance use, evidenced by three (or more) of the following symptoms occurring at any time in the same twelve-month period:

---

[21] *Diagnostic and Statistical Manual of Mental Disorders,* Fourth Edition, American Psychiatric Association, 1994.
[22] Ibid., p. 181.

- Tolerance by either markedly increased amounts to achieve intoxication or to achieve the desired effect, or having a diminished effect with continued use of the same amount.
- Withdrawal symptoms appear when the substance is removed, or some other similar substance is used to avoid withdrawal symptoms.
- Substance is taken in larger amounts over longer periods than was intended.
- A desire, or unsuccessful efforts, to reduce or control substance use.
- Significant time is given over to activities related to obtaining or using the substance.
- Important activities are reduced or given up because of the substance use.
- Use is continued despite knowledge of problems stemming from the use or activity.

With two years of continued abstinence and participation in a twelve-step organization, the first five criteria (specific to using and acting out) become non-issues. Regarding the last two criteria: important activities would be resumed or new ones created, and there would be no problems from use or activity.

Criteria for Substance Abuse[23]

Clinically significant impairment or distress from a maladaptive pattern of substance use, as evidenced by one (or more) of the following symptoms occurring within a twelve-month period:

- Recurrent substance use resulting in a failure to fulfill obligations.
- Recurrent substance use in hazardous/harmful situations, including driving.
- Recurrent substance use resulting in legal problems.
- Continued substance use despite persistent or recurrent social or interpersonal problems arising from the effects of substance use.

---

[23] *Diagnostic and Statistical Manual of Mental Disorders,* Fourth Edition, American Psychiatric Association, 1994, p. 182, 183.

The situation is basically identical here. After two years of abstinence and twelve-step work, there would be no impairment, no recurring hazardous situations or consequences, and no recurring distress or problems related to substance abuse. Hence: recovered.

From another medical perspective, two years of abstinence would allow time to address the physical/medical problems from use or abuse: physical health would be reestablished and stabilized; detoxification would be finished. General health would be largely regained within two years. Granted, there may be long-range complications like HIV or hepatitis, but two years of abstinence and responsible twelve-step participation would allow time for these to be properly assessed and managed. Continued commitment to abstinence and a twelve-step program would qualify as being recovered from the symptoms outlined within the DSM-IV.

(4) Psycho-Social

A general pattern of symptoms in a psycho-social model of addictions (closely related to the mental health perspective) might be:

- substance abuse and destructive or harmful behaviour
- deceit
- arrogance and blaming
- selfishness
- noticeable social/personal irresponsibility

These five would manifest in a consistently noticeable pattern, over an extended period of time, with increasing persistence or frequency. Therefore, in order to become recovered, addicts [alcoholics] must extricate themselves from, and eliminate, the symptoms in some permanent manner, over an extended period of time.

Assume, for at least two years, an addict participates in a twelve-step program, maintains abstinence, and sincerely follows instructions through Step Nine. Throughout this period, the substance abuse and self-harm cease; and deceit, arrogance, selfishness, blaming, and irresponsibility are reduced to within "socially acceptable" limits. There would be a generally non-destructive participation in life. In achieving all this, the addict in a twelve-step program would have eliminated all of these symptoms and demonstrated responsibility. This would qualify them as having recovered from addiction from a psycho-social viewpoint.

(5) Spiritual

For this point of view, I'll begin by reminding you of the five spiritual principles: respect for the body-temple, veracity, humility, charity, and responsibility and obedience.[24] And, the behaviours of a practicing addict, the symptoms, if you will, can be grouped into five major (opposite) categories:

- self- and other-destructive acting out (causing harm and mood altering);
- dishonesty, withholding, manipulation;
- arrogance and pride to the detriment of themselves and others;
- selfishness in a way that detracts from the rights and well being of others, or casts doubt on their innocence; and,
- general irresponsibility and willfulness or defiance.

These unspiritual behaviours are altogether the classic aspects of addiction. Some health specialists might refer to these as symptom constellations.

Maintaining abstinence and following precisely the original instructions eliminates these symptoms. The original twelve steps, when followed exactly, enable an addict to transform from unspiritual (addict) to basically spiritual (recovered). *"Well, that's exactly what this book* [Alcoholics Anonymous] *is about. Its main object is to enable you to find a Power greater than yourself which will solve your problem."*[25]

The twelve steps don't "treat" addiction; they resolve spiritual corruption, which makes the phenomenon of addictions disappear. The first nine steps, done meticulously, eliminate the attitudes and behaviours of spiritual corruption (which is/was your addiction). By completing the steps *as instructed*, addicts achieve a sincere spiritual ambience to their life, which the maintenance steps are designed to continuously enhance. From a spiritual perspective, completing the steps properly allows you to become recovered.

(6) The (Original) Twelve Steps

There are many references to being recovered in *Alcoholics Anonymous*, some of which are noted in this book. The original twelve-step reference texts, in the midst of pages of explanation, advise that to be recovered there are essentially two things to accomplish: overcoming the obsession to drink [act out], and eliminating the insane thinking.[26] By the time you finish Step Nine, these two general conditions are gone. Achieving a life with no obsession and no insane thinking removes the five main

---

[24] See Appendix II.

[25] *Alcoholics Anonymous*, p. 45.

[26] This was discussed earlier at The Doctor's Opinion.

symptom constellations (noted in the bullet list on p. 396 under Spiritual). Steps One to Nine allow you to become recovered. Steps Ten to Twelve allow you to maintain and enhance it.

Being Recovered (Responsibility in Spirituality)

It's easier to stay recovered than it is to get recovered, and within a few days of inattention to spiritual principles, it's easy to lose what progress you've made. Study the original reference texts *extensively*. Practice doing what you are told rather than self-serving interpretation or debating "whys and wherefores". Wear out the books and fill up many pads of paper with cross-referenced notes, all the while constantly focusing your willpower on creating a sincerely spiritual mindset. Tell no one you are working so hard, and eventually, regardless of how you look at it, you will become recovered. You, and anyone who associates with you (lovers, spouses, children, work mates, friends, family) will benefit.[27]

Many things prevent people from becoming recovered. The *most* significant is probably dishonesty, closely followed by an absence of, or misunderstanding about, sincere spiritual commitment. Another prevalent obstacle, heretofore unstated, is contained in the unhealthy ego-posture of "perfectionism". Some people repeat the steps in an effort to get them done perfectly fearfully believing their salvation depends upon not missing the minutest detail of any task. [Conversely: It is also true that many of the litanies of magnificent failure, and the grim determination to maintain a squalid life, are a dramatic twist on overachieving under achievement.]

For perfectionists, any level of achievement that's generally acceptable to the majority of their culture is *un*acceptable to them. Just because perfectionists don't believe they are recovered doesn't mean that they aren't; it means they're perfectionists. Or, just because people are insecure about their own capabilities, or don't believe being recovered is possible for themselves, doesn't mean it isn't possible. It means they are insecure.

Being subjected to the tyranny of an inner, relentless, demand for perfection is sometimes an emotional issue that's independent of addictions. There's a great deal of misdirected emotional energy in struggling to achieve perfection within the steps, which perpetuates the abysmal mindset of self-castigation and failure.

Should you misunderstand what serenity means, or misperceive how the steps accomplish what they are intended to accomplish, you may believe that today's turmoil or conflict is evidence of yesterday's "poorly completed" steps. In many cases this may be accurate; however, completing the steps with an attitude that demands perfection doesn't allow for an eventually conflict-free life; it promotes conflict. This process promises "recovered and serene", but does not imply an absence of error or misadventure. As a perfectionist, if any time you encounter turmoil, and are left with the sense (fleeting or otherwise) that somehow you didn't do something right within the steps, your perfectionism and insecurity will then prompt you to repeat them.

The significant condition of serenity is feeling comfortable that, with help from a higher power, while relying on the five spiritual principles— especially rigorous honesty and responsibility, you are competent to respond to whatever life throws at you. In the midst of turmoil and misadventure, there may well be indecision and disagreement. However, you will carry an abiding faith that if you choose an honest, "maintenance-step" orientation to life, meaning that you view life spiritually and not culturally, you'll always succeed in being abstinent and serene, regardless of the outcome.

Out of this mindset comes this truth: You don't have to be wise or powerful—the maintenance steps are. You can therefore focus on obedience rather than dominance, and humility rather than self-importance. You never again have to figure out "how" to live, you only have to adhere to the five spiritual principles. [That's "how" to live, but what you actually do with your life is another matter entirely.]

Is My Step Work Good Enough?

When you went through school and passed from grade to grade, rarely did you get perfect marks in all subjects. Your marks were sufficient to progress into the next year. Bs or Cs may not have been sufficient for your caregivers or yourself, but they were sufficient for the educational system. As an adult, should you decide to return to school, I suspect you would not be required to repeat grade five in an effort to get perfect grades because you only managed a C+ when you were there the first time. The passing marks from years gone by were sufficient then, and they are still sufficient today.

So it is with the steps in the program. If Step Four rates a metaphysical B, so be it; if it rates an A, that's fine too. With willingness, patience, and labor, be thorough; make a sincere and honest effort; be diligent. Trust in the spiritual integrity of what's written in the original twelve-step literature, and in the firm, gentle guidance of a spiritually wise mentor. The mainte-

---

[27] By the same token, you, and anyone who associates with you, will be hurt by your half-measures. Everything costs something.

nance steps, when approached properly, are revealed in such a way that they compensate for our less-than-perfect (all too human) efforts. Struggle against perfection, which masks insecurity, and be satisfied with being confidently ordinary. Should you ever manage to live within the five spiritual principles, and be confidently ordinary, you'll be remarkable for that.

The first two sentences of Step Ten are: *"As we work the first nine Steps, we prepare ourselves for the adventure of a new life. But when we approach Step Ten we commence to put our AA way of living to practical use, day by day, in fair weather or foul."*[28] This points to the clear separation between getting recovered and being recovered. There is also this: *"We have entered the world of the spirit,"*[29] which implies that before Step Ten, you weren't "in" the world of the spirit, you were preparing for it. At Step Ten, you've entered it. There are profound implications in these sentences regarding the major shift that occurs after Step Nine.[30]

Being recovered, and maintaining that spiritual state, requires a steady, gentle, persistent effort towards responsibility and spiritual fitness. People make mistakes—it goes with being human. Living in the maintenance steps doesn't carry the requirement to be above your humanity.[31]

Being recovered entails living a life of ups and downs, and sometimes missing the mark of spiritual soundness. When success and misadventure befall you, compass your behaviour with the maintenance steps and spiritual principles. Responsibly address any irresponsibility. Being recovered is frightening to many people because there is so much responsibility attached to it, but remember, you were [supposed to have been] trained for living responsibly through the process of meticulously doing the steps. Maintain your commitment to your higher power; seek trenchant, percipient guidance from a well-informed spiritual advisor; and be honest about *every*thing. Being human doesn't remove your entitlement to being recovered.

In examining the invisible, perennial themes of spirituality, I've come to believe that for an addict to get to the maintenance steps is to attain only a very elementary competence in spiritual endeavor. Certainly they are recovered, but that's only novice-level spirituality. Going beyond to the next level of being Spiritual through true humility and devotion to spiritual principles—becoming someone who is an insightful, wise, and humble spiritual

---

[28] *Twelve Steps and Twelve Traditions*, p. 88.

[29] *Alcoholics Anonymous*, p. 84.

[30] In this book, in Chapter 10 on Step Eleven, I examine meditation in some detail. After reading that section, consider returning to this point and meditate on what I offer here regarding being recovered.

[31] What might serve us well is recognizing that our modern-day culture embraces fantasy, illusion, greed, power, violence, blaming, accumulation of shiny things, sexual dysfunction, status, fame, character assassination, notoriety, tabloid gossip, racism, and sexism. All of this actually denies our humanity.

advisor to other pilgrims, is another matter entirely. That's why there are so very few bona fide saints and spiritual gurus—it's such hard work. (From my experience and from what I'm told, the rewards are legion and beyond anything an unregenerate person can imagine.)

With willingness, patience and labor; with Right Effort, Right Association, Right Conduct, etc., and wise counsel, you can become and stay recovered (maintain spiritual integrity)—all within the guidelines of the original twelve-step program. *Alcoholics Anonymous* refers to drinking as only a small part of the problem. Drinking or acting out are only a symptom; character defects are only a symptom. The purpose of the original twelve steps appears to be to relieve you of your addiction and character defects; but not really. At a deeper level, they're to repair the spiritual corruption in your human condition, which will enable you to embrace sincere self-discipline regarding spiritual principles.

As *Alcoholics Anonymous* leads into the promises, you are advised: *"For by this time sanity will have returned."*[32] There is nothing unclear about that, but it's dependent upon the following observation: *"Rarely have we seen a person fail who has* thoroughly *followed* our *path."*[33] If you do a Step One from a recovery house, Steps Two and Three from some treatment centre, and then an AA Step Four and Five; if you use the NA guide for Steps Six and Seven, and a self-help book for Eight and Nine, I don't know what you'll end up with, but it won't be The Promises as outlined in *Alcoholics Anonymous*.

Another observation about being recovered is this: Read the promises several times, very slowly. Meditate on their *all*-encompassing nature. Reflect carefully on how they are the antithesis to any and all of the symptoms of addiction. They represent virtues and attributes that, with continued right effort, etc., will be present in *every* aspect of your existence from the first time you appreciate them to the moment you die. The promises are universal in their scope and soulful in their depth. They contain respect, veracity, humility, charity, and responsibility—the essence of spirituality—deep within the experience of them. Should you authentically achieve these promises, how could you not be recovered?

Maintaining a Spiritual Aspect to Life — Stages of Learning

Your exploration of your own addictions—three-dimensional spider's web, described in The Manner of Presentation[34], has, in concert with the

---

[32] *Alcoholics Anonymous,* p. 84.
[33] Ibid., p. 58, emphasis added.
[34] The Prologue to this book.

mysterious machinations of Providence, allowed you to acquire certain abilities. Acquiring these abilities, and learning in general, always follows these four stages, which I've explained by example:

- 1ˢᵗ Stage - *Unconscious Incompetence*: A newborn baby doesn't know that bicycles exist (unconscious) and doesn't know it cannot ride one (incompetent).
- 2ⁿᵈ Stage - *Conscious Incompetence*: One day, when still very young, the infant learns of the existence of bicycles, or sees a child riding a bike. It now knows there are bicycles (conscious), and realizes that it is incapable of riding one (incompetence).
- 3ʳᵈ Stage - *Conscious Competence*: When older, after diligent practice, by carefully concentrating on exactly what they're doing (conscious), the child can ride a bicycle (competence). They must focus carefully on riding and can't pay attention to the scenery or chat with friends as they ride along.
- 4ᵗʰ Stage - *Unconscious Competence*: After years of riding a bicycle the child takes no notice of its skills and ability (unconscious), and is able to chat with friends and notice the scenery as it rides along (competence).

For a moment, consider playing the guitar. To play a guitar well requires a wide range of finger and arm movements, mastery over a certain amount of musical knowledge, and the ability to coordinate these things to achieve competence in this art form.[35] These various elements might be broken down into these categories:

- <u>Notes</u>: chord positions, octaves, scales, fret use.
- <u>Tuning and Strings</u>: open tunings, number of strings (usually between four and seven), number of frets (usually between seventeen and twenty-four).
- <u>Plucking</u>: multiple string plucking, strumming, movement of fingers, using a plectrum, different kinds of plectra, slide bars, or any combination of these.
- <u>Music Theory</u>: playing melody lines, chords, lead lines, chord structures, riffs, chops, scales, "comping", harmonies, accompaniment, and arrangements.

---

[35] It is the same for all skills that have to be mastered, from acting (film or theatre) and music, through to performing surgery, teaching, pounding a nail, paddling a canoe, or making spaghetti sauce.

- The Instrument: acoustic, electric, solid-body, hollow-body, semi-hollow body, wood, metal, synthetic, pickups, amplification systems.
- Music Genre: Jazz, Pop, Blues, Rock, Fusion, Country, Folk, Classical, Spanish, R & B, Grunge, Ska, Heavy Metal, Soul, Punk Rock, Blue Grass, etc.

Prior to their first lesson, want-to-be guitarists don't know what it is they don't know because they don't know. Unconscious incompetence. As novices, guitar students are told and shown what the basic elements are, but they still can't do them. Conscious incompetence. In other words, they now know some of what they don't know. This stage is always identified by the universal proclamation: "Hey! I can't do *that!*" Under expert guidance they are taught, and for a long time they select one skill and focus on it in isolation from other skills.

To focus in isolation is what happens when a guitar student concentrates on what their chord-hand is doing and ignores or forgets what their plectrum-hand is supposed to do. Or, they concentrate on singing lyrics and forget a chord change. They learn C, F, and G, and when asked about B-flat, they look puzzled as they count up the neck to find it. They have to concentrate on "one thing" in isolation from everything else they've learned until they command all of it. Then, one day, they play gracefully through a scale or blues turn-around, and are thinking self-congratulatory thoughts— "Wow! I did it," and miss the modulation two bars later. All of this is the beginning of Conscious Competence.

After years of study and practice, they multitask. Guitar players or musicians choose from many alternatives without thinking too specifically about any one of them—Unconscious Competence. Here's the application to getting recovered:

(1) Immediately *prior* to entering a twelve-step program, a newcomer doesn't know what it is they don't know about addictions, the steps, spiritual principles, or regeneration, nor do they know how to achieve any of this. They are unknowing of, and unable to live, a spiritually principled life. Unconscious Incompetence.

(2) Shortly after their arrival in a twelve-step group, they [hopefully] observe recovered people behaving spiritually, but realize they're unable to do it themselves. "Hey, I can't do that!" Conscious Incompetence.

(3) The steps, through to the end of nine, require an extraordinarily concentrated effort, to the exclusion of other spiritual tasks. Each step is focused on, and completed, in isolation from the others—one at a time and in sequence. A very basic, spiritual lifestyle (Conscious Competence) is

realized at the completion of Step Nine with the acquisition of The Promises—entry-level serenity. This requires a diligent, focused effort. Since
they've become recovered through the completion of the first nine steps,
they are then able to undertake the maintenance steps without too much
discomfort—entry-level spirituality.

(4) Years later, and I mean *years*, with continued devotion to the maintenance steps and the spiritual principles embodied therein, and being
spiritually mentored, they really don't notice their willing obedience to a
spiritually principled life. Unconscious Competence. [What I say next may
sound like a contradiction, but it really isn't: Being truly spiritual is most
often lived at the level of Conscious Competence.]

A New Perspective of the Maintenance Steps

There is a subtle and important perspective attendant to the last three
steps, and how they arise in your personality, that's remarkably different
from the first nine steps. This new perspective allows you to live *in* the integrated ambiance of a spiritual life. Without this, the maintenance steps
will be ineffectively viewed as three somewhat independent spiritual exercises—independent of each other and of you.[36]

Steps Ten, Eleven, and Twelve are not independent of each other,
they're *inter*dependent and completely *inner*-dependent—they happen together, in concert, at the same time, and inside you. Even though you'll be
intellectually focusing on one of them at any given moment of your life, the
other two will be operating in the background. They are infused within each
other and [should be] infused within you.

Another way of representing this truth is throughout the first nine regeneration steps you acquired insight and rudimentary spiritual discipline
that, within those nine steps, were noticeably independent of each other. For
example, what you learned in accomplishing Step Four was, in some clear
way, independent of what you learned in accomplishing any other of those
nine steps. The individual themes and tasks of each of the first nine steps—
the regeneration steps—were completed as individual exercises, with spiritual insights particular to that step.

Conversely: "Doing" the maintenance steps aren't each an independent, specific course of study in themselves. For example: You realize you
must make an amend to someone and you do this promptly. Attendant to the
amend, you're demonstrating each of the five spiritual principles (in the

---

[36] We are human beings, not human doings. The phrase may be worn out from overuse (psychobabble), but spirituality is not a thing you do, it is actually a state of being. Seeing the
maintenance steps as independent "tasks" leaves them splintered from each other and leaves
you with a subtly dislocated sense of spiritual unity. This results from an error of application—
a misalliance of commitment—doing the maintenance steps instead of being them.

amend itself, you are respectful, honest, humble, charitable, responsible); *and* by making the amend, you are also practicing a meditation on the wisdom of others (Step Eleven), and practicing the principles in all your affairs (Step Twelve). This deep *inter*connectedness is equally true for the other two maintenance steps. Any one of the three embodies the other two, and each embodies all the spiritual principles, all at the same time.

What you learned about a spiritually principled life in Steps One to Nine merges together in the maintenance steps. They both preserve and enhance a spiritual way of life, the basics of which you "should" have already established. In maintaining, you aren't learning any specific new thing. You aren't so much learning about a spiritual life; you are a spiritual life.[37] [I referred to this from the perspective of language on p. 203.]

Here's a similar perspective regarding another behaviour. Consider, for a moment, breathing. Only occasionally do people think about breathing. They simply breathe. In the midst of *extra*ordinary exertions, people notice their breathing, and probably concentrate on some aspect of it (depth, regularity, muscle movement). But for the most part, most people don't notice their breathing.

Spirituality, breathing, and loving never need to be taught. Truly spiritual people throw off (abandon and become unattached to) the selfish trappings of culture and addictions, and apprehend the reality that the ability to be spiritual naturally resides within them. In times of *extra*ordinary circumstances these people may have to concentrate more diligently on spiritual principles (it's how they get through trying times), but otherwise, being spiritual is simply the nature of their life.

The prominent themes of any one maintenance step are always noticeably influenced by the themes of the other two maintenance steps, which themes always hover in the background. Spiritually, you can do none of them independent unto themselves. Focusing your attention on any one of them naturally entails the background presence of the spiritual elements of the other two. Maintenance steps are *inner*-dependent.

In *any* circumstance in your life, you can incorporate the themes of all three maintenance steps (the five spiritual principles) at the same time. You will examine only your own behaviour as it relates to the service of a higher power. In the midst of making love, eating dinner, resolving misunderstandings, paying taxes, driving a car, going through divorce, undergoing surgery, or dying, you can gracefully behave, speak, and *think* (which is the hard one because no one can see your thoughts and many of us are good actors) in a way that demonstrates the five principles.

---

[37] *"...when they are logically related and interwoven, the result is an unshakable foundation for life." Twelve Steps and Twelve Traditions*, p. 98.

You evince a life of spiritual principle without ever mentioning a higher power or spirituality or maintenance steps. In the special circumstance of carrying the actual message of a spiritual awakening to another person (when invited) there's the added responsibility of discussing specifically a higher power and the attendant spiritual work involved. Outside of that, however, you live in the moment, in all the maintenance steps, evincing the spiritual principles, all at the same time, in every circumstance, and never mention spirituality at all.

This is what it means to *"...practice these principles in all our affairs."*[38] Simple, eh?

---

[38] *Alcoholics Anonymous*, p. 60, and *Twelve Steps and Twelve Traditions*, p. 106.

Chapter 9

Step Ten: Responsible For Truth

*Everything I do for my private wellbeing adds an-
other layer to my ego, and in thickening it insulates
me more from God.*

Huston Smith[1]

Be advised at the outset: Should you harm someone, in setting things
right and repairing harms you caused, inconvenience to yourself in making
it right is of no account in the matter. Step Ten: *"Continued to take personal inventory and when we were wrong promptly admitted it."*[2]

Throughout this step, a tone of immediacy prevails. This urgency
comes from the words *continued*, which implies a gentle relentlessness, and
promptly, which implies a gentle urgency. Taken together, these define the
spontaneous immediacy of your ongoing personal inventory and your admissions of wrongs done. Within the framework of this step, there are two
aspects to *continue*; one is to continue to take your own inventory, and the
other is to continue to admit the results of that inventory regarding *your*
character defects when you harm someone. In regard to the spiritual principles contained within Step Ten, there is:

Respect For The Physical Body
When others are emotionally or physically wronged by you it affects their physical well-being. To repair a harm done—to amend
a wrong—shows respect and consideration for their body-temple.
(And your subsequent inner peace contributes to your own physical health.)

Veracity
In circumstances where others have been harmed, to withhold the
truth about your own accountability aggravates relationships
through suspicion, cynicism, and ill will. When people have been

---

[1] *The World's Religions,* by Huston Smith, HarperSanFrancisco, p. 38.
[2] *Alcoholics Anonymous,* p. 59, and *Twelve Steps and Twelve Traditions,* p. 88.

hurt, they'll often withhold kindness or gentleness, and become reluctant to be honest themselves. People who have been lied to will oftentimes become suspicious of others generally (we do project) and your dishonesty may be a contributing cause to their suspicions directed at innocent persons. Prejudices sometimes develop. Veracity is fostered and encouraged in others when you take responsibility for the harms you've caused.

Humility
In its aspect of being egalitarian, the decision to comply with Step Ten contains an admission of human ordinariness (imperfection), which is an element of humility. No one is above doing wrong and to honestly admit your humanity is an exercise in humility. The second aspect of humility, honoring a deity by whatever name or cultural manifestation, is evident in your continuous effort to abide by spiritual principles. Any sincere effort to amend harm, without external coercion to do so, demonstrates spiritual grace.

Charity (of spirit)
In its purest form, charity is enveloped by willingness. It's charitable to spread the bounty of the world, and so it is with promptly making amends—generously providing peace and serenity to others by smoothing the disruptions caused by your character defects. It is charity of spirit to admit wrongs.

Responsibility & Obedience
Responsibility is an obvious component of making amends, especially in never finding fault elsewhere, and the requirement to examine only your own conduct. Taking responsibility within Step Ten demonstrates obedience to spiritual principles and to the tenets of all the maintenance steps.

All five principles are clearly evident within the action of Step Ten. Over a long period of diligent application, it becomes easier to apprehend the depth of what's spiritually afoot here. It follows that the more continuous your personal inventory taking is, the more graceful your admissions will be, and the less often you'll have to make amends.

Observations About Words and Phrases

"Continued to take" is very straightforward. In using everyday language to describe spiritual principles, "continued" means repetitive and

ongoing, or extended without interruption. Certainly, yes, if someone takes a personal inventory the first Saturday of every third month they could claim to be continuing to take a personal inventory. However, when you appreciate the tone of the suggestions, and the nature of spiritual principles, a *continuous* personal inventory, once every three months, or once at the end of the day, doesn't fit with sincere commitment, or within the context of Step Ten, or comply with the word promptly.

This *"personal inventory"* is your own, never others', which reflects the previously established theme of taking responsibility for your self-imposed crisis. Step Ten demonstrates what was learned in Steps Four, Eight, and Nine. You repeatedly examine your insecurities, how you harmed others, and fix it... and leave *un*analyzed anything that anyone else is or isn't doing.

"...and when we... " This leaves no doubt that you will be wrong—the human factor. You are going to make mistakes. Humility is the virtue that allows for acceptance of our own (and others') fallibility.

"...were wrong... " Wrong encompasses any conflict you participate in, any harm you cause, and any behaviour or thought motivated by a character defect of yours. You learned, in Steps Four and Eight, the nature of character defects, how they arise in your personality, and the broad scope of harm. All of this applies here.

"...promptly" Especially notice the step does not say, "...and when we were wrong, promptly, provided we weren't too tired or too busy or too inconvenienced, admitted it." Promptly means what it means.

"...admitted it." Admitting you were wrong (and by association, amending any harm) is the task at hand. The step doesn't say to admit being sorry, sad, bad, mean, or angry. Neither does it advise you to announce any mitigating circumstances in your own defense, or to expound at all regarding the real or imagined character defects of the other person.[3]

"...there is a long period of reconstruction ahead. We must take the lead. A remorseful mumbling that we are sorry won't fill the bill at all."[4] This maintenance step does not allow you to rest on your laurels from the hard work of the first nine steps. Yes, you have completed the primary phase of major reconstruction. There is still much work to be done, and you must take the lead in this. Don't wait until someone else catches you in a defect; don't wait until calamity forces you to act. Take the lead; be proactive, not reactive.

---

[3] All of this seems so straightforward, it's almost patronizing to explain it in this detail, yet the original author(s) found it necessary to write eight pages of explanation. (*Twelve Steps and Twelve Traditions*, pp. 88-95.) Why? Probably to identify and eliminate as many of the evasive strategies and excuses that unspiritual people can dream up.

[4] *Alcoholics Anonymous*, p. 83.

Being sorry and apologizing are entirely insufficient. What lies ahead isn't only making amends and repairing damage. There is also reconstructing how you view apologies, amends, and responsibility; modifying how you interact with others, and how you view spiritual principles; and reconstructing your personality to embody all of this gracefully.

There are various kinds of inventories.[5] The focus here is: *"A spot-check inventory... aimed at our daily ups and downs, especially those where people or new events throw us off balance..."*.[6]

Take a few minutes right now and think about the last thirty people you interacted with: a person at the grocery store, a neighbor, a child, an accountant, a person selling something through a phone survey, a driver of another car, a loud person in the movie theater, your spouse, someone from your twelve-step group. Were you mean, harshly judgmental, disrespectful, or unkind? Did you take advantage of your authority? Were you unfair, abrupt, angry, or inconsiderate? Were you silently mean spirited, racist, or sexist, but overtly behaved otherwise? Have you gossiped? If *any* of these questions have a "yes" answer, regardless of who they are, whether or not they know it, how old they are, where they are, or how inconvenient or embarrassing it may be for you, an amend *may* be in order.[7]

Consider that if it takes you several hours or days to make an amend, you have all that time of irresponsibility and awkwardness building up, and both you and the person you harmed lose serenity. This always impacts your conscious contact with your higher power (as you understand this). If left unattended, this delay subsequently jeopardizes your abstinence. Equally as important, when you are harming others, you are not being gov-

---

[5] See the paragraph: *"Although all inventories...."* *Twelve Steps and Twelve Traditions*, p. 89.
[6] Ibid., pp. 90-91.
[7] If your unspiritual behaviour is *silent* harsh judgment, rage, racism, sexism, etc., but doesn't involve any overt demonstration of such, you might not have to make an amend to the other person. However, you must take the lead in resolving this silent spiritual corruption. You will be required to discuss this in honest detail with a therapist or spiritual advisor—with a single view to eliminating *your* unspiritual attitude. In this context, it is acceptable, when discussing your behaviour in relation to another person, to make mention of someone else, including their (apparently) unspiritual behaviour or character defects, *provided* it is done (1) in the strictest confidence, to only one person who themselves doesn't behave this way, and is also wise enough to assist and facilitate you changing your behaviour; (2) with the single view of challenging only yourself; (3) with someone who'll understand your intent; and (4), with an advisor who is spiritual enough in their own character, and far enough removed from the circumstances, to not have their view of the third party affected by your disclosure. Discussing the misdemeanors of others, outside of these conditions, is gossip—unspiritual behaviour, motivated by a character defect of yours, and facilitated by a character defect in anyone who'll listen to you, or anyone else who promotes it. Being truly spiritual demands attention to detail. It is complicated, but once you have some self-discipline and an experience of humility, it's an enjoyable quest. You must do everything possible to avoid gossip and any hint of character assassination (your own or others') when trying to sort out your own unspiritual conduct.

erned by spiritual principles.[8] The other people in your life will affected by the meanness or cruelty of your character defects and your irresponsibility in not addressing your defects promptly.

"... *we need self-restraint, honest analysis of what is involved, a willingness to admit when the fault is ours... .*"[9] Balking at continuous responsibility, or finding fault with this literal interpretation of the original instructions, means you aren't willing "...*to go to any length to get* [what we have]." Nor have you "...*decided to go to any lengths for a spiritual experience.*"[10]

Here are some related concepts that are difficult for many people to grasp:

- When you have hurt someone or wronged them, they are the injured party. The fact that you are sorry, or you think you have a "good" reason, or that you feel guilty about it, may not mean too much to them. The amend isn't about you, it's about them. Don't justify it—fix it.
- Avoid telling them you are bad or stupid for what you did in the midst of making your amend. Don't demean yourself or apologize for your humanity.
- Don't, at any time, focus on whatever it is the other person may have done—it's irrelevant. Identify and focus on what you are responsible for in the conflict and harm done.
- Some people report they may be too angry to make an amend promptly. Being angry is a choice you make to attempt to dominate and control other people or the circumstances. Take a time out[11], i.e. force yourself to temporarily excuse yourself and in the interlude, direct yourself to examine both what you did to cause the harm, *and* how you are irresponsible in being so angry.
- In an anecdote related by Joseph Campbell to Bill Moyers, a Japanese Shinto priest was overheard offering this response to a question about ideology, theology, and life: "*I think we don't have ideology,*" the [Shinto] *priest said. "We don't have theology. We dance.*"[12] Like people on a crowded dance floor, we move through life to the song we hear, bumping into each other, interacting, and moving on. Sometimes we

[8] *Alcoholics Anonymous*, p. 85.
[9] *Twelve Steps and Twelve Traditions*, p. 91.
[10] *Alcoholics Anonymous*, pp. 58 and 79, respectively.
[11] Time Out will be described in some detail in *Facets of Personal Transformation*.
[12] *The Power of Myth*, Joseph Campbell with Bill Moyers, Betty Sue Flowers, Editor, Doubleday, 1988, p. xix.

dance alone, sometimes with a partner, and sometimes our dance is to sit on the sidelines watching everyone else. Some people make up their own music, and others dance their whole life to someone else's song.

- **The Two Step Dance** is something my friend Leonard Shaw talks about.[13] Most people think that life is a two step dance. The first step is when something happens or doesn't happen, or when someone else does or doesn't do something. The second step is the reaction: the first person is upset, hurt, or angry and they can't help it. Ask them and they'll emphatically tell you their reaction couldn't be helped. However, life is really a three-step dance. The first step is that something happens. The second step is an instant perception of the event, and the fact that the event is assigned *both* a meaning in terms of emotions (happy, sad, pleased, angry, bad, good, they deserved it, I didn't deserve it, etc.), and it's also assigned a value in intensity (i.e. low – medium – high). The third step is the person's visible reaction. They're upset or in some other emotional state that's related to the meaning and intensity they assigned at the second step. *The second step (perception) of assigning meaning and value is always present, even if the person's unaware of it*. The perceptions, values, and intensity assigned to a circumstance are always the responsibility of the one who's assigned them. If you don't want to be upset, take responsibility and change your perceptions at the second step.[14]

- The "original" four noble truths of Buddhism are the living philosophy of achieving non-attachment and of being responsible. According to this path of self-discipline, which was in its original presentation *not* a religion, every time you are disturbed there is something wrong with you because of your attachment to some particular value or perception. *Twelve Steps and Twelve Traditions* advises, similarly, that *"... every time we are disturbed, no matter what the cause, there is something wrong with us."*[15] What's "wrong" is the meaning and value that is assigned at the second step of the dance.

---

[13] Leonard Shaw, M.S.W., A.C.S.W., a therapist in Seattle, with whom I had the privilege to work, wrote a short and impactful book called *Love and Forgiveness*, available through Leonard Shaw, Seattle, WA, Ph. 206-322-5785.

[14] Changing expectations and perceptions about people was a major theme of the discussion in the section Contracts & Reciprocity, Forgiveness & Covenants, in Chapter 6. It's also discussed in Appendix IV regarding perception and filtering.

[15] *Twelve Steps and Twelve Traditions*, p. 90, emphasis theirs.

Humility at Step Ten

Recall that Step Seven explored the importance and acquisition of humility. When humility is a desirable quality, and something you willingly pursue, the maintenance steps are graceful. At Step Ten, admitting wrongs will carry an element of spiritual joy when done in concert with humility. It's the absence of humility (in other words, the presence of arrogance and righteousness) specifically within Step Ten, that's one cause of people continuously repeating Step Four for the rest of their lives.

Here's a view of fear and irresponsibility, which perpetuates the need to repeat the steps. For ease in explanation, I've described completing the twelve steps in relation to a period of one calendar year.

In January a person does Steps One, Two, and Three. In February they do Steps Four and Five. In March and April they do Steps Six to Nine and claim to be at the maintenance steps and appear to have recovered. However, this person was impatient and didn't really understand the spiritual requirements, and has completed the steps with a misalliance of commitment (described in Chapter 6). They missed the crucial importance of humility at Step Seven.

This leaves them with a self-serving attitude towards the maintenance steps and amends. They'll strive for personal exoneration (guilt reduction); in any conflict will portion out accountability, and are neither in service to their higher power nor living a spiritual lifestyle. When this person is wrong or harms others, they will then be lax in spiritual self-discipline. If they, themselves, aren't affected by the harm they caused others, the necessity of making an amend appears minor. They'll be wrongly focused—more on what the other person did, and will then disregard *continued* and *promptly*.

So, in May they hurt a dozen people and don't promptly take full responsibility for this. In June and July they harm twenty more people, and mumble an insufficient "I'm sorry." In August it may be twenty-five people, and they avoid admitting their wrongs and fixing the harm. In September they hurt a dozen more and from October to December twenty-six more. In those eight months, from May to December, they've wronged or harmed about ninety-five people—the accumulation since completing Step Nine in April.

There is now another "wreckage of their past" that resulted from a superficial spiritual focus (*Acedia*; see fn. p. 326). Because they missed the profound import of humility and charity of spirit, which was because of negligence in the first seven steps, they focus more on portioning out responsibility (blaming) and social atonement, than spiritual responsibility. This causes a rapid accumulation of harmed people. As a result, from anxiety, guilt, and anger, they have to repeat the steps clean up the wreckage of their past (the ninety-five incidents from April to December); hence they "need" to repeat the steps, and start all over again (which reflects the Myth of Sisyphus).[16] In January they start Step One... and so it goes.

Any misalliance of commitment when doing Steps One to Nine won't allow for spiritual integrity. Addicts cannot then incorporate *continued* and *promptly* at Step Ten. Their lack of spiritual accountability makes them incapable of maintaining the level of self-examination required. If this person had valued humility, and done Step Ten *each* time they were selfish or mean from April to December, there would be no wreckage of their past.

The Mechanics of Step Ten

Alcoholics Anonymous describes, in succinct detail, the mechanics of Step Ten where it begins: *"This thought brings us to Step Ten... ."*[17] All of the quotations immediately below come from that one paragraph.

"... continue to take personal inventory..." identifies the task at hand, which you learned previously at Steps Four and Eight.

"... continue to set right any new mistakes as we go along." This identifies how you are to do it—continuously; the gentle relentlessness needed for setting things right (amend making), which was practiced at Step Nine.

"... grow in understanding and effectiveness." This identifies the ongoing process which was explored from different perspectives at Steps Two, Four, Six, Seven, and Eight.

"Continue to watch for selfishness, dishonesty, resentment, and fear." This requires ongoing vigilance—being observant for the insecurities, fears, and sexual selfishness you identified in Step Four.

"When these crop up, we ask God at once to remove them." The ability to do this is a result of a thorough investigation at Step Two and a sincere decision at Step Three. It's also a variation of the theme of Step Seven, bringing you back to humility, which effectively underlies Step Ten.

---

[16] Repetitive cycles of step completion are now-a-days almost standard procedure. This inefficiency results from an ineffective attempt to manage addictions by recasting the twelve steps from a spiritual discipline into psychology (again, a misalliance of commitment). Regarding sponsors who encourage recycling through the steps, or who deny the possibility of being recovered, in addition to their own spiritual sloth, they camouflage their insecurity and lack of faith, and reassure themselves by enrolling naïve newcomers into a complex system of ersatz recovery. This creates more shame and results in all manner of spiritual dislocation. A grudging or intermittent effort at Step Ten is the direct result of an insincere or non-existent desire for humility. This will inevitably require a return to Step Four. In order to camouflage the shame that's generated from going "backwards" and repeating the steps (repetitive inadequacy), there's an automatic defiance to, and slick defenses against, being recovered. The only way to get off this merry-go-round of repetitive inadequacy (which generates shame) is to *plant* yourself in Step Two and stay there for a *very long* time.

[17] *Alcoholics Anonymous*, p. 84, emphasis theirs.

"*... discuss them with someone immediately...*" Here is the practice of humble and non-blaming disclosure that you practiced in Step Five.

"*... make amends quickly if we have harmed anyone.*" This is what you practiced at Step Nine. Notice: It's done quickly.

"*... resolutely turn our thoughts to someone we can help.*" Here you incorporate charity of spirit and service work on behalf of your higher power, which unites Steps Ten and Twelve. "Someone" isn't limited to those in your recovery program.

"*Love and tolerance of others is our code.*" Love and tolerance are now two identified standards of conduct, which you began to appreciate as far back as Step One, which are also attributes of humility.

This one paragraph in *Alcoholics Anonymous* describes the process of making amends during the normal course of your day. Doing "Step Ten" embodies the themes and practices of Steps Two to Nine, and is, in itself, united with Steps Eleven and Twelve. With humility as the fundamental operating principle, and the degree of thoroughness that is described in these Step Ten instructions, what need is there to repeat the steps?

Here's a very true imaginary story:

The Story of Lee

A long time ago, for a couple of years, Lee had been in a twelve-step program. Lee was divorced at the time, a single parent, and someone who seemed to be doing fine. I remember Lee being invited to some big AA house party. 'What?' Lee exclaimed, 'A party? Sober? Do people do this? What a concept!' We laughed. Lee was very nervous about meeting new people and socializing sober, but Lee went anyway.

At the party, Lee asked someone to dance, but they said: 'No thanks. I don't feel like dancing. Thank you for asking.' Lee told me about smiling awkwardly and feeling silly, and someone from the group sniggering and saying something sarcastic. Lee said something sarcastic in response to this other person and didn't stay much longer. The next morning Lee felt depressed and awkward, but didn't call anyone. At a twelve-step meeting the next night, as people were recalling how much fun they had at the party, Lee was quiet.

On Monday morning, driving to work, Lee got cut off and was a little angry. At the office, Lee ignored the receptionist's greeting, and later, in a meeting, noticed people seemed quite re-served. Driving home, Lee thought: 'I don't know if I really like working at that place.' By the next weekend, Lee hadn't called anyone and couldn't get organized enough to pick up the literature for the group. A few days later, while hurrying to work depressed and late, Lee got a speeding ticket. By that time Lee was hardly speaking with anyone.

No one in the group knew anything about this. Lee hadn't told anyone, and was convinced that nobody really understood, and daydreamed a lot about the 'old days'. Lee's partner had left about a year earlier. Lee had been neglecting spirituality and prayer for a while and finally, quite fed up (I could see it coming), said: 'I've had it!' and bought a bottle of liquor.

Lee only blacked out for a few hours, and only missed three or four days of work in the next month. Eventually, though, arriving late and hung over, one morning, Lee was fired, had to find another job (at half the salary), and had to give up the house. Lee's children went to live with their grandparents and six months later, Lee was down to casual employment and getting drunk several times a week.

That's when Lee started getting picked up by the police—drunk, disorderly, shoplifting, and ended up sleeping in some tiny welfare-room. Last winter Lee caught double pneumonia and was found passed out behind a garbage dumpster. The police had to make an arrest. I guess Lee was covered with body ulcers, underweight, and almost dead then. When I was called a month later to identify Lee's body, I hardly recognized him.

I spoke with the constable who made that last arrest. Apparently, as Lee was being rolled into the back of the paddy-wagon, I guess the cop was puzzled by the whole thing—maybe a little disgusted—and apparently said: 'You're killing yourself. You're in terrible shape. What happened to you? What's wrong with your life?' The cop told me that Lee started to cry—just couldn't hide the shame and pain anymore. Through the crying and sobbing, Lee could only say: 'I was at a party two years ago and someone wouldn't dance with me.'

I guess it was a nice funeral, but not too many people were there.

Many "in recovery" addicts interpret Step Ten so that it dovetails with their thinly disguised self-serving agendas. This is evident in people who do "a Step Ten" at night, only at the end of their day. These people examine their daily relationships in hindsight, many hours after the fact, and then decide which interactions require admissions of personal wrongdoing. There are three concerns with this.

First: An inventory at the end of each day, practiced over the long term, may satisfy the definition of "continued", but done at the end of the day prohibits an amend being made promptly. Consider what would happen if, during an interaction with someone early in the morning, they do harm in some manner, and then before bed that night realize an amend is required (if they remember the interaction at all). The person they have wronged sixteen hours before, would have been carrying the hurt all day. And now there the added the complications of locating them, diffused memory, and explanations. Any commitment to doing an amend the next day may be minimally adequate in theory, but decidedly lacking in devotion and promptness.

Second: There is the added risk that the addict's late evening, good intentions to make an amend the next day will get lost in the demands of a chaotic and busy new day. No one can reliably predict "tomorrow". They will then accumulate another wreckage of their past, in spite of otherwise good intentions. In spirituality, good intentions don't count.

Third: Many twelve-step participants confuse Step Ten, i.e. continuously reviewing their behaviour, identifying wrongdoings, and making prompt amends, with something similar, but that is a specific part of Step Eleven. In *Alcoholics Anonymous,* on page 86, is a paragraph that begins *"When we retire at night, we constructively review...."*[18] This Step Eleven paragraph encourages a meditative review of the *entire* day, and would include a review of amends that were made earlier that day, and possibly uncover harms that were missed or amends that were insufficient. This Step Eleven daily, evening review would *also* include meditating on fears that were encountered and addressing them, noticing where indifference was practiced rather than compassion, noticing silent anger, racism, sexism, etc., *and* also observing the successes of the day. All of this requires attention, but this is a part of attending to Step Eleven, not Step Ten.

At the time I was personally discovering the complex beauty of this, I was employed in the traffic-monitoring consumer-relations and complaints division in a large department of a municipal government. My spiritual advisor commented that, while being at work, it would be a fine opportunity for me to practice Step Ten. My immediate reaction was mildly defensive—I was at work and they were just complaints.

He observed there were probably times when I was sarcastic or belligerent when encountering an irate citizen. I shrugged, and vaguely allowed that I might possibly, sometimes, occasionally, be only slightly less than considerate. (!) We chuckled at my evasiveness. He observed that Step Ten required promptness and was explicit about righting wrongs to everyone,

---

[18] *Alcoholics Anonymous*, p. 86.

meaning at work or not. Should I realize, long after any interaction, that I had in some way harmed someone, been rude or inconsiderate, etc., it would be difficult for me to then contact the person to make an amend (which was clearly required if I were to thoroughly follow the instructions).

He suggested I take a brief moment to examine my behaviour at the conclusion of *each* encounter, with *every* person, during the course of my entire day. When I realized I was wrong or had harmed someone, I could immediately make an amend in the moment, and start the next encounter with a fresh attitude. It was obviously a good idea, clearly within the suggestions of Step Ten, definitely in line with spiritual principles, and over time would make my life more graceful. So being the cooperative person I was at the time, I became evasive and thought it over for a week or so.

It soon came about that I would briefly examine my conduct near the conclusion of each interaction and make amends if required. In a matter of weeks, I had made progress in curbing my surly attitude and soon had to make amends less often. I was more considerate and sincere in my dealings with people. More importantly, I modified my interaction with people I didn't like, so the encounter was at least respectful. I was much more aware of my conduct during each interaction and was no longer developing a wreckage of my past.

It didn't take too long for me to realize how much energy I had formerly invested in keeping my resentments at the forefront of my mind. Maintaining anger, rationalizing disrespect for others, and justifying blame are exhausting. Over a period of weeks, as I explored the nuances of what was afoot, two profound realizations were (a) how much easier I could make other people's lives; and (b), how much less exhausted I was at the end of the day. My life was subsequently more graceful, and I became less invested in controlling others and winning arguments.[19]

Whenever you make an amend immediately after you've harmed someone you don't have to carry that queasy, upset-guilty feeling. Neither do you become inattentive to this present moment nor exhausted from constantly revisiting the memory and justifying or concealing your neglect of spiritual principles. You experience the serenity that comes from never having a wreckage of your past. The other person doesn't have to feel insulted or

---

[19] Arguments are either disagreements over facts: The longest river is… , The correct spelling is… , The population of Ireland is… ; or arguments are disagreements over opinions: Blue is a nicer color than red… no it's not. Asparagus tastes better than chocolate cake… no it doesn't. If it's an argument over a fact, don't argue go to the library. If it's an argument over an opinion, it's an opinion, and so there's no point in arguing. A truly spiritual lifestyle can never justify arguing—over anything. Now, I offer one exception from *How To Be A Gentleman*, by John Bridges, Rutledge Hill Press, 1998. On page 67, Mr. Bridges advises that a gentleman *"…argues only over an issue that could save a life."*

hurt, and they have no need to feel defensive. Certainly people get wrapped up in the chaos of a busy day, and at times some encounter isn't examined with the scrutiny that spirituality requires. When you realize this omission, promptly address it. As the years go by, you will make amends more promptly and less often.

When you think an amend is in order and the other person sees the circumstance as being of no consequence, don't force the issue, and still live your life by your standards. Quietly and *politely* say something like: "Well, thanks for your generosity. I think I was a little _(insert defect)_, but maybe I wasn't. Thanks for talking about it," and then get on with the business at hand. Establish your own integrity and move on.[20]

Sometimes when making an amend the other person may reply with anger: "Yes, you're wrong. You're inconsiderate too... and nasty and mean! You're horrible." The spiritual task, at this moment, is for you to buy out of the conflict, thank them kindly for telling you what they think (*no* sarcasm), and get on with your business. Don't argue. If the business is concluded, politely excuse yourself (*no* sarcasm).

The spiritual rationale for not arguing is their perspective of your behaviour is their personal opinion. Their opinion is right for them. It may or may not be accurate; you no doubt have a different opinion of your behaviour. Trying to argue that your view of your behaviour is more accurate than their view of your behaviour is pointless. It's what they believe.[21] To not argue is going beyond forgiveness to acceptance and compassion.

The message in the first two paragraphs on page 88 of *Twelve Steps and Twelve Traditions* is obvious. A continuous inventory is frequent and without interruption. This might be called micro-awareness of yourself. In the beginning, this requires a significant amount of focused, conscious energy, and can only be sustained with spiritual support.

No longer can you slide through your day living in ignorance of the moment and hoping for wisdom in hindsight. Through Step Ten you will very quickly start living in the present, listening to others with less prejudice, and responding with acceptance. *"More experienced people, of course, in all times and places have practiced unsparing self-survey and criticism. For the wise have always known that no one can make much of his* [or her] *life until*

---

[20] Addicts generally find that life is more serene when they develop an expertise at taking their own inventory rather than honing their skills at taking others'. Too many addicts instantly calculate the "Conflict Responsibility Factor"—what percentage of any conflict is their own fault (49.5% or less is the desired amount) and what percentage is the other person's fault. In unregenerate people, the end result is decidedly self-serving.

[21] Keep this in context. If it's necessary to defend yourself legally, then do that; but even then, don't engage in petty squabbles or name-calling. In the realm of personal relationships, what someone else thinks of you is none of your business. The more you try to debate people out of their cherished beliefs, the more they'll cling to them.

self-searching becomes a regular habit... and until he [or she] *patiently and persistently tries to correct what is wrong."*[22]

One of the AA cofounders described his own early views of Christ: *"His moral teaching—most excellent. For myself, I had adopted those parts which seemed convenient and not too difficult; the rest I disregarded."*[23] Many twelve-step people have a similar view regarding the moral and spiritual teachings of *Alcoholics Anonymous*[24]—selective convenience.

What suggestions, which go against your more cherished and justified prejudices, do you neatly avoid? How do you slyly promote only those principles that do not entail too much social, emotional, or financial inconvenience? In my experience, sadly, most people in twelve-step programs are too busy with "social" things to be concerned with the nuances of continuous spiritual self-examination. Yet regarding human relations, a person undergoing spiritual transformation is clearly told:

- *"Learning how to live in the greatest peace, partnership, and brotherhood with all men and women, of whatever description, is a moving and fascinating adventure."*
- *"...no field of investigation could yield more satisfying and valuable rewards than this one."*
- *"...[no] need to wander morbidly around in the past; ...[strive for the] admission and correction of errors now; ...settle with the past; ...made peace with ourselves..."*
- *"Once this healthy practice has become grooved, it will be so interesting and profitable..."*
- *"...[to quiet] stormy emotions..."*
- *"...see what real love for our fellows actually means..."*
- *"...[express* gratitude] *for the blessings we have received..."*[25]

With all the popular and various declarations about peace, love, and gratitude, what is it that makes so few people willing to eagerly seek these out? It's fear. So, they abandon a spiritual objective for the more easily attainable and popular social objective. When people other-examine rather than self-examine, and amend wrongs less than continuously, they miss out

---

[22] *Twelve Steps and Twelve Traditions*, p. 88.
[23] *Alcoholics Anonymous*, p. 11.
[24] *"That means we have written a book..."* Ibid., p. 45.
[25] All taken from *Twelve Steps and Twelve Traditions*, pp. 77, 80, 89, 89, 90, 92, 95, respectively, emphasis theirs.

on the serenity that arises from being spiritual in the moment, which, in turn, only arises from a sincere dedication to the well-being of others.

Many people in twelve-step programs blatantly ignore the responsibility inherent in *continued* and *promptly*. They don't relapse; however, they do stay mean, moody, and miserable—and they're often secretly racist, spiteful, dishonest, sexist, etc.[26] Spiritual principles are remarkably absent, and various other socially approved addictions (work, sex, anger, violence, tobacco, righteousness, relationships) are remarkably present. As a consequence, serenity will be forever distant, chaos is always close-to-hand, and abstinence is dependent upon belligerence and the cooperation of Fate.

For the most part, addicts in recovery are excellent at surviving the big calamity and managing major crises. Such people don't relapse because their house burns down or war is declared; it's because someone didn't hang up their coat. They rise to the challenge of Armageddon, but don't anyone buy the wrong kind of toothpaste. Their personality traits, which accumulate petty annoyances and ignore their own wrongdoings, are exactly what's counteracted by *continued* and *promptly*. Step Ten, when approached with obedience to the spiritual principles it embodies, prevents everyday misdemeanors from escalating into relapse and death.

In order to live like this you will need *"In all... situations... self-restraint, [an] honest analysis of what is involved, a willingness to admit when the fault is [yours], and an equal willingness to forgive when the fault is elsewhere."*[27] You acquired the wherewithal to do this in Steps Four, Eight, and Nine, and the willingness and humility to be interested in doing this at Steps Six and Seven. You learned everything you needed to know before you arrived here.

Clues to Self-righteousness

There are four styles of behaviour that demand careful scrutiny. Even though they may appear to be well intended, they actually conceal unspiritual/selfish motives. These self-righteous behaviours, and the common justifications for them, are:

- constructively criticizing someone who is present and who "needs" the criticism to help them understand their own

---

[26] It appears that many people automatically assume that sexism is the degradation of women by men. Sexism is as equally prolific regarding women towards men. For an important, although for some people a controversial perspective, see *The Myth of Male Power,* by Warren Farrell, Simon & Schuster, 1993.
[27] *Twelve Steps and Twelve Traditions*, p. 91.

character, when, in fact, we're trying to win a useless argument or feel superior;

- constructively criticizing someone who isn't present, claiming we're trying to help others understand this person, or
  warning people so they won't be hurt, when, in fact, we're
  trying to feel superior, and hurt the person we are criticizing; or trying to impress or endear ourselves to someone and
  collect allies;

- teaching someone a lesson and "helping" them to be smarter
  or wiser, when, in fact, we're only trying to punish them;
  and,

- telling others how we're sick, depressed, tired; how we're
  forced to contend with life's difficulties and "dysfunctional"
  people—"sharing"—when, in fact, we're trying to elicit
  sympathy, get a break, and get attention.[28]

The original literature is rather specific: *"...this perverse wish to hide
a bad motive underneath* [an apparent] *good one, permeates human affairs
from top to bottom. This subtle and elusive kind of self-righteousness can
underlie the smallest act or thought."*[29] Your task, regardless of whatever
anyone else is doing, is to eliminate this perverse trait from your character
through diligent effort at Step Ten, and to discipline only yourself to be
obedient to the spiritual principles.

Spirituality In Action

Step Ten is the realization of living inside the mandate of the Step
Seven prayer. Doing "Step Ten" properly actually eliminates whatever
"...stands in the way of my usefulness to you and my fellows."[30] Step Ten
keeps your defects out of the way so you can *"...carry the vision of God's
will into all* [your] *activities."*[31] Humility is the crucible out of which you
do spiritual work. Using your willpower to continue to promptly attend to
Step Ten *"...is the proper use of the will."*[32] It's the single, most effective
way of attracting rather than promoting a spiritual lifestyle.

Any benefits to yourself become secondary to taking responsibility for
the well-being of others and carrying "God's vision" into your life. Yes,
you may have a good day, but that's not the primary purpose of doing this.
Besides, if you've done your homework, and approach this right, you won't

---

[28] *Twelve Steps and Twelve Traditions*, p. 94.
[29] Ibid., pp. 94, 95.
[30] Part of the Step Seven prayer, *Alcoholics Anonymous*, p. 76.
[31] Ibid., p. 85.
[32] Ibid.

really be interested in what you get out of it. If you insist on pinpointing some personal reward, it's this: Experiencing the essence of humility in making amends is winning the spiritual lottery. Making amends becomes easy and self-searching becomes enjoyable. It's at this point that you begin to understand what Mr. Camus was referring to when he described appreciating the implacable grandeur of life exactly as we have been given it.[33]

When humility becomes more important than being right, making amends promptly is no trouble at all. When making amends promptly becomes no trouble at all, you never build up a wreckage of your past. When you never build up a wreckage of your past, you get to stay in the maintenance steps. When you stay in the maintenance steps, you stay recovered and consistently appreciate the promises.

The original literature advises we're meant to be joyous and free, but not without taking responsibility, and we must (of course) still be human and therefore make mistakes, and sometimes serious ones. How can we make mistakes and hurt others, and be hurt by others, and still be joyous and free? When we seek out humility in both its aspects. It is very simple. It is also very complicated and profound.

It is important to note the grammar and syntax of the following sentence: *"For the readiness to take the full consequences of our past acts, and to take responsibility for the well-being of others <u>at the same time</u>, is the very spirit of Step Nine."*[34] Pay especial attention to the words *"at the same time"*. This is embodied in Step Ten, which is, in fact, a combination of examining yourself for instincts gone awry (that are evident in the harming of others through your character defects) and promptly making amends (thereby taking responsibility for the wellbeing of others).

By using the phrase *"at the same time"* the author(s) of the original literature point out that these two apparently separate actions—taking the full consequences of our acts, and taking responsibility for the well being of others—happen together. They're embodied entirely within each other and within Step Ten. It's rare that anyone could reasonably accomplish either of these, with any amount of sincerity, with the resistance attendant to spiritual endeavor in this day and age. But, to have a formerly self destructive, nonspiritual, selfish person act this way, and be able to do it at all gracefully, is more rare still. It's a great blessing to be able to choose this as a way of life.

A subtle and devastating result, which arises from being forever "in recovery" is the sense that you end up being on the road to recovery for so long that you forget you're trying to get somewhere. An almost subcon-

---

[33] *The Myth of Sisyphus and Other Essays,* Albert Camus, Vintage Books, 1991.

scious despair develops that is too often interpreted as depression. Addicts struggle through getting abstinent, through coming to believe, and then through inventories that require taking complete responsibility, changing values, and making amends. Should they repeat the steps very year or two, the constant and repetitive effort of trying to heal, trying to grow, "trying" to get through the steps, and then to start all over again with yet another set of steps, becomes a frustrating, never-ending morass of minimal accomplishment. The road to repetitive mediocrity.

One unstated and powerful derivative benefit of being recovered is that you realize that you finally did "get somewhere". With the proper approach, at some unexpected moment in the middle of some amend, you will suddenly realize how sincerely graceful and stable your life is. To regenerate yourself from active addiction into being recovered, and at the same time into being spiritual, allows you to realize that you have actually become a different person. For a formerly practicing alcoholic/addict to achieve any of this is profound. However, for them to achieve it to the depth that is available, after only several years of very hard work, is true evidence of spiritual grace and the bounty of providence.

Your quest for a spiritual life has become a comforting reality. *"But we must go further…."*[35]

---

[34] *Twelve Steps and Twelve Traditions*, p. 87, emphasis added.
[35] *Alcoholics Anonymous*, p. 85.

Chapter 10

Step Eleven: Responsible For Humility

"There is a principle which... cannot fail to keep a [person] *in everlasting ignorance—that princi-ple is contempt prior to investigation."*

Herbert Spencer[1]

"As we have seen, self-searching is the means by which we bring new vision, action, and grace to bear upon the dark and negative side of our natures. It is a step in the development of that kind of humility that makes it possible for us to receive God's help."[2] One implication is that the dark, negative side of your personality prevents deep inner awareness, which (in turn) prevents finding the Great Reality deep within you.[3] What this means is that anything you may accomplish by way of prayer and meditation, within Step Eleven, is directly dependent upon your willing and continuous *self*-examination within Step Ten.

In order to be effective in prayer and meditation you must first notice your own dark nature i.e. subtle self-righteousness, subtle character defects and selfishness, and subtle participation in socially approved addictions, and commit to continuously challenging these—which is Step Ten. This nur-tures the development of a special kind of humility that makes it possible to receive your higher power's help through Step Eleven, which is: *"Sought through prayer and meditation to improve our conscious contact with God* as we understood Him, *praying only for knowledge of His will for us and the power to carry that out."*[4]

Should you believe you are sincerely praying and meditating, a few times a day, on a regular basis, and over some months you notice that your

---

[1] As quoted in *Alcoholics Anonymous*, p. 570.
[2] *Twelve Steps and Twelve Traditions*, p. 98.
[3] *Alcoholics Anonymous*, p. 55.
[4] Ibid., p. 59, and *Twelve Steps and Twelve Traditions*, p. 96, emphasis theirs. I personally do not subscribe to a religious traditional "God", nor do I believe *It* is a him or a her. This is a quoted passage from a reference text.

spiritual serenity isn't more apparent, then you are not praying or meditating properly and you're not diligent and relentless in self-examination.[5]

Regarding the spiritual principles contained within Step Eleven...

Respect for the Body-Temple: With frequent and regular prayer and meditation, your body will relax and carry less tension — healing benefits for your body. Your own reduced tension, through prayer and meditation, has a calming effect on people who associate with you. Prayer and meditation on your part shows respect for the body-temple — your own and others'.[6]

Veracity

Veracity's aspect of honesty is strengthened through prayer by truth telling to your higher power, and its aspect of gentle trustworthiness is enhanced through the nature of meditation.

Humility

Regarding the spiritual aspect of humility: In both prayer and meditation, you recognize your dependence on a higher power, and demonstrate a desire to be constantly guided (governed) by spiritual principles. Regarding the egalitarian aspect of humility: In prayer, you reveal your ordinary, fragile humanness (universal equality with all people); in meditation, you seek the wisdom of the spiritual masters (demonstrating that you are teachable).

Charity

Charity is a valid spiritual endeavor only when it carries no pity, sorrow, self-advertisement, or other selfish ego-agenda.[7] During

---

[5] Should you have achieved a sincere spiritual ambience in your life and then become lax in self-examination, the defects-side of your character will increase its influence and eventually block your conscious relationship with your higher power. You will then begin to accumulate a wreckage of your past. Should this happen, until you reestablish diligent self-examination, your conscious contact with your higher power and any effort at prayer and meditation will be ineffective because you will be controlled by your character defects. The maintenance steps are linked to each other in incredibly intricate patterns. To skimp on any one of them is to prevent yourself from doing the other two.

[6] Two related views of God residing within us are found in *Mysticism In Religion,* by Rev. W.R. Inge, University of Chicago Press, 1948. In Chapter 3, p. 35, attributed to St. Paul. Rev. Inge offers: *"...the Spirit dwelling in us, or of our bodies as the temple of God... ,"* and *"'the body' as the 'tabernacle' of the soul while we live here."* And, from Rev Inge, himself: *"The body must be reverenced and preserved from defilement because it is the temple of the Holy Spirit."* Many other, similar perspectives are found in all the major religious philosophies.

[7] *"The* [pilgrim] *should also bestow* [charity], *uninfluenced by any preconceived thoughts as to self and other* [persons] *and for the sole purpose of benefiting sentient beings"*; and *"...in* [the] *practice of charity* [have] *no arbitrary conceptions of the attainment of the blessing* (cont'd)

prayer and meditation you are actively reorganizing your personality to remove any selfish agenda. Without selfish agendas underneath charity you benefit because there's no manipulation and other people benefit because for them there's no obligation arising from your charity. All sincere prayer and meditation is charity to others before the fact.[8]

Responsibility & Obedience

The continuous seeking of "God's" will through Step Eleven demonstrates both of these attributes at the same time. Responsibility is inherent in prayer and meditation, and these are the crucibles out of which greater responsibilities arise and expand into your life. Obedience has two aspects within Step Eleven. One is being obedient to the principle of prayer and meditation, and the other is being obedient to the spiritual obligations that arise *from* your prayer and meditation. Should you regularly pray and meditate, over time, you will be rewarded with spiritual tasks that require greater responsibility and obedience.

All of the spiritual principles are evident within the action of Step Eleven. Over a *long* period of *diligent* application (ten years or more), it becomes easier to apprehend what's spiritually afoot here. The more continuous your prayer and meditation is, the more graceful your life will be. The more graceful your life is, the less often you'll face indecision or turmoil. Thusly, the more aware you'll be about what the will or your higher power is for you, and you will receive the power to carry that out.

Observations About Words and Phrases

"Sought…" [Seek]: *1. To attempt to locate or discover; search for. 2. To endeavor to obtain or reach: seek a* [higher power]. *3. To inquire for; request: to seek direction* [from a spiritual advisor].[9] The central theme of these definitions involves making an effort to find something. Sought is an action word that has within it a sense similar to "continued" as used in Step Ten—expend energy in an ongoing (continuing) effort to find something. Sought implies a gentle relentlessness.

---

and merit which [you will] *will attain by such practice…". A Buddhist Bible,* edited by Dwight Goddard, Beacon Press, 1994, pp. 90-91.

[8] My observation is dependent upon your prayer and meditation being absent of selfishness, righteousness, and self-serving rationalization.

[9] Excerpted and abridged from *The American Heritage® Dictionary of the English Language, Third Edition,* © 1996, Houghton Mifflin Company. Electronic version.

If you are a person who likes to refinish old furniture, you first have to find the old furniture. *How* do you look—drive around to yard sales, walk to stores, read newspaper ads, telephone friends? *Where* do you look: newspaper ads, yard sales, retail stores, garage sales, estate sales, auctions? Which of these alternatives of "How" and "Where" provide the best results for acquiring old furniture? In Step Eleven you are advised "How" to seek—through prayer and meditation. At other places in the literature, you are advised "Where" to seek:

- *We found the Great Reality deep down within us;*[10] and,
- We reduce the influence of our defects and enable prayer by self-examination. In other words, we look inside ourselves.[11]

So, "where" to look is inside yourself. How to look is two-fold—by first doing Step Ten—eliminating defects, which enables spiritual insight; and then, "how" you look, is through Step Eleven. The effective methods of prayer and meditation are explained later in this chapter. These have been proven to be the most effective process for spiritual transformation.

These instructions, regarding spiritual endeavor, prevent you from becoming frustrated with ineffective or otherwise scattered efforts such as doing service work, being a circuit speaker, chairing meetings, or having a good sponsor (which are all inadequate for the task at hand). Do not permit yourself to seek easier ways that suit your fancy, meaning light-hearted efforts that look and sound good, but accomplish little. A higher power is like honesty: It may be appreciated in others, but only found within yourself.[12]

If you've been in a twelve-step program for some period of time, and aren't making a regular, noticeable effort to pray and meditate in some fashion approximating what you've been advised through the literature, you're cheating yourself and harming others. Years ago, I was annoyed that a mentor had kindly pointed out this truth about me. I responded with irritation. At that point, he gently informed me that he was more interested in saving my life than in whether or not I liked what he had to tell me.

For an addict/alcoholic to recover and achieve sincere personal fulfillment, the phenomenon of addictions has taken away any other options,

---

[10] *Alcoholics Anonymous*, p. 55.

[11] *Twelve Steps and Twelve Traditions,* p. 98. The passage begins, *"As we have seen... "*.

[12] Some philosophies suggest that personal transformation is primarily by a vaguely defined transcendental meditation—stressing meditation more than deliberate self-examination. This more "eastern" approach is at odds with the specific approach suggested here: detailed self-examination independent of meditation and prayer, *and* meditation through contemplation of the wisdom of others. Eastern meditation practice doesn't appear to be an effective substitution for authentic recovery. Other meditation practices (TM, yoga, Qi Gong, etc.,) are designed for everyone. Sincere spiritual transformation has very specific requirements that are dictated by the phenomenon of addictions and cultural issues, which together preclude generic approaches.

other than obedience to spiritual principles, which other options they might have had in the some-time distant past. Their addiction may well require that they obey the original twelve-step instructions or die.

"*...to improve...*" is the goal. At the beginning, you had to eliminate your acting out, and then later, your character defects, selfishness, and irresponsibility, in order to let your higher power work within you. You did this through to Step Nine, and developed a very basic relationship with a higher power and a rudimentary understanding of what God's will is for you.

By the time you finished Step Nine, you should have created a very basic spiritual tone to your life. Here, within the maintenance steps, you're not creating a belief about whether or not you have a higher power, or creating a conscious cooperation with spiritual principles; you should have already done these. At Step Eleven, the orientation of effort is to improve this foundation, not to establish it.

"*...conscious contact...*" does not mean that God is going to appear to you personally. Conscious, in this context, means awake and deliberate, not haphazard or accidental, on *your* part. An analogy may be that you can wander aimlessly in the wilderness and accidentally see a bear, or you can study the bear's habits, study the terrain, and walk quietly and carefully searching for it. One event is not conscious or deliberate; the other one is. A deliberate search will have decidedly better results than a haphazard one; hence, *conscious* contact.

How you ended up in a twelve-step program in the first place, when you were blinded by your addictions and still in monumental denial, indicates there was some (forever unknowable) relationship with "positive coincidence". Providence, it seems without your conscious intention, rolled over in your favor. Early in your transformation, contact with a higher power was largely unconscious and sporadic. Step Eleven is intended to eliminate this haphazard relationship with a deity and to create a conscious, deliberate one. This doesn't imply that you will be conscious of your higher power in your life like you are conscious of someone walking into a room.

Conscious contact can only arise from a regular and continuous effort. Through self-discipline, ritual, and regular wise counsel, you become capable of noticing subtle, unexplainable shifts that enhance virtue and make you mindful of spiritual principles. Sensing these shifts is conscious contact, and they enhance trust in a higher power. Sometimes I describe this as an awareness of the benevolence of the universe.[13]

---

[13] For the atheist, these principles are easily recast as principles of ethical behaviour or principles of harmony. For atheists, "spiritual" principles are codes of personal conduct, absent of "god". In Appendix II, the third spiritual principle, Humility, would be edited to be sincere egalitarianism. With that change, all five apply. Atheism, tentative or adamant, is more common in modern (technological) cultures than many people will admit. On a tangent to all of this: Some sociologists and psychologists posit the striking migration to structured (cont'd)

This is never noticeable in sporadic effort, or in a life with addictions or chaos, or if your recovery efforts are psychologically oriented. It only arises and appreciated out of a continuous, sincere, and properly focused effort in spiritual discipline. This is rooted in a deliberate and planned effort on your part, hence, "conscious". Because of the propensity of addicts to create drama and chaos, only ongoing rituals of prayer, meditation, and wise counsel allow you to develop a mindset where you can be aware of spiritual influence without seeing *or needing to see* your higher power.

"*...as we understood* [God]*...*" Understood is past tense. This relates back to how you came to understand and believe at Step Two. The chapter on Step Two in *Twelve Steps and Twelve Traditions* ends in the present tense with: "*...is the rallying point,*" and "*...we can stand...*". At Step Three, and thereafter, the grammatical tense in relation to God changes from present to past: it becomes under*stood*. When you reach Step Eleven, you completed Step Two some timer ago, and so at Eleven it is how you under*stood* God. This again points to the idea that at Step Eleven, you aren't creating the relationship; you're enhancing it.

Step Eleven in particular, and the original twelve-step program in general, allow you complete freedom in identifying the symbols around which you organize your beliefs. The image of *That Which Art* that appears in your mind, the name you assign, the metaphors you employ, are how this higher power manifests in your consciousness; it is particular to you. Do not shove your interpretation of god down anyone else's throat.

Believing in spiritual principles and having no image of a higher power is quite satisfactory, and probably more effective than trying to create an image. Beware of idolatry. Our minds, restricted by Time and Space, must perceive everything, including a higher power, in some image, but when the image (or concept or picture or statue) is itself imbued with spiritual power, that's idolatry. All manner of spiritual misadventure, like religious wars and persecution, is the result.

· *Signs and Symbols*

Carl Jung differentiated between *symbol* and *sign*.[14] The distinction is worth knowing. A *symbol* is a thing, or an image, that represents a link to

---

religions at the end of the last century (c. 1980 – 2000) as a reflection of our unmet need for ethics and principled interaction. However, this will eventually fail because organized religions are, in themselves, styled after the needs of the religious political bureaucracy, not the individual.

[14] *Man and his Symbols,* Carl G. Jung, Anchor Books, 1964, pp. 20-21, p. 55. This delineation is also important in mythology—cf. *Transformation of Myth Through Time,* Joseph Campbell, Harper and Row, 1990, p. 132. This concept was apprehended 2500 years ago, and, in a slightly different sense, is referred to in The Diamond Sutra, as translated in (cont'd)

deity: one part here in Time and Space that represents connection to the mysterious unknowable dimension of life, transcendent of Time and Space. A symbol offers a link that represents a way for people to conceive of something that, by definition, is beyond conception. The wise spiritual pilgrim is ever mindful that the image is not God, the picture is not the thing; it's a symbolic conception of something, only linking Time and Space to The Transcendent. That's a symbol.

A *sign,* however, doesn't transcend—it's something here, concrete and knowable. When you imbue any image, thing, or person with what are assumed to be God-like powers, or attempt to organize God's "powers" around any logical or rational construct (meaning something within Time and Space, like the twelve steps) there is idolatry. This most often feeds into righteousness.

People in recovery programs should not confuse "the program" with "a higher power". The steps or other transformation processes are only a self-imposed discipline that enables an awareness of a higher power. Many pages ago, I wrote that Step Two is coming to believe that a higher power could restore you to sanity. The steps, sponsors, service work, meetings, recovery conventions, are not this higher power.

Also beware of clinging to temporal or social constructions of a higher power: your cat, your support group, Nature. These are all finite and limited, leaving you at the mercy of charismatic people and Fate. Some reactionary religious views may suggest that temporal realities, like a sunset or Nature, contain some manifestation of God or God-like attributes. Should this be the case, those people are then imbuing signs with God-like powers, and that's idolatry. At another level, yes, your children are some genetic extension of you; or your home that you decorated entirely by *your*self may be an extension of your personality; but these are not you. I concede, because it's not provable, Nature, in all it's vicious magnificence, may be God's handiwork, but Nature isn't God.[15]

There is compassionate guidance offered in this matter in the original twelve-step literature. *"To certain newcomers and to those one-time agnostics who still cling to the A.A. group as their higher power, claims for the power of prayer may... still be unconvincing or objectionable. Those of us who once felt this way can certainly understand and sympathize. We well remember... rebelling against the idea of bowing be-*

A *Buddhist Bible,* edited by Dwight Goddard, Beacon Press, 1994, p. 89. The Buddha's words are figures of speech. The metaphors are symbols, not signs. And elsewhere, the chapter Idolatry, in *Huxley and God, Essays,* cited at an earlier footnote, is well worth extensive reflection.
[15] In *The Bhagavad-Gita,* Lord Krishna says to Arjuna: *"The whole universe is pervaded / by my unmanifest form; / all creatures exist in me, / but I do not exist in them."* *The Bhagavad-Gita,* The Ninth Teaching / The Sublime Mystery, Translated by Barbara Stoler Miller, Bantam Books, 1986, p. 83. This is arguably the best translation I have read.

fore any God." The next paragraph encourages going beyond clinging to a group as a higher power and includes this passage: *"almost the only scoffers at prayer are those who never tried it enough."*[16] This statement tells any twelve-step participant, without a specific reference to the definitions of sign and symbol noted earlier, that with the right effort and concentration, they could go beyond a sign (the AA group) to a symbol of God, and thereby create a more dependable relationship with a higher power.[17]

Beware of getting caught in the self-aggrandizing posture of superlative comparisons: my symbol for God is better than yours, or my path to God is better than your path; my group is the best in the city. Any time you hear anyone talk about people needing to find "the one true way", or the very best group, trouble is brewing. Having one true way for you alone is quite acceptable, but don't adorn your path with righteous superlatives. This builds *you* up and not spiritual principles.[18]

The original twelve-step program offers complete freedom by encouraging you to choose your own personal understanding of your higher power (Step Two) when you voluntarily submit yourself to that spiritual pilgrimage (Step Three). But, as with all freedoms, there are dangerous pitfalls. Be alert to the ones noted above.

"...praying only for knowledge of [my higher power's *will for* [me]...*"* The purpose of prayer is quite limited in this context. You pray for only that one thing, which, of course, begs the question: "What is God's will for me?" There is endless and pointless debate about "God's will" in twelve-step meetings. Here are ten phrases from the original twelve-step literature that suggest what God's will is, as it manifests in the process of getting recovered. These aren't specifically cited within Step Eleven; they're taken at random from *Alcoholics Anonymous*.

- *"...to perfect and enlarge* [your] *spiritual life through work and self-sacrifice for others..."*
- *"...tolerance of other people's shortcomings and viewpoints and a respect for their opinions..."*
- *"...constant thought of others and how we may help meet their needs."*

---

[16] *Twelve Steps and Twelve Traditions*, pp. 96-97.

[17] If you struggle with imagery and are fearful in this regard, it may be wise to choose a neutral image when praying. Review the information on a "limitless blue-black nothingness" in Chapter 3. When addressing religious addictions, it is necessary to help addicts deconstruct the *signs* of God they used that are imbued with power, and help them create symbols that can transcend secular or temporal limits. This is incredibly complex cross-over work.

[18] There is a succinct and related perspective to this written by Thich Nhat Hanh in The Introduction to *Contemplative Prayer*, by Thomas Merton, Image Books, 1996, p. 6. The paragraph begins: *"But many Christians and many Buddhists...."*

- *"...to be of maximum service to God and the people about us."*
- *"...to do the right thing, no matter what the personal consequences may be."*
- *"Helping others is the foundation stone..."*
- *"...to be at the place where you may be of maximum helpfulness to others..."*
- *"...to think of what you can put into life instead of how much you can take out."*
- *"Giving, rather than getting, will become the guiding principle."*
- *"...transcended by the happiness they found in giving themselves for others. They shared..."*[19]

Each of these is about how you conduct yourself and not what you do.

It would appear that social status, sexual relationships, wealth, and collecting shiny things aren't a part of "God's" will. But, to debate at all what "God's" will is (or isn't) is certainly an expression of what your will is. According to these quotations, neither is it God's will for addicts to agonize in dubious intellectual battle about the efficacy or credibility of "God's" design—it's beyond our comprehension, just as "God" is. [Recall the analogy at the end of Chapter 5 about The President and The Janitor. The janitor is incapable of understanding anything the CEO is doing, and, quite possibly, the CEO doesn't understand much about floor cleaners.]

If you are one who believes "God" created the universe, then debating with others who differ, or debating with God because you think it should have been designed differently, is rooted in a lack of faith and absence of humility. So many people in the world spend *so* much time trying to "figure out" either what God's will is for them, or what The Grand Plan of the Universe is, and of course debate how they'd improve it or what they disapprove of in others' points of view, they have scarcely any time to pray for the courage to challenge their short-comings and racism, or to acquire simple virtues.

However, in a spirit of fairness, since *no one* has verifiable, direct access to God Transcendent of Time and Space, I concede that for some people, God's will might be:

- to accumulate vast wealth and power, with a caravan of servants, in a blissful fulfilling relationship, growing old gracefully, in a magnificent palace, on a huge tropical plan-

---

[19] *Alcoholics Anonymous*, pp. 14-15, 19, 20, 77, 79, 97, 102, 120, 128, and 159, respectively.

tation (with no mosquitoes and a good internet connection), forever free from pain in paradise; or God's will may be...

• to rise above being merely mortal and act as God's personal advisor on how to improve the general conditions of human existence. Or, if not that, to at least advise everyone on which of the religious and political views [in certain geographical areas] are, according to them, rooted in lunacy and deserving of immediate modification.

Okay... Either of these could be God's will for some people, but I'm skeptical. [Of course, my exaggerations were facetious.] However, do *not* be fooled by the excess. The defects of spiritual racism, greed hidden under charity, arrogance in prayer, and religious elitism, are rampant in the routines of everyday spiritual and cultural religious life.

From the experience and wisdom of the ages, it would appear that fiscal concerns and social advantage are at odds with the benefits and blessings of authentic spiritual endeavor. I'm not intending this as a criticism of people who have significant financial resources or social influence. Nothing in and of itself makes these wrong. There are, however, important considerations and implications regarding power and wealth if your desire is to be sincerely spiritual.[20]

There is yet another important caution for those involved in spiritual transformation. Abuse, violence, punishment, spiritual elitism, gossip, racism, brain-washing children, indoctrination, homophobia, sexism, greed, etc., are perpetrated and justified as "God's will" by fanatics and neurotics. This abuse arises from all manner of fear and insecurity, and often indicates an addiction to religion (distraction) and self-righteousness (adrenaline).

Notice: *"Quite often, however, the thoughts that <u>seem</u> to come from God are... well-intentioned unconscious rationalizations."* And *"[there is] ...the possibility that [a person's] own wishful thinking and the human tendency to rationalize have distorted [their] so-called guidance."* Asking for things via petitionary prayers *"...[is] based upon a supposition that we know God's will...".*[21] Be especially cautious and reserved about what you

---

[20] It is spiritually corrupt to be powerful or wealthy and claim more entitlement to life than others because of this. However, it's equally corrupt to insist you're spiritual, and to be arrogant in prayer and meditation, claiming you're better or wiser than those who aren't ("spiritual"); and again, equally corrupt, to claim you are "more spiritual" because you eschew wealth and power and hide in righteous mediocrity or poverty or dogmatic servitude. These hypocrisies, concealed in elitism and righteousness, stem from fear and lack of compassion and humility They are prevalent in politics, religion, and twelve-step programs when the discussion is how "their way" is what the world needs, and how much nicer it would be if *every*body did what they're doing.

[21] *Twelve Steps and Twelve Traditions*, pp. 103, 104, emphasis theirs.

think "God's will" is for you if it falls outside of the original literature's guidelines, or what you think it is for others in any circumstance.

Alcoholics Anonymous offers specific counsel on how people should conduct themselves (noted above), which are an excellent reflection of spiritual principles. Meditate less on what God's will may or may not be for you, and more on how you can be more generous and kind, and less inclined to selfish petulance, annoyance, and gossip. Pray frequently for the courage to challenge your own unspiritual behaviour and everyone around you will benefit.[22] (Maybe this is all that God's will needs to be.)

"...and the power to carry that out." Earlier I explored the relationship between an increase in honesty and spiritual help. There is abundant anecdotal evidence from millions of twelve-step pilgrims that a higher power and the relationship therewith are the sources of change. Having only good intentions from the addict, although laudable, are insufficient to the task of getting recovered.

The phenomenon of addictions precludes sincere recovery without obedience to spiritual principles. Within the context of Step Eleven,*"...and the power to carry that out,"* is a request of your higher power to provide the courage and perseverance to enable you to live by spiritual principles. This is of long-term and permanent benefit to everyone around you.

There's an interesting book that identifies an insidious hypocrisy in Western culture. *Resentment Against Achievement*[23] advises that as much as we encourage and applaud the acquisition and possession of wealth, influence, power, beauty, and fame, those who acquire it are resented. This also applies to those people, without fame or wealth, who are decidedly assertive and live life by their own values, caring little for popular sentiment. The *"...one thing that enrages people trapped by their lives is the flaunted freedom of outsiders."*[24]

Out of this resentment arises the popularity of tabloid papers, magazines, TV shows, and entire books that smear the characters, demean the accomplishments, and exaggerate into character assassination the ordinary foibles of famous or powerful people. It's a manifestation of resentment and bitterness against assertive, passionate, successful people who aren't necessarily flaunting anything, but who are just being successful. Our culture is

---

[22] *"Every active force produces more than one change—every cause produces more than one effect." Herbert Spencer on Social Evolution,* Herbert Spencer, Edited by J.D.Y. Peel, The University of Chicago Press, 1972, p. 47. Prayer and meditation have a ripple effect; so do character defects.

[23] *Resentment Against Achievement – Understanding the Assault Upon Ability,* Robert Sheaffer, Prometheus Books, 1988.

[24] This quote is taken from *The Great Movies,* by William Bayer, The Ridge Press, Inc., and Grosset & Dunlap, Inc., 1973, p. 161. It was related to an insightful and well-merited classification of *Easy Rider* (directed by Dennis Hopper and released by Columbia Pictures, 1969), as a great film.

overloaded with insecure people—successful or not. This insecurity under-lies the power of peer pressure and the neurotic need for compliance. Those who aren't compliant are envied and resented.[25]

It's the same in twelve-step programs. Be advised: Should you go be-yond the social comfort zone and be diligent in your adherence to spiritual principles, in *all* your affairs, you will be successful at it, and soon stand apart from the crowd. You will then be resented. People will gossip about you and malign your integrity. If you're truly spiritual, it won't bother you beyond a poignant sadness, but it will affect how you act in the world, and how you are treated.

The Myth of Ego Reduction as Humility [26]

Historically, a desire for political power, religious arrogance, and so-cial or cultural wealth, have allowed insecure religious leaders, and more recently "health gurus", to present self-serving interpretations of spiritual principles and religious doctrine. This includes many recovery people and therapists misrepresenting what the bona fide spiritual masters tried to teach (a very common misdemeanor), and includes people amending the original twelve steps to suit their convenience (either financial or emotional; or both). Challenging the status quo established by the religious or mental-health power-elite is dangerous business.

George Santayana recognized this in his comment about the self-serving nature of politics in religion:

> *"My atheism is true piety towards the universe and denies only gods fashioned by men in their own image, to be servants of their human interests."*

---

[25] This works both ways. I also write screenplays. Years ago, I offered two film scripts to two different director/producers. These producers were successful by cultural standards, known in the film industry, and often resented for their success—they were the subjects of tabloid, cof-fee-room gossip. The producers wanted to develop the scripts I had given them, but they also wanted the endings changed as a condition of development. What one described as a too-bleak ending about families in one script, and the other a too-macabre ending about mothers and sons in the other script, were to me only realities of the plots and extensions of the characters. Whether bleak or macabre, both producers told me I'd probably do well in the film industry. However, because of their insistence on drastically revised endings, I politely turned down both offers. I'd decide differently today, but that's what I decided then. The endings stayed as written and the film scripts sit on my shelf today, still undeveloped.

Here's the point: Both producers were resentful that I said no to the deals they offered. By *their* standards, I chose "non-success" when I was offered "success" in the form of being a (compliant) working scriptwriter, receiving a sizable amount of money, having a lucrative income, and the opportunity to become established in the film industry. Be advised: Anyone in our culture of compliance who assertively insists on adhering to a personally established code of conduct, with polite disregard for the sensibilities of others, will meet with resentment and end up as tabloid-gossip for insecure people.

[26] It may be appropriate to review Appendix IV.

In the last fifty years, it's generally represented that a spiritual pilgrim, people in therapy, and people in relationship "power struggles" have to knock their egos down to size to be healthy, content, humble, or spiritual. Variations of the following statements are made all the time: "He's got a big ego; that's his problem." "She's got to get her ego in check, otherwise, she'll never be happy." "You've got to get your ego down to size." And then there's the professional observation: "If you really want to become more spiritual... or serene or content," said by the therapist (or doctor or minister or sponsor) with a quiet tone of rebuke or a patronizing air of superior insight, "you'll have to get rid of your ego. It's too big."[27]

These indicate strong-willed people somehow threaten the person who made the judgment; or they're at a loss for how to respectfully interact by utilizing the focus of the other person's will power. Making a demand for "ego reduction" immediately creates a power struggle in the dynamic of the relationship. It also implies that a "small" ego is present in humble/spiritual people, and significant ego-reduction is necessary for spiritual or psychological health. These are patently false. It's a myth that becoming truly spiritual (or healthy) is an exercise in ego reduction or ego annihilation.

Consider a person who's independent and decidedly assertive; they refuse to be manipulated. They could easily be labeled as having a big ego. From the rationale of "reduce your ego", it appears that assertive, independent people cannot then be spiritual or happy because they're willful and have "big" egos. Yet, on the flip side, other people who are passive, and "helplessly victimized" or manipulated by predators, are told to get independent, get strong, get assertive, be more willful or bold... which could be easily construed to mean "get a bigger ego".

My own investigation repeatedly reveals that any great saint or spiritual leader who evinces humility has an ego that is "comparatively at par" with any tyrant or ruthless dictator who's the model of arrogance. (Don't get caught up in arguing with this just yet.) The difference between the saint and the tyrant is not in the size of their egos, or the force of their willpower, but what their egos and willpower are directed towards. One of these people has their ego and all their considerable willpower set on the five spiritual principles or serving their version of God. The other, equally strong "personality" is focused on selfishness, anger, and domination.

---

[27] The place someone is assigned to on the spectrum "Passive -> Assertive -> Aggressive" is decided by the ego-posture of the person doing the assigning. i.e. An aggressive person will probably be labeled a variation of dangerous/nasty/frightening by a decidedly passive person; and they, being passive, may view an assertive person as "safer" but somewhat bossy. An assertive or aggressive person would have different views of the other two types. It's all relative.

This interpretation applies to anyone. What any individual focuses on: sex, winning, harmony, righteousness, humility, mediocrity, dominance, money, being right, passivity, is what they present to the world. The character traits people consistently display and the values they defend represent an accurate reflection of the focus of their ego. Since, (i) our instinct for survival naturally resists annihilation; and (ii), our willpower/ego exists to facilitate survival, it is more effective to applaud our ego's strength and get it focused differently rather than eliminate it (which is impossible, anyway).

If your ego—if you, they're the same thing, believe that spirituality and, attendant to that, humility, is dependent upon chopping your ego down to size, then praying and being humble will always be subconsciously threatening (an inner struggle). I've seen time and again that people resist "ego reduction".

I know many people who, after years of being a therapist or spiritual advisor (minister, priest, etc.), or after years of therapy as a client, still talk like the death of their ego is the ultimate objective. They batter themselves with recrimination for not annihilating, subduing, reducing, eliminating, killing, whittling down, chopping up, shrinking, or erasing their ego.

Attempts at ego reduction in the pursuit of spirituality, humility, or health, should that ego reduction actually happen (which, by the way, I've *never* seen any evidence of), would leave the person at the mercy of tyrants, predators, and abusive partners because of the weakening of their ego boundaries. Mental-health professionals are long familiar with the theories that refer to the development of strong ego boundaries.

Nowhere in Step Seven or Eleven does it say that you are required to annihilate or even reduce your ego. Addicts are told they will have to get rid of arrogance and the like, and adopt spiritual virtues, but that doesn't require killing your ego. By adhering to the theory of ego reduction, spiritual pilgrims will forever have to drag themselves kicking and screaming to the alter of spiritual principles. The original program implies, in many places, that being recovered is only sincerely available to people with a strong and devoted commitment to a spiritual lifestyle. How, then, could someone with weak ego boundaries, or a "small" ego, accomplish this?

The traditional, popular theories almost invariably present that strong or "big" egos are fatal to serene health or spirituality. This is not true. I have met, or have had the privilege to be instructed by, people whom I consider to be authentically Spiritual. These women and men, who were obviously living deep within the five spiritual principles, each had a strong, fine character: sincere, articulate, confident, assertive. There was nothing weak or small about their egos.

This also appears to be true in the writings of the spiritual masters I've studied. In fact, it appears to me that through prayer, meditation, and devotion, spiritual people actually strengthen their character, and develop a strong ego focused on spiritual pursuits. Strong ego boundaries are what keep them spiritually on track.

This isn't semantics. The "small/reduced ego" views on health and spirituality, and that theory's place in therapy and transformation, are seriously at odds with human nature and the dynamics of spirituality. Being truly spiritual, i.e. respectful, honest, egalitarian, compassionate, responsible, exists at the core of human nature. Becoming spiritual must therefore be (somehow) consistent with health. If I am told that a strong ego prevents emotional or relationship harmony and bliss, and at another time I am told to have a strong, well-defined ego for self-protection (assertive and independent for personal fulfillment), there are subtle and confusing contradictions that must be examined closely.

Our culture embodies everything unspiritual. It denigrates compassion, love, and humility, and encourages racism, wealth, privilege, religious elitism, greed, violence, and sexism. How can anyone be truly spiritual, or emotionally "balanced", or maintain inner-harmony in this culture, without a strong and well-focused ego? It's hard enough to stand up to addictions, but to live spiritually is to be generally opposed to modern culture. This requires tremendous ego strength. When I add to this my observations and learning about the characters of the bona fide spiritual masters, and the strong characters of recognized peace-oriented leaders of the world, the theory of "small egos for bliss and humility" is untenable.

Becoming humble and spiritual, or sincerely loving someone (especially romantic loving) requires a strong, well-defined ego. In our culture, there is so little that supports the significant commitment and effort needed for truly spiritual endeavor, that it couldn't be accomplished by anyone with a "small" ego. Authentic transformation (spiritual or emotional) that must stand against addictions and culture requires a strong ego for a fulfilled life of love, spirituality, and serenity.

Recognizing this truth has allowed three changes for me. The first is that all of the contradictions and puzzles I had regarding ego theories and transformation immediately evaporated. The second is that my own inner life and spiritual work (such as it is) became smoother. The third is that my work helping others (and their own experience of themselves) became clearer, not necessarily easier emotionally, but less tangled.

Here it is in a nutshell: It's not necessary to change the size of your ego to become spiritual. This perspective has profound implications for the generally accepted views of personality, humility, love, relationship contentment, individuation, and personal change. Within the crucibles of genetics, family, personal temperament, intellect, and culture (social rituals, education, politics, religion), we adopt values. Those values—about everything, which are very delicately balanced and carefully prioritized—are the manifestation of our egos. This forms the core of our beliefs and perceptions. At a conscious level, this shows up as the organization of our personality and governs what we focus our considerable willpower upon.

One person focuses their ego-willpower on passive behaviour, another on charitable works, another on the acquisition of fame or wealth, yet another on dominating others or violence. People who are extremely passive actually dominate those around them with their ego's powerful focus on passive behaviour. All our egos are the same size [sic], but are focused differently. Our "egos" are focused on however we *self*-perceive we must be to survive.

Investing all your creative energy, intellect, and willpower, in music or painting isn't that much different than investing it in creative bank robbing, or creative stock swindling. The purpose of Steps Two, Six, and Seven (probably the least talked about steps), is to change the most basic thing about an addict's personality: the focus of their values and perceptions—their ego.

So, what's this got to do with praying? Strong ego boundaries are important to a fulfilling life. People instinctively resist ego-reduction ("ego-death"). At a very deep level our psyches resist ego annihilation, which would leave a person at risk. If you even remotely believe that humility requires an elimination of your ego, and praying does require humility, you'll resist prayer. If you have a hard time praying or approaching humility, part of that difficulty may be concealed in the belief that you need to "chop" your ego down to size (akin to self-annihilation) as a prerequisite to being humble or spiritual. It's a short step to believe if you're humble you'll be taken advantage of.

Many mystics and spiritual masters write of self-mortification and "the self" dying to the "will of God". Reading these works as prose (literally), not as poetry (metaphorically), is one source of major corruption. The metaphor of death implies changing yourself so that your values are prioritized differently. Look at self-mortification ("dying" to the will of God) this way: Notice the powerful focus of energy on "self" and "selfishness", and with the same intensity, refocus that energy on service to spiritual principles. The "I" of selfishness "dies"—self-mortification—in a symbolic way. Ego-willpower stays strong but is directed elsewhere. It's not about ego death; it's about ego redirection.

Monks, saints, and thousands of others, who proved themselves to be humble and spiritual, were strongly opinionated and had powerful personalities (strong egos). Many were murdered rather than abandon their values, commitment to their own understanding of God, or spirituality. This is not evidence of weak or small egos. These people had powerful egos directed at spiritual things.

Great humility is the direct result of an ego's unrelenting focus on spiritual principles.[28] The task of a person in spiritual transformation is changing the focus of their ego from self-destructive, non-spiritual behaviour to devoted obedience to the five spiritual principles. *"Every day is a day when we must carry the vision of God's will into all of our activities. 'How can I best serve Thee—Thy will (not mine) be done.' ...We can exercise our willpower along this line all we wish. It is the proper use of the will."*[29] It would require a well-organized and willful ego to comply with this.

Should you do this in some way similar to what the spiritual masters did, as advised in Step Eleven (which encapsulates the themes of Steps Two, Six, and Seven, and reprioritize your values with spiritual principles are at the top of the list), you will never again have to force yourself to pray or meditate. Ever. The irony is your ego will be just as big as it ever was.

Prayer

People getting recovered often experience an automatic belligerence towards prayer. Sometimes it's vicious enough to prohibit them from praying, and they relapse and die because of their refusal to pursue spirituality. Very often, however, people stay just on the very edge of spirituality, only dipping their toes in the waters of prayer (and meditation). This reluctance to pray, or demonstrating an intermittent effort, is evident in all manner of mediocre recovery and socially approved addictions like sex, shopping, relationships, exercise and in long bouts of depression, irresponsibility, moodiness, and petulant complaining.

Prayer is: *1. a. A reverent petition made to God or another object of worship. b. The act of making a reverent petition to God or another object of worship. 2. An act of communion with God or another object of worship, such as in devotion, confession, praise, or thanksgiving. 3. A specially worded form used to address God or another object of worship.*[30] In order to explore prayer, it is important to start from a place of grounded orientation.

---

[28] In counselling and any "spiritual" work, I work at having clients develop not small, whittled-down egos, but powerful egos focused on truly ethical, spiritual endeavor. In this manner, much resistance to the idea of spirituality decreases because the ego isn't threatened with annihilation.

[29] *Alcoholics Anonymous*, p. 85.

[30] *The American Heritage® Dictionary of the English Language, Third Edition,* © 1996, Houghton Mifflin Company. Electronic version.

I've divided prayer into three broad classifications to provide a basic sense of structure, so that the student at prayer can more wisely choose a focus for their interior life. The three classifications are Prayers of Petition, Contemplation, and Gratitude.

Prayers of Petition

Dear God:
Because of this __insert circumstance__, and these itemized, righteous "good" reasons: __insert one or more justifications__, may I (and/or __insert name__) please have __insert desired gift(s)__."

> *Thank you very much,*
> *__(insert name & address)__*

These prayers are styled after the suppliant asking their higher power for specific things. It's a one sided conversation with requests.

"Our immediate temptation will be to ask for specific solutions to specific problems, and for the ability to help other people as we have already thought they should be helped."[31] Even with devotion to a higher power, and integrity based in the five spiritual principles, all petitionary prayer runs the risk of complications, even though it's necessary in one convoluted context.

There are many drawbacks to petitionary prayer. If you "miraculously" get what you want, it tends to lead you to be self-righteous and self-congratulatory, and for you to then rest on your laurels or become greedy. If you pray and don't get what you want, it tends to lead into feeling forsaken; that you're doing something wrong; that God is punishing you, or God likes those others more that hint or brag their prayers were answered. This undermines faith, and may lead to abandoning God and pouting: "I'm not praying any more. I never get what I want." You may increase your efforts to the point of being obsessive: "When I get this prayer-thing perfect, then I'll get what I want," or "When I finally get rid of all my character defects, then God will listen to me." Any time you superimpose God on Santa Claus, you set yourself up to flatter your selfishness or slander your own character; there is no escape from this.

"In [asking for specific solutions] *we are asking God to do it our way. Therefore, we ought to consider each request carefully to see what its real merit is."*[32] Any petition to your higher power (whether sign or symbol) contains your suggested solution for a situation you've assumed is a problem: your uncle gets over the cancer, your friend gets through the housing crisis, the twins have a nice camping trip, your spouse comes home safely. These petitions are a grocery list for God's Supermarket. Or, you seek some

---

[31] *Twelve Steps and Twelve Traditions*, p. 102.

message from "God", to you personally, that you should or shouldn't move, quit, marry, divorce, leave, stay, hide, run, or buy something.[33] You're asking the deity of your choice to intervene on your personal behalf, to keep you out of pain, or in happiness, or to rescue you out of responsibility.[34]

The moral value, which lies underneath the petition, is rooted in fear, selfishness, or moral righteousness and lies at the core of this risky style of prayer. Within that moral value is the trap you set for yourself in how you righteously justify your prayer wish list. Praying righteously is always spiritually dangerous. Praying that someone dies in a fiery car crash because they were late for your party would be a morally "bad" thing; you can't justify it. Praying it doesn't rain on the day of the orphans' picnic has an ambience of moral uprightness—unless you're the farmer in the next field who's praying for rain for his crops. Praying a child recover from cancer is easily justifiable—it's "righteous". A perceived or justified moral righteousness rationalizes petitions to "God".

Petitionary prayer isn't necessarily wrong; it's dangerous. Those desiring spiritual transformation, and those with weak faith, righteous spiritual intent, or pronounced character defects need to be very cautious regarding its use. It's often a compensation for temporal laziness, or an effort to thwart disappointment and control life. Regardless of any apparently ethical or altruistic agenda, all petitionary prayer is to some degree self-serving. It can't *not* be—we're human.

The novice at prayer usually misperceives prayer-time with God as similar to an audience with royalty, or a job interview with the head of the corporation: have your shoes shined, fingernails clean, hair combed, and be on top of the agenda—get it right. Don't make mistakes and don't waste time; God's busy. This is indicative of God being seen as a sign, the CEO of the Universe, and not a symbol. This creates needless anxiety and all manner of corruption in spiritual principles.

Most well-intentioned people live in perpetual dislocation within the disciplines of prayer and meditation. They're confused, live with doubt, and worry they weren't eloquent, or might have said the wrong things to "God". I remember speaking about this with a monk. I was living in a monastery at

---

[32] *Twelve Steps and Twelve Traditions*, p. 102.

[33] In a truly spiritual life, there are no problems: there are only opportunities to work on humility. Remember the Two-Step Dance, p. 407.

[34] The motivation for most petitionary prayer, albeit well disguised, is rooted in selfishness. It is the same with pursuing a relationship with The Divine Spirit, or the desire to acquire faith—both are most often rooted in selfishness. *"Some believe that spiritual achievement will bestow temporal authority; others, that it will compensate for weaknesses of character; and still others, that it will make available to them... the material objects of their desires. While such ulterior motives are present, true faith is not possible." The Mystical Christ,* Manly P. Hall, The Philosophical Research Society, Inc., 1993, p. 17.

the time, preparing for residency, and we were walking along a trail in the woods on the monastery grounds. I told him of my anxiety about not getting my prayers "right". I remember him smiling reassuringly. As I recall it today, many years after it happened, this is my perspective of what he advised:

> Be kind to yourself. Accept your ever-present, human limitations as an important part of the unfolding of the universe, and graciously stop trying to understand "God". A higher power isn't anything that I can conceive of, ever, and neither can you. There are only metaphors and symbols that are always inadequate, and can never do more than magnificently misrepresent whatever is God's true nature. You don't accept this yet.
>
> Experiencing gratitude and love are gifts from the universe (or a higher power) that become our prayers. For myself, I wish my life to become a total prayer to God; that my whole being and existence is the prayer; and so, when I experience doubt or confusion or anxiety that is my prayer to God, too.
>
> Pray your confusion and your anxiety to your higher power just as sincerely as your love and gratitude. These are as important as anything else we offer. Contained within this is humility, and your faith and trust that your higher power will understand your prayer as you giving yourself completely. The greatest gift we can offer "God" is everything.

In life, and especially in the midst of your prayers, should you become lost or anxious, or feel guilty for some perceived fault, then *that* becomes your prayer' pray your confusion to God, too. In prayer, don't search for fancy words—that's Impression Management, and insincere. If you're angry with God because you've misperceived God's "participation" in your life, offer that anger in prayer, too. Should you have turned your will *and life* over to the care of God, all of these are in your prayers because they are you.

If a person in spiritual transformation prays for reduced character defects or another day of sobriety and abstinence so they can have a peaceful life (which are petitions for gifts), they have may have recast God as Santa Claus. What is spiritually appropriate is requesting these "gifts" so as to be of service and thereby reduce or eliminate the chaos and pain you inflict on others. With this motive for prayer, certainly the secondary effect will be serenity for you. Serenity is not for your personal pleasure, it's so you can help bring peace to other troubled souls. When deciding to petition your higher power for *any*thing, do *every*thing to ensure that it is from humility, and of benefit to others (the primary reason), and of secondary benefit to yourself.

Prayers of Contemplation

This style of prayer is sometimes called Prayer of Quiet, where suppliants become still within their heart, and peaceful in reverence. They communicate to their higher power *without doing*. In using some wisdom from Taoism it might be described as *Wu Wei* in prayer—accomplishing without action; acting deliberately but with deliberate non-purpose. This unique, prayerful meditation takes you to rest with the knowing of God.[35] This is a close cousin to some meditative practice.

Prayers of Gratitude

These are [supposed to be] a communication from a person to their higher power offering gratitude and praise, and asking for nothing for themselves. In the spiritual perspectives that superimpose God and Santa Clause, when something "nice" happens, like your drunken relative is well behaved at the wedding reception, or someone survives their surgery... well, you've received "a present" and polite people say thank you. As regards this particular type of prayer, you're essentially telling your higher power you're pleased and grateful for getting your own way. There is no humility in these prayers.

For people with a different spiritual perspective, prayers of gratitude mean gratitude for everything, including "hardship" (calling anything "hardship" is only an arbitrary, self-serving interpretation of some circumstance). In Chapter 11, there is reference to Boethius, and his view of spiritually "troubled" times, which applies here.

Prayers of gratitude are not to be offered because the bus was on time or somebody found their lost wallet. Prayers of gratitude are offered as an active recognition of the perpetually available state of love and grace, and an appreciation for the implacable grandeur of the experience of our humanness through spirituality, regardless of the circumstance. This embodies humility.

Incidental to this, the more a person submits to humility on behalf of a higher power of their own understanding, the *less* emotional pain they will feel, regardless of what happens. The realization of a true spiritual state of being is through devoted, humble obedience to spiritual principles. If stated

---

[35] *Contemplative Prayer*, by Thomas Merton, Image Books, Doubleday, 1996, although sometimes esoteric, is a valuable guide to contemplative prayer, which makes it a fine volume for learning about prayer through Meditations on Wisdom (which is discussed in the section on Meditation that follows).

in non-theological terms, this touches the essence of Buddhism: the absence of dukkha (dislocation) through compassionate non-attachment.

When prayers are primarily of contemplation and gratitude, you eventually pray only because "God" is worthy of being prayed to. Consider reducing petitionary prayer and increasing prayers of contemplation and gratitude, which are closer to the heart of ethical spiritual endeavor. When assessing your commitment to prayer, ask yourself: "Do prayers interrupt my life, or does life interrupt my prayers?"

Meditation

Meditate: 1. To reflect on; contemplate. 2. To consider or reflect at length. 3. To engage in contemplation, especially of a spiritual or devotional nature.[36]

I've arbitrarily divided meditation into two categories: (i) Meditations *of* Transcendence (there are two subtypes: Intellectual and Physical); and (ii), Meditations *on* Wisdom. These two general categories are only to help clarify the issues of meditation within Step Eleven, and to enable you to more clearly appreciate what the original twelve-step program advises. *It's important to remember*: You can explore meditation in the context of the Eastern traditions, Transcendental Meditations (TM), or in the context of Step Eleven, Meditations on Wisdom. They are different, require a different mind-set, and offer different results.[37]

As you explore meditation in the context of the original twelve-step literature, that literature was written long *before* North American culture experienced any noticeable presence of Eastern philosophy. Step Eleven, written c. 1937, was at least twenty-five years before the work of Alan Watts, Ram Dass, Aldous Huxley, D.T. Suzuki, Thomas Cleary, Dwight Goddard, and many others, fostered a conscious presence of Eastern philosophy in North America. Additionally, the TM movement that took root in the 1960's was at least twenty-five years after the meditation instructions for Step Eleven were written.

---

[36] *The American Heritage® Dictionary of the English Language, Third Edition,* © 1996, Houghton Mifflin Company. Electronic version.

[37] There is actually a third style of meditation—Meditations of Safety (Guided Meditation). This is usually offered in some therapeutic context. You sit relaxed and a meditation tour guide (therapist, counsellor, or seminar leader) tells you what to think by creating images that they suggest. It's an imaginary story with a specific goal: to create a sense of safety, to reduce anxiety, or to realize dreams. A specific path is created by someone else to get you there. This is valuable in some situations (very therapy-oriented) and harmful in others, but it is not what is required for liberation through Step Eleven or Siddartha-Buddhist meditation. As an aside, what appears to be more effective than guided meditation for anxiety and tension is to understand and become skilled at body energy healing.

(i) Meditations of Transcendence - TM

Transcendence, as a discipline meditation, originates out of the Eastern religious philosophies of Hinduism and ancient Asian disciplines similar to Taoism. Generally, Transcendental Meditation (TM) is to rise above, and, at the same time disable, the distractions of mind-stuff and sentient chaos. When done effectively, TM takes you beyond your pain or above the dislocation of your life to achieve a state of "blissful absence". TM, in one way, is intended to create harmony that resides beyond the broken images of perceived truth. There are two basic approaches to TM — Intellectual and Physical.

TM — Intellectual: These would be meditations that require no movement and focused intellectual concentration: sitting quietly, generally immobile, concentrating on breathing, and/or concentrating on *OM* or other mantras, and chanting. With years of due diligence, the meditator achieves transcendence. This would include some types of stationary yoga.

Mantras and intellectual meditation are to replace the chaos and broken images of thought-truth with a rhythm of focused awareness. The rhythm is established within the mantra or the pattern of concentration. Depending on the skill and intent of the meditator, and the style and rhythm of the mantra, it can elevate you into transcendence, *but* you may also just remain at the level of rhythmic, focused awareness.

When done well, the meditator "leaves" chaos and distraction and goes into a state of absence and pseudo-harmony. This is not necessarily transformation, it could be just avoidance.

TM — Physical: In this group are Tai Chi, Qi Gong, and those types of Yoga that incorporate movement and balance. These include focused breathing and sometimes include mantras. These physical disciplines aren't necessarily intended to transcend the spontaneous mind-chaos (which is the specific intent of the intellectual style of TM). They are to bring harmony and grace to our physical *and* mental condition. When done well, the meditator "leaves" chaos and distraction and goes into a state of absence and pseudo-harmony.

When you practice TM or any similar discipline, with wise discipline, there's a "leaving" from what you are at the beginning, and a "going" to another conscious state. When the practice is over, you most often return to the previous state, where you were before you left. Sometimes the only thing that's really accomplished is a short vacation from you, which is a glib metaphor for what addicts tried to do in their addictions.[38] [And, too,

---

[38] This is one aspect of a subtle corruption that is sometimes present in "spiritually minded" people—their spiritual endeavors are brief vacations from their greed or selfishness. (cont'd)

some TM can be a justified-by-righteousness, mind-altering experience that isn't spiritual — it depends.]

Since the 1960s, Transcendental Meditation and mantra work have become very well known, and these are what people usually think of when someone speaks of meditation. However, *the original twelve-step literature teaches a uniquely different style of meditation*, which is rarely appreciated, because of the more popular awareness of TM. Not all meditation is transcendental. TM is valuable, but it should not, and in fact, cannot, substitute for what is suggested in Step Eleven. Addicts have to transform their personalities, not transcend them.

What needs to be clarified is the meditation suggested within the original Step Eleven is not TM. It's a Meditation *on* Wisdom, which is a crucial practice that challenges the recovered addict's self-limiting beliefs and prejudices. If recovered addicts are to reduce their defects of character, and enhance their spirituality so they can improve their conscious contact with their higher power, they must *consciously* let go of their old ideas. This is accomplished by forcing themselves to appreciate the wisdom of others through thoughtful reflection (Meditations *on* Wisdom), not TM. Transcendental Meditation is also important — but in a very different context.

(ii) Meditations on Wisdom

Rather than transcending the human condition, Step Eleven advises to *"improve our conscious contact..."* — to deliberately develop an awareness that promotes insight and humility. Meditations on Wisdom are how addicts detach from self-limiting ideas, dismantle old defense mechanisms, and alter perceptions. It's a spiritually focused, deliberate, self-initiated reorganizing of themselves through the wisdom of others, which is tough for addicts because of their well-concealed arrogance. Meditations on Wisdom are active humility, which creates inner vision.

There isn't a Step Eleven prayer, *per se*. The original twelve-step literature provides an example of a Meditation on Wisdom and offers instruction at the same time. The author(s) chose a prayer written by St. Francis of Assisi to demonstrate the technique of a Meditation on Wisdom.

They go to a church, a meeting, a therapist, a meditation retreat, thereby escaping their guilt and corruption and feel good about the impression they're making (mostly on themselves), and then return from the spiritual outing (like a picnic), to be themselves again, changing nothing. There is a well-concealed and self-righteous Impression Management scheme operating in this lifestyle. Challenging this widespread behaviour is incredibly complicated.

The Instructions for Meditations on Wisdom

"Well, we might start like this. First let's look at a really good prayer. We won't have far to seek...." And, *"The world's libraries and places of worship are a treasure trove for all seekers."*[39] First: find a prayer or spiritual writing that attracts you, and then *"As beginners in meditation... "* [Here are the instructions...]

"...reread [it] *several times very slowly savoring every word..."*
"...trying to take in the deep meaning of each phrase and idea..."
"...drop all resistance..." and *"...debate has no place."*
"...rest quietly with the thoughts of someone who knows..."
"...ponder what its mystery is", and
"...seek all those wonders still unseen..."

The goal is to *"...experience and learn* [and to]... *be strengthened and lifted up,"*[40] which has little in common with TM, and much to do with re-education and being open-minded. Again, this creates inner vision.[41]

"It is to be hoped that every A.A. who has a religious connection which emphasizes meditation will return to the practice of that devotion as never before."[42] Many people may not have a religious connection that encourages meditation, or you may wish to distance yourself from your earlier religious associations regarding this quote; however, there is this perspective: For those addicts without a prior religious connection, being voluntarily involved in a process that strongly emphasizes a connection to a higher power of your understanding and encourages meditation, regardless of whether or not you ever had a previous association that encouraged meditation, you have one now.

The Example for a Meditation on Wisdom

"The actual experience of meditation and prayer across the centuries is... immense."[43] The original AA literature offers an example and explains how to apply this style of meditation to your spiritual life—which *is* your life. The example, from St. Francis of Assisi, begins: *"Lord, make me a channel of thy peace..."* Granted, the example is a Christian prayer, but the

---

[39] *Twelve Steps and Twelve Traditions*, pp. 98, 99.
[40] Ibid., pp. 99-100.
[41] Thich Nhat Hanh asks for meditation on wisdom in the writing of Thomas Merton: *"I hope you will read the words of this wise visionary slowly and mindfully, in a way that your reading will itself be a contemplation, a meditation, a prayer of the heart."* The Introduction, by Thich Nhat Hanh, *Contemplative Prayer*, by Thomas Merton, Image Books (Doubleday), 1996, p. 7.
[42] *Twelve Steps and Twelve Traditions*, p. 101.
[43] Ibid., p. 98.

teaching of meditation on wisdom isn't meant to be restricted to meditations on Christian doctrine.

After quoting that prayer, *Twelve Steps and Twelve Traditions* applies that example to the instructions for meditations on wisdom (noted above). The book advises that you reread it several times, savor each word, take in the deep meaning, drop any resistance, relax, be strengthened, use constructive imagination, focus undisturbed, find the inner essence, take a good look at where you stand now, try to glimpse the ideal, and decide what would happen if you moved closer to that ideal. The text refers to all of this as *"...a fragment of what is called meditation."*[44] By doing all of this you are meditating *on* the wisdom of a spiritual master. That's a Meditation on Wisdom (Simple, eh?)

Meditation on any spiritual or philosophical writing that pushes you to challenge your self-limiting thoughts tends to draw you closer to a higher power (as you understand this). This is how you abandon your old ideas and secret prejudices. Learn about yourself and about spirituality. Adopt new values; don't cling to carefully reconfigured old ones. What do the spiritual masters (from any spiritual tradition) know that you don't know? According to Step Eleven, you are charged with the responsibility to find out.

Consider how these instructions for meditation apply in the context of understanding great artistic endeavor. Meditate on the applicability of what I am about to offer. Great actors, musicians, philosophers, scientists, writers, poets, painters, dancers, social activists, film directors, sculptors, etc., contain, within their work, some symbolic connection to humanity at large *and* to the transcendent. This isn't always easily visible in their work, but there's a symbolic connection to transcendence for the meditative observer. That connection is its quality of greatness.[45]

When people witness great creativity, or hear a profound spiritual insight they don't understand, oftentimes there's an immediate tendency to dismiss it. They create a shallow argument to conceal their ignorance or laziness; or dismiss the artist through racism, sexism, or character assassination. The task for an authentic spiritual pilgrim is to not do this. At the minimum, be accepting, and if you're interested then listen, study, call yourself to task, discover, and savor the transforming connection. Rest quietly with the insight of someone who knows. Ask, "What are they teaching me?" Do not lose the opportunity to be enlarged by humility.

---

[44] *Twelve Steps and Twelve Traditions*, pp. 99-101, emphasis added.
[45] The list of endeavors stated here is certainly incomplete. As I encourage you to meditate on endeavors of great merit, I do not endorse consuming gratuitous violence, pornography, hate literature, religious elitism, and the like.

"When there's something you don't understand, you have to go humbly to it. You don't go to school and sit down and say 'I know what you're getting ready to teach me.' You sit there and you learn. You open your mind. You absorb. But you have to be quiet, you have to be still."

John Coltrane, Musician[46]

Lao Tse is reported to have said: *"To venerate without understanding, to worship without inner vision, is blasphemy and vain."* Creating inner vision is through Step Eleven meditation and is enabled by devoted self-examination at Step Ten. Step Eleven meditation is not TM and it's not to transcend the human condition (which most addicts tried to do, and eventually failed miserably, in acting out). It's to challenge your own prejudices and defects, *and* to deepen your awareness and commitment to a spiritual life by absorbing the wisdom of others.

Through this, you plumb the depths of your own character, and go past "yourself" into the universal soul that resides within you. This takes... *devotion: 1. Ardent, often selfless affection and dedication, as to a person (or a process). Sometimes a synonym for love. 2. Religious ardor or zeal; piety. 3. Often: devotions: acts of religious observance or prayer.*[47]

Seven Odds and Ends

(1) Meditate on the Step Eleven instructions for meditation.

(2) The process of understanding and completing Steps One to Nine actually involves doing Meditations on Wisdom on each step. At Step Eleven, the spiritually transformed person is instructed to meditate on the wisdom of the spiritual masters, whose insights will enhance but may not necessarily be particular to, the original twelve-step philosophy.

(3) Include some meditation on those points of view you see as different from yours. Contemplate another view *from* the other point of view. For example, if you're a Muslim, study Christianity; if Jewish, study Buddhism for a while; and likewise for Christians—be respectfully informed about other perspectives. Work to appreciate the wisdom of the parallel. There are no opposites; there are only parallels. *"Be quick to see where religious peo-*

---

[46] Years ago I clipped this out of a magazine, and have only a small piece of glossy paper with this quote on it. It appears to be from a mail-order club of some description, but I don't know which one. To the editor who included it in the magazine, thank you.
[47] *The American Heritage® Dictionary of the English Language, Third Edition,* © 1996, Houghton Mifflin Company. Electronic version.

ple are right."[48] This is not to convert yourself to another belief; it's to temper any prejudice with compassion and awareness. This is difficult. Belligerent, out-of-hand rejection of a different viewpoint is arrogant. At the level of mystic, there are no religious enemies.

It's easy to attend lectures and read books by people who agree with you, but that practice is disastrously limiting. Joseph Conrad wrote: "[people] *learn wisdom with extreme slowness, and are always ready to believe promises that flatter their secret hopes...*".[49] I add: they prefer to cater to their coveted prejudices. Meditations on Wisdom in Step Eleven counteract this dangerous tendency.

(4) To proselytize without invitation advertises arrogance and insecurity. Avoid offering opinions unless they're invited, and only then if they can be offered without belligerence, *and only* if you aren't benignly indifferent to others agreeing or disagreeing with you.

(5) Twelve-step people often suggest that praying is talking to God and meditating is listening for an answer. According to Step Eleven, Meditations on Wisdom are to seek the spiritual wisdom of others, not to listen for the voice of God. In Transcendental Meditation people seek the bliss of nirvana or peaceful-nothingness. Either way, hearing the voice of God isn't a part of meditation. A person can wait for an awfully long time to hear "God", and besides, waiting and listening isn't seeking

(6) Create a place for Meditations on Wisdom for yourself. Because of preconceived ideas about meditation in the Eastern traditions i.e. the lotus position, mudras, incense, and sitting on a cushion or a floor mat, what I suggest will be remarkably different from what many people might think a meditation place is.

Step Eleven meditation is to quietly contemplate the wisdom of the insights and philosophies of the spiritual masters. You'll need a comfortable chair—but not too comfortable, you don't want to fall asleep; a decent reading lamp, a nearby bookshelf, at least one dictionary (with etymology), writing paper, writing implements, and several spiritually oriented books, the content of which you would like to explore and meditate on.

If you want to meditate on *The Bhagavad-Gita*, *The Koran*, *The Upanishads*, or any other translated writing, get two different translations (at least a decade apart in terms of the publication date) and compare them.

---

[48] *Alcoholics Anonymous*, p. 87. Also, on p. 48 is this: "*...we often found ourselves handicapped by obstinacy, sensitiveness, and unreasoning prejudice* [and] *...spiritual things made us bristle with antagonism. This sort of thinking had to be abandoned.*"
[49] The quote is from Part III of *Nostromo*, by Joseph Conrad, Wordsworth Classics, 1996.

That's a part of acquiring wisdom—the wisdom of the writing, and of the translator. If you're meditating on the writings of T. Merton, F. Nietzsche, C. Jung, or some other similar author, consider beginning with a "Best of..." collection. Create a meditation place for Step Eleven where you can quietly read and study. Allow yourself to be taught.

(7) You entered a twelve-step program blind to the machinations of the universe that placed you there. After a few months of abstinence and participation, should you think you are still "in" your group because your higher power put you there, you are externalizing responsibility and, in a sense, holding "God" accountable for yourself.

Recognize that at some point after arriving, it was *you* who decided to stay. You may have asked for spiritual help, but it was you who decided to ask. As you make progress, there are those moments you cannot explain, that you may interpret as the hand of Providence, but it is you who decided to notice (or ignore) them. You also choose to pray and meditate (or not). Inherent in all of these is the responsibility of choice. An appropriate self-respect arises from the spiritual choices you've made.

Consider breathing and thinking. You don't necessarily take pride in these behaviours; however, you can choose to be reasonably physically fit and thus choose how you breathe, or through devotion to spirituality, you can choose how you think. Often I've written that you are completely re-sponsible for the chaos and turmoil in your life. Wise choices are the seeds of healthy self-respect. This work is a *voluntary* choice on your part—don't complain.

Step Eleven is specifically designed to enhance your intimate relation-ship with *That Which Art*.[50] And, with Step Eleven, you continuously challenge whatever level of spiritual fitness you find yourself at. Its design is to establish a standard set by spiritual principles and not by you. It will also maintain, within you, a consistent, conscious awareness of your higher power beyond what you might otherwise, accidentally comprehend.[51] If you let it, it will take you out of yourself and put you into the spiritual wisdom of the ages. Prayers of Contemplation and Gratitude, and Meditations *on* Wisdom (not TM) lead and cause you to descend into a soulful awareness of your higher power.

---

[50] *That Which Art* is a representation, in the symbolism of words, for the Great Reality, the Animating Principle, the Ground of All Being, the Clear Light of the Void... and a thousand other names.
[51] After people become firmly rooted in the practices of Prayer and Meditations on Wisdom, Meditation of Transcendence will be easier to master. In the beginning it may be judicious to spend more time trying to change your limiting defects rather than trying to transcend them.

Through the disciplines of prayer and meditation you *"...let go of old ideas,"*[52] and rest quietly with the thoughts of someone [else] who knows. There are no accidents in authentic spiritual enlightenment.

Prayer and meditation on wisdom require significant self-discipline, especially in the beginning. You will struggle. Your addicted, self-centered personality will categorize these new and unfamiliar practices as decidedly threatening. Why bother? The end of Step Eleven reads: *"Perhaps one of the greatest rewards of meditation* [on the wisdom of others] *and prayer is the sense of belonging that comes to us."*[53] This is not about belonging in your family, belonging in your meeting, or belonging in your workplace. It's about you belonging *in* the world and *to* the universe.

From a different perspective, but with a similar sense, Ram Dass represented this nicely in *The Only Dance There Is*. Regarding the concept of "home", he relates that during a road trip, he met a man at a gas station and unexpectedly ended up visiting with the man and his family. Ram Dass writes: *"So I stay for lunch... and we're all settling in, and we've all got our feet up and we're all home. I realize this is my home. Am I going to say, 'Well, I gotta go home?' ...we're all here."*[54]

One of many interpretations of his book revolves around the implication that *everyone* is our family. Throughout the book, Ram Dass describes a spiritual mindset where the universe is our home, not some geographical location behind an imaginary, politically defined boundary. By doing Prayer and Meditations on Wisdom, in the manner suggested, you will recognize you belong in this universal family.

The vast scope of what can be accomplished within Step Eleven is a testament to the devotion and insight of the cofounders of the original twelve-step program. The AA reference texts impart effective guidance and direction regarding the nature of transformation, prayer, meditation, conscious contact with your higher power, knowledge of "God's" will for you (which at its most practical is obedience to spiritual principles), and the power to carry that out. At the best of times, too many people see these as contentious, which is only the result of their own Two-Step Dance.[55]

An Existential Summary

Life, to me, often seems to be a reality-based mirage that envelops people through the eternity between birth and death. It's real because we exist, but a mirage because nothing is ever as it seems. Spiritual pilgrims enlist some version of a higher power, through prayer and meditation, to

---

[52] From How It Works, *Alcoholics Anonymous*, p. 58.
[53] *Twelve Steps and Twelve Tradition*, p. 105, emphasis added.
[54] *The Only Dance There Is*, Ram Dass, Anchor Books (Doubleday), 1973, pp. 7, 8.

assist them in their passage through this temporary existence. To appreciate the passage through this reality-based mirage with serenity—with compassion—is the result of obedience to spiritual principles.

At Step Eleven, Prayer (not petitionary) and Meditations on Wisdom (not TM) are nourishment to the life of your soul exactly as food and exercise are nourishment to the life of your body. Recovered addicts—and remember the wide range of addictions—have a purpose now, and it's a great purpose: to pray and meditate to improve their conscious contact with their higher power, which in turn brings peace to other troubled souls. For a formerly self-destructive, selfish, frightened person to have a great purpose, and to embrace it in a way that brings harmony to the world, is a magnificent accomplishment.

> *"But, this is not all… there is more*
> *action. Faith without works is dead."* [56]

---

[55] The Two-Step Dance was discussed in Chapter 8.
[56] *Alcoholics Anonymous*, p. 88.

Chapter 11

Step Twelve: Responsible for Charity of Spirit

Discussing Spiritual Transformation: Art Form or Proselytizing?

"Having had a spiritual awakening as the result of these steps, we tried to carry this message to alcoholics, and to practice these principles in all our affairs."[1]

What points to Step Twelve's importance is that it's the only step within *Alcoholics Anonymous* that has an entire chapter devoted to it. This would seem to be consistent with the frequency of various phrases that appear throughout the writing indicating that "God's will" for people in twelve-step programs is to primarily be of service to others. However, this is not a blanket injunction, there are some very specific limitations.

Step Twelve explains two different contexts within which you are to be spiritual: "carrying the message" and "in all your affairs". And, of course, in either context, the primary requirement is to role model and actually practice a life governed by spiritual principles. Regarding Step Twelve:

Respect for the Physical Body
An obvious observation is there are two perspectives to this—respect for your own body-temple, and respect for others'. Practicing spiritual principles in a responsible manner i.e., being attentive to your own and others' physical well being, allows you to peacefully integrate sensation, emotion, and behaviour within yourself.[2] When sharing your experience, strength, and hope this balance (in you) is evident in your demeanor and tends to have a calming affect on others. This avoids causing others undue stress, and makes their lives more peaceful; hence you are respectful of their physical body.

---

[1] *Alcoholics Anonymous*, p. 60, and *Twelve Steps and Twelve Traditions*, p. 106.
[2] Being appropriately attentive to diet and health is essential to a well-rounded life. From a Buddhist perspective, the path is moderation: The Middle Way.

Veracity

If you embody honesty and gentle trustworthiness in all your affairs, whether carrying the message or not, you will present yourself as being sincere. These three—honesty, gentle trustworthiness, and sincerity will arguably become the most apparent qualities in your character, whether or not anyone knows about your obedience to spiritual principles.[3] When acting in the capacity of carrying the message, these qualities allow others greater ease in making choices and encourage participation by attraction.

Humility

There are two aspects to humility: egalitarian and spiritual, and two aspects to Step Twelve: carrying the message of a spiritual awakening, and practicing spiritual principles in all your affairs.

By adhering to the egalitarian aspect of humility in all your affairs, which includes carrying the message, everyone you encounter will feel respected. This allows them to relax and, regardless of the social circumstance, they can retain their dignity and not feel demeaned or controlled. Their life will be graceful in their association with you.

If the spiritual aspect of humility isn't offered in carrying the message then it becomes proselytizing; that's promotion not attraction. The newer person will feel patronized and demeaned (even if they can't articulate it, it will be there). Spiritual humility, in whomever carries the message, allows others freedom in choosing their conception of their higher power, freedom in adopting the style of relationship with that higher power, and leaves them the sense that access to serenity isn't dependent on obedience to someone else.

Charity

Step Twelve is the second of two never-ending exercises in being generous and graceful. (The first is Step Ten.) Giving away

---

[3] Some people see "truth" as a method to correct someone's behaviour, to justify meanness, to manipulate people, or to autocratically impose values and limitations on others. This is using truth as a weapon to control others, or to establish some pecking order of entitlement, which prohibits veracity. The offering of truth will be seen as trustworthy when you're not trying to maneuver some situation to your own advantage, and you speak the truth without any manipulation. *Your truths must be presented as a lonely effort to develop your own integrity,* not as a tactic to gain external reward or control. Only then is your truth trustworthy, because it applies only to you, and can be heard by others without threat. This will be discussed at length in *Facets of Personal Transformation* regarding communication skills.

your hard-won wisdom and knowledge about the steps and spirituality, and offering serenity and acceptance, benefits everyone: authentic charity of spirit. Charity is "distributed" by your abiding by the spiritual principles, regardless of whom you come into contact with. If, in carrying the message, or in any of your affairs, there is a selfish agenda (seeking gratitude, living up to a reputation, collecting salvation points, impressing others with your devotion) you defeat charity.

Responsibility & Obedience
In making an effort to be spiritual all the time—being governed by spiritual principles in *all* your affairs, you would be exercising and demonstrating responsibility as you participate in life. When you are responsible, regardless of the inconvenience to yourself, you demonstrate obedience to spiritual principles.

As with the other two maintenance steps, a long period of diligent application is necessary to be able to apprehend what's spiritually afoot here. The more consistently you devote yourself to practicing the principles in *all* your affairs, the more graceful life will be. You'll rarely (and probably never) face indecision or turmoil. You'll be very clear about what spiritual behaviour is required of you, and without realizing it, you'll create opportunities for other people to bring harmony to their world.

Observations About Words and Phrases

"Having had…" I've discussed that becoming recovered happened in the first nine steps. Therefore, by Step Twelve, a substantive personality change should have already occurred. Step Twelve facilitates improving upon the already established changes. Similarly, "continued" from Step Ten and "to improve" from Step Eleven also refer to something that has already happened. In Step Twelve, *"Having had"* is consistent in that it, too, refers to spiritual awakenings that have already happened.

"…a spiritual awakening…" When reading the first printing of the first edition of *Alcoholics Anonymous,* many people got the impression that there had to be some sudden, profound awareness of God, otherwise, they weren't doing it right. This misperception was corrected in subsequent printings by the addition of the appendix Spiritual Experience.[4] A spiritual awakening is any change in your personality, *however small,* sufficient to bring about recovery from addictions. There isn't anything noteworthy or

---

[4] *Alcoholics Anonymous*, p. 569.

spectacular in the subtle, slow, small changes that are overlooked in the face of a busy, spiritually oriented lifestyle.

Your spiritual experiences are most often revealed in the fact that you are a little bit more willing to be honest, a tiny bit more willing to give charitably, and a little more willing to pray or meditate. They are usually noticed weeks (or months) after the fact: spiritual awakenings all, and primarily the slow, transformative type.[5]

If you're not praying and meditating regularly, there won't be slow, subtle changes there'll be no changes. But out of arrogance and pride (fear), and almost subconsciously, you'll create the impression there are changes to keep your reputation abreast of your abstinence seniority. It's pretty hard to attract people to sponsor, or have any influence in your peer group, or be taken seriously, if you're five or fifteen years sober and still acting like a newcomer. Impression Management hides neglect of spiritual principles. If you aren't regularly praying and meditating as suggested, there are no spiritual experiences. You're just pretending there are.

"*...as the result...*" There is only one result—the spiritual awakening—not the job, the relationship, the new furniture, or getting your name in the phonebook. These things will appear in a sober life, but however pleased you may be with social success these self-satisfying accomplishments are not the intent of ethical step work.

"*...of these steps...*" The result isn't from any steps, or some steps, it's from *these* steps. The result isn't from being a sponsor or going to meetings, or doing service work. Treatment centres, self-help books, therapists, sponsors, your own personal reorganizations of these steps, and any variation of these steps, aren't *these* steps. Becoming recovered isn't a matter of rocket science or creative genius; it's a matter of obedience... to *these* steps.[6]

"*...we...*" Throughout this book, I've suggested that the "we" and "our" in the original AA literature are only a grammatical representation of what each individual did (or must do). Here, the same grammatical representation applies. Under most circumstances, it is spiritually correct to interpret "we" as you, personally who is being charged with the responsibility of carrying the message and practicing the principles. However, there is this advisory:

---

[5] This is referred to as a conversion experience, detailed in *The Varieties of Religious Experience*, Lecture IX, by William James, The Modern Library, Random House, 1994. "*In the volitional type the regenerative change is usually gradual...* ," p. 228. The second type is "*...the type by self surrender...* ," which, although much less common, is, as a rule, startling and much more interesting. It isn't difficult to appreciate that addicts of any stripe, having a decided tendency to live in drama, ignore the slow and look (or wait impatiently) for the startling conversion experience.

[6] I spoke to this idea regarding The Promises: to get these promises, you must complete *these* steps.

In the instance of your speaking to a raw newcomer, in the first few encounters, it's wise to attend those discussions with someone else. Should two people attend the twelve-step call, or even three, there's a greater opportunity for the new person to relate to the information presented.

However, in the situation where you attend to yet another one of the several relapses of a person you've sponsored for some time, how effective is it to rehash the same issues you've both discussed so many times before? Obviously, what you both are doing isn't working. Encourage them to seek a fresh approach with someone else. Do not get caught up in the underlying drama (yours or theirs).[7]

It takes experience and humility to know when it's more effective to "carry the message" alone, when to insist on bringing someone, or when to excuse yourself entirely from someone else's drama. If you're ever in doubt, err of the side of humility and seek wise spiritual counsel. Bear in mind, too, if the person doesn't want what you have, even though they proclaim otherwise, nothing you say or do will work.

From what I've seen, not often enough do helpers excuse themselves from the drama of someone else's life. It takes great humility for the sponsor or counsellor to recognize that they, the "helper", are at the end of their own dead-end street, and that they must set someone free from their own limitations, and do this without blaming and with compassion.

"*...tried to carry...*" It doesn't say succeeded, it says tried. It's very clearly written that you "*...don't waste time trying to persuade* [them]." "*If* [they are] *not interested in your solution... ,*" or "*If* [they think they] *can do the job in some other way,*" Note: "*We find it a waste of time to keep chasing* [someone]... ".[8]

If someone doesn't want some reasonably close approximation of sobriety by taking the spiritual twelve-step path, move on. A newcomer, or someone returning after one of many relapses, may certainly want what you have, but is determined to attain it by some other means, which is fine (for them). They may die in the effort, but that isn't your concern, it's theirs. As advised in the original literature, invite them to try some controlled drinking

---

[7] Almost invariably in these situations, when the same sponsor tries to help the same person through many relapses, the helper, sponsor, or family member has taken a willing but unwitting role in the drama of the person who continuously relapses. The helper or sponsor (or sometimes therapist) may have taken a martyr role, or have subtly defined themselves as a hero/savior. This is an enabling role in the melodrama of the practicing addict's life. To exit this style of relationship requires a very deep self-examination on the part of the helper, compassion without pity, and often a kind, firm exit from the drama. Here are two important references to this aspect of the helper-relationship: *The Only Dance There Is*, Ram Dass, Anchor Books, 1973, p. 73; and *Back To One, A Practical Guide for Psychotherapists*, Sheldon Kopp, Science and Behaviour Books, 1977, p. 113.

[8] *Alcoholics Anonymous*, pp. 90, 95, 95, 96, respectively.

or acting out.[9] I have often invited obviously unwilling people to try some controlled acting out, quietly adding, "I hope, however, that you don't die in the experiment, or even worse, kill someone else."

Over-explaining, cajoling, brow-beating, lecturing, threatening, hinting, declaring, arguing, enticing, entreating, or giving ultimatums is entirely unspiritual behaviour on your part. I've worked with some people who paid money to newcomers to get them to go to meetings. If they don't want *both* what you have and how you got it, move on. Some people are shocked by my apparently calloused approach to this. *Alcoholics Anonymous* advises this course of action. People who disregard it are themselves relationship addicts. They're overly invested in saving souls to hide insecurity, look good, and collect social or spiritual brownie points.

"*...this message...*" The message you are to carry is specifically stated within the step: "*Having had a spiritual awakening as the result of these steps...* ". If you carry the message that meetings are fun, or people get a good life, or people get to have sober sex, or get their family back, then (according to Step Twelve) you're not carrying the message. Bragging about various social accomplishments has a very subversive effect on getting recovered. It creates a misalliance of commitment—switching the theme of step work from spirituality to psychology and social success (discussed in Chapter 6.

Yes, people enjoy twelve-step meetings (usually), and it's fine to talk about the pleasure of your fellowship, and it *is* important to socialize within your fellowship. I do not quarrel with these truths. However, the primary message to convey is that if people become spiritual, they will heal and become recovered from the seemingly hopeless state of mind and body that is destroying them. There are a significant number of sober or otherwise abstinent addicts who are still being destroyed by a hopeless state of mind and body in socially approved addictions, *and* are completely unaware that (a) this is optional; and (b), that it can be resolved by sincere spiritual self-discipline.

Carrying "this message" means discussing spirituality (these steps) in friendly, attractive terms. If you think you're going to scare a newcomer away with spiritual talk, their acting-out will scare them back (if it doesn't kill them). How they respond to you, when you quietly and respectfully speak about spirituality, is not your concern. Besides, if you don't tell them about spirituality, and its preeminent position within recovery, you're dishonest, which means the newcomer's first twelve-step encounter is with a liar, and how spiritual is that? "*Stress the spiritual feature freely.*"[10]

---

[9] *Alcoholics Anonymous*, p. 31.
[10] Ibid. p. 93.

"...to alcoholics [addicts]*..."* The twelve-step spiritual process is for people who are addicted (to anything), and addictions are rampant in this culture. It doesn't say we tried to carry this message to schizophrenics, abusive partners, bad drivers, or corrupt politicians. The treatment for the phenomenon of addictions is twelve-step spirituality. The treatment for other "issues" is something else. Carrying this message is not for...

Saving the World

It's often apparent that some twelve-step participants believe that the world would benefit from what twelve-step programs offer: peace, serenity, love, tolerance, honesty, etc. They've decided the world is sadly lacking in virtue, and is in horrific trouble because of this. Getting this wonderful "twelve-step message" out to everyone would save the world, "Hooray for our side!"

Regardless of how laudable the intent, it's arrogant to view this process as applicable or superlative to other lifestyles, regardless of whether they harbor addictions. Should you proclaim that everyone be given this to better their world, that's uninvited proselytizing.[11] However true it may be that the world is in dire straits, it certainly requires arrogance to view these twelve steps as the panacea for the ills of the human race.

I admit there's violence we could well do without, but is there a shortage of love and harmony, or a shortage of press coverage? "Bad" people and violent sports get the front page; "saints" get Section Three, Page Two, Column Four. The public reads the front page. That's what they [you] want to read, so that's what they get. If you change your personality, you change the front page of your own newspaper.

Remember: The treatment for the phenomenon of addictions is twelve-step spirituality. The treatment for other "issues" is something else.

"...and," There are two assignments within Step Twelve. There is carrying the message (the first assignment) and practicing the principles in all your affairs (the second assignment). Since carrying the message is now a

---

[11] Consider these points: (i) Racism, sexism, conflict, prejudice, resentments, and the abstinence not-available addictions, are rampant in many twelve-step meetings, or in group business meetings, or at service committee meetings... all of which are often very feisty. If there's such a lack of spiritual focus in meetings supposedly devoted to spiritual principles, there isn't much possibility of saving the world. (ii) The original twelve-step process is only effective for addictions. If a significant portion of our population is addicted, and addictions are increasing (both of which are true), then twelve-step programs may "change the world" (sic); but not because they are a panacea for all human ills, but only because of the huge number of addicts. (iii) Because you see a value for yourself in this process does not mean it is of value to everyone. To impose what you value on others, is abusive—no different from your sponsor or your parents imposing something "that's good for you" onto you, that you don't want or believe in.

part of your affairs, it means that practicing the principles will be done all the time.

"*...to practice...*" *Practice (verb):* *1. To do or perform habitually or customarily; make a habit of. 2. To do or perform (something) repeatedly in order to acquire or polish a skill: practice a dance step. 3. To work at, especially as a profession: practice law. 4. To carry out in action; observe: She practices her* [meditation] *regularly.*[12] In practice, you are charged with the responsibility of demonstrating...

"*...these principles...*" in relation to sharing and carrying the message. Don't practice the principles of good storytelling, or of a good comedy routine. Don't hone your debating skills or social skills. Practice the maintenance steps and the spiritual principles that are embodied within them.[13]

As I've discussed elsewhere, there are many contentious discussions about what spiritual principles actually are, and also about how these should, or should not, be spoken about when working with new people. *Alcoholics Anonymous* advises: "*Stress the spiritual feature freely,*" and that the main object of that book "*is to enable you to find a Power greater than yourself which will solve your problem.*"[14] This doesn't leave too much room for debate.

"*...in all our affairs.*" This is about being spiritual in the check-out line at the store, in the movie theater, at the party, at the dentist's office, when someone interrupts your movie with a telephone survey, when someone you don't like wins the lottery, when dinner is late, and when you're late. In all your affairs includes when your spouse has an affair *and* during the ensuing divorce or reconciliation. Being spiritual is required in snowstorms, rainstorms, traffic jams, and mismanaged hotel reservations.

Practicing spiritual principles is also required when you lose your investments, your job, your parking spot, your dog, or your wallet; or sit beside noisy people in the movie theater; and when you get a speeding ticket, a sunburn, the flu, or a tax notice. Spiritual principles should be evident when you share at your twelve-step meeting, miss your plane, get fired, get hired, get laid (or don't); and especially when you don't get your own way.

---

[12] From *The American Heritage® Dictionary of the English Language, Third Edition,* © 1996, Houghton Mifflin Company. Electronic version.

[13] Elsewhere I have remarked that the steps are not principles, they are tasks to be performed. I have also observed that maintenance steps (10 – 12) are remarkably different in context from the regeneration steps (1 – 9). The regeneration steps are the on-the-job apprenticeship that trains you how to apply spiritual principles to your life. The maintenance steps are the graceful and practical embodiment of a life governed by the five spiritual principles.

[14] *Alcoholics Anonymous,* pp. 93 and 45, respectively.

Being spiritual *"in all* [your] *affairs"* is no mean feat. Spiritual transformation does not allow for friends and lovers receiving preferential
treatment. It's easy to be spiritual towards someone when that someone is
being nice. It's easy to be "spiritual" when you get your own way. Twelve-
step people are to carry the principles of spirituality out to the world, regardless of what the world and the people in it are doing to them. They may
be the only version of *Alcoholics Anonymous* that anybody ever sees, so
let's hope it's the spiritual version and not the victim/petulant version. By
investigating and volunteering for a spiritual life (respectively Steps Two
and Three), you take on a great responsibility and have a great purpose: to
be an attractive advertisement for a spiritual life, all the time.

The Especially Unique Person

We've all seen characters in movies, heard of, read about, or witnessed
first-hand people who exhibit rare talent. The uniquely quirky and tenacious
detective must catch the brilliant, unique jewel thief. Someone has an especially complex problem, so they track down and hire the uniquely trained
and especially talented therapist, accountant, doctor, carpenter, business
consultant, meditation guru, or mountain climber who is their last hope.

Everyone cheers when the Especially Unique Person (EUP) saves...
the town, the puppy, the children, the beautiful girl, the space ship, the
friendly alien, or the treasure map. We all understand that the fate of democracy, the world, the relationship, the skier lost in the avalanche depends
on some EUP, somewhere, who will make sure that the ship doesn't sink,
the skier doesn't freeze to death (they just get very cold), the town isn't
flooded, the mad scientist is thwarted, the criminal is arrested, the secret
code is broken, and... the bridegroom makes it to the church on time!
Thank goodness for the Especially Unique Person—wherever would we be
without them? However, being an EUP can carry a tremendous burden.

If the Especially Unique Person doesn't deliver the goods, thwart the
evil plot, save the day, find the kitty cat, defuse the bomb, or deliver the
computer chip then someone dies, the house burns down, the evil-doers get
the secret formula, and the world blows up—not nice prospects. And, *of
course,* it's always better if they save it, her, him, them, or us at the last possible moment. (Is there any other time to be saved?) If "we" were saved at
the first possible moment, many feature films would be seven minutes long.
Everyone cheers except the cynics, who are often only jealous because they
aren't the EUP (hence, the birth of the critic). Being an Especially Unique
Person means you automatically take a place of importance in the lives of

others. The more unique an EUP is, the more good they can do, but the more harm they can also do, too. [15]

Sponsorship

"So cooperate; never criticize,"[16] which is a pretty tall order for addicts, even sponsors, whom, I understand, are to share only their experience, strength, and hope (which does not include making up recovery rules and imposing their values). It's amazing how, in the midst of a friendly social conversation that is called "fellowship" or sponsorship, so many people conveniently forget the injunction to never criticize. Along with the injunction to never criticize, there is this observation: *"...because of your own drinking experience you can be uniquely useful to other alcoholics* [addicts]."[17]

A sponsor is an especially unique person, who is supposed to do special and important work, called sponsorship, with a charitable spirit, on behalf of a higher power, and without fanfare. It would appear logical that sponsors would willingly adhere to the tenets of the twelve steps, and encourage but never demand similar behaviour from those they help. Sponsors, and twelve-step pilgrims in general, are EUPs: *"You can help when no one else can." "You can secure their confidence when others fail." "...you can be uniquely useful to other alcoholics."*[18]

This unique ability to help carries with it an important caution *and* a significant obligation. Because of being especially unique and useful, spon-

---

[15] Being especially unique or having great talent or devotion isn't always to be appreciated in relation to calamity or misadventure. It is to be noticed and valued elsewhere. In acting: Richard Burton and Elizabeth Taylor in *Who's Afraid of Virginia Woolf*; Nicole Kidman in *Moulin Rouge*; Sidney Poitier in *In The Heat of The Night*; Bruno Ganz in *Downfall*; there are *many* others. In medicine: Louis Pasteur or Marie Curie. In politics and civil rights: Nelson Mandela, Gandhi, Dr. Martin Luther King, Jr., Rosa Parks, Malcolm X, James Reeb; there are *many* others. In music: Bach, Mozart, Louis Armstrong, Charlie Parker, Miles Davis, Ella Fitzgerald, Lenny Breau, and Eric Clapton. Mr. Clapton offered a personal perspective of his life and playing blues music that relates to this theme: *"I have tried to play folk music, play country and western, play even jazz, and a lot of pop music, but I don't do it well. I* [play the blues] *best and that's been given me to do. And as much as I've questioned it, and railed against it, and been stubborn about my path, I'm back on it. For better or for worse. I'm happier doing this."* From *The Rehearsal* (video) ©Drumlin Ltd., New York, NY, 1994. Mr. Clapton's unique ability is in music, and according to him, even though he has resisted it at times, it is most apparent within blues music; and again, there are *many* others. This is equally evident in art, dance, science, world peace (such as it is), literature, teaching, parenting, and in expressions of great love: Heloise & Abelard for example. Bill Wilson and Dr. Bob Smith qualify for being especially unique. At some time or other, the burden of being an Especially Unique Person— and it can be a burden—falls on each of us. Our unique talents or devotion may not be witnessed or appreciated on a grand scale, but the magic of the human condition is that we all harbor greatness.
[16] *Alcoholics Anonymous*, p. 89.
[17] Ibid.
[18] Ibid., p. 89.

sors must strive for genuine integrity; otherwise, those they help will become an extension of the unspiritual impression management schemes at play in the sponsor. When a sponsor, or a therapist or caregiver lives with conflicted values and spiritual negligence, is unethical, or in any addiction, those they help will not be able to get recovered. It's difficult enough to face abstinence, the steps, and spirituality without having to negotiate through any hypocrisy in people who hold themselves out as helpers. In these circumstances, to blame or hold the client/newcomer responsible for all their difficulty is reprehensible and ignores the program injunction to never blame.[19]

Yes, sponsors and therapists are human, and certainly everyone is completely responsible for their own abstinence, confusion, and relapses. We *must* each attend to our own disease, and above all, attend to it without blaming anyone or anything. But none of that absolves a helper from the responsibility to demonstrate devotion to spiritual integrity, to do no harm, and to make a noticeable effort to not impose or inject their own chaos and insanity into the lives of others.

As a sponsor, share your experience, strength, and hope, not your opinions. Rather than dispensing advice, demonstrate your own obedience to spiritual principles. Never demand obedience from anyone. When you offer advice or create and impose rules you go from sponsor to parent/personality consultant. This, indirectly and subtly, leads you to assume the role of rescuer, which demonstrates that you have an emotional investment in them getting recovered, which is entirely unwise.

When a sponsor shares their experience, strength, and hope they remain a sponsor. Sponsors can't really go wrong if they follow the instructions, sponsor people "out of the book", and relate all discussions and struggles back to spirituality and spiritual principles—some relevant passage from the AA reference texts. It's not up to the sponsor to solve the newcomer's problems; that's the newcomer's job. A sponsor doesn't have to be precocious, prescient, wise, powerful, or amazing; they have to be humble and willing to follow the instructions. The sponsor's "job" is to (a) demonstrate spiritually-focused problem solving; and (b), to teach those they help how to identify any passages in the original twelve-step literature that relate to any "problem". This means sponsors show other people how to depend on the original literature and on their higher power—on spiritual principles embodied in the maintenance steps, and not to depend on the sponsor or meetings or anything else. Spiritual transformation is an inside job and is independent of anything external, except good role modeling.

---

[19] *Twelve Steps and Twelve Tradition*, p. 47.

There's no place at all for arguing when carrying the message. None. You demonstrate sincere spirituality, and share your experience, strength, and hope. The other person either wants what you have, or they don't. What's to argue?

"Practical experience shows that nothing will so much insure immunity from drinking as intensive work with other alcoholics [addicts]. *It works when all other activities fail."*[20] It's important to notice that this statement insures immunity from drinking (abstinence), but doesn't insure a meaningful relationship with a higher power. Prayer and Meditations on Wisdom develop a relationship with a higher power, not carrying the message.

Working with other addicts will keep you sober; it won't get you spiritual. If you want to guarantee your abstinence, work with other addicts—not just ordinary work, intensive work. However, "intensive work" isn't arguing with those who don't want what you have, or intensely trying to persuade those who aren't convinced (that's browbeating and debating), or "intensely" imposing any arbitrary rules about recovery, relationships, or sex. Intensive work is being available, charitable, accepting, dependable, generous with your time, quietly open about your experience, wise about teaching them to rely on the maintenance steps (i.e. spiritual principles) not on you, and patient—being a spiritual role model.

From infancy we are taught by example that what we love is what we give our time to. If you play with your dog more than you watch TV, or talk about sports more than about spirituality, you demonstrate your priorities of affection.[21] If you don't have time to commit to sponsorship (and some people don't), then don't say yes to it. If you're chaotic and undisciplined in your life when it comes to commitments, prayer, honesty, meditation, attending meetings, etc., give someone the gift of not making their life more awkward than it already is by *not* introducing your insanity into their life. Don't let them sense they are not cared for by your lack of attention, negligence, or unavailability. Do them a favor and say no to the relationship. Charity and kindness is keeping your insanity out of their life.

Should your sponsor have little group-meetings of all their sponsees[22], take you through the steps as a group, dispense advice and opinions on rela-

---

[20] *Alcoholics Anonymous*, p. 89.

[21] I will go into this in some detail in *Facets of Personal Transformation*.

[22] *Sponsees*, a term that has come into twelve-step vogue in the last decade or so, refers to people that someone sponsors: people with less abstinence and more naiveté, whom are offered help and mentored into a twelve-step lifestyle. In recent years, that help appears to be predominately concerned with indoctrinating them into the social etiquette, psychological jargon, and shallow political correctness that prevails in meetings. Sponsors often speak about their sponsees—how many they have, how hard they work on their sponsees' behalf, how strict (cont'd)

tionships, sex, employment, finances, etc., enforce rules, or promote or use various outside step-guides for everyone's edification, then everyone's in trouble, especially your sponsor. You'll end up with a pocketful of clichés that you don't really understand, with no clear sense of yourself, of your higher power, or of how the steps apply to you personally.

If you attend meetings flirting with newcomers to collect people to sponsor, you're in trouble. If you're asked and agree to being someone's sponsor, you'd better pay attention to this: By saying "Yes," you have held yourself out to be caring, interested in another's welfare, available, generous of spirit, willing to help, knowledgeable about the program and spirituality, and respectful. You should be capable of demonstrating a visible presence of program spirituality and capable of minding your own business. This is what you imply by saying "yes" to sponsorship.

Being a sponsor is *not* being a therapist, a sexuality monitor, a personality consultant, a relationship counsellor, a financial advisor, or the sobriety police. Don't betray anyone who puts their trust in you, or misrepresent the twelve steps, or avoid spirituality; don't you create a misalliance of commitment. Especially do not betray whatever limited faith the newer person has in the program (or in you) by being a flake about your sponsorship commitment. The cost is too great. You may not relapse, but they almost certainly will.

I was a passenger in a car in a large car park one Christmastime in the early 1980s. The driver was a person who promoted himself in meetings as being quite peaceful, and who often spoke of his own spirituality. We were slowly exiting the car park because of the heavy holiday traffic. I observed the driver demonstrating impatience, anger, and racism. We got out in about fifteen minutes, but with the driver's belligerence and mean spirit, it seemed an hour. Coincidentally, later that same week, I was in the same circumstances, in the same parkade, with someone else driving. This second driver was letting people in, waving and smiling, chatting with me about something festive, and simply appreciating a sober life in the busy holiday season. It seemed like we got out of the same parkade, in the same heavy traffic, in no time at all.

In remembering the first driver, I asked the second driver what he did to have such an attitude. He quietly shrugged and we started talking about

---

they are with sponsees, how wise they are in the rules they impose upon them, how foolish their sponsees are for not complying, and flagrantly breach their sponsees anonymity by sharing details of their struggles and stories—all in tones of self-importance and phony humility. The term sponsees always seems to be used in a subtly pejorative sense (like *Normies*, which was discussed earlier), and designed to self-advertise and self-promote the sponsor at the expense of newer members. From a spiritual perspective, I can see no reason for someone to ever say anything about anyone they sponsor.

kindness, and meditating, and expectations, and cooperation. That's sponsorship.[23]

> *"Setting an example isn't the main means to influence others, it's the only means."*
>
> Albert Einstein[24]

Epilogue on "Maintenance"

There is a healthy process in the acquisition of values. In brief, it is this: Out of your rights and freedoms, discussed briefly in Chapter 2, you choose what you value. You choose it from alternatives, and when making choices, you have some knowledge of what each alternative entails. You choose what you value freely and voluntarily. What makes a value authentic is when appropriate, you announce or state what you value and live by it. You are prepared to adhere to the value in the face of opposition and personal consequence. If you aren't willing to pay for it, it isn't a value; it's a political convenience.

Since you began these steps, and especially while completing the first nine steps, you've been changing the context of your life—transforming your values. You've adopted the spiritual principles that are embodied in the maintenance steps, in (roughly) the process I outlined above. However, *"Principles only mean something if you stick by them when they're inconvenient."*[25]

The maintenance steps are in a particular order for a particular reason. In maintenance, self-examination (Step Ten) must come first. All spiritual transformation begins, and deepens, with self-awareness and responsibility by first clearing the blockages to your inner spiritual nature, which blockages were created *by* your character *in* your character. Only by reducing your defects can you access a higher power through prayer and meditation—Step Eleven. With both of these well established, only then are you capable of imparting (a) something of spiritual substance to a fellow pilgrim, and (b) able to practice these principles in all your affairs—Step Twelve.

Notice the similarity of themes in the way the first nine steps are sequenced, as compared to the way the maintenance steps are sequenced:

---

[23] Ram Dass describes a different scenario that has a similar theme in *The Only Dance There Is*, Anchor Books, 1973, p. 1. The reference begins: *"But there is the story of a monk… ".*

[24] This quote was told to me by an acquaintance. It may be apocryphal; I've been unable to find a reliable reference source.

[25] This line is a quote from the feature film, *The Contender*, written and directed by Rod Lurie, © Cinecontender Internationale, 2000.

- Steps One to Five are concerned with your character and the blockages to inner awareness: One is personality and addiction. Two is recognizing the limitations of your personality and your own willpower. Three is deciding to change the focus of your personality. Four is identifying inner defects, fears, and selfishness, and taking responsibility for them. Five is sharing information about yourself. (All this is represented in Step Ten: being aware of your character defects, admitting them, and being responsible for them.) Steps One to Five are the training ground for Step 10.

- Steps Six and Seven develop your willingness and humility in relation to your higher power: deepening your trust of, and dependence upon, God. (Represented in Step Eleven: Prayer and Meditations on Wisdom to develop faith.) Steps Six and Seven are the training ground for Step 11.

- Steps Eight and Nine focus on caring for the well being of others, charity of spirit, and responsibility. (Represented in Step Twelve: practicing the principles in all your affairs and sponsorship.)[26] Steps Eight and Nine are the training ground for Step Twelve.

Steps Ten, Eleven, and Twelve are designed to both maintain and deepen the spiritual orientation to your life, that you've supposedly established in the first nine steps. Your devotion to them is a reflection of how highly you value your relationship with your higher power.

A Fable

"Once upon a time there dwelt an old king in a palace. In the centre of a golden table in the main hall, there shone a large and magnificent jewel. Each day of the King's life, the jewel shone more resplendently.

One day a thief stole the jewel and ran from the palace, hiding in a forest. As he stared with deep joy at the stone, to his amazement the image of the King appeared in it.

'I have come to thank you,' said the King. 'You have released me from my attachment to Earth. I thought I was freed when I acquired the jewel, but then I learned that I would only be released when I passed it on, with a pure heart, to another.

---

[26] This theme will be picked up again in the next chapter "Relapse Prevention."

'Each day of my life I polished that stone, until finally this day arrived, when the jewel became so beautiful that you stole it, and I have passed it on, and am released.

'The jewel you hold is Understanding. You cannot add to its beauty by hiding it and hinting that you have it, nor yet by wearing it with vanity. Its beauty comes of the consciousness that others have of it. Honor that which gives it beauty.'"[27]

Make spirituality so beautiful that others will want to steal it from you; there's plenty to go around.

Having spiritual values like believing in kindness, not participating in or supporting violence or racism, adhering to the spiritual principles, and believing in some version of a higher power, are meaningless unless you're willing to face the consequences of adhering to those values without complaint (because you volunteered; they were freely chosen). Yes, being spiritual is very demanding, and expensive to your pride, and it does take a *very* long time to achieve, and many people will secretly view you with suspicion and possibly envy. In active addiction, the disease required that you pay with your life, and being spiritual requires that you volunteer to give your life—all of it.

Nothing is free. Everything costs something.

---

[27] *The Lazy Man's Guide to Enlightenment*, Thaddeus Golas, Bantam Books, 1981, p. 78.

Chapter 12

Relapse Prevention:
The Routine Of Spiritual Commitment

Understanding why Relapse Prevention is so simple is rather complicated. (i) There is relapse. (ii) There is relapse prevention. (iii) As you attain a deeper commitment to spirituality, and enhance your spiritual integrity, what constitutes relapse and what is required for relapse prevention will change. What is required in the first nine steps to prevent relapse is quite different from what is required in the last three steps. Should addicts getting recovered not appreciate this significant difference, they may attempt the maintenance steps but always be living in addiction, and therefore stymie all their efforts to be spiritual.

- *Relapse: verb (relapsed, relapsing, relapses) 1. To fall or slide back into a former state. 2. To regress after partial recovery from illness. 3. To slip back into bad ways; backslide.* Relapse is to go "backwards" to such a degree that the symptoms of addiction reappear, which is usually thought of, but not limited to, overt acting out.
- *Prevent: verb (prevented, preventing, prevents) 1. To keep from happening: took steps to prevent the [relapse]. 2. To keep (someone) from doing something; impede: prevented [me] from [cheating].*
- *Prevention: noun 1. The act of preventing or impeding. 2. A hindrance; an obstacle.* [1]

From these definitions it appears that relapse prevention is work or effort directed towards stopping the symptoms of addiction from returning. In Chapter 2, the symptoms of an addiction were identified as acting out and life-damaging consequences, neurosis, denial, disproportionate fear, repression, isolation (from self and others), assumptions, shame, dishonesty,

---

[1] Remind yourself to use the ordinary definitions of ordinary words when describing spiritual principles. The three definitions on this page are taken from *The American Heritage® Dictionary of the English Language, Third Edition*, © 1996, Houghton Mifflin Company. Electronic version.

withholding, selfishness, irresponsibility, arrogance, some types of fantasy and obsession, and cynicism—all chronic and entrenched, and addicts are largely blind to them. These general symptoms are often buried under slick justifications. They show up in a multitude of ways and will be evident in any of the five main categories (which are called symptom constellations), which are the general opposite of the five spiritual principles:

Symptom Constellations of Addictive Behaviour	Spiritual Principles
1) Self-destructive or harmful behaviour to self and others, including emotional disregard.	1) Thoughtful and considered self-care and respect for others.
2) Dishonesty and manipulation.	2) Veracity, regardless of the situation.
3) Arrogance, cynically superior, living with double standards. Argumentative or belligerent about things "spiritual".	3) Humility: egalitarianism *and* some considered respect for a higher power of your understanding.
4) Generally selfish, manipulation for undeserved advantage, or acting charitable with various hidden agendas.	4) Charity of spirit, which would include compassion.
5) Generally irresponsible or defiant; argumentative.	5) Responsibility and obedience to these principles.

Relapse Prevention is a deliberately focused effort, on your part, to stop these symptoms (left column) from returning. Ultimately, relapse prevention is an inside job—nudging yourself into obedience to the proven principles of spiritual behaviour.

Someone has pneumonia. The doctor advises medication (six pills a day for fourteen days), and to also do this, and that, and some other thing. A week later, the person feels much better, becomes less diligent about following the doctor's instructions, and soon the pneumonia returns. This isn't a matter of "slipping". It's defiance or irresponsible neglect. The doctor gave reliable advice about the treatment of pneumonia and the patient didn't follow instructions; it isn't a slip, it's "a deliberate". Think about what irresponsibility is concealed by using the word slip. If the patient ignores any of the physician's instructions, they invite relapse. Why aren't doctors surprised in these situations?—because they know.

In the same manner, *Alcoholics Anonymous* knows. Once you're advised that the recovery strategy is to become "spiritual", and come to reasonably believe this at Step Two, if you subsequently ignore spirituality any relapse isn't a slip, implying an accident; it's "a deliberate". A decision to ignore spiritual principles, or to ignore the step instructions, is a decision to not recover. A decision to not embrace frequent, sincere prayer and meditation is a decision to embrace addictions and turmoil.

You have manifested the phenomenon of addictions. If you are obedient to spiritual principles, which according to *Alcoholics Anonymous* are the proven remedy, the symptoms will not return. There's nothing magic about Relapse Prevention.

Relapse Prevention Plans

Treatment centres and recovery houses are proliferating, and to my knowledge, virtually all of them have some document or treatment protocol that comes under the general heading of a Discharge Plan, or a Relapse Prevention Outline. Too often these plans set up confusion, create unnecessary burdens, promote misdirection, and actually contribute to relapse. As you read this, bear in mind that:

- Addict/alcoholic newcomers are desperate, and will necessarily place great stock in their counsellors and sponsors; and,
- Caregivers in general (counsellors, doctors, psychiatrists, therapists, gurus, ministers, priests, rabbis, and especially sponsors) carry an air of mystery and authority. They *apparently* have what the newcomer wants—the insight, knowledge, and experience that contain the keys to a new life.

Caregivers and treatment programs have great influence. Not only must they have integrity, they must be seen to have integrity. Whatever they propose, like Relapse Prevention Plans, must stand up under scrutiny. The following five examples that I comment on are real examples culled from the dozens I've seen over the years. I chose these not because they are the worst (they're not. I've seen much worse), but because they reflect the more common, confusing themes present in many treatment-discharge plans.

Relapse Prevention Plan #1

This plan begins with general statistics that break down, into various categories, the projected 95 percent relapse rate after discharge from treatment. It takes the position, and not subtly, that relapse will occur, and largely ignores the possibility that newcomers may remain abstinent. It contains considerable explanation about there being no shame when you relapse; it's an expected part of the "recovery". This plan focuses almost exclusively on the steps to take after a relapse happens, making it an emergency response to relapse rather than a relapse prevention plan. (Relapses aren't earthquakes; they're preventable.) Newcomers are told that after a relapse. they are to never give up hope, to return to meetings, return to treatment, and to believe that eventually something will happen: they'll "catch on".

This plan is seven pages long and advises, several times, that to err is human (it is), and to return to acting out is akin to making a mistake (it isn't). I agree that relapse by someone very early in their pilgrimage may simply be an error out of confused ignorance; but the sentence *"Rarely have we seen a person fail who has thoroughly followed our path,"*[2] implies that relapse is optional. Once a person is established in abstinence beyond a few weeks, relapse isn't about mistakes, and it certainly isn't inevitable.

Getting recovered isn't as haphazard as this plan implies. Staying abstinent isn't a matter of chance; it's a matter of well-informed counsel, proper support, and determined effort. What attitude must there be in whoever wrote this plan, that sees newcomers as bound to relapse and spirituality as a matter of luck? Aside from the obvious cynicism, they've implied relapse is nothing more than an inevitable mistake. It isn't.

Newcomers are desperate. They'll believe what they are told. If they are told, by someone who is seen to be knowledgeable that relapse is in their destiny, it will be. Reporting that addicts are bound to fail, regardless of their efforts, is cynical and mean-spirited. It foments discouragement. This perspective allows an addict to blame the machinations of the universe, and conveniently ignore their own defiance and irresponsibility in the face of spiritual truths.

Relapse Prevention Plan #2

Here, to prevent relapse, newcomers are advised to not intellectualize. Over the first two pages there is a lengthy discourse against "intellectualizing". Then, over the last four pages, newcomers are instructed, *in noticeable detail*, to understand their denial; analyze their minimizing; examine closely their blaming; understand their rationalizations, justifications, and diversions; and through self-monitoring, think about what pain they are avoiding through their fantasies.

Overall, there are two pages telling addicts to not intellectualize, and four pages teaching them how to do just that. With no explanation offered for this contradiction, clients can't follow the instruction for relapse preven-

---

[2] *Alcoholics Anonymous*, p. 58.

tion (don't intellectualize) without ignoring the instructions to prevent relapse (intellectual analysis)—a double bind.

The other interesting contradiction is, this treatment centre represents itself as based on the twelve steps and the "Minnesota Model" of addictions treatment (spiritually based). It refers to step work and spirituality and achieving a spiritual life, in two short sentences in six pages of instruction.

Relapse Prevention Plan #3

In this example, on the first page, the plan strongly counsels clients to avoid being obsessive and preoccupied about any one area of their life. It is explained this could set up an easy segue into being obsessive about acting out and lead to relapse.

On the other side of the same page, and continuing for five pages, it advises them to: (i) talk as often as possible to people who are supportive of their relapse prevention, (ii) express as much as they can about what they're feeling, (iii) stay focused on relapse prevention by asking questions of others so they can understand their own denial and behaviour, (iv) contemplate their relapse prevention strategies at preset times each day, (v) examine their own non-compliance with these strategies, (vi) analyze anything that didn't work well to learn what other options they might consider in the future in similar circumstances, (vii) to do all of this regularly throughout the day; and (viii), it concludes with this evening exercise: Write an overall summary of their day: how they feel about it, what they might have missed, and what they might do to improve on the following day.

As with plan #2, this one sets up another double bind: Being advised not to be preoccupied, followed immediately by extensive instruction that creates preoccupation. The final page refers, in one paragraph, to twelve-step meetings, sponsorship, and spirituality.

Relapse Prevention Plan #4

In this one, newcomers are told that minor depression, daydreaming, and wishful thinking are indicative of pending relapse. These newly discharged clients are warned against defensiveness; tendencies towards loneliness (what's a *tendency* towards loneliness?), and loneliness itself; idle daydreaming (as opposed to active daydreaming? There's no clarification.); an immature wish to be happy (with no description of what a mature wish to be happy is); periods of confusion; irregular eating patterns; irregular sleep; wishful thinking; dissatisfaction with life; experiencing self-pity; and having unreasonable resentments. [Considering the general twelve-step caution against having any resentments what would a reasonable resentment be?] There is minimal explanation about any of this, and the inference to people reading this plan is that (a) these behaviours or feelings are optional, and (b) if you have them, you're in trouble.

To varying degrees, during early transformation struggles, the experiences of defensiveness, loneliness, idle daydreaming, wishing to be happy, confusion, irregular eating and sleeping patterns, dissatisfaction, some self-pity, and resentments, are not optional. Experiencing these is a necessary part of getting recovered. To instill a fear of imminent relapse regarding these routine experiences of early recovery creates problems. What's needed is to normalize these experiences, because they are normal, to encourage perseverance, and to teach response strategies.

The centre that uses this particular plan advertises that it is based on a twelve-step model of treatment. At the end of their relapse prevention plan they advise that should the newcomer begin the controlled use of any drug or alcohol, relapse is imminent. In twelve-step programs, where abstinence is vigorously encouraged, controlled use of chemicals isn't a warning sign of relapse—it is relapse.

Relapse Prevention Plan #5

This example is twenty-five pages long. There are instructions for finding a therapist, sitting in yoga postures, and TM meditating for relaxation (four pages). There's a list of twenty-three emotions, why people have them, and why they shouldn't have some of them (two pages). There are three pages of advice on diet and exercise. Spirituality and twelve-step meetings are encapsulated on one page. Sexual relationships are discouraged (one page). The plan insists all families are blatantly dysfunctional, with flow charts and stick figures to prove it (two pages). It also requires writing a Personal Recovery Timetable Chart, which plots moods, emotions, and conflicts at two-hour intervals throughout the day; using extra paper if needed (one page). The newcomer is advised to carry the plan with them as much as possible and to refer to it frequently (one page).

The client is strongly warned that over the coming year, there will be seven predictable times of probable relapse. These are: just after leaving treatment, birthday, twelve-step anniversary, Christmas, family occasions, sexual encounters, and changing jobs or residences. Each situation gets its own page of analysis, with space to start immediately writing plans for these impending dangerous times.

The final three-column exercise is in three phases (one page per phase). The client is instructed to enter the calendar dates of the first twenty-one days of their immediate post-treatment abstinence in Column One. In Column Three, they're to enter the dates for the twenty-one days between day one of week six and day seven of week eight of their abstinence. The assignment is to write in Column Two a day-by-day comparative analysis of these two three-week periods of their abstinence. They are told that *if* they make it to six months abstinence, they are then to repeat this exercise, comparing and analyzing the first twenty-one day period of the sixth month of abstinence and the twenty-one days at the end of the second month; and then again (*if* they remain abstinent for ten months), comparing the first twenty-one days of the tenth month to the sixth month's twenty-one days.

The degree of rhetoric and detail would prove a burden to a seasoned client in therapy, let alone an addict with a few days of abstinence. This plan contains far too many assumptions, has no direct association with being spiritual, and firmly entrenches a misalliance of commitment in the life of a newcomer. Additionally, a newcomer wouldn't have the insight to accurately self-observe, and is therefore encouraged to invest energy in a daunting, primarily irrelevant exercise that has no chance of success.

In these five "relapse prevention plans", clients are not supported in responding to their own fears and experience, whatever these may be. They're indoctrinated into the fears and misalliance of commitment harbored by the authors and the treatment centres that present them. Each of these five plans is a complicated psychological instrument of very questionable merit and represent a misalliance of commitment.

The people who wrote them have little understanding of twelve-step programs and little faith in spirituality. Spirituality and spiritual advisors are only very briefly mentioned, even though each program claims to be based on "a twelve-step model of treatment".

The original twelve-step program is a program for spiritual transformation. There is no other aspect to them. These treatment centres and relapse prevention plans obviously aren't. They decidedly down play or ignore: "*...being willing to believe in a Power greater than myself. Nothing more was required...*", "*...to accept spiritual help*", "*...they outlined the spiritual answer...*", "[Your] *defense must come from a higher power.*" "*...a Power greater than yourself which will solve your problem.*" "*Our ideas did not work. But the God idea did.*"[3]

These plans are a poorly disguised rehashing of ideas that don't work. In spite of their faults, and offering the benefit of the doubt, the authors are sincere; however, they are trapped in a psychological orientation (misalignment of commitment), and themselves don't trust a spiritual solution — spiritual principles. At some level they think they're wiser than the original program. This invites, rather than prevents, relapse.

---

[3] *Alcoholics Anonymous*, pp. 12, 25, 42, 43, 45, 52, respectively.

According to Dr. Silkworth, Dr. Jung, Dr. Tiebout, the cofounders of AA, human oriented efforts like psychology were (or are) are not effective and insufficient. The original twelve-step program, in its first three decades, reported a remarkable 50% of new people stayed sober at the first serious attempt and 25% after a few setbacks. That success was based on spiritual transformation, not psychological integration.

Dr. Harry Tiebout (a psychiatrist) was a specialist in addictions treatment, who was closely associated with Alcoholics Anonymous in its early years. He wrote and published a pamphlet: *Conversion as a Psychological Phenomenon.*[4] In it, Dr. Tiebout described a conversion experience, in a manner similar to what William James described 25 years earlier.

A conversion experience, called a spiritual experience in *Alcoholics Anonymous* at Appendix II to that book, would be that personal transformative moment, sometimes dramatic or sudden, but most often silent and hardly noticeable, that originates in relation to spirituality, and embodies a healing change in an addict. With continued right effort and concentration, it facilitates a theretofore-unavailable new perspective that makes recovery from addiction possible. Regarding a conversion experience, Dr Tiebout offered it was a *"...communion with God, man, and all the creative forces of the universe."*

In his pamphlet, he quoted one of his alcoholic patients as saying: *"Something has taken place in me. I cannot put my finger on it... I am grateful that my mind is able to accept the necessity of treatment that logically I cannot understand."* The patient was implying a spiritual connotation. These next quotes are also from Dr Tiebout's monograph.

- *"Religion provides the cultural media to the attainment of the affirmative outlook upon life."*
- *"Religion should function so as to permit the budding and flowering of the positive potential which resides in the deep unconscious..."*
- *"Too often religion has been identified with its dogma and not with its essence of spirituality."*
- *"Because religion often fails signally in its function is no reason to deny that that function exists, or with that denial of*

---

[4] *Conversion As A Psychological Phenomenon*, a pamphlet, ©Dr. Harry M. Tiebout, M.D., The National Council on Alcoholism, Inc., New York (c. 1943). The pamphlet was read before the New York Psychiatric Society, April 11, 1944. In it Dr. Tiebout made these observations about the characteristics of an alcoholic: *"(1) Tense and depressed, (2) Aggressive, or at least quietly stubborn, (3) Oppressed with a sense of inferiority, at the same time secretly harboring feelings of superior worth, (4) Perfectionistic and rigidly idealistic, (5) Weighed down by an overpowering sense of loneliness and isolation, (6) Egocentric and all that implies in the way of a basically self-centered orientation, (7) Defiant, either consciously or unconsciously; and (8), Walled off and dwelling, to a large extent, in a world apart from others."*

*function to deny the existence of the inner forces which re-
ligion is designed to set in motion."*

- *"We as psychiatrists* [or counsellors or therapists or spon-
sors] *must always be alert to the constructive forces residing
in every individual. I am sure that without them, we... can do
nothing."*

Reread The Doctor's Opinion in *Alcoholics Anonymous*. Notice where
Dr. Silkworth describes how the best efforts of medicine and psychiatry
didn't work. Read the passage where Dr. Jung advises *"a certain American
business man"* it is hopeless unless there's a *"...vital spiritual experience."*[5]
The passage goes on to explain what Dr. Jung meant. There are additional
worthwhile expositions of this view by Dr. Silkworth and Dr. Tiebout in the
appendices to *Alcoholics Anonymous Comes of Age.*[6] Be advised: Psychological endeavor has no long-term substantive value in resolving addictions
issues. Psychology does not and cannot prevent relapse.

Do not let your recovery efforts be diverted away from spirituality because someone's extensive education in psychology or medicine presents a
powerful looking relapse prevention scheme that isn't spiritually oriented.
Don't be fooled into believing that modern, "human-oriented" ideas are any
more effective in combating addictions today than they were seventy years
ago. They weren't then; they aren't now.

For addressing addictions, nothing that's been tried thus far is an improvement on spirituality. It's hard for most people to accept the idea that as
far as addiction is concerned (not the psychological symptoms that manifest
out of it, but the addiction itself), psychology is impotent to affect recovery.
The best plan you can have is to be determined to enhance your conscious
contact with your higher power. Entrench an attitude that makes spiritual
principles a living presence in your life, and you'll be fine (as far as addiction goes). Be ever mindful of *"...the discovery that spiritual principles
would solve all problems."*[7]

> *"My Lord God, I have no idea where I'm going. The fact that I
> think I am following your will does not mean that I am actually
> doing so... But I believe that the desire to please you does in fact
> please you. I will trust you always though I may seem to be lost
> and in the shadow of death."* [I add: or in the shadow of relapse.]
>
> Thomas Merton[8]

---

[5] *Alcoholics Anonymous*, The Doctor's Opinion, p. xxiii, and p. 26-27.
[6] *Alcoholics Anonymous Comes of Age*, Alcoholics Anonymous Publishing, Inc., 7th printing,
1977, pp. 302 and 309.
[7] *Alcoholics Anonymous*, p. 42.
[8] An excerpt from *Thoughts in Solitude,* Thomas Merton, The Noonday Press, 1996, p. 83.

The Process of Relapse

One of the symptoms of addiction that operates as an aspect of denial is that you don't know you're sick. One of the goals, then, is to get yourself to the point where you know "I am sick," [sic] and you *believe* it. Only then are you capable of relapse, and not before. Because of the profound difference between getting recovered and being recovered, which I've referred to many times, relapse prevention when completing the first nine steps is remarkably different from relapse prevention that relates to the maintenance steps.

Relapse Prevention: Steps One to Nine

In early recovery, relapse prevention is a matter of exerting your will to do what you're told as far as the original twelve-step program advises: get involved, pray for sobriety and the determination to be spiritual, study *Alcoholics Anonymous* and *Twelve Steps and Twelve Traditions* (often), and don't act out one day or one minute at a time. Because of what you became convinced of at Step Two, you should be taking the literature at face value.

If you debate the importance of being thorough, or are doing other than those steps, or fail to maintain a relationship with your higher power as you understand this; it these are not the priorities, then (i) you never came to believe; or (ii) you do believe, but for whatever reasons, don't care enough to work hard; or (iii) you're defiant and searching for an easier way by hiding in psychology; or (iv), you have other addictions you're refusing to address.

Recall, in this book, at Step One the discussion about "admitting" or "accepting", and a newcomer's limitations regarding acceptance, which are imposed by their defects. There's a similar limitation regarding "understanding" spirituality. During the first nine steps, and especially in the first four, a person's self-insight and ability to understand is drastically limited because their character defects are prominent, which doesn't allow for a deep understanding of anything, especially the nuance of spiritual awakenings.

Trying to understand the spiritual nuances of the instructions—their "enlightened" deep meaning, prior to Step Seven, is futile because character defects stand in the way. Granted, defects are [supposed to be] gradually reduced over the course of completing the steps; however, the strong presence of defects is what renders ineffective a newcomer's attempts to "understand" the deep meaning of the original literature. This is no reflection on character or intellectual astuteness; it's the truth of addictions.

Until there is reasonable proficiency at continuous *self*-examination (Step Ten), and regular applications of prayer and meditations on wisdom

(Step Eleven), relapse prevention is largely limited to taking responsibility, identifying and following the twelve-step instructions, and identifying and reducing spiritual defiance.

Trust, obedience, and determination are the primary requirements of relapse prevention for the early phases of all spiritual pilgrimages because of the defect-imposed inability to understand the nuance and depth of authentic spiritual practice. Only after someone is well established in the maintenance steps, and has many *years* of consistent effort, can one achieve deep spiritual insight.[9]

Through to Step Nine, the purpose of attending a twelve-step literature study-group (which is itself relapse prevention) is to clarify what the exact assignments are, and to complete them.[10] When you notice you *didn't* do whatever you were advised to do in the literature, ask yourself "Why am I not doing what I am told?" rather than "Why do they want me to do this?" Challenge your resistance, not the instructions. Should you challenge the instructions, you never came to believe. When you often ask yourself why you are not doing what you are told, your studying never becomes an opportunity to memorize knowledge and act precocious; it remains an exercise in obedience and faith (which is humility).

In early recovery, relapse means simply returning to overt acting out. Relapse Prevention is limited to the following: don't drink, go to meetings, get honest, force yourself to pray, breathe in, breathe out, don't act out. Between Steps One and Nine, relapse prevention is obedience to the suggestions. Exert your will to complete the steps as they are written; pray; and reduce your dishonesty, pride, greed, irresponsibility, and selfishness. The result is the acquisition of virtue by default; it's the only way to acquire spiritual virtues.

"Some of us have tried to hold on to our old ideas and the result was nil until we let go absolutely."[11] Among other things, this refers to old ideas about relapse. By the time you have largely completed Step Nine, you're told in the original literature that insane thinking has been removed and

---

[9] An analogy: When a child is being taught addition, they are not also taught the theories of the relationships between the signs that represent quantitative value (Numbers Theory). Children have to master the basics like adding and subtracting first; otherwise, they will never understand advanced theory—obedience first, insight second. It's the same here. Up to Step Nine a spiritual novice *cannot* understand the spiritual philosophy of regeneration that lies underneath the instructions—they aren't yet spiritually fit enough. Your work to Step Nine is the "adding and subtracting" of spirituality. That's why the instructions for Meditations on Wisdom (which is the on-going homework assignment for understanding spiritual theory) come after you've developed some mastery over the basics, meaning the first nine steps. Only after a long and persistent effort (above ten years) at Step Ten are twelve-step people reasonably successful at Meditations on Wisdom. They need to have completed the prerequisite work.

[10] I discussed this in Chapter 3, and it is part of what's meant by *"...thoroughly followed our path." Alcoholics Anonymous*, p. 58.

[11] Ibid.

alcohol, drugs, etc., are no longer a problem. It follows after Step Nine, then, if these problems have been removed, relapse and its prevention must be something different than just not acting out.

Relapse Prevention: Steps Ten, Eleven, and Twelve

First, something about enlightenment: As discussed earlier, denial is an ego-defense mechanism and a subconscious dynamic for surviving trauma. Too many people think that knowledge or awareness resolves denial. Even though people report they are aware (meaning well-informed about psychology and their own personal history), debilitating and controlling defects still flare up and repetitive, destructive behaviour is often still prevalent. They'll be facing some other calamity in a few months.

How many times have you heard (or said) after some calamity: "I'll find a book or go to therapy for a few sessions. I'll increase my meetings for a while." Over time, the pain slowly hides itself, but there is rarely any substantive change to the person's inner nature—except for the addition of another layer of emotional scar tissue.

Recovery programs and therapist's offices are full of people who've skimmed hundreds of self-help books, attended several treatment centres, participated in dozens of awareness-oriented workshops, attended 243 lectures, and gone to a thousand meetings. They're "aware" and repeat the rhetoric flawlessly. Under close examination, they still participate in subtle addicted or symptomatic behaviour.

People who struggle with addictions may be aware that their life is erratic and painful, aware of shame, and know about their "family issues", yet they continue to act out, evince little joy, and evade spiritual principles. This all proves that awareness and insight, and "getting in touch with your feelings" are inadequate solutions to addictions. Being aware of the content of your "dark side" isn't the same as turning the light on.[12]

The true antidote to addictions is spiritual enlightenment. Once enlightened, the denial that concealed whatever you realized through the enlightened moment is eliminated. Once addicts transcend, with enlightened awareness, the denial that concealed some aspect of painful reality, trans-

---

[12] Dark sides, light sides, masculine and feminine sides, inner children, inner critics, inner warriors, inner parents, [I've known people who created inner babysitters and inner pets], and various other similar metaphors, are only metaphors. They are illusory symbols and only representative of a vague idea and not signs, or a reality in and of themselves. Everyone is unified; there are no sides, and we are each an indivisible 'It'. These metaphors represent incredibly complex, and often self-serving interpretations of personality dynamics; they are symbols. When these are used in character analysis as signs rather than symbols, as labels in trendy workshops, or in coffee table/lunch room conversations, additional complex problems are created. Their over-use and misapplication have rendered them ineffective to the point of being dangerous.

formation becomes possible. For the addict, only spiritual enlightenment guarantees recovery.[13]

One particular Buddhist discourse explores the task of delivering sentient beings from delusion. Hui-Neng (c. 550 CE) taught that: *"The false will be delivered by truthfulness; the delusive by enlightenment; the ignorant by wisdom... such is genuine deliverance."*[14] Very generally: Delusion is subscribing to a persistent false belief about ourselves, presented from the inside out. Delusion, always associated with denial, is an inside job that conceals some unbearable or unacceptable reality.

Addiction embodies the delusions that addiction is caused by outside factors, and that "addiction" is the problem. Both of these delusions conceal the reality that inner spiritual dislocation is actually the problem. Enlightenment is associated with spiritual integrity not psychological astuteness.

After Step Nine, some measure of spiritual integrity exists within you (the rudiments of which were obtained by completing the first nine steps). A new perspective of relapse is now required. It is thus: When you knowingly allow your character defects to harm or importune another, you are in relapse. Relapse no longer means just drinking or watching porn or your other obvious destructive behaviour. Being intentionally dishonest, mean, selfish, blaming, arrogant, irresponsible, etc., are evidence that you are *in* relapse. Once you are willingly committed to spirituality, which is as much your effort to be spiritual as it is your actually embodying the principles, any non-spiritual behaviour will then be experienced as relapse.

Spiritual integrity, for a recovered addict, means in part to accept that to knowingly ignore character defects is to relapse. To accept this as truth takes many years of devoted attention to spiritual principles under the intimate guidance of a wise spiritual mentor. For anyone to attempt to describe how wonderful and rewarding this level of willingness is, would be ill-advised promotion rather than attraction. Either you'll believe this and willingly pursue it (because you came to believe), or you won't. Either way, there's a high price tag attached.

When you're recovered and solidly in the maintenance steps, the purpose of then studying the literature, which in itself would constitute Relapse Prevention, becomes two-fold: (i) to remind yourself to do what you are told; and (ii), to engage in the regular practice of Meditation on Wisdom that enables you to reflect on the deep nuance of transformational or spiri-

---

[13] Be mindful of the difference between denial and belligerence that was discussed earlier. Here, belligerence i.e. intellectual arguing, is the antithesis to "surrender". And Meditations on Wisdom is the vehicle to surrender. Many therapists are skilled at fostering awareness and insight, but laying the groundwork for enlightenment is another matter entirely. This is the stumbling block / inadequacy of most well-intentioned addictions-related therapy.

[14] Sutra Spoken by the Sixth Patriarch, *A Buddhist Bible*, edited by Dwight Goddard, Beacon Press, 1994, p. 510.

tual literature. In this meditation style, studying becomes an exercise in faith (trust the program), obedience (to the instructions), and an exercise in surrendering to the wisdom of others (the material you're meditating on) which all are exercises in humility.

After you become recovered (spiritual), relapse occurs when you don't gently challenge your indifference to your own character defects, or when you're not abiding by spiritual principles. Relapse Prevention becomes, with due vigilance, conforming to the five spiritual principles as embodied in the maintenance steps, with Meditations on Wisdom and prayer being a noticeable part of your routine.

When In Doubt, Start Inside

As I wrote in the Epilogue On Maintenance, p. 469, all spiritual transformation begins and deepens with self-awareness and personal responsibility—clearing away character defects that block access to our inner spiritual nature. Step Ten comes first. Only thereafter can there be access to a higher power through prayer and meditation—Step Eleven. Once these two practices are established, you are then capable of imparting something of spiritual substance to a fellow pilgrim, and can practice spiritual principles in all your affairs—Step Twelve.

When you're spiritually lost, the impulse will often be to pray harder, take a course, or attend a spiritual retreat. You may impress yourself with your willingness to "spend thousands" and sit in a cave in the mountains or at a silent retreat spa with a hot tub and vegetarian meals. But, without forcing yourself to be more diligent about Step Ten, it's only impression management. For the addict (for anyone, actually) they must *first* identify their dishonesty, their spiritually crippling sense of entitlement, and various defects related to pride, righteousness, etc., and amend any and all wrongs and misdemeanors they've left unattended, (and there will be many.)

Self-examination and amends always come first in maintaining spiritual fitness. *It is never external conditions that initiate spiritual sloth or relapse; it's always internal conditions and lack of due diligence regarding defects and amends.*

More on the Advanced View of Relapse

To establish a context for the advanced view of relapse, I will make some observations about the secular concerns of careers and ethics. In order to become a professional in some endeavor, a person must achieve some pre-established level of education and proficiency. Police academies, law schools, and teacher's colleges—all professions—set basic qualifications. When these are met, people would then enter their chosen profession and be entitled to call themselves a chiropractor, a dental technician, or a librarian (whatever it is they've trained for).

Professional associations also establish ethical standards. Usually there are committees, or governing bodies to oversee their members' conduct, and because they've been trained, the members know what behaviour is expected of them. Consider these parallels...

When acting out in your addictions, you were (unknowingly) completing the entrance requirements to a twelve-step program. You were paying your admission fee before you joined. *After* you joined a twelve-step program [the "Academy of Getting Recovered"], you started your spiritual basic training. By meticulously completing the regeneration steps, you became informed about the basics of spiritual principles, responsibility, self-examination, and amends. You completed this basic training, and thereby earned the right to qualify as recovered—a new member of the "Recovered Spiritual Pilgrim's Association".

However, in this particular spiritual association, unlike most professional or religious associations, there's no ethics committee or appointed official to monitor your conduct (which is good). You can interpret your twelve-step program any way you want and you can't be fined, suspended, excommunicated, ordered to do penance, or denied membership. Only you can demand of yourself your own standard of spiritual integrity. No one has the authority to impose, nor are they to "suggest" rules for relationships, sexual conduct, step completion, meeting attendance, sharing, praying, bedtime, making decisions, diet, or anything else.

Regardless of how articulately they defend whatever their assumed authority is for imposing rules and opinions, they have no authority. Sponsorship is role modeling, not bossing around or criticizing. The AA literature and this book are to advise on what appears to be the most effective procedure to get recovered. The choice is yours. In twelve-step programs, the right to a *self*-assigned standard of behaviour is inalienable.

Knowing people's penchant for resistance and sloth in authentic spiritual endeavor, however, and by way of offering wise counsel, the original twelve-step program advises members to aspire to a standard set by "God", and not by themselves or their peer group. The higher the spiritual standard you aspire to, the more you demonstrate your devotion to spiritual principle and the better off you'll be. Ask yourself this, and meditate on the answer: "Is my level of spirituality enough to stay sober and be popular, or is it high enough to rate as truly spiritual?" The upshot of this is: You are your own twelve-step (spiritual) ethics committee, and no one else's, which is good.

Being a month sober and not acting out is something to be proud of. It's easy to notice what requires attention when you wake up in bed with a stranger, drive drunk, buy prostitutes, or gamble with the rent money. Once you've accumulated several years of abstinence, however, should you still think relapse is simply a matter of returning to blatant acting out (drinking, drugs, sex), you live with the mentality of a newcomer? With this view, you've given yourself permission to ignore spiritual principles. Even after years of sobriety, your character defects will be hurting others, but you'll perceive yourself as not being in relapse. However, you are—all the symptoms, including some self-destructive behaviour, will be present.

Self-assigned spiritual standards are rooted in, and maintained by, fear and arrogance. Self-assigned standards leave coveted prejudices, anger, defects, pride, etc., unchallenged. For someone with long-term abstinence, they often act like a newcomer, but aren't seen as one because long-term abstinence is perceived as "proof" of being spiritual. There's a global, implicit assumption, within twelve-step programs that because someone is sober for a long time they must "somehow" be spiritual; but being sober for a long time only means long-term sobriety.

People who don't maintain a high standard of spiritual behaviour, within the maintenance steps, live with their character defects controlling themselves and harming others. This is always the result of belligerence towards spiritual principles. They need to maintain an Impression Management scheme to keep themselves looking good.

When you do the steps as advised in *Alcoholics Anonymous*, you willingly (and voluntarily) assume responsibility for always striving for deeper spirituality. This is the ever-present, underlying condition of the decision made at Step Three. The responsibilities attendant to being spiritual become ever more intricate. Through devotion to Steps Ten and Eleven, you'll notice minute spiritual impurities like tiny lies, exaggerations, small incidents of showing off, subtle sarcastic thoughts about all manner of things, and the invisible silent ways you're fearful, arrogant or righteous.

By the time you reach the maintenance steps, you should have trained yourself to realize that any time you ignore a spiritual principle you're in relapse. Deliberate dishonesty, arrogance, selfishness, and the like, are all relapse. Once recovered, what constitutes "relapse" has a much greater scope than the early-abstinence idea of just acting out.

Your concept of relapse and its prevention will reflect your spiritual condition. You have to gently nudge yourself into deeper levels of accountability. Everything you say, think, or do is up for detailed scrutiny. You are your own ethics committee and, as you gently, firmly, and kindly drag yourself into embracing new truths, you must also reorganize your definitions of relapse to match new levels of spiritual insight. The shades and shadows of spiritual corruption are astonishingly subtle. That's why you must ever increasingly turn to a higher power—the source of courage—in order to go deeper into a life governed by spiritual principles.

Newcomers vs. Old-timers

Here, I refer to those rare twelve-step old-timers who are *authentically,* spiritually self-disciplined. Consider that newcomers and old-timers are both supposed to go to meetings, read the literature, be abstinent one day at a time, meditate and pray, and otherwise endeavor to be spiritual. Even though these basic requirements and obligations are remarkably similar, there are two main differences between newcomers and authentically spiritual old-timers.

The first difference is a matter of faith. Someone with a few months of abstinence who reads the original twelve-step literature will wonder: "Will spirituality really keep me sober through *every*thing: divorce, unemployment, sex, deaths, illnesses, dancing, dentists' appointments, blind dates, flat tires?" Unlike newcomers, these old-timers *know* that spirituality works—they have faith.

To develop faith in spiritual principles, newcomers have to test and examine them. They can't acquire faith in *Alcoholics Anonymous* and *Twelve Steps and Twelve Traditions,* which teach the process of how to acquire faith, if they do some treatment centre's or recovery house's version of the steps, or if they make half-hearted or psychologically-oriented efforts. Not only must people follow the original instructions, they must painstakingly follow them. Developing a strong faith is hard work. Without apparent rhyme or reason, the Spirit Of The Universe [sic] may have put a person *in* a twelve-step program, but that person has to work to stay in it. Good, solid, authentic spiritual recovery is never accidental and never a gift.

People "in recovery" will experience The Promises weakly or intermittently because they resist spiritual obedience. If they recycle through the steps, they have little faith. They made ill-advised step-substitutions or didn't work exactly as is suggested. No matter who designed the in-depth, important-looking, step guides, they aren't the real deal. Do them if you must, but realize that for disobedience to spiritual principles it may be you who pays with your life, not whomever wrote them. If you don't follow the instructions in the original literature, you may stay sober, but while you're harming others with substitute addictions, are burdened with ongoing character defects, and live a narrowly circumscribed life, you'll get to petulantly claim that spirituality doesn't work. Unlike newcomers, old-timers *know* that spirituality works—they have faith without belligerence.

The second difference between a spiritual old-timer and a newcomer is that an old-timer who regularly practices prayer and meditations on wisdom is often sensitive to the appearance of their character defects (a relapse out of spirituality), well before they actually cause harm. If people with any length of sobriety are mean-spirited, brag, gossip, curse and swear routinely, are racist or sexist, smoke, are demanding or intrusive, or are dishonest in any way, they cannot be sensitive to impending trouble.

Truly spiritual people can sense in advance when to be careful, and can govern themselves accordingly. Newcomers aren't sensitive to impending emotional calamity; they "wake up" in trouble and wonder how they got there. A newcomer has only hindsight. Spiritually oriented old-timers have hindsight, insight, *and* foresight (about themselves).

Mental Relapse Patterns

In addition to the given condition that prior to relapse, an addict will have been dishonest, there are identifiable thinking patterns that set up any relapse. When you are aware of these patterns, and can identify them in yourself, it's easier to maintain a fit spiritual condition. Said in differently, this means that by having done the prerequisite inner-homework, you will be able to recognize and change whatever destructive trajectory you may have placed yourself on because of some passing thought or misadventure, *before* it damages you or someone else. These mental set-ups for relapse are in two main categories: *Falling From Grace* (a four step process) and *Isolation Thinking* (four different types).

Falling From Grace... Relapsing

By definition, this would be that process of losing whatever self-determined level of spiritual fitness you have established. In present-day, traditional religious terms, "sinning" implies some breach of religious or moral law. Several hundred years ago it found favor as an archery term meaning, "to miss the mark". When you aim for some standard or goal, and fall short or miss the mark, you have "sinned". Granted, sinning is associated with religion, but it's important to balance the present-day sense of moral turpitude with the idea of missing the mark.

In an effort to legislate behaviour and codify punishment for "missing the mark", some religions that incorporate the concept of sin have categorized sins this way: regarding religious endeavor, they are cardinal (big), or ordinal (little); and regarding mercenary-social endeavor, they are venal. Defining sin, and legislating the appropriate ecclesiastical punishment, is complicated and arbitrary at the best of times.[15]

---

[15] The related and important discussion of why righteousness and punishment are intrinsic to organized religion, or why self-appointed religious authorities (they're all self-appointed) need to punish people, is left for another time. As an aside: for those of a more discerning (cont'd)

In your desire to be spiritual, you would aspire to evince certain virtues like humility, kindness, charity, etc.[16] In a purist sense, should you fail to achieve or maintain these (i.e. miss the mark) you've "sinned". However, because you miss the mark of perfect virtue, which in absolute terms is sinning, it doesn't mean that contrition or penance is required. In a gentler view of spirituality, it isn't necessary to do penance for being human; it's only necessary to fix any harm caused. Being deliberately negligent or cruel on the other hand, is something altogether different.

After attaining enough "virtue" by reducing defects to be considered recovered; by living *in* the maintenance steps, you need only remain gently vigilant in order to avoid falling from grace (called relapsing). Falling From Grace is that mental process of...

Thought, Form, Fascination, Fall

Thought: Initially you have a thought that falls short of integrity or fidelity—a fleeting idea of something *un*spiritual. In the midst of an ordinary day, at some inconsequential moment, the corrupt idea might be to steal something, have an affair, cheat, lie, go on a shopping spree, or get drunk.

Kim has been pleasantly married and living with someone for a few years. Kim is walking home from work and notices their new neighbor, Lee, and stops to say hello. Lee is rather attractive—really quite sexy. Kim wonders what it would be like to have sex with Lee, and ponders this. Their social talk continues for a few minutes.

There's the fleeting, destructive thought: the hit. Next comes...

Form: The passing "inconsequential" thought gets stuck in your mind. For any number of reasons, summed up in your not doing enlightened inner work on insecurities, denial, and spiritual values, the fleeting unspiritual/corrupt thought is held onto. By thinking about it, it's given a structure and Form. The passing thought becomes a recurring mental presence.

Kim thinks: "I never noticed our new neighbors. They live just down the block. Very nice body. I wonder what they do for a living?" The initial

---

temperament, it's worthy to note that the presence of guilt isn't necessarily evidence of doing wrong or being bad.

[16] Humility, kindness, and charity are attributes that might be referred to as virtues—laudable personality traits that govern and guide conduct. From an uncomplicated perspective, virtues would be generally opposite to the seven deadly sins (listed in *Twelve Steps and Twelve Traditions*, p. 48). The Catholic-Christian view of virtues is that there are two main categories: Cardinal (or Human) Virtues: prudence, justice, fortitude, and temperance; and Theological Virtues: faith, hope, and charity. [*Catechism of the Catholic Church*, Publication Services, Canadian Conference of Catholic Bishops, 1994, beginning at p. 381.] Cardinal virtues are to orient thoughts and behaviour in relation to social endeavor and the world, while (cont'd) theological virtues orient thoughts and behaviour in relation to The Church and God. In *being* virtuous, the test is to act thusly in difficult times. (See Boethius, p. 502.)

thought of sexiness persists, but it's gently obscured and hidden in the Form of "being a good neighbor"—the "good neighbor" justification is camouflage; a ruse. In any casual, subsequent conversation about the new neighbor there will be dishonesty.

Lee and Lee's spouse have a housewarming party and invite their new neighbors. Kim and Kim's spouse attend. When leaving, Kim will conveniently forget a jacket or scarf, or make some subtly unnecessary offer of "friendship" (another ruse) *and will soon call Lee and make the necessary arrangements. In their conversation there will be a subtle sexual or romantic innuendo, some dishonesty about their respective situations, various compliments and too-personal personal disclosure—socially acceptable flirting—that can be easily defended as "friendly conversation".*

An astute friend may notice and challenge Kim. Kim defends the desire and flirting within the socially approved form of being neighborly and friendly. Kim is incapable of challenging this invisible game and the original sexual thoughts are left unexamined. Kim is in denial about the illicit, destructive trajectory that's now been established.

Recall the World Health Organization's definition of addiction: *"A pathological relationship with a mood altering experience that has life damaging consequences."* The naughty excitement and impending illicit romance and sex is the mood altering experience. Some need, concealed by denial and repression, has triggered this behaviour and is holding Kim captive in the destructive path that is now established. This is beginning of Kim being manipulated by mood-altering, *un*examined subconscious issues, which lead to…

Fascination and Fantasy: The form of "friendly neighbor", which was built around the original unchallenged, destructive thought, escalates to Fascination and Fantasy. There'll be preoccupation, anticipation, distraction, dishonesty, intrigue, and allure. Fascination will be a noticeable part of conscious thought, with justifications for the established destructive path.

These justifications will be relative to other life circumstances and rooted in blaming, a false sense of entitlement, an exaggerated, romanticized sense of unhappiness, and irresponsibility. Fascination and fantasy are designed to, and will always, minimize the harmful consequences, romanticize and exaggerate the expected pleasure, and categorize the situation as harmless, or worth it, or manageable. At this stage, people (like Kim) convince themselves they don't care; it's harmless; no one will get hurt, and especially that they can control the outcome.

Self-destructive behaviour is designed to serve some unknown (but with proper work, knowable) need the behaviour is compensating for. This oversimplified diagram may make you aware of this process, but remember that awareness isn't healing.

visible behaviour (compensation)
denial - repression
subconscious unmet need or wound

A person living with unhealed wounds *must* compensate for them. The visible, compensating behaviour is always a metaphor for what the problem actually is. Fascination is what mood-alters and compensates for the subconscious unmet need or unhealed wound. The person trapped in this fantasy-cycle cannot understand it (they aren't smart enough for their own good) because its origin is subconscious, but for some unexplainable reason to them the destructive behaviour feels necessary and offers relief.[17]

Kim creates fantasies (about Lee's character, having sex, romantic dinners, getting away with it, or that it's of no consequence) and may suspect they aren't wise, but there's a silent, unavoidable need to ignore this suspicion. Kim also justifies and rationalizes this by dredging up "reasons and justifications" from the past, creating illusions and drama about the present, and forming various fantasies about the future. Kim's method of self-reassurance is to naively classify all of this harmless and controllable. Kim remains powerfully preoccupied and is thereby forced into calamity.

If, in this scenario, Lee participates at all, Lee has also established some similar destructive trajectory. If Lee refuses to participate, Kim will continue wandering around in denial, unconsciously trying to create another scenario and be unaware of what's happening.

A person is blind to these subconscious machinations. Limbic brain energy signatures associated with trauma (see Appendix II), and instant mood altering through fantasy, are what give this destructive path its power. At this point, a person is entirely incapable of preventing disaster. Whatever is hidden by repression and denial is in charge and, because the motivation for the behaviour exists underneath denial and repression, it can't be challenged at a conscious level.[18]

The impending calamity isn't always horrific, but it is always damaging, emotionally expensive, and inevitable. The actual fall from grace (the calamity) is only a matter of time and circumstance. It always appears out-

---

[17] The example I use here, for destructive behaviour, is sexual, but it could be spending, eating, gambling, drug use, alcohol, righteousness (especially anger), substances, violence... whatever. The destructive behaviour is rarely a direct reflection of the nature of the unmet need or wound. In the process of being externalized from subconscious to conscious, the need is transformed and reframed into something else.

[18] Recall the earlier discussion about Unconscious Incompetence. "Thought – Form – Fascination – Fall" is Unconscious Incompetence in a destructive form.

rageous or unnecessary because the motivation exists subconsciously, underneath denial. People who witness the disaster in someone will express this by saying something like: "I can't believe they did that! It was so senseless. There's no reason for that!" No one, especially the person trapped in this relapse pattern, can understand why.

Fall: *Kim will retrieve the "forgotten" item when Lee is home alone. If not that, some other "innocent" meeting scenario will be orchestrated, pushed by whatever is under the denial.* [By now it's too late, and the puppet plunges into disaster.[19]] *Sex "just happens" between Kim and Lee.*

The romantic/sexual fantasy will evaporate with the destructive behaviour—the harmful consequences, be that binge eating, pornography, shopping sprees (from CDs and clothes to cars and houses), more affairs, disease, impulsive divorce or marriage, violence, cruelty, substance abuse, illness, righteous rage or indignation, crime and more. These are the visible consequences of an un-examined interior life.

Thought, Form, Fascination, Fall can happen in the span of a minute, a month, or a year. The time frame depends upon how available the opportunity is, how elaborate the ruse needs to be in order for it to appear harmless or controllable, and the "power" of the subconscious wound. The prerequisite conditions for this cycle of self-destruction were established long before the actual event.

Don't be fooled into a false sense of superiority because this example of adultery appears outrageous to your values. The destructive behaviour is unique to each person and can be as innocuous as committing to a diet and then going grocery shopping, and coming home with $45.00 worth of junk food; or going into a book store for one book and leaving with seven you didn't plan on buying. It can be needing only new ski boots and leaving the store with $3,000 worth of new gear; or wanting one CD and buying ten; or planning to watch TV for one hour and later realizing you've watched TV for five hours and accomplished nothing. Immediately after the behaviour ends, there'll be fused realizations of fear, shame, indecision, and guilt.

Fate and circumstance will act in concert with an unexamined life to abet Thought, Form, Fascination, Fall. Our culture of consumerism and disposability foments spiritual alienation (crucial elements of this dynamic). That's partly why there's so much calamity and misadventure in personal relationships in modern culture. People cannot change or control fate or circumstances, they can only become enlightened unto themselves, and thereby reasonably influence their destiny in non-harmful ways.

---

[19] Consider further the metaphor of a puppet: A puppet isn't conscious and is controlled by strings it's unaware of: helpless to respond independently of the puppet master. An unenlightened person is unaware of the disasters they create which control their destiny.

People's *un*preparedness for commitment to an ethical or compassionate life through unresolved shame, a need for revenge, insecurity that demands power over others, greed, a self-destructive orientation, or an exaggerated view of entitlement, is all too common. People are responsible for the calamities they orchestrate, but will be confused about their culpability, and be incapable of preventing disaster. Without proper, long-term work, they're perpetually blind to their irresponsibility. Ending up in calamity, not knowing what happened, blaming someone else, and deflecting responsibility, are so entrenched as normal that people don't consider there might be alternatives, let alone the disasters can be successfully challenged and stopped.

Many people are in committed and notoriously unfulfilling relationships as a consequence of living an unexamined life. This is absolutely true for *un*spiritual addicts, alcoholics, and people in related programs like Ala-non, Naranon, CODA and ACOA. The degree of calamity is irrelevant. The poignancy of this all too-common situation is that whatever the disaster is, it's perceived as "the way life is".

This pattern is portrayed astonishingly well in the film *Unfaithful*.[20] The lead character, Connie Sumner (played by Diane Lane), without having done the prerequisite inner work, is trapped in this specific process of Falling From Grace (losing integrity, committing adultery—call it what you will), as is her husband, Edward Sumner (played by Richard Gere). The reality of this process is poignant in the excellent writing and both actors' excellent portrayals of their characters' blind helplessness, and the resulting crises. On the commentary track of the DVD-release of the film, Diane Lane offers these observations:

> "*When you know your own boundaries and what you're capable of being around or not being around,* [you can extricate yourself] *long before* [the character] *Connie did. Why is she capable of this affair? Because a lot of homework has not been done in their relationship. When you find yourself stymied because of what you are discovering...* [about] *betraying the person you are with... it's too late to go back and do the homework.*

---

[20] *Unfaithful*, directed by Adrian Lyne, ©2002 "Unfaithful" Film Produktion Co. and Twentieth Century Fox Film Corp. The film is an uncanny representation of the psychology that's under examination here. It's worthy of note that both main characters go through two cycles of Thought, Form, Fascination, Fall within the film, although from different perspectives and with different motivations. This is so common in modern culture—we are so alienated from truth—the Impression Management schemes we present have to be immaculately constructed.

"It's very funny because it can be an umbrella you leave at somebody's house. It can be muffins that you say you're bringing. It's a ruse. Your subconscious is ruling you. If you want to know what people are up to, look at the end result. Don't even look at the end result, look at the trajectory you're on. You're drawing closer to someone or you're pulling away from someone. Period.

"There's a lot of denial... something to hide. The feelings are a betrayal to the inner church of what a relationship is founded on. Once you start to wander—once you start to allow yourself that on a daydream level—then you've already done it." [21]

"[It's by] not doing your homework on your inner life in your relationship that you're vulnerable to an invasion." [22]

Diane Lane

The consequences to any cycle of Thought, Form, Fascination, Fall may appear outrageous to the extant circumstances, or they may appear to be inconsequential. The consequences are never outrageous or inconsequential. They only appear so because of the absence of enlightened awareness, which allows people's lives to be completely manipulated by whatever "unfinished business" lurks beneath their conscious awareness.

"Perhaps your definition of your self-system lacks authentic boundaries. You've erected a precarious structure of personality on unconscious factors over which you have no control."[23]

The dynamic of Thought, Form, Fascination, Fall, as portrayed in the movie, is also a parallel to falling out of a relationship with your higher power, and finding that you have relapsed. If you are caught in the cycle of Thought, Form, Fascination, Fall, there will be a deeply entrenched and operating Impression Management scheme.[24] Integrity and abstinence are then dependent upon Fate not presenting circumstances that hook into any unresolved needs. For recovering/recovered addicts, this is always the result of not doing inner-work: the steps exactly as suggested, living by the five

---

[21] Diane Lane's comments quoted here were part of her commentary track on the *Unfaithful* DVD. I've used what's pertinent to the topic at hand.

[22] This last observation is on the *Unfaithful* DVD, in the interview with Charlie Rose, ©CharlieRose.com Inc., ©2000.

[23] *UBIK*, Philip K. Dick, Bantam (Science Fiction), 1977, p. 45.

[24] Impression Management, which I've referred to several times, operates on two levels. At the conscious level, it could be as simple as getting dressed up, using fancy words, and acting other than as you are, in order to impress (manage) people. At the unconscious level, it's automatic behaviours that you are unaware of that are unconsciously created to compensate and maintain denial and repression.

spiritual principles, and seeking authentic long-term therapeutic and spiritual guidance.[25]

Life is ongoing change, and as life changes, so must you. Ongoing vigilance and commitment must keep spiritual integrity abreast of change and circumstance. If not, a person will be at risk of being impelled into destructive behaviour because of resistance to ever-changing circumstances. This is why ongoing participation in spiritual counsel is wise. Even though some spiritual pilgrims have thoroughly and sincerely done their inner-homework, should they not continue to be gently vigilant, they'll slowly lose whatever integrity they've gained.

The Dance	gentle vigilance to integrity and
	abandon concern for success.
	disgrace lurks in shadows of negligence;
	in delusions of preparedness
	Calamity smiles
	dislocated mysteries, deeply layered.
	the Abyss
	at the edge the pilgrim dances
	never hearing music
	parading fragrant ignorance.
	Disaster floats patiently

Thought, Form, Fascination, Fall is a process that results in "waking up" in the middle of disaster or relapse—falling into the abyss and never knowing you were standing on the edge. In what seems like a puzzling mess, and all too fast, once again you're buying sex, smoking, calling your drug dealer, spending money you don't have, waking up in bed with a stranger, getting drunk, buying eleven books you won't read, binging on junk food, using pornography, getting married, getting divorced, lecturing someone righteously, in a fit of rage, or betraying your spouse.

There are two conditions that will exist prior to and during Falling From Grace. The first is you will have been dishonest. You will not remember when the dishonesty actually started, but you cannot relapse out of being recovered without being dishonest.[26] The second condition, and

---

[25] With the dramatic increase of abstinence not-available addictions, it would appear that seeking out well conducted, long-term therapy is now, more than ever before, necessary. As cultural dislocation increases, so does that affect the quality of therapy that is readily available since many therapists are not as divorced from cultural insanity as they would like to think.

[26] In *all* relationships—those that are some manifestation of addiction, those that are symbiotic, and those that appear for the most part to be truly fulfilling and intimate, the partner (cont'd)

probably the most destructive trap there is for defeating spirituality, is the belief that you can handle it yourself (the justification for non-disclosure and dishonesty). You will cling to the devastating delusion that you are smart enough for your own good.

Jackson Pollock, the American abstract painter, said of abstract painting that for him there were no accidents. He believed that, even though he, the artist (or the recovered addict, or the two main characters in the movie *Unfaithful*) may not understand what's happening, there's an unconscious structure to it. Mr. Pollock "denied" the accident. There are no accidents in relapse, either.

Spiritual fitness, embodied in a commitment to the maintenance steps and the five spiritual principles, *and* a requisite amount of well conducted therapy, will prevent *un*spiritual transient thoughts from going farther than being transient. You'll never be free of troublesome thoughts, but you'll certainly have fewer of them, they will be less intense, and they'll always be manageable before they lead to disaster.

Isolation Thinking

Isolation Thinking is the other common process for relapsing out of being recovered, back to being "in recovery", and then from "in recovery" (without much effort), back into overt addiction. There are four types.

To start: One simplified perspective of spiritual transformation might be that it's a four-fold task: (i) overcome isolation-from-self and eliminate self-destruction; (ii) appreciate and achieve individuality; (iii) continuously honor and respect another's rights and freedoms (which includes making amends); and (iv), revere the spiritual unity that underlies everything beyond Time and Space. Mystics and spiritual masters advise that beyond the limits of consciousness, we are all *That Which Art*.

At the same time, the nature of our conscious existence within Time and Space requires that we each strive for independence. We are, within Time and Space, required to be "an individual" and must stand alone. In your present manifestation as "*I*", you're unique, and this, coupled with the phenomenon of addictions, both enables and entrenches destructive isolation.

---

that isn't first captured by Thought, Form, Fascination, Fall, will sense something is amiss as their partner descends into calamity. In addictive and symbiotic relationships the partner who isn't first caught in the Thought Form Fascination Fall cycle (the non-instigating one), will be triggered into their own destructive trajectory by sensing that something is amiss in their partner, but will be unable to address it. Only in the truly intimate, trusting relationship, where the inner work has been done, will either person be able to bring either the "thought" *or* the sense that something is amiss out for discussion soon enough to prevent the calamity.

Unregenerate addicts isolate from themselves, from others, and from a higher power, both (i) consciously, in a deliberate attempt to conceal things; and (ii), unconsciously—motivated by some compensation strategy underneath repression and denial. In addition to these dynamics of isolation, with all relapse there'll be two other associated conditions. (a) The person will have been dishonest; and (b), they'll think they are smart enough for their own good.

These are the four types of Isolation Thinking that set up relapse:

(1) *Isolation Through Mental Arguing*

You'll be sitting in a meeting, listening to someone at a lecture, or talking with a friend or your partner, and you'll think: "You're wrong," or "That's stupid," and leave the accusation silent and yourself unchallenged. Anything like this represents mental belligerence—mental arguing—and separates you from others. The resulting isolation is not about the other person's behaviour; it's about your attitude through which you filter their behaviour.[27] What insecurity motivated you to need to be right or condemn them, and thereby leave yourself silently isolated? In one way, condemnation, racism, sexism, prejudice, etc., are all isolation tactics.

Even though you may be convinced that your view is true, or more spiritually tenable, it's your condemnation and overt rejection of others that isolates you. Your "silence" is extremely manipulative behaviour. You're self-righteous about your own perceptions and, whether vocal or not, your mental argument will leave you separated from others. This applies equally when someone silently justifies obviously unspiritual behaviour like violence or smoking, or some character flaw like greed or arrogance.

The point of noticing your mental arguing isn't to encourage you to voice all your disagreements with everyone. Addicts/alcoholics can be rather argumentative. It's oftentimes wiser to say nothing (otherwise many addicts would be arguing with everyone all the time). It is, however, very important to discuss this belligerence with a mentor, or better still a good therapist, and to eventually eliminate it through self-disciplined commitment to spiritual principles.

(2) *Isolation Through Unique Suffering*

"If they had *my* problems," or "Nobody understands!" are isolation tactics, and of the four isolating attitudes presented here, Unique Suffering is the most easily justified. The truth is, regardless of the degree of anyone's compassion and empathy, no one can ever truly understand the *exact* depth

---

[27] This will be discussed in detail in Emotions and Communications in *Facets of Personal Transformation*, and is discussed in this book in both Appendix IV, and The Two-Step Dance in Chapter 9.

of another's pain (and this is especially so for The Suffering Victim). Nevertheless, understanding and compassion are available. As soon as you insist that no one could ever understand, or that no one cares, you place a glass wall between you and everyone else. You're in the world on your own, completely alone, and no one understands.

The Tree of Sorrows is an Hasidic tale about how, on the Day of Judgment, we each place our sorrows in a bag and hang our bag of sorrows from the Sorrow Tree's branches. Everyone then walks slowly around the tree looking for another set of problems that appeal more than their own. The story goes that, at day's end, everyone takes back their own sorrows.[28] Sorrows are uniquely our own.

When you describe your problems as unique, you're accurate. Circumstances may be similar, but our personalities make them unique. Compassion for others must necessarily have a personal slant. However, when you introduce drama, and claim that your problems are *so* unique that *no one* could understand, or no one ever experienced these before, or that no one cares, you're wrong and you live isolated.

(3) *Isolation Through Superlative Comparisons*

"I'm sicker than they are," or "They're sicker than I am," or "I'm the sickest person in the room." And, for the self-righteous, there's the vicious game of silently comparing newcomers and deciding who are the sickest, and which ones will make it and which ones won't.

Many people in recovery live with the idea that, as far as addictions are concerned, some people are sicker than others. That *may* be so; however, there's a dangerous potential in that line of reasoning. As soon as you decide you're sicker than anyone else, or that others are decidedly sicker than you, there's a character defect in you arising out of insecurity that needs to be addressed. In the face of harsh judgments about who are the sickest, there's isolation.

Some people do have grave emotional and mental disorders, but they are able to recover (from addictions) if they have the capacity to be honest.[29] Helping them discover their capacity to be honest may require extra compassion and empathy from others. Does that make them "sicker" as far as addiction goes, or simply place a greater demand on you for spiritual compassion? They may appear to be "the sickest" because no one has ever offered them compassion, or you may classify them as sicker because you have to be kind and offer charity of spirit when you're feeling tired, lazy or selfish.

---

[28] *If You Meet The Buddha on The Road, Kill Him,* Sheldon Kopp, Bantam Books, p. 17.
[29] *Alcoholics Anonymous*, p. 58.

You're in charge of how accepting you are of others, so you therefore have the ability to enable and encourage honesty in others by offering acceptance. That makes it easier for others to be honest, and to therefore get recovered. People may not be as far along in their pilgrimage as you, but does that make them sicker or just not in the same place as you? Addicts are notorious for isolating by creating a sick-sicker-sickest mentality.[30]

(4) *Isolation Through Withholding*

People will attend therapy and talk for a long time. They won't disclose everything that's going on, which guarantees that the therapy will be ineffective, then they quit therapy and blame the therapist. It's the same with physical fitness, relationships, almost any endeavor—especially a spiritual one: Your success will be commensurate with your commitment and emotional investment. Blaming anyone other than yourself for your mundane accomplishments, in the face of your own half-hearted efforts, or blaming inefficiency or conflict on others while concealing your own mistakes or defects, is grossly irresponsible. Withholding constitutes a half-hearted effort in and of itself. It will ensure that you maintain whatever sense of isolation you are experiencing, and enable you to justify cynicism.

Mental arguing, claiming unique suffering, being self-righteous, living with "comparison recovery", and withholding, guarantee isolation and relapse will be forever near to hand. These are partly what motivate an exaggerated and belligerent participation in meetings. Addictions wait patiently, and are nurtured in Isolation Thinking.

Alcoholics Anonymous points out "...*some of the mental states that precede a relapse...*" and "*What sort of thinking dominates...*" prior to relapse.[31] Be aware of thoughts and feelings that dominate your attitude. Relapse Prevention is an "inside job" and ultimately begins and ends within you. On a conscious level:

- Be vigilant for Thought, Form, Fascination, Fall—those persisting thoughts and fantasies about unspiritual/acting out behaviour that set up a cycle leading to calamity. Seek wise counsel to discuss these.
- Notice and challenge your own Isolation Thinking.
- Be very wary of the ultimate arrogance: believing you are smart enough for your own good; and,

---

[30] This superlative-comparison thought process relates to the exaggerated tales of one-upmanship and bragging that happens during "sharing" at meetings, which was discussed earlier.

[31] *Alcoholics Anonymous*, p. 35.

- Undertake whatever course of action is necessary to maintain a commitment to spiritual principles.

Six "Simple" Things

On a conscious level, there are six things you can do to make it easier to challenge how you think.

1) <u>Obedience</u>: The original twelve-step literature provides precise instructions on how to get recovered. There are guarantees and promises that, if you painstakingly do what you're told, you'll become recovered. Willingness, patience, and labor, under the umbrella of obedience, are all that's required. Doing what you're told within the books *Alcoholics Anonymous* and *Twelve Steps and Twelve Traditions* is relapse prevention. Don't follow any instructions—follow *those* instructions. Go to the source. This is difficult. Do it anyway.

2) <u>Spirituality</u>: Make a visible effort to live by spiritual principles embodied within the maintenance steps. Someone's late for an appointment— as they rush out the door they're abrupt, short-tempered, and drive dangerously cutting people off and speeding to get somewhere. The line is long and you don't get into the movie. Your hair isn't cut exactly how you want it. Someone forgets your anniversary or birthday. Someone you love dies. You can petulantly crash around making life worse or you can abide by spiritual principles. This is difficult. Be determined.

3) <u>Commit to Integrity</u>: Seek guidance from, and desire to become, a spiritually oriented person. Attend meetings quietly. Don't show off. Be respectful. Don't lie—ever. Seek wise *long*-term spiritual counsel. Consider well-conducted long-term therapy, and pay for it yourself. Do it.

4) <u>Prioritize</u>: If spirituality and establishing a relationship with a higher power (via the steps) isn't first on your list of priorities, you've missed the point of the entire exercise. Establish your priorities and maintain them. This is very difficult.

5) <u>Never Blame/Stop Complaining</u>: Blaming and complaining imply you can only become happy or recovered if "they" or "it" changes. If you're blaming anyone for anything, then getting recovered or being joyous is dependent on them. Maybe someday they'll agree that your misery is their fault, and they'll give you money, move away, be sorry, or do an act of contrition, thereby allowing you to finally become happy. You may think:

"Yes, I shouldn't blame, but in *my* case, it was *so* horrific that it *is* partly their fault that I'm unhappy/unfulfilled/miserable." No, it isn't.

Your addictions, or bad moods, or anger, or petulance, poor health, or divorces, or bad marriages, or stupid jobs, or unhappiness, or lack of fulfilling sex is *your* fault. It's completely self-defeating, and totally ineffective to put someone else in charge of any aspect of your life. In our culture, it is difficult to never blame anyone for anything. We are advised in the original literature that we are to drop the word blame from our speech and thought.[32] Don't ever blame.

As far as complaining goes, anyone pursuing spiritual transformation volunteered for this work. Spirituality, honesty, Step Eight... whatever, may be difficult but there are never grounds for complaint. You volunteered. You may need extensive therapy to figure out how not to complain or blame—even then, don't complain about the therapy, you will have volunteered for that, too.

"So a wise [person] ought no more to take it ill when [they] clash with fortune than a brave [person] ought to be upset by the sound of battle. For both of them their very distress is an opportunity, for the one to gain glory and the other to strengthen [their] wisdom. This is why virtue gets its name, because it is firm in strength and unconquered by adversity."[33] This theme applies to spirituality as well. Any perceived difficulty is only an opportunity to celebrate your spiritual life. That was Boethius' point.

6) The Declarations: Meditate upon and abide by, Declaration II, which is discussed in Chapter 3.

Some Odds and Ends

We all have complicated problems, get mixed messages, and live with conflict. Albert Camus, in *The Myth of Sisyphus*, wrote about the absurdity of life. At times we're overwhelmed and confused. Not everyone will understand or care about your pilgrimage. Life appears tough. Sometimes. But when you're authentically spiritual, the difficulty vanishes and life becomes a place of grandeur.

By being spiritual, you offer the people in your life a special gift—not making their life worse by inflicting your defects on them. This kindness will set you apart, and you'll be cherished by some and resented by others. Being spiritual in all circumstances doesn't mean that calamity will pass you by. People die, break legs, get sick, and lose jobs. Big chunks of life happen to everyone in particular, and some people deeply resent that life

---

[32] Twelve Steps and Twelve Traditions, p. 47.
[33] *The Consolation of Philosophy*, Boethius, by V.E. Watts, Penguin Books, 1969, p. 144.

takes up so much of their time. We're all susceptible to missing the mark and mishandling the daily ups and downs of life.

People can't develop habits of devotion when they're in crisis; and neither can they complete the subtle therapeutic work that signals permanent change when they're in calamity. Spiritual transformation is impossible in a life of reaction. In times of relative peace, maintain deeply committed routines of prayer and meditation. Seek out well-conducted therapy when nothing's wrong. If you don't, then the steps or therapy become crisis management tools, which is exactly what they are not. If you think spirituality is expensive, try addictions. If you think therapy is expensive, try adultery, divorce, abuse, anger, denial, etc.[34] Force yourself to participate in wise and insightful counsel, and stay in it for a *very* long time.

Addictions are cunning, baffling, and powerful. Life is indifferent to everything. Being Spiritual offers you a gift—it disarms whatever is cunning, baffling, and powerful and allows an appreciation for the grandeur of life exactly as you have been given it. Be always sensitive to, and curious about, the beauty and powerful nature of a spiritual lifestyle (i.e. living a life governed by the five spiritual principles).

Being recovered and living in the maintenance steps doesn't mean you're not at risk of being dishonest, mean, arrogant, proud, selfish, etc. It does mean that moments of indecision are easily governed by spiritual principles and you will therefore stay out of relapse. Indecision about how to conduct yourself doesn't happen when you're entrenched in the maintenance steps and rigorous honesty.

Initially, while searching for peace and looking for "God", newcomers will wander through their personality like it's a foreign, hostile territory. Getting recovered is possible and insanity is optional, but we never know beforehand how difficult the job of getting recovered is actually going to be. We are to be congratulated for this undertaking. The more senior, spiritual members of twelve-step programs should take some time to gently inform others about this truth.

"Furthermore, we have not even to risk the adventure alone, for the heroes of all time have gone before us. The labyrinth is thoroughly known. We have only to follow the thread of the hero path, and where we had thought to find an abomination, we shall find a

---

[34] These are my modification of a quote from Derek Bok, former President of Harvard University, who said: *"If you think education is expensive, try ignorance."* As reported in *1,911 Best Things Anybody Ever Said*, compiled by Robert Byrne, Fawcett Columbine, 1988, p. 158. Regarding therapy and the steps becoming crisis management tools: That is not what they are designed for and using them thusly renders them ineffective.

god. And where we had thought to slay another, we shall slay ourselves. Where we had thought to travel outward, we will come to the centre of our own existence. And where we had thought to be alone, we will be with all the world."

Joseph Campbell[35]

At the outset this is very difficult, but you volunteered, so don't complain (too much), and do it anyway. Persevere.

The Addict's Secret Desire

How many times have you thought: "When am I going to be normal? I just want to be normal." This desire isn't limited to addicts or alcoholics, and has nothing to do with gender, sexual orientation, religion, or culture. Quentin Crisp wrote:

"From time to time, every mature homosexual man should issue a solemn warning to all his young gay friends that they must never adopt, even unconsciously, an exile's view of normality. To this day, in spite of all that gay pride stuff, many of us who stand in the street, knee-deep in the snows of rejection, press our noses to the cold windowpanes of establishment and imagine that the carpet slipper setup that we see dimly on the other side of the glass is permanent, cozy, and peaceful.

"In fact, those who are on the inside are frantically trying to get out."[36]

Many people in recovery talk about the twelve steps like they're a treasure map—secretly coded directions to the lost city of Normal. People naively hope for "normal" as the reward for a successful hunt for "God". Like other misunderstood or oppressed members of subcultures, alcoholics and addicts too often make the big assumption: getting recovered is getting to Normal (some vague place or state that they're supposed to arrive at). In the first place, Normal doesn't exist. In the second place, anything that a recovering addict could conceive of as normal isn't.

People trapped in mediocrity often resent the flaunted freedom of outsiders.[37] Some people envy the destructive flamboyance of addicts and alcoholics, who interpret that reckless self-destruction as freedom (the reactive antidote to their own denied desperation). Pining away, waiting for

---

[35] *The Power of Myth*, Joseph Campbell with Bill Moyers, Doubleday, 1988, p. 123.
[36] *How To Go To The Movies*, Quentin Crisp, St. Martin's Press, 1988, p. 127.

admission to Normal, is often the deeply secret emotional posture of members of any troubled subculture like recovering addicts. They idealize the establishment from the outside-in. As Quentin Crisp says, we *"...press our noses to the cold windowpanes of establishment..."*.

Avoid the destructive assumption that becoming normal is the goal. Don't be normal: be sincerely spiritual, which, in this culture, is clearly abnormal. Ask: "What is 'normal' and, if I could figure out what that is, do I really want it? Is there within me a creative, spiritual person whom I will suffocate by being normal?"

Oftentimes I'm seen as a malcontent, a social outcast if you will, within the culture at large and within twelve-step programs. And yet, all I do is politely ignore peer pressure and live by applying the five spiritual principles to *my* values, *my* desires, and *my* preferences. I've received no end of condemnation for this. And yet, I've no intention of surrendering me to them. I've worked too hard for too long, and I'm too precious to give up "me" for popular approval.

The original twelve-step program isn't designed to make you normal. It's designed to make you spiritual. The more spiritual you are, the less normal you'll be. Inherently, we all know this, but carbon-based life forms blessed with intellect and inundated with technology, cherish their preoccupation with mood-altering experiences, fornication, and shiny things.

Insecure people often live with the illusion that compliance with popular opinion will someday be fulfilling or meaningful. This is because they have decided social success and obedience to cultural values equals fulfillment. Within this faulty perception, they will have labeled relationship addiction as normal, violence as acceptable, greed as good, people as disposable, and sexuality as dirty, bad, or *un*spiritual. They know they'll be ostracized for being truly unique.

> *"Difficulty at the beginning works supreme success.*
> *Furthering through perseverance.*
> *Nothing should be undertaken*
> *It furthers one to appoint helpers."*

---

[37] This refers to the earlier quote of William Bayer about the film *Easy Rider* (directed by Dennis Hopper), in *Great Movies*, The Ridge Press, Inc., Grosset & Dunlap, Inc., 1973, p. 161.

"No plain not followed by a slope.
No going not followed by a return.
He who remains persevering in danger
Is without blame.
Do not complain about this truth;
Enjoy the good fortune you still possess." [38]

After years of self-annihilation in active addiction, some addicts getting recovered take life very seriously. At the outset, they should. But that often extends into a permanent mindset that everything's a chore and it's all hard work. Others make light of everything and refuse to appreciate the life-or-death nature of addictions. After years of hard work and self-discipline, when addicts have finally recovered and are spiritual, they end up being able to evince a spiritual harmony; a benign indifference and joy, in any life circumstance. We can't take it too seriously, after all it's just life. And for addicts, life is easiest to manage when it's devoted to spiritual principles.

---

[38] These poetic aphorisms are taken from *If You Meet The Buddha on The Road, Kill Him,* Sheldon Kopp, Bantam Books, pp. 3 and 187 respectively. The original translation is by Cary F. Baynes, *The I Ching or Book of Changes*, Princeton University Press, 1950, pp. 16 and 116.

Appendix I

AA & Traditions

If a man does away with his traditional way of living and throws away his good customs, he had better first make certain that he has something of value to replace them.

Basuto Proverb[1]

There are three general purposes for this appendix. The first is to en-able you to understand how to examine and challenge traditions. You may find yourself experiencing guilt, or a sense of failure, and be unable to es-tablish its origin. Unless people, who are exiting addictions and chaos, understand the double bind that often arises from conflict between new emerging value systems and established traditions, they'll relapse and often stay rooted in a cycle that approximates: Desire—Action—Guilt—Aversion—Regression (explained on p. 512).

The second purpose is to provide a *brief* over-view of the two main temperance philosophies that predate AA. The third is to offer some discus-sion about the short-sighted perceptions, within some recovery groups, that traditions exist *only* for the organization of groups. At first look, this is what they appear to be for, but this categorizes the AA traditions as separate from the individual member (which actually renders the groups ineffective). I will establish the basis for an alternate view of the AA traditions; a view that perceives them as an expression of the five principles of spirituality. The AA traditions actually represent how to conduct yourself spiritually, in the context of community, anywhere in your life.

Forming Traditions

There are two basic ways that traditions originate. The first is from the long-range collective experience of the people involved. The Hindu and Aboriginal religious traditions evolved over a few thousand years and were formed out of *both* the evolving mythology and the experience of people in the communities, without the dominant influence of any single leader. They

---

[1] *Something of Value*, Robert Ruark, Doubleday & Company, Inc., 1955.

are the result of a collective experience over a *long* time. The other way is when they're formed around the charisma of an inspired teacher like Buddha, Jesus, Moses, or Mohammed. Some individual's powerful philosophy motivates people to rally around them or the philosophy they espouse. This group then traditionally celebrates the insights or anniversaries that arise from identifiable, specific events.[2]

A newly married couple will negotiate how to celebrate birthdays, Halloween, etc. Their traditions will evolve and become some collaboration of what they've each done in the past. Over the course of five or ten years the new couple develops a collective experience of how to celebrate their life—from sharing food and lovemaking to anniversaries and funerals. This takes a long time.

The overall difficulty in surrendering to spiritual principles (which embody new "traditions") arises from being unsure of their viability. This is similar to becoming willing to let go of character defects at Step Six. It's hard to let go of, or modify, your old traditions if you don't trust they'll be replaced with something of value. People in transformation often get trapped in debilitating limbo between the old and new ways. Here are two definitions (abridged for this discussion):

> <u>Tradition:</u> *1. The passing down of elements of a culture from generation to generation, especially by oral communication. 2. a. A mode of thought or behaviour followed by a people continuously from generation to generation; a custom or usage. b. A set of such customs and usages viewed as a coherent body of precedents influencing the present: followed family tradition in dress and manners. 3. A time-honored practice or set of such practices.*

> <u>Custom:</u> *1. A practice followed by people of a particular group or region. 2. A habitual practice of a person: my custom of reading a little before sleep. 3. Law. A common tradition or usage so long established that it has the force or validity of law.* [3]

What's the point of having traditions?

- They create structure and cohesiveness in groups.
- They bring people together and create unity.

---

[2] "Traditions" or powerful philosophies that collect adherents or motivate people to some end can also be dangerous (i.e. Ku Klux Klan, Jim Jones, Adolf Hitler); or in another context like Carl Rogers (therapy), Martin Luther King Jr. and Gandhi (social activism), or Steven Hawking (science and speculation).

[3] Both from *The American Heritage® Dictionary of the English Language, Third Edition,* © 1996, Houghton Mifflin Company. Electronic version.

- They can be used for problem solving—if you don't know what to do in a given situation, do the traditional thing.
- They can offer both a personal and a collective identity.
- Life and the calamities it presents are bigger than any individual. Traditions, within families and communities, allow people to face the enormity of life with a greater expectation of success.

Mom's Birthday

The family next door religiously gathers together to celebrate Mom's birthday (just like for Grandmother's birthday). Mom expects it, and Dad says so. It's so entrenched it seems like "Mom's Birthday" has parliamentary approval, and besides, it's a tradition—everyone just always does it.

A week before Mom's birthday, two of her adult children get in a very nasty argument. One decides they're never talking to the other again. Ever. Dad hears about the fight and phones each one. He says: "Mom's birthday is coming up. I'm looking forward to seeing you at the party." Each of the adult-children protests. Dad says: "Patch it up for the party. You can continue fighting after. *Be here* next Saturday at noon. It's *Mom's birthday.*" The kids show up. (If they don't, there'll be a heavy price to pay.)

Granted, rigidly adhering to tradition can be unwise. But clearly, tradition can often be used to foster harmony and resolve conflict.

Traditions operate on different levels: nuclear family, social, corporate, community, province, state, country, and international. They operate from many different perspectives: ethnic heritage, gender, geographic area, political association, and religious denomination. Family and local customs vary, i.e. Christmas in rural Quebec is very different from Christmas in California or Scotland; a grandparent's birthday celebration is different from a grandchild's. As you read the following short list of traditions, realize that as much as they operate on different social and cultural levels, they are also uniquely personalized.

- birthdays, opening presents, eating and food customs;
- funerals, memorial services, anniversaries, weddings, stags, stagettes, graduations, class reunions, vacations, holidays, summer camp, spring break, visiting relatives;
- special-interest group celebrations, business conventions, Stonewall, Halloween, Valentine's Day, Labor Day, New Year's Eve, Independence Day, Canada Day, Remembrance Day, Armistice Day, Women's Day, awards ceremonies, Gay Pride, community festivals, pageants;

- celebrations in agriculture, technology, beauty, strength, art, any of the four seasons, amateur sports, theater, music, animal husbandry, hobbies, swap-meets, rodeos;
- family: Dad's chair, Mom's chair, Dad at the head of the table, TV rituals, chores, responsibilities, codes of family loyalty, codes of conduct, manners, the division of work;
- rituals and traditions at mosque, synagogue, cathedral, monastery, retreat centre, cloister, temple, sweat lodge, feast, coven, or church (any denomination), AA, NA, CA, SLAA, CODA;
- celebrations of the life, work, or death of famous people; and,
- Sports: Hockey Night in Canada, World Cup Soccer, Monday Night Football, Kentucky Derby, The World Series, Grand Prix, golf, tennis, The Olympics, etc.

Traditions and customs carry tremendous influence and have powerful social expectations regarding their celebration. One result of them remaining unexamined is they often end up appearing to have the force and validity of law, but they really aren't anything more than tradition. People know that if they want to stay out of trouble, they should do the traditional thing. As soon as people start breaking traditions, other people give them a hard time (and can be quite vicious), so people comply with tradition to avoid rejection or mistreatment. They'll be "accepted" and fit in, even though it may be against one of their secret beliefs; they'll comply, but at what cost?

Here's an awareness exercise: On paper, list thirty traditions/customs that affect your life. Now reflect carefully and evaluate each one for Participation/Interest, and then again separately for Spiritual Conflict.

Participation/Interest	Spiritual Conflict
• enjoy the tradition; look forward to it and participate eagerly: + 10	• the tradition embodies spiritual integrity and offers support: + 10
• pleasantly involved; not eager: + 5	• some spiritual value but not a lot: + 5
• not affected; notice it only in passing: 0	• no noticeable spiritual value, but nothing contrary to spiritual principles: 0
• dislike it but participate because of pressure to comply; reluctantly go along and put on a happy face: - 5	• noticeable, but not severely detrimental effect on spirituality: - 5
• strong dislike and participate with concealed disdain and anger: - 10	• decidedly contradicts spiritual principles; obviously detrimental: - 10

The last two choices from either column, the -5 and -10, indicate an Impression Management Scheme and will be detrimental to your well-being.

Reflect carefully and evaluate how each one does or does not conflict with your emotional well being in getting recovered. What's your level of interest? Be aware of how it may or may not be in conflict with spiritual principles and getting recovered.

Guilt and Tyranny Under Tradition

Before we get into "guilt", a few words about fear and shame, which precede guilt in the hierarchy of developmental dependency needs. Fear and shame are respectively the predominant emotional characteristics of the first and second stages of childhood development. Guilt is predominant in the *third* stage of development, and the major emotional consideration when children become capable of talking in sentences. When you feel *guilty*, you've broken a rule.[4] Fear and shame are primarily associated with pre-verbal developmental issues; guilt is post-verbal (after about 3 years old).

A person can say "tree" or "sex" but the word is not the thing. As much as language is powerful and emotionally charged, it is abstract. Rules are also abstract and arbitrary. Children must be able to "think" before they can negotiate and comprehend rules. Talking in sentences is representative of a certain stage of intellectual development. When children can articulate and understand simple word ideas they can comprehend simple rules.

In other words, for a person to understand the relationship between rules and behaviour and feelings of guilt, it's necessary to be able to articulate ideas—a function of words and sentences (language and the intellect). Being able to articulate ideas requires a certain level of intellectual-verbal acuity; only then can rules be understood.

When children are forced to endure the consequences of breaking rules *before* they're capable of understanding the concept of rules (using language), then shame and fearful confusion are the result. Punishing people for not following rules, before they can understand rules is shaming, frightening and harmful. This is never more evident than in the deep healing work of people who, when young children, were indoctrinated into complex religious theology, or who survived caregivers and parents who were petty tyrants or demanding about obedience.

Rules are the situational preference of some authority figure. The transgression of rules, which often merits censure, is specific to some arbitrary circumstance, and punishment is meted out at the discretion of the authority figure. Guilt is the sensation of "bad" that arises when rules are broken. In a healthy person, when you feel *guilty*, you've broken a rule.

---

[4] This explanation of these aspects of developmental dependency needs is over simplified. They are presented here to help understand some of the more complex issues (cont'd)

As an adult, if you feel shame and/or fear when you unknowingly or *un*intentionally break a rule, there's more than likely a developmental dislocation present. In addicts, they'll feel shame and fear when they unintentionally break a rule. In addicts, however, this may be indicative of childhood development problems (just as it is with others who have unresolved developmental issues), and it will *also* be derivative of their addiction—from the fusion or over coupling of emotional experiences and the breaking of rules in their self-annihilating acting out. Aside from any personal dynamics and their acting out, this "double-jeopardy" is also related to culturally imposed guilt that I spoke to earlier. It's very complicated.

The value of a rule is relative to the circumstance it governs. The rule may be a good rule, like honesty; but to a thief, honesty is a bad rule (in relation to thievery). If your family tradition is blood-loyalty and codes of silence, should you become open and honest about family secrets, you'll feel guilty because you're breaking the established family tradition of silence. In the transition from addicted, dysfunctional traditions (codes of silence or dishonesty) to the spiritual principle of veracity, you'll feel guilty for being honest until you've properly oriented yourself to the new rules of conduct. This takes a *long* time.

Desire—Action—Guilt—Aversion—Regression

Earlier I mentioned the cycle of Desire—Action—Guilt—Aversion—Regression. It is in relapse and prevention this comes into play.

(1) Desire (to heal): I'm sick and exhausted. I'm dying from my destructive behaviour. I want to change my life. I want to get recovered. I'm really going to do it this time. I'm serious.

(2) Action (towards the desire): I'll quit acting out, stop attending addictive social events, change social groups, go to meetings (do whatever). I'll tell the truth. I will *not* attend events where there is drug use, heavy alcohol use, disrespect, etc. This may require I leave an abusive or addicted relationship, change jobs, or not attend family or social events. These are difficult changes with noticeable consequences (guilt, punishment, shame, fear) but I'll do them. I'm determined.

(3) Guilt/Fear (about breaking tradition): I'm not going home for Christmas. (I feel ashamed and guilty.) I'm not going to my best friend's drunken birthday. (I feel guilty.) I'm not attending the company summer

---

regarding addictions and recovery. There are other considerations that will be explored in *Facets of Personal Transformation*, but for this discussion, these generalities are sufficient.

picnic. (I feel afraid and guilty.) I have to leave my spouse. (I feel stupid, ashamed, and guilty.)

(4) Aversion (to the guilt, fear, and shame at #3): Getting recovered, not acting out, being honest, is *too* hard! What about my family? friends? career? social life? reputation? I can't handle recovery (meaning can't handle the fear, guilt, shame, and other consequences of new, non-traditional behaviour).

(5) Regression: Abandon the original desire for healing, spirituality, honesty, integrity (at #1) to avoid the struggle/pain of changing behaviour, rules and traditions (at #2 & #3). This requires excuses: Therapy is too expensive. I'll wait until after the party. I'll give my boyfriend-girlfriend-spouse-boss another chance. I'll wait until my parents die. I'll start after Christmas. I'll quit after I've pirated all the software I need; *then* I'll be honest. Next month I'll... leave, grow up, throw away the porn, quit the affair, stop stealing, quit chocolate, get sober, move, or confess. I'll try again, after the snow melts. I will. Honest.

Regression at #5 is a complex and harbours a very deep experience of failure. It becomes an additional, invisible burden—another layer of emotional scar tissue molded around shame and guilt. This is associated with a double-bind dilemma—feeling guilty for participating in some activity because they're breaking recovery guidelines or spiritual principles; or feeling guilty for adhering to spiritual principles and refusing to participate in established but unhealthy traditions. (This cycle is a close parallel to the relapse cycle that is described on p. 23.)

The person becomes more deeply entrenched in self-annihilation. They'll invariably relapse. Time passes and they experience another desperate desire to change, so they create another #1 scenario. The cycle starts over and they develop a fatalistic acceptance of recidivism and relapse. The mindset of repetitive inadequacy becomes entrenched in "recovery", which is partly rooted in the difficulty of abandoning old rituals and traditions.[5]

In many families, the dominant authority figure imposes the family's traditions by edict. Conflict often results. "Underlings" seeking autonomy will revolt, especially when either the authority figure or the traditions are perceived as restrictive—the more restricting the traditions or autocratic the authority, the more likely the revolt.

---

[5] In Chapter 12, I spoke about Relapse Prevention Plans. Plan #1 presented relapse as almost inevitable. This cycle is the dynamic that has set up that particular fatalistic view of recovery.

Families that are molded on dictatorships (benevolent or otherwise) always carry an element of tyranny.[6] In these closed systems, saying "No" to any tradition because you don't want to, meaning trying to assert personal preference, is never sufficient reason for the authority figure to excuse you from participation. These autocratic environments, where children are not allowed to say no, often extend into adulthood. People end up participating in certain marriages, careers, and lifestyles, even though they really don't want to. This has all manner of consequences from trivial to horrific.

The amazing misperception is when addicts in recovery are unable to say "No" in a way that establishes boundaries or appropriate levels of participation, it's too quickly assumed this is a family or pre-addictions issue. However, addicts often have periods of intellectual clarity in their addiction and realize they want to say no to their addiction, but cannot. To personify this: The addiction is the dominant authority figure of the addict's life and the addict wanting to say "No" to it (i.e. assert personal preference) is insufficient.

The repetitive inability to say "No" in addiction is a condition that may appear to have its origin in childhood that was carried through their addiction into recovery. Yes, that may have originated in childhood but not necessarily so. It *will* have some origin in addiction. Regardless, the resulting behaviour and consequences are the same. Do not too-quickly assume the cause of "poor boundaries" is a developmental/pre-addiction concern. [Note: For abstinence not-available addictions (p. 21) the inability to say "No" is a seriously complicating factor in maintaining abstinence.]

Society makes demands on everyone. As much as there may be comfort in knowing that most people do as you do, and democracy may be the best form of government for trying to get it right most of the time, "majority rule" is risky. Popularity is nothing more than a guarantee of popularity. There is no moral correctness in popularity, but there is questionable safety in knowing you probably won't be criticized for compliance. Being noticeably different is threatening to the insecure power elite.

Democracy ends up with whatever most people think is right (the popular perspective) being imposed on those who differ. As soon as most people in a group do a given thing, there's the very real probability of tyranny of the majority.[7]

A tradition is self-perpetuating and is proof only of itself. The assumption that traditional behaviour is right is what justifies exorbitant peer

---

[6] This is not meant to include age-appropriate prohibitions that speak to the considered safety of children.
[7] For a slightly different perspective see *Blues ain't nothing but a good soul feeling bad,* Sheldon Kopp, Fireside/Simon&Schuster, 1992, entry for Dec 6.

pressure to ensure compliance and punishment for non-compliance. Should someone surrender to peer pressure and participate in a tradition they'd rather not (or participate differently than the power brokers would prefer), or participate under duress, there's resentment or bitterness that underlies begrudging compliance with tradition. This can motivate all manner of cruelty towards others.

Regarding participation in traditions, there are these two considerations: (1) If you suddenly stop doing something you've done for a long time, it may seriously disrupt your family, friends, or coworkers. It will have a major impact on others and on yourself. If you're going to change your life, be considerate when the change will be an imposition on other people.[8] Expect long periods of adjustment. (2) Carefully examine your motives for not participating in some tradition. Sometimes "I will not" is defiance for its own sake (dysfunctional independence). This defiance may be an unkind cover-up for something else, like trying to punish.

It's important you understand which traditions you're interested in, which ones you're not, and what motivates you to participate in them (or not). Knowing this allows you to evaluate the spiritual, emotional, and social cost of participation or abstention, and to choose accordingly.

Traditions embody rules. Guilt arises from breaking rules. To resolve guilt, examine *both* the tradition (the rule) that you broke, *and* your behaviour. Decide which you need to change, the rule or your behaviour. If it's a good rule or tradition, stop breaking it; if it's a dysfunctional rule or unhealthy tradition, change your rule (don't participate). This is the process, but it's a lot more arduous and complicated than the equation presented here. It may be wise to consider well-conducted long-term therapy when challenging traditions.

Following a tradition fosters acceptance and popularity within the group that promotes the tradition. Defying a tradition foments rejection, but may be what is necessary to acquire spiritual integrity.

Faith and Trust

Faith: 1. Confident belief in the truth, value, or trustworthiness of a person, an idea, or a thing. 2. Belief that does not rest on logical proof or material evidence. 3. Loyalty to a person or thing; allegiance. 4. The theological virtue defined as secure belief in God and a trusting acceptance of God's will.

---

[8] Adherence to spiritual principles requires this to be true: I cannot "succeed" in any endeavor when my success is built on abuse, dishonesty, or detracts from another's dignity.

Trust (noun): 1. Firm reliance on the integrity, ability, or character of a person or thing. 2. Reliance on something: in the future; in another's character. Trusted (verb): 1. To have or place reliance; depend upon: Trust in... the Lord, destiny. 2. To be confident; hope. 3. To expect with assurance; assume: I trust that you will be on time.[9]

There are three ways for people to acquire faith. The first is to adopt the proclamations of some higher authority who says: "This is good (or bad or right or wrong)," and to have faith because of who said it. This can prove to be a weak basis for faith because as soon as some more impressive authority figure appears on the scene, faith can be undermined and confusion results.

In an over-simplified view of this, for Christians prior to 1860, there was the bible (New Testament) and the church. Faith imposed by the edict of an authority figure. Since Darwin's *Origin of the Species* the new authority figure has become the microscope. This has undermined the original authority figure (church doctrine) and there's been on-going squabbling and conflict about faith ever since.

The second way faith is acquired is through personal experience and research—individual trial and effort, and the rejection of all outside authority. The resulting values and beliefs are valid, but for one person. This tends to create another individual morals dictator and very often defeats community participation. Charity and egalitarianism are unavailable.

The third, and what appears to be the most reliable and satisfying avenue to faith and belief, is by combining historical tradition and personal experience. This third way establishes the context for the traditions of AA.

"Henceforth we would have to rely upon spiritual principles, as set forth in the Twelve Traditions."[10] Why rely on these traditions? There are four sources of authority that altogether make the AA traditions a dependable and reliable basis for spiritual transformation.

1) The experience of active addiction—self-destruction, dishonesty, fear, shame, guilt, pain, failure, arrogance, selfishness, and your awareness of the continuous and consistent results of acting out, proves acting out was unreliable for life-management. You may not know what to do to make your life better, but you certainly know what will make it worse. That experience is something you can rely on, and is included in molding your behaviour to the AA traditions.

---

[9] Abridged definitions from *The American Heritage® Dictionary of the English Language, Third Edition*, © 1996, Houghton Mifflin Company. Electronic version.

[10] *Alcoholics Anonymous Comes of Age*, Alcoholics Anonymous Publishing, Inc., 1977, p. 213.

2) The subtle changes you notice in yourself as you painstakingly complete the steps and abide by traditions—those consistent personal changes are an authority you can rely on. What you're doing is not just "the steps". What you're doing is, by completing the steps and adhering to principles, you are experiencing the importance of these traditions.

3) Noticing the improvement in others who are behaving according to the steps and traditions, and noticing also the absence of improvement in those who aren't applying themselves to this. This promotes right association and through observation of others, you come to rely on traditions that have spiritual integrity.

4) As you complete this work, after several years beyond the level of spiritual newcomer, there's an intrinsic realization of the obvious universal value of the twelve traditions (rules) that embody spiritual principles. You can rely on the innate truth about the inherent good that's beyond any person or personal ideology. Once you access this *a priori* knowledge through experience and meditation, it becomes an authority you can rely on.

These four sources of authority are actually a delicate combination of personal and social traditional experience, which was outlined (a few paragraphs above) as the third option for acquiring faith and belief. With these, your faith will become quite unshakable and you'll come to rely on spiritual principles in the traditions.

Values & Tradition

The situation: Lou is well known in a twelve-step program, has years of abstinence, and talks about a higher power, prayer, and the importance of honesty and respect for others. Lou (and Lou's spouse) are friends with another married couple. One member of the other couple tells Lou privately they're having an extramarital affair. Lou is now privy to the lying, manipulation, and betrayal in the other couple's relationship. Several days later, when Lou's spouse notices an unexplained tension and initiates a private conversation with Lou about this, Lou is evasive. Lou's spouse now becomes quietly anxious. Lou doesn't confront the adulterer, doesn't say anything to the betrayed spouse who is also a friend; Lou's spouse remains noticeably troubled by the mysterious tension. Lou continues to share at meetings about the importance of rigorous honesty, respect, and spiritual principles.

What identifies spiritual people is not only that they value spiritual principles, but also abide by them in the face of personal cost. Values are a belief about the worthiness of something or somebody. If a person doesn't adhere to their values; if there's no personal investment in upholding the "value", it's not a value, it's a convenience. Addicts who remain "in recovery" are long on conveniences and short on values. People cannot proclaim that honesty is of high value, and maintain integrity, while they continue to lie or participate in behaviour that's deceitful; or, where deceit affects their life, to allow that dishonesty or disrespect to go unchallenged.

A *value* is a principle or a belief in something you hold in high regard. Whatever it is you value, i.e. honesty, kindness, literature, your love relationship, swimming, etc., governs your investment of time and money. If you claim to value honesty, but are at times dishonest, then you don't value honesty unless it's convenient to some selfish, favorable circumstance.

To identify what you value, notice what you give your time to. How tenaciously do you defend some behaviours? What's the discrepancy between your thoughts and secret behaviour and what you present to others? On any day of leisure, should you spend four hours on the golf course, two hours watching a film, ten minutes playing with your children, and three minutes praying, you've identified your values and priorities. No amount of protest will alter the truth of this statement: What you love or what you value, *is* what you give your time to. What you love is what captures your energy.

What fear causes you to be duplicitous? What addiction causes you to deceive others about the values you claim to embrace? What shame or guilt motivates your hypocrisy? These questions are worthy of careful examination so you can challenge yourself. Authentic integrity is expensive.

Addictions and Traditions

What I'm going to describe next aren't traditions in a sociological sense. I'm going to describe addictive, symptomatic behaviour as "traditional", using that as a metaphor to create some clarity about one aspect of the task that awaits a person in spiritual transformation. There is a group of standard, "traditional" behaviours that addicts or alcoholics display, which represents the symptoms of the phenomenon. A successful alcoholic/addict will act out, otherwise self-destruct, lie, cheat, intimidate, manipulate, be violent, defiant, or compliant, and sound convincing as they blame others to extricate themselves from responsibility. These comprise the behaviours that addicts traditionally display.

The more a person participates in these "traditional" addictive behaviours, the more they are successful at self-annihilation. It takes a lot of practice, talent, and determination for people to beat themselves into the all-encompassing mess that they do, and to blame others for the mess they, themselves, create.

The goal of getting recovered is to live with minimal personal cost and greater spiritual rewards — to abandon traditional/destructive behaviours and adopt spiritual behaviours.[11] As addicts transform through their own hard work, they come to have faith in new principles and values that are reflected in behaviours that are traditionally spiritual in nature. Only then can they confidently abandon their old lifestyle (old traditions), because they have something of value with which to replace it.

Washington Temperance Society

The temperance movement in the United States (most prominent c. 1826–1836) was focused entirely on alcoholism and drunkenness, and generally geared toward keeping drinkers away from alcohol. Practicing alcoholics were believed to be doomed sinners unless they completely and vigorously immersed themselves in fundamental Protestant-Christian values.

The Washington Temperance Society ("The Washingtonians"[12]) started in April 1840, in Baltimore, Maryland, intending to prove that a drunk could, in fact, be saved. It was *"...in a spirit of fun to challenge the now waning temperance movement..."*[13] that six men (while drinking in a local tavern) formed a group, and, on the spot, paid twenty-five cents in dues, elected officers, and each agreed to bring a new person to the meeting they planned for the following week. They each signed a pledge to create *"...a society for our mutual benefit, and to guard against a pernicious practice which is injurious to our health, standing, and families, and do pledge ourselves as gentlemen that we will not drink any spiritous or malt liquors, wine, or cider."*[14]

At the first anniversary there were about 1,000 *"reformed drunkards"* and 5,000 other members and friends. In three years, their membership grew to over 100,000 *"...recovered sots"*. Splinter organizations sprang up with varied political or temperance-related agendas. However, according to Dr. Milton Maxwell, the movement declined quickly because its *"membership, purposes and ideology were inextricably mixed with those of the temperance movement, and it turned into something it did not start out to*

---

[11] Destructive behaviour is as much hurting or harming others as it is yourself.
[12] The Washingtonians are referred to in *Alcoholics Anonymous Comes of Age*, Alcoholics Anonymous Publishing, Inc., 1977, p. 124.
[13] From the AA newsletter, *Box 459,* Vol. 34, No. 5 / October-November 1987; Fate of Washingtonians..., p. 6. That article uses as its source a monograph by Milton A. Maxwell, Ph.D., former chairperson of the AA General Service Board, and professor of sociology, Center of Alcohol Studies, Rutgers University, New Jersey.
[14] Ibid. p. 6.

be. ...the original purpose of rehabilitating alcoholics was lost to sight."[15] By 1845 the Washingtonian movement had largely disappeared.

The article in *Box 459* goes on to point out these five distinct differences between the Washingtonians and AA, which until recently allowed AA to remain effective: *"1. Exclusively alcoholic membership. 2. Singleness of purpose. 3. An adequate, clear-cut program of recovery. 4. Anonymity. 5. Hazard-avoiding Traditions."*[16] From the Washingtonians in 1845, leap ahead about 80 years to England.

The Oxford Group

The Oxford Group embodied *"...a campaign for the renaissance of the practice among men of the truths of simple Christianity...".*[17] It was in a large part focused on alcoholism, but anything under the general heading of "sin" was included. The Oxford Group began with Dr. Frank Buchman (a Lutheran minister twice nominated for the Nobel Peace Prize). He was in England in 1908 when *"he caught a vision of a Christ-led world untrammeled by Sin."*[18] Dr. Buchman traveled the world carrying this message. Eventually, at Oxford in England, his message found energetic support. In the mid-1920's his vision caught on and expanded rapidly from there.

The Oxford Group adhered adamantly to the view that Christianity, through Jesus Christ, was the only acceptable avenue to redemption. Redemption, here, meant to recover a Christian soul that was pawned or mortgaged for the pleasures in sin. [Sin in this context contains some Christian righteousness and prohibitions regarding morality. Here, it's much more than simply "missing the mark" as discussed earlier.]

The four points of the Oxford Group were *"1. Absolute Honesty. 2. Absolute Purity. 3. Absolute Unselfishness. 4. Absolute Love."*[19] These four points were to be demonstrated in *"four practical spiritual activities: (1) The sharing of our sins and temptations with another... ; (2) Surrender of our life, past, present, and future... ; (3) Restitution to all whom we have wronged directly or indirectly... ; and (4), Listening to, accepting, relying on God's Guidance and carrying it out in everything we do or say, great or small."*[20]

The Oxford Group's four points and the related spiritual activities (certainly from a traditional Christian perspective, and adamant about the

---

[15]. AA newsletter, *Box 459,* Vol. 34, No. 5 / October-November 1987, p. 6.

[16] Ibid., p. 7.

[17] *What Is The Oxford Group?*, by The Layman With A Notebook, Oxford University Press, 1933, p. 3.

[18] Ibid. p 13.

[19] Ibid. p. 7.

[20] Ibid. p. 8-9.

hegemony of Christianity) have a thematic similarity to the Twelve Steps. The *"early A.A. got its ideas... straight from the Oxford Groups and directly from Sam Shoemaker, their former leader in America, and from nowhere else."*[21]

"At the [1955 AA] *Convention it was widely appreciated for the first time that nobody had <u>invented</u> Alcoholics Anonymous, that many streams of influence and many people, some of them non-alcoholics, had helped, by the grace of God, to achieve AA's purpose."*[22] That the cofounders didn't invent the AA process is not a criticism of AA or its cofounders, nor does it demean what they figured out or wrote. They, with much gracious help from non-alcoholics, and certainly some inspiration, made clear two things: (1) recovery from addictions depended upon achieving and maintaining a spiritually principled life; and (2), the exact path that made recovery possible for the alcoholic [or addict] who really wanted it, *and* was willing to go to any lengths to get it.

Addicts struggle to make some kind of sense out of life. They secretly despair at the senseless, destructive behaviour they inflict on themselves, and search for some meaning to their apparently pointless existence—no differently than billions of other people over thousands of years. One truth that was implied in 1935 was that *while in any addiction, it is not possible to give meaning to life*. This can only be done when an addict is abstinent and lives governed by spiritual principle.

People with addictions (and there are a lot of them) have to start their spiritual transformation from inside an addiction. [This requires a different focus of effort from a non-addict who wishes to be spiritual.] At the outset, it makes for a more arduous journey. *Alcoholics Anonymous* offers a path to transformation that [virtually] guarantees results. People with addictions are not pariahs; they too, belong in the world, but not all of them will find their way to a twelve-step program. And, sadly, many addicts in twelve-step programs never touch the true potential of what the original twelve steps and traditions have to offer.

Alcoholics Anonymous & Tradition

I offer only a few very brief comments on the development of the traditions of AA. This section is intended as neither an exposition of the origin of the traditions, nor an analysis of their obvious content. *Twelve Steps and Twelve Traditions* and *Alcoholics Anonymous Comes of Age* contain a

---

[21] *Alcoholics Anonymous Comes of Age*, Alcoholics Anonymous Publishing, Inc., 7th printing, 1977, p. 39.

wealth of information on the traditions' content and origin. Here, the purpose is to encourage Meditations on Wisdom in order to unveil the spiritual principles within the traditions themselves.

The traditions are usually presented as "rules for groups", which is important. However, they are much more than guidelines for group organization. They are a guide for spiritual living that "should" govern your behaviour. The twelve steps create spiritual integrity in your personality. The twelve traditions create spiritual integrity in your behaviour while participating in the communities that inform your world.

"Even as early as 1945, the solution to group problems by correspondence had put a large volume of work on [AA] *Headquarters. ... The basic ideas for the Twelve Traditions of Alcoholics Anonymous came directly out of this vast correspondence."*[23] Thousands of letters, over fifteen years or so, formed the basis of the Twelve Traditions. The collective, successful experiences of the members, which reflected the most effective ways to overcome addictions and role model spiritual behaviour in a group, were distilled into guidelines for a successful spiritual *community* experience. [These are a parallel to the maintenance steps that are the guidelines for a successful spiritual *personal* experience.] In carrying the message to others, service to a higher power could now be demonstrated in our social behaviour.

Throughout the AA twelve-step literature, there is never an obscuring of the truth that: *"Unless each A.A. member follows to the best of his ability the suggested Twelve Steps of recovery, he almost certainly signs his own death warrant. We must obey certain principles or we die. The same stern threat applies to the group itself. Unless there is approximate conformity to A.A.'s Twelve Traditions, the group too can deteriorate and die. So we of A.A. do obey spiritual principles, first because we must and ultimately because we love the kind of life such obedience brings."*[24] This refers to spiritual principles inherent in the steps *and* the traditions.

The phrase *"...ultimately because we love..."* is a direct reference to the transformation of attitude regarding humility that happens at Step Six. In this context, a love of obedience (to the maintenance steps) is rooted in humility. That passage also contains an implied reference to the difference between awareness and enlightenment. Awareness only allows humility to be perceived as a "must", and enlightenment through prayer and meditations on wisdom allows humility to become a cherished value.

---

[22] *Alcoholics Anonymous Comes of Age*, Alcoholics Anonymous Publishing, Inc., 7th printing, 1977, p. 2 emphasis theirs.
[23] Ibid., p. 203.
[24] Ibid., p. 119-120, emphasis theirs.

Addicts who ignore any aspect of any tradition are acting in an *un-spiritual* manner. Notice those who dominate business meetings, family or social gatherings, or push personal agendas in twelve-step groups. With this happening, it's impossible for the group to carry the message of a spiritual awakening because the group becomes representative of the will of the dominant members and not representative of spiritual principles.

Just as the maintenance steps keep individuals spiritual in their private relationship with their higher power, the traditions keep individuals spiritual in their relationships with each other. The steps create spirituality inside you in your relationship with yourself. The traditions create spirituality inside you in your external relationships and groups. The traditions are not "for the group"; they're for the people who are in the group.

"Implicit throughout A.A.'s Traditions is the confession that our fellowship has its sins …these defects threaten us continually… But the twelve traditions also point straight at <u>many of our individual defects</u>… The Traditions guarantee the equality of all members and the independence of all groups."[25] How do you reconcile (a) the sins of the fellowship, (b) group-threatening defects, (c) individual defects, (d) equality of all members; and (e), the independence of all groups? These are reconciled through obedience to spiritual principles that are embodied in the traditions.

Try this exercise: Obtain a small reprint of the Twelve Traditions; write out your rights and freedoms, and another sheet with the five spiritual principles. Hang these on the wall in your kitchen and discuss them with your family or partner. Create a spiritually based relationship based on those traditions and principles. You'll be surprised at two things—how hard it is, and the sense of fulfillment when you accomplish it.

"Henceforth we would have to rely upon spiritual principles, as set forth in the twelve traditions."[26] This doesn't mean there are twelve principles. Recall that a tradition is a guideline or a "rule of conduct" that carries authority because of its (apparent) historical efficiency in problem solving and its ability to create social harmony. There are five spiritual principles embodied in twelve traditions.

Recall that *Alcoholics Anonymous* advises that the purpose of that book is to help alcoholics find a power greater than themselves which will solve their problem (p. 45). Both the steps and the traditions are of a single view: to re-educate a person in how to become spiritual and maintain obedience to spiritual principles—but one is from an inner-personal perspective (the steps), and the other from a social perspective (the traditions). The traditions are designed to veto politics and impression management at the

---

[25] *Alcoholics Anonymous Comes of Age*, Alcoholics Anonymous Publishing, Inc., 1977, p. 96, emphasis added. *"…the equality of all members…"* is egalitarianism. See App. II, Humility.
[26] Ibid., p. 213.

group level (relationships), and maintain a spiritual purpose in people, while they organize the group's chores and carry out its responsibilities.

Some Specifics

Each tradition, like each step, has specific tasks and conduct guidelines associated with it. The obvious intent is to harmonize the relationships within groups. However, immediately under the surface of the group's operation is the ever-present obligation to carry the message of a spiritual awakening. The traditions are guidelines that ensure the visible presence of spiritual principles.

Each member is [supposed to] represent some version of a spiritual awakening, which "should" be reflected in the group's (or family's) organization and operation. Groups are a public forum for carrying the message of spiritual awakening and getting recovered (and no other message). A pleasant social life often results from abstinence, but a pleasant social life is neither the message to carry, nor the goal of membership. Every time a tradition is *not* followed in a group's operation, the message of a kindness, acceptance, compassion, etc., is obscured, and politics and personality (impression management) are placed above principle.

The AA traditions[27] are presented here for convenient reference. *Twelve Steps and Twelve Traditions* has a detailed explanation of their organizational intent.

> "1. Our common welfare should come first; personal recovery
> depends upon A.A. unity.
> 2. For our group purpose there is but one ultimate authority—a
> loving God as he may express himself in our group conscience.
> Our leaders are but trusted servants; they do not govern.
> 3. The only requirement for A.A. membership is the desire to stop
> drinking.
> 4. Each group should be autonomous except in matters affecting
> other groups or A.A. as a whole.
> 5. Each group has but one primary purpose—to carry its message
> to the alcoholic who still suffers.
> 6. An A.A. group ought never endorse, finance, or lend the A.A.
> name to any related facility or outside enterprise, lest problems of
> money, property, and prestige divert us from our primary pur-
> pose.

---

[27] *Twelve Steps and Twelve Traditions*, Alcoholics Anonymous World Services, Inc., 1995, pp. 9-13.

7. Every A.A. group ought to be fully self supporting, declining outside contributions.

8. Alcoholics Anonymous should remain forever non-professional, but our service centres may employ special workers.

9. A.A. as such, ought never be organized; but we may create service boards or committees directly responsible to those they serve.

10. Alcoholics Anonymous has no opinion on outside issues; hence the A.A. name ought never be drawn into public controversy.

11. Our public relations policy is based on attraction rather than promotion; we need always maintain personal anonymity at the level of press, radio, and films.

12. Anonymity is the spiritual foundation of all of our traditions, ever reminding us to place principles before personalities."

Spiritual behaviour towards others reflects service to a higher power. It's humility in action; the foundation of all of AA's Traditions. With the work you've done to understand what meditations on wisdom are, it'll be fairly straightforward to study and discover which spiritual principles are prominent and which are subordinate within each tradition.

The five spiritual principles are demonstrated in relationships and groups by surrendering personal agendas to spiritual agendas. Twelve-step groups are too easily converted into drama clubs and soapbox arenas for spiritually undisciplined people.

In recent years, as devotion to personal spirituality has been disintegrating regarding the twelve steps, so has group integrity regarding the twelve traditions. This disintegration arises from a misalliance of commitment and an unhealthy influence of psychology.

This is a variation of the idea of the Evil Blue Meanies that I spoke of earlier: No one outside of my group can understand me. I am so unique. AA, NA, CA, SLAA, SAA, SA, EA, MA, etc., all exclude "those other addicts" because they won't understand. However, this limiting and false belief is now manifesting inside twelve-step groups. i.e. Very few people inside "the program" can understand *me*, so I'll start my own special "recovery group", just for *my own* unique problems, because "that other kind" can't understand (me): women's groups, men's groups, young people's groups, gay or lesbian groups—where does the terminal uniqueness and internal splintering stop? This is an arrogant perception of terminal uniqueness.[28] This internal splintering can be stopped only by reliance upon, and obedience to, the traditions and the spiritual principles they embody.

The Myth of "The Movement"

One noticeable aspect of the mess that twelve-step programs are in is related to the subtle perception of many people that they are a "movement". A movement, in a sociological sense, is some organized effort or a series of organized activities where people promote some objective. The Suffragettes, Greenpeace, the Washingtonians, and Recycling are movements.

Twelve-step meetings are places where people can remind themselves of, and develop and enhance, their spiritual orientation to life. Meetings are (supposed) to provide a place to do this, or when invited, to help other people do this. Addicts getting recovered have, or should have, nothing to prove to anyone, and nothing to convince anyone of. They should work towards being spiritual, minding their own business, avoiding gossip, and not willfully debating the "issues". There's no planet to save, no axe to grind, no fundraising drives, no delegates to represent, no people to convert, no slogans to chant, no issues to debate, and no morality to promote.

Proselytizing is against the steps and the traditions. So are debates and arguments. Twelve-step programs are not movements. Thinking that they are assigns to them a political agenda that has no place in authentic spiritual endeavor.

Self Supporting

Addicts getting recovered must pay their own way: rent, books, coffee, pamphlets, and all by donations during twelve-step meetings. This is such a sacred trust, there are limits as to what amounts can be bequeathed through wills and inheritance to AA. However, with the changes in our culture, "self-supporting" has become a more complex and much broader issue. What follows is subtle and worthy of careful consideration, especially regarding the first and fifth spiritual principles.

---

[28] (1) Earlier in this chapter, and in Chapter 1, I discussed the shame and insecurity underneath flamboyant "sharing" of tales of excess and debauchery. Those dramatically expressed feelings of inferiority contribute to the group splintering I describe here. (2) Recall the discussion of Four Big Topics in Chapter 5. In a psychologically oriented program, addiction of preference, acting-out and self-harm, detoxing, and abstinence remain important because of the grand "I". Within AA, this creates an unnecessary need for special-admission groups for just old-times, only newcomers, only women or men or gays or lesbians, etc. Within NA there's regular NA, and Cocaine Anonymous, and Marijuana Anonymous. The creation of special membership twelve-step groups within twelve-step groups (internal splintering) is how disintegration and lack of spiritual commitment shows up.

Modern government requires an important separation between church and state. This separation may not be as great as some would like, but it is there.

Government grants are not awarded to organizations wanting to help people find God. Asking a government-funding agency for money for spiritual pursuits will not be successful. However, asking for funding so people afflicted with the "medical disease" of addictions can be rehabilitated members of society (meaning law-abiding taxpayers) has proven successful, even though the success rate for rehabilitation is notoriously low. Receiving government or corporate funding to treat addictions requires a significant suppression of spirituality in favour of psychology and social rehabilitation. The modern, vague euphemism "a twelve-step model of treatment" hides all manner of reframing and misrepresentation to get money. [This abets a misalliance of commitment.]

As a result, recovery houses and treatment centres that solicit government funding (whether it's applications for grants or for social allowance cheques), or treatment centres that solicit corporate sponsorship, are political organizations. These agencies must necessarily suppress spirituality to ensure financial support, and these have become a *major* source of dislocation and problems that twelve-step groups must contend with. Government or corporate funding of "the twelve-step model of treatment" [sic] has now clearly established detoxification and treatment centres as powerful twelve-stepping agencies.

Literally tens-of-thousands of rehab-clients are discharged each year from government, union, or corporate funded treatment centres straight into twelve-step programs. This guarantees chaos within the groups and drastically increases the probability of newcomer relapse.

These centres, as much as they *may* be helpful, must by financial mandate, present three subtle and powerful messages: (a) psychology is the main vehicle to recovery, (b) "rehabilitation" (implying recovery) should be paid for by someone else; and (c), the time-consuming and frustrating work of early recovery will be handled by treatment centres and professionals. All three are sweet music to the irresponsible nature of addicts.

For those people already in twelve-step programs: Rather than the difficult job of role-modeling spirituality or of being held accountable for your disinterest; rather than being truly generous of spirit and accepting; rather than challenging your own impatience and having your life interrupted by some frightened, confused newcomer, when a new person relapses today, it's easy to deflect from your own lack of commitment by telling them they need to go to rehab. "Phone me back when you're done treatment."

The original AA reference texts are, at their core, focused on spiritual transformation. They "demand" personal responsibility for a self-imposed crisis where the word blame must be dropped from speech and thought. This is at odds with psychologically oriented treatment centres. In an important aside, religiously oriented treatment centres may claim to be more in tune with the AA philosophy of spirituality, but there, they must impose, by religious mandate, a specific interpretation of "God", and are therefore equally ineffective because they will deny freedom in the choice and orientation of a higher power.

Altogether, these profound influences are at play:

(1) The deification of self-help psychology.

(2) The prevalence of a quick-fix mentality and disposable consumerism.

(3) Professional agencies, funded by governments, corporations, and private agencies are taking responsibility for carrying the message to newcomers. Corporations don't award grants for addicts to find God, they want tax-paying consumers—whomever pays the band calls the tune. This, by necessity, must down play spirituality.

(4) Religious organizations funding treatment centres will, by mandate, expect compliance to the "God rules" that define the religion.

(5) Medical experts aren't maintaining only a supportive role in treating the derivative physical damage, detoxing etc., which was the wisdom that assisted AA in it's first thirty years. There's the ever-increasing takeover by medicine and science of "addictions treatment", with a related massive profit from that treatment. There is reported evidence that the original "AA twelve-step protocol" is more effective. In the original AA text, based on their early AA membership surveys, they report that 50% of people who sincerely attempted recovery stayed sober and recovered on the first attempt, and that 25% more stayed sober after a few attempts. That's a 75% recovery rate, significantly higher than treatment centers and AA groups of today.

(6) The increase of greed and dislocation in culture; the greater disparity in the distribution of wealth; the greater levels of consumerism; the drastic increase in addiction; and having the trinkets of psychology become status-jewellery, makes for "high-end" elitist treatment; and,

(7) The drastic change in age demographics in meetings.

Professionals often and generally promote treatment centres in order to create patients, clients, and incomes.[29] They're also promoted to obtain government or corporate funding, and it's all endorsed by the addict's irresponsible nature. Altogether, these influences reinforce the internal splintering of twelve-step groups. The original literature stands opposed to these recent trends in addictions recovery. Meetings are evolving into spiritually bereft social circles and dating agencies.

Treatment-centre recovery that's primarily psychological, paid for by someone other than the addict, fostered in our blaming, victim culture, *and* endorsed by irresponsible addicts in recovery, foments disaster. In many recovery groups there are now prominent but vaguely defined political alliances with recovery houses, detoxification centres, and treatment centres. Within these environments, there are many people, some with very marginal training, acting as professionals paid to do twelve-step work.

These dynamics of treatment and "rehab" require a disastrous realignment of priorities and a reduction of twelve-step spiritual responsibility. Government and corporate funding largely controls the "twelve-step model" of helping newcomers. Taken altogether, these influences have orchestrated an insidious shift in the mindset of people in recovery—there's an overwhelming misalliance of commitment (discussed in Chapter 6). Although much slower, and of an indirectly different focus, and slickly justified under the righteous declaration of "helping", this has clearly put twelve-step groups on a course that's parallel to The Washingtonians and The Oxford Groups: alliances with political, corporate, or religious agencies.[30] Twelve-step programs are glaringly less effective than in decades past, and rapidly getting worse.

The steps and traditions weren't designed to serve anyone in any social context, which is what a movement does. Government/corporate funding will not be awarded to help people "find God". If it's religious funding, the religious organization will of course expect you to find "their" God. It's a short step from there to the spiritually defeating view that twelve-step programs are movements and recovery is a psychological issue.

---

[29] There are several texts and reports about this dynamic of health care professionals. One credible source, with a wealth of reference material cited, is *Manufacturing Victims*, Dr. Tina Dineen, Robert Davies Publishing, 1996.

[30] This closely parallels the massive realignment of expectations regarding therapeutic services. As many therapists raise their rates and make their services inaccessible to the majority of our society, insurance companies, social and religious organizations, employee assistance programs, government agencies, etc., are in higher demand. It bears reflection as to why addicts in the midst of their *self*-imposed crisis should expect others to pay for any therapy that might be required. Additionally, since insurance/government plans have severely limited amounts that can be claimed for therapy, participants never have sufficient time to accomplish anything significant. This sets up a serpentine list of harmful expectations and consequences. I will explore this in my next book, *Facets of Personal Transformation*.

Now that someone else largely pays for "twelve-stepping" and rehabilitation, not spirituality is the intent twelve-step programs will (eventually) experience the fate of The Washingtonians and The Oxford Groups.

If you're a person getting recovered, consider carefully that twelve-step programs aren't designed to change the worldview of addictions or to change anyone's view of you. They're to change your inner perception of yourself, and to thereby enable you to create a devoted relationship with a power greater than yourself. There's nothing "social" about the intent or the process of twelve-step programs. They were designed to teach you how to live by spiritual principles so you could rid yourself of addictions and humbly (anonymously) serve a higher power.

I'm not suggesting that twelve-step meetings aren't supposed to be friendly or enjoyable. Social occasions outside of meetings are important. I'm *not* suggesting that treatment agencies are necessarily wrong. They might have a very important part to play. However, when (i) twelve-step meetings are social occasions, (ii) spiritually oriented traditions aren't the guiding authority; and (iii), a non-spiritual approach to newcomers is underwritten with outside "rehab" agencies in control, meetings become ineffective. This is often talked about (in whispers) but it is rare that anyone ever says anything out loud. In my work and experience, many people suspect that something isn't right, but are unsure of what to do about it.

Meditate on the wisdom of the AA traditions. See for yourself, they're much more than rules that govern the operation of groups. Learn how the traditions embody spiritual principles and make them personal.

The traditions are guidelines for your attitude and behaviour in all your group activities. [An intimate relationship is a group activity.] Interacting with your family, your lover, your leisure-activity companions, your friends, your coworkers, and your twelve-step associates are group activities. In your commitment to a spiritual way of life, the maintenance steps keep you in personal-spiritual harmony with your higher power; the traditions keep you in social-spiritual harmony with people.

Appendix II

The Five Spiritual Principles

These are principles that appear to me, to govern ethical spiritual endeavor. I understand that, underneath the complex beauty of parables,
metaphors, and mysticism, spirituality is very practical.

There are five universal principles that, when willingly complied with
and taken altogether, create spiritual integrity in a spiritual pilgrim. "Willingly" complied with means to be voluntarily obedient to them. These
principles would also comprise the underlying, inherent qualities that would
be required for an organization, or an applied philosophy, to be spiritually
ethical.

I refer again to the Manly Hall quote cited at p. 197: *"The unfolding of
a man's spiritual nature is as much as exact science as mathematics…"*.
Yes, the varied manifestations of *The Ground of All Being* may be mysterious, and the debates and discussions about god and religion may be
esoteric, but the everyday application of spirituality is neither of these.

The Fundamental Qualities of a Principle

"Principles, unlike values [or rules], *are objective and external. They
operate in obedience to natural laws, regardless of conditions."*[1]

A spiritual principle would be an authentic truth, and hold within itself
a universal theme applicable beyond personality or culture. It would also be
the foundation out of which arise beliefs and attitudes that would enable a
person to rise above (be spiritual), or descend below (be soulful), the ego-
constructions of self-serving convenience.

Spiritual principles must take us beyond psychology and the related,
limited vision of personal insight. They should also be above the pettiness
of politics and culture. Additionally, a bona fide spiritual principle would be
universal enough to embrace all of the generally recognized virtues, regardless of the folk-tradition through which they are perceived, and include (in
this instance) whatever virtues recovering addicts would evince to be recov-

---

[1] *Principle-Centered Leadership,* Stephen R. Covey, A Fireside Book, Simon & Schuster,
1992, p. 19.

ered. And finally: A spiritual principle would have to be authentic enough to hold up under close scrutiny.

The general chaos and confusion around spirituality occurs most often when people take something as fundamentally universal as "spirituality" or "a higher power", slant interpretations to cater to their coveted prejudices and insecurities, then claim that their own personal interpretation is superior to others' interpretations. Spiritual principles must be broad and flexible enough to be available to everyone at a deeply personal level. Therefore, to allow something to qualify as a spiritual principle (as opposed to a rule, which is secular and limited) is no mean feat. Each of these five spiritual principles is a *principle* because it is:

- <u>Universal</u> enough to accommodate and embrace all spiritual endeavor, beyond the narrow limits of culture;
- <u>Respectful</u> of any personal symbolism of deity;
- <u>Broad</u> enough to encompass the generally recognized virtues;
- <u>Restricted</u> enough to exclude the more universal vices;
- <u>Tested</u> enough over the centuries to be trusted;
- <u>Simple</u> enough to comprehend;
- <u>Complex</u> enough to perpetually require attention;
- <u>Demanding</u> enough to require continuous effort to evince it;
- <u>Idealistic</u> enough to be always worthy of respect, and just out of reach—to keep people humble in their pursuit of it,
- <u>Specific</u> enough that it can be approached with confidence;
- <u>Achievable</u> to a degree that people can demonstrate or realize personal progress; and,
- <u>Profound</u> enough to be above pettiness.

Each of the five principles I recommend satisfy the twelve qualifications noted above. Additionally, because there are only five, there are few enough of them so people can apprehend their interrelatedness. What may be more important is these five allow the adherents of different faiths to peacefully interact, while maintaining different beliefs. These principles can be internalized and become the governing values of truly spiritual people.

Regardless of the circumstances people find themselves in, they would aspire to demand of themselves adherence to these principles as non-negotiable standards of behaviour. To the uninitiated, the principles are probably overwhelming, and for addicts they are often viewed with disbelief and thought to be untenable. However, with willingness, patience, and labour (or desire, devotion, and diligence), and right association, they are within reach of anyone who is desirous of a truly spiritual way of life beyond the conventionally enlightened.[2] The five principles are:

Principle #1: Respect for the Physical Body and Respectful Self-Care

It is long known in the perennial philosophies that the Atman-Brahmin resides within, and access to *It* is through ourselves.[3] Our souls, from one perspective, are the access point to, and the residence place of, the dark void out of which we arise. From there, we are animated in a manner that allows integrity in two seemingly opposite directions. People can be drawn into an appreciation of the dark, sublime mysteries of primal life and love (soulful) or can rise above to the call of light and spirit (spiritual). Harmonizing these may the intended journey of life.

Either way, the selfish trappings of personality and culture must be left behind. Being soulful is quite a bit different than being spiritual. Spirituality might be described as manifesting the action of a deity within each of us "out" towards the world. Soulfulness is sincerely demonstrating and honoring the strength, frailty, mystery, and power at the core of our being.

Because all access to "God" ultimately begins with us challenging ourselves, and ends *within* ourselves, it is our bodies, our emotions, and our thoughts through which this is appreciated. Our bodies are the temples within which the essence of a higher power resides. Contact with the soul or the spirit *begins* through and within our own physical being. Your body is literally the home of your soul and spirit, as is everyone else's the home of their own. The body must be cared for.

Respect for the body, as demonstrated by respect and healthy caring for our physical being—for others as much as ourselves—is essential. Not

---

[2] Marshall Frady, in his book *Martin Luther King, Jr.*, Viking/Penguin Books, 2002, p. 186, offered this observation about Dr. King: *"King was indeed passing now into that far country of all true prophets ultimately: that lonely region beyond the conventionally enlightened...."*
People in twelve-step programs don't have to be prophets; however, the decision at Step Three has no limits attached to it. It was voluntary, and so the standard to aspire to is that set by the principle itself and not by mediocre social conventions (meaning socially acceptable levels of spiritual irresponsibility associated with twelve-step psychobabble). Go beyond the pale; it's worth it.

[3] According to *Alcoholics Anonymous*, in the final analysis, it is deep within us that the Great Reality is found (p. 55). Additionally, as was mentioned earlier, there are two similar views of God residing within us, found in *Mysticism In Religion*, by Rev. W.R. Inge, University of Chicago Press, 1948, Chapter 3: Attributed to St. Paul: *"...the spirit dwelling in us, or of our bodies as the temple of God... 'the body' as the 'tabernacle' of the soul while we live here* [on earth].*"* And, from Rev Inge: *"The body must be reverenced and preserved from defilement... it is the temple of the Holy Spirit."* I do not intend Christian hegemony in this. *The Kabalah* teaches similarly, that what we consume or use (good or not good), so it is that we become. Many other religious traditions, and particularly Buddhism, promote respectful self-care with equal style and grace.

damaging ourselves or others through squalid living, toxic diets, violence, addictions, greed, irresponsibility, selfishness, or physical or emotional abuse is crucial. Nurturing the residence of the spirit is the starting place for all spiritual transformation. If you're damaging or neglecting the care of the body (your own or another's physical and emotional health), you are damaging the home of the *Atman-Brahmin*, and therefore cannot be spiritual.

Principle #2: Veracity

This is a certain style being honest, and describing your perception of truth that incorporates gentle trustworthiness. For many years, with the advent of the social movement towards health and enlightenment in the 1960s, truth was quite rightly encouraged. "Let it all hang out" became a euphemism for honesty—blunt, brutal, or otherwise. Venting was the order of the day; however, being honest and presenting your truths without regard for others is cruel and not a part of veracity.

Honest communication that is angry or without respect and consideration for others will be received as abusive. The speaker will be viewed as selfish or rude, and the truth, or any wisdom in the truth, will be held suspect because of the manner in which it's delivered. Angry people who are honest are seen as more angry and righteous than honest.

Spiritual people always speak the truth as they see it—they are consistently and *gently* honest—with all people, in all situations, at all times, regardless of the cost to themselves. This disables impression management, which is crucial to any sincere spiritual endeavour.

In microscopic truth telling, spiritual people always offer respect, courtesy, and dignity to others, regardless of the nature of what needs to be told.[4] You cannot be spiritual and dishonest, or be spiritual and mean while being honest. Being spiritual always requires gentleness, trustworthiness, and courtesy in microscopic truth telling; no exceptions. That is veracity.

Principle #3: Humility

Often largely misunderstood, especially by people seeking spiritual transformation, humility is rare and elusive, and becoming ever more so. As soon as anyone talks about humility as a personal endeavor, it slips away. There are two aspects of humility that must be incorporated in both behaviour and attitude in order for it to have integrity.

The **first** (too often ignored) requirement for humility involves adhering to a sincerely egalitarian philosophy as the foundation of all interaction.

---

[4] Microscopic truth telling is a descriptive phrase that I find particularly applicable. It is from *Conscious Loving*, Gay Hendricks, Ph.D., & Kathlyn Hendricks, Ph.D., Bantam Books, 1990, Chapter 4.

Being sincerely egalitarian, in attitude and outlook, must be universal, and operate generously and willingly regarding gender, age, health, ability, talent, culture, religion, politics, and affluence; egalitarian about *every* category that people use to classify people and animals. [This extends out to other living things and the earth as a matter of respect and stewardship.]

Humility requires that the fundamental prerequisite to all interaction be sincere egalitarianism. To interact with anything other than this is evidence of racism, elitism, sexism, expecting privilege, etc., and fails to honor the universal truth of unity that underlies all intellectual categorizations of life. An egalitarian philosophy for *all* of life is a crucial component to humility and the spiritual requirement at hand.

The **second** requirement for humility—which is the usual focus of any discussion about humility, which is itself an ego tactic to avoid egalitarianism—is participating in the sincere honoring of some form of "higher power" (*very* broad definition), by whatever cultural manifestation. Your interpretation of this is entirely a personal choice. You decide; you honor it.

Granted, in my own experience, some concepts in the long term appear to be more effective than others regarding spiritual transformation. Those that embody generosity and acceptance; those with an absence of dogma and structure, seem to be more effective in fostering serenity.

Recognizing there is a universal spirit (by many names), and willingly incorporating a devoted and regular appreciation of *It* in your private and social behaviour, is the second requirement. For some people, this might simply be a modern interpretation of a universal, governing energy harmony to the universe. (Meditate on the quote of George Santayana, p. 436.)

A "higher power", which is the common, socially safer phrase now in vogue, is left to the interpretation of the beholder. Your idea may be clear and structured, or not. Regardless, have some notion of what that is, however vague, and honor it.

Humility is the primary prerequisite for judicious participation in community. Humility requires a deeply willing participation in an egalitarian lifestyle *and* the regular and sincere appreciation of a Universal Cohesiveness that animates life, without regard to the inconvenience or awkwardness that this requires of you. As an aside: If you are truly humble, there is never any awkwardness or inconvenience. [Humility is discussed further at Step Seven, p. 292.]

Principle #4: Charity

Charity, common in the jargon of religious people, is generally understood to be some variation of "giving things away"—giving away your time, giving away money, volunteering your expertise, donating old clothes.

What qualifies or disqualifies charity as having spiritual integrity is the ego agenda underneath the "charitable" behaviour, which agenda is often *in*visible to the individual in self-introspection.

When charity is offered as a social grace, or with any underlying agenda of personal advancement or salvation, or getting a tax break, or for good publicity, then the charity lacks spiritual integrity. Yes, it's generous, but it's spiritually suspect. Charity, in other words, may be socially admirable but unspiritual when offered because the giver feels guilty; feels sorrow or pity for the recipient; tries to impress anyone (most often and especially themselves); wants a tax break; rescues the recipient out of some responsibility that is the recipient's to meet; tries to collect salvation points with God; offers charity with self-serving personal distinctions of who's worthy of charity and who isn't; offers charity to live up to other people's expectations (especially shadow-expectations from the past); or vies for social admiration through the charity. The unrecognized *un*spiritual ego machinations that motivate "charity" are insidious.[5]

"St. John of the Cross put the whole matter [of charity] *in a single question and answer. Those who rush headlong into good works without having acquired through contemplation the power to act well—what do they accomplish? Little more than nothing, and sometimes nothing whatever, and sometimes even harm."*[6] For the giver of charity, without appropriate self-love/respect, veracity, and both aspects of humility (which are the first three spiritual principles), as sincere prerequisites to the charity, the charity is selfish manipulation (impression management), and harmful to both the giver and the receiver.

Being generous (charitable) with your experience, wisdom, time, kindness, or spiritual courage through role modeling, will be more advantageous in the long run for those concerned with spiritual transformation. There's no tax deduction for compassion or respect, but these, rather than money, offer dignity and generate a healing relationship.

Principle #5: Responsibility & Obedience

These two attributes, which comprise the final spiritual principle, are usually abhorrent to addicts in general, to angry people, and to victims. This principle doesn't harbor well in our culture of victim-hood, disposable consumerism and greed. Certainly these two attributes are easily viewed as separate qualities, but in regards to spirituality they are so closely related and interdependent that I present them together.

---

[5] Joshua Loth Liebman, in his book *Peace of Mind*, Simon and Schuster, 1946, speaks to this in an anecdote about "victims of humility," pp. 38-39.

[6] *Huxley and God Essays*, Aldous Huxley, cited earlier, p. 175.

If people value an idea, and are obedient to that value (adhere to it), then they would be responsible in relation to it; and if someone is responsible, then they would be *willing* to be held accountable for not following the values they proclaim they have.[7] For example: If people hold kindness as an important value, then they "should" be obedient to that temporal virtue. They would be kind. They would be responsible (to themselves) to offer kindness in trying or awkward circumstances. More importantly, they would hold themselves fully accountable if they weren't kind. If they were kind only when it was convenient, or only to certain people, or only when people were watching, or were unwilling to be taken to task when they weren't kind, then kindness wouldn't be a value, it would be only a convenience and used for Impression Management.

In Chapter 12, I referred to Boethius' statement that *"A wise* [person] *ought no more to take it ill when* [they] *clash with fortune than a brave* [person] *ought to be upset by the sound of battle. This is why virtue gets its name, because it is firm in strength and unconquered by adversity."*[8] I add this: A person who willingly pursues a relationship with a higher power, or tries to live in harmony with the universe, ought not to take it ill or complain when they clash with their human nature and defects. Someone who volunteered at Step Three, and became willing at Step Six, would view all inner-personal struggles with their unspiritual impulses and temptations only as an opportunity to be devoted—an opportunity to gain faith.

You are responsible for things that belong to you. If you are given a magnificent gift that you declare you value highly, you are [would be] responsible to take care of it. Your life was given to *You*. As a person in recovery, your "recovery life" was also given to you, and not to anyone else. Your life, your health, your transformation, your cherished mementos and shiny things, your lover, all "belong" to you, and only you are responsible to take care of them. More importantly, since you volunteered for the job of being spiritual (at Step Three), all the related responsibilities and hard work are all self-imposed.

Responsibility: Truly spiritual people are willingly and completely responsible for themselves, their conduct, their thoughts, and their feelings— for their very life, and everything in it—*without complaint*. Granted, at times you are not responsible for what is done to you (calamity is random), but you are responsible for cleaning up after it—again, without complaint. Always hold only yourself responsible for the entire state of affairs in your life, and never surrender this responsibility. Anything less defeats your being spiritual and denies you serenity.

---

[7] Willingness is explored in detail in Chapter 6.

Obedience: If you aspire or claim to be spiritual, then you will desire to adhere to these five principles, which are embodied within the maintenance steps of the original twelve-step program. Obedience is mandatory because it's only obedience that proves you hold them of value and proves that you are spiritually responsible. Principles and values are only what they are *if* you adhere to them through adversity. Be completely responsible for yourself and obedient to the principles of spirituality; otherwise, you're not obedient, responsible, or spiritual.[9]

These five spiritual principles are applicable to every aspect of every situation and relationship in your life. Haphazard adherence to them is not evidence of spirituality; it's evidence of convenience and Impression Management. For people getting recovered, they are not negotiable or optional unless you're willing to embrace shallowness and hypocrisy. Then, in short order, your abstinence will be at risk. A person cannot disregard any part of any one of these principles and claim spiritual integrity.

A concomitant truth is whenever a spiritual pilgrim's own life is unsatisfying, conflicted, or lonely they're not (consistently) living within these principles.[10] They're being ignored in favor of influence, affluence, petulance, sex, blaming, revenge, or power. That's the paradigm of the human condition in modern culture.

Being spiritual, beyond the usual social constructs, seems monumentally difficult. Social cooperation, or in other cases corruption, appears easier, but that's an illusion, only because these are more popular and we're trained early to live that way. It's the transformation into a spiritual life that seems insurmountable. Once you are well on the way to achieving it, being spiritual is much easier and more graceful than corruption.

It appears that these principles are innate and exist *a priori* to intellect. When children are allowed to be spontaneous, they eat when they're hungry, stop doing something when it hurts, and sleep when they're tired. The impulse to self-care and self-respect is innate. Honesty is natural and makes sense — it takes no effort. Truth is graceful and the facts are friendly.[11]

Children are taught how, why, and when to deceive. Often I've heard an adult counselling a child to be dishonest and the child asks innocently:

---

[8] *The Consolation of Philosophy*, Boethius, Penguin Books, 1969, p. 144.
[9] St. Augustine wrote that spirituality is not efficient. It is the most difficult journey that anyone can undertake. And, as explained by Aldous Huxley in *Huxley and God: The Essays* (cited at an earlier footnote), that's why there are so few saints.
[10] One of the more unique and exasperating facets of any addiction is the ego-posture that tells an addict their unhappiness or conflicted life is someone else's fault. In order to be spiritual you will be required to willingly and definitively abandon this mindset.
[11] "The facts are friendly" is an expression attributed to the American psychotherapist Carl Rogers, referred to in an earlier footnote.

"But why can't I tell?" It's also very natural to be egalitarian. People are taught racism and prejudice. They're taught arrogance about culture and beliefs about god: "My way is better; you're wrong."

Likewise, people are often taught to disbelieve the mysterious power of unity that underlies everything. Humility is natural; arrogance is cultural. Greed is taught. Responsibility is as natural as honesty: "Who did this?" "I did." Through fear, people learn how to blame others and minimize their accountability. It seems to me that being spiritual is innate and doesn't really need to be taught.

Being spiritual often generates insecurity in other people, especially regarding veracity. Rather than examine their own dishonesty, they justify their own insecurity and attack someone else. Be wary of the unregenerate person whose propensity to blame and disrespect others creates a dark labyrinth that keeps them off of the path of spiritual transformation, even though it appears (to them) that they're on it. A spiritual lifestyle is all encompassing—a state of existence. You will miss the mark, which is the nature of being human, but you only have to make amends and diligently refocus your energy and intellect onto these principles. According to *Alcoholics Anonymous*, this is the proper exercise of willpower.

As I said in the Manner of Presentation, from wherever you are right now, at this immediate point in your own transformation, you are a newcomer to the rest of your life. This is the inherent uncertainty in life. In the face of this uncertainty, in order to appreciate the implacable grandeur of life, exactly as you have been given it, consistently and voluntarily demonstrate respect for the physical body, veracity, humility, charity, and responsibility and obedience.

As I reflect on how these five principles coalesced in my mind, I'm very aware of my gratitude to the monks, mystics, imams, priests, ministers, and rabbis I have the pleasure of knowing, who were very generous with their knowledge and wisdom. I'm also grateful to the authors of the many books I've studied.[12]

---

[12] Worthy of special note are: William James, for his book *The Varieties of Religious Experience*, (various publishers)—my most recent edition is Modern Library Classics, 2002; to Huston Smith, for his book *The World's Religions*, HarperSanFrancisco, 1991; to Aldous Huxley, for two of his books: *The Perennial Philosophy*, recently by Harper Collins, 1994, and *Huxley and God Essays*, Jacqueline Hazard Bridgeman editor, HarperSanFrancisco, 1992; and to Gerald May, for his book *Will and Spirit*, Harper Collins, 1982.

Appendix III

Energy & Body Healing[1]
(A too-brief overview)

In addition to the spiritual dislocation (which must be addressed), that underlies addictions; any acting-out may be an attempt to calm traumatized, dysregulated body-energy. This is often evident when people achieve abstinence from socially *dis*approved-of addictions like pornography, alcohol, or drugs and make a quick transition to the socially approved addictions like exercise, romance, relationships, greed, spending, or work.[2] Because of the significant amount of trauma that's experienced during addiction, and the cravings associated with addictions, the energy treatments I describe here can be an incredibly valuable and effective part of any spiritual transformation process.

First, there are three general categories of trauma.

Developmental trauma (including fetal development): This occurs when developmental, emotional, or physical needs are not met through physical or psychological abuse or neglect. This can include biogenealogical and environmental trauma that occurs during the early stages of emotional or physical development. This is usually, but not always, during the period between conception and thirteen or fourteen years of age.

Shock trauma, which occurs from some defined physical event like accidents, violence, surgery, misadventure, or sudden ruptures in established perceptions and beliefs.

Psychological trauma results from both other types of trauma *and* from illness, significant upheaval, significant loss, drastic change, etc.

Some events aren't necessarily "bad" *per se,* but do cause trauma. i.e. There are harmful, traumatic effects from undergoing a general anesthetic and surgery (which are both severe physiological shocks), even though surgery can be good and certainly saves lives, it still results in ancillary,

---

[1] Read the disclaimer at the end of this appendix. This appendix is much too-brief an explanation of trauma and body-energy. This is only to provide a very general outline, to encourage curiosity, so readers will explore these other avenues to healing. At www.gracewfultransformation.ca there is a free forty-five page manual (download) that explains this in some detail

[2] Recall, in Chapter 2, the observation of Terry Kellogg that the most common solution to an addiction is another addiction. The attempt to self-regulate is one component of this.

harmful trauma. The trauma from successful surgery can often result in other ailments that will require attention.

Trauma can be related to developmental concerns, emotional issues, abuse, or physical injury, and is often greatly complicated by toxins. Trauma, and subsequent illness, occurs when body energy is disrupted and left out of balance (referred to as dysregulated)—when a person is detrimentally, but not necessarily overwhelmingly, impacted by some event.

This is creates a cycle or recurring trauma, especially for the self-destructive behaviour of addicts.

---

(1) Some circumstance or event that results in trauma, injury, or emotional distress...

(2) This causes physiological dysregulation or disruption in the body's energy patterns—the generation of traumatic energy in body tissue and nerves, which is complicated by toxins and generally poor cellular health. Next, is one of two options, either 3(a) Best Scenario or (b) Worst Scenario:

(3a) <u>Best Scenario</u>: Healing—a naturally occurring process augmented by formal trauma recovery (treatment) "should" compensate and rebalance the energy dysregulation from the trauma (go to #4); or,

(3b) <u>Worst Scenario</u>: Additional recurring trauma; extended traumatic episodes that result in extended energy imbalance or dysregulation that eventually results in illness, disease, physical impairment, addictions substitutions, emotional disorders, mental health issues. This means a life of repeating: 1 –> 2 –> 3b... go directly back to #1 (worst-case scenario).

(4) A reestablished, balanced energy flow in the energy meridians, and a physiological homeostasis at an energy-cellular level — reestablished good health. Life is unpredictable and at some point another traumatic event occurs. Go to #1. This means a life of repeating 1 —> 2 —> 3(a) — 4, (best-case scenario).

If the healing process at 3(a) is not undertaken or is defeated by more trauma before the body can reestablish proper energy patterns; if stress, trauma, and toxins are left unaddressed and on-going, [as in 3(b)] and body-energy isn't realigned through treatment, energy dysregulation becomes established as "normal". The longer this is left unaddressed or untreated, the more pronounced are the subsequent symptoms of dysregulation—an astonishing array of health problems that range from chronic illnesses, panic attacks, weight problems, phobias, headaches, attention disorders, physical disabilities, chronic pain, cancers, environmental illnesses, and addictions.

The following two approaches to good health have been shown to be quite effective, especially when applied in conjunction with each other:

Meridian Energy Work *

Meridian energy work, which largely follows the protocols and recommendations of Emotional Freedom Techniques, balances body energy. This is very similar in theory to acupressure or acupuncture, but is done by light finger tapping on energy meridians.

The energy work described at www.gracefultransformation.ca or through the Emotional Freedoms Techniques website has been shown to be very effective for many health concerns. People (should) usually begin with training from a properly trained and skilled EFT practitioner. After an introductory period of acquiring basic skills and treatment people are expected to self-administer the tapping.

Organic Sulfur and pH Catalyst Altered Water *

Organic sulfur (often referred to as MSM) and pH water (Catalyst Altered Water) are not diet supplements. These are foods that must be consumed in certain quantities for optimum health. The West Coast Organic Sulfur Study has been collecting information since 2005.

Organic sulfur is a food that is crucial for good health, and it is substantially lacking in our diet. Catalyst Altered Water is a patented water formula—water that has been altered at the molecular level into long-chain water molecules with a stable pH level of 10.4. For various reasons these are important for cellular gas balance transfers, amino acid manufacture, detoxification, and oxygen transport at the cell membrane.

We now have valid, reported information on the benefits of these foods. Amazing and permanent health improvements are regularly and consistently reported. The reported benefits are explained in detail at www.organicsulfur-msm.ca

At first view, because the methods are so unconventional, many people are suspicious and doubt their effectiveness. Creating energy harmony and the healing that results, although still considered by many to be in the experimental-research phase, demonstrates a remarkable success rate for emotional, physical, and environmental illnesses, healing after surgery, and resolving trauma. They are proving to be *very* effective aides to addicts getting recovered.

These treatments are respectful of a person's physiological and psychological needs and capabilities. These three, altogether, promote the body's natural ability to heal itself. When done in a skilled and persistent manner, in addition to the probable reduction or elimination of the original issues, there's a newly developed ability to self-monitor personal health. This creates an enhanced level of sensation awareness, confidence, and physiological and emotional stability.

*DISCLAIMER

These self-help treatments described at www.organicsulfur-msm.ca and at www.gracefultransformation.ca do have an amazing record of success, but also should be considered to be in their research stage. As with all therapeutic endeavors, and especially here, common sense is required. We are not physicians or psychologists and make no claims as to these treatments' guaranteed effectiveness or of their success. The benefits reported at the websites are accurate quotes from people who participate in this type of healing. Results vary. No all people experience the same degree of positive results. Both practitioners and the public must take complete personal responsibility and use judicious common sense in undertaking any of these self-help, self-applied treatments or therapy for health issues. Check the noted websites for information.

Appendix IV

The Ego — "I" Am It

There are many interpretations and definitions of what an ego is, some are quite confusing and esoteric. I don't believe my ego and understanding it needs be as complicated as I am led to believe.

I offer the following perspective not to imply other views are wrong, but to make the ego a more tangible concept. This won't necessarily make becoming spiritual (or any personal transformation) easier, except it may only prevent forays into unproductive ventures, and become more viable when "working with your ego" is no longer vague nor punitive.

Neutralizing the Self-Attack

It's common in discussions about spirituality, psychology, or self-help to hear phrases similar to these: "She's got to get her ego down to size." "He's an ego-maniac and has got to get his ego under control." "You've got to get rid of that ego if you're going to be spiritual." "You've got to cut your ego down to size if you're going to be happy in your relationship." Among the many observations that might be made about these sentences, three are relevant here.

- They reflect the tendency of technological cultures to attach a negative connotation to words of neutral character (similar to the words "criticize" and "animosity").[1]
- These involve some element of attack or punitive judgment.[2] They're very non-accepting of "self". In this vein, egos are represented as bad.

---

[1] *Criticize* is to analyze or make observations on the value or worth of a thing. Paying compliments or giving praise is to criticize. *Animosity* originally meant having high spirits and great energy. Both of these words have taken on negative connotations, and so it is with *ego*. This negative perspective, that egos are bad, limits our perceptions, and limited perceptions are fatal to spirituality. (The observation on *animosity* is from *Brewer's Dictionary of Phrase & Fable,* Revised Edition, Edited by Ivor H. Evans, Cassell Ltd., 1981.)

[2] Whenever you're spiritually lost in character defects, it is ineffective to cut yourself down to size, or hack away at your ego, or slap yourself back into spirituality. Psychological violence, self-rejection, or harsh criticism implied rhetorically or otherwise, won't contribute to transformation—these prevent it. You simply need to recognize you're human (that's why you have an ego, and why you're off course), and lovingly nudge yourself in another direction.

Cutting your ego down to size, or any other euphemism that implies self-attack, isn't a loving nudge by any standard. Too often, our socially appointed mentors like doctors, therapists, teachers, priests, counsellors, social workers, parents, older siblings, religious leaders, or sponsors are themselves the purveyors of character assassination camouflaged as (cont'd)

- The self-rejecting nature of these perspectives; their disapproval of the human condition, makes them spiritually
  untenable. They're at odds with the first spiritual principle,
  the aspect of egalitarianism in the third spiritual principle,
  and they do not embody charity.

In relation to alcoholics and addicts, and spirituality in general, neu-
tralizing this commonly accepted negative connotation to "ego" enables a
smoother transition into spirituality. In perceiving your ego as I am about to
suggest, a spiritually based life becomes possible, and it becomes more palatable.

The Premise

Each person has two fundamental and non-modifiable realities to contend with. I call these the **Matrix of the Soul** and the **Corporeal Universe**.

The Matrix of the Soul is comprised of that inherent set of instinctual
drives and emotions that are here generally categorized as fear, joy,
sexuality, hunger, survival, social association, and some awareness of a
higher power (by whatever name). These exist "within our soul" and, are
altogether the apparently mandatory, deeply subconscious state of affairs in
everyone.

These instincts exist in everyone like a multi-dimensional matrix.
Whatever animates into life these aspects of our soul may arrive from beyond, but exists in, Time and Space. The Matrix of the Soul is the unknown,
animating energy of humanity—the "every person" in each of us, regardless
of age, gender, or cultural heritage.

These attributes of the soul collide and negotiate with each other. At
an unknowable level fear, sexuality, social association, joy, survival (food,
shelter), the dynamic of love, the essence and origin of life-energy, all interact *within* our souls. This is why any healing or recovery is an inside job,
and has nothing to do with anyone or anything "outside" you.

The Matrix of the Soul constitutes that unknowable place inside from
which we originate (collectively and individually). It's a lattice of interacting, fundamental life-energy that impels us to *be*. It cannot *not* exist.
Everyone who is alive has, and must respond to, the nature of their soul. It
motivates life—the never knowable source of our instincts and origin-point
to our spiritual nature. The Matrix of the Soul exists independently of all
things "material". This is one reality with which we must all contend.

---

guidance or help. It's so often true that people pounce like jackals on the humanness of others,
thinking that this cruelty will contribute to someone else's transformation.

The Corporeal Universe, which is the other experience of reality, is everything that isn't the Matrix of the Soul—literally *any*thing and *every*thing that can in any way be referred to as material, extant, or measurably present. The Corporeal Universe is other people, animals, and all material things of any description, cultural and religious values and expectations, and it includes your body and its physical needs, which are "external" to the Matrix of the Soul. Your own physical existence is not a part of what it is that impels you to *be*. Nerves and flesh and blood are only things that support the brain, in which the Matrix of the Soul mysteriously resides.

Everything in the Corporeal Universe (all of the things outside of our soul) must influence and negotiate with each other. The Corporeal Universe requires and demands interaction. There's an inherent, unavoidable imperative in and for relationship: fish and water; food and people; people with people; intellect and emotion; the environment and all living things; safety and joy. Reality in the Corporeal Universe is composed of different manifestations of energy and requires interaction.

The Corporeal Universe is quantifiable reality—anything you can see, evaluate, or measure. This is our other experience of reality.

The Problem

The Matrix of the Soul and the Corporeal Universe are completely and mutually exclusive. They are each a different reality with nothing in common. They each have independent aspects that negotiate within themselves, and these two realities must act upon each other. They often appear to be, and are often actually, at odds with each other, but life demands they coexist.

Another way of saying it is "I" must find some way to get these two opposing forces to cooperate to "my" satisfaction—

a) Someone feels sexual, hungry, lonely, or cold (internal reality), so

b) They negotiate with external reality for a partner, food, companionship, or shelter.

That mandatory coexistence; the balancing act, between The Matrix of the Soul and The Corporeal Universe, is where lies the problems of every individual.

In order for anyone to "be" or to exist, there must be an operating agent or system that facilitates the interaction and balancing of instinct and reality (The Matrix of the Soul vs. The Corporeal Universe). Your life, as you know it, is the result of the interaction between the matrix of *your* soul and the corporeal universe you are exposed to.

Being born into a rich family in Thailand or a poor family in Ireland, or a religious family in the Middle East will expose you to different realities. Every person has sexual, companionship, and other "survival" needs. You, as a living person, must somehow negotiate between these two mutually exclusive realities, or contend with these opposing forces. The job of balancing these two realities falls to...

The Ego

The operating agency (of your mind) that coordinates or mediates that relationship, and creates harmony or disharmony between The Corporeal Universe and The Matrix of the Soul, is your ego. Your ego, encapsulated in your mind—which is an emergent property of "being"—is both a funnel and a teeter-totter. Your ego is the filtering balance point where everything is organized and mediated. But... you can't see your ego, you can only see the results of it. Your ego is only visible in its derivations, not in its reality. The end result of your ego's balancing act is Your Life.

Your ego is the organized conscious mediator between your unknowable, instinctual soul and the reality you are exposed to, as it exists outside of your soul.

Your ego is actually a solution to a problem. It's the solution to the existential problem of balancing the reality of your soul and the reality of the universe. The problem isn't your ego; it's how your ego balances the interaction of these two realities.

Matrix of the Soul	EGO	Corporeal Universe
	∧	
fear, joy, love, sexuality, hunger, social association, awareness of a higher power (by what-ever name or definition	**My Personality** the invisible mind-agency that negotiates, mediates, and balances these opposing realities	*Every*thing in reality including your own physical being

Your interpretation of the reality you are exposed to is your ego at work. That interpretation is rooted in your ego's filtering and balancing, and was molded by your genetics, by your developmental stages, by how your caregivers influenced your perceptions of your own Matrix of the Soul and your own Corporeal Universe, by your temperament, and by the haphazard circumstances that befell you. Your ego was also molded by how your caregiver's egos manifested and organized their own balance in their own lives. It all combines to become *you* (your personality is your ego).

A soft generalization is the psychological problems that people experience, which is the content of most therapy, i.e. anxieties, neuroses, anger, despair, conflict, sex, depression, unhappiness, and complaints about the unpleasantness of everyday life, is representative of this balancing act. Recall these earlier discussions: hopeless and helpless (Chapter 2); the committee that wants to help the old woman (Chapter 7); and, the overlooked middle step of the Two-Step Dance (Chapter 8). These are all representative of the ego's balancing and funneling.

Finish the Sentence

- You're given $50,000 to spend so you...
- You get any book in a bookstore for free. You choose...
- Someone prays nine times a day and you think...
- Your favorite sexual partner is (or was)...
- It's a warm summer day. An acquaintance stays inside *all* day, watches five movies and eats popcorn. You think...
- You're late and stuck in heavy traffic behind a confused and timid driver, so you...
- You're *exhausted* and under *terrific* pressure at work. That evening your spouse starts caressing and flirting. You...
- You have to spend the day by yourself, so you...
- Your idea of a physically attractive, sexy person is someone who looks just like the movie star...

Your answers represent the filtering and balancing of your ego. Your response to *any* circumstance is your ego in action, which is sometimes conscious (people act deliberately), or sometimes subconscious (people act without clear awareness). Perceived as evil or good, ordinary or magnificent, your ego is the solution to the problem of mediating between two unyielding, opposing realities. To try to eliminate or reduce it is akin to self-annihilation. Your spirit will resist, and transformation into a spiritual lifestyle will not be possible.

One crucial problem that addicts must address is their ego modifies and filters everything destructively. It negotiates and balances the relationship between these two realities *anti*-spiritually.[3]

---

[3] When offering resolution strategies for addiction, if the addict's damage to other people (you have to change because you're hurting others) is prioritized over *self*-damage, a socially directed treatment plan is mandated. That would then be a reflection of a sentimental perspective that arises from relationship addiction (which is rampant in our culture). With addictions, "outer/socially-directed" treatment modalities always fail. A spiritually directed life is, at its core, never a socially directed exercise.

Self-destruction &
Comparative Character Assassination

Personal Assassination of Self – the extra variable for addicts

What follows may be one of the most difficult things to understand about addictive behaviour. Non-addicted people contend and balance their instinctive desires and their corporal universe—the two realities, and in their balancing (in their life), their view of themselves is such that they aren't "separated" from themselves or their realities.

An addict, on the other hand, has to contend with external reality, and with their instincts as everyone else does, but there is an extra third variable—a strange aspect of their mind perceives "itself" as separate or independent of "itself". Their own mind sees some part of itself (of their own mind) as independent or "separate" from the rest of themselves and independent of life. This is evident when an addict's mind, in the midst of their self-destructive life, very subtly excuses itself from reality.

That part of the mind which values-and-judges, for an addict, embodies a curious and destructive characteristic: It views itself as not a part of the destruction, or capable of escaping unscathed. For addicts, it is thus: Their mind thinks "the addict" may die but "it" (an aspect of how their mind perceives itself) will escape and still go on living. "I know I'm killing myself but I'll be okay." "I know this is stupid or dangerous but I'll escape." There's a part of an addict's mind that views itself as separate from the destruction.

The addict's mind thinks *to itself*, like a sub-conscious, internal dialogue, as if it's talking to the addict's body: "Go ahead, you can destroy yourself by acting out, but I'll get through this. I can force the destructive reality of this to be different and not affect me." The addict's *mind* perceives, to itself, it can continuously do destructive things and somehow squeeze out unscathed.

This mindset of addiction is the *Velcro* set up for rescuing on the part of codependent, relationship addicts. The first addict (alcohol, food, shopping, sex) has a mindset of "I can destroy myself but escape alive." (One half of a *Velcro* strip.) The second addict—relationship-addict hero rescuer, witnesses this and their insecurity, and arrogance that conceals this insecurity, convinces themselves they alone can and must save the first addict from the self-destruction (the other half of a *Velcro* strip).

The (self-destructive) hero rescuer destroys themselves in the attempt to "save" the first addict, but the rescuer also believes they can escape unscathed the self-destruction of rescuing. They *Velcro* onto each other because they both believe they can escape the destructive behaviour. The trap for the rescuer is, their self-destruction is motivated by moral superiority (which is itself rooted in carefully concealed insecurity). Fun, eh?

This is sometimes evident when addicts refer to themselves in the third person. Other people may occasionally refer to themselves in the third person in wry humor; for an addict it can have particularly sinister implications. People without addictions don't have this third aspect to their personality. For non-addicts, generally it's different: The part of their mind that views the nature of their personality sees themselves as included in the part that judges.

In the personality of an addict (the ego) there are these four dynamics operating:
(i) The Matrix of the Soul—their instinctual drives;
(ii) The Corporeal Universe)—the reality they are exposed to;
(iii) How they balance and negotiate these two realities (for the most part destructively); and,
(iv) That part of their mind that perceives itself as removed from the consequences—a peculiar mindset, which believes itself to be independent of the self-destruction.

Every time an addict says something like this: "I didn't think I'd get hurt." "I never thought I'd get caught." "I never believed it would get this bad." "I always got away with it before," this dynamic is what they refer to. Eliminating this style of dissociation from the reality of their life is one crucial aspect to treating addictions.

Comparative Character Assassination & Relationships
Even though it often appears that one half of a couple is "healthier" than the other half, this isn't the truth of the matter. The appearance of one person being healthier is the end result of a mind game that I call Comparative Character Assassination.

Comparative Character Assassination is an ego gambit that goes like this: One half of a couple compares themselves to the other half of that couple and, for any number of reasons, decides, through assassinating the other person's character, that the other person is less "healthy" (whatever that means).[4] This is announced at every reasonable opportunity, i.e. "I'm more in touch with my feelings than you because..." or "I'm more committed to the relationship than you because..." or "You're not as emotionally healthy as me because...." None of this is true.

---

[4] One person in a relationship takes a morally superior position (I'm healthier than you...) because of their own well concealed insecurity, superficial self-help jargon, superficial application of psych-101 courses, or inaccurate information from social stereotyping (i.e. women are more in touch with their feelings than men; men are more angry than women).

Any partner that you're with, in any longer-term relationship, will have a mirroring personality-structure that compliments or "fits" with yours.[5] You will each have approximately the same capacity or incapacity to bring conflict, commitment, intimacy, or love to the relationship. If one person was actually and significantly more "emotionally healthy" than the other one, they wouldn't be in the relationship. Neither person is healthier than the other, even though it may appear otherwise. And, even if the *apparently* unhealthier person in the relationship agrees with the accusations of the "healthier" person, or if one half voluntarily condemns themselves as unhealthier, it still isn't true.

Intimate relationships are carefully pre-arranged, choreographed dances, and most are initiated as personal salvation strategies. They're compensations for unknown dislocation. This was very briefly touched upon in Thought, Form, Fascination, Fall (Chapter 11), and in the poem *The Dance* p. 496.

The five rules of relationship, which appear to be universal, are:

1) You cannot be "out" of relationship. Not being in a relationship is a fool's delusion. All that's available is to define how you participate *in* relationships. Your life is the active dynamic of relationships. Period.

2) Whatever dynamics are present in one relationship are present to some degree in all your relationships. Every relationship is to some degree a mirror of (or it's reaction to) *all* your relationships. We are subtly, universally consistent.

3) We choose long-term, intimate partners that will bolster our compensations and, over the long-term demand that we expose our deepest insecurities. If you are in repetitive, short term relationships and "can't commit" that's also an exposure of your deepest insecurities.

4) Our intimate partners will reflect our deeply cherished self-judgments. This is largely subconscious and primarily a subtle and complex reflection or mirror of the relationship with the parent you have the most unresolved conflict with. Gender is irrelevant. No one can escape this truth.

5) In any on-going relationship of intimacy, each person is equally capable of bringing love and harmony or conflict and fear to the relationship. This is the unalterable fact: Neither person is

---

[5] Dating is actually that process of going "people shopping" for a complimentary personality structure. When you find the one that matches what your ego requires, that's the one you'll want. If you've asked eleven consecutive, different people out on a *second* date and they all say 'No,' your ego is deliberately (subconsciously) choosing these people because its balancing and mediation policy is rooted in rejection. Whatever you get is what you want, regardless of your verbal protestations to the contrary.

emotionally healthier that the other, *regardless of how obvious it appears otherwise*.

If you select a mate who, over time, starts to love you more or differently than your own ego can accommodate; or if after the relationship is established, your partner (their ego) modifies the relationship contract (changes the dance) without your cooperation, i.e. changes the level of emotional disclosure or accountability/responsibility, without your ego making an accommodating, voluntary ego-shift, you'll not be able to tolerate or accept the change. You'll precipitate a struggle to change your partner back to the rules you agreed on. The machinations and needs of your personality will dominate the situation regardless of your intellectually good intentions.

Additionally, there are traits that attract you to a person in the first place: He's so outgoing. She's so assertive and independent. He's so neat and tidy. She's so financially organized. These qualities will eventually be recast by your ego to be a source of complaint. These very qualities, that were once attractive, will become: He's a flirt. She's stubborn. He's a neat freak. She's cheap. This is the testing phase of a relationship.

All of this *self*-generated conflict was orchestrated before the fact, (i.e. you actually set up the divorce *before* you meet your partner) and may result in an end to the relationship. Separation brings immediate relief, but without significant inner work, the parties will sooner or later orchestrate another similar relationship scenario. Or, if they "can't" separate (another self-generated, self-serving perception), they'll remain in perpetual struggle, or completely smother and eradicate the vulnerable parts of their personality, eventually abandoning themselves and remaining forever unfulfilled.[6]

Self-condemnation that someone harbors, of which they are unaware, is so powerful that life situations and partners will be chosen so their relationships are a parallel reflection (a metaphor) of the unrealized self-condemnation. This is often reflected in parenting. All abuse of children, or of anyone, or anything, is *never* about the abused, it's always about the perpetrator.

These are all machinations of your personality. In relationships, nothing is accidental. People get exactly what they want, regardless of passionate speeches and public declarations to the contrary.

---

[6] Without expert help, meaning much more than an adequately trained addictions counsellor, many people can't change a situation that's intolerable, or separate from isolation, unfulfilling careers, conflict, or self-destruction. Their ego continues to choose these because of a subconscious contextual view that life *is* conflict, and/or an unresolved *self*-perception of unworthiness or personal incompetence, or because the perceived loneliness and fear attendant to being alone or independent is horrific. Without changing the underlying context, the possibility of a peaceful life is non-existent. Ask yourself and your spouse: "Do we want a divorce @ $250,000 and bitterness for 25 years or do we want three years of therapy @ $25,000?"

The Only Variable

Everyone has an instinctual soul that is what it is—the unalterable core of existence: The Matrix of the Soul. Also: Everyone was born into reality, and reality is what it is—unyielding, resistant, and capricious—The Corporeal Universe. The only variable is how you negotiate between these unalterable realities—how you dance yourself through their interaction. Your cooperation with or defiance to reality; your respect or disregard for yourself; the way you participate in life; and especially, the love or absence of love you have for your own authentic self, are all demonstrations of your ego.

As an adult: your parents, your spouse, your job, your life, your childhood, your children, are not the problem, although to you it looks like they are. The problem may also appear to be the size of your ego, but even that isn't really the problem, it just looks that way because that's how other (insecure) egos have defined "the problem". The core issue is how your ego is organized, and how it funnels information between the matrix of your soul and the corporeal universe that you are exposed to.

Your own ego's balancing act—its interpretations and perceptions, are what generates your own psychological state of affairs. Your ego is the organizer of your psychology, be it aggressive, atheistic, charitable, chaste, dramatic, domineering, self-destructive, other-destructive, generous, kind, mean, passive, pompous, promiscuous, quiet, rude, selfish, sexual, shy, spiritual, submissive, violent... *whatever* (and any and all combinations and permutations of these attributes). Every thought you have, every emotion you experience, every word you utter, is some aspect of your ego.

The Solution

You can't change the Matrix of the Soul. You can't change the Corporeal Universe. You can't reduce or increase your ego. All attempts to do any of these only redefines the dynamics and results in some new type of relationship, therapeutic, or spiritual disaster. The only effective, long-range plan is to modify the mandate of your ego—to adjust how it perceives and interprets information in the relationship between the matrix of your soul and your corporeal universe.

If you don't have a strong, well-defined ego that can harmonize and balance the relentless demands of these two realities, and have no doubt the demands are relentless, you will founder and become lost.[7] Chaos in self-awareness cannot balance powerful forces like instincts and external reality. When you are lost and foundering, or unfulfilled (the manifestation of an

---

[7] For additional explanation see The Myth of Ego Reduction in Chapter 10.

external locus of control), you will attach yourself to strong, controlling egos like an abusive partner, a cult leader, or an overbearing counsellor, therapist, or sponsor. You may become involved in a rigid religious structure, or participate in a group with strong peer-pressure values, or simply abandon yourself to the whims and coincidences of the universe.

Your personality is actually a visible demonstration of the manner and pattern of your attempt to balance the matrix of *your* soul and the reality to which *you* are exposed. How your ego facilitates this interaction is "life" as you know it, which is the operational status of your personality. You are not your potential: you are you. You life is your ego in action.

Egos & Addiction & Relationships

People with addictions live in desperate, self-destructive dislocation. Regardless of how much they remember they were loved, or thought they were loved, or really were loved, or were not loved, or were abused, or were not abused, the fact is, they are attempting to solve their own spiritual dislocation through self-annihilation (called addiction). In a desperate reaction to life to save themselves they capture people—other addicts—in friendships, marriages, and sexual relationships.

These fractured relationships are an externalized metaphor to the addict's dislocated, interior life, and a skewed, holographic image of their ego. Along with the usual relationship problems of sexually destructive/harmful behaviour, power-struggles, anger, neglect, deceit, greed, a need to dominate or be victimized, betrayal, irresponsibility, etc., these relationships embody isolation and loneliness.

Life is Relationship.

The addict approaches relationships as a game of blame, control, and manipulation, and life is experienced in such a way as to perpetuate alienation from everything. That's what is accomplished in the acting out rituals. If you resolve spiritual dislocation, you resolve addictions. If you're spiritual, that will become the paradigm for your relationships with people, which will be the opposite of the list of problems in the paragraph immediately above. The original twelve-step program was designed to reorganize and refocus your ego's focus and thereby create spiritual integrity. Without spiritual integrity addicts and alcoholics remain unfulfilled.

The task in spiritual transformation is to deliberately modify your interpretations and perceptions of how reality impacts on the components of your soul, and how your instincts interrelate and make demands on the universe. Spiritual integrity requires a well-defined, strong ego (not a reduced ego) that filters and balances these two opposing realities according to spiritual principles.[8]

Everyone is created without flaw, without prejudice or mean judgment, and capable of love in its purest form. However, at birth, that "purity" must be immediately abandoned on behalf of instinctual survival and obedience to the circumstances of the reality into which we are born. Over time, recapturing that spiritual essence is the task human beings are presented with—to reorganize their perceptions of the universe and to reclaim the spiritual principles that naturally exist within them. The original twelve steps have brought us (back) to an historical, subtle truth that was so succinctly stated by Aldous Huxley: *"God is. That is the primordial fact. It is in order that we may discover this fact for ourselves, by direct experience, that we exist."*[9]

"God" may not be a word you are comfortable with. The fact is, there is a harmony to the universe and you (or I) can disrupt that harmony or cooperate with it. It is in order that we may discover how to dance in harmony with the universe, by direct experience, that we exist. That is the stewardship we offer the world.

---

[8] This is discussed in Chapter 10—The Myth of Ego Reduction as Humility.

[9] *Huxley and God, Essays,* Aldous Huxley, Edited by Jacqueline Hazard Bridgeman, Harper San Francisco, 1992, p. 17, (quoted at the beginning of this book).

Epilogue

A Lot of Work to Go Not Very Far

It began with severe spiritual dislocation in you, and it really wasn't your fault that you ended up with an addiction, but neither was it anyone else's fault. Then Providence, or Grace, or The Energy of the Universe, in some mysterious machination, offered you the opportunity to reconstruct yourself. The condition attached to you achieving a fulfilling life was that it must be rooted in a non-addicted lifestyle governed by spiritual principles.

There was the realization that you were spiritually sick, and a decision to live by the will of your higher power, as you came to understand this. As you slowly reorganized your life around spiritual principles, you realized that the crisis called "Your Life" was your fault, and admitted this. You abandoned willfulness and other destructive attributes you had formerly cherished, and sought willingness. Humility became a desired character trait, adopted not through fear but through appreciating its inherent beauty. Life was becoming graceful.

It was with some eagerness, and no regret, that you examined your own life, and quietly made amends to repair the holes you tore in the fabric of the universe. You became truly responsible. You realized you had achieved what you were promised you could achieve, and volunteered to continually deepen your devotion to a spiritual way of life, which became your life.

In transforming from self-destructive to spiritual, you've progressed along this approximate spectrum of emotion: hopeless, angry, despairing, angry, confused, bitter, frustrated, suspicious, reluctant, resigned, curious, hopeful, interested, willing, serious, committed, devoted, and (finally) sincerely spiritual. If you painstakingly follow the original twelve-step instructions you end up with new values, new priorities, new traditions: a new life. And even after all that, nothing "out there" will have changed much. The four critical decisions you made—to remain abstinent, to never complain because you volunteered for this, to work hard on your own behalf, and to live governed by the five spiritual principles have altered your destiny. This is no mean feat.

Herakleitos the Obscure was of this view:

> *"The wise* [person] *must make tremendous efforts to grasp*
> *"the unexpected": that is to* say [they must keep themselves]
> *alert, and constantly* [seek for themselves] *and not fear to*

strive for the excellence that will make [them] *an object of ha-*
tred and mistrust in the eyes of the conventional majority...."

"[Herakleitos] *preferred loneliness to the warm security of*
[the] *collective illusion... It takes humility to confront the*
prejudice and the contempt of all, in order to cling to an un-
popular truth."[10]

For Spiritual Transformation

What I offer is this: Humans are very bitter sweet, and are not disposable. A spiritual life is never about the result. It's never about getting some
honesty "thing", or some prayer issue, or this relationship "problem" out of
the way. If you don't fully explore it, understand it, or appreciate it, your
life will end up being just good enough, and life will never be satisfying or
fulfilling. You will miss the meaning of your own life.

In spiritual endeavor, as in love, refuse to be restricted by time. What
you love is what you give your time to. What you love is what captures
your spiritual integrity. Don't walk away from some relationship, or some
spiritual commitment, before you feel like you've really challenged yourself. Explore every avenue, every nuance, and then live your life based on
that. Your time and living by spiritual principles are the precious jewels that
you offer to the world.

"So what's your life about?" "Where do you really want your life to
end up?" "What are you doing with your life?" Smile gently and don't answer. Never justify yourself. Don't complain. Believe in something. Believe
passionately in it. Devote yourself to it... completely, utterly.[11]

"*Of all forms of caution, caution in love is perhaps most*
fatal to true happiness."[12]

The Movie Scene

Pretend you're watching a movie. The scene is set in 1937, in a cozy
den. There are some worn, comfortable armchairs, bookshelves, a small
fireplace, an oak desk and typewriter. Sitting at the desk is Bill Wilson. Sitting on the corner of the desk is Dr. Bob Smith. The cofounders of AA are
wearing casual clothes, or maybe suits with their collars and ties loosened.

---

[10] *A Thomas Merton Reader,* Revised Edition, edited by Thomas P. McDonnell, Doubleday
Image Books, 1974, pp. 264-267.
[11] Here I have recast, from film making to spirituality, the views expressed by Nicole Kidman
that were discussed in Chapter 5.
[12] Bertrand Russell, as quoted in *The Blues ain't nothing but a good soul feeling bad,* Sheldon
Kopp, Fireside Books, Simon & Schuster, 1992, entry for Sep. 17.

It's late at night. The table lamps are on, and it's quiet. A clock ticks in the background.

"What can we say to these people to give them hope?" Bob asks.

"I don't know exactly," Bob replies, "but I guess they'll have to at least do what we did. How do we get them to persevere?" They both sigh.

Bill Wilson shakes his head. "We're at the end of the book. We've got to end it with something. But what?" He fiddles with a pencil on the desk.

Dr. Bob paces about the room, finally sitting in one of the armchairs. With his face in shadow, he asks Bill, "What was it that *we* wanted to know when we were all jittery and alone?" There's a long pause, and then Bob quietly asks, "What did you want, Bill? What did *you* want to know?"

Bill Wilson is startled by an idea. He shifts closer to the desk and types a few sentences, then pulls the paper out of the typewriter and smiles at Bob, who's half hidden in the shadows. Bill turns to the camera and looks directly at *you*.

"Bob and I '...*know what you are thinking. You are saying to yourself: "I'm jittery and alone. I couldn't do that." But you can. You forgot that you have just now tapped a source of power much greater than yourself. To duplicate, with such backing, what we have accomplished is only a matter of willingness, patience and labor.*'"[13]

On this pilgrimage you have been required to make many difficult choices, often wandering through the hostile areas of your own personality, always on faith, always pushing yourself deeper into spiritual principles. This has not been easy. The author W. Somerset Maugham was reported to have said that if you refuse to settle for nothing but the best, you very often get it. What will you settle for?

Here we are at the end of this book but not of our pilgrimage. Love and fear are not the opposite of each other. They are parallel. People can lose their fears and that doesn't necessarily leave them experiencing love. People can stop loving and not necessarily end up experiencing fear. They are perfectly parallel paths of the same thing—life.

> *I shall be telling this with a sigh*
> *Somewhere ages and ages hence:*
> *Two roads diverged in a wood, and I—*
> *I took the one less traveled by,*
> *And that has made all the difference.*[14]

---

[13] *Alcoholics Anonymous*, p. 163.
[14] The Road Not Taken, *The Poetry of Robert Frost*, Robert Frost; Edited By Edward Connery Lathem, Holt, Rinehart and Winston, 1969, p. 105.

The paths of love and fear are so close together you can change from one to the other and move nowhere. Traversing that very short distance from fear to love and compassion, and staying there, is how spiritual transformation is accomplished. You've worked hard and changed a great deal to accomplish this, and yet haven't gone very far at all.

M. Scott Peck was reported to have said when future generations look back on the twentieth century, it won't be nuclear fission they'll remark on; it will be Alcoholics Anonymous. From my own perspective, it will be *Alcoholics Anonymous* and *Twelve Steps and Twelve Traditions*, not because of their meaning to alcoholics but because of their astonishing insight into the human condition.

Remember: You are a sexual being, in a physical body, trying to be a spiritual entity, in a human context, within a limited but unknown segment of eternity. Even without dysfunction and abuse, or addictions and a destructively oriented ego, it's incredibly complicated.

As an addicted person now recovered, somehow realize within yourself that simply learning and doing will not guarantee your remaining spiritual. Knowledge and action are not the solution. In its broadest sense, and by whatever definition, authentic living by spiritual principles is.

Labour with patience and devotion. Live intimately with trusted loved ones. Develop compassion and respect for the earth and all living things. Maintain an intimate, *long* relationship with a spiritually oriented mentor or therapist. And, in all of this, hold respect, veracity, humility, compassion, charity, personal responsibility, and non-violence as the highest values. Labor with devotion and patience only to this end: Through the maintenance steps, be forever governed by the five spiritual principles.

You will have crossed some ubiquitous line and sense in hindsight, and only by continuing to embrace your ever-present frailties, that you're recovered. Some might call you wise, many will resent you, and you'll smile gently because, for you alone, it will be sufficient to quietly repose in the safety of knowing that the mysterious machinations of The Universe are beautiful.

Words cannot describe everything.
The heart's message cannot be delivered in words.
If one receives words literally, they will be lost.
If one tries to explain with words, they will not
attain enlightenment in this life.[15]

As for myself...

As I traverse the eternity between my own birth and death, I am forever encased in the *being* of my own life. I must remind myself that I unfold into only a supporting role. At my own last exit I will face a final curtain, the closing of which always comes before the end of the play. And as for encores, if there are any... probably none that I'll remember.

---

[15] *Zen Flesh, Zen Bones, A Collection of Pre-Zen Writings,* complied by Paul Reps, Anchor Books, 1989, p. 120, (quoted with minor editing of pronouns).

About the Author

Richard Clark was born in 1950, in Ontario, Canada. He wandered through the 1960s and college in a manner of 'protest and experimentation', and traveled widely throughout North America. He was known to lean heavily on a quote from William Blake: *"The road to excess leads to the palace of wisdom."*[16] Certainly the excess part was true, but some people might question where that excess led him. He's been a construction worker, miner, soldier, military policeman, security guard, driving instructor, police constable, seniors' outreach worker, teacher, writer, artist, musician, therapist, seminar leader, consultant, and counsellor.

Richard trained in addictions treatment and many of the issues related to addictions at several colleges and private training centres. He's a certified addictions counsellor (CAC II) through the Canadian Council of Professional Certification and trained in several energy healing modalities.

He's offered seminars and lectures to over twenty thousand people on topics that include addictions, sexuality, violence, relationships, change, stress and trauma, religion, spirituality, Buddhism, applied problem solving, gender issues, therapy, life skills, counselling, energy healing, interpersonal communications, and twelve step programs.

As a therapist and educator, Richard's worked in colleges, First Nations' communities, the sales industry, prisons, monasteries, non-profit agencies, and treatment centres. He's offered seminars and lectures in Canada, the United States, China, and Russia, and has been a therapist and addictions counsellor since 1986.

www.richardwclark.com

www.gracefultransformation.com

Facets of Personal Transformation

The first-draft of this project counted in at above 800 pages. In it, I had said all I wanted to say about addictions, twelve-step programs, personal transformation, and spirituality. When I talked about this with my friend Michael, to whom this book is dedicated, for various reasons he suggested I divide the material into two volumes. *Addictions & Spiritual Transformation* is the first book of a set.

---

[16] This William Blake quote comes from Proverbs of Hell, which begins: *"In seed time learn, in harvest teach, in winter enjoy. / Drive your cart and your plow over the bones of the dead. / The road of excess leads to the palace of wisdom. / Prudence is a rich, ugly old maid courted by Incapacity. / He who desires but acts not, breeds pestilence..."* From: The Portable Blake, Edited by Alfred Kazin, Viking Portable Library, p. 252.

Throughout this book there are references to *Facets of Personal Transformation*. This companion volume will discuss family, personality, psychology, gender, the dynamics of relationships, applied personal problem solving, therapy, emotions, communications, Buddhism, ethics and values, religion, and spirituality. These topics will be of interest to people in general, but there will also be specific information for people committed to spiritual transformation.

Facets of Personal Transformation is scheduled for publication in late 2011. Together, these two books will comprise a detailed examination of the dynamics and process of self-directed personal transformation and spirituality.

Index

1

F

G

H

I

Index of Subsections by Title